A Text Book Of

MECHANICAL OPERATIONS

Fundamental Principles and Applications

ENLARGED AND REVISED THIRD EDITION

FOR DEGREE COURSES IN CHEMICAL, PETROCHEMICAL, PETROLEUM, POLYMER ENGINEERING AND BIOTECHNOLOGY

Covering the Revised Syllabus of:

University of Pune, University of Mumbai, Shivaji University, North Maharashtra University, North Gujarat University, Dr. Babasaheb Ambedekar Technological University, Lonre (Dist-Raigad), Jawaharlal Nehru Technological University, Hyderabad, University of Kerla, University of Osmania, University of Bangalore, University Of Delhi

DR. KIRAN D. PATIL

M.E. (Chemical Engineering), Ph.D. (Chemical Engineering)
Professor in Chemical Engineering,
Department of Petrochemical and Petroleum Engineering,
Maharashtra Institute of Technology, PUNE - 411 038 (MS)

Price ₹ 330.00

NIRALI PRAKASHAN

N1014

MECHANICAL OPERATIONS: FUNDAMENTAL PRINCIPLES AND APPLICATIONS ISBN : 978-93-80064-00-0
Third Edition : September 2012
© : Author

The text of this publication, or any part thereof, should not be reproduced or transmitted in any form or stored in any computer storage system or device for distribution including photocopy, recording, taping or information retrieval system or reproduced on any disc, tape, perforated media or other information storage device etc., without the written permission of Author with whom the rights are reserved. Breach of this condition is liable for legal action.

Every effort has been made to avoid errors or omissions in this publication. In spite of this, errors may have crept in. Any mistake, error or discrepancy so noted and shall be brought to our notice shall be taken care of in the next edition. It is notified that neither the publisher nor the author or seller shall be responsible for any damage or loss of action to any one, of any kind, in any manner, therefrom.

Published By :
NIRALI PRAKASHAN
Abhyudaya Pragati, 1312, Shivaji Nagar,
Off J.M. Road, PUNE – 411005
Tel - (020) 25512336/37/39, Fax - (020) 25511379
Email : niralipune@pragationline.com

Printed By :
RACHANA PRINTS
Plot No. E-54, Market Yard, Gultekdi,
PUNE - 411 037
Tel - (020) 2426 8680 / 4480

DISTRIBUTION CENTRES

PUNE
Nirali Prakashan
119, Budhwar Peth, Jogeshwari Mandir Lane
Pune 411002, Maharashtra
Tel : (020) 2445 2044, 66022708
Fax : (020) 2445 1538
Email : bookorder@pragationline.com

MUMBAI
Nirali Prakashan
385, S.V.P. Road, Rasdhara Co-op. Hsg. Society Ltd.,
Girgaum, Mumbai 400004, Maharashtra
Tel : (022) 2385 6339 / 2386 9976,
Fax : (022) 2386 9976
Email : niralimumbai@pragationline.com

DISTRIBUTION BRANCHES

NAGPUR
Pratibha Book Distributors
Above Maratha Mandir, Shop No. 3, First Floor,
Rani Jhanshi Square, Sitabuldi, Nagpur 440012,
Maharashtra, Tel : (0712) 254 7129

BENGALURU
Pragati Book House
House No. 1, Sanjeevappa Lane, Avenue Road Cross,
Opp. Rice Church, Bengaluru – 560002.
Tel : (080) 64513344, 64513355,
Mob : 9880582331, 9845021552
Email:bharatsavla@yahoo.com

JALGAON
Nirali Prakashan
34, V. V. Golani Market, Navi Peth, Jalgaon 425001,
Maharashtra, Tel : (0257) 222 0395
Mob : 94234 91860

KOLHAPUR
Nirali Prakashan
New Mahadvar Road,
Kedar Plaza, 1st Floor Opp. IDBI Bank
Kolhapur 416 012, Maharashtra. Mob : 9855046155

CHENNAI
Pragati Books
9/1, Montieth Road, Behind Taas Mahal, Egmore,
Chennai 600008 Tamil Nadu, Tel : (044) 6518 3535,
Mob : 94440 01782 / 98450 21552 / 98805 82331
Email : bharatsavla@yahoo.com

RETAIL OUTLETS
PUNE

Pragati Book Centre
157, Budhwar Peth, Opp. Ratan Talkies,
Pune 411002, Maharashtra
Tel : (020) 2445 8887 / 6602 2707, Fax : (020) 2445 8887
Pragati Book Centre
Amber Chamber, 28/A, Budhwar Peth,
Appa Balwant Chowk, Pune : 411002, Maharashtra,
Tel : (020) 20240335 / 66281669
Email : pbcpune@pragationline.com

Pragati Book Centre
676/B, Budhwar Peth, Opp. Jogeshwari Mandir,
Pune 411002, Maharashtra
Tel : (020) 6601 7784 / 6602 0855
Pragati Book Centre
917/22, Sai Complex, F.C. Road, Opp. Hotel Roopali,
Shivajinagar, Pune 411004, Maharashtra
Tel : (020) 2566 3372 / 6602 2728

PBC Book Sellers & Stationers
152, Budhwar Peth, Pune 411002, Maharashtra
Tel : (020) 2445 2254 / 6609 2463

MUMBAI
Pragati Book Corner
Indira Niwas, 111 - A, Bhavani Shankar Road, Dadar (W), Mumbai 400028, Maharashtra
Tel : (022) 2422 3526 / 6662 5254
Email : pbcmumbai@pragationline.com

www.pragationline.com info@pragationline.com

Dedicated

To My Parents

and

To My Wife, Varsha, Son, Aditya

For inspiring, encouraging, and sustaining

PREFACE TO THIRD EDITION

I am happy to note that the earlier edition of this book was well received by members of engineering community. We are thankful to all those students, professional engineers and academicians who sent me critical comments and feedback for future improvements of this book.

The feedback received from different sources has been incorporated. All possible efforts have been made to enhance further the usefulness of the book. The revised edition is going to press with a few modifications. All the printing errors that inadvertently appeared in the previous editions have been corrected. The new material has been included in keeping with current need and demands of students. In this book there are numerous line diagrams and illustrations included, but very few pictures. Instead, web addresses are provided for equipment manufactures and interested students should access these sites to see the equipment offered. The other highlights of this revised edition are (i) the subject contents has been developed, refined and restructured at several points; (ii) several new problems have also been added at the end of various chapters for the benefit of the students; and (iii) every page of the book has been read carefully so as to improve its quality. Fifteen to twenty problems at the end of each chapter ensure that students will remain actively engaged with the course material presented in this revised edition of the book. Every practicing chemical engineer, whether in industry or academics, who reads this book, will find that his own specialty has been inadequately treated.

I express my appreciation and gratefulness to my publisher, Shri Dineshbhai Furia and Shri. Jignesh Furia and his entire team of Nirali Prakashan, Pune for bringing out the third edition of this book with a very attractive manner.

I am grateful to all those who have helped me directly and/or indirectly in preparing this revised edition. I firmly believe that there is always scope for improvement and accordingly I shall look forward to receive suggestions for further enriching the quality of the text.

Pune
5th September 2012
Teacher's Day

Prof. (Dr.) Kiran D. Patil
E-mail: kiran.patil@mitpune.edu

PREFACE TO FIRST EDITION

In view of revised syllabus of Chemical Engineering in all the Universities in Maharashtra, Gujarat and other states, there is an urgent need to have standard textbooks for various Chemical Engineering Subjects. When I set to write this book, only a very limited number of books are available books on Mechanical Operations were available in the Indian market. Also based on the market survey on available books in Chemical Engineering, it is observed that the books are written foreign authors (with a few exceptions), and are often very costly.

Therefore, it is not possible for undergraduate students to understand the basic theory and principles of various Chemical Engineering Subjects to the depth they should. As a result their preparation is not upto the mark. This I have observed, often, in oral examinations. Thus, there is a need of good quality undergraduate textbooks in Chemical Engineering subjects which : (i) cover topics in the syllabus upto appropriate details, (ii) discuss adequate problems, (iii) useful to all Chemical Engineering students in Maharashtra, and (iv) are inexpensive. I hope that the students studying Chemical Engineering will find the book useful for self-study.

This book presents on elementary treatment of the principles of Mechanical Operations. Presentation of the subject follows classical lines of separate discussions for Properties and Handling of Particulate Solids, Size Reduction, Mixing and Agitation, Screening, Filtration, Sedimentation. Fluidization, Beneficiation Processes. Throughout the book emphasis has been placed on visualization of physical processes. Theory alone won't do, particularly from the point of view of examination in Indian Universities and Engineering Colleges. Hence, emphasis is given on numerical examples in this book. A liberal number of numerical examples are given.

Exercises are included at the end of each chapter and devised to extend the subject- matter by requiring students to apply the basic principles to new situations and develop their own operations. For the serious students, then, the end-of-chapter references offer an open door to the literature of Mechanical Operations that can pyramid upon further investigation. In several chapters, the number of references offered is much larger than necessary and older citations of historical interest have been retained freely. The author feels this is a luxury that will not be intrusive on the reader or detract from the utility of the text.

I am grateful to Prof. (Dr.) V. D. Karad, Director, Maharashtra Institute of Technology (MIT), Pune for his content encouragement and moral support during the presentation of this book. I am very thankful to Prof. (Dr.) L. K. Kshirsagar for his guidance and suggestions during the preparation of this book. Thanks are due to Prof. Datta B. Dandge for constructive criticism of the text. I am very thankful to my Publisher M/s Nirali Publishers, Pune and especially to Shri. Dineshbhai Furia for giving the present form to the book in minimum possible time.

I am also thankful to efficient and professional staff of M/s Nirali Prakashan, Mr. Malik Shaikh, Mrs. Anagha Kaware (Proof Reading), Mrs. Anjali Muley (Figure Artist), Pune. I am immensely grateful to the members of my family who were encouraging, tolerant, totally supportive and generous. I am overwhelmingly happy to acknowledge, how much I owe them and how inadequate this sounds from the heart. I would express my sincere gratitude to my parents, who have always been a major source of encouragement in all my academic pursuits. Finally, my wife Varsha gives me a wonderful rich life.

Finally to say, though I have made possible attempts to make this book flawless, yet some errors may surprisingly creep into. Suggestions from the readers regarding improvement of the utility of this book will be gratefully acknowledged and acted upon. I am confident that this book will be definitely useful to the teachers and students of Chemical Engineering. My efforts will be successful only to that extent to which it receives patronage from the wider section of the students and teachers of Chemical Engineering.

Date : 5th September, 2002
Place : Pune.

Mr. Kiran D. Patil
Email : kiran.patil@mitpune.edu.in

FOREWORD

The subject of "Mechanical Operations" forms an essential part of the syllabi of the undergraduate courses in Chemical Engineering and other diversified courses such as Polymer Engineering, Petroleum Engineering and Petrochemical Engineering. A textbook on "Mechanical Operations" is therefore always welcome, if it is comprehensive and yet easy to understand.

Many basic fundamental concepts in various Chemical Engineering Unit Operations such as Size Reduction, Filtration, Sedimentation, Mixing and Agitation etc. and their mathematical relationships are usually difficult to understand for an average student. However, without understanding the basic principles and construction details of various chemical engineering equipment, it is difficult to appreciate their applications in Chemical Industry, including their design and maintenance.

Only a few books on "Mechanical Operations" are available in the Indian market, and most of these books are written by foreign authors (with a few exceptions), and are often very costly and their orientation and presentation may not always suit the needs of Indian students community. The author of the present book, Mr. Kiran Patil has very nicely explained each concept in the most logical and systematic manner. Solutions of numerical problems and large number of exercises given at the end of the each chapter illustrate the application of theoretical concepts. The author has taken care to incorporate every concept in a logical sequence and developed it step by step to its final form. This will facilitate self-learning by the reader and satisfy the long felt need of the students for such a standard textbook.

Mr. Kiran Patil is Professor in Chemical Engineering, Department of Petrochemical and Petroleum Engineering, Maharashtra Institute of Technology, Pune, (M.S.) India. His industrial and teaching experience and ability to effectively communicate with the students is amply revealed in each chapter of this book. I congratulate Mr. Patil for his untiring efforts and dedication in preparing this textbook.

I hope and feel confident that this book will prove to be quite helpful to the engineering students community at large in the long run and it will also be quite useful as a noteworthy standard text book on the subject of "Mechanical Operations" for Chemical Engineering and allied degree courses in the various Universities of India.

(Prof. Dr. Vishwanath D. Karad)
Executive President and Director General,
MAEER'S, Maharashtra Institute of Technology,
Pune – 411 038, Maharashtra, India.

CONTENTS

1. Properties and Handling of Particulate Solids — 1.1 – 1.86

- 1.1 Introduction to Particle Technology — 1.1
  - 1.1.1 Introduction and Classification of Mechanical – Physical Separation Processes — 1.11
  - 1.1.2 Solid Processing Operations — 1.12
  - 1.1.3 Solids/Liquid Separations — 1.13
  - 1.1.4 Driving Forces used to separate Particles from Liquids — 1.15
- 1.2 Characterization of Solid Particles: Particle Shape and Size — 1.16
- 1.3 Classification of Solid Materials — 1.20
  - 1.3.1 Introduction — 1.20
  - 1.3.2 Particle Size and Shape — 1.20
    - 1.3.2.1 Particle Shape — 1.20
  - 1.3.3 Size Distributions — 1.22
  - 1.3.4 Mean Particle Sizes — 1.23
  - 1.3.5 Particle Size Measurement Methods — 1.25
    - 1.3.5.1 Microscopic Examination — 1.26
    - 1.3.5.2 Sieve Analysis — 1.27
    - 1.3.5.3 Methods based on Differential Terminal Velocity — 1.27
    - 1.3.5.4 The Gamma Distribution — 1.28
    - 1.3.5.5 Gamma Distribution Maths — 1.29
    - 1.3.5.6 Log-Normal Distribution — 1.30
- 1.4 Screen Analysis: Cumulative and Differential — 1.31
  - 1.4.1 Differential Analysis — 1.31
  - 1.4.2 Cumulative Screen Analysis — 1.31
  - 1.4.3 General Procedure for Screen Analysis — 1.32
  - 1.4.4 Methods of Reporting Screen Analysis — 1.32
  - 1.4.5 Size Distribution Equations — 1.34
- 1.5 Specific Surface of Mixture — 1.34
  - 1.5.1 Average particle size — 1.35
  - 1.5.2 Number of particles in mixture — 1.36
- 1.6 Standard Screen Series — 1.36
- 1.7 Properties of Particulate Masses — 1.40
  - 1.7.1 Distinct properties of solid masses — 1.40
  - 1.7.2 Pressure in masses of particle — 1.40
  - 1.7.3 Angle of Internal friction and Angle of Repose — 1.41
- 1.8 Storage of Solids — 1.42
  - 1.8.1 Bulk Storage — 1.42
  - 1.8.2 Bin Storage — 1.42
  - 1.8.3 Stresses in Hoppers and Silos — 1.42
- 1.9 Grade Efficiency — 1.45
  - 1.9.1 Why do we classify particles ? — 1.46
  - 1.9.2 Measuring Efficiency — 1.46
  - 1.9.3 Cut Size and Sharpness of Cut — 1.49
  - 1.9.4 Construction of the Grade Efficiency Curve — 1.50
- 1.10 Solved Examples — 1.51
- Exercise for Practice — 1.81
- Nomenclature — 1.86

2. Conveyors   2.1 – 2.18

  2.1 Introduction   2.1
  2.2 Belt Conveyors   2.2
      2.2.1 Belt Construction   2.3
      2.2.2 Belt-Conveyor Drives   2.3
      2.2.3 Belt-Conveyor Supports   2.4
      2.2.4 Belt-Conveyor take-ups   2.4
      2.2.5 Feeders   2.4
  2.3 Chain Conveyors   2.5
      2.3.1 Scraper Conveyors   2.5
      2.3.2 Apron Conveyor   2.5
      2.3.3 Bucket Conveyors and Bucket Elevators   2.6
  2.4 Screw Conveyors (Flights)   2.7
  2.5 Pneumatic Conveyors   2.9
      2.5.1 Pneumatic Conveying   2.10
  2.6 General Field of Conveyors   2.14
  2.7 Solved Example   2.15
      Exercise For Practice   2.17
      Nomenclature   2.18

3. Mixing of Solids and Pastes   3.1 – 3.24

  3.1 Introduction   3.1
  3.2 Theory of Solid Mixing   3.2
  3.3 Characteristics of Mixtures   3.2
  3.4 Measurement of Mixing   3.3
  3.5 Particle Mixing   3.4
  3.6 Equipment for Solid Mixing   3.5
  3.7 Mixers for Pastes and Plastic Masses   3.6
  3.8 Mixers for Dry Powders   3.12
  3.9 Power Requirements   3.14
  3.10 Mixing Index in Blending Granular Solids   3.15
  3.11 Rate of Mixing   3.16
  3.12 Criteria of Mixer Effectiveness: Mixing Index   3.16
  3.13 Solved Examples   3.18
      Exercise for Practice   3.22
      Nomenclature   3.23

4. Size Reduction   4.1 – 4.46

  4.1 Introduction   4.1
      4.1.1 Size Reduction   4.1
            4.1.1.1 Mechanisms of Size Reduction   4.5
      4.1.2 Factors Influencing Choice of Size Reduction Equipment   4.6
      4.1.3 The Value of Size Reduction   4.6
      4.1.4 Product Factors Influencing Equipment Selection   4.7
  4.2 Principles of Comminution   4.7
      4.2.1 Criteria for Comminution   4.7
      4.2.2 Characteristics of Comminuted Products   4.8
  4.3 Energy and Power Requirements in Size Reduction   4.8
  4.4 Laws of Size Reduction   4.9
      4.4.1 Empirical relationships – Rittinger's and Kick's Law   4.9
      4.4.2 Bond Crushing Law and Work Index   4.10
  4.5 Size Reduction Equipments   4.10
      4.5.1 Crushers   4.11
      4.5.2 Relative Merits of the Jaw Crusher and Gyratory Crusher   4.14

	4.5.3 Hammer Mills and Impactors	4.15
	4.5.4 Ball Mill	4.16
4.6	Equipment Operation	4.18
	4.6.1 Open-Circuit and Closed-Circuit Operation	4.18
	4.6.2 Feed Control	4.20
	4.6.3 Mill Discharge	4.20
	4.6.4 Energy Consumption	4.21
	4.6.5 Removal or Supply of Heat	4.22
4.7	Comparison between Crushing and Grinding Operations	4.22
4.8	Principles of Size Enlargement	4.23
4.9	Solved Examples	4.26
	Exercise for Practice	4.42
	Nomenclature	4.45

5. Mechanical Separations: Screening — 5.1 – 5.20

5.1	Mechanical Separations	5.1
5.2	Screening (Sieving)	5.2
5.3	Types of Screening Equipment	5.3
5.4	Comparisons of Ideal and Actual Screens	5.6
5.5	Material Balance Over Screen	5.7
5.6	Screen Effectiveness	5.8
5.7	Capacity and Effectiveness of Screen	5.9
5.8	Solved Examples	5.9
	Exercise for Practice	5.18
	Nomenclature	5.20

6. Filtration — 6.1 – 6.52

6.1	Introduction	6.1
6.2	Factors Affecting on Rate of Filtration	6.3
6.3	Clarifying Filters	6.4
	6.3.1 Gas Cleaning	6.4
	6.3.2 Liquid Clarification	6.4
6.4	Cake Filters	6.5
6.5	Classification of Filters	6.5
	6.5.1 Discontinuous Vacuum Filters	6.6
	6.5.2 Continuous Vacuum Filters	6.6
6.6	Equipment for Filtration	6.6
	6.6.1 Plate and Frame Filter Presses	6.6
	6.6.2 Leaf Filters	6.9
	6.6.3 Continuous Rotary Filters	6.9
6.7	Filter Media	6.11
6.8	Filter Aids	6.11
6.9	Principles of Cake Filtration	6.12
6.10	Principles of Clarification	6.12
	6.10.1 Membrane Filtration	6.13
6.11	Pressure Drop through Filter Cake	6.14
6.12	Compressible and Incompressible Filter Cake	6.16
6.13	Filter Medium Resistance	6.16

6.14	Constant Pressure Filtration	6.16
6.15	Empirical Equation for Cake Resistance	6.17
6.16	Constant–Rate Filtration	6.17
6.17	Filter-Cake Compressibility	6.18
6.18	Rate of Washing	6.18
6.19	Principles of Centrifugal Filtration	6.19
6.20	Fundamentals of Microfiltration	6.20
	6.20.1 Basic Principles of Microfiltration	6.21
	6.20.2 Particle Retention	6.23
6.21	Introduction to Biofiltration	6.24
	6.21.1 Principles of Biofiltration	6.24
	6.21.2 Advantages of Biofiltration	6.25
	6.21.3 Disadvantages of Biofiltration	6.25
	6.21.4 Commercial Applications	6.25
6.22	Design of Filtration Units	6.26
6.23	Solved Problems	6.28
	Exercise for Practice	6.47
	Nomenclature	6.51

7. Separation Based on Motion of Particles through the Fluids 7.1 – 7.70

(A) Gravity Settling Process

7.1	Introduction	7.1
7.2	Relative Motion between Particles and Fluids	7.1
7.3	Gravity Settling Processes	7.5
	7.3.1 Gravity Classifiers	7.6
	7.3.2 Sorting Classifiers	7.7
	7.3.3 Sink and Float Method	7.7
	7.3.4 Differential Settling Methods	7.8
7.4	Free and Hindered Settling	7.9
7.5	Sedimentation	7.11
	7.5.1 Introduction	7.11
	7.5.2 Batch Settling Tests	7.14
	7.5.3 Application of Batch Settling Tests to Design of Continuous Thickeners	7.20
	7.5.4 Equipments for Settling and Sedimentation	7.21
	7.5.5 The Kynch Theory	7.23
	7.5.6 Determination of Thickener Area	7.25

(B) Centrifugal Settling Processes

7.6	Cyclone Separator	7.29
7.7	The Hydrocyclone	7.40
7.8	Centrifugal Settling	7.41
7.9	Selection of Separation Equipment	7.42
7.10	Solved Examples	7.42
	Exercise for Practice	7.67
	Nomenclature	7.70

8. Mixing and Agitation   8.1 – 8.32
    8.1 Introduction   8.1
    8.2 Agitation Equipment   8.2
    8.3 Impellers and their Characteristics   8.3
    8.4 Power Requirements for Agitation   8.7
    8.5 Selection of Impellers   8.9
    8.6 Scale-Up of Mixing System   8.10
    8.7 Liquid Mixing   8.13
    8.8 Design of Mixing System   8.14
    8.9 Agitator Design   8.14
    8.10 Agitator Selection   8.19
    8.11 Solved Examples   8.24
    Exercise for Practice   8.31
    Nomenclature   8.32

9. Fluidization   9.1 – 9.28
    9.1 Introduction   9.1
    9.2 Principles of Fluidization   9.1
    9.3 Flow through Packed Beds   9.2
    9.4 Pressure Drop in Packed Beds   9.7
    9.5 Pressure Drop-Flow Diagrams   9.10
    9.6 Types of Fluidization   9.11
       9.6.1 Particulate Fluidization   9.11
       9.6.2 Aggregative Fluidization   9.12
       9.6.3 Determination of Minimum Fluidizing Velocity   9.12
       9.6.4 Observation of General Bed Behavior   9.13
    9.7 Applications of Fluidization Techniques   9.15
    9.8 Design of Fluidized Beds   9.16
       9.8.1 Comparison of Contacting Methods   9.18
       9.8.2 Advantages and Disadvantages of Fluidized Beds   9.18
       9.8.3 Uses of Fluidized Beds   9.19
    9.9 Pneumatic Conveying   9.19
    9.10 Solved Examples   9.20
    Exercise for Practice   9.27
    Nomenclature   9.28

10. Beneficiation Process   10.1 – 10.30
    10.1 Introduction   10.1
    10.2 Which Beneficiation Process is Right for your Plant ?   10.1
    10.3 Filters   10.3
       10.3.1 Bag Filters   10.3
       10.3.2 Fibrous or Deep-bed Filters   10.4
    10.4 Jigging   10.5
    10.5 Tabling   10.9

10.6	Magnetic Separation	10.11
	10.6.1 Magnetic Separation of Free Metals	10.15
10.7	Electrostatic Separation	10.16
10.8	Gravity Concentrator	10.19
10.9	Froth Floatation	10.22
	10.9.1 Hydrophobic and Floatation	10.26
	10.9.2 Physical Processes in Floatation	10.27
	10.9.3 Floatation Machines	10.28
10.10	Flocculation	10.28
	Nomenclature	10.30

Appendix A : Units for Particulate Measurements — A.1 – A.2

Appendix B : Frontiers in Particle Technology — B.1 – B.24

Appendix C : Bulk Solids for Storage and Handling — C.1 – C.4

Appendix D : Bin and Hopper Design — D.1 – D.12

Appendix E : The Value of Size Reduction — E.1 – E.4

Appendix F : Elutriation of Particles from Fluidized Beds — F.1 – F.6

Objective Questions — O.1 – O.22

Question Bank — Q.1 – Q.14

Reference Books — R.1 – R.2

***

Unit 1

Chapter 1: PROPERTIES AND HANDLING OF PARTICULATE SOLIDS

1.1 Introduction to Particle Technology

The term *"Particle Technology"* deals with techniques for processing and handling particular solids. It plays a major role in the production of materials in the chemical industry. In the most of processing operations in the chemical industry, solids may appear in a variety of forms – continuous sheets, angular pieces, finely divided powders. In general solids are more difficult to handle than liquids or gases. They may be hard and abrasive, tough and rubbery, soft or fragile, dusty, cohesive, free flowing or sticky. So it is necessary to find a method to manipulate the solids as they occur and thus to improve the handling characteristics.

Of all the shapes and sizes that may be found in solids, the most important from a chemical engineering standpoint is the *small particles*. An understanding of the characteristics of masses of particular solids is necessary in designing processes and equipment for dealing with streams containing such solids.

Particle technology may be described as being the study of materials dispersed within a continuous fluid. The particles may be solid, but they can also be oil droplets in water, water droplets in air etc. So, by a particle we mean any dispersed material within a fluid. In many cases deformable particles have a slightly different behaviour to rigid ones, but the starting point for the description of deformable particles is that of the rigid, and simpler, case. Hence, particle technology includes the understanding of raindrops, oil emulsions, powders, slurries etc., and just about every industrial process uses the subject at some stage. For example, in petrol production the catalytic cracking of petroleum is achieved in fluidized beds of catalyst particles. An understanding of fluidization relies upon knowledge of particle characterization and fluid flow through porous media. The petroleum processing is performed in the vapour phase, not the liquid, hence the fluidized beds require appropriate gas cleaning equipment for recycling and retention of the catalyst particles. The catalyst is stored and conveyed into the system and, of course, due care must be exercised over powder hazards.

There is a reputed saying that a liquid is a hen-pecked husband whereas a solid particle is a male chauvinist pig. The hint behind this statement is obvious. A liquid does not have any definite shape, it takes the shape of its container; whereas every solid particle has a specific shape of its own. Thus, whenever we handle any system involving solid particles, which we encounter' quite often in chemical process industries, for defining the system, first we have to specify the size and shape of the particles involved. The task however, is not an easy one.

If the particle conforms itself to any of the standard configurations we are familiar with such as spherical, cubical, cylindrical etc., then its size can be easily specified. For example, the size of a spherical particle is nothing but its diameter and that of a cubical particle the length of its side. However, many of the particles commonly encountered in industrial practices do not conform any of these standard configurations. We can call them, in general, irregular particles. How to define the size of such an irregular particle is now the question before us.

During the early stages of development of particle technology, a number of authors proposed empirical definitions to particle size. For example, Martin (1931) defined the size of an irregular particle as the length of the line bisecting the maximum cross-sectional area of the particle. Similarly, Feret (1929) defined particle size as the distance between the two most extreme points on the particle surface. The limitations of such definitions are obvious.

An even greater reliance on particle technology is provided by the increasing trend towards high value batch processing in the chemical and pharmaceutical industries. A prime example is the production of a tablet. In many cases a reactant is provided in a solid form and product recovery involves nucleation and then crystallization of the product. The crystals may be settled, to increase the slurry concentration going on to a filter, or filtering centrifuge; the resulting cake will need washing free of reaction products and unreacted feed material and mechanically dried, to minimize the amount of thermal energy required to complete the drying. After thermal drying, there is likely to be a need for product storage, crushing and classification, solid/solid mixing, conveying and agglomeration for the purpose of forming the tablet. Any one of these processes may be the cause of a process bottleneck, or throughput limitation, and the intention of this book is to provide a sound understanding of the underlying principles behind these operations to enable reliable operation and appropriate decisions to be drawn.

Prerequisites and Objectives:

In common with most engineering subjects particle technology requires a basic competence in calculus and algebraic manipulation. A first course in fluid mechanics would also be helpful, as it will be assumed that the reader is familiar with concepts such as Reynolds number, Bernoulli's equation, Hagen–Poiseuille, Newton's law (F=ma), friction factor and flow regimes. Knowledge of very basic statistics would be useful for a complete understanding of solid/solid mixing. Likewise, the concepts of mean, median and mode are used when discussing particle size distributions. Particle technology is a very broad subject and there have been many very good books describing specialized aspects of the subject published over the last twenty years. (See bibliography for such references).

The Micron:

All sizes in microns	
Fine sand	20 to 200
Hair diameter	100
Clouds/fog:	30
Red blood cells	8
Silt	2 to 20
Clays	< 2
Tobacco smoke	< 1
Bacteria	0.2 to 40
Viruses	< 0.5

Most industrial processing is performed on small particles with a diameter typically in the range of 10^{-6} to 10^{-3} m; i.e. 1 to 1000 microns or µm. The box provides some sizes, i.e. particle diameters, of commonly encountered materials. We will become very familiar with working in a length scale of microns in particle technology. However, there are often times when the centimeter, gram, second (cgs) system of units may be easier to apply.

Outline of Particle Technology:

The topics noted below included are currently part of the engineering curriculum but deal with only continuous phases (not particulates or droplets). Some of these topics are discussed in detail in this book.

1. **The Significance of Particle Technology:**
   - In Industrial Processes
   - In the Environment
   - In Research Opportunities

2. Making, Merging, and Breaking Particles

Chemical Methods to Make Particles:
- Precipitation from a Gas Phase - condensation, evapouration, effect of nuclei, crystallization, agglomeration/sintering.
- Precipitation from a Liquid Phase - nucleation, precipitation, dissolution, Ostwald ripening, crystallization, agglomeration/sintering, precipitation in emulsions, effect of secondary solutes.
- Mutation from another solid phase.
- Encapsulation - physical, precipitation, chemical transmutation.

Physical Methods to Make Larger Particles:
- Compaction - application and propagation of impact forces
- Sintering
- Granulation
- Agglomeration - liquid bridges, solid bridges (formation and removal), diffusion, mixing, local shear

Physical Methods to Make Smaller Particles
- Comminution
- Attrition
- Extrusion
- Chopping
- Application and propogation of uni-axial slow forces

3. Physics of Particles

Particle Contact Interactions (Tribology)
- Particle-Particle Interaction - contact forces; Van der Waal's, charge, magnetic etc.
- Particle-Field Interaction (Gas and Liquid Phase) - thermal diffusion, sedimentation (gravity, centrifugal), electro drift (zeta potential), magnetic, radiation pressure for particle trapping, light scattering (Mie, Rayleigh etc.)
- Effect of Loading on Particle-Field Response - hindered settling etc.

Particle-Wall Interactions, Use in Characterization:
- Particle-wall impact, attrition, and wear.
- Tribo-charging
- Surface stress generation, mechanochemistry

- Electrochemical cell formation due to deposition
- Detergency and removal of wall deposits
- Gas-phase wall deposition and re-entrainment (time effects)
- Fouling, sediment beds and resuspension (time effects)

Physical Methods for Characterizing Particles:
- Sampling techniques (flow, whole stream, changes on standing, problems due to segregation based on composition or size)
- Density (specific gravity)
- Hardness
- Tribocharging
- Size Distribution
    ... light scattering (Mie, Rayleigh etc.)
    ... sedimentation
    ... electro transport
- Pore Size Distribution
- Shape, Surface Roughness
- Crystal habit, domain size
- Evaluation of Chemical Composition (bulk, surface)

4. Storage and Transport of Particles
Piles, Silos, and Bins (fill, stand, discharge)
- Angle of Repose
- Bulk Density (Consolidation, packing, and time effects)
- Special Distribution of Bulk Density
- Level, shape of top during fill, discharge
- Mohr circle, wall friction, stresses in bulk and on wall consolidation
- Design and testing, level detection

Bin Flow Problems:
- Arch formation, cohesive strength, heel in silo
- Flow function, flow factor, discharge flow patterns
- Bin design, testing, discharge rate and pattern indicators
- Flow discharge aids
- Explosive aerators, vibrators, arch breakers, delumpers
- Effect of vibration and condensation cycling in rail cars
- Valves and flow restricting (metering) devices (feeders)

Bed Transport - trucks, belts, bucket elevators
Cascade Transport - chute flow, screw feeders
Flow Aids - agglomeration, additives, coatings, surface treatments

Fluidized Transport:
- Permeability to Flow (gas, liquid).
- Measuring special distribution of particulates (tomography).
- Fluidization (non-cohesive, cohesive).
- Pneumatic conveying (saltation, dune flow, dense phase conveying, choking flow), standpipes.
- Blower selection and operation with powders.
- Measurement and control of effective fluidized viscosity.
- Pressure drop, monitoring flow and pressure.

Transport and Storage of Powders:
- Conveying in slurry form
- Measurement and control of Rheology
- Pump selection and operation with slurries
- Pressure drop, monitoring flow and pressure
- Stirred tanks, agitator blade design and placement
- Agitator motor selection for startup and settled conditions
- Distribution of solids due to settling and centrifugation
- Effect of vibration and Ostwald ripening in rail cars

5. **Mixing and Separation of Particles:**
Mixing Powders:
- Quantitative theory, implications for analysis
- Powder mixers
    .. Mechanical, power requirements
    .. Pneumatic, (batch, continuous)
    .. Metering and monitoring flows and composition
    .. Methods for assessing mixing
- Liquids
    .. Points of addition, points for sampling (batch, continuous)
    .. Methods for assessing mixing

Mixing With a Gas:
- Fluidization (gas)
    - .. Bed expansion, bubbling, distributors
    - .. heat and mass transfer
- Feeders and distributors into gas systems

Mixing With a Liquid:
- Wetting into liquids
- Feeders and distributors into liquid systems
- Fluidization in liquids

Separation from a Gas Phase:
- Filters, cyclones, electrostatic, magnetic
- Grade efficiency curves
- Blockage, abrasion, fouling, bypass
- Series and parallel operation

Separation from a Liquid Phase:
- Sedimentation (batch, continuous), thickening, flocculation
- Centrifugation (batch, continuous), cake compression, washing
- Filters, cyclones, electrostatic, magnetic
- Selective flotation
- Selective extraction to a second liquid phase
    - .. Emulsion, coated wire/drum
- Selective capture on a solid surface
    - .. Second powder, wire, sheet

Separation from Solids of Differing Composition:
- By Size Classification
    - .. Screens, cyclones etc

Dispensing and Distributing Solids (on top of another phase)
- Sifters, sprayers, settlers, electro pinning
- Suspension coaters, spin coaters, electro coaters
- Adhesion strength, binders

6. **Thermal interactions in Particles:**
    - Radiant Energy Exchange at Dilute and Dense Loadings
    - Thermal Conduction in Packed Beds
    - Thermal Transfer from the Fluid Phase
    - Mixing Hot and Cold Particles
    - Wall - Bed Heaters (Screw, Plate)
    - Thermophoresis
    - Sintering, glass-crystal, melting, freezing, evapouration
    - Drying, condensation, adsorption, stripping

7. **Chemical Interactions in Particles:**

Particle-Solute Interaction
- Surface Chemistry
- Effect of the Surface on Attraction/Repulsion
- Surface Thermodynamics, Microcalorimetry
- Adsorption, Quantifying Its Rate and Extent
- Polymer Thermodynamics
- Entropy and Steric Effects
- Dispersants, Flocculants, Wetting Agents
- Cohesion, adhesion, impurity-diffusional sintering, agglomeration

Reactivity of Fine Powders
- Significance of large area and small particle separation
- Combustion
- Evaluation and control of dust explosion hazards
    .. Test methods
    .. Vent panels, crushable environment
    .. Inerting and suppression measures
- Evaluation and control of run-away slurry reactions
    .. Test methods
    .. Quenching and discharge to thin film area
- Tribocharging, mechanochemistry, optical trapping

Water - Very Special Stuff
- Gross, Loose, Wicked, Adsorbed, Bound
- Rheology as Moisture Increases (sand, silica spheres, Teflon fluff)
- Drying, dryer selection, case hardening
    .. Vacuum drying, phase displacement, supercritical

8. Mathematical Techniques for Particulate Systems
MATHEMATICAL TECHNIQUES: Modelling and Simulation Techniques
- CFD, DEM, FEM etc.
- Single particle physics (breakage)
- Bulk powder (compaction)
- Electrostatic interaction
- Scattering (light, sound)
- Chemical speciation and phase equilibria
- Polymer conformation statistics
- Slurry Rheology

9. Health, Safety, and Environmental Concerns
Health Implications of Particulates
- Inhalation
- Ingestion
- Adhesion effects
- Effects on the eye

Safety Implications of Particulates:
- Overflow due to excessive foaming
- Inoperative instrumentation due to sediment, foam, or dispersions
- Failure to flow due to high loading of particulates
- Valve, blade, and wall erosion
- Pipeline plugs from saltation or jamming
- Pressure buildup from screen or filter blinding
- Runaway thermal reactions and explosions

Environmental Implications of Particulates
- Albedo of the earth
- Penetration of light into the ocean
- Saltation
- Entropy and mineral resources
- Inactive dust impact on leaf and lung functions
- Spread and effect of toxic dusts (lead, etc.).
- Aerosol effect on greenhouse gases

10. Specific Applications of Particle Technology:

Specific Industrial Operations:
- Recovery of fines
- Water clarification
- Sewage treatment
- Coal combustion
- Pharmaceutical pill compaction
- Stack gas cleanup

Why Study Particle Science?

Some 75% of chemical manufacturing processes involve small solid particles (fine particles) at some point. Proper design and handling of these fine particles often makes the difference between success and failure. Careful attention to particle characteristics during the design and operation of a facility can significantly improve environmental performance and increase profitability by improving product yield and reducing waste.

In the early stages of product and process R and D, as the process is scaled-up from bench-top glassware to several-gallon, then hundred-gallon and finally production scale, technologists should explicitly consider how the particulate material in the system will behave in the sequence of unit operations and in the equipment for processing, storage, and transport.

For each particulate material - raw material, intermediate, final product or co-product consider the following:
- **Sampling and analysis:** To charactersize the particles, you need a good samling protocol, sound analytical procedures, and photographs that allow you to monitor the particles continuously on-line (best case) or through grab samples taken while trying to resolve a problem.
- **Size distribution:** The particle size distribution should be carefully controlled and consistent from batch to batch, or over time (in continuous reactors). It should be optimized to give the least trouble during processing and the best product characteristics.
- **Shape, state of aggregation, area:** The particle shape, state of aggregation and surface area per gram should be characterized after each key processing stage. Understanding and controlling the conditions that produce the particles can help you to optimize them for their intended use.

- **Flow, sedimentation, bed density:** Flow characteristics (powder or slurry), sedimentation rates (in liquid or gas), and bed density (shifted, settled, or packed) significantly affect processing, so you should characterize them and understand how changes in these parameters will affect the process.
- **Attrition:** Attrition resistance (resistance to breakage) should be known, well controlled and optimum for the task. Keep in mind that particle breakdown during processing can destroy carefully developed characteristics.
- **State of dispersion (in liquids):** Particles suspended in liquid may flocculate, agglomerate, float, fail to wet-in, foul the walls, or stabilize foam.
- **State of dispersion (in gases):** Particle suspended in gas may pick-up a charge, explode, form agglomerates, or coat the walls.
- **Safety, health, and environment:** It is prudent (and generally required) that you evaluate and minimize hazards related to explosion or fire (of a dust cloud or fluidized bed or pneumatic conveying line or dust buildup on equipment or walls) inhalation or contact with dusts or mists from the process discharge to the environment of dusts particles or sprays.

The study of particle technology has many interesting technical facets and many rewarding economic aspects. Failure to consider the particle science involved in a process can result in very expensive or unpleasant consequences.

1.1.1 Introduction and Classification of Mechanical – Physical Separation Processes

Introduction: In this book a group of separation processes will be considered where the separation is not accomplished on a molecular scale nor is it due to the differences among the various molecules. The separation will be accomplished using mechanical-physical forces and not molecular or chemical forces and diffusion. These mechanical-physical forces will be acting on particles, liquids or mixtures of particles and liquids themselves and not necessarily on the individual molecules. The mechanical-physical forces include gravitational and centrifugal, actual mechanical and kinetic forces arising from flow. Particles and/or fluid streams are separated because of the different effects produced on them by these forces.

Classification of Mechanical-Physical Separation Processes:
These mechanical-physical separation processes are considered under the following classifications. These separations are described in detail in this book in subsequent chapters.

(1) **Filtration:** The general problem of the separation of solid particles from liquids can be solved by using a wide variety of methods, depending on the type of solids, the proportion of solid to liquid in the mixture, viscosity of the solution and other factors. In filtration a pressure difference is set-up and causes the fluid to flow through small holes of a screen or cloth, which block the passage of the large solid particles, which, in turn, build-up on the cloth as a porous cake.

(2) **Settling and Sedimentation:** In settling and sedimentation, the particles are separated from the fluid by gravitational forces acting on the various size and density of the particles.

(3) **Centrifugal Settling and Sedimentation:** In centrifugal separations the particles are separated from the fluid by centrifugal forces acting on the various size and density particles. Two general types of separation processes are used. In the first type of process, centrifugal settling or sedimentation occurs.

(4) **Centrifugal Filtration:** In this second type of centrifugal separation process, centrifugal filtration occurs which is similar to ordinary filtration where a bed or cake of solids builds up on a screen, but centrifugal force is used to cause the flow instead of a pressure difference.

(5) **Mechanical Size Reduction and Separation:** In mechanical size reduction, the solid particles are broken mechanically into smaller particles and separated according to size.

1.1.2 Solid Processing Operations

Solid processing is a area that can cover a very wide range of processes. Processes could include:

particle sizing and shaping	crushing/grinding	catalytic reactors
flocculation	particle classification	settling
pastes	(separation by size)	agglomeration
packing and compassion	caking	drying
absorption/desorption	crystallization	digestion
mixing	separations	floatation
Brownian motion	fluidization	surface phenomena
leaching	filtration	ion exchange
theological applications	slurry flow	packed beds

Solids processing is an important part of industrial operations. In the chemical process industry roughly 60% of the products are particulate in form. When we add in products that at some intermediate step are in particulate form then 80 to 90% of all chemical processes used in industry require application of solids processing either directly or indirectly.

Partial List of Industries that Use Fluid/Particle Processes:

water conditioning	environmental clean-up
coal chemicals	glass industry
industrial carbon	phosphorous production
ceramics	potassium production
paints	nuclear industries
explosives and propellants	food and food processing
agriculture	sugar and starch
fermentation	wood chemicals
pulp and paper	plastics
synthetic fibres	rubber industries
petrochemicals	pharmaceuticals

List of Operations found in the Industrial Processes:

crushing and screening	oven bin
conveyor	storage bins
vibrating feeders	classifiers and screens
flotation cells	pebble mills
thickeners	filters
dryers	pneumatic conveying
grinding mills	slurry mixers
rotary kiln	dust collector
classifiers	cyclone separators
screw conveyors	cake washing
leaching	crystallizers
digesters	beaters
fourdrinier	

1.1.3 Solids/Liquid Separations

There are large varieties of separation equipment available to industry for Solid/Liquid separations. A frequent question is: *"Which is the right choice for my application"?* A number of authors have published selection guides to help the practicing engineers. Because of complexity an number of approaches have been developed.

There are four stages to solid-liquid separations. Not all of these stages are present in all processes. These stages are:

Pretreatment
Solids Concentration
Solids Separations
Post treatment

Pretreatment	To increase particle size, reduce viscosity.		
	CHEMICAL	PHYSICAL	
	coagulation	crystallization	
	flocculation	aging	
		freezing/heating	
		filter aid admix	
SOLIDS Concentration	To reduce the volume of material to process.		
	CLARIFICATION	THICKENING	
	gravity sedimentation	gravity sedimentation	
		cross-flow filtration	
		cyclones	
		periodic pressure filters	
SOLIDS SEPARATION	To separate the solids from the liquid; to form cakes of dry solids or to produce particulate free liquid.		
	CLARIFICATION	FILTRATION	CENTRIFUGATION
	granular bed	vacuum	sedimenting centrifuge
	precoat drum	gravity	filtering centrifuge
		pressure	cyclone
		expression	
POST TREATMENT	To remove solubles, remove moisture, reduce cake porosity, or prepare material for downstream processes.		
	PHYSICAL		
	washing		
	drying		
	repulsing		
	deliquoring		

The cost of solid/liquid separations is directly related to the volume of material that must be processed. Pressurized equipment such as pressure filters are more expensive to operate than thickeners, for example, hence, there is incentive to optimize the process by setting-up the equipment in series.

For example, suppose we have slurry feed that is 1% solids. You run this slurry through a thickener that concentrates it to 10% solids, followed by a filter centrifuge that filters is to 25% solids. The centrifuge is then used to deliquour the cake with a resulting cake of 50% solids. In each of these steps how much of the original slurry is processed and how much liquid is removed?

Basis: 100 unit volumes of slurry feed:

Step	Solids Volume %	Volume of Solids	Volume of Liquid in Mixture	Volume of Liquid Removed	% Liquid Removed From Feed	Volume of Mixture (After Treatment)
Feed	1	1	99	0	0	100
Thickener	10	1	9	90	90/99 = 90.9	10
Filter	25	1	3	6	6/99 = 6.1	4
Deliquoring	50	1	1	2	2/99 = 2.0	2

Hence, we can see that even though the thickener only concentrated the solids from 1 to 10%, 91% of the liquid was removed and the mixture yet to be treated was only 10% of the volume of the original feed. This is show in Figure 1.1.

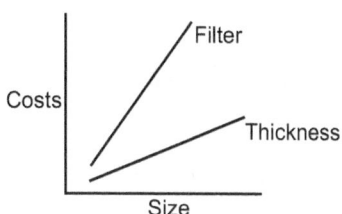

Fig. 1.1: Cost v/s Size diagram

1.1.4 Driving Forces Used to Separate Particles from Liquids

There are four primary driving forces that are used to separate particles from liquids. The choice of which method to use in any particular application must take into account many diverse factors. The following generalisations may be of assistance.

Gravity: Simple
              Low Operating Cost
              Very Bulky
              Still High Volume of Liquid After Separation

Vacuum: Vacuum is Easy to Produce
              Effective up to ΔP of about 0.8 atm
              Improved Rates Over Gravity
              Equipment is Simple, But Bulky and Expensive
              Compared to Pressure Filters, Output is Low
              Moisture Content of Cake May Be High
              Volatile Liquids Difficult to Handle

Pressure: Greater Output Per Unit Area
              Smaller Equipment, Low Cake Moisture Content
              Difficult to Continuously Discharge Cake
              Equipment is Expensive, High Operating Costs

Centrifugal:	Maximum Separating Forces (High-Gravity)
	Construction is simple for Cyclones:
	– Compact, Low Operating Costs
	– Efficiently Falls for Particles < 10 μm
Centrifuges:	Have Longer Residence Time:
	– More Efficient, Even for Fine Particles
	– High Throughputs
	– Low Residual Moisture
Other:	Sonic, Electrokinetic

1.2 Characterization of Solid Particles : Particle Shape and Size

Particle characterization:

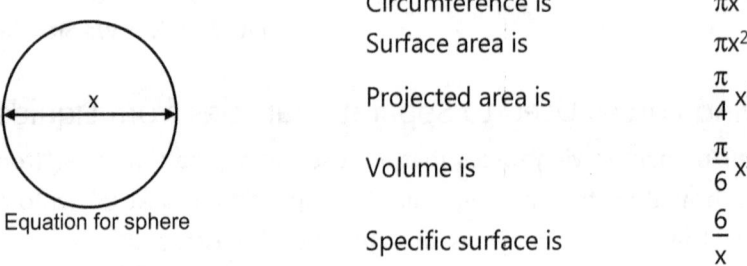

Circumference is	πx
Surface area is	πx^2
Projected area is	$\dfrac{\pi}{4} x^2$
Volume is	$\dfrac{\pi}{6} x^3$
Specific surface is	$\dfrac{6}{x}$

Equation for sphere

Fig. 1.2

An obvious question to ask is, 'What is the particle diameter of my powder?' However, the answer is not so simple. Firstly, most materials are highly irregular in shape, as can be seen in Fig. 1.2, where should one make the measurement? Also, if we turn a particle on its side it is likely that the measurement would be different. When we have to verbally provide this information to someone, who cannot see the particle, it becomes almost impossible to describe the particle simply. In engineering, we wish to perform calculations using the diameter; so, we need some simple basis for describing the irregularly shaped particle that can be used in communication and calculations. This is the origin of the concept of the equivalent spherical diameter, in which some physical property of the particle is related to a sphere that would have the same property. For example, the same volume. Volume is easily measured. If the particle is big enough, water displacement would work and the particle volume can be equated to the volume of a sphere. Note that we shall use diameter rather than radius and the symbol x rather than d. Also, it is common practice to talk about particle size, which really means particle diameter.

A sphere is a readily understood geometric shape and characterized by a single dimension: its diameter. Note that for the same particle, the equivalent spherical diameter depends upon the property selected for the equivalence. Unless, of course, the particle is spherical in shape. Hence, it is a sphere that all particles are related to and not some other simple geometric shape, for example, a cube. Even though we can relate a measured property of our particle to that of a sphere we should still consider particle shape, as it can have an important influence on processing requirements. One simple way to quantify shape is using Wadell's sphericity (ϕ).

$$\phi_S = \frac{\text{Surface area of sphere of equal volume to the particle}}{\text{Surface area of the particle}} \quad \ldots (1.1)$$

This uses the property that a sphere has the smallest surface area per unit volume of any shape. Hence, the value of sphericity will be fractional, or unity in the case of a sphere. There are a variety of accepted shape descriptors and some of these are provided in Table 1.1.

Table 1.1: Common Particle Shape Descriptions

Descriptor	Wadell's sphericity	Example
spherical	1.000	glass beads, calibration latex
rounded	0.82	water worn solids, atomised drops
cubic	0.806	sugar, calcite
angular	0.66	crushed minerals
flaky	0.54	gypsum, talc
platelet	0.22	clays, kaolin, mica, graphite

Table 1.2

Material	Sphericity, (ψ_s)
Sand (rounded)	0.83
Fused flue dust	0.89
Fused flue dust (aggregates)	0.55
Tungsten powder	0.89
Sand (angular)	0.73
Pulverised coal	0.73
Coal dust (upto 10 mm)	0.65
Flint sand (jagged flakes)	0.43
Mica flakes	0.28
Berl saddles	0.3 (average)
Raschig rings	0.3 (average)

Particle size analysis equipment is of fundamental importance in particle technology, as it provides the values used in the calculations. However, there are many different types of equipment and they typically provide equivalent spherical diameters based on: volume, projected area, chord length, area related to the light scattering properties of the particle, etc. A table of selected devices, the equivalent spherical diameter measured and links to appropriate images and descriptions are included in Table 1.3.

Table 1.3: Commonly Used Particle Size Analysis Equipment

Name	Equivalent spherical diameter	Example URL (www)
microscope	projected area	
sieve	mesh size	www.atmcorporation.com
Lasentec™ (particle chord length FBRM)	length	www.lasentec.com
Falvern™ (Fraunhofer diffraction)	area – light scattering properties	www.malvern.co.uk
Coulter Counter™ (electric zone sensing)	volume	www.beckman.com see Multisizer
Sedigraph™ and Andreasen pipette	sedimentation	www.micromeritics.com see Sedigraph

Size, shape and surface area are the most important properties of all the particulate systems. Properties of homogeneous solids have the same density as the bulk material. Particles obtained by breaking-up a composite solid, such as a metal-bearing ore, have various densities, usually different from the density of the bulk material. In case of solid particles size specification is very important. However, the characterization of the size is not as easy as it appears to be. This is because of irregular shapes. Also there is a distribution of sizes, with particle sizes as small as 0.1 mm and as large as 1 m or more. Size and shape are easily specified for regular particles such as spheres, cubes etc.

Particle Size:

In general, "diameters" may be specified for any equidimensional particle. Particles, which are not equidimensional, i.e., which are longer in one direction than in others, are often characterized by the *second* longest major dimensions. For needle like particles, for example, D_p would refer to the thickness of the particles, not their length. By convention, particle sizes are expressed in different units depending on the size range involved. Coarse particles are measured in inches or millimeters, fine particles in terms of screen size, very fine particles in micrometers. Ultrafine particles are sometimes described in terms of their surface area per unit mass, usually in m^2/gm.

More on Sphericity:
We represent a bed of non-spherical particles by a bed of spheres of diameter D_{eff} such that a bed of spheres and a bed of non-spheres have,

This representation would ensure almost the same flow resistance in both beds. In typical use of the Ergun Equation, the effective diameter of the particle is replaced with the sphericity times the defined diameter based on sphericity;

$$D_{eff} = \phi \, D_{sph} \quad \text{...(1.2)}$$

The specific surface area of particles in either bed is found to be

$$a_s = \left(\frac{\text{Surface area of one particle}}{\text{Volume of one particle}} \right)$$

$$= \frac{\pi D_{sph}^2 / \phi}{\pi D_{sph}^3 / 6}$$

$$= \frac{6}{\phi D_{sph}} \quad \text{...(1.3)}$$

For the whole bed:

$$a = \left(\frac{\text{Surface of all particles}}{\text{Total Volume of Particles in the Bed}} \right)$$

$$= \frac{6(1-\epsilon)}{\phi D_{sph}} \quad \text{...(1.4)}$$

Since there is no general relationship between D_{eff} and d_p (particle diameter corresponding to a sphere of the same volume), the best we can do without running experiments is as given on next page.

- ✓ The same total surface area, a in a given volume of the bed.
- ✓ The same fractional voidage, ϵ_{bed}.
- ✓ For irregular particles with no seemingly longer or shorter dimensions (hence isotropic in irregular shape).
$$D_{eff} = \phi \, D_{sph} = \phi d_p$$
- ✓ For irregular particles with one longer direction, but with a length ratio not greater than 2 : 1 (eggs for example)
$$D_{eff} = \phi D_{sph} = d_p$$

- ✓ For irregular particles with one dimension shorter, but with a length ratio not less than 1 : 2 (peanut, for example)

$$D_{eff} = \phi D_{sph} = \phi^2 D_p$$

- ✓ For very flat or needlelike particles, estimate the relationship between d_p and D_{eff} from ϕ values for corresponding disks and cylinders.

1.3 Classification of Solid Materials

1.3.1 Introduction

Solid materials are involved in a great many chemical process. Most primary feedstocks other than oil, water and air are dug out of the ground as solids. Catalysts and materials such as molecular sieves, other absorbent materials and filter aids are solids. Many products are produced as dry powders, granules, pastes or slurries, all involve solids.

The nature of solid materials makes analysis of their behaviour much more difficult than the equivalent analysis of fluids. The basic problem is the non-homogeneity of particulate solids. It is very unusual to find a solid material where all the particles are the same size and shape; extruded and shaped polymers and some supported catalysts are perhaps the closest approximations to uniformity in solids commonly met in the process industries.

The characterization of a particulate solid material is the first step in defining how it can be processed and transported. A fluid can be defined by a reasonably small set of properties for example, for fluid flow calculations density and viscosity are often sufficient to define the fluid's behaviour. Other properties relevant to heat and mass transfer, solubility etc. are usually defined by the chemical composition of the fluid. For a solid material however, the physical characteristics i.e. size and shape may be equally as important as its chemical composition. The possibility of different forms of chemically similar materials can also complicate estimation of the solid's properties.

1.3.2 Particle Size and Shape

1.3.2.1 Particle Shape

Aside from physical form of the solid the two important factors, which must be defined for a solid material, are size and shape. These are related since in order to define a size one has to make some assumption about shape. For some shapes there is a single measurement, which completely defines the particle, for example, if the diameter of a sphere or side length of a cube is known the volume and surface area may be uniquely calculated. For other shapes more than one measurement is required; cylinders require two, diameter and length; cuboids require length, breadth and depth. For irregular shapes some 'typical' dimension must be defined.

The simplest three-dimensional shape is the sphere. The shape of solid particles is often described by their *Sphericity*, Φ, i.e. how similar they are to spheres. For spheres Φ is equal to 1, for non-spherical particles sphericity is defined as:

$$\Phi = \frac{6v_p}{D_p s_p} \qquad \ldots (1.5)$$

where, D_p is the equivalent diameter or nominal diameter of particle
s_p is the surface area of the particle
v_p is the volume of the particle

Some typical sphericities are shown in Table 1.4. This does not help very much since a particle diameter is still required. The equivalent diameter of a particle is sometimes defined as the diameter of a spherical particle with the same volume, the same surface area or the same ratio of volume to surface area. Strictly, in the definition of above the diameter, D_p, is the diameter of a sphere with the same volume as the particle. This definition then gives the sphericity as,

$$\Phi = \frac{\text{Surface area of sphere of same volume as particle}}{\text{Surface area of particle}}$$

However, it is generally difficult to measure exact volumes and surface areas of individual particles and often D_p is determined by microscopic examination or screen analysis. It is possible to determine the total volume and surface area of a sample of a particulate material and these measurements, with the some mean diameter of the material can be use in [1.5] to determine Φ. Mean diameter are discussed later.

The term 'diameter' is normally used for particles, which are roughly equidimensional, for those which are non-equidimensional, i.e. those which are longer in one direction than in the others, the *second* largest dimension may be used. Needle-shaped particles would be characterized by the thickness of the particle, not its length. This relates to sieve analysis where particles will pass only through meshes of size equal to their second largest dimension or greater.

Table 1.4: Sphericity of Some Materials

Material	Sphericity	Material	Sphericity
Spheres, cubes	1.0	Ottawa sand	0.95
Cylinders (L = D_p)	1.0	Rounded sand	0.83
Raschig rings (L = D_p)	1.0	Coal Dust	0.73
L = D_o, D_i = 0.5 D_o	0.58	Flint sand	0.65
L = D_o, D_i = 0.75 D_o	0.33	Crushed glass	0.65
Berl saddles	0.3	Mica flakes	0.28

Particle sizes are given in millimeters for large particles, either micrometers (microns, 10^{-6} m) or standard screen size for fine particles and microns or nanometers (10^{-9} m) for very fine particles.

1.3.3 Size Distributions

As mentioned before it is most unusual to find a particulate material where all the particles are the same size, there is almost always a distribution of sizes within the material. This is often represented by a histogram, where the area of the bar on a histogram represents the fraction of particles within a range of sizes. The fraction may be a weight fraction or a number fraction, depending on the measurement method. Another common representation of the distribution is the *cumulative curve*, this is produced by adding successive fractions to give the total fraction below a size and plotting these values. This would be an *undersize curve*. An *oversize curve* is produced when the fractions are successively subtracted from 1.

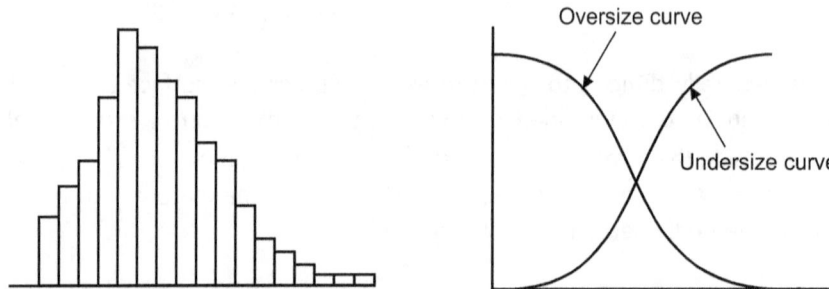

Fig. 1.3: Size Distribution Histogram and Over-and Undersize Curves

The particle size distribution may be described mathematically by a *frequency function* f(d) where the number of particles or (more usually) the number of fraction particles in a sample between sizes d and d + d(d) is given by f(d) d(d). A smooth curve drawn through the points on the histogram would approximate this frequency function. The histogram is in fact a discrete approximation to this function i.e. the number fraction of particles between sizes d and d + Δd is approximated by Δ(d) Δd so that:

f(d) ≃ height of histogram column/Δd.

The sum of the fractions must always sum to unity,

$$\int_0^\infty f(d)\, d(d) = 1 \qquad \ldots (1.6)$$

We can also define a function O(d), the fraction of particles with size greater than d, and U(d) the fraction of particles with size smaller than d:

$$O(d) = \int_{d}^{\infty} f(d)\, d(d) \qquad \ldots (1.7)$$

$$U(d) = \int_{0}^{d} f(d)\, d(d) \qquad \ldots (1.8)$$

So that,

$$f(d) = \frac{d}{d(d)} U(d) = -\frac{d}{d(d)} O(d) \qquad \ldots (1.9)$$

1.3.4 Mean Particle Sizes

It is useful to be able to define a *mean diameter* to characterise the material, this mean diameter can be defined in several ways. The most common mean diameters are: Linear Mean Diameter, Area Mean Diameter, Volume Mean Diameter and Surface Volume Mean Diameter. The linear mean diameter $\bar{d}_L$ (which is often known simply as $\bar{d}$) is given by:

$$\bar{d}_L = \frac{\text{Total sum of all particles diameters}}{\text{Total number of particles}} \qquad \ldots (1.10)$$

$$\bar{d}_L = \frac{\int_{0}^{\infty} (\text{Diameter} \times \text{Number of particles with diameter d})\, d(d)}{\text{Total number of particles}}$$

So, remembering that f(d) is defined in terms of number fraction.

$$\bar{d}_L = \int_{d=0}^{\infty} d\, f(d)\, d(d) \qquad \ldots (1.11)$$

This is usually the simplest mean diameter to calculate from size analysis data. To calculate the area and volume mean diameters we must define two shape factors:
ψ_V is a shape factor such that

$$\text{Volume of particle} = \psi_V\, d^3 \qquad \ldots (1.12)$$

Similarly, another shape factor ψ_A can be defined such that

$$\text{Surface area of particle} = \psi_A\, d^2 \qquad \ldots (1.13)$$

The area mean diameter $\bar{d}_A$ is found from:

$$\psi_A \bar{d}_a^2 = \int_{d=0}^{\infty} \psi_A d^2 f(d)\, d(d) \qquad \ldots (1.14)$$

Assuming that ψ_A is not a function of size then:

$$\bar{d}_A = \left\{ \int_{d=0}^{\infty} d^2 f(d)\, d(d) \right\}^{\frac{1}{2}} \qquad \ldots (1.15)$$

Similarly, the volume mean diameter $\bar{d}_V$ is given by:

$$\bar{d}_V = \left\{ \int_{d=0}^{\infty} d^3 f(d)\, d(d) \right\}^{\frac{1}{3}} \qquad \ldots (1.16)$$

Finally, the surface-volume mean diameter $\bar{d}_{VS}$ is given by:

$$\bar{d}_{VS} = \frac{\int_{d=0}^{\infty} d^3 f(d)\, d(d)}{\int_{d=0}^{\infty} d^2 f(d)\, d(d)} \qquad \ldots (1.17)$$

The surface-volume mean diameter is important in processes such as dissolution, crystallization and solid-fluid reactions.

The mean diameters are defined above for continuous functions, however, size distribution data is usually in discrete form, i.e. as a series of weight fractions w_i in size ranges with mean size d_i. For a sample of total mass M the mean diameters may be calculated as follows, where the shape factors and particle density, are assumed to be constant for all sizes of particle:

By definition:

$\psi_A \bar{d}_A^2 \times$ Number of particles in sample = Total surface area in sample and

Total surface area = $\sum_i$ surface area in range i

$= \sum_i$ number of particles in range i $\times \psi_A d_i^2$

$$= \sum_i \frac{\text{Mass in range}}{\text{Mass of 1 particle}} \times \psi_A d_i^2$$

$$= \sum_i \frac{Mw_i}{\rho \psi_v d_i^3} \times \psi d_i^2$$

So, Total surface area $= \dfrac{M\psi_A}{\rho \psi_v} \sum \dfrac{w_i}{d_i}$ ... (1.18)

Total number of particles in sample $= \sum_i \dfrac{Mw_i}{\rho \psi_v d_i^3}$

Total surface area in sample $= \psi_A \bar{d}_A^2 \sum \dfrac{Mw_i}{\rho \psi_v d_i^3}$ ... (1.19)

Equating (1.18) and (1.19) gives

$$\psi_A \bar{d}_A^2 \frac{M}{\rho \psi_v} \sum \frac{w_i}{d_i^3} = \frac{M\psi_A}{\rho \psi_v} \sum \frac{w_i}{d_i}$$

$$\bar{d}_A = \left\{ \frac{\sum_i w_i/d_i}{\sum_i w_i/d_i^3} \right\}$$

Similarly,

$$\bar{d}_L = \frac{\sum w_i/d_i^2}{\sum w_i/d_i^3} \qquad \ldots (1.20)$$

$$\bar{d}_V = \left\{ \frac{\sum w_i}{\sum w_i/d_i^3} \right\}^{\frac{1}{3}} \qquad \ldots (1.21)$$

$$\bar{d}_V S = \frac{\sum w_i}{\sum w_i/d_i} \qquad \ldots (1.22)$$

1.3.5 Particle Size Measurement Methods

Other Methods:

(1) Coulter Counter:

In this type of machine the powder is suspended in an electrolyte solution. This suspension is then made to flow through a short insulated capillary section between two electrodes and the resistance of the system is measured. When a particle passes through the capillary there is a momentary peak in the resistance, the amplitude of the peak is proportional to the particle size. Counting is done by a computer.

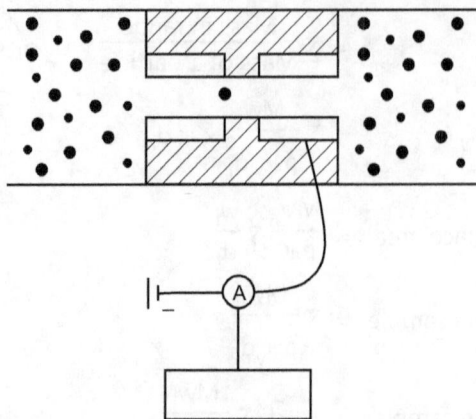

Fig. 1.4: Coulter Counter

(2) Laser Beam Diffraction Methods:
One of the most common classes of size measurement equipment used now is that using laser diffraction measurement. The material is suspended in a suitable liquid; the difference in refractive index between the liquid and the solid should be as great as possible. A laser beam is then passed through the suspension. The pattern of fringes produced by the suspended solids can be analyzed to produce a size distribution for the material.

Comparison of Different Methods:
The method used to determine size distribution will depend on many factors; the coarseness of the material, the precision required, time available, equipment available. One thing, which is important to remember, is that in most cases size distributions are not reproducible using different techniques. Thus sieve analysis will not produce the same mean particle diameter as a Coulter counter. This is partly due to the different methods measuring different types of diameter (see above). Some devices will calculate distributions based on area, volume etc. which can aid comparisons. However in general only measurements using the same equipment should be compared directly.

The method used will also depend on the purpose of the measurement, for example, sometimes the amount of under or oversize in a sample is important, in which case a single sieve may give the required information.

1.3.5.1 Microscopic Examination
The simplest method of determining the size distribution of a sample of particulate material is to measure the sizes of a large number of individual particles. This can be done using a microscopic and graticule, but it is extremely tedious when done by hand. Computer techniques exist which automate the process so that it is practical. Even so only a relatively small number of particles can be analysed in this way.

1.3.5.2 Sieve Analysis

Probably, the most common method of particle-sized analysis used is sieve analysis. Standardised sieves are available to cover a wide range of sizes. These sieves are generally round and designed to sit in a stack so that material falls through smaller and smaller meshes until it reaches a mesh, which is too fine for it to pass through. The stack of sieves is mechanically shaken or tapped to promote the passage of the solids. The finest material is caught in an unperforated pan at the bottom of the stack. The fraction of the material between pairs of sieve sizes is determined by weighing the residue on each sieve.

When carrying out sieve analysis, it is important to maintain a standard method. The result achieved will depend on the duration of the agitation and the manner of the agitation. Care is needed when collecting the fractions from the sieves that the meshes are not damaged by rough handling.

There are four sets of standard sieves: USS and Tyler in the USA, IMM and BSS in the UK. Tyler is the most comprehensive, successive meshes vary by a factor $4\sqrt{2}$. This is usually too fine a division for practical purposes so only every other sieve is used.

1.3.5.3 Methods based on Differential Terminal Velocity

Different sizes of particle settle at different terminal velocities, this phenomenon can be used in several ways to determine the size distribution of a sample. The terminal velocity of particle can be calculated by equating the gravitational and drag forces acting on it. It is assumed that the particles are all of equal density and that they are spherical. The gravitational force is,

$$= \frac{\pi}{6} d^3 (\rho_s - \rho_f) g \qquad \ldots (1.23)$$

where, d is the particle diameter
ρ_s is the solid density.
ρ_f is the fluid density.

According to Stoke's Law the drag force is given by:

$$3\pi\mu d v \qquad \ldots (1.24)$$

where, μ is the viscosity of the fluid.
v is the velocity of the particle relative to the fluid.

Equating these gives the following expression for the terminal velocity of the particle:

$$v = v_t = \frac{d^2}{18\mu} (\rho_s - \rho_f) g \qquad \ldots (1.25)$$

Thus, the terminal velocity of the particle is proportional to the squares of its diameter (i.e. to its projected area).

There are two basic techniques of size measurement based on the relationship between terminal velocity and diameter. Differential settling methods allow the particle to fall through a fluid (usually a liquid), while elutriation methods blow the fluid up through the particles, the size of particles leaving with the fluid depends on the fluid velocity.

There are several specific pieces of apparatus, which use this principle; two of the best known are the Andreasen Pipette and the Air Elutriator.

1.3.5.4 The Gamma Distribution

A much better approximation is given by the *Gamma Function* size distribution, given by:
$$f(d) = a d^m e^{-bd} \qquad \ldots (1.26)$$

Remembering that
$$\int_0^\infty f(d)\, d(d) = 1 \qquad \ldots (1.27)$$

and that the gamma function is defined by:
$$\Gamma(m+1) = \int_0^\infty x^m e^{-x}\, dx \qquad \ldots (1.28)$$

gives the constant a equal to $b^{m+1}/\Gamma(m+1)$. The gamma function then only depends on two parameters, b and m. At the most common diameter d_{max}, i.e. the maximum of the curve (where there is a clear maximum), we can put,
$$\frac{df(d)}{d(d)} = 0 \qquad \ldots (1.29)$$

which gives,
$$d_{max} = \frac{m}{b} \qquad \ldots (1.30)$$

If we can now evaluate m, the distribution will be completely defined. It is possible to evaluate m by plotting log f(d) against log d. This graph tends to a straight line with gradient m at small d. This property is useful for determining m and also for estimating the frequency at very small diameters from experimental data for larger particles. The fit is best for freshly ground particles. The value of m gives an idea of how 'flat' the distribution is, the greater the value of m, the sharper the peak in the distribution.

The gamma distribution has some further useful properties:
$$\bar{d} = \frac{a\Gamma(m+2)}{b^{(m+2)}} = \frac{1}{b}\frac{\Gamma(m+2)}{\Gamma(m+1)} = \frac{m+1}{b} \qquad \ldots (1.31)$$

(For integers $\Gamma(m + 1) = m\Gamma(m)$ i.e. $\Gamma(m) = (m - 1)!$)

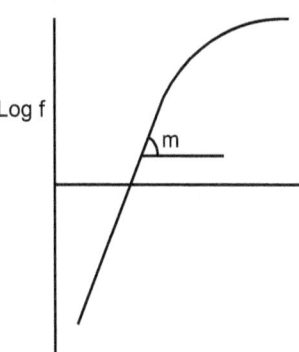

Fig. 1.5: f(d) vs. d

More on the derivation of the expressions for most common size, constant a and the mean diameter is given here as below.

1.3.5.5 Gamma Distribution Maths

(a) Maximum of Distribution

$$f(d) = ad^m e^{-bd}$$

$$\frac{df(d)}{d(d)} = mad^{(m-1)} e^{-bd} - bad^m e^{-bd} \qquad \ldots (1.32)$$

At the maximum $\dfrac{df(d)}{d(d)} = 0$

$$mad^{(m-1)} e^{-bd} = bad^m e^{-bd}$$

$$\frac{m}{b} = \frac{d^m}{d^{(m-1)}} = d \qquad \ldots (1.33)$$

(b) Value of a

$$f(d) = ad^m e^{-bd} \qquad \ldots (1.34)$$

$$\int_0^\infty f(d)\, d(d) = 1 = \int_0^\infty ad^m e^{-bd}\, d(d)$$

Using the substitution $x = bd$ gives

$$\frac{dx}{d(d)} = b \text{ and } d(d) = \frac{dx}{b}$$

$$1 = a \int_0^\infty d^m e^{-bd}\, d(d) = a \int_0^\infty \left(\frac{x}{b}\right)^m e^{-x} \frac{dx}{b}$$

$$1 = \frac{a}{b^{m+1}} \int_0^\infty x^m e^{-x} dx = \frac{a}{b^{m+1}} \Gamma(m+1)$$

$$a = \frac{b^{m+1}}{\Gamma(m+1)} \qquad \ldots (1.35)$$

(c) Mean diameter value

$$\bar{d} = \int_0^\infty d f(d)\, d(d) = \int_0^\infty a d^{m+1} e^{-bd}\, d(d)$$

$$\bar{d} = a \int_0^\infty \left(\frac{x}{b}\right)^{m+1} e^{-x} \frac{dx}{b} \quad \text{where, } x = bd$$

$$\bar{d} = \frac{a}{b^{m+2}} \int_0^\infty x^{m+1} e^{-x} dx$$

$$\bar{d} = \frac{a}{b^{m+2}} \Gamma(m+2) \quad \text{but } a = \frac{b^{m+1}}{\Gamma(m+1)}$$

$$\bar{d} = \frac{b^{m+1}}{\Gamma(m+1)} \cdot \frac{\Gamma(m+2)}{b^{m+2}}$$

$$\bar{d} = \frac{\Gamma(m+2)}{b\,\Gamma(m+1)} = \frac{m+1}{b} \qquad \ldots (1.36)$$

1.3.5.6 Log-Normal Distribution

The other commonly used distribution is the Log-Normal Distribution given by:

$$f(d) = \frac{1}{d S_G \sqrt{2\pi}} \exp\left\{-\frac{(\log d - \log d_{GM})^2}{2 S_G}\right\} \qquad \ldots (1.37)$$

where, d_{GM} is the geometric mean diameter.
and S_G is the geometric standard deviation.

This approximation is used in size reduction calculations. When $U(d)$ is plotted against d, with $U(d)$ on a probability scale and d on a logarithmic scale a straight line is produced. (On a probability scale the distance from 50% is proportional to $\int_0^\infty e^{-x^2} dx$). The standard deviation S_G of the distribution is given by:

$$S_G = \frac{d_{84.1}}{d_{50}} = \frac{d_{50}}{d_{15.9}} \qquad \ldots (1.38)$$

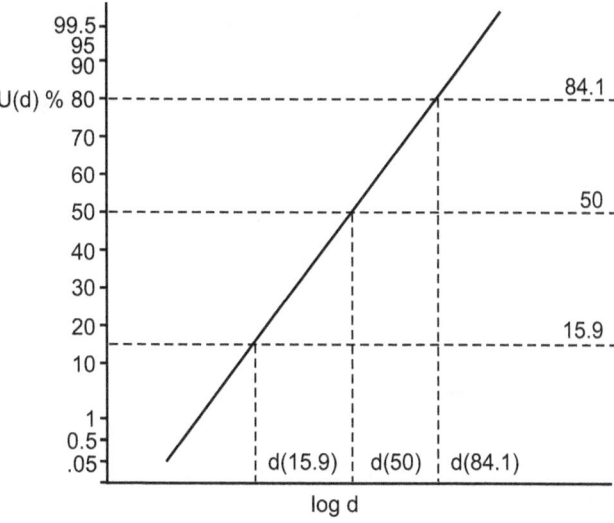

Fig. 1.6

1.4 Screen Analysis : Cumulative and Differential

1.4.1 Differential Screen Analysis

Information from a particle size analysis is tabulated to show the mass or number fraction in each size increment as a function of the average particle size (or size range) in the increment. An analysis tabulated in this way is called as a *differential analysis*. The results are often presented as a *histogram* as shown in Fig. 1.7 (a), with a continuous curve like the dashed line used to approximate the distribution.

1.4.2 Cumulative Screen Analysis

A second method to present the information is through *cumulative analysis* obtained by adding, consecutively, the individual increments, starting with that containing the smallest

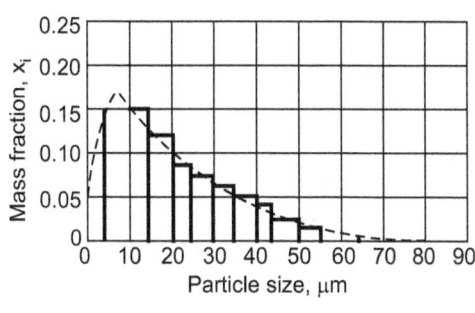

(a) Differential analysis

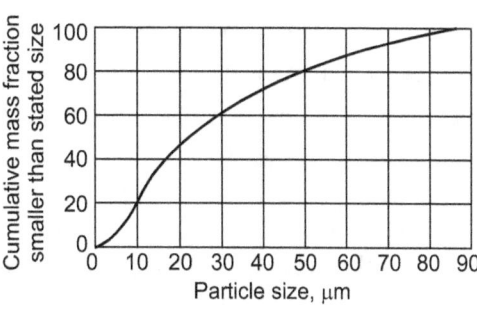

(b) Cumulative analysis

Fig. 1.7: Mass Fraction, x_i: Particle Distribution for Powder

particles, and tabulating or plotting the cumulative sums against the maximum particle diameter in the increment. In a cumulative analysis the data may appropriately be represented by a continuous curve. Fig. 1.7 (b) is a cumulative-analysis plot of the distribution shown in Fig. 1.7 (b).

Calculation of average particle size, specific surface area or particle population of a mixture may be based on either a differential or cumulative analysis. In principle, methods based on the cumulative analysis are more precise than those based on the differential analysis, since when the cumulative analysis is used, the assumption that all particles in a single fraction are equal in size is not needed. The accuracy of particle-size measurements, however, is rarely accurate enough to warrant the use of the cumulative analysis, and calculations are always based on the differential analysis.

1.4.3 General Procedure for Screen Analysis

To perform screen analysis, a set of standard screens are arranged serially in a stack, with the smallest mesh at bottom and largest at the top. The sample is placed on the top screen and then the stack is shaken mechanically for a definite time, usually 20 min. The particles retained on each screen are removed and weighted and the masses of the individual screen increments are converted to mass fractions or mass percentages of the total sample. Any particle that pass the finest screen are caught in a pan at the bottom of the stack.

The results of a screen analysis are tabulated to show the mass fraction of each increment as a function of the mesh size range of the increment. Since the particles on any one screen are passed by the screen immediately ahead of it, two numbers are needed to specify the size range of an increment, one for the screen through which the fraction passes and other one which it is retained. Thus, the notation 14/20 mean "through 14 mesh and on 20 mesh". (Sometimes the notation −14 + 20 may be employed).

1.4.4 Methods of Reporting Screen Analysis

The screen analysis is reported in tabular form or a graph or alternatively in the form of appropriate distribution equations. A typical screen analysis is shown in Table 1.5.

Table 1.5: Screen Analysis

Mesh	Screen Opening D_{pi}, mm	Mass Fraction Retained, x_i	Average Particle Diameter in Increment, $\bar{D}_{pi}$, mm	Cumulative fraction smaller than D_{pi}
4	4.699	0.0000	–	1.0000
6	3.327	0.0251	4.013	0.9749
8	2.362	0.1250	2.85	0.8499
10	1.651	0.3207	2.007	0.5292
14	1.168	0.2570	1.409	0.2722
20	0.833	0.1590	1.001	0.1132
28	0.589	0.0538	0.711	0.0594
35	0.417	0.0210	0.503	0.0384
48	0.295	0.0102	0.356	0.0282
65	0.208	0.0077	0.252	0.0205
100	0.147	0.0058	0.178	0.0147
150	0.104	0.0041	0.126	0.0106
200	0.074	0.0031	0.089	0.0075
Pan	–	0.0075	0.037	0.0000

As the range of particle sizes covered different from increment to increment, a differential plot of the data in the columns 2 and 3 of Table 1.5 gives a wrong impression of the particle-size distribution. A typical differential screen analysis is shown in Fig. 1.7 (a) and (b). Cumulative plots are made from results shown columns 2 and 5 of Table 1.5. When the overall range of particle size is large, such plots show the diameter on a logarithmic scale. A semilogarithmic cumulative plot of the analysis shown in Table 1.5 is given in Fig. 1.8.

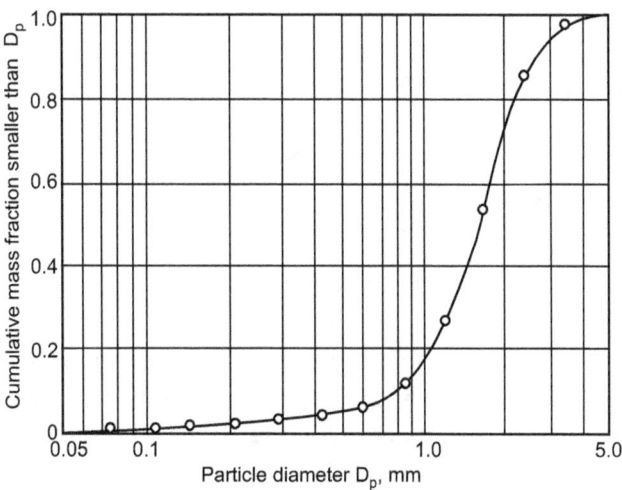

Fig. 1.8: Cumulative Screen Analysis

Cumulative plots may also be made on logarithmic probability paper on which the abscissa scale is divided as per Gaussian probability distribution.

1.4.5 Size Distribution Equations

The usual statistical distribution functions do not apply to one distribution of particle sizes. Following simple distribution equations have been proposed and are widely used.

(i) Gates – Gaudian – Schumann Equation:

$$Y = 100 \left(\frac{x}{k}\right)^m \quad \ldots (1.39)$$

where, Y = The cumulative weight percent undersize
x = Particle size
k = Size modulus k is that size for which Y = 100
i.e. it represents the size of the coarest particle
m = Distribution modulus.

It increases with closeness of size range.

(ii) Rosin – Rammler Equation:

$$Y = 1 - e^{-bx^n} \quad \ldots (1.40)$$

where, b and n are characteristic terms. This equation applies in the coarser size range. Note that the above equations give Y as a function of particle size x and are easier to handle.

1.5 Specific Surface of Mixture

In a sample of uniform particles of diameter D_p, the total volume of particles is m/ρ_p, where, m is mass of sample, ρ_p is density. Since the volume of one particle is V_p, the total number of particles in the sample is,

(1) Number of particles in the sample N:

$$N = \frac{m}{\rho_p V_p} \quad \ldots (1.41)$$

(2) The total surface area of the particles:

$$A = N S_p = \frac{6m}{\phi_s \rho_p D_p} \quad \ldots (1.42)$$

To apply the above two equations to mixtures of particles having various size and densities, the mixture is sorted into fractions, each of constant density and approximately constant size. If the particle density ρ_p and sphericity ϕ_s are known, the surface area of particles in each fraction may be calculated from equation (1.42) and the results for all fractions added to give A_W, *the specific surface* area A_W (the total surface area of a unit mass of particle).

If ρ_P and ϕ_S are constant, Aw is given by:

$$A_W = \frac{6x_1}{\phi_S \rho_P D_{P_1}} + \frac{6x_2}{\phi_S \rho_P D_{P_2}} + \cdots \frac{6x_n}{\phi_S \rho_P D_{P_m}}$$

$$= \frac{6}{\phi_S \rho_P} \sum_{i=1}^{n} \frac{x_i}{\overline{D}_{P_i}} \qquad \ldots (1.43)$$

Where, subscripts = individual increments
x_i = mass fraction in a given increment
n = number of increments
$\overline{D}_{P_i}$ = Average particle diameter, taken as arithmetic average of smallest and largest particle diameters in increment.

1.5.1 Average Particle Size

(a) Volume-surface mean diameter ($\overline{D}_S$): The average particle size for a mixture of particles is defined in several ways. The most widely used is *volume-surface mean diameter*, ($\overline{D}_S$), which is related to the specific surface area Aw. It is defined by equation:

$$\overline{D}_S = \frac{6}{\phi_S A_W \rho_P} \qquad \ldots (1.44)$$

Substitution from equation (1.43) in equation (1.44), gives,

$$\overline{D}_S = \frac{1}{\sum_{i=1}^{n} \left(\frac{x_i}{\overline{D}_{P_i}}\right)} \qquad \ldots (1.45)$$

(b) Arithmetic Mean Diameter ($\overline{D}_N$):

$$\overline{D}_N = \frac{\sum_{i=1}^{n} N_i \overline{D}_{P_i}}{\sum_{i=1}^{n} N_i} = \frac{\sum_{i=1}^{n} N_i \overline{D}_{P_i}}{N_T} \qquad \ldots (1.46)$$

Where N_T = Number of particles in the entire sample.

(c) Mass Mean Diameter ($\overline{D}_W$):

$$\overline{D}_W = \sum_{i=1}^{n} x_i \overline{D}_{P_i} \qquad \ldots (1.47)$$

(d) Volume Mean Diameter ($\bar{D}_V$):

$$\bar{D}_V = \left[\frac{1}{\sum_{i=1}^{n} \frac{x_i}{D_{P_i}^3}} \right]^{1/3} \qquad \ldots (1.48)$$

1.5.2 Number of Particle in a Mixture

For a given particle shape, the volume of any particle is proportional to its "diameter" cubed.

or
$$v_p = a D_p^3 \qquad \ldots (1.49)$$

Where, a = Volume shape factor.

Assume that 'a' is independent of size, then,

$$N_W = \frac{1}{a\rho_P} \sum_{i=1}^{n} \frac{x_i}{D_{P_i}^3} = \frac{1}{a\rho_P \bar{D}_V^3} \qquad \ldots (1.50)$$

1.6 Standard Screen Series

It has been the custom in the past to specify screens merely by the number of meshes per linear inch. Thus, a screen analysis may show the weight-percentage of the material that passes through 10 mesh and remains on 20 mesh, through 20 and on 30, through 30 and on 40 etc. Such a presentation is absolutely meaningless and should not be used unless the screens themselves are specified. The reason for this is that wire cloth with any given number of meshes per inch is made with a wide variety of wire diameters and as the wire diameter varies the clear aperture of the screens. This is shown in Table 1.6. This shows how meaningless such a specification as "30 mesh screen" may be, and it also shows how, by choice of wire diameter screen from 20 to 35 meshes per inch are made with nearly the same clear openings.

Table 1.6: Variations of Screen Openings with Mesh and Wire Diameter

Mesh	Wire Diameter, in.	Clear Opening in.
30	0.017	0.0163
30	0.014	0.0193
30	0.012	0.0213
30	0.010	0.0233
30	0.008	0.0253
20	0.032	0.0180
22	0.028	0.0175
26	0.020	0.0185
28	0.018	0.0177
30	0.015	0.0183
35	0.011	0.0176

To overcome this situation various standard screen scales have been proposed, in which both the diameter of the wire and number of meshes per inch are specified so as to give a definite ratio between the openings in one screen and the next succeeding screen in the series.

Table 1.7: Tyler Standard Screen Scale

Sieve Opening		Nominal Wire Diameter		Tyler Equivalent Designation
mm	inch. (approximately equivalents)	mm	inch. (approximately equivalents)	
26.9	1.06	3.90	0.1535	1.050 in.
25.4	1.00	3.80	0.1496	
22.6	0.875	3.50	0.1378	0.883 in.
19.0	0.750	3.30	0.1299	0.742 in.
16.0	0.625	3.00	0.1181	0.624 in.
13.5	0.530	2.75	0.1083	0.525 in.
12.7	0.500	2.67	0.1051	
11.2	0.438	2.45	0.0965	0.441 in.
9.51	0.375	2.27	0.0894	0.371 in.
8.00	0.312	2.07	0.0815	2 1/2 mesh
6.73	0.265	1.87	0.0736	3 mesh
6.35	0.250	1.82	0.0717	
5.66	0.223	1.68	0.0661	3 1/2 mesh
4.76	0.187	1.54	0.0606	4 mesh
4.00	0.157	1.37	0.0539	5 mesh
3.36	0.132	1.23	0.0484	6 mesh
2.83	0.111	1.10	0.0430	7 mesh
2.38	0.0937	1.00	0.0394	8 mesh
2.00	0.0787	0.900	0.0354	9 mesh
1.68	0.0661	0.810	0.0319	10 mesh
1.41	0.0555	0.725	0.0285	12 mesh
1.19	0.0469	0.650	0.0256	14 mesh
1.00	0.0394	0.580	0.0228	16 mesh
0.841	0.0331	0.510	0.0201	20 mesh
0.707	0.0278	0.450	0.0177	24 mesh
0.595	0.0234	0.390	0.0154	28 mesh
0.500	0.0197	0.340	0.0134	32 mesh
0.420	0.0165	0.290	0.0114	35 mesh
0.354	0.0139	0.247	0.0097	42 mesh
0.297	0.0117	0.215	0.0085	48 mesh
0.250	0.0098	0.180	0.0071	60 mesh
0.210	0.0083	0.152	0.0060	65 mesh

Sieve Opening		Nominal Wire Diameter		Tyler Equivalent Designation
mm	inch. (approximately equivalents)	mm	inch. (approximately equivalents)	
0.177	0.0070	0.131	0.0052	80 mesh
0.149	0.0059	0.110	0.0043	100 mesh
0.125	0.0049	0.091	0.0036	115 mesh
0.105	0.0041	0.076	0.0030	150 mesh
0.088	0.0035	0.064	0.0025	170 mesh
0.074	0.0029	0.053	0.0021	200 mesh
0.063	0.0025	0.044	0.0017	250 mesh
0.053	0.0021	0.037	0.0015	270 mesh
0.044	0.0017	0.030	0.0012	325 mesh
0.037	0.0015	0.025	0.0010	400 mesh

Table 1.8: Comparison Table of Standard Sieve Series

U.S.A. Aperture	Mesh No.	Tyler Mesh No.	British Aperture	Mesh No.
4.75 mm	4	4	–	–
4.00 mm	5	5	–	–
3.35 mm	6	6	3.35 mm	5
2.80 mm	7	7	2.80 mm	6
2.36 mm	8	8	2.40 mm	7
2.00 mm	10	9	2.00 mm	8
1.70 mm	12	10	1.68 mm	10
1.40 mm	14	12	1.40 mm	12
1.18 mm	16	14	1.20 mm	14
1.00 mm	18	16	1.00 mm	16
850 µm	20	20	850 µm	18
710 µm	25	24	710 µm	22
600 µm	30	28	600 µm	25
500 µm	35	32	500 µm	30
425 µm	40	35	420 µm	36
355 µm	45	42	355 µm	44
300 µm	50	48	300 µm	52
250 µm	60	60	250 µm	60
212 µm	70	65	210 µm	72
180 µm	80	80	180 µm	85
150 µm	100	100	150 µm	100
126 µm	120	115	125 µm	120
106 µm	140	150	105 µm	150
90 µm	170	170	90 µm	170

U.S.A. Aperture	Mesh No.	Tyler Mesh No.	British Aperture	Mesh No.
75 µm	200	200	75 µm	200
63 µm	230	250	63 µm	240
53 µm	270	270	53 µm	300
45 µm	325	325	45 µm	350
38 µm	400	400	–	–

In the above screen analysis table, the first two column represent the mesh size and width of opening of the screen; the third column is the mass fraction of the total sample that is retained on the designated screen. This is x_i, where i is the number of screen starting at the bottom of stack; thus i = 1 for the pan and the screen i + 1 is the screen immediately above screen i. The symbol D_{p_i} means the particle diameter equal to mesh opening of screen i. The last two column of Table 1.6 show the average particle diameter $\bar{D}_{p_i}$ in each increment and the cumulative fraction smaller than each value of D_{p_i}. In screen analysis cumulative fractions are written sometimes starting at the top of the stack and are expressed as the fraction *larger than* a given size.

Standard Screen Series:

Standard screens are used to measure the size (and size distribution) of particles in the size range between about 3 and 0.0015 inch (76 mm and 38 µm). Testing sieves are made of woven wire screen, the mesh and dimensions of which are carefully standardized. The openings are square. Each screen is identified in meshes per inch. The actual openings are smaller than those corresponding to the mesh numbers because of the thickness of the wires.

The characteristics of one common series *Tyler standard screen series*. This set of screen is based on the openings of the 200-mesh screen, which is established at 0.074 mm. The area of the openings in any one screen in the series is exactly twice that of the openings in the next smaller screen. The ratio of the actual mesh dimension of any screen to that of smaller screen is then $\sqrt{2}$ = 1.41. For closer sizing, intermediate screens are available, each of which has a mesh dimension $\sqrt[4]{2}$ = 1.189 = 1.189 times that of the next smaller standard screen. Normally, these intermediate screens are not used in actual practice. Tyler standard screen series is as shown in Table 1.6. Also comparison of standard screen series are shown in Table 1.7.

1.7 Properties of Particulate Masses

When the particles are dry and not sticky, masses of particles have many of the properties of fluid. They exert pressure on the sides and walls of a container, they flow through openings or down a chute. They differ from liquids and gases in several ways. Unlike most fluids, granular solids and solid masses permanently resist distortion when subjected to a moderate distoring force.

1.7.1 Distinct Properties of Solid Masses

(1) The pressure is not the same in all directions. In general, a pressure applied in one direction create some pressure in other directions, but it is always smaller than the applied pressure. It is a minimum in the direction at right angles to the applied pressure.
(2) A shear stress applied at the surface of a mass is transmitted throughout a static mass of particles unless failure occurs.
(3) The density of mass may changes, depending on the degree of packing of the grains. The density of a fluid is a unique function of temperature and pressure as is that of each individual solid particle, but the bulk density of mass is not. The bulk density is *minimum* when the mass is "loose", it rises to a maximum when the mass is packed by vibrating or tamping.

Depending on their flow properties, particulate solids are divided into two classes:

(a) Cohesive solid: Wet clay is characterized by their reluctance to flow through openings.
(b) Non-cohesive solids: Grain, sand and plastic chips readily flow out of a bin or silo.

1.7.2 Pressure in Masses of Particle

The minimum pressure in a solid mass is in the direction normal to that of the applied pressure. In a homogenous mass, the ratio of the normal pressure to the applied pressure is constant K', which is characteristic of the material. K' depends on the shape and interlocking tendencies of the particles, on the stickiness of the grain surfaces, and on the degree of packing of the material. It is nearly independent of particle size until the grains become very small and the material is no longer free flowing.

The ratio of normal pressure to the applied pressure $\dfrac{p_L}{p_V}$ equals K'

$$\sin \alpha_m = \frac{1 - K'}{1 + K'} \qquad \ldots (1.51)$$

$$K' = \frac{1 - \sin \alpha_m}{1 + \sin a_m} \qquad \ldots (1.52)$$

where, α_m = Angle of internal friction of material

1.7.3 Angle of internal friction and angle of repose

Angle of Repose: The angle of repose is a characteristic the piling or stacking nature of the particles. The way that particles stack when poured into a pile is a function of the size/shape, particle intrinsic density, surface forces (stickiness, electrostatic) and roughness of the particles. Many factors can influence the way particles stack hence it is difficult to predict; normally a simple measurement can be made to determine the angle of repose.

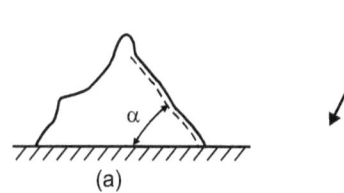 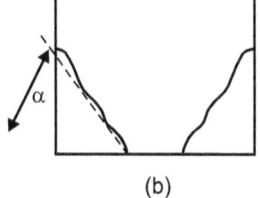 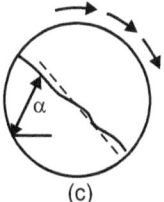

Fig. 1.9: Angle of repose, α, of (a) A Pile of Powder, (b) Powder in a Container and (c) Powder in a Rolling Drum

The angle of repose is considered to be mostly a measure of the internal friction between the particles as a whole, but not between individual particles. It is used in a number of correlations and estimates for the behaviour properties of the bulk solids. One example given in Coulson and Rcihardsons's text relates the angle of repose to the height of the longest movable plug in a piston. The angle of repose may is often incorrectly be used to estimate the angle required for the bottom of a hopper to ensure proper discharge.

The angle α_m is the angle of internal friction of the material. The tangent of this angle is the coefficient of friction between two layers of particles. When granular solids are piled up on a flat surface, the sides of the pile are at definite reproducible angle with horizontal. This angle α_r is the angle of repose of the material. It is useful for determining the capacity of a bin or a pile.

Ideally, if the mass were truly homogenous, $\alpha_m = \alpha_r$. In practice, the angle of repose is smaller than the angle internal friction because the grains at the exposed surface are more loosely packed than those inside the mass and often drier and less sticky. The angle of repose is low when the grains are smooth and rounded, it is high with very fine, granular or sticky particles. K' approaches zero for a cohesive solid. For free flowing granular materials K' which means that α_m is between 15 and 30°.

1.8 Storage of Solids

1.8.1 Bulk Storage

Coarse solids like gravel and coal are stored outside in large piles unprotected from weather. When hundreds or thousands of tons of material are involved, this is the most economical method. The solids are removed from the pile by dragline or tractor shovel and delivered to a conveyor or to the process. Outdoor storage can lead environmental problems such as dusting or leaching of soluble material from the pile. Dusting may necessitate a protective cover of some kind of stored solid, leaching can be controlled by covering the pile.

1.8.2 Bin Storage

Solids that are too valuable or too soluble to expose in outdoor piles are stored in bins or silos. These are cylindrical or rectangular vessels of concrete or metal. A silo is tall and relatively small in diameter, a bin is not so tall and usually fairly wide. A hopper is a small bin with slopping bottom, for temporary storage before feeding solids to a process. A major problem in bin design is to provide satisfactory discharge.

1.8.3 Stresses in Hoppers and Silos

Consider the equilibrium of forces acting on a differential element, dz, in a straight sided cylindrical silo (Fig. 1.10). In the stationary situation the surrounding fluid (air) pressure acts uniformly on all solid particles throughout the silo.

However, there are compressive normal stresses, P_V, acting on the cross-sectional area, A, due to the overburden of material above the volume element. There are also shear stresses, τ_R, of the solid phase acting on the silo walls. We list the various components contributing to the force in the z-direction.

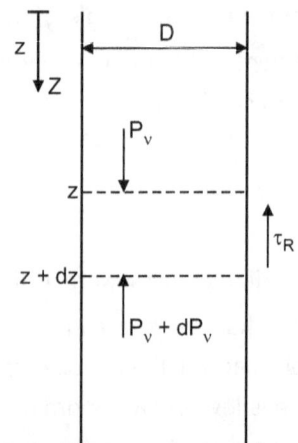

Overburden normal stress acting downward on the surface at z.	$P_V A$
Normal stress acting upward on the surface at $z + \Delta z$	$-(P_V + dP_V) A$
Shear stress acting on the silo walls acting upward	$-\tau_R \pi D\, dz$
Gravity force acting downward on the differential element	$\rho^o A\, dz\, g$

Fig. 1.10 : Differential force Balance on a Cylindrical Storage Bin

At steady state (no accelerations, or neglecting inertial terms) the sum of the forces must equal to zero. This gives the balance of forces as,

$$A(P_V) - A(P_V + dP_V) - \tau_R \pi\, Ddz + \rho^o Adz\, g = 0 \qquad \ldots (1.53)$$

which reduces to

$$-A(dP_V) - \tau_R \pi\, Ddz + \rho^o Adz\, g = 0 \qquad \ldots (1.54)$$

From Physics, we relate the shear stress at the wall to the lateral normal stress acting in the radial direction at the wall, P_W, with the coefficient of friction, μ,

$$\tau_R = \mu P_W \qquad \ldots (1.55)$$

Substituting equation (1.55) into (1.54) gives,

$$-A(dP_V) - \mu P_W \pi\, Ddz + \rho^o Adz\, g = 0 \qquad \ldots (1.56)$$

which has both P_W and P_V terms.

Janssen solved this equation (H. A. Janssen, Versuche uber Getreidedruck in Silozellen, Verein Deutcher Ingenieure, Zeitschrift, 39, August, 1985, 1045-1049) by assuming that the vertical normal stress is proportional to the lateral normal stress, where,

$$P_W = KP_V \qquad \ldots (1.57)$$

Substituting equation (1.36) into (1.35) and rearranging, where, $A = \dfrac{\pi D^2}{4}$, we get,

$$dP_V = -\frac{4\mu K}{D}\left(P_V - \frac{\rho^o gD}{4\mu K}\right) dz \qquad \ldots (1.58)$$

Equation (1.37) is integrated with the boundary condition that $P_V = 0$ at $z = 0$, to obtain,

$$\boxed{P_V = \frac{\rho^o gD}{4\mu K g_c}\left(1 - \exp\left(-\frac{4\mu Kz}{D}\right)\right)} \qquad \ldots (1.59)$$

where, the g_c is the gravity constant conversion factor to convert the result from units of mass to units of force. This latter expression is known as the *Janssen Equation*. When we plot the pressure in the silo as a function of depth from the free surface of the granular material at the top we get a plot shown in Fig. 1.11.

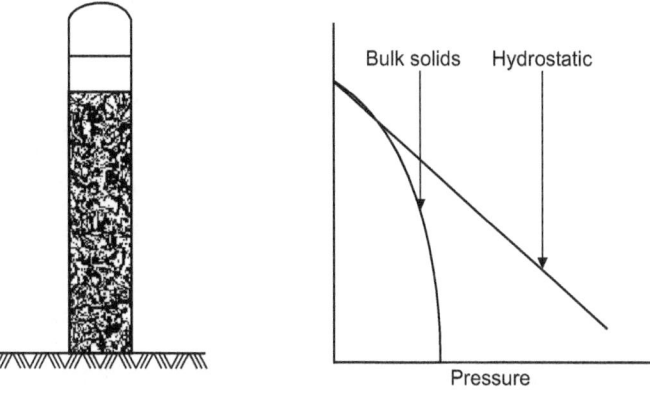

Fig. 1.11: Vertical Normal Stress Profile in a Silo

Note that in Fig. 1.11 the asymptotic pressure for large depth is only a function of the silo diameter and not on depth. This is one reason why commercial silos are designed tall and narrow rather than short and squat.

At the bottom of the silo is the converging hopper section. Andrew Jenike (A. W. Jenike, Storage and Flow of Solids, Bulletin No. 123, Utah Engineering Experiment Station, University of Utah, Salt Lake City, Utah, 1964) postulated that the magnitude of stress in the converging section is proportional to the distance from the hopper apex (as well as a dependence on the angle). The stress is written as

$$\sigma = \sigma(r, \theta) \qquad \ldots (1.60)$$

As indicated in Fig. 1.12.

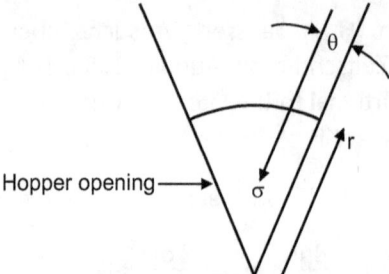

Fig. 1.12: The stress σ, in the Hopper is a Function of Position (r, θ)

The rigorous calculations applying the radial stress field assumption are beyond the scope of this discussion. However, the results of those calculations shown in Fig. 1.13 give us insight as to the conditions at the bottom of the silo at the hopper discharge. Fig. 1.13 shows that there is essentially no stress at the hopper outlet. This is good because it allows dischargers such as screws and rotary valves to turn easily.

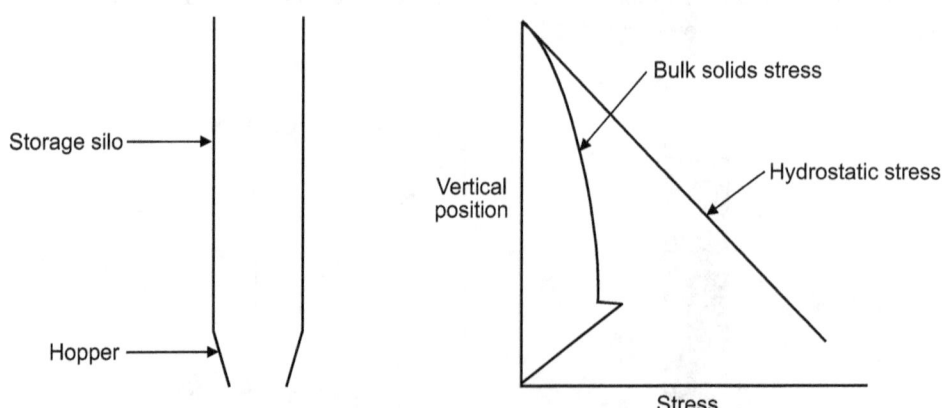

Fig. 1.13: Hopper Stress Field Including the Stresses in the Converging Hopper Discharge Section

Janssen's Coefficient (K):

Janssen's coefficient is defined as

$$K = \frac{\sigma_{rr}}{\sigma_{zz}} \qquad \ldots (1.61)$$

where, σ_{rr} and σ_{zz} are the stress components in the r and z directions. These stresses are the total stresses acting on the multiphase material. These stresses are the sum of the fluid phase and solid stresses. Hence, this definition applies whether the material is totally liquid, totally solid, or mixture in-between.

This coefficient represents the ratio of the measurable stresses, as can be measured with a strain gauge to measure the force acting on a defined probe surface. For a pure liquid, we know that the probe would measure an equal pressure in all directions within the liquid at a given point within the liquid at stagnant conditions. Hence, for a pure liquid K = 1. For a totally solid material K = 0 because we can set a weight on top of a solid block and all of the stresses within the block are aligned vertically.

Fig. 1.14 gives a rough correlation showing the Janssen's coefficient approximate values for several fluid-solid mixture materials. This correlation is crude, it only gives a rough approximation. For most granular materials we can take Janssen's coefficient to be approximately 0.4.

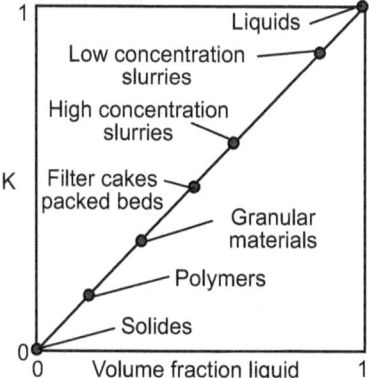

Fig. 1.14: Janssen's Coefficient of Various Materials

1.9 Grade Efficiency

Classification is the art of separating solid particles in a mixture of solids and fluid into fractions according to particle size or density by methods other than screening. Most methods of separation are not 100% effective. There is usually a range of particle sizes that are separated with varying degrees of efficiency. The variation in the efficiency is referred to as the Grade Efficiency Curve.

The grade efficiency is a way of characterising how well particles are separated according to size (density, or some other desired property). Separation of particles by size is referred to as *classification*.

1.9.1 Why do we classify particles?

We classify particles to remove contaminants and unlike particles (wheat from chaff, or metal particles from polymers). We classify to remove unwanted parts of a size distribution. In Fig. 1.15, it indicates the tailings and oversize particles that may be removed from a material for a particular purpose.

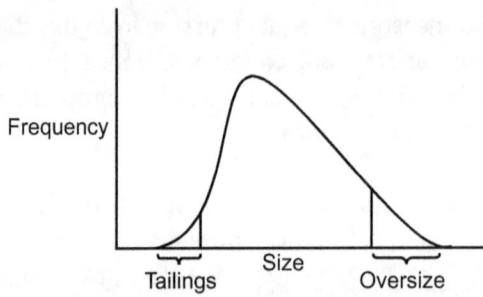

Fig. 1.15: Size Distribution Indicating Undesired Tailings and Oversize Particle Ranges

There are many processes that may be used to classify particles.

Screening	These methods are effective, but rate of production may be low.
Sieving	
Air or water classification	These methods take advantage of different drag forces acting on different size particles.
Physical separations • Magnetic • Gravity • Electrostatic • Radiation • Colour	These methods rely on physical properties other than differences in fluid drag to classify.

1.9.2 Measuring Efficiency

Separation efficiency is directly related to processing costs. Most separations are not 100% efficient. The outlet streams of the separation may be concentrated in the desired or undesired products, but may not be pure. The challenge is to determine the best way to define and measure the efficiency of the separation.

The method of separation considered here is called **The Grade Efficiency**. A black box powder separation process is shown in Fig. 1.16. The total mass balance gives,

$$M = M_c + M_f \qquad \ldots (1.16)$$

The total separation efficiency, E_T, is defined as

$$E_r = \frac{M_c}{M} = 1 - \frac{M_f}{M} \qquad \ldots (1.63)$$

We assume that there is no agglomeration or comminution in the separator. For a particle size, x, the masses of size x in each stream are noted by M_x, M_{fx}, M_{cx}. By analogy with equation (1.63), the grade efficiency of separation of size x is defined as,

$$G_x = \frac{M_{cx}}{M_x} \qquad \ldots (1.64)$$

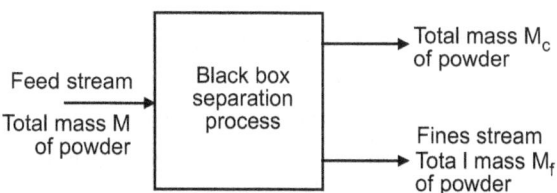

Fig. 1.16: Black Box (Hypothetical) Separation Process to Separation Coarse Particles from Fine Particles

We know from the definition of frequency distributions that the mass and mass components of each stream are related by

$$\begin{aligned} M_x &= M \text{ (Fraction of size x)} \\ &= M\, f_x dx \\ &= M\, dF_x \end{aligned} \qquad \ldots (1.65)$$

Similarly, $\qquad M_{cx} = M_c\, f_{cx}\, dx = M_c\, dF_{cx} \qquad \ldots (1.66)$

Hence, the grade efficiency is related to the size distribution functions by,

$$G(x) = \frac{M_c f_{cx}}{M f_x} \qquad \ldots (1.67)$$

A typical plot of the grade efficiency versus the particle size is shown in Fig. 1.16. The area under the curve plotted in Fig. 1.17 represents the coarse cut (the stream with the larger particles) and the area above the plotted curve represents the fines cut.

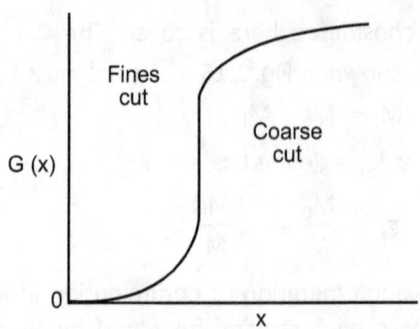

Fig. 1.17: Typical S-Shaped Grade Efficiency Curve

At a point, x, on the curve, G(x) represents the fraction of particles of size x that are separated out of the feed stream and contained in the fines product stream. For a continuous steady process the curve in Fig. 1.17 is steady. For an unsteady process such as filtration, the curve changes with time, as shown in Fig. 1.18.

In a typical cake filtration, as the filter cake depth increases, the cake itself improves the separation and the grade efficiency shifts with increasing efficiencies for smaller particles. In depth filtration, initially the filter may perform very well. Gradually, the capture sites in a typical depth filter are occupied (though other mechanisms such as straining may occur) and the fine particles start to bleed through. Hence, in depth filtration the grade efficiency curve shifts towards larger particles as the filter becomes less efficient at capturing small particles.

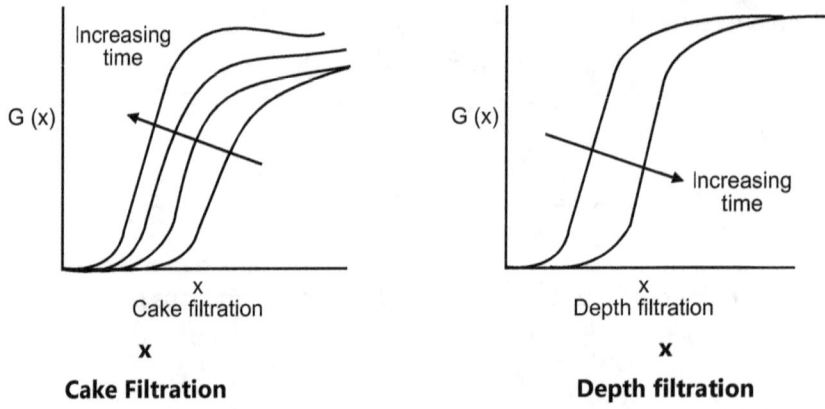

Cake Filtration   **Depth filtration**

Fig. 1.18: Comparison of Typical Grade Efficiency Curves for Cake Filtration and Depth Filtration

1.9.3 Cut Size and Sharpness of Cut

To compare efficiencies between steady state processes, we define cut size and sharpness of cut. Normally, cut size refers to 50% cut size, denoted x_{50}. This is the particle size for which 50% of the particles exit the separation process in the coarse product stream and 50% exit in the fines product stream.

Sharpness of cut is defined as a ratio of particle sizes specified at two efficiencies, typically at 20% and 80%. The sharpness of cut is defined as,

$$I_{80/20} = \frac{x_{80}}{x_{20}} \quad \ldots (1.68)$$

By this definition and because the grade efficiency is a monotonically increasing curve, the sharpness must be greater than or equal to unity. In an idealized case in which there is a perfect separation, where all particles less than the 50% cut size exit in the fines stream and all particles greater than the cut size exit in the coarse stream, the sharpness of cuts equals unity. Real separation processes have a sharpness of cut greater than unity. These concepts are shown in Fig. 1.19.

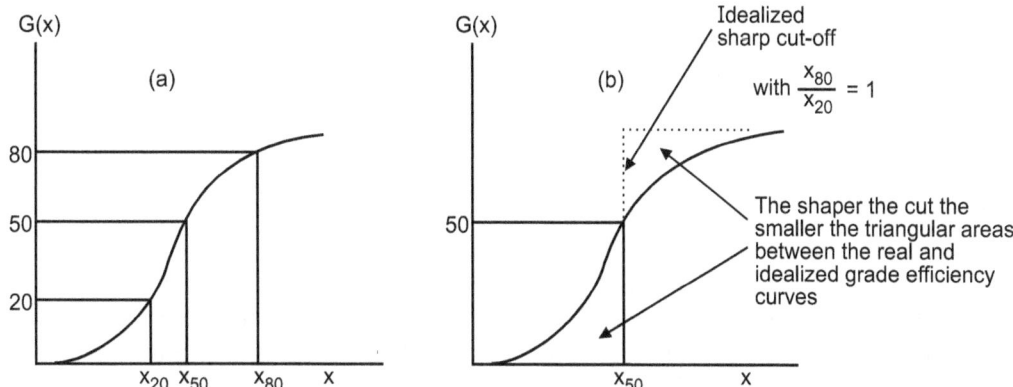

Fig. 1.19: (a) Typical Grade Efficiency Curve with the Particle Sizes Indicated for which the Separation is 20, 50, and 80 percent Efficient. (b) The Idealized sharp Cut-off Grade Efficiency Curve is a Vertical Line

Other definitions of sharpness of cut are also used, including.

1. $I_{20/80} = \dfrac{x_{20}}{x_{80}}$ which is the inverse $I_{80/20}$. x values such as 90/10 could also be defined.

2. Variance in the slope, $\dfrac{dG}{dx}$.

3. Slope of the grade efficiency curve, $I_x = \dfrac{dG(x)}{dx}$.
4. Sum of the triangular areas in Fig. 1.19 (b).

1.9.4 Construction of the Grade Efficiency Curve

In the ideal case you would feed into your separator a material with a monodispersed particle size distribution (of size x).
You would –
- Measure M_x, M_{cx}, M_{fx}
- Calculated G(x).
- Repeat for other size x (until you have enough points to construct your curve or you loose patience).

This approach is not very realistic because of the difficulty in obtaining monodispersed materials (especially in the very small particle size range) and because of the time and effort required.

In real applications you need to measure two of the following:
- Feed rate,
- Coarse product, rate,
- Fines product rate.

and you need atleast two of the following:
- Feed particle size distribution,
- Coarse particle size distribution,
- Fine particle size distribution.

It is best to have data from the smaller of the two product streams because errors in sampling are smaller than when you subtract two larger streams to get the smaller stream. As indicated in Fig. 1.20, the flow rate of the smaller stream may be less than the error of measurement of the larger streams.

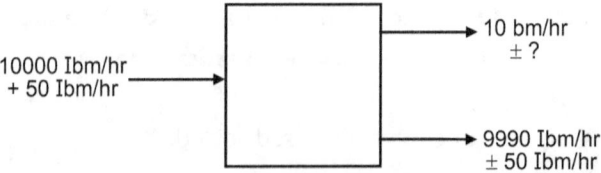

Fig. 1.20: Example in which the other size of the smaller product stream is smaller than the error in measurements of the other two steams. Due to the error, it is better to measure the smaller stream directly instead of calculating it from the two larger streams

1.10 Solved Examples

Example 1.1:
The size analysis of a powdered material on a weight basis is represented by a straight line from 0% weight at 1 µm particle size to 100% weight at 101 μ_m particle size. Calculate the mean surface diameter of particles constituting the system.

Solution: The surface mean diameter is given by:

$$\bar{D}_s = \frac{1}{\sum_{i=1}^{N}(x_1/d_1)}$$

Since the size analysis is represented by continuous line:

$$d = 100x + 1$$

$$\bar{D}_s = \frac{1}{\int_0^1 dx/d} = \frac{1}{\int_0^1 \frac{dx}{(100x+1)}} = \frac{100}{\ln 101}$$

$$\boxed{\bar{D}_s = 21.7 \ \mu m} \qquad \text{(Ans.)}$$

Example 1.2:
Calculate the surface volume mean diameter for the following particulate material. Show the detailed calculations.

Size Range (µm)	Mass of particles in the range (gm)
−704 + 352	25
−352 + 176	37.5
−176 + 88	62.5
−88 + 44	75
PAN	50

Solution: Surface-volume mean diameter $\bar{D}_s$ is given by,

$$\bar{D}_s = \frac{1}{\sum_{i=1}^{N}(X_i/\bar{D}_{Pi})}$$

where, X_i = Mass fraction of material retained on the screen

$\bar{D}_{Pi}$ = Average size of the particle on the screen.

Total mass of particles = 25 + 37.5 + 62.5 + 75 + 50 = 250 gm

$$\text{Mass fraction} = \frac{\text{mass}}{\text{total mass}}$$

Size range (μm)	$\bar{D}_{Pi}$ (μm)	Mass of particles (gm)	Mass fractions (X_i)	$\dfrac{X_i}{\bar{D}_{Pi}}$
−704 + 352	(704 + 352)/2 = 528	25	25/250 = 0.1	0.1/528
−352 + 176	264	37.5	0.15	0.15/264
−176 + 88	132	62.5	0.25	0.25/132
−88 + 44	66	75	0.30	0.3/66
PAN	(44 + 0)/2 = 22	50	0.20	0.2/22

$$\sum_{i=1}^{N} (X_i/\bar{D}_{Pi}) = \frac{0.1}{528} + \frac{0.15}{264} + \frac{0.25}{132} + \frac{0.3}{66} + \frac{0.2}{22}$$

$$= 163 \times 10^{-4}$$

$$\therefore \quad \bar{D}_S = \frac{1}{\sum_{i=1}^{N} (X_i/\bar{D}_{Pi})} = \frac{1}{163 \times 10^{-4}} = 61 \text{ μm}$$

∴ Surface volume mean diameter = 61 μm   (Ans.)

Example 1.3:
Calculate the sphericity of a cuboid with dimensions 1 × 2 × 3. Use as the equivalent diameter of a sphere with the same volume.

Solution: The volume of the cuboids is 6 units. The diameter of the sphere of equivalent volume is therefore,

$$d = \left(\frac{6v_p}{\pi}\right)^{\frac{1}{3}} = \left(\frac{36}{\pi}\right)^{\frac{1}{3}} = 2.25 \text{ units}$$

Sphericity is defined as,

$$\Phi = \frac{6v_p}{d_p s_p}$$

The surface area of the cuboids is 22 units so the sphericity is,

$$\Phi = \frac{6 \times 6}{2.25 \times 22} = 0.2727 \quad \text{(Ans.)}$$

Example 1.4:
Repeat 3 but using an equivalent diameter based on surface area.

Solution: Repeat 3 but using an equivalent diameter based on surface area.
The diameter of a sphere with surface area 22 units² is 2.646 units hence the sphericity is given by,

$$\Phi = \frac{6 \times 6}{2.646 \times 22} = 0.618 \quad \text{(Ans.)}$$

MECHANICAL OPERATIONS — PROPERTIES AND HANDLING OF PARTICULATE SOLIDS

Example 1.5:

Repeat 3 but using an equivalent diameter based on the ratio of surface area to volume.

Solution: Repeat 3 but using an equivalent diameter based on the ratio of surface area to volume. The ratio of surface area to volume of the cuboids is 3.667. For a sphere the ratio of surface area to volume is given by,

$$\frac{\pi d^2}{\frac{\pi d^3}{6}} = \frac{6}{d}$$

So the equivalent diameter is 1.636 units, which gives a sphericity of 1. **(Ans.)**

Example 1.6:

For a cube with dimensions 5.00 × 5.00 × 5.00 mm, calculate the following parameters:

(a) Equivalent volume diameter
(b) Equivalent surface diameter
(c) Sauter diameter, and
(d) Corresponding sphericities. **(8 marks)**

Solution:

Equivalent volume diameter:

$$d_{volume} = \sqrt[3]{\frac{6V}{\pi}} = \sqrt[3]{\frac{6 \times 5^3}{\pi}} = 6.2 \text{ mm}$$

Equivalent surface diameter:

$$d_{surface} = \sqrt{\frac{A}{\pi}} = \sqrt{\frac{6 \times 5^2}{\pi}} = 6.9 \text{ mm}$$

Sauter diameter:

$$d_{Sauter} = \frac{6V}{A} = \frac{d_{sphere}^3}{d_{surface}^2} = 5.0 \text{ mm}$$

Volume sphericity: $\psi_V = \pi (d_V)^2 / A = 0.81$

Surface sphericity: $\psi_A = \pi (d_A)^3 / 6V = 1.38$

Sauter-diameter sphericities:

$$\psi_{VA} = \pi (d_{32})^2 / A = 0.52$$

$$\psi_{AV} = \pi (d_{32})^3 / (6V) = 0.52$$

MECHANICAL OPERATIONS — PROPERTIES AND HANDLING OF PARTICULATE SOLIDS

Example 1.7:

Below is the result of a particle size analysis:

Aperture size (mm or μm)		Amount retained (g)
-10 mm	+9.5	0.36
-9.5	+6.8	5.16
-6.8	+4.75	24.36
-4.75	+3.4	50.04
-3.4	+2.36	83.64
-2.36	+1.7	115.08
-1.7	+1.18	131.28
-1.18	+850 μm	129.6
-850	+600	118.92
-600	+425	101.04
-425	+300	85.44
-300	+212	73.2
-212	+150	62.76
-150	+106	52.56
-106	+75	46.2
-75	+53	34.92
-53	+38	25.68
-38	0	59.76

(a) Determine the mass fractions of the amounts retained, the (arithmetic) mean diameter (using the mid-point diameter for each size range), and the standard deviation. Show your table.

(b) Determine the cumulative oversized and undersized, and complete the following table.

Size range	Mid-point	Mass retained	Mass fraction	Cumulative Undersized	Cumulative Oversized
(micron) d_i	(micron)	(g)	Y_i	P	Q
0-38		0			
38-53		59.760			
53-75		25.680			
75-106		34.920			
106-150		46.200			

Size range (micron) d_i	Mid-point (micron)	Mass retained (g)	Mass fraction γ_i	Cumulative Undersized P	Cumulative Oversized Q
150-212		52.560			
212-300		62.760			
300-425		73.200			
425-600		85.440			
600-850		101.040			
850-1180		118.920			
1180-1700		129.600			
1700-2360		131.280			
2360-3400		115.080			
3400-4750		83.640			
4750-6800		50.040			
6800-9500		24.360			
9500-10000		5.160			
sum		0.360			
		1200			

(c) Plot the particle size distribution as a histogram, normalised histogram and continuous distribution (normal axes and lognormal axes), cumulative oversized and undersized products (normal axes and lognormal axes).

(d) Determine the most frequent (mode) diameter and median diameter of the particles. You can use the available tables and diagrams in the answers to the above questions. Show your answers on the diagrams.

(e) Determine the volume-equivalent, surface-equivalent, and Sauter-equivalent diameters of the particles (using the mid-point diameter for each size range). Show your table.

Solution:

(a) The table is shown below.

Size range (micron)	Mid-point d_i (micron)	Mass retained (f)	Mass fraction (γ_i)	Mean diameter $d_i * \gamma_i$	Standard deviation $(d_i - \bar{d})^2 \gamma_i$	$d_i^2 * \gamma_i$
00-38	19	59.76	0.050	0.946	65561.804	17.978
38-53	45.5	25.68	0.021	0.974	26886.804	44.303
53-75	64	34.92	0.029	1.862	35364.126	119.194
75-106	90.5	46.2	0.039	3.484	44565.201	315.325
106-150	128	52.56	0.044	5.606	47227.448	717.619
150-212	181	62.76	0.052	9.466	50782.880	1713.400
212-300	256	73.2	0.061	15.616	50557.324	3997.696
300-425	362.5	85.44	0.071	25.810	46012.140	9356.125
425-600	512.5	101.04	0.084	43.153	36001.491	22115.656
600-850	725	118.92	0.099	71.848	19307.105	52089.438
850-1180	1015	129.6	0.108	109.620	2475.220	111264.300
1180-1700	1440	131.28	0.109	157.536	8189.995	226851.840
1700-2360	2030	115.08	0.096	194.677	71524.476	395194.310
2360-3400	2880	83.64	0.070	200.736	204671.388	578119.680
3400-4750	4075	50.04	0.042	169.928	352782.688	692454.563
4750-6800	5775	24.36	0.020	117.233	431157.649	677017.688
6800-9500	8150	5.16	0.004	35.045	209714.522	285616.750
9500-10000	9500	0.36	0.000	2.85	20834.720	27075.000
sum		1200	1.00	1166.389	1723616.981	3084080.864

The mass fractions of the amounts retained are shown in the fourth column.

The calculation of the mean diameter is shown by the fifth column, which gives,

$$\bar{d} = \sum_{i=1}^{m} \gamma_i \, d_i = 1166.389 \; \mu m$$

The standard deviation can be calculated in two ways which are shown by the last two columns.

The first gives,

$$\sigma = \sqrt{\sum_{i=1}^{m} \gamma_i (d_i - \bar{d})^2} = \sqrt{1723616.981} = 1312.866 \; \mu m$$

The second way gives

$$\sigma = \sqrt{\left\{\sum_{i=1}^{m} \gamma_i (d_i)^2\right\} - (\bar{d})^2} = \sqrt{3084080.864 - 1166.389^2} = 1312.866 \; \mu m$$

The two calculations give the same result.

(b) The completed table is shown below.

Size range (micron)	Mid-point d_i (micron)	Mass retained (g)	Mass fraction γ_i	Cumulative Undersized P	Cumulative Oversized Q
	0	0	0	0	1.000
0-38	19	59.76	0.050	0.050	0.950
38-53	45.5	25.68	0.021	0.071	0.929
53-75	64	34.92	0.029	0.100	0.900
75-106	90.5	46.2	0.039	0.139	0.861
106-150	128	52.56	0.044	0.183	0.817
150-212	181	62.76	0.052	0.235	0.765
212-300	256	73.2	0.061	0.296	0.704
300-425	362.5	85.44	0.071	0.367	0.633
425-600	512.5	101.04	0.084	0.451	0.549
600-850	725	118.92	0.099	0.550	0.450
850-1180	1015	129.6	0.108	0.658	0.342
1180-1700	1440	131.28	0.109	0.768	0.232
1700-2360	2030	115.08	0.096	0.864	0.136
2360-3400	2880	83.64	0.070	0.933	0.067
3400-4750	4075	50.04	0.042	0.975	0.025
4750-6800	5775	24.36	0.020	0.995	0.005
6800-9500	8150	5.16	0.004	1.000	0.000
9500-10000	9500	0.36	0.000	1.000	0.000
sum		1200			

(c) The histogram for the particle size distribution is obtained by plotting the third versus first column in the table shown in the answer.

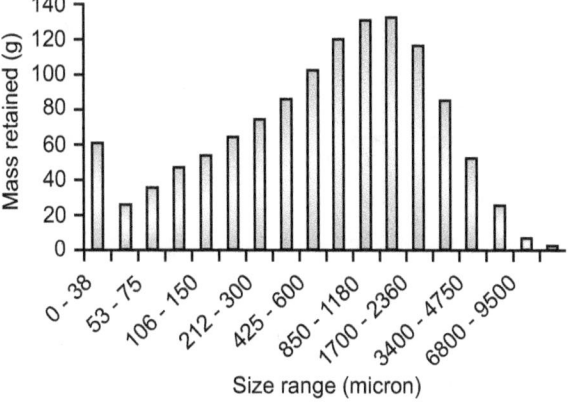

Fig. 1.21: Particle Size Distribution

The normalized histogram for the particle size distribution is obtained by plotting the fourth versus first column in the table shown in the answer.

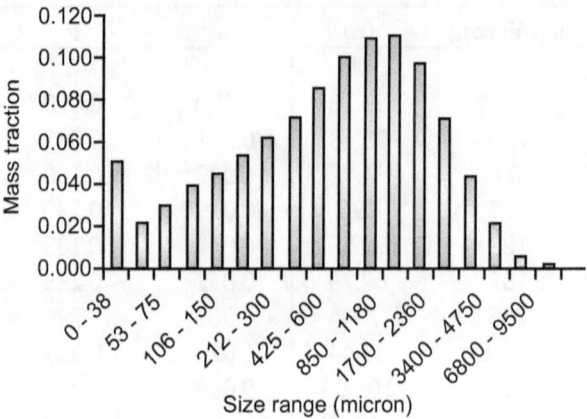

Fig.: 1.22: Particle Size Distribution

The continuous distribution is obtained by plotting the fourth versus second column in the table shown in the answer. The horizontal axe can be in either the normal or lognormal scale.

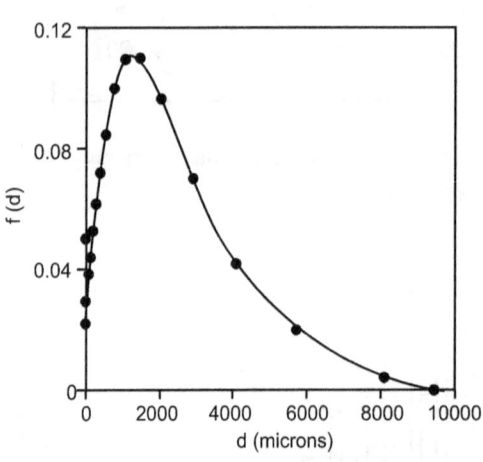

Fig. 1.23: Continuous Distribution Plot

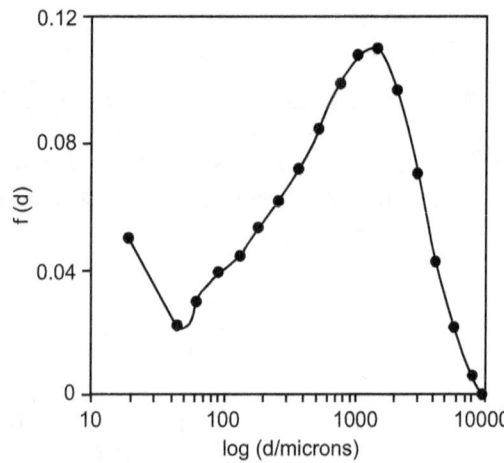

Fig. 1.24: Continuous Distribution Plot

The curves for cumulative oversized and undersized products can be obtained by plotting the fifth and sixth versus second column in the table shown in the answer to Q. 7 (b). The horizontal axe can be in either the normal or lognormal scale.

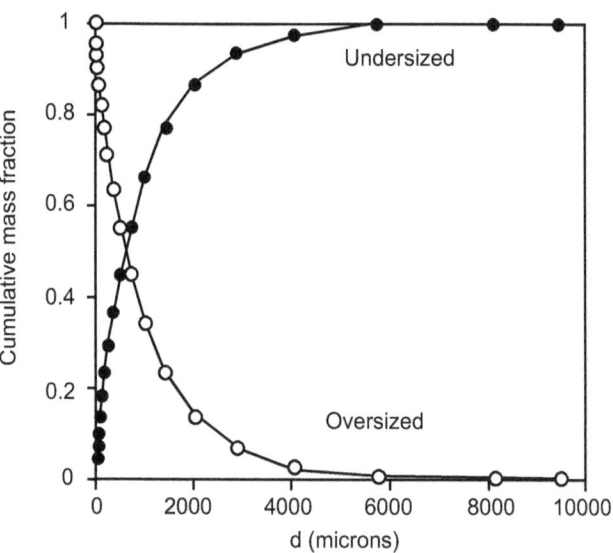

Fig. 1.25: Curves for Cumulative Oversized and Undersized Products

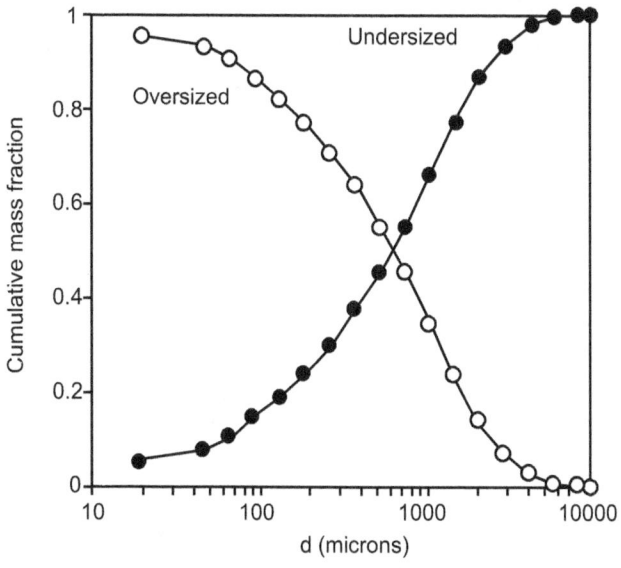

Fig. 1.26: Curves for Cumulative Oversized and Undersized Products

(d) The mode diameter can be best determined at the maximum frequency distribution which is about 1400 ± 50 mm (see the column for mass retained or mass fraction in the answer to Q. 7 (a) or (b). The diameter on the horizontal axis of the frequency distribution is shown by the arrow in the following diagram.

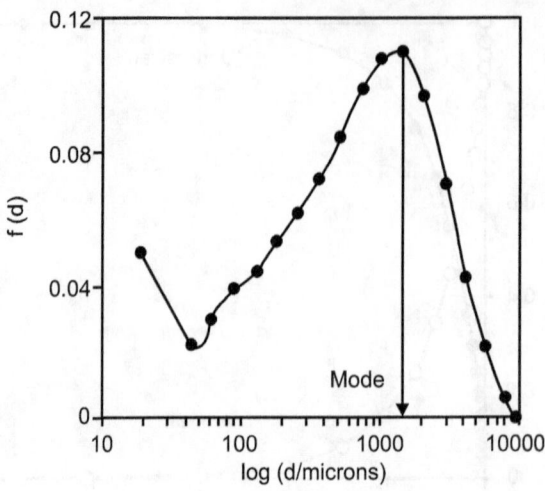

Fig. 1.27: Frequency Distribution Plot

The median diameter can be best determined at the 50% of cumulative oversized or undersized production distribution which is about 618 ± 5 mm (see the column for mass retained or mass fraction in the answer to Q. 7 (a) or Q. 7 (b). The diameter on the horizontal axis of the frequency is shown by the red arrow in the following diagram.

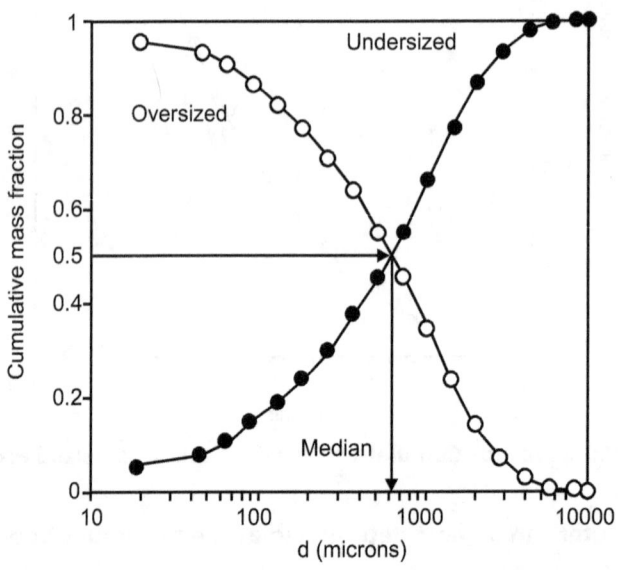

Fig. 1.28: Cumulative Oversized and Undersized Product Distribution

MECHANICAL OPERATIONS — PROPERTIES AND HANDLING OF PARTICULATE SOLIDS

(e) The table showing the calculation is given below.

Size range (micron)	Mid-point d_i (micron)	Mass retained (g)	Mass fraction γ_i	Surface Equivalent $d_i^2 \gamma_i$	Surface Equivalent $d_i^3 \gamma_i$
	0	0	0	0	0
0-38	19	59.76	0.050	17.978	341.578
38-53	45.5	25.68	0.021	44.303	2015.802
53-75	64	34.92	0.029	119.194	7628.390
75-106	90.5	46.2	0.039	315.325	28536.879
106-150	128	52.56	0.044	717.619	91855.258
150-212	181	62.76	0.052	1713.400	310125.454
212-300	256	73.2	0.061	3997.696	1023410.176
300-425	362.5	85.44	0.071	9356.125	3391595.313
425-600	512.5	101.04	0.084	22115.656	11334273.828
600-850	725	118.92	0.099	52089.438	37764842.188
850-1180	1015	129.6	0.108	111264.300	112933264.500
1180-1700	1440	131.28	0.109	226851.840	326666649.600
1700-2360	2030	115.08	0.096	395194.310	802244449.300
2360-3400	2880	83.64	0.070	578119.680	1664984678.400
3400-4750	4075	50.04	0.042	692454.563	2821752342.188
4750-6800	5775	24.36	0.020	677017.688	3909777145.313
6800-9500	8150	5.16	0.004	285616.750	2327776512.500
9500-10000	9500	0.36	0.000	27075.000	257212500.000
Sum		1200		3084080.864	12277302166.666

Volume equivalent diameter:

$$d_V = \sqrt[3]{\sum_{i=1}^{m} \gamma_i d_i^3} = \sqrt[3]{12277302166.666} = 2306.929 \ \mu m$$

Surface equivalent diameter:

$$d_A = \sqrt[3]{\sum_{i=1}^{m} \gamma_i d_i^2} = \sqrt[3]{3084080.864} = 1756.155 \ \mu m$$

Sauter diameter:

$$d_{Sauter} = \frac{\sum_{i=1}^{m} \gamma_i d_i^3}{\sum_{i=1}^{m} \gamma_i d_i^2} = \frac{12277302166.666}{3084080.864} = 3980.863 \ \mu m$$

Note: The surface area and volume for each fraction should be $\frac{\pi d_i^2}{4} \gamma_i$ and $\frac{\pi d_i^3}{6} \gamma_i$, respectively. For simplicity, the numerical factors have been dropped-off in the above calculation. If the full expressions for the surface area and volume are used, the equivalent diameters should be calculated in the same way i.e.,

$$\frac{\pi d_A^2}{4} = \sum_{i=1}^{m} \frac{\pi d_i^2}{4} y_i$$

$$\therefore \quad d_A = \sqrt{\frac{4}{\pi} \sum_{i=1}^{m} \frac{\pi d_i^2}{4} y_i}$$

and

$$\frac{\pi d_V^3}{6} = \sum_{i=1}^{m} \frac{\pi d_i^3}{6} y_i$$

$$\therefore \quad d_V = \sqrt{\frac{6}{\pi} \sum_{i=1}^{m} \frac{\pi d_i^3}{6} y_i}$$

If the full expressions for the surface area and volume are used, the numbers in the last two columns should be different but the results for the equivalent diameters should be the same as those shown above.

Example 1.8:

Estimate the specific surface and sauter diameter of a sample of galena (specific gravity = 7.43) having the screen analysis below:

Mesh	Mass fraction
− 570 + 480	0.01
− 480 + 340	0.04
− 340 + 240	0.081
− 240 + 160	0.115
− 160 + 120	0.160
− 120 + 85	0.148
− 85 + 60	0.132
− 60 + 40	0.081
− 40 + 30	0.062
− 30 + 20	0.041
− 20 + 15	0.036
− 15 + 10	0.022
− 10 + 8	0.019
− 8	0.053

Assume Gaudin-Schumann distribution is valid for sizes below 8 mesh.

Solution: The Specific surface of the sample can be computed from equation

$$S_m = \frac{6}{\rho_s} \sum_i \frac{n_i x_i}{d_{avg_i}}$$

where, ρ_s = 7.43 gm/cc

MECHANICAL OPERATIONS — PROPERTIES AND HANDLING OF PARTICULATE SOLIDS

If D_{vs} is the volume surface diameter (sauter diameter) of the sample, then by definition,

$$s_m = 6/(\rho d_{vs})$$

or

$$D_{vs} = 1 \Big/ \sum_i \frac{n_i x_i}{d_{avg_i}}$$

The values of specific surface ratio n can be obtained from the standard plot given in Fig. 1.27. The average size d_{avg} of each fraction is computed from the aperture sizes of screens given in table. The results are given below.

Mesh	Average size, d_{avg} (cm)	Specific surface ratio, n	Mass fraction, x
−570 + 480	$\dfrac{0.566 + 0.476}{2} = 0.521$	4.0	0.01
− 480 + 340	0.4056	3.8	0.04
− 340 + 240	0.2876	3.55	0.081
− 240 + 160	0.19995	3.2	0.115
− 160 + 120	0.14005	2.8	0.160

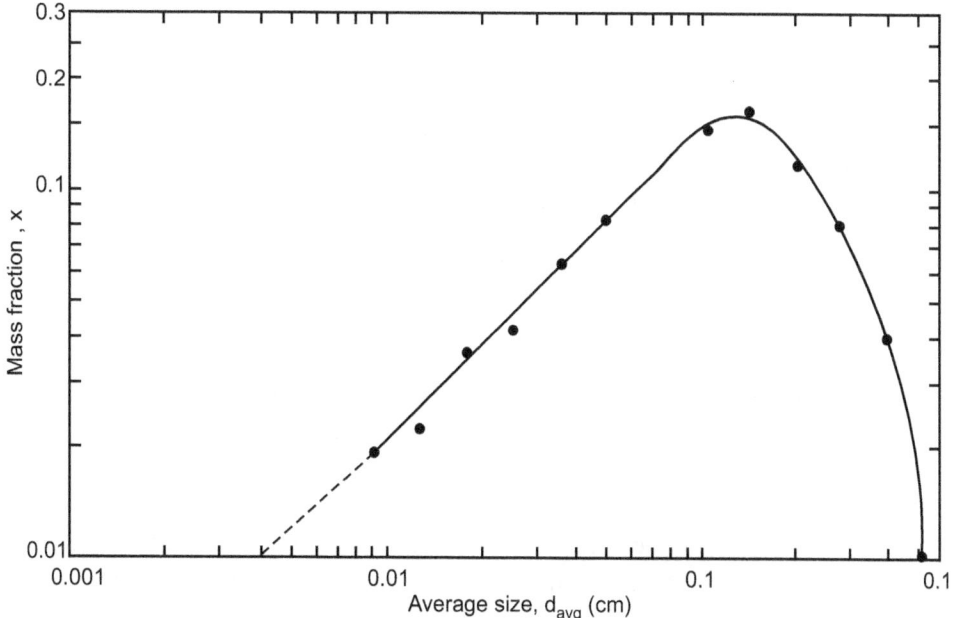

Fig. 1.29: Log-Log Plot of Mass Fraction Versus Average Particle Size

Mesh	Average size, d_{avg} (cm)	Specific surface ratio, n	Mass fraction, x
− 120 + 85	0.10215	2.7	0.148
− 85 + 60	0.0717	2.5	0.132
− 60 + 40	0.0506	2.3	0.081
− 40 + 30	0.0358	2.1	0.062
− 30 + 20	0.02535	2.0	0.041
− 20 + 15	0.0181	1.85	0.036
− 15 + 10	0.01275	1.75	0.022
− 10 + 8	0.00895	1.70	0.019

Since it is given in the problem that for sizes below 8 mesh, Gaudin-Schumann size distribution law is applicable, we can plot x versus d_{avg} on log-log co-ordinates and then extrapolate back the lower portion of the graph (corresponding to low size range) since the plot within this portion must be linear. The plot is given in Fig. 1.29. From the figure, the average slope of the extrapolated portion is,

$$m = 0.7777$$

We can therefore write equation as,

$$\log x = 0.7777 \log d_{avg} + \log B$$

or

$$x = B (d_{avg})^{0.7777}$$

It can be seen that the screen data reported above follows a screen interval of $(2)^{1/2}$ and not $(2)^{1/4}$. Therefore, in applying above relation, we must use d_{avg} in the interval of $(2)^{1/2}$. Thus, at $d_{avg} = \dfrac{0.0895}{1.41} = 0.063475$ mm, the mass action (x) from the graph is 0.0142. Using these two values, we can compute the value of constant B as,

$$0.0142 = B (0.063475)^{0.7777}$$

or

$$B = 0.21$$

The relation between x and d_{avg} for sizes below 8 mesh thus becomes,

$$x = 0.121 (10 \, d_{avg})^{0.7777}$$

where, d_{avg} is in cm.

To compute the size distribution below 8 mesh, we proceed to calculate x for different values of d_{avg} (without forgetting to maintain the screen interval of 1.41) from the above correlation until all the computed values of x add closely to 0.053 (that is, total mass fraction of − 8 material). The results are given below.

d_{avg}, cm	x	Specific Surface Ratio (n)
0.0063475	0.0142	1.65
0.0045	0.0108	1.60
0.00319275	0.0083	1.5
0.002264	0.00636	1.5
0.001606	0.00486	1.45
0.0011389	0.003725	1.40
0.000810	0.002852	1.35
0.000573	0.002183	1.30

Having thus made the size distribution complete, let us now compute (nx/d_{avg}) for all the fractions.

Mass Fraction (x)	(nx/d_{avg})
0.01	0.07677
0.04	0.37475
0.081	0.9998
0.115	1.84046
0.160	3.1988
0.148	3.9120
0.132	4.6025
0.081	3.6818
0.062	3.6368
0.041	3.2347
0.036	3.6795
0.022	3.0196
0.019	3.6089
0.0142	3.6912
0.0108	3.84
0.0083	3.8995
0.00636	4.2138
0.00486	4.3879
0.003725	4.579
0.002852	4.759
0.002183	4.9527
	$\Sigma \dfrac{n_i x_i}{d_{avg_i}} = 70.18378 \text{ cm}^{-1}$

MECHANICAL OPERATIONS — PROPERTIES AND HANDLING OF PARTICULATE SOLIDS

Specific surface of sample, $S_m = \dfrac{6}{7.43}[70.18378]$
$= 56.676 \text{ cm}^2/\text{gm} = 5.667 \text{ m}^2/\text{kg}$

Sauter diameter, $D_{vs} = 1/\Sigma \dfrac{n_i x_i}{d_{avg_i}} = \dfrac{1}{[70.18378]} = 0.14248 \text{ mm}$

Example 1.9:

In the above example, estimate the total number of particles per kg of the sample, if the volume shape factor (λ_v) of the material is 2.0 and may be assumed to be essentially constant within the size under consideration.

Solution: The number of particles per unit mass of the sample can be computed from the following equation.

$$(N/M) = \dfrac{1}{\lambda_v \rho_s} \sum_i \dfrac{x_i}{d_{avg_i}^3}$$

where, $\lambda_v = 2.0$ and $\rho_s = 7.43$ gm/cc. Let us therefore compute the value of (x/d_{avg}^3) for all the fractions.

x	d_{avg}, cm	$[x/d_{avg}^3]$, cm^{-3}
0.01	0.521	0.0707
0.04	0.4056	0.5995
0.081	0.2876	3.405
0.115	0.19995	14.386
0.16	0.14005	58.247
0.148	0.10215	138.850
0.132	0.0717	358.110
0.081	0.0506	625.221
0.062	0.0358	1351.27
0.041	0.02535	2516.807
0.036	0.0181	6071.09
0.022	0.01275	10,614.318
0.019	0.00895	26,502.352
0.0142	0.0063475	55,523.928
0.0108	0.0045	118,518.50
0.0083	0.00319275	255,037.29
0.00636	0.002264	548,059.50
0.00486	0.001606	1,173,274.50
0.003725	0.0011389	2,521,560.20
0.002852	0.00081	5,366,540.30
0.002183	0.000573	11,603,524.0
		$\Sigma \dfrac{x_i}{d_{avg_i}^3} = 21{,}690{,}292.0$

Therefore, $(N/M) = \dfrac{1}{(2.0)(7.43)} [21{,}690{,}292.0] = 14{,}59{,}643$ per gm.

Number of particles per kg = **1459.643 × 10⁶**. (Ans.)

Example 1.10:

The screen analysis shown in the following table applies to a sample of crushed quartz. The density of the particles is 2650 kg/m³ and the shape factors are a = 2, spherecity = 0.571. For the material between 4 - mesh and 200 - mesh in particle size, calculate:

(a) A_w in square millimeters per gram and N_w in particles per gram.

(b) ($\bar{D}_v$) Volume mean diameter.

(c) ($\bar{D}_s$) Volume surface mean diameter.

(d) ($\bar{D}_w$) Weight mean diameter.

(e) (N_i) for the 150/200 - mesh increment.

Mesh	Screen Opening D_{Pi}, mm	Mass fraction retained, x_i	Average particle diameter in increment, $\bar{D}_{Pi}$, mm	Cumulative fractions smaller than D_{Pi}
4	4.699	0.0000	–	1.0000
6	3.327	0.0251	4.013	0.9749
8	2.362	0.1250	2.845	0.8499
10	1.651	0.3207	2.007	0.5292
14	1.168	0.2570	1.4009	0.2722
20	0.833	0.1590	1.001	0.1132
28	0.589	0.0538	0.711	0.0594
35	0.417	0.0210	0.503	0.0384
48	0.295	0.0102	0.356	0.0282
65	0.208	0.0077	0.252	0.0205
100	0.147	0.0058	0.178	0.0147
150	0.104	0.0041	0.126	0.0106
200	0.074	0.0031	0.0889	0.0075
PAN	–	0.0075	0.037	0.0000

Solution: To find A_w and N_w we have equations,

$$A_w = \dfrac{6}{\phi_s \rho_p} \sum_{i=1}^{N} \dfrac{x_i}{\bar{D}_{Pi}} \quad \ldots (1)$$

where, subscripts indicates individual increments

x_i = Mass fractions in a given increment

n = Number of increments

$\overline{D}_{Pi}$ = Average particle diameter taken as arithmetic average of smallest and largest particle diameters in increment.

Thus, $$A_w = \frac{6}{0.5 + 1 \times 0.00625} \sum \frac{x_i}{\overline{D}_{P_i}} = 3965 \sum \frac{x_i}{\overline{D}_{P_i}}$$

and for a finding N_w, we have equation,

$$N_w = \frac{1}{a\rho_p} \sum_{i=1}^{n} \frac{x_i}{\overline{D}_{P_i}^3} = \frac{1}{a\rho_p \overline{D}^3 V} \quad \ldots (2)$$

Thus, $$N_w = \frac{1}{2 \times 0.00625} \sum \frac{x_i}{\overline{D}_{P_i}^3} = 188.7 \sum \frac{x_i}{\overline{D}_{P_i}^3}$$

(a) For the 4/6 mesh increment, $\overline{D}_{P_i}$ is the arithmetic mean of the mesh openings of the defining screens or from screen analysis table, we have,

$$\frac{4.699 + 3.327}{2} = 4.013 \text{ mm}$$

For this increment, $x_i = 0.0251$

and hence, $\dfrac{x_i}{\overline{D}_{P_i}} = \dfrac{0.0251}{4.013} = 0.0063$

and $x_i \overline{D}_{P_i}^3 = 0.0004$

Corresponding quantities are calculated for the other 11 increments and summed to give $\sum \dfrac{x_i}{\overline{D}_{P_i}} = 0.8284$ and $\sum \dfrac{x_i}{\overline{D}_{P_i}^3} = 8.8296$

Since the pan fraction is excluded, the specific surface and number of particles per unit mass of particles 200 - mesh or larger are found by dividing the results from equations (1) and (2) by $1 - x_1$ (since i = 1 for the Pan) or $1 - 0.0075 = 0.09925$.

Then, $$A_w = \frac{3965 \times 0.8284}{0.9925} = 3309 \text{ mm}^2/\text{gm} \quad \textbf{(Ans.)}$$

and $$N_w = \frac{188.7 \times 8.8296}{0.9925}$$

$$= 1679 \text{ Particles/gm} \quad \textbf{(Ans.)}$$

(b) The Volume – Mean Diameter ($\bar{D}_V$) is given by,

$$\bar{D}_V = \left[\frac{1}{\sum_{i=1}^{n}\left(\frac{x_i}{\bar{D}_{P_i}^3}\right)} \right]$$

$$= \frac{1}{(8.8296)^{1/3}}$$

$\bar{D}_V = 0.4238$ mm **(Ans.)**

(c) The volume-surface mean diameter ($\bar{D}_S$) is given by,

$$\bar{D}_S = \frac{1}{\sum_{i=1}^{n}\left(\frac{x_i}{\bar{D}_{P_i}}\right)}$$

$$= \frac{1}{0.8284}$$

$\bar{D}_S = 1.207$ mm **(Ans.)**

(d) Mass mean diameter $\bar{D}_W$ is given by:

$$\bar{D}_W = \sum_{i=1}^{n} x_i \bar{D}_{P_i}$$

$\bar{D}_W = 1.677$ mm **(Ans.)**

(e) The number of particles in the 150/200 mesh increment is given by,

$$\frac{1}{a\,\rho_P}\sum_{i=1}^{n}\frac{x_i}{\bar{D}_P^3} = \frac{x_2}{a\,\rho_P\,\bar{D}_{P_2}^3} = \frac{0.0031}{2 \times 0.00265 \times 0.089^3}$$

$N_W = 836$ particles/gm **(Ans.)**

Example 1.11:
Calculate the sphericity of a cylinder of a diameter 1 cm and height 3 cm.

Solution: Let r_c = Radius of cylinder
r_s = Radius of sphere

Volume of particle = $\pi r_c^2 h = p \times 0.5^2 \times 3 = 2.356$ cm³

Radius of sphere of volume 2.356 cm³:

$$\frac{4\pi r_s^3}{3} = 2.356$$

$r_s = 0.8255$ cm.

Chp 1 | 1.69

Surface area of sphere of same volume as the particle
$$= 4\pi r_s^2 = 4 \times \pi \times 0.8255^2$$
$$= 8.563 \text{ cm}^2$$

Surface area of particle $= 2\pi r_c (h + r_c) = 2 \times \pi \times 0.5 \times (3 + 0.5) = 10.996 \text{ cm}^2$

Sphericity $(\phi_s) = \dfrac{8.563}{10.996} = 0.779$

Sphericity could also be found from the formula,

$$\text{Sphericity } (\phi_s) = \dfrac{6 V_p}{(D_p S_p)}$$

Where,
V_p = Volume of particle.
D_p = Equivalent diameter of particle.

(Equivalent diameter is defined as the diameter of a sphere of equal volume)

S_p = Surface area of particle
$V_p = \pi r_c^2 h$
$\quad = 2.356 \text{ cm}^3$
$D_p = 2 r_s$
$\quad = 2 \times 0.8255$
$\quad = 1.651 \text{ cm}$
$S_p = 2\pi r_c (h + r_c)$
$\quad = 10.996 \text{ cm}^2$
$\phi_s = \dfrac{6 \times 2.356}{(1.651 \times 10.996)}$
$\quad = 0.779.$

∴ Sphericity $= \phi_s = 0.779$ **(Ans.)**

Example 1.12:

Calculate sphericity of a solid particle of cubical shape.

Solution:
$$\phi = \text{sphericity} = \dfrac{\text{Surface area of sphere of same volume as the particle}}{\text{Surface area of particle}}$$

Volume of particle $= a^3$

Volume of sphere $= a^3 = \left(\dfrac{4}{3}\right)\pi r^3$

∴ $r = \sqrt[3]{\dfrac{3}{(4\pi)}}$

Surface area of sphere $= 4\pi r^2$

$$= 4\pi \left[\frac{3}{(4\pi)}\right]^{2/3} \cdot a^2$$

$$= (4\pi)^{1/3} \cdot 3^{2/3} \cdot a^2$$

Surface area of sphere $= 6a^2$

Hence, from equation (1), we get,

$$\phi = \frac{(4\pi)^{1/3} \cdot 3^{2/3} \cdot a^2}{6 \cdot a^2}$$

$$= \left(\frac{4\pi}{3}\right)^{1/3} \cdot \frac{3}{6}$$

$$\phi = \left(\frac{\pi}{6}\right)^{1/3} \qquad \text{(Ans.)}$$

Example 1.13:

A large welded steel silo 4 meters in diameter and 20 meters high is to be built. The silo has a central discharge on a flat bottom. Estimate the pressure on the wall at the bottom of the silo if the silo is filled with (a) plastic pellets, and (b) water. The plastic pellets have the following characteristics:

$$\rho° = 560 \text{ kg/m}^3$$
$$\phi = 20°$$

Solution: (a) The Janssen equation is for silos of circular cross-section. Diameter and height are given in the problem statement. The coefficient of wall friction is obtained by inverting equation as,

$$\mu = \tan(20°) = 0.364$$

K, the Janssen coefficient, is assumed to be 0.4. The Janssen coefficient can vary with material as indicated in Fig. 1.12, but is not often measured. Substituting these quantities into equation (1.38), we get the vertical stress at the bottom of the silo:

$$P_v = \frac{\rho° gD}{4\mu K g_c}\left(1 - \exp\left(-\frac{4z\mu K}{D}\right)\right)$$

$$= \frac{(560 \text{ kg/m}^3)(9.807 \text{ m/s}^2)(4m)}{4(0.364)(0.4)(1 \text{ kg m/Ns}^2)}$$

$$\left(1 - \exp\left(\frac{-4(20 \text{ m})(0.364)(0.4)}{4m}\right)\right)$$

$$= 35{,}668 \text{ N/m}^2 \text{ (or 5.2 psi)}$$

To estimate the normal stress on the wall we apply Janssen's assumption.

$$P_w = kP_v$$
$$= 0.4 (35{,}668 \text{ N/m}^2)$$
$$= 14{,}267 \text{ N/m}^2 \text{ (2.1 psi)} \qquad \text{(Ans.)}$$

(b) If the silo was filled with water instead of granular solids, the pressure at depth H is given by,

$$P = \frac{\rho g H}{g_c}$$

$$= \frac{1000 \text{ kg/m}^3 \, (9.807 \text{ m/s}^2) \, (20 \text{ m})}{1 \text{ kg m/Ns}^2}$$

$$= 196{,}140 \text{ N/m}^2 \, (28.4 \text{ psi})$$

The result in (b) is a factor of about 13 times greater than the normal wall stress calculated in (a). This is due to the wall friction exerting a vertical upward force on the granular solids.

Example 1.14:

A large welded steel silo 12 ft. in diameter and 60 feet high is to be built. The silo has a central discharge on a flat bottom. Estimate the pressure of the wall at the bottom of the silo if the silo is filled with (a) plastic pellets, and (b) water. The plastic pellets have the following characteristics:

$\gamma = 35$ lb/cu ft, $\phi' = 20°$.

Solution: The Janssen equation is,

$$P_V = (\gamma g D/4\mu K)(1 - \exp(-4H \mu K/D))$$

In this case:

$D = 12$ ft

$\mu = \tan \phi' = \tan 20° = 0.364$

$H = 60$ ft

$g = 32.2$ ft/sec^2

$\gamma = 35$ lb/cu ft

K, the Janssen coefficient, is assumed to be 0.4. It can vary according to the material but it is not often measured.

Substituting we get, $P_V = 21{,}958$ lb$_m$/ft - sec^2.

If we divide by g_c, we get $P_V = 681.9$ lb$_f$/ft^2 or 681.9 psf

Remember that $P_W = K P_V$, so $P_W = 272.8$ psf.

For water P, $= \rho g H$ and this results in P = 3744 psf, a factor of 14 greater. **(Ans)**

MECHANICAL OPERATIONS — PROPERTIES AND HANDLING OF PARTICULATE SOLIDS

Example 1.15:

A sample of the feed, coarse, and fines streams for a separation of a material 'Hexamethyl chicken wire" is screened with the following results:

Screen size (microns)	Average particle size	Feed size mass fraction retained on screen	Mass rate of particles size x in feed stream	Coarse size mass fraction retained on screen	Mass rate of particles size x in coarse stream	Fines size mass fraction retained on screen	Mass rate of particles size x in fines stream	$G(x) = \dfrac{M_{cx}}{M_x}$
		ΔF_x	M_x	ΔF_{cx}	M_{cx}	ΔF_{fx}	M_{fx}	
850		~0		~0		~0		
600	725	0.30		0.45		0.075		
425	512.5	0.40		0.45		0.325		
300	362.5	0.20		0.09		0.365		
212	256	0.10		0.01		0.235		
Total		1		1		1		

The stream rates are:
- Feed rate = 100 lbm/hr
- Coarse product rate = 60 lbm/hr
- Fines product rate = 40 lbm/hr

Plot the grade efficiency curve and calculate $I_{20/80}$.

Solution: A sample of the feed, coarse, and fines streams for a separation of a material "Hexamethyl chicken wire" is screened with the following results:

Screen size (microns)	Average particle size	Feed size mass fraction retained on screen	Mass rate of particles size x in feed stream	Coarse size mass fraction retained on screen	Mass rate of particles size x in coarse stream	Fines size mass fraction retained on screen	Mass rate of particles size x in fines stream	$G(x) = \dfrac{M_{cx}}{M_x}$
		ΔF_x	M_x	ΔF_{cx}	M_{cx}	ΔF_{fx}	M_{fx}	
850		~0	0	~0	0	~0	0	0
600	725	0.30	30	0.45	27	0.075	3	0.9
425	512.5	0.40	40	0.45	27	0.325	13	0.68
300	362.5	0.20	20	0.09	5.4	0.365	14.6	0.27
212	256	0.10	10	0.01	0.6	0.235	9.4	0.06
Total		1	100	1	60	1	40	

The stream rates are:
- Feed rate = 100 lb,/hr
- Coarse product rate = 60 lbm/hr
- Fines product rate = 40 lbm/hr

Plot the grade efficiency curve and calculate $I_{20/80}$.

$$\text{Recall that, } M_x = M \Delta F_x$$
$$M_{cx} = M_c \Delta F_{cx}$$
$$M_{fx} = M_f \Delta F_{fx}$$

Using these equations and a basis of 1 hour, the table is filled in.

The calculated points for the Grade Efficiency are plotted on the graph and a curve is fitted to the points. From the curve the x_{20}, x_{50} and x_{80} values are estimated to be 330, 450 and 625 microns respectively.

The sharpness of cut is calculated to be

$$I_{20/80} = \frac{330}{625} = 0.528$$

Note, mass retained on the 850 microns screen is zero. In the limit G_x approaches 1 at this size (G_x = 1 at the size for which all the particles exit the separator in the coarse stream).

Plot G_x vs the average particle size to determine the x_{20}, x_{50} and x_{80} values.

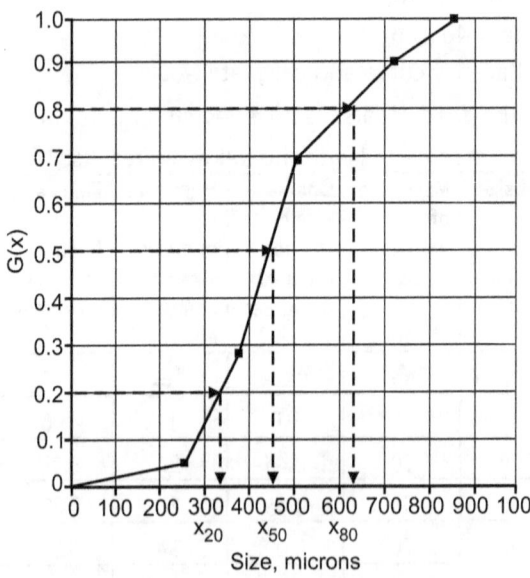

Fig. 1.30: Average Particle Distribution

Example 1.16:

The grade efficiency represents the fractional amount of particles by mass size x in the feed stream that exists the separator in the coarse stream. Derive a formula in terms of grade efficiencies for determining the fractional amount of particles of size x in the coarse stream existing separator 2 in the compound process shown in Fig. 1.31.

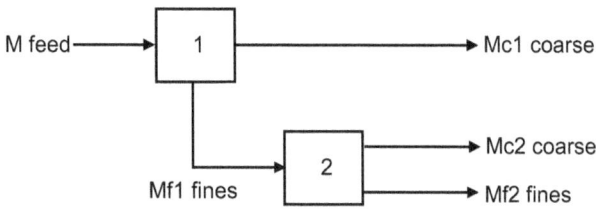

Fig. 1.31: Coarse Stream Separator

Solution: The fractional amount of size x in the coarse stream existing separator 2 can be determined by,

Mass balances

$$M_{f1} = M_{c2} + M_{f2}$$
$$M = M_{c1} + M_{f1}$$

Definitions

$$G_1 = \frac{M_{c1}}{M}$$

$$G_2 = \frac{M_{c2}}{M_{f1}}$$

Fractional amount of feed existing separator 2 is given by,

$$\frac{M_{c2}}{M} = \frac{M_{c2}}{M_{f1}} \cdot \frac{M_{f1}}{M}$$

$$= G_2 \frac{M - M_{c1}}{M}$$

$$= G_2 (1 - G_1) \qquad \text{(Ans)}$$

Example 1.17:

You have 10,000 sphericals particles, 50% by weight of these particles are 25 μm in diameter, the other 50% are 75 μm in diameter. How many of the smaller particles do you have?

Solution: The mass of a particle with diameter 75 μm will be 27 times greater than the mass of a particle of diameter 25 μm. Hence, there will be 27 times as many as particles as there are large ones. Hence, $\frac{1}{28}$ of the particles will be large i.e. 357 (to the nearest whole number) leaving 9,643 small particles.

The number fraction of small particles is 96.4% as compared to a mass fraction of 50%.

MECHANICAL OPERATIONS — PROPERTIES AND HANDLING OF PARTICULATE SOLIDS

Example 1.18:
If a particle of diameter 1 unit has a terminal velocity of 1.2 m/s what is the terminal velocity of a particle with diameter 2 units?

Solution: Terminal velocity varies with the square of the diameter of a particle, hence a particle with double the diameter will fall with a terminal velocity 4 times greater i.e. 4.8 ms^{-1}, all other factors being the same.

Example 1.19:
An Andreasen pipette apparatus was filled to a depth of 5 cm above the pipette tip with an initially homogeneous suspension of power station fly ash in water. At intervals 10 ml samples of the suspension were withdrawn, dried and weighed to find the quantity of suspended solids in the liquids sample.

Time (min)	0	0.5	1	2	10	20	30	60	360	1080
mg solid	100	97	91	79	52	43	28	19	8	4

The density of fly ash is 2400 kgm^{-3}.

Draw a cumulative oversize size distribution curve.

Solution: Maximum particle diameter in a sample is given by,

$$d_{max} = \left\{\frac{18\mu\,(h/t)}{(\rho_s - \rho_p)g}\right\}^{\frac{1}{2}} = \left\{\frac{18 \times 10^{-3} \times 0.05}{(2400-1000) \times 9.81\,t}\right\}^{\frac{1}{2}}$$

$$= \frac{2.56 \times 10^{-4}}{t^{1/2}}\,m = \frac{256}{t^{1/2}}\,\mu m$$

Weight fraction of solids with terminal velocity less than h/t is given by $C(t)/C_0$. The oversize fraction, $O(d_{max})$ is given by $\left(1 - \frac{C}{C_0}\right)$. Thus, a table can be produced.

Time (s)	30	60	120	600	1200
$d_{max}/\mu m$	46.7	33	23.4	10.5	7.4
C/C_0	0.97	0.91	0.79	0.52	0.43
$O(d_{max})$, %	3	9	21	48	57

Time (s)	1800	3600	21600	64800
$d_{max}\,\mu m$	6.0	4.3	1.7	1
C/C_0	0.28	0.19	0.08	0.904
$O(d_{max})$, %	72	81	92	96

The oversize curve is a plot of $O(d_{max})$ vs. d

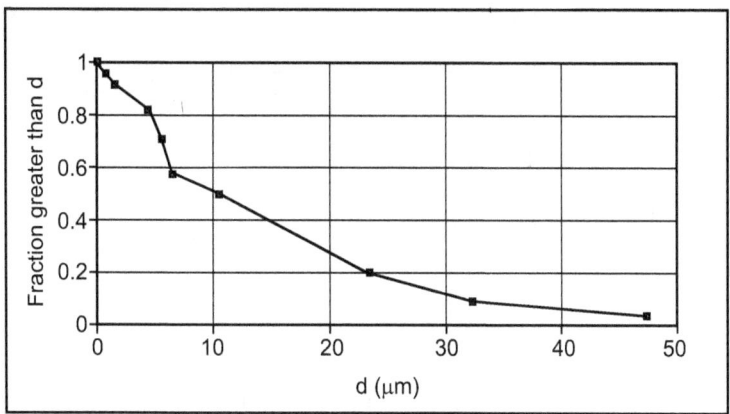

Fig. 1.32: Oversize Curve

Example 1.20:
The table below gives the results of a microscopic size analysis of a particulate solid sample. The lower limit of resolution of the instrument was 40 μm. By plotting the data logarithmically, find whether the size distribution corresponds to the gamma distribution and, if so, of what order. Estimate the percentage of particles in the 20-40 μm range.

Size range (μm)	Number % of particles
40-60	0.996
60-80	2.025
80-100	3.189
100-120	4.314
120-140	5.275
140-160	6.003
160-180	6.474
180-200	6.695
200-220	6.697

Solution: The log-log graph of the data is appended. The graph does tend to a straight line at small values of d implying that it is a gamma distribution. The gradient of the straight part of the line is 2.04, so the value of m can be assumed to be 2.

The percentage of particles in the 20-40 μm range can be estimated from the graph by reading the % in range value for d = 30 μm which is 0.325%.

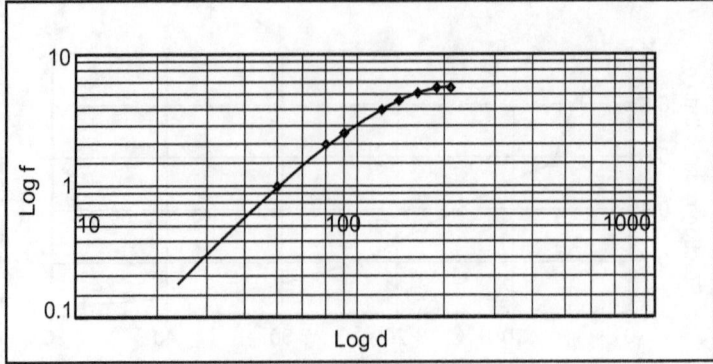

Fig. 1.33: Plot of log f vs. log d

Example 1.21:

The size distribution function of a sample of freshly ground material is given by,

$$f(d) = 1.35 \times 10^{-7} d^3 e^{-0.03d}$$

Data: For integral values of m.

$$\int_{d_1}^{d_2} a d^m e^{-bd} d(d) = e^{-bd_1}\left\{1 + \sum_{j=1}^{m} \frac{(bd_1)^j}{j!}\right\} - e^{-bd_2}\left\{1 + \sum_{j=1}^{m} \frac{(bd_2)^j}{j!}\right\}$$

where, d is the particle diameter in μm.

Solution: Find: (a) The most common particle size.

This question can easily be answered from first principles by finding the maximum of the distribution. This is, of course done by differentiating the function and setting the derivative equal to 0,

$$f(d) = 1.35 \times 10^{-7} d^3 e^{-0.03d}$$

$$\frac{df(d)}{dd} = 1.35 \times 10^{-7} \{3d^2 e^{-0.03} - 0.03 d^3 e^{-0.03}\}$$

Setting this equal to 0 and cancelling gives,

$$3d^2 - 0.03 d^3 = 0$$

$$3d^2 = 0.03 d^3$$

$$d = \frac{3}{0.03} = 100 \text{ μm}$$

Alternatively you can take a short cut and simply use the relationship for a Gamma function, which this clearly is, where m = 3, b = 0.03 and a = 1.35 × 10⁻⁷.

The most common size is therefore given by,

$$\frac{m}{b} = \frac{3}{0.03} = 100 \text{ μm}$$

(b) The length mean particle size

The length mean diameter

$$\bar{d} = \frac{m+1}{b} = \frac{4}{0.03} = 133.3 \text{ μm}$$

(c) The fraction of particles below 75 μm in diameter

The fraction below 75 μm is equal to the integral from 0 to 75 μm of the expression given for the size distribution frequency function. We can use the integral given with following values: $d_1 = 0$, $d_2 = 75$ μm, $m = 3$, $b = 0.03$.

Hence, $bd_1 = 0$ and $bd_2 = 2.25$, so the fraction below 75 μm is,

$$e^0 \{1 + 0 + 0 + 0\} - e^{-2.25}\left\{1 + 2.25 + \frac{(2.25)^2}{2 \times 1} + \frac{(2.25)^2}{3 \times 2 \times 1}\right\} = 1 - 0.8094 = 0.190$$

(d) The fraction of particles between 125 and 175 μm in size.

Similarly, the fraction with diameter between 125 and 175 μm is given by the integral of the frequency function between these limits:

$d_1 = 125$ μm, $bd_1 = 3.75$, $d_2 = 175$ μm, $bd_2 = 5.25$

Hence, the fraction in this range is,

$$e^{-3.75}\left\{1 + 3.75 + \frac{(3.75)^2}{2} + \frac{(3.75)^3}{6}\right\} - e^{-5.25}\left\{1 + 5.25 + \frac{(5.25)^2}{2} + \frac{(5.25)^3}{6}\right\}$$

$$= 0.4838 - 0.2317 = 0.2521$$

Example 1.22:

A sieve analysis of a sample of sand yielded the following results:

BSS No. Sieve	Aperture Size (μm)	Weight Retained (%)
100	152	0.41
120	125	2.36
150	104	48.30
170	89	40.00
200	76	5.93
Pan		3.00

In a separate experiment the density of the sand was determined as follows:

A 25 ml density bottle was weighed, carefully filled with the sand and reweighed. Benzene was then poured into the bottle until no more could be accommodated and the bottle was weighed again. The weights recorded were:

Weight of empty bottle	15.3600 g
Weight of bottle and sand	50.0835 g
Weight of bottle, sand and benzene	58.0806 g

Find the linear, surface area, volume and surface-volume mean diameters of the sand as well as its bulk and true density, voidage and specific surface area.

Data: Density of benzene is 872.4 kgm^{-3}.

Solution: The mean diameters are best calculated using a spreadsheet, since tedious and repetitive calculations are involved! The table below shows all the intermediate values, which are needed to calculate the mean diameters.

In this case, we do not know the mean size for the fractions, which are greater than 100 mesh size. Since this only accounts for 0.41% of the total material it will make little difference if we ignore this fraction. It is necessary however to adjust the other fractions so that the total is still 100%.

For the materials less than 200 mesh, we can assume that the mean size is 38 μm i.e. the average of 0 and 76 μm.

Mesh range	Mean size μm	Corr. wt.%	w_i/d_i	w_i/d_i^2	w_i/d_i^3
100-120	138.5	2.37	0.01711	1.2354×10^{-4}	8.920×10^{-7}
120-150	115	48.50	0.42173	3.667×10^{-3}	3.189×10^{-5}
150-170	96.5	40.165	0.4162	4.313×10^{-3}	4.470×10^{-5}
170-200	83	5.954	0.07174	8.643×10^{-4}	1.0414×10^{-5}
0-200	38	3.01	0.07927	2.0861×10^{-3}	5.4898×10^{-5}
Sums	–	–	1.0061	1.1054×10^{-2}	1.4279×10^{-4}

Hence, the mean diameters are as follows:

$$\bar{d}_L = \frac{\sum w_i/d_i^2}{\sum w_i/d_i^3} = 77.42 \ \mu m$$

$$\bar{d}_a = \left(\frac{\sum w_i/d_i}{\sum w_i/d_i^3}\right)^{\frac{1}{2}} = 83.94 \ \mu m$$

$$\bar{d}_v = \left(\frac{\sum w_i}{\sum w_i/d_i^3}\right)^{\frac{1}{3}} = 88.80 \ \mu m$$

$$\overline{d_{vs}} = \frac{\sum w_i}{\sum w_i/d_i} = 99.40 \ \mu m$$

Weight of sand in bottle = 34.7235 g
Weight of benzene = 7.9941 g
Volume of benzene = 9.1668 ml
Volume of sand = 25.0000 − 9.1668 = 15.8322 ml

MECHANICAL OPERATIONS   PROPERTIES AND HANDLING OF PARTICULATE SOLIDS

True density of sand = 34.7235/15.8322 = 2.1931 g/ml
Bulk density = 34.7235/25.0000 = 1.3889 g/ml
Voidage = 9.1668/25 = 0.3667

$$\text{Surface per unit mass} = \frac{\pi \bar{d}_{vs}^2}{\frac{\pi}{6}\rho_s \bar{d}_{vs}^3} = \frac{6}{\rho_s \bar{d}_{vs}}$$

$$= \frac{6}{2193.1 \times 99.40 \times 10^{-6}}$$

$$= 27.49 \text{ m}^2/\text{kg}$$

$$= 275 \text{ cm}^2/\text{g}$$

(Assuming the particles are spherical).

EXERCISE FOR PRACTICE

(1) The size analysis of the screen underflow from a rod mill is as follows:

Plus 6 mesh	Weight % retained on each size	Plus 6 mesh	Weight % retained on each size
8	–	10	–
14	–	20	3
28	6	35	8.3
48	8.7	65	8.1
100	8.4	150	7.6
200	8.1	325	8.8
400	7.5	Plus 400	24.5

Do as follows:
(a) Plot weight % retained (cumulative) against particle size.
(b) Estimate 80% passing size.
(c) Make a log-log plot of cumulative weight % finer against particle size.
(d) From the log-log plot, estimate the weight percent of material finer than 16 microns.

(2) Find out the specific surface of (a) a sphere of diameter 4 cm and density 5 gm/cm³ (b) cube with a side 5 cm and density 2.6 gm/cm³.

(3) Show that the vertical static pressure at the base of a cylindrical hopper is,

$$p_B = \frac{r\rho_b g}{2\mu K'}\left(1 - e^{-\frac{2\mu K' z_t}{r}}\right)$$

where, r is the hopper radius.
ρ_b is the solid bulk density.
μ is the coefficient of friction between solids and wall.
K' is the ratio of lateral to vertical pressure.
and z_t is the total height of solids above the base.

Why would the design pressures in a hopper be greater than those calculated from the above equation?

(4) A hopper contains coffee beans with a true density of 1200 kgm^{-3} and voidage of 0.35. The hopper is cylindrical, diameter 1.5 m, height 5m.
The coefficient of friction between the coffee and the hopper wall is 0.4 and the ratio of lateral to vertical pressure in this material is 0.3 What are the maximum vertical and horizontal static pressures in this vessel?

(5) By using a force balance on a horizontal layer of solids of differential thickness show that the vertical pressure at the base of a hopper containing particulate solids is given by:

$$P_b = \frac{r\rho_b g}{2\mu K'}\left(1 - e^{-2\mu K' z_t / r}\right)$$

where,

P_b = Vertical pressure at hopper base
r = Hopper radius
ρ_b = Bulk density
K' = Ratio of normal pressure to applied pressure
μ = Coefficient of friction between solids and wall
z_t = Total depth of solids

Clearly state all assumptions.

(6) A cylindrical hopper of diameter 1m is filled to a depth of 4m with solids with true density 2200 kgm^{-3} and voidage 0.4. For this material the coefficient of friction between the solids and the wall is 0.45 and the ratio of normal to applied pressure is 0.50. Calculate the vertical and horizontal pressures at the base of the hopper.

(7) Fine sand with a bulk density of 1,560 kg/m³ and angle of internal friction of $\phi = 24.1°$ is stored in a tall cylindrical bin of diameter $D = 2$, $b = 1.8$ m and an angle of wall friction of $\phi_w = 20.2°$. Take $g \approx 10$ m/sec.
(a) Calculate the maximum vertical stress in the bin assuming active state of stress.
(b) Use Janssen's equations to determine the depth at which the vertical stress reaches 99% of its maximum value; also calculate the wall pressure at this point.
(c) Compare the hydrostatic pressure at the point calculated in question (b) to the actual stresses present in the powder.
(d) Recalculate questions: (a), (c) for the case of passive stress in the bin.

(8) A mixture of spherical particles consists of 60% number fraction 1 mm diameter particles and 40% number fraction 2 mm particles. Both sizes of particle have the same density.
(i) What is the mass fraction of large particles?
(ii) Describe, in words, what is meant by the volume mean diameter of a mixture of particles. What is the volume mean diameter of the mixture described in (1) above?

MECHANICAL OPERATIONS   PROPERTIES AND HANDLING OF PARTICULATE SOLIDS

(iii) 100 kg of the mixture is sieved on a sieve with nominal aperture size 1.5 mm. The smaller particles are the desired material in this case. The recovery of this sieve is 87% and the rejection is 95%.

(iv) What mass of material passes through the sieve?

Table 1.9

Mesh	Screen opening, mm	Mass retained, g
4	4.699	0
6	3.327	0.251
8	2.362	1.250
10	1.651	3.207
14	1.168	2.570
20	0.833	1.590
28	0.589	0.538
35	0.417	0.210
48	0.295	0.102
65	0.208	0.077
100	0.147	0.058
150	0.104	0.041
200	0.074	0.031
Pan	–	0.075

(9) Plot the cumulative distribution of the data given in above Table 1.6 on semilog paper. Is the plot linear over any range of particle sizes? How does the amount of fine material (smaller than 20 mesh) differ from what would be predicted from the size distribution of the coarser material?

(10) Suppose you have a cube shaped particle (all three sides are equal length L).
  (a) What is the equivalent sphere diameter what would pass through the smallest screen that the cube can pass?
  (b) What is the equivalent sphere diameter of a sphere of the same volume as the cube?
  (c) What is the equivalent sphere diameter of a sphere with the same projected area of the cube when the cube sits on a flat surface and the projected area is upward (such as on a microscope)?
  (d) What is the equivalent sphere diameter with the same projected area of the cube for the largest possible projected area of the cube (i.e. the cube in part c may rotate to a position that gives the largest projected area).

(11) A particle analysis is shown in Table.
  (a) Determine the median particle size and mode for the mass distribution.
  (b) Compare the arithmetic, quadratic, cubic, geometric, and harmonic mean particle sizes of the given mass distribution data where the means are defined by –

$$\overline{g(x)} = \int_0^1 g(x)\, dF$$

Table 1.10: Cumulative Percentage Undersize Distribution (by mass, Sieve Analysis)

Sieve size mm	Cum. % undersize
0.038	1.4
0.043	9.8
0.061	17.9
0.074	32
0.104	50
0.147	64.5
0.175	76
0.246	87.4
0.295	93.9
0.351	98.1
0.417	99.4
0.495	99.9

(12) Determine the mass arithmetic, quadratic, and geometric means from the following particle size distribution:

Cumulative % undersize by mass	Particle size (um)
0.7	20
5.0	30
15.0	40
27.5	50
42.0	60
53.0	70
64.0	80
72.5	90
80.0	100
90.0	125
95.0	150
98.5	200
99.6	250

(13) The size distribution of a particulate material can be approximated to a Gamma function size distribution where f(d), the frequency function of the distribution, is given by:

$$f(d) = a d^m e^{-bd}$$

d is the particle diameter.
a, b and m are constants for a particular sample.

(a) By differentiating (1) show that the most common particle diameter d_{max} can be expressed as a function of m and b for a sample, which is well described, by a gamma function of this type.

(b) Show that for integer values of m

$$a = \frac{b^{m+1}}{\Gamma(m + 1)}$$

(**Hint:** The gamma function is defined as

$$\Gamma(m + 1) = \int_0^\infty x^m e^{-x} dx$$

For integers $\Gamma(m + 1) = m\Gamma(m)$ i.e. $\Gamma(m) = (m - 1)!$
Use the substitution $x = bd$ when integrating).

(c) The data below was obtained by size analysis of a sample of material from a milling process. Use this data to obtain values of a, b and m by plotting appropriate graphs or otherwise.

(d) The mean particle diameter, $\bar{d}$, of a distribution is given by,

$$\bar{d} = \int_0^\infty df(d)\, d(d)$$

Show that for the gamma distribution given in (1),

$$\bar{d} = \frac{m + 1}{b}$$

and evaluate the mean diameter for the data provided. You may approximate m to the nearest integer.

DATA: Two tests were carried out: a counter test to determine the distribution of the coarser fractions and a laser diffraction test to determine the size distribution of the fines (< 10 μm).

Coulter Counter			
Size interval (μm)	Number of Percentage in interval	Size interval (μm)	Number of Percentage in Interval
<10	0.074	250-280	4.95
10-40	3.57	280-310	3.49
40-70	9.92	310-340	2.40
70-100	14.04	340.370	1.62
100-130	15.02	370-400	1.08
130-160	13.83	400-430	0.71
160-190	11.58	430-460	0.46
190-220	9.10	460-490	0.30
220-250	6.83	> 490	1.026

Laser Diffraction	
Size interval (μm)	Number of Percentage in Interval
0-2	0.621
2-4	5.589
4-6	15.293
6-8	29.721
8-10	48.776

(14) A mixture of spherical particles consists of 60% number of fraction 1 mm diameter particles and 40% number of fraction 2 mm particles. Both sizes of particle have the same density.

(a) What is the mass fraction of large particles?
(b) Describe, in words, what is meant by the volume mean diameter of a mixture of particles.
What is the volume mean diameter of the mixture descibed in (a) above?
(c) 100 kg of the mixture is sieved on a sieve with nominal aperture size 1.5 mm. The smaller particles are the desired material in this case. The recovery of this sieve is 87% and the rejection is 95%.
What mass of material passes through the sieve?

NOMENCLATURE

Symbol	
A	Area, m^2; total surface area of particles
A_W	Specific surface are of particle, m^2/gm
a	Volume shape factor [Equation (1.49)]
D	Diameter, mm; D_p, particle size; D_{p_i}, mesh opening in screen i
$\bar{D}$	Average particle size, mm, μ_m; $\bar{D}_N$, arithmetic mean diameter [Equation (1.46)], arithmetic mean of D_{p_i} and $D_{p_{i+1}}$; $\bar{D}_S$, mean volume-surface diameter [Equation (1.8)]; $\bar{D}_V$, volume mean diameter [Equation (1.48)]; $\bar{D}_W$, mass mean diameter [Equation (1.47)].
g	Gravitation acceleration, m/s^2
i	Number of fraction or increment; also screen number, counting from smallest size
K'	Ratio of pressures, p_V/p_L
N	Number of particles; N_T, total number; N_W, number per unit mass
p	Pressure, N/m^2
S_p	Surface area of particle, mm^2
t	Time, s
V_p	Volume of particles, mm^3
x_i	Mass fraction of total sample in increment
Greek Letters:	
α	Angle; α_m, angle of internal friction; α_r, angle of repose.
θ	Angle; θ_m, maximum value in stress analysis.
ρ	Density, kg/m^3, ρ_b, bulk density; ρ_p, particle density.
ϕ_S	Sphericity of particle, defined by Equation (1.1).

***

Unit II

Chapter 2: CONVEYORS

2.1 Introduction

This chapter covers the transportation of particles by fluids. It considers hydraulic, pneumatic and mechanical conveying means. The former uses liquids the second gases and an example of the latter is a conveyer belt. A basic course in fluid mechanics will equip the reader with sufficient knowledge to calculate the pressure drop for a given flow rate of a uniform, or homogeneous fluid.

The transportation of particulate solids is an important consideration of most processes involving solids. Often equipment selection is based on process considerations such as the need to void contamination from the environment of the valuable solid such as a pharmaceutical product. If required throughput is high, normally associated with low value products such as minerals, then a mechanical device is appropriate such as a belt conveyor. If the material is sticky, due to moisture or temperature softening, then a chain conveyor may be required. For most chemical and food processes pneumatic conveying is preferred because it is enclosed and controllable. Using a rotary valve to meter the solid input into the system the solid mass flow rate can be easily relayed to the control room, and changed by it, if the valve is controlled by an inverter.

The transport of solids variously described as *conveying*. Although it is easier to handle material in the form of fluids or slurries. In many situations materials are required to be taken from one place to the other within the factory. The choice of transportation equipment depends on the following factors:
(i)   Type of material transported.
(ii) Capacity necessary.
(iii) Shape and Size of Material.
(iv) Whether the material is to be transported horizontally, vertically or on an incline.

In general, the equipment used is normally designed on the basis of empirical experience rather than by any rational methods of calculations. This is due to the inherent variation of properties of the materials transported and also the very wide range of processes where material handling is involved. The following is the classification of some of the more important conveyors:

(1) Belt Conveyors
(2) Chain Conveyors:
    (a) Scraper Conveyors
    (b) Apron Conveyors
    (c) Bucket Conveyors
    (d) Bucket Elevators
(3) Screw Conveyors
(4) Pneumatic Conveyors.

2.2 Belt Conveyors

The belt conveyor consists of an endless belt moved on two pulleys at the two ends rotating with the help of suitable source of power as shown in Figure 2.1. The belts are made-up of rubber of special grade. The rubber is generally reinforced with appropriate cords to give more strength to the belt. Since the belt is very long it is supported on rollers called idlers. As shown in Figure 2.1 the idlers are troughed so as to allow the belt to be depressed at the center. This permits the belt to carry more material without spillage. There is a possibility of a change of length due to heavy loads or due to seasonal changes in temperature and humidity. Therefore, a tightener is provided so maintain even tension in the belt so that it remains tight.

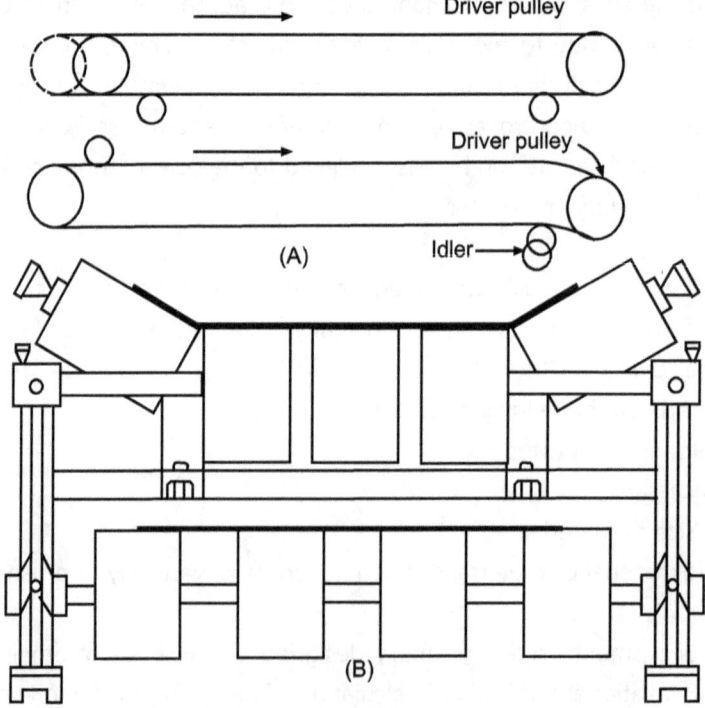

Fig. 2.1: Belt Conveyor

The capacity of a belt conveyor is dependent on the cross-section of the load and on the speed of the belt. The power required to run a belts depends on its width. Some typical values are given in Table 2.1.

Table 2.1: Horse power for One Tripper

Width of the belt (inch)	Plain bearings	Roller bearings
12	0.75	0.50
14	1.00	0.75
16	1.00	0.75
18	1.50	1.25
20	1.50	1.25
24	1.75	1.25
30	2.50	1.75

2.2.1 Belt Construction

The common material of construction for belt conveyor is rubber. It essentially consists of a core or carcass, of several piles of cotton duck, each impregnated with rubber and bonded together with rubber. Over the carcass is a covering of rubber that binds the whole together. Generally, the top cover is usually thicker than the undersize. Special grades of rubber may be employed to withstand excessively abrasive conditions higher temperature (upto 120°C), chemical attack. Safe working stress on such belts rounds from 25 to 40 lb/in per ply special constructions are available for temperature above 120°C.

2.2.2 Belt–Conveyor Drives

Various methods of driving belt conveyors are shown in Fig. 2.2.

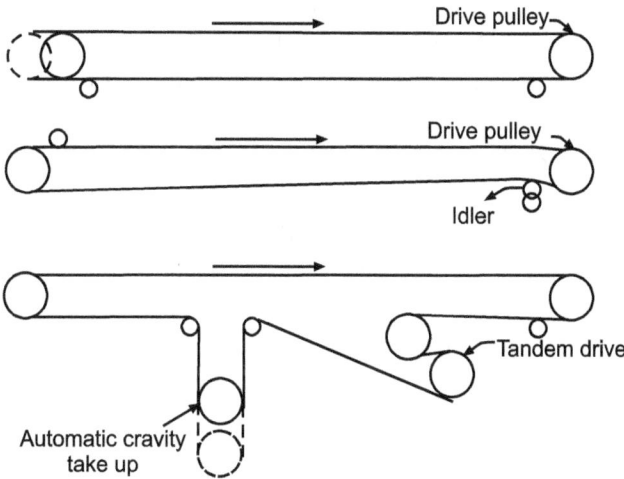

Fig. 2.2: Belt Conveyor Drives

The simplest possible drive is a bare steel pulley actuated by some source of power. This method is found best suitable when the power that must be transmitted is low enough to be carried by the friction of the belt on the pulley. In this type of drive, both the area of contact between the belt and pulley and the coefficient of friction are small.

2.2.3 Belt-Conveyor Supports

Typically, the supports for the belt are rollers and supported and are usually *idlers*. They are built in a large variety of forms. The most expensive are carried on roller bearings equipped with pressure-grease-gun lubrication. The cheaper ones are carried on ordinary bushings and lubricated with grease cups. The idlers are toughed so as to allow the belt to be depressed in the center and edges to be raised. This permits a belt of a given width to carry more material per linear meter without spillage.

2.2.4 Belt-Conveyor Take-Ups

For the shortest conveyors, changes in load or in weather, especially in temperature and humidity, result in a variation in belt length of sufficient magnitude to give an uneven tension if there is no provision for keeping the belt taut. Therefore, take-up must be installed to maintain an even tension on the belt under all conditions.

2.2.5 Feeders

The simplest method of feeding a belt conveyor is by means of a hopper. When hopper is used, the slope of the side should be such that the horizontal component of the velocity of material as it slides onto the belt is nearly the same as that of the belt itself. Other feeding devices includes short belt or apron conveyors discharging onto main conveyors, shaking screens, rotary-drum feeders, reciprocating – plate feeders and rotary-vane feeders. The types of chains available are so varied that it is difficult to bring them all into one simple classification. The major types may be classified as:

1. Malleable detachable chain.
2. Malleable pintle chain.
   - (a) Plain
   - (b) Interlocked
   - (c) Plain bushed
   - (d) Ley bushed
   - (e) Roller bushed
   - (f) Special forms such as sawdust, transfer etc.
3. Combination Chain
4. Steel Chain
   - (a) Ice Chain
   - (b) Flat and Round
   - (c) Roller Bushed
   - (d) Straight-Side-Long-Pitch

2.3 Chain Conveyors

A large number of conveyors is built around chains, these include scraper conveyor, apron conveyor, bucket conveyor and bucket elevators. The chain conveyors are cheaper and are simple to install as compared to the belt conveyors.

2.3.1 Scraper Conveyors

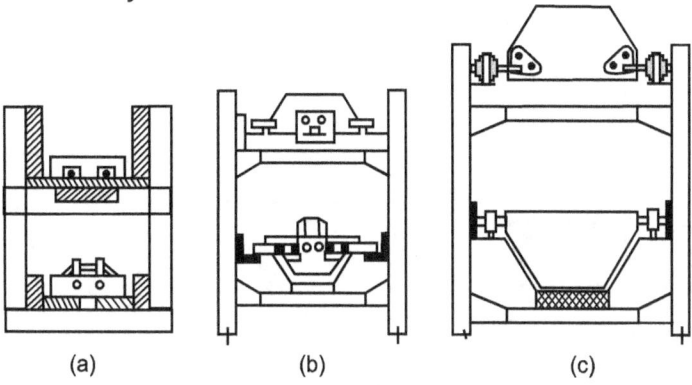

Fig. 2.3: Scraper Conveyor

The simple scraper conveyor using malleable chains and wooden flights are shown in Figure 2.3. The conveyor runs in a wooden trough. In the figure the upper run is the conveyor and the lower run acts as a return. The scraper conveyor is the cheapest and inexpensive type of conveyor. However, it consumes more power and needs frequent repairs if run continuously on heavy loads.

2.3.2 Apron Conveyor

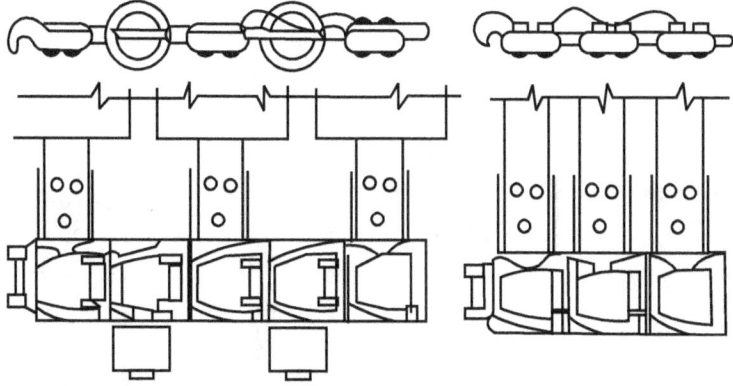

Fig. 2.4: Apron Conveyor

Apron conveyors are more useful for short runs and heavy loads. It consists of two chains made entirely of malleable detachable links. Wooden bars are fastened to the attachments of the chains and the whole conveyor moves on supports. For heavy use, steel plates replace wood bars. More elaborate constructions are also available. In such cases, it involves the use of long-pitch straight-side chains that carry steel plates with a depression stamped in each.

2.3.3 Bucket Conveyors and Bucket Elevators

Bucket conveyors are used for handling coal in powerhouses. Cast iron or stamped steel buckets are pivoted between two long pitch straight side steel chains. On a horizontal run the buckets overlap each other so that a continuous stream of material is formed. The buckets are so pivoted that on a vertical run they hang freely between chains and the conveyor acts as an elevator.

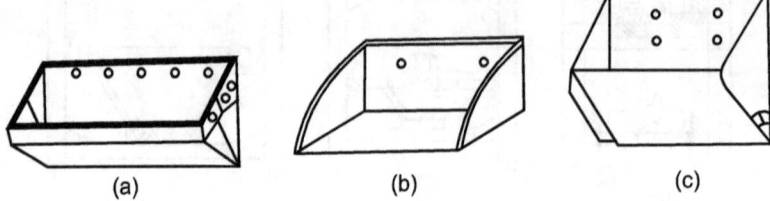

Fig. 2.5: Types of Buckets

The buckets used in conveyors are of several forms. Some of these are shown in the Fig. 2.5. The Minneapolis type buckets are used for the dry granular material. For sticky material flat buckets are used whereas for large heavy lump sheaves tamped steel buckets are used. The bucket elevators are operated at a speed of 150-250 feet per minute. At this speed the material is usually thrown from the bucket at the top of the elevator so that a spout placed to clear the head sprocket will receive all the discharged material. For lower speeds and heavy loads the so-called "perfect discharge" may be used. In this arrangement an idler sprocket, bends the chain back under the heat sprocket so that the buckets turn completely upside down over a spout placed under the head sprocket.

Elevators are driven from the head sprocket put because of the weight of the conveyor and the stretching of the chain under heavy loads devices are provided for altering the position of the sprocket at the boot of elevator located at the lower part. The buckets fill in the material by scooping into the loose material kept at the lower end. A typical elevator boot construction is shown in Fig. 2.6. The elevators are generally completely covered.

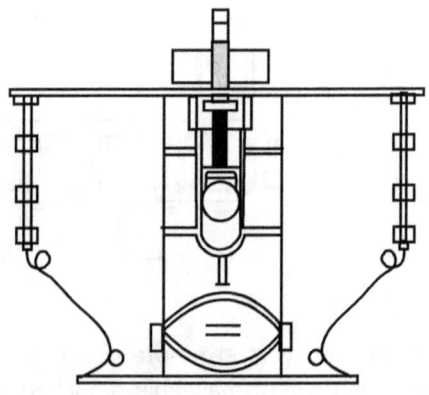

Fig. 2.6: Elevator Boot

2.4 Screw Conveyors (Flights)

Screw conveyor is extensively used to transport finely divided material and pastes. The conveyor essentially consists of a U-shaped trough in which a spiral blade round a horizontal axis is made to rotate. The screw element is called a flight and may be sectional, helical or of a special shape as shown in Fig. 2.7.

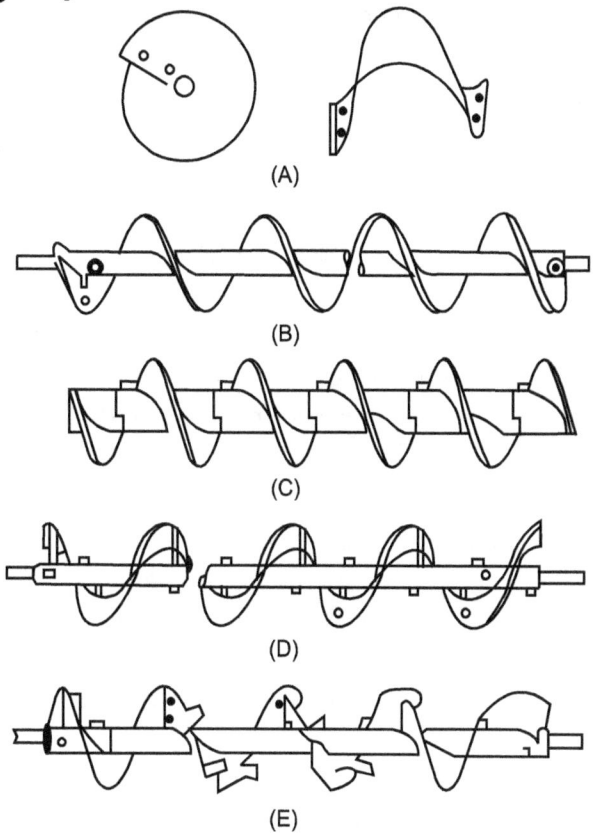

Fig. 2.7: Screw Conveyor Flights

The trough is ordinarily made of sheet metal and a typical trough is shown in Fig. 2.8.

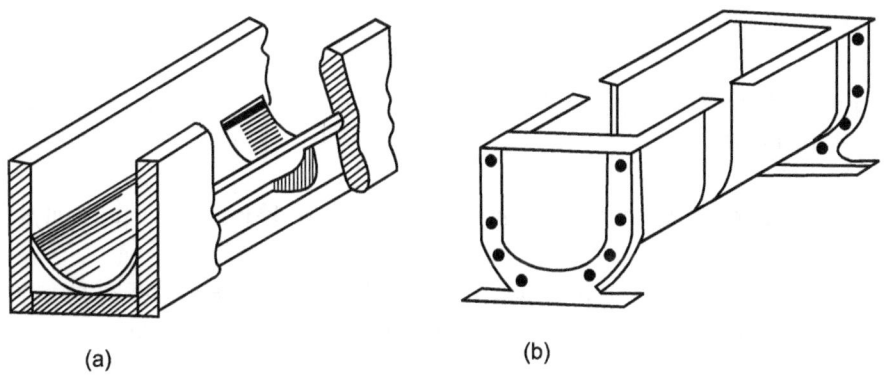

Fig. 2.8: Screw Conveyor Trough

Screw Conveyors:

The power requirement for a screw conveyor may be estimated from the sum of the power required to turn the empty screw and the additional power required to move the solids.

$$\text{Empty power} = 2.45 \times 10^{-6} \, LNF_D F_B \text{ kW} \quad \ldots (2.1)$$

where,
$\quad$ L is the screw length in m.
$\quad$ N is the rotating speed in rpm.
$\quad$ F_D is a function of the screw size, usually about 5.
$\quad$ F_B is a bearing factor, about 4.
$\quad$ Material motion power = $5.39 \times 10^{-6} \, LCW \, F_M F_F F_P$

where,
$\quad$ C is the capacity in m³/h
$\quad$ W is the material density in kg/m³
$\quad$ F_M is a material factor (usually 1.0)

F_F and F_P are a flight factor and a paddle factor respectively, both usually 1 for standard screws.

C the capacity can be estimated from

$$\frac{\pi}{8}(D_S^2 - D_A^2) \, N \times (P - t) \quad \ldots (2.2)$$

(i.e. assuming the screw is half full) D_S is the screw diameter.

D_A is the axle diameter.

P is the pitch of the screw (normally equal to the diameter of the screw) and t is the thickness of the blade.

In addition if the screw is inclined there will be a term for work done against gravity.

The torque available at the drive limits the length of the screw. The pitch sometimes decreases from the feed end to the discharge end to condition the powder.

Some control of the flow rate can be achieved by setting the speed of the screw.

2.5 Pneumatic Conveyors

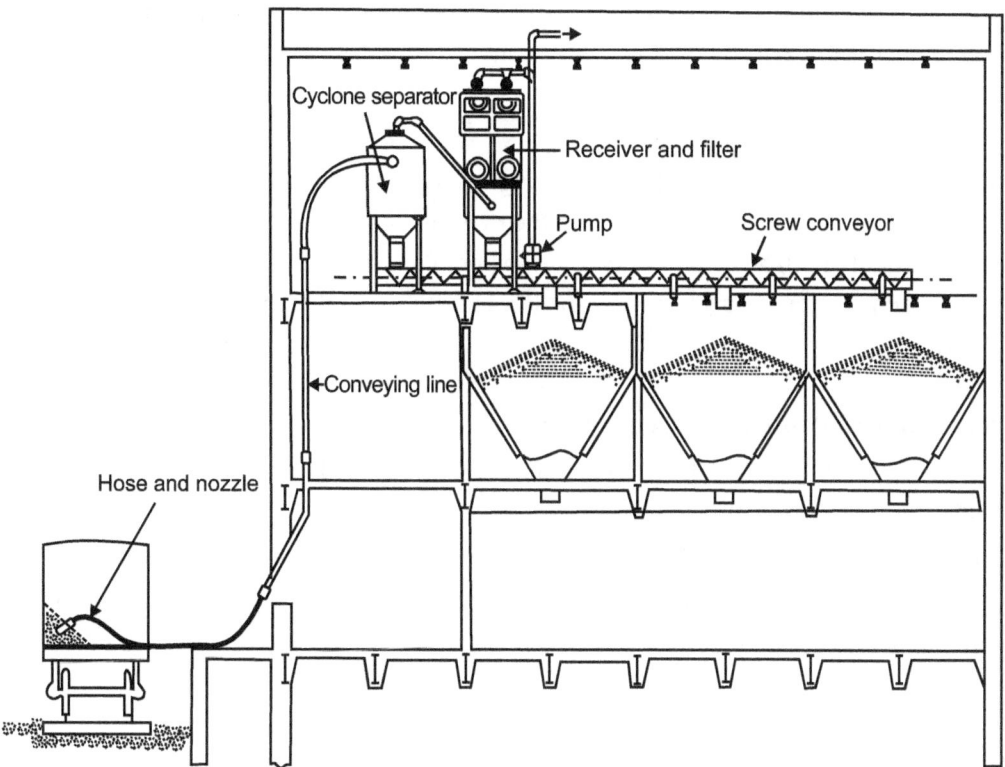

Fig. 2.9: Pneumatic Conveying System and Auxilliary Equipment

A method extensively used for the conveying of light and bulky materials is the *pneumatic conveying*. In pneumatic conveying consists of transporting relatively light material by suspending it in air and then moving the air borne solid by producing moderate vacuum. A typical pneumatic system is illustrated in figure 2.9. It essentially involves a pump or fan for producing a stream of air, a cyclone for removing larger particles and bag filter for removing the dust so that it does not cause any harm to the pump. Pneumatic conveying is recommended for materials that are required to be kept clean and without contamination such as food grains; that would be unpleasant or injurious, such as pulverized soda ash; or pulversized materials containing such poisonous constituents as lead or arsenic. It also suitable for bulky materials such as wood chips, dried beet pulp and other similar items. It is also recommended where the path of transport involves many turns and lifts. It is easier to construct the piping work with frequent turns. The typical velocity of air required for transport varies from 3,000 fpm to 20,000 fpm. About 50 to 200 cfm of air is required to transport one ton per hour of material depending on the nature of the material, the distance conveyed, lift, turns etc. The power requirement for a pneumatic handling system is rather high. The calculations of pneumatic conveying systems is entirely empricial and involves factors not available outside of equipment manufactures files.

2.5.1 Pneumatic Conveying

One of the most popular methods of moving solids in the chemical industry is pneumatic conveying. Pneumatic conveying refers to the moving solids suspended in or forced by a gas stream through horizontal and/or vertical pipes. Pneumatic conveying can be used for particles ranging from fine powders to pellets and bulk densities of 16 to 3200 kg/m^3 (1 to 200 lb/ft^3).

Dilute Phase vs. Dense Phase Conveying:

The specifying engineer typically has four choices in specifying a pneumatic conveying system.

1. Dilute phase vacuum operation.
2. Dilute phase pressure operation.
3. Dilute phase pressure-vacuum operation.
4. Dense phase pressure operation.

Vacuum systems allow multiple product inlets through the use of simple diverter valves. However, it becomes costly to have multiple destinations because each must have its own filter receiver with partial vacuum capability. Vacuum systems are also more "distance sensitive" than pressure systems due to the maximum pressure differential of 5.5 to 6.0 psi. Dilute phase pressure systems can easily achieve pressure differentials of 12 psi. Pressure-vacuum operation (utilizing both methods) are sometimes ideal for a given conveying set-up. A very common application is the unloading of a standard railcar. Since, the cars cannot be pressurized, air is pulled from the outside, through the car (carrying solids with it) to a filter. Then after the filter, a blower can be used to forward the solids to the final receiver.

The choice between dilute and dense phase operation is typically dependent on the solid properties. For example, the lower velocity bulk phase operation is popular for highly abrasive products or for those that degrade easily. For example, this method is popular in transporting kaolin clay.

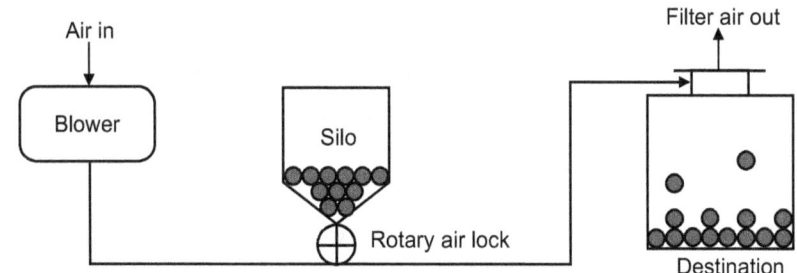

Fig. 2.10: Dilute Phase Pressure Operation

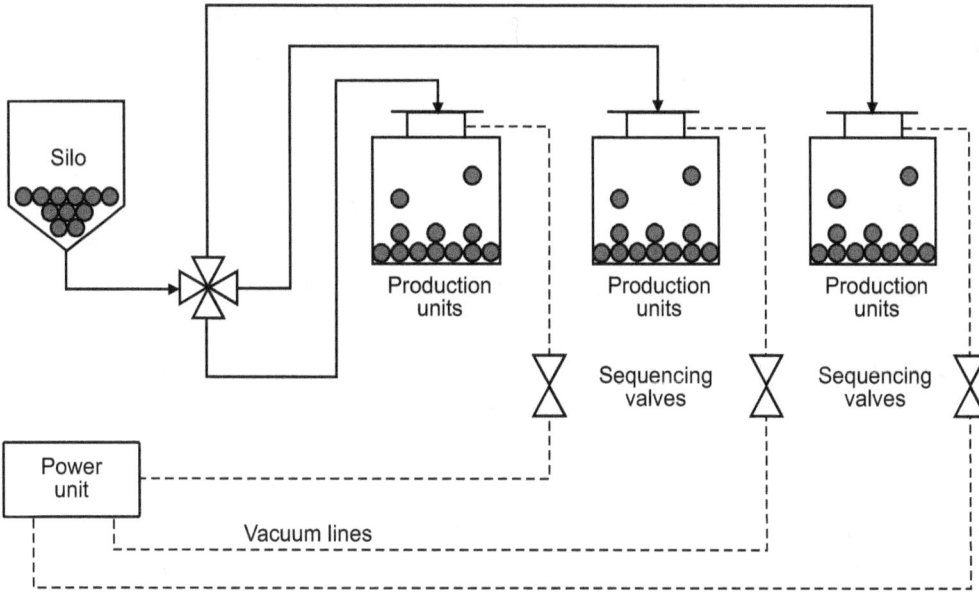

Fig. 2.11: Dilute Phase Vacuum Operation

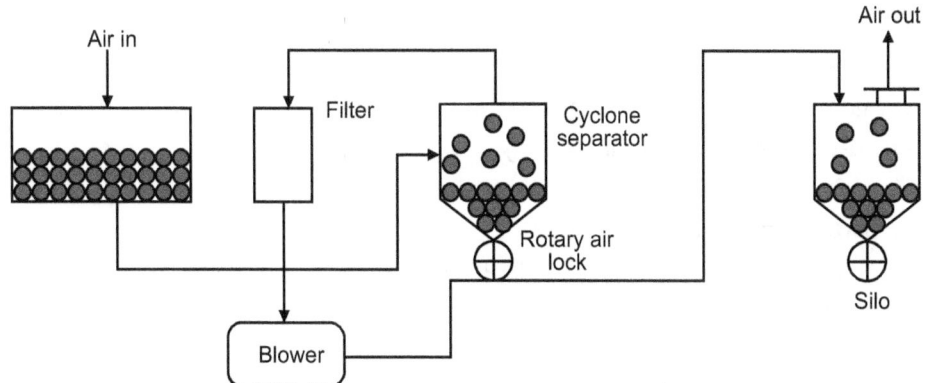

Fig. 2.12: Dilute Phase Pressure-Vacuum Operation

Pneumatic Conveying:

Pneumatic conveying eliminates the need for mechanical equipment in contact with the solids. The material is carried by a stream of air or gas, so the only moving part need be a compressor, which can be situated in a clean area.

The fluid has to exert a hydrodynamic force sufficient to counter act the effect of gravity on the solids.

In **vertical** conveying the direct drag forces of the upward moving gas keep the particles suspended. Additional work must be done to overcome frictional resistance; particle-particle and particle-wall, to accelerate the particles from rest and to provide the potential energy gained.

In **horizontal** conveying gravity is counteracted by the transverse components of the fluid velocity due to turbulence. There is therefore a minimum Reynold's Number to be maintained. The effect of decreasing the gas: solid ratio is as follows:

Vertical Conveying the increased pressure drop due to increased solid holdup eventually matches the reduced pressure gradient. Further decrease leads to choking and unstable (slugging) flow.

Horizontal Conveying: As the gas flow decreases dunes are formed on the duct bottom. At first these particles are still carried from one dune to the next by the gas flow.

Further reduction in gas flow leads to the dunes progressing in a slow "crawling" motion. Eventually, if the gas flow is low enough, the dunes grow to fill the duct and it clogs.

In conveying the fluid-particle force is taken as being proportional to the square of the relative fluid-particle velocity or *slip velocity*.

$$U_{sl} = (u_f - u_s) \qquad \ldots (2.3)$$

The fluid-particle force is then,

$$F_p = k\rho_f (u_f - u_s)^2 \qquad \ldots (2.4)$$

where, ρ_f is the fluid density.

It is assumed that the constant of proportionality, k, is the same as that at the terminal velocity u_t in a fluid of density ρ, not necessarily the same as the conveying fluid.

MECHANICAL OPERATIONS — CONVEYORS

$$(F_p)u_t = m\left(1-\frac{\rho}{\rho_s}\right)g = k\rho u_t^2 \qquad \text{... (2.5)}$$

i.e.
$$k = \frac{mg}{\rho u_t^2}\left(1-\frac{\rho}{\rho_s}\right) \qquad \text{... (2.6)}$$

so,
$$F_p = mg\frac{\rho_f}{\rho}\left(1-\frac{\rho}{\rho_s}\right)\left(\frac{u_f - u_s}{u_t}\right)^2 \qquad \text{... (2.7)}$$

If the transport line has length 1, the residence time of particles is l/u_s where u_s is the solids velocity relative to the walls of the pipe.

$$\text{Mass of particles in the line} = \frac{Wl}{u_s}$$

where, W is the solids federate.

$$\text{Number of particles in the line} = \frac{Wl}{mu_s}$$

Where, m is the mass of one particle, so the total force exerted by the fluid on the particle is,

Number of particles × Force on 1 particle

$$= \frac{Wl}{mu_s}mg\frac{\rho_f}{\rho}\left(1-\frac{\rho}{\rho_s}\right)\left(\frac{u_f-u_s}{u_t}\right)^2$$

$$= \frac{Wl}{u_s}g\left(1-\frac{\rho}{\rho_s}\right)\frac{\rho_f}{\rho}\left(\frac{u_f-u_s}{u_t}\right)^2 \qquad \text{... (2.8)}$$

In a **horizontal** pipe this force overcomes the frictional forces between the particles and the pipe wall and between the particles themselves.

If ΔP_s is the pressure drop of gas required to exert his force, then,

$$\Delta P_s A = \frac{Wl}{u_s}g\left(1-\frac{\rho}{\rho_s}\right)\frac{\rho_f}{\rho}\left(\frac{u_f-u_s}{u_t}\right)^2 \qquad \text{... (2.9)}$$

where, A is the pipe area.

In a vertical duct there is an additional pressure drop due to the weight of the particles, the frictional element is the same as in horizontal conveying.

$$(\Delta P_s A)_{vert} = \frac{Wl}{u_s}\left(1-\frac{\rho}{\rho_s}\right)\frac{\rho_f}{\rho}\left(\frac{u_f-u_s}{u_t}\right)^2 + \frac{Wl}{u_s}g\left(1-\frac{\rho}{\rho_s}\right) \qquad \text{... (2.10)}$$

u_s is not normally known but can be estimated as half the fluid velocity.

A relationship has been proposed which relates slip velocity to voidage ε.

$$\frac{u_{sl}}{u_t} = 1 - 1.209\,(1-\varepsilon)^{2/3}$$

ε is related to W and u_s by,

$$Al(1-\varepsilon)\rho_s = \frac{Wl}{u_s}$$

$$\varepsilon = 1 - \frac{W}{A\rho_s u_s} \quad \ldots (2.11)$$

In the above no account is taken of the work done in accelerating the solids to u_s. The pressure gradient is shown, comparing gas-solids pressure drop to that with gas flow only.

Graphs of ΔP/l vs. fluid velocity using solid flow rate as a parameter give a phase diagram of the gas-solids flow. There are some advantages to working in the dense phase region since the pressure drop is lowest, airflow is low therefore, energy requirement is lower, less fluid has to be separated. Solid velocities are also low, so there is low particle attrition and lower wear on the ducting. However, dense phase conveying is much more difficult to control than lean phase.

2.6 General Field of Conveyors

The following table gives a brief summary of general fields of usefulness of conveyor types.

Table 2.2: General Fields of Usefulness of Conveyor Types

	Belt Conveyor	Apron Conveyor	Flight Conveyor	Drag Chain	Screw Conveyor
Carrying paths	Horizontal to 18°	Horizontal to 25°	Horizontal to 45°	Horizontal or slight incline, 5-10°	Horizontal to 15°; may be used up to 90° but capacity falls off rapidly
Capacity range, tons/hr. material weighting 50 lb/cu ft	2160	100	360	20	150
Speed range, fpm	600	00	150	20	100 rpm

	Belt Conveyor	Apron Conveyor	Flight Conveyor	Drag Chain	Screw Conveyor
Location of loading point	Any point	Any point	Any point	Any point	Any point
Location of discharge point	Over and wheel and intermediated points by tripper or plow	Over end wheel	At end of trough and intermediate points by gates	At end of trough	At end of trough and intermediate points by gates
Handling abrasive materials	Recommended	Recommended	Not recommended	Recommended with special steels	Not preferred

2.7 Solved Examples

Example 2.1:

In an experiment, 1 kg/s of a particulate material was transported 4 m through a horizontal 0.038 m I.D. pipe by an air stream with mean velocity 5.0 m/s. The material had a density of 2000 kg/m³ and a terminal velocity in atmospheric air of 1.5 m/s. The pressure drop in the pipe was found to be 0.38 bar. Find the mean particle velocity and the voidage of the solid-air mixture.

What pressure of air supply would be necessary to transport the same solid flow rate to a hopper on the roof of a building 30 m high? What would be the air consumption (std m³/min) for this service ?

Solution:

W = Solid rate = 1.0 kg/s

l = 4 m

ρ = Density of atmosphere in which v_t was determined

v_t = Terminal velocity = 1.5 m/s

ρ_f = Density of air in experiment

ρ_s = 2000 kg/m³

u_f = Fluid velocity = 5.0 m/s

If the pipe discharges to atmosphere, (1.0 bara) entering air pressure = 1.38 bara and mean pressure = 1.19 bara. If the operation is isothermal:

$$\frac{\rho_f}{\rho} \simeq \frac{P_f}{P} = 1.19$$

$$\frac{\rho}{\rho_s} \simeq 0$$

so, $\dfrac{\pi}{4}(0.038)^2 \times 0.38 \times 10^5 = \dfrac{1 \times 4}{u_s} \times 9.82 \times 1 \times 1.19 \left(\dfrac{5 - u_s}{1.5}\right)^2$

$$2.076\, u_s = (5 - u_s)^2 = 25 - 10\, u_s + u_s^2$$

$$u_s^2 - 12.076\, u_s + 25 = 0$$

$$u_s = \frac{12.076 \pm (145.84 - 4 \times 25)^{1/2}}{2}$$

$$= 9.42 \text{ or } 2.65 \text{ ms}^{-1}$$

Since the first of these is greater than the gas velocity u_s must be 2.65 m/s.

Mass of solids per m of tube = $\dfrac{W}{u_s}$ = 12.65 = 0.377 kg

Volume of solids = $\dfrac{0.377}{2000}$ = 1.885×10^{-4} m³

Volume of 1 m of pipe = $\dfrac{\pi}{4}(0.038)^2$

$$= 1.134 \times 10^{-3} \text{ m}^3$$

so

$$\varepsilon = \frac{1.134 \times 10^{-3} - 1.885 \times 10^{-4}}{1.134 \times 10^{-3}}$$

$$= 0.834$$

For vertical transport the pressure drop will be the scaled-up pressure drop from the horizontal experiment.

$$0.38 \times \frac{30}{4} = 2.85 \text{ bar}$$

Plus a contribution due to the hydrostatic head of suspended solids equal to

$$\frac{Wl}{u_s} g\left(1 - \frac{\rho_f}{\rho_s}\right) \div \frac{\pi}{4}(0.038)^2 = 9.8 \times 10^4 \text{ Nm}^{-2}$$

$$= 0.98 \text{ bar}$$

So the total pressure drop = 2.85 + 0.98

= 3.83 bar

In order to have a velocity at the pipe entry of 5 m/s under these conditions gas flow rate must be,

$$5 \times \frac{\pi}{4}(0.038)^2 \times 4.831 \times 60 = 1.64 \text{ stdm}^3/\text{minute}$$

EXERCISE FOR PRACTICE

(1) Show that in pneumatic conveying in a horizontal duct of length l the pressure drop ΔP due to solids flow in the duct is given by:

$$\Delta P = \frac{Wl}{u_s A} g \left(1 - \frac{\rho}{\rho_s}\right) \frac{\rho_f}{\rho} \left(\frac{u_f - u_s}{u_t}\right)^2$$

Where u_s and u_f are the solid and fluid velocities, ρ_s and ρ_f are the solid and conveying fluid densities and W is the mass flowrates of solids through the system.

You may assume that the drag coefficient in this situation is equal to that for a particle at terminal velocity u_t in a fluid of density ρ.

(2) Pulverized coal is to be pneumatically conveyed from a storage facility to a burner in a power station. 2,000 kg per hour is to be fed to the burner. The terminal velocity of the coal dust in air at atmospheric pressure has been measured as 1.65 ms^{-1}. It is to be delivered to the burner at 2 barg through a 10 cm diameter pipe. If the maximum pressure at the inlet of the pipe is 6 bar (g) and the pipe is 35 m long can the required flow be achieved? The velocity of the solids is to be 6 ms^{-1} at the burner. The gas velocity may be assumed to be twice the solid velocity. Assume all temperatures to be 293 K.

It is decided to modify the process by moving the burner to a position 5 m above its present position. What is the maximum throughput of coal that the existing conveying system will be able to provide in this new layout? The horizontal section will still be 35 m long and the delivery velocity is to be maintained.

Data: The density of the coal is 2000 kgm^{-3}. Density of atmospheric air may be taken to be 1.2 kgm^{-3}.

NOMENCLATURE

Symbol	
A	Pipe area, m^2
C	Capacity of Screw Conveyor m^3
D, d	Diameter, m
F_P	Paddle factor
F_B	Bearing factor
F_D	Function of screw size
F_F	Flight factor
h_p	Horsepower
L	Length
P	Pull, kg force
N	Rotating speed, rpm
W	Weight of conveyor alone or of material conveyed, solid rate, kg/s
α	An angle
ρ	Density, kg/m^3
V_t	Terminal velocity, m/s
u_f	Fluid velocity, m/s
m	Mass of particle, kg
g	Acceleration due to gravity, m/s^2
ϵ	Voidage
ΔP_s	Pressure drop of gas, defined by equation (2.9)

***

Unit III

Chapter 3: MIXING OF SOLIDS AND PASTES

3.1 Introduction

Mixing is an important, even fundamental, operation in nearly all-chemical processes. Mixing dry solids and heavy, viscous pastes resembles, to some extent, the mixing of liquids of low viscosity. Both processes involve intermingling two or more separate components to form a more or less uniform product. Some of the equipment normally used for blending liquids may, on occasion, mix solids or pastes, and vice versa.

There are significant differences between these two processes. Liquid blending depends on the creation of flow currents, which transport unmixed material to the mixing zone adjacent to the impeller. In heavy pastes or masses of particulate solids no such currents are possible, and mixing is accomplished by other means. In consequence, much more power is normally required in mixing pastes and dry solids than in blending liquids.

Another difference is that in blending liquids a "well-mixed" product usually means a truly homogeneous liquid phase, from which random samples, even of very small size, all have the same composition. In mixing pastes and powders the product often consists of two or more easily identifiable phases, each of which may contain individual particles of considerable size. In the mixing of solid particles, three mechanisms may be involved:
(a) *Convective mixing*, in which groups of particles are moved from one position to another.
(b) *Diffusion mixing*, where the particles are distributed over a freshly developed surface.
(c) *Shear mixing*, where slipping planes are formed.

These three mechanisms will occur to varying extents in different kinds of mixers and with different kinds of particles.

Mixing heavy pastes, plastic solids and rubber is more of an art than a science. The properties of the materials to be mixed vary considerably from process to another. Intermediate properties of the materials such as stiffness, tackiness and wetability are as significant as viscosity and density in mixing problems. Mixers for pastes and plastic masses must be versatile. In a given problem the mixer chosen must handle the material when in its worst condition and may not be so effective as other designs during other parts of the mixing cycle. In general, as with other equipment, the choice of a mixer for heavy materials is often a compromise.

3.2 Theory of Solids Mixing

It is not possible to achieve a completely uniform mixture of dry powders or particulate solids. The degree of mixing achieved depends on:
- The relative particle size, shape and density.
- The efficiency of the particular mixer for the components being mixed.
- The tendency of the materials to aggregate.
- The moisture content, surface characteristics and flow characteristics of each component.

Generally, materials similar in size, shape and density are able to form the most uniform mixtures. Differences in these properties can also cause unmixing or segregation during mixing or mechanical jiggling of the mixture. Experience shows that materials with a size greater than 75 μ_m will segregate readily during mechanical jiggling of the mixture, but those below 10 μ_m will not segregate appreciably.

Means of overcoming segregation and poor mixing include:
- Communication to smaller sizes.
- Use of powders with a narrow size distribution.
- Use of the same volume-average diameter for all components.
- Granulation.
- Coating processes.
- Controlled continuous mixing.

3.3 Characteristics of Mixtures

Ideally, a mixing process begins with the components, grouped together in some container, but still separate as pure components. Thus, if small samples are taken throughout the container, almost all samples will consist of one pure component. The frequency of occurrence of the components is proportional to the fractions of these components in the whole container. As mixing then proceeds, samples will increasingly contain more of the components, in proportions approximating to the overall proportions of the components in the whole container. Complete mixing could then be defined as that state in which all samples are found to contain the components in the same proportions as in the whole mixture. Actually, this state of affairs would only be attained by some ordered grouping of the components and would be a most improbable result from any practical mixing process. Another approach can then be made, defining the perfect mixture as one in which the components in samples occur in proportions whose statistical chance of occurrence is the same as that of a statistically random dispersion of the original components. Such dispersion represents the best that random mixing processes can do.

3.4 Measurement of Mixing

The assessment of mixed small volumes, which can be taken or sampled for measurement, is what mixing measurement is all about. Sample compositions move from the initial state to the mixed state, and measurements of mixing must reflect this.

The problem at once arises, what size of sample should be chosen? To take extreme cases, if the sample is so large that it includes the whole mixture, then the sample composition is at once mean composition and there remains no mixing to be done. At the other end of the scale, if it were possible to take samples of molecular size, then every sample would contain only one or other of the components in the pure state and no amount of mixing would make any difference. Between these lie all the practical sample sizes, but the important point is that the results will depend upon sample size.

In many practical mixing applications, process conditions or product requirements prescribe suitable sample sizes. For example, if table salt is to contain 1% magnesium carbonate, the addition of 10 kg of magnesium carbonate to 990 kg of salt ensures, overall, that this requirement has been met. However, if the salt is to be sold in 2 kg packets, the practical requirement might will be that each packet contains 20 g of magnesium carbonate with some specified tolerance, and adequate mixing would have to be provided to achieve this. A realistic size to take from this mixture, containing 1000 kg of mixture, would be 2 kg. As mixing proceeds, greater numbers of samples containing both components appear and their composition tends towards 99% salt and 1% magnesium carbonate.

It can be seen from this discussion that the deviation of the *sample compositions* from the mean composition of the overall mixture represents a measure of the mixing process. This deviation decreases as mixing progresses. A satisfactory way of measuring the deviation is to use the statistical term called the standard deviation. This is the mean of the sum of the squares of the deviations from the mean, and so it gives equal value to negative and positive deviation and increasingly greater weight to larger deviations because of the squaring. It is given by:

$$s^2 = 1/n \, [(x_1 - \bar{x})^2 + (x_2 - \bar{x})^2 + \ldots + (x_n - \bar{x})^2] \quad \ldots (3.1)$$

where, s is the standard deviation, n is the number of samples taken, $x_1, x_2, ... x_n$ are the fractional compositions of component X in 1, 2 ... n samples and $\bar{x}$ is the mean fractional composition of component X in the whole mixture.

Using equation (3.1) values of s can be calculated from the measured sample compositions, taking the n samples at some stage of the mixing operation. Often it is convenient to use s^2 rather than s, and s^2 is known as the variance of the fractional sample compositions from the mean composition.

3.5 Particle Mixing

If particles are to be mixed, starting out from segregated groups and ending up with the components randomly distributed the expected variances (s^2) of the sample compositions from the mean sample composition can be calculated.

Consider a two component mixture, consisting of a fraction p of component P and a fraction q of component Q. In the unmixed state, virtually all the small samples taken will consist either of pure P or of pure Q. From the overall proportions, if a large number of samples are taken, it would be expected that a proportion p of the samples would contain pure component P. That is their deviation from the mean composition would be (1 − p), as the sample containing pure P has a fractional composition 1 of component P. Similarly, a proportion q of the samples would contain pure Q, that is, a fractional composition 0 in terms of component P and a deviation (0 − p) from the mean.

Summing these in terms of fractional composition of component P, and remembering that p + q = 1:

For n samples

$$s_0^2 = 1/n \, [pn(1-p)^2 + (1-p)\, n\, (0-p)^2]$$
$$= p(1-p) \quad \quad \quad ...(3.2)$$

When the mixture has been thoroughly dispersed, it is assumed that the components are distributed through the volume in accordance with their overall proportions. The probability that any particle picked at random will be component Q will be q, and (1 − q) that is not Q. Extending this to samples containing N particles, it can be shown, using probability theory, that:

$$s_r^2 = p(1-p)/N = s_0^2/N \quad \quad \quad ...(3.3)$$

This assumes that all the particles are equally sized and that each particle is either pure P or pure Q. For example, this might be the mixing of equal sized particles of sugar and milk powder. The subscripts 0 and r have been used to denote the initial and the random values of s_2, and inspection of the formula, equation (3.2) and equation (3.3), shows that in the mixing process the value of s^2 has decreased from $p(1 - p)$ to $1/N^{th}$ of this value. It has been suggested that intermediate values between s_o^2 and s_r^2 could be used to show the progress of mixing. Suggestions have been made for a mixing index, based on this, for example:

$$(M) = (s_o^2 - s^2)/(s_o^2 - s_r^2) \qquad \ldots (3.4)$$

which is so designed that (M) goes from 0 to 1 during the course of the mixing process. This measure can be used for mixtures of particles and also for the mixing of heavy pastes.

3.6 Equipment for Solid Mixing

Selection of mixers must take into account any tendency towards segregation. This may be evaluated form a "*heap test*", in which a well-mixed material is poured through a funnel to form a heap. If the composition of samples taken from the outside varies significantly from compositions of samples from the centre of the heap, the material is likely to segregate during mixing or later processing. Mixers can be classed into two groups with respect to segregation.

Segregating mixers have mainly *diffusive mechanisms*, encouraging the movement of individual particles, making segregation more significant. Non-impeller type mixers tend to be of this type.

Less segregating mixers have mainly *convective mixing* mechanisms. These are typically impeller types in which blades, screws, ploughs etc., sweep groups of particles through the mixing zone.

Tumbler Mixers:
- Operate by tumbling the solids inside a revolving vessel.
- May be fitted with baffles etc., to assist mixing, or with internal rotating devices to break-up agglomerates.
- Operate at speeds up to about 100 rpm (about half the critical speed – at which the centrifugal force on the particles exceeds the pull of gravity).
- Working capacity is about 50 to 60% of volume.

- Best suited to gentle blending of particles with similar physical characteristics, segregation can be a problem.
- Equilibrium is generally reached in about 10 to 15 minutes.

Horizontal Trough Mixers:
- Consist of semi-cylindrical horizontal vessels in which one or more rotating devices (such as screw conveyors or a ribbon mixer) are located.
- In a typical ribbon mixer one ribbon moves the material slowly in one direction, while the other moves it quickly in the opposite direction, so there is a net movement of material and the system can be used as a continuous mixer.
- Particle damage can occur due to the small clearance between the ribbon and the vessel wall and the mixer has a high power requirement.
- Segregation is less of a problem.

Vertical Screw Mixers:
- A rotating screw located in a cylindrical or cone shaped vessel.
- The screw may be mixed centrally or may rotate around the vessel near the wall.
- Quick and efficient and good for mixing a small quantity into a larger one.
- Good for materials prone to segregation.

Fluidised Bed Mixers:
- Effective for materials that will fluidise and with similar settling characteristics.
- Added jets of air that produce "spouting" are said to be effective in decreasing the time required to achieve good mixing.
- Very rapid – 1 to 2 minutes compared with around 15 minutes for a tumbler.

Other Types:
- Examples include heavy paddle mixers, pan mixers and Z-arm blenders.
- Injecting additives into pneumatic lines carrying solid particles can be effective.
- Continuous mixers – for example Littleford Day.

3.7 Mixers for Pastes and Plastic Masses

Mixers described in this section are change - can mixers; kneaders, dispersers, and masticators; continuous kneaders; mixer-extruders; mixing rolls; mullers and pan mixers; and pug mills.

(a) Change-can mixers: These devices blend viscous liquids or light pastes, as in food processing or paint manufacture. A small removable can 5 to 100 gal in size holds the material to be mixed. In the pony mixer shown in Fig. 3.1 (a) the agitator consists of several vertical blades or fingers held on a rotating head and positioned near the wall of the can. The blades are slightly twisted.

The agitator is mounted eccentrically with respect to the axis of the can. The can rests on a turntable driven in a direction opposite to that of the agitator, so that during operation all the liquid or paste in the can is brought to the blades to be mixed. When the mixing is complete, the agitator head is raised, lifting the blades out of the can; the blades are wiped clean; and the can is replaced with another containing a new batch.

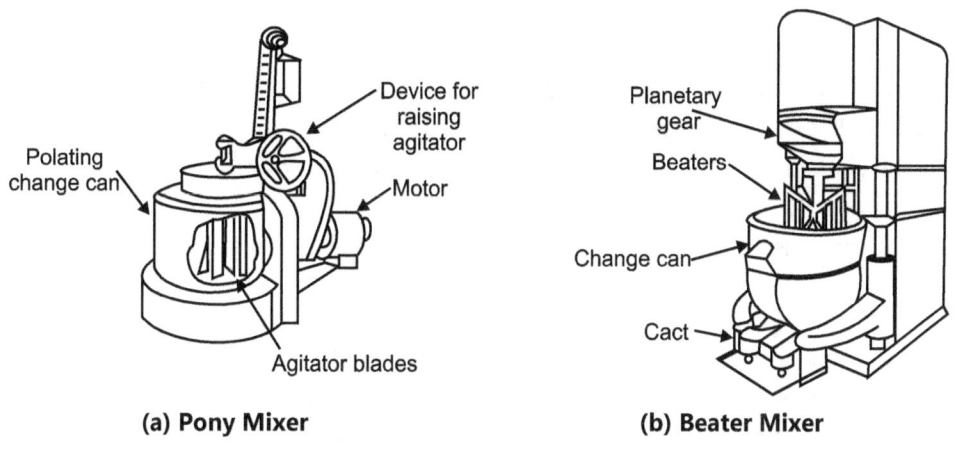

(a) Pony Mixer   (b) Beater Mixer

Fig. 3.1

In the beater mixer in Fig. 3.1 (b) the can or vessel is stationary. The agitator has a planetary motion; as it rotates, it processes, so that it repeatedly visits all parts of the vessel. Beaters are shaped to pass with close clearance over the side and bottom of the mixing vessel.

(b) Kneaders, dispersers, and masticators: Kneading is a method of mixing used with deformable or plastic solids. It involves squashing the mass flat, folding it over on itself, and squashing it once more. Most kneading machines also tear the mass apart and shear it between a moving blade and a stationary surface. Considerable energy is required even with fairly thin materials, and as the mass becomes stiff and rubbery, the power requirements become very large.

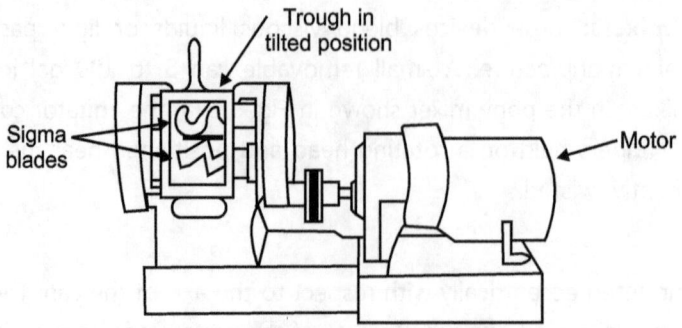

Fig. 3.2: Two Arm Kneader

A *two-arm kneader* handles suspensions, pastes, and light plastic masses. Typical applications are in the compounding of lacquer bases from pigments and carriers and in shredding cotton linters into acetic acid and acetic anhydride to form cellulose acetate. A disperser is heavier in construction and draws more power than a kneader; it works additives and coloring agents into stiff materials. A masticator is still heavier and draws even more power. It can disintegrate scrap rubber and compound the toughest plastic masses that can be worked at all. Masticators are often called *intensive mixers*.

In all these machines the mixing is done by two heavy blades on parallel horizontal shafts turning in a short trough with a saddle-shaped bottom. The blades turn toward each other at the top, drawing the mass downward over the point of the saddle, then shearing it between the blades and the wall of the trough. The circles of rotation of the blades are usually tangential, so that the blades may turn at different speeds in any desired ratio. The optimum ratio is about $1^1/_2 : 1$. In some machines the blades overlap and turn at the same speed or with a speed ratio of 2 : 1. A small two arm kneader with tangential blades is sketched in Fig. 3.2, with the trough tilted upward from its normal position to show the blades.

In many kneading machines the trough is open, but in some designs, known as internal mixers, the mixing chamber is closed during the operating cycle. Thus, a cover, the underside of which conforms to the volume swept out by the blades, can be used on the kneader shown in Fig. 3.2. Such mixers do not tilt. This type is used for dissolving rubber and for making dispersions of rubber in liquids. The most common internal mixer is the Banbury mixer, shown in Fig. 3.3. This is a heavy-duty two-arm mixer in which the agitators are in the form of interrupted spirals. The shafts turn at 30 to 40 r.p.m. Solids are charged in from above and held in the trough during mixing by an air-operated piston under a pressure of 1 to 10 atm. Mixed material is discharged through a sliding door in the bottom of the trough.

Banbury mixers compound rubber and plastic solids, masticate crude rubber, devulcanize rubber scrap, and make water dispersions and rubber solutions. They also accomplish the same tasks as kneaders but in a shorter time and with smaller batches. The heat generated in the material is removed by cooling water sprayed on the walls of the mixing chamber and circulated through the hollow agitator shafts.

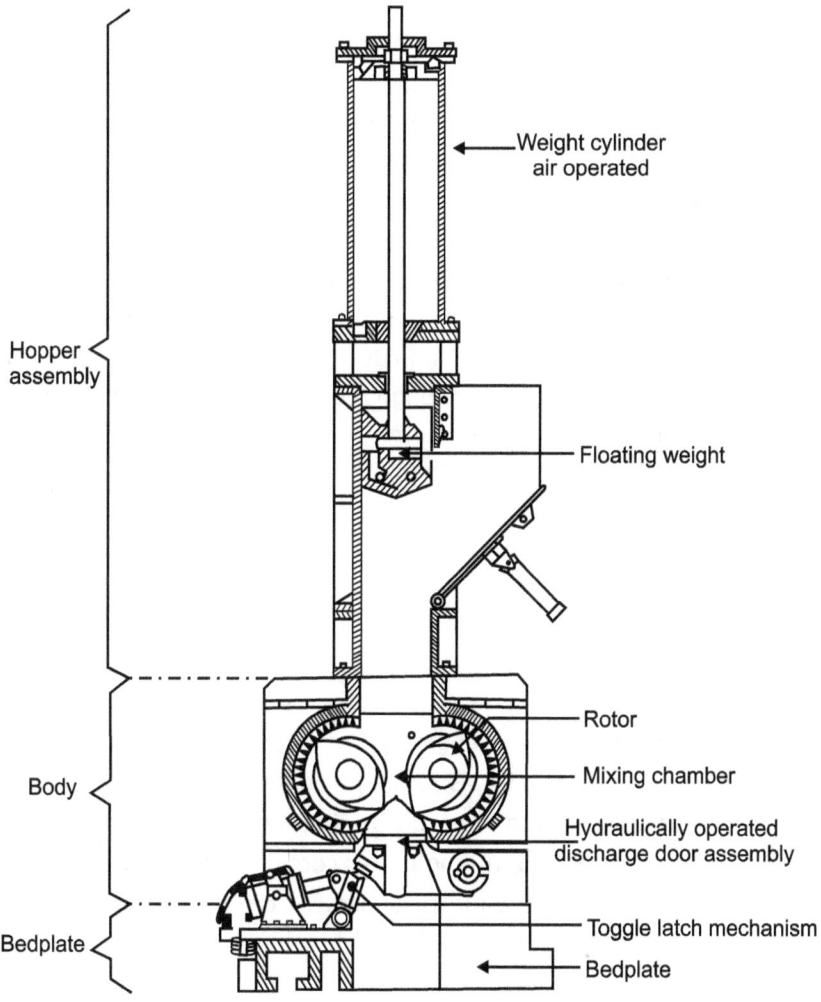

Fig. 3.3: Banbury Mixer

(c) Continuous kneaders: The machines discussed above operate batchwise on relatively small amounts of material. The more difficult the material is to mix, the smaller the batch size must be. Many industrial processes are continuous, with steady uniform flow into and out of units of equipment; into such processes batch equipment is not readily incorporated.

Continuous kneading machines have been developed which can handle light to fairly heavy materials. In a typical design, the Ko-Kneader, a single horizontal shaft, slowly turning in a mixing chamber, carries rows of teen arranged in a spiral pattern to move the material through the chamber, carries row of teeth on the rotor pass with close clearance between stationary teeth set in the wall of the casing. The shaft turns and also reciprocates in the axial direction. Material between the meshing teeth is therefore smeared in an axial or longitudinal direction as well as being subjected to radial shear. Solids enter the machine near the driven end of the rotor and discharge through an opening surrounding the shaft bearing in the opposite end of the mixing chamber. The chamber is an open trough with light solids, a closed cylinder with plastic masses. These machines can mix several tons per hour of heavy, stiff, or gummy materials.

(d) Mixer-extruders: If the discharge opening of a continuous kneader is restricted by covering with an extrusion die, the pitched blades of the rotor build up considerable pressure in the material. The mix is cut and folded while in the mixing chamber and subjected to additional shear as it flows through the die. Other mixer-extruders function in the same way. They contain one or two horizontal shafts, rotating but not reciprocating, carrying a helix or blades set in a helical pattern. Pressure is built up by reducing the pitch of the helix near the discharge, reducing the diameter of the mixing chamber, or both. Mixer-extruders continuously mix, compound, and work thermoplastics, doughs, clays, and other hard-to-mix materials. In some designs heating jacket and vapor-discharge connections are provided to permit removal of water or solvent from the material as it is being processed.

(e) Mixing rolls: Another way of subjecting pastes and deformable solids to intense shear is to pass then between smooth metal rolls turning at different speeds. By repeated passes between such mixing rolls, solid additives can be thoroughly dispersed into pasty or stiff plastic materials. Continuous mills for mixing pastes contain three to five horizontal rolls set one above the other in a vertical stack; the paste passes from the slower rolls to successively faster ones.

Rubber products and pastes can be compounded on batch roll mills with two rolls set in the same horizontal plane. Solids are picked up on the faster roll, cut at an angle by the operator, and folded back into the "bite" between the rolls. Additives are sprinkled on the material as it is being worked. Batch roll mills require long mixing times and careful attention by the operator, and have largely been displaced by internal mixers and continuous kneaders.

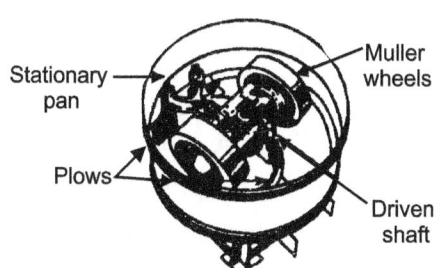

Fig. 3.4: Muller Mixer

(f) Muller mixers: A muller gives a distinctly different mixing action from that of other machines. Mulling is a smearing or rubbing action similar to that in a mortar and pestle. In large-scale processing this action is given by the wide, heavy wheels of the mixer shown in Fig. 3.4. In this particular design of muller the pan is stationary and the central vertical shaft is driven, causing the muller wheels to roll in a circular path over a layer of solids on the pan floor. The rubbing action results from the slip of the wheels on the solids. Plows guide the solids under the muller wheels, or to an opening in the pan floor at the end of the cycle when the mixer is being discharged. In another design the axis of the wheels is held stationary and the pan is rotated; in still another the wheels are not centered in the pan but are offset, and both the pan and the wheels are driven. Mixing plows may be substituted for the muller wheels to give what is called a *pan mixer*. Mullers are good mixers for batches of heavy solids and pastes; they are especially effective in uniformly coating the particles of granular solid with a small amount of liquid. Continuous muller mixers with two mixing pans connected in series are also available.

(g) Pug mills: In pug mill blades do the mixing or knives set in a helical pattern on a horizontal shaft turning in an open trough or closed cylinder. Solids continuously enter one end of the mixing chamber and discharge from the other. While in the chamber, they are cut, mixed, and moved forward to be acted upon by each succeeding blade. Single-shaft mills utilize an enclosed mixing chamber; open-trough double-shaft mills are used where more rapid or more thorough mixing is required. The chamber of most enclosed mills is cylindrical, but in some it is polygonal in cross-section to prevent sticky solids from being carried out with the shaft. Pug mills blend and homogenize clays, break-up agglomerates in plastic solids, and mix liquids with solids to form thick, heavy slurries. Sometimes they operate under vacuum to air form clay or other materials. They are also provided with jackets for heating or cooling.

3.8 Mixers for Dry Powders

Many of the machines can blend solids when they are dry and free flowing as well as when they are damp, pasty, rubbery, or plastic. Mullers, pan mixtures, and pug mills are examples. Such versatile machines are needed when the properties of the material change markedly during the mixing operation. In general, however, these devices are less effective on dry powders than on other materials and are heavier and more powerful than necessary for free-flowing particulate solids.

The lighter machines discussed here handle dry powders and sometimes-thin pastes. They mix by mechanical shuffling, as in ribbon blenders; by repeatedly lifting and dropping the material and rolling it over, as in tumbling mixers and vertical screw mixers; or by smearing it out in a thin layer over a rotating disk or impact wheel.

(a) Ribbon blenders : A ribbon blender consists of a horizontal through containing a central shaft and a helical ribbon agitator. A typical mixer is shown in Fig. 3.5. Two counteracting ribbons are mounted on the same shaft, one moving the solid slowly in one direction, the other moving it quickly in the other. The ribbons may be continuous or interrupted. Mixing results from the "turbulence" induced by the counteracting agitators, not from motion of the solids through the trough.

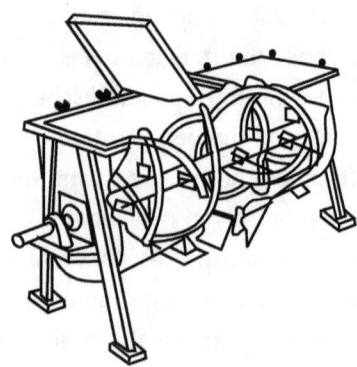

Fig. 3.5: Ribbon Mixers

Some ribbon blenders operate batchwise, with the solids charged and mixed until satisfactory; others mix continuously, with solids fed in one end of the trough and discharged from the other. The trough is open or lightly covered for light duty, closed and heavy-walled for operation under pressure or vacuum. Ribbon blenders are effective mixers for thin pastes and for powders that do not flow readily. Some batch units are very large, holding up to 9,000 gal (34 m^3) of material. They require moderate power.

(b) Internal Screw Mixers: Free-flowing grains and other light solids are often mixed in a vertical tank containing a helical conveyor, which elevates and circulates the material. Many different designs are commercially available. In the type shown in Fig. 3.6, the double-motion helix orbits about the central axis of a conical vessel, visiting all parts of the mix. Mixing is generally slower than in ribbon blenders, but the power required is somewhat less.

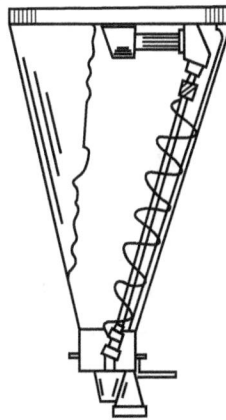

Fig. 3.6: Internal Screw Mixer (Orbiting Type)

(c) Tumbling mixers: Many materials are mixed by tumbling them in a partly filled container rotating about a horizontal axis. The ball mills are often used as mixers. Most tumbling mixers, however, do not contain grinding elements.

Tumbling barrels, for example, resemble ball mills without the balls; they effectively mix suspensions of dense solids in liquids and heavy dry powders. Other tumbling blenders, such as those illustrated in Fig. 3.7, handle lighter dry solids only. The double-come mixer shown at (a) is a popular mixer for free-flowing dry powders. A batch is charged into the body of the machine from above until it is 50 to 60 percent full. The ends of the container are closed and the solids tumbled for 5 to 20 min. The machine is stopped; mixed material is dropped out the bottom of the container into a conveyor or bin. The twin-shell blender shown at (b) is made from two cylinders joined to form a V and rotated about a horizontal axis. Like a double-cone blender, it may contain internal sprays for introducing small amounts of liquid into the mix or mechanically driven devices for breaking up agglomerates of solids. Twin-shell blenders are more effective in some blending operations than double-cone blenders. Tumbling mixers are made in a wide range of sizes and materials of construction. They draw a little less power than ribbon blenders.

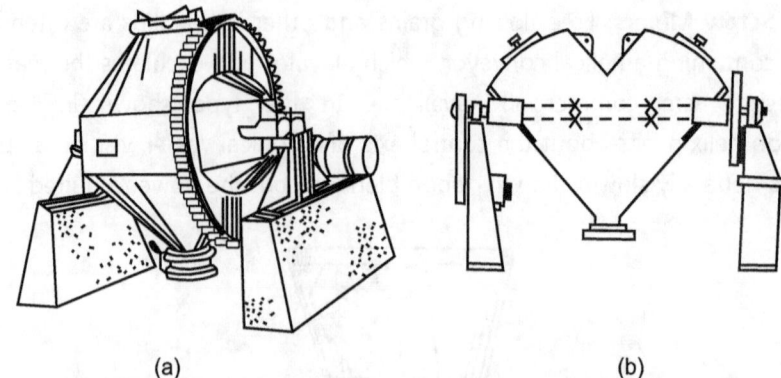

Fig. 3.7: Tumbler Mixer: (a) Double Cone Mixer; (b) Twin-Shell Blender

One method of scaling-up such mixers is based upon keeping the Froude number, n^2L/g constant, where L is a characteristic length of the equipment, n is the rate of rotation, and g is the gravitational acceleration. Scale-up procedures for tumbling mixers are discussed in detail by Wang and Fan.

(d) Impact wheels: Fine, light powders such as insecticides may be blended continuously by spreading them out in a thin layer under centrifugal action. A premix of the several dry ingredients is fed continuously near the center of a high-speed spinning disk 10 to 27 inches in diameter, which throws it outward into a stationary casing. The intense shearing forces acting on the powders during their travel over the disk surface thoroughly blend the various materials. The attrition mill is an effective mixer of this type. In some devices, designed for mixing and not size reduction, the premix is dropped onto a horizontal double rotor carrying short vertical pins near its periphery to increase the mixing effectiveness. A 14-inches disk turns at 1,750 rpm for easy problems and 3,500 rpm for materials that are hard to mix. Sometimes several passes through the same machine or through machines in series are necessary. For good results the premix fed to an impact wheel must be fairly uniform, for there is almost no hold-up of material in the mixer and no chance for recombining material that has passed through with that which is entering. Impact wheels blend 1 to 25 tons/hr of light free-flowing powders.

3.9 Power Requirements

For mixing heavy plastic masses, large amounts of mechanical energy are needed. The material must be sheared into elements that are moved relative to one another, folder over, recombined and redivided. In case of continuous mixers the material must also be moved through the machine. Only part of the energy is directly useful for mixing, and many machines that useful part is small. In general mixers that work intensively on small quantities of materials, dividing it into very small elements, make more effective use of energy than those that work more slowly on large quantities. Machines that weight little per kilogram of material processed waste less energy than heavier machines. Regardless of the design of machine, the power needed to drive a mixer for pastes and deformable solids is many times greater than that needed by a mixer for liquids. The energy supplied appears as heat. This must be removed to avoid damaging the machine or the material.

3.10 Mixing Index in Blending Granular Solids

The effectiveness of a solids blender is measured by a statistical procedure much like that used with pastes. Spot samples are taken at random from the mix and analyzed. The standard deviation of the analysis S about their average value $\bar{x}$ is estimated, as with pastes from equation,

$$S = \sqrt{\frac{\sum_{i=1}^{N}(x_i - \bar{x})^2}{N-1}} = \sqrt{\frac{\sum_{i=1}^{N} x_i^2 - \bar{x}\sum_{i=1}^{N} x_i}{N-1}} \qquad \ldots (3.5)$$

The value of S is a relative measure of mixing valid only for tests of a *specific material* in a specific mixer. With granular solids the mixing index is based, not on conditions at zero mixing, but on the standard deviation that would be observed with a completely random, fully blended mixture. With pastes, assuming the analysis are perfectly accurate, this value is zero. With granular solids it is not zero.

Consider a completely blended mixture of salt and sand grains from which N spot samples, each containing n particles, are taken. Suppose the fraction of sand in each spot sample is determined by counting particles of each kind. Let the overall fraction, by number of particles, of sand in the total mix be μ_p. If n is small (say about 100), the measured fraction x_i of sand in each sample will not always be the same, even when the mix is completely and perfectly blended; there is always some chance that a sample drawn from a random mixture will contain a larger (or smaller) proportion of one kind of particle than the population from which it is taken. Thus for any given size of spot sample there is a theoretical standard deviation for a completely random mixture. This standard deviation σ_e is given by

$$\sigma_e = \sqrt{\frac{\mu_p(1-\mu_p)}{n}} \qquad \ldots (3.6)$$

For granular solids the mixing index I_s is defined as:

$$I_s = \frac{\sigma_e}{S} = \sqrt{\frac{\mu_p (1-\mu_p)(N-1)}{N \cdot n \sum_{i=1}^{n} 1 (x_i - \bar{x})^2}} \qquad \ldots (3.7)$$

3.11 Rate of Mixing

In mixing, as in other rate processes, the rate is proportional to the driving force. The mixing index I_s, is a measure of how far mixing has proceeded toward equilibrium. It has been found that for short mixing times the rate of change of I_s is directly proportional to $1 - I_s$

or, $$\frac{dI_s}{dt} = k(1 - I_s) \qquad \ldots (3.8)$$

where, k is a constant. The equilibrium value of I_s is 1; therefore the driving force for mixing at any time can be considered to be $1 - I_s$. With rearranging and integrating between limits, equation (3.8) becomes,

$$\int_0^t dt = \frac{1}{k} \int_{I_{s,0}}^{I_s} \frac{dI_s}{1 - I_s} \qquad \ldots (3.9)$$

From which, $$t = \frac{1}{k} \ln\left(\frac{1 - I_{s,0}}{1 - I_s}\right) \qquad \ldots (3.10)$$

The mixing index at zero time is given by,

$$I_{s,0} = \frac{\sigma_e}{\sigma_0} = \frac{1}{\sqrt{n}} \qquad \ldots (3.11)$$

Substitution from equation (3.11) gives,

$$t = \frac{1}{k} \ln\left(\frac{1 - 1/\sqrt{n}}{1 - I_s}\right) \qquad \ldots (3.12)$$

Equation (3.12) can be used to calculate the time required for any desired degree of mixing; provided k is known and unbending forces are not active.

3.12 Criteria of Mixer Effectiveness : Mixing Index

The time required, the power load, and the properties of the product judge the performance of an industrial mixer. Both the requirements of the mixing device and the properties desired in the mixed material vary widely from one problem to another. Sometimes a very high degree of uniformity is required; sometimes a rapid mixing action; sometimes a minimum amount of power.

MECHANICAL OPERATIONS — MIXING OF SOLIDS AND PASTES

The degree of uniformity of a mixed product, as measured by analysis of a number of spot samples, is a valid quantitative measure of mixing effectiveness. Mixers act on two or more separate materials to intermingle them, nearly always in a random fashion. Once a material is randomly distributed through another, mixing may be considered to be complete. Based on these concepts, a statistical procedure for measuring mixing of pastes is given as below:

Consider a paste to which has been added some kind of tracer material for easy analysis. Let the overall average fraction of tracer in the mix by. Take a number of small samples at random from various locations in the mixed paste and determine the fraction of tracer x_i in each. Let the number of spot samples be N and the average value of the measured concentrations be $\bar{x}$. When N is very large, $\bar{x}$ will equal; when N is small, the two may be appreciably different. If the paste were perfectly mixed (and each analysis where perfectly accurate), every measured value of x_i would equal $\bar{x}$. If mixing is not complete, the measured values of x_i differ from $\bar{x}$ and their standard deviation about the average value of $\bar{x}$ is a measure of the quality of mixing. This standard deviation is estimated from the analytical results by the equation:

$$S = \sqrt{\frac{\sum_{i=1}^{N}(x_i - \bar{x})^2}{N-1}} = \sqrt{\frac{\sum_{i=1}^{N} x_i^2 - \bar{x}\sum_{i=1}^{N} x_i}{N-1}} \quad \ldots (3.13)$$

The value of S is a relative measure of mixing, valid only for tests of a specific material in a specific mixer. Samples from the first layer would have the analysis $x_i = 0$; in the other layer $x_i = 1$. Under these conditions the standard deviation is given by:

$$\sigma_0 = \sqrt{\mu(1-\mu)} \quad \ldots (3.14)$$

Where, μ is the overall fraction of tracer in mix. The mixing index for pastes I_p is then, given by,

$$I_p = \frac{\sigma_0}{S} = \sqrt{\frac{(N-1)\,\mu(1-\mu)}{\sum_{i=1}^{N} x_i^2 - \bar{x}\sum_{i=1}^{N} x_i}} \quad \ldots (3.15)$$

In any batch mixing process I_p is unity at the start and increases as mixing proceeds.

3.13 Solved Examples

Example 3.1:
A silty soil constaining 14% moisture was mixed in a large muller mixer with 10 weight percent of a tracer consiting of dextrose and picric acid. After 3 minutes of mixing 12 random samples were taken from the mix and analyzed colorimetrically for tracer material. The measured concentration in the sample were in weight percent tracer, 10.24, 9.30, 7.94, 10.24, 11.08, 10.03, 11.91, 9.72, 9.20, 10.76, 10.97 and 10.55. Calculate the mixing index.

Solution: Mixing Index is given by equation:

$$I_p = \sqrt{\frac{\sum_{i=1}^{N}(x_i - \bar{x})^2}{(N-1)\mu(1-\mu)}}$$

Here,
$N = 12$
μ = Overall fractions of tracer in the mix = 0.10

Calculations of $\bar{x}$ and $(x_i - \bar{x})^2$ are given in the following table:

Sample No.	x_i	$x_i - \bar{x}$	$(x_i - \bar{x})^2 \times 10^4$
1	0.1024	+ 0.008	0.0064
2	0.0930	− 0.0086	0.7396
3	0.0794	− 0.0222	4.9284
4	0.1024	+ 0.0008	0.0064
5	0.1108	+ 0.0092	0.8464
6	0.1003	− 0.0013	0.0169
7	0.1191	+ 0.0175	3.0625
8	0.0972	− 0.0044	0.1936
9	0.0920	− 0.0096	0.9216
10	0.1076	+ 0.0060	0.3600
11	0.1097	+ 0.0081	0.6561
12	0.1055	+ 0.0039	0.1521
Total	1.2194	−	11.89

$\sum x_i = 1.2194$

$\therefore \quad \bar{x} = \dfrac{1.2194}{12} = 0.1016$

$\sum (x_i - \bar{x})^2 = 11.89 \times 10^{-4} = 0.001189$

$$I_p = \sqrt{\frac{0.001189}{(12-1)\,0.1\,(1-01)}} = 0.0347$$

The mixing index is 0.0347. **(Ans.)**

Example 3.2:

Data on the mixing of sand and salt particles in an air-fluidized bed are given below. Assuming that the mixing process is first-order calculate the time taken for the mixing index to reach 0.95. In each run, the charge to the mixer was 254.4 g salt on top of 300.0 g of sand. The average number of particles in each sample was 100.

Run No.	Mixing Time(s)	Data on mixing of 35/48 mesh sand in a 2 inch air-fluidized mixer									
		Number fraction of sand in spot samples									
1	45	0.64	0.68	0.74	0.63	0.73	0.81	0.59	0.65	0.62	0.70
		0.66	0.64	0.77	0.70	0.67	0.58	0.60	0.65	0.87	0.60
		0.49	0.52	0.49	0.54	0.64	0.38	0.32	0.34	0.49	0.52
		0.25	0.32	0.33	0.35	0.48	0.23	0.16	0.32	0.44	0.39
		0.26	0.26	0.21	0.32	0.38	0.22	0.24	0.22	0.15	0.36
2	87	0.53	0.54	0.60	0.60	0.60	0.55	0.56	0.60	0.69	0.63
		0.48	0.67	0.65	0.63	0.62	0.46	0.63	0.58	0.48	0.59
		0.49	0.53	0.46	0.49	0.58	0.34	0.52	0.45	0.50	0.47
		0.42	0.35	0.43	0.49	0.59	0.38	0.39	0.45	0.52	0.39
		0.35	0.36	0.37	0.49	0.48	0.37	0.49	0.32	0.32	0.36

Solution: The mixing index is calculated from following equation:

$$I = \sqrt{\frac{\mu(1-\mu)(N-1)}{n \sum_i (x_i - \bar{x})^2}}$$

For the 45s result $\bar{x} = 0.483$ and

$$\sum_i (x_i - \bar{x})^2 = 1.83085$$

The easy way to calculate $\sum_i (x_i - \bar{x})^2$ is to use the fact that:

$$\sum_i (x_i - \bar{x})^2 = \sum_i x_i^2 - \frac{(\sum_i x_i)^2}{n}$$

At 87s $\bar{x} = 0.497$ and $\sum_i (x_i - \bar{x})^2 = 0.5005$

N, the number of samples is 50 and n the number of particles in each sample is 100.

The true mean, µ, is not known but one could assume that it is close to the value of $\bar{x}$ at 87s, 0.497, it is true number fraction had been given, or could be calculated then this approximation would not have been made.

Using the equation above gives,
$$I_{45} = 0.2587$$
and
$$I_{87} = 0.4947$$

The first order equation for mixing is,
$$\frac{dI}{dt} = k(1 - I)$$

This integrates to
$$\ln\left(\frac{1 - I_{45}}{1 - I_{87}}\right) = k(87 - 45)$$
$$k = 9.125 \times 10^{-3} \text{ s}^{-1}$$

Further time required to get to I = 0.95 is
$$\frac{1}{9.125 \times 10^{-3}} \ln \frac{1 - 0.4947}{1 - 0.95} = 253.5 \text{s} \quad \text{(Ans.)}$$

Example 3.3:

After a mixer mixing 99 kg of salt with 1 kg of magnesium carbonate had been working for some time, ten samples, each weighing 20 g, were taken and analysed for magnesium carbonate. The weights of magnesium carbonate in the samples were 0.230, 0.172, 0.163, 0.173, 0.210, 0.182, 0.232, 0.220, 0.210, 0.213 g. Calculate the standard deviation of the sample compositions from the mean composition.

Fractional compositions of samples, that is the fraction of magnesium carbonate in the sample, are respectively:

0.0115, 0.0086, 0.0082, 0.0087, 0.0105, 0.0091, 0.0116, 0.0110, 0.0105, 0.0107 (x)

Solution: Mean composition of samples, overall = 1/100 = 0.01 ($\bar{x}$)

Deviations of samples from mean, (0.0115 − 0.01), (0.0086 − 0.01) etc. $(x - \bar{x})$

$$s^2 = 1/n\ [(x_1 - \bar{x})^2 + (x_2 - \bar{x})^2 + \ldots + (x_n - \bar{x})^2]$$
$$s^2 = 1/10\ [(0.0115 - 0.01)^2 + (0.0086 - 0.01)^2 + \ldots]$$
$$= 2.250 \times 10^{-6}$$
$$s = 1.5 \times 10^{-3}$$

At some later time samples were found to be of fractional compositions: 0.0113, 0.0092, 0.0097, 0.0108, 0.0104, 0.0098, 0.0101, 0.0094, 0.0098, giving:

$$s = 3.7 \times 10^{-7} \quad \text{(Ans.)}$$

Note: Showing the reducing standard deviation. With continued mixing the standard deviation diminishes further.

The process of working out the differences can be laborious, and often the standard deviation can be obtained more quickly by making use of the mathematical relationships, proof of which will be found in any textbook on statistics:

$$s^2 = 1/n \left[\sum(x_1^2) - \sum(\bar{x})^2\right]$$
$$= 1/n \left[\sum(x_1^2) - n(\bar{x})^2\right]$$
$$= 1/n \left[\sum(x_1^2)\right] - (\bar{x})^2$$

Example 3.4:

For a particular bakery operation, it was desired to mix dough in 95 kg batches and then at a later time to blend in 5 kg of yeast. For product uniformity it is important that the yeast be well distributed and so an experiment was set up to follow the course of the mixing. It was desired to calculate the mixing index after 5 and 10 min mixing.

Sample yeast compositions, expressed as the percentage of yeast in 100 g samples, were found to be:

After 5 min	0.0	16.5	3.2	2.2	12.6	9.6	0.2	4.6	0.5	8.5
After 10 min	3.4	8.3	7.2	6.0	4.3	5.2	6.7	2.6	4.3	2.0

Solution: Fractional compositions:

5 min	0.0	0.165	0.032	0.022	0.126	0.096	0.002	0.046	0.005	0.085
10 min	0.034	0.083	0.072	0.06	0.043	0.052	0.067	0.026	0.043	0.020

$$s^2 = 1/n \left[\sum(x_1^2)\right] - (\bar{x})^2$$

Therefore,
$$s_5^2 = 3.0 \times 10^{-3} = 0.3 \times 10^{-2}$$
$$s_{10}^2 = 3.8 \times 10^{-3} = 0.38 \times 10^{-2}$$

The value of
$$s_0^2 = 0.05 \times 0.95 = 4.8 \times 10^{-2}$$

and $s_r^2 \approx 0$ as the number of "particles" in a sample is very large,

From equation (3.4)
$$M = (s_0^2 - s^2)/(s_0^2 - s_r^2)$$
$$(M)_5 = (4.8 - 0.3)/(4.8 - 0)$$
$$= 0.93$$
$$(M)_{10} = (4.8 - 0.04)/(4.8 - 0)$$
$$= 0.99 \quad \text{(Ans.)}$$

EXERCISE FOR PRACTICE

(1) Below is a table of results showing the values of mixing indices for different mixing times. What mixing time would you choose for this process, explain your choice in terms of the experimental results. Mixing times are in minutes.

Mixing Time	I	Mixing Time	I
2.5	0.254	5	0.381
7.5	0.487	12.5	0.648
15	0.708	17.5	0.603
20	0.520	52	0.482

(2) The equation below is used to estimate mixing times by assuming a first order process with "rate constant" k:

$$\frac{dI}{dt} = k(1 - I)$$

In the full scale equipment which the experiments described above were intended to model two mixing trials were carried out, for 5 minutes and 12.5 minutes mixing. The resulting mixing indices were 0.247 and 0.520. Estimate the length of mixing time required to produce a mixing index of 0.700, clearly stating any assumptions.

(3) Laboratory blending experiments were carried out to investigate mixing of different sized particles. In order to do this supplies of a material were produced in two particle sizes. The size distributions of the two sizes of material were very narrow and each may be assumed to have contained only one particle size.

Show that for a mixture of two particle diameters the number fraction of size d_1 may be determined from its weight fraction using the following equation:

$$x_1 = \frac{m_1 d_2^3}{m_1 d_2^3 + d_1^3 - m_1 d_1^3}$$

where, x_1 is the number fraction of particles of size 1, d_1 and d_2 are the two particle diameters and m_1 and m_2 are the respective mass fractions of the different sizes in the mixture.

(4) In the experiments particles of diameter 1 mm and 2 mm are used. Equal masses of each size of particle were initially placed in the mixer and mixed for a period of time. The objective of the experiments was to find the optimum mixing time, i.e. the time, which gives the nearest approach to random mixing, with a view to applying this to a full-scale mixer processing the same materials.

At the end of each experiment 10 samples of the mixture are taken and the mass fractions of each size of particle were measured and corresponding number fractions calculated. One experiment, for 10 minutes of mixing, produced the following results.

Sample No.	Number fraction 1 mm particles	Sample No.	Number fraction 1 mm particles
1	0.782	6	0.937
2	0.911	7	0.853
3	0.889	8	0.917
4	0.893	9	0.954
5	0.812	10	0.867

(a) The average of these experimental number fractions is 0.881. What value would you expect? Explain any difference between your expected average and the experimental average.

(b) Calculate the expected and experimental standard deviations and the mixing index for this experiment. The number of particles in each sample may be taken to be 100.

(5) Below is a table of results showing the values of mixing indices for different mixing times. What mixing time would you choose for this process, explain your choice in terms of the experimental results. Mixing times are in minutes.

Mixing Time, t	Mixing Index, I	Mixing Time	Mixing Index, I
2.5	0.254	5	0.381
7.5	0.487	12.5	0.648
15	0.708	17.5	0.603
20	0.520	52	0.482

NOMENCLATURE

Symbol	
E	Diffusivity in axial mixing, m²/s
g	Gravitational acceleration, m/s²
I_P	Mixing index for pastes, σ_o/s
I_S	Mixing index for granular solids, σ_e/s;
	$I_{S,O}$, at zero time or zero mixing
i	Number of fraction or increment
m	Mass of fraction or increment
k	Constant in equation (3.8)

Symbol	
N_{Pe}	Peclet number for axial mixing, UL/E, dimensionless
n	Number of particles in spot sample
S	Estimate of standard deviation, [Eq. (3.9)]
t	Time, Second
U	Longitudinal velocity of material through mixer, m/s.
x_i	Measured fraction of tracer in spot sample; $\bar{x}$ average measured fraction of tracer.
Greek Letters:	
μ	True average fraction of tracer in mix; $μ_p$, true average number fraction of tracer particles.
ρ	Density, kg/m^3; $ρ_b$, bulk density; $ρ_p$, particle density.
σ	Standard deviation; $σ_e$, equilibrium value for complete mixing of granular solids; $σ_o$, at zero time or zero mixing.

Unit IV

Chapter 4: SIZE REDUCTION

4.1 Introduction

4.1.1 Size Reduction

Estimates vary, but it is generally accepted that of all the energy used in the World something like between 1 and 10% is in comminution, i.e. the processes of crushing, grinding, milling, micronising etc. Changing the size of the particles by crushing creates many important industrial products. An example is sugar, which has three different grades: granular, castor and icing; chemically they are the same material the main difference is their particle size. So, grinding followed by *classification* (Classification is the term for industrially sorting particles into different size fractions or grades) is all that is needed to produce the three different products.

The production of particles by crushing and grinding is a very important operation throughout the world. In most cases mechanical classification is also required, to return the oversize material to the mill. Common classification equipment includes sieves, or when used on an industrial scale these are called screens. In some cases decks of screens may be used to fractionate the product: the largest screen size on the top deck. Slotted screens are often used to minimize screen blinding, or blockage. Historically, grinding became a mechanized industrial process with the advent of water and wind powered mills to process wheat, barley, animal feed etc. The mills used a flat stationary stone with a moving mill wheel revolving on top. A derivative of this type of mill, an edge-runner mill, can still be found in use today, albeit electrically driven. In old mills classification was important to separate the flour from the husk, this was often achieved by sieving. Modern mills often combine classification and milling within the same device by having an up draught to carry the finer particles away from the milling section. These are known as air swept devices.

Milling of minerals has been an important part of the recovery of metals and industrial minerals for many centuries. Often a mineral of interest is surrounded by rock of a different type, which may be worthless; i.e. a gangue mineral. The grain boundary between the desired mineral and the gangue will be the weakest mechanical point and the most likely to break. Thus, grinding to the liberation size will release the valuable mineral so that it may then be separated from the gangue. This is a process that is employed for metal ore mining as well as precious minerals recovery – see the box below Table 4.1. In the table the Moh's scale of hardness is shown. It is based on the mineral lower in the table being able to scratch the mineral above. 'Soft' minerals are 1 to 3, 'medium' are 4 to 6 and 'hard' are 7 to 10. However, the hardness value is entirely arbitrary, it is merely a ranking of the described minerals.

Table 4.1: Moh's Scale

Material	Moh's hardness	Bond Work index (kWh to n⁴)
Talc	1	
Gypsum	2	7
Calcite	3	
Fluorite	4	10
Glass	Scratches above	11
Apatite	5	
Orthoclase Feldspar	6	12
Quartz	7	14
Topaz and beryl	8	
Carborundum	9	26
Diamond	10	

An initial size reduction from material several centimeters in diameter down to one centimeter, or so, is often termed primary crushing. This may be followed by further size reduction, secondary crushing, and then pulverizing, or fine grinding. The term micronising has become popular for the reduction of particle size to this dimension. Thus, coal being fed into a pulverized fuel burner for electricity generation will undergo the first three grinding operations. Primary crushing normally takes place close to the mine head and relies on equipment with very large throughputs, usually having two surfaces approaching and retreating from each other. Examples include Jaw and Cone Crushers. Secondary crushing can be by rotating surfaces such as swing hammer mills, for brittle materials, and roll crushers. Finer grinding usually takes place in rotating vessels, such as ball and rod mills. Very fine grinding, to sizes less than 10 µm, requires high energy and attrition mills are often used. These have much lower throughputs than the primary crushers. These are usually found in the fine chemical industry. Examples of these and other types of machines can be easily found on The Internet.

The term "size reduction" is applied to all the methods in which particles of solids are cut or broken into smaller pieces. Solid materials such as minerals are extensively used in process industry as raw materials. Chunks of crude ore are crushed to workable size; synthetic chemicals are ground into powder; sheets of plastics are cut into tiny cubes. Also several commerical chemical products are solids and these have to be supplied to the consumers in desired size range. Unfortunately, the original solids, whether these are raw materials or finished – products, are seldom available in a desirable size range. Thus, it is necessary to either reduce the size or increase it using various techniques. In general size reduction is carried out in process industry for the following purposes:

(i) Size reduction is usually carried out to increase the surface as, in most reactions involving solid particles, the rate is directly proportional to the area of contact with a second phase. Thus the rate of combustion of solid particles is proportional to the area presented to the gas. Again in leaching, not only is the rate of extraction increased by virtue of increased area of contact between the solvent and the solid, but the distance the solvent has to penetrate into the particles in order to gain access to the more remote pockets of solute is also reduced. This factor is also important in the drying of porous solids.

(ii) By reducing the particle size also increases the reactivity of solids.

(iii) It permits separation of unwanted ingradients by mechanical methods.

(iv) It reduces the bulk of fibrous materials for easier handling and for waste disposals. There are four commonly used methods for size reduction: (i) compression, (ii) impact, (iii) attrition or rubbing, and (iv) cutting. A nutracker a hammer, a file and a pair of shears constitues these four types of action.

Comminution means size reduction or the crushing and grinding of solids. In general, crushing involves the production of coarse solids from larger pieces whereas grinding refers to the production of fines from relatively small-sized feed. Crushing and grinding play a vital role in the chemical engineering industry. Some applications include:

(a) The crushing of limestone and clay from about – 10 mesh size (obtained from preliminary crushing) to about – 200 mesh before sending it to the rotary kiln, in the manufacture of cement;

(b) The crushing and grinding of phosphate rock to about – 100 mesh size before sending it to the digestor where sulphuric acid is present – in the manufacture of super phosphate fertilizers;

(c) Crushing and grinding of bauxite ore to – 100 mesh size before mixing it with sodium hydroxide – in the manufacture of Alumina;

(d) The grinding of pigments in paints.

In the first three cases, size reduction of the solids leads for example, to a decrease in the residence time required for subsequent reaction besides giving better heat transfer characteristics, whereas in the fourth example, smaller size particles give good coverage of the paint when applied over any surface.

Normally, large-sized rocks are crushed in several stages. In primary crushing, the larger pieces from the mines are broken down to about 15 cm (6 in.) sizes (which itself may be achieved in several stages). Thereafter, secondary crushing is used to obtain solids of about 1.3 cm (0.5 in.) sizes. Size reduction below this range is referred to as *grinding*.

In the design of a crushing and grinding unit, a chemical engineer must:
(a) Select the proper equipment. The choice is based on the characteristics (primarily hardness) of the solids and on the sizes of the feed and products;
(b) "Size" the equipment' usually, specification of the power required is sufficient; and
(c) Estimate the fixed and running costs. This is necessary for an economic analysis of the plant and for optimization. Normally, correlations between equipment costs and the power required are available in literature. As such, once the power requirements for crushing and grinding are estimated, both fixed and running costs may be easily obtained.

In this chapter, some common equipment is described along with criteria for their selection and power requirements for size reduction machines. More exhaustive descriptions are available in the literature. The mechanical design of communication equipment, however, falls primarily in the realm of mechanical engineering.

In general most solids begin their processing as large lumps of material, because they are dug out of the ground as such. Alternatively they may have been produced from a liquid; by precipitation, crystallisation or by drying off a solvent. In these latter cases methods exist to control the process of solid formation to produce material of the correct size. However, in many cases the solids must be processed to produce the correct size distribution. It is very difficult to control particle shape since chemical processes largely govern this.

The majority of materials require *size reduction* although the opposite process *size enlargement* is not uncommon. Indeed some processes have both reduction and enlargement stages. This will be discussed towards the end of this section under Integrated Particle Production.

4.1.1.1 Mechanisms of Size Reduction

The reason that size reduction or *comminution* is usually carried out is to increase the surface area of the material. This will maximize the area of solid in contact with the liquid or gas phase around it, which enhances reaction, dissolution, catalytic effect etc. and is therefore desirable. It should be noted however that very small particles are more difficult to handle, more dangerous in terms of toxic effect and explosive hazard and have other problems such as increased resistance to flow through them.

There are four mechanisms by which size reduction may be achieved.

Impact:
Particle concussion by a single rigid force.

Compression
Particle disintegration by two rigid force.

Shear:
Produced by a fluid or by particle-particle interaction.

Attrition:
Arising from particles scraping against one another or against a rigid surface. Size reduction obviously requires energy input but the energy is consumed in size reduction apparatus at a much higher rate than would be predicted from the new surface area created, by a factor of about 1,000. This 'lost' energy is consumed in,
(1) Deforming the particle to its elastic limit.
(2) Compacting particles after fracture.
(3) Overcoming friction between particles.
(4) Elastically deforming milling surface.
(5) Deformation of fractured particles.

This energy is dissipated as heat. There are also significant mechanical losses in the milling machinery.

It is interesting that around 5% of the world's energy consumption goes to size reduction. Whereas, it is impossible to predict from any theory the energy consumed in size reduction there are a number of empirical rules which allow data from one process to be extrapolated to another.

4.1.2 Factors Influencing Choice of Size Reduction Equipment
1. Feed and Product Size

	Feed Size	Product Size
Coarse Crushers	1500 - 40 mm	50 - 5 mm
Intermediate Crushers	50 - 5 mm	5 - 0.1 mm
Fine Crushers, Grinders	5 - 2 mm	< 0.1 mm
Fine Milling	< 0.2 mm	Down to 0.01 μm

2. Nature of Material:
   (a) Hardness - Very hard materials are better in low speed or low contact machines.
   (b) Structure - Fibrous materials need tearing or cutting action.
   (c) Moisture content - Materials with 5-50% moisture do not flow easily and can be difficult to process.
   (d) Friability.
   (e) Stickiness: Stickly materials need easily cleaned machines.
   (f) Soapiness: If coefficient of friction is low crushing may be difficult.
   (g) Explosives: Need inert atmosphere.
   (h) Hazardous to health: Need good confinement.
   (i) Closeness of distribution.

4.1.3 The Value of Size Reduction
The breakdown of solid materials by the application of mechanical forces is also referred to as comminution. Size reduction operations can include grinding and cutting.

Size reduction in liquid foods (for example homogenisation) is covered in the "emulsification" topic in the series of articles.

The value of size reduction comes from:
- Aiding the extraction of a constituent from a composite structure - for example in making sugar from sugarcane.
- Satisfying consumer or functional requirements - for example in manufacturing of icing sugar, pineapple rings or pieces.
- Increasing the ratio of surface area to volume so as to
   - reduce drying time.
   - increase extraction rate.
   - decrease heating, cooking time etc.
- Improving mixing/blending - for example in packaged soups, cake mixes etc.

4.1.4 Product Factors Influencing Equipment Selection

Hardness and Abrasiveness of Feed: In general harder materials require more energy to comminute, therefore, a longer residence time (lower throughput) or higher capacity equipment will be required. More robust construction is also required. Hard material also tends to be more abrasive, so that more wear resistant materials may be desirable (for example, manganese steel) and wearing parts should be easily replaceable. Slower speed is also desirable to reduce wear.

Internal Structure of Feed: If the material is crystalline or friable in nature, compressive forces are likely to be suitable. If few lines of weakness are present and new "cracks" have to be formed, impact or shear may be more effective.

Moisture Content: Moisture can either aid or hinder comminution. With some materials, moisture above 2-3% may cause clogging of the mill, or agglomeration may occur. Too dry a condition can result in excessive dust. For some products milling may be carried out as a free flowing slurry for example, wet milling of maize.

Temperature Sensitivity: The heat generated by grinding can result in loss of heat sensitive components. Softening or melting may also be important - leading to clogging. In some cases cryogenic comminution may be necessary - cooling during milling using liquid nitrogen or dry ice for example, in milling spices or size reduction of meat.

4.2 Principles of Comminution

4.2.1 Criteria for Comminution

Comminution is a generic term for size reduction; crushers and grinding are the types of comminuting equipment. An ideal crusher or grinder would:
- (1) have a large capacity;
- (2) require a small power input per unit of product;

and (3) yield a product of the single size or the size distribution desired.

The standard method of studying the performance of process equipment is to set up an ideal operation as a standard, compare the characteristics of the actual equipment with those of the ideal unit and account for the difference between the two. When this method is applied to crushing and grinding equipment, the difference between the ideal and actual are very great and in such situations, we depend on the empirical equations available in literature for predicting equipment performance.

4.2.2 Characteristics of Comminuted Products

The main purpose of any crushing and grinding operation is to produce small particles from larger ones. Smaller particles are desired either due to their large surface or due to shape, size and number. The efficiency of the operation is based on the energy required to create new surface. The surface area of a unit mass of particles increases greatly as the particle size is reduced.

An actual equipment does not give a uniform product, whether the feed is uniformly sized or not. The product consists of a mixture of particles, ranging from a definite maximum size to very small particles. The grinding equipments are designed to control the magnitude of the largest particles in their products, but the fine sizes are not under control. In some types of grinders fines are minimised, but they are not completely eliminated.

The ratio of the diameters of the largest and smallest particles in a comminuted product is of the order of 10^4. Because of this extreme variation in the sizes of the individual particles, relationships adequate for uniform sizes must be modified when applied to such mixtures. The term *average size*, is meaningless until the method of averaging is defined. For compact grains, the largest dimension or apparent diameter is generally taken as the particle size. For particles that are platelike or needlelike, two dimensions should be given to characterize their size.

4.3 Energy and Power Requirements in Size Reduction

An interesting feature of crushing and grinding is the extremely high in efficiency of the process. By multiplying the amount of new surface generated in comminution by the specific surface energy of the solids, we can estimate the total useful work done in crushing and grinding. The actual energies needed are almost 100 to 1000 times larger than these values. This means that efficiencies based on surface energy vary from 0.1 to 1%.

The remaining energy is wasted in:

(a) The elastic deformation of solid particles before fracture occurs, this stored energy being dissipated as heat and sound at fracture;
(b) The elastic deformation of the equipment;
(c) Friction between solid particles and also between the particles and the equipment walls.

These losses manifest themselves primarily as heat through a small part of it shows up as noise and vibration of the equipment. Such high-energy losses may raise the temperature of the solids considerably and cooling is often required to prevent damage to the equipment as well as to the product (if it is heat sensitive).

Crushing Efficiency: It is defined as the ratio of the surface energy created by crushing to the energy absorbed by the solid is called as crushing efficiency. It is denoted by η_c.

Let, e_s = surface energy per unit area, in meter times kilogram force per square meter.

A_{wb} and A_{wa} = Areas per unit mass of product and feed respectively.

Then the energy absorbed by a unit mass of the material W_n is given by:

$$W_n = \frac{e_s (A_{wb} - A_{wa})}{\eta_c} \qquad \ldots (4.1)$$

The surface energy created by the fracture is small in comparison with the total mechanical energy stored in the material at the time of rupture and most of latter is converted into heat. Hence, crushing efficiencies are low. (Typically range from 0.06 to 1%).

Three laws have been proposed to correlate the power requirement for crushing and grinding with the feed and product sizes. All the three involve modeling of the energy required to actually break the solids (the total surface energy required being one). The total energy required is expressed as a product of this computed energy and an efficiency, which is assumed to be independent of the size of the solids. These laws are discussed below.

4.4 Laws of Size Reduction

4.4.1 Empirical Relationships: Rittinger's and Kick's Law

The work required in crushing is proportional to the new surface created. This is equivalent to the statement that the crushing efficiency is constant and for a giving machine and mateiral, is independent of the sizes of feed and product. If the sphericities ϕ_a (before size reduciton) and ϕ_b (after size reduction) are equal and the machine efficiency is constant, then

(i) Rittinger's law can be written as:

$$\frac{P}{\dot{m}} = K_r \left(\frac{1}{\bar{D}_{Sb}} - \frac{1}{\bar{D}_{Sa}} \right) \qquad \ldots (4.2)$$

where, P is the power required, $\dot{m}$ is the feed rate to crusher, $\bar{D}_{Sa}$ is the average particle diameter before crushing, $\bar{D}_{Sb}$ is the average particle diameter after crushing and K_r is Rittinger's coefficient or constant.

(ii) Kick's law: The work required for crushing a given mass of material is constant for the same reduction ratio, that is the ratio of the initial particle size to the finial particle size:

$$\frac{P}{\dot{m}} = K_k \ln \frac{\bar{D}_{Sa}}{\bar{D}_{Sb}} \qquad \ldots (4.3)$$

where, K_k is Kick's coefficient or constant.

4.4.2 Bond Crushing Law and Work Index

(i) Bond's Law: The work required to form particles of size D_p from very large feed is proportional to the square root of the surface-to-volume ratio of the product s_p/v_p. Since $\phi_s = 6/D_p$, it follows that:

$$\frac{P}{\dot{m}} = \frac{K_b}{\sqrt{D_p}} \qquad \ldots (4.4)$$

where K_b is a constant that depends on the type of machine and on the material being crushed.

(ii) Work Index (W_i): The work index, w_i, is defined as the gross energy required in KWH per ton of feed to reduce a very large feed to such a size that 80% of the product passes a 100 μm screen. If D_p is in millimeters, P in KW, and $\dot{m}$ in tons per hour, then

$$K_b = \sqrt{100 \times 10^{-3}}\, w_i = 0.3162\, w_i \qquad \ldots (4.5)$$

If 80% of the feed passes, a mesh size of $\bar{D}_{pa}$ millimeters and 80% of the product, a mesh of $\bar{D}_{pb}$ millimeters, it follows that:

$$\frac{P}{\dot{m}} = 0.3161\, w_i \left(\frac{1}{\sqrt{D_{pb}}} - \frac{1}{\sqrt{D_{pa}}}\right) \qquad \ldots (4.6)$$

4.5 Size Reduction Equipments

Size-reduction equipment is divided into crushers, grinders, ultra fine grinders, and cutting machines. Crushers do the heavy work of breaking large pieces of solid material into small lumps. a primary crusher operates on run-of mine material, accepting anything that comes from the mine face and breaking it into 6 to 10 in. (150-to 250- mm) lumps. A secondary crusher reduces these lumps to particles perhaps 6 mm in size. Grinders reduce crushed feed to powder. The product from an intermediate grinder might pass a 40-mesh screen; most of the product from a fine grinder would pass a 200-mesh screen. An ultra fine grinder accepts feed particles no larger than 1/4 in. (6 mm); the product size is typically 1 to 50 μm. Cutters give particles of definite size and shape, 2 to 10 mm in length. The principal types of size-reduction machines are:

(A) Crushers (coarse and fine):
1. Jaw crushers.
2. Gyratory crushers.
3. Crushing rolls.

(B) Grinders (intermediate and fine):
1. Hammer mills; impactors
2. Rolling-compression mills.
   (a) Bowl mills.
   (b) Roller mills.

3. Attrition mills.
4. Tumbling mills.
   (a) Rod mills.
   (b) Ball mills; pebble mills.
   (c) Tube mills; compartment mills.

(C) Ultrafine grinders:
1. Hammer mills with internal classification.
2. Fluid-energy mills.
3. Agitated mills.

(D) Cutting machines:
1. Knife cutters; dicers; slitters.

These machines do their work in distinctly different ways. Compression is the characteristic action of crushers. Grinders employ impact and attrition, sometimes combined with compression; Ultrafine grinders operate principally by attrition. A cutting action is of course characteristic of cutters, dicers, and slitters.

4.5.1 Crushers

Crushers are slow-speed machines for coarse reduction of large quantities of solids. The main types are jaw crushers, gyratory crushers, smooth-roll crushers, and toothed-roll crushers. The first three operate by compression and can break large lumps of very hard materials, as in the primary and secondary reduction of rocks and ores. Toothed-roll crushers tear the feed apart as well as crushing it; they handle softer feeds like coal, bone, and soft shale.

(1) Jaw Crusher: In a jaw crusher feed is admitted between two jaws, set to form a V open at the top. One jaw, fixed, or anvil, jaw, is nearly vertical and does not move; the other, the swinging jaw, reciprocates in a horizontal plane. It makes an angle of 20 to 30° with the anvil jaw. It is driven by an eccentric so that it applies great compressive force to lumps caught between the jaws. The jaw faces are flat or slightly bulged; they may carry shallow horizontal groves. Large lumps caught between the upper parts of the jaws are broken, drop into the narrower space below, and are recrushed the next time the jaws close. After sufficient reduction they drop out the bottom of the machine. The jaws open and close 250 to 400 times per minute.

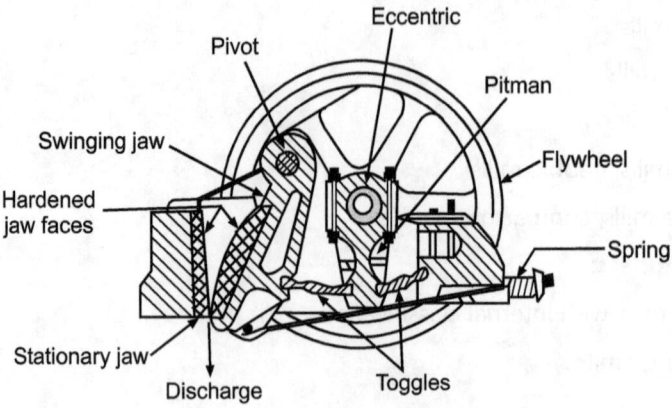

Fig. 4.1: Blake Jaw Crusher

(a) Blake-Jaw Crusher: The most common type of jaw crusher is the Blake crusher, illustrated in Fig. 4.1. In this machine an eccentric drives a pitman connected to two toggles, one of which is pinned to the frame and the other to the swinging jaw. The pivot point is at the top of the movable jaw or above the top of the jaws on the centerline of the jaw opening. The greatest amount of motion is at the bottom of the V, which means that there is little tendency for a crusher of this kind to choke. Some machines with a 1.8 by 2.4 m feed opening can accept rocks 1.8 m in diameter and crush 1,000 tons/h to a maximum product size of 250 mm. Smaller secondary crushers reduce the particle size of precrushed feed 6 to 50 mm at much lower rates of throughput.

(b) The Dodge-Jaw Crusher: In the Dodge Crusher, the moving jaw is pivoted at the bottom. The minimum movement is thus at the bottom and a more uniform product is obtained. However this type of crusher is not commonly used due to its tendency to choke. The larger opening at the top enables it to take very large feed and to effect a large size reduction. This crusher is usually made in smaller sizes than the Blake-Jaw Crusher due to high fluctuating stresses that are produced in the members of the machine.

(2) Gyratory Crushers: The gyratory cursher was invented by Charles Brown in 1877. The name gyratory comes from the fact that while the spindle is revolving around the axis of the frame generating a conical surface, at the same time it rotates about its own axis due to frictional drag. A gyratory crusher may be looked upon as a jaw crusher with circular jaws, between which material is being crushed at same point at all times. A conical crushing head gyrates inside a funnel-shaped casing, open at the top. As shown in Fig. 4.2, the crushing head is carried on a heavy shaft pivoted at the top of the machine. An eccentric drives the bottom end of the shaft. At any point on the periphery of the casing, therefore, the bottom of the crushing head moves toward, and then away from, the stationary wall. Solids caught in the V-shaped space between the head and the casing are broken and rebroken until they pass out the bottom. The crushing head is free to rotate on the shaft and turns slowly because of friction with the material being crushed.

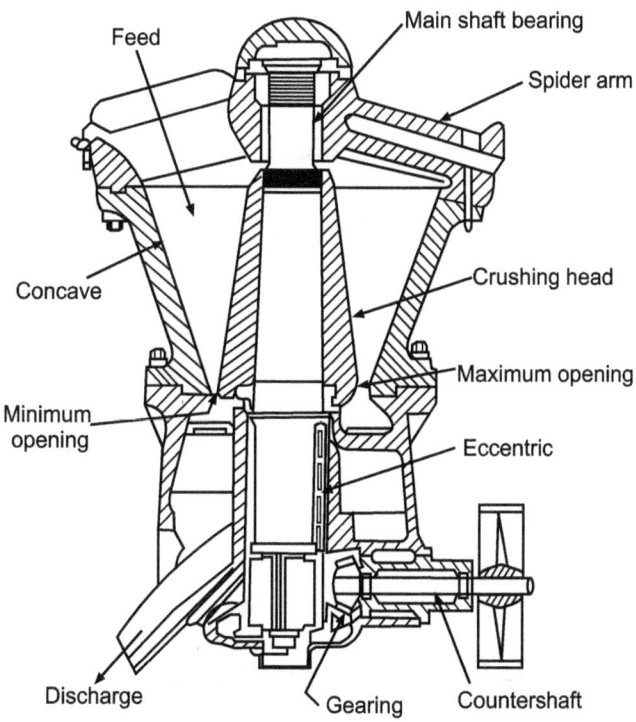

Fig. 4.2: Gyratory Crusher

The speed of the crushing head is typically 125 to 425 gyrations per minute. Because some part of the crushing head is working at all times, the discharge from a gyratory is continuous instead of intermittent as in a jaw crusher. The load on the motor is nearly uniform; less maintenance is required than with a jaw crusher; and the power requirement per ton of material crushed is smaller. The biggest gyratories handle up to 3,500 tons/h. The capacity of a gyratory crusher varies with the jaw setting, the impact strength of the feed, and the speed of gyration of the machine. The capacity is almost independent of the compressive strength of the material being crushed.

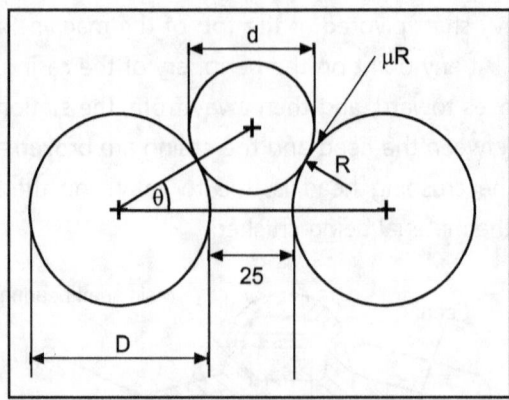

Fig. 4.3: Crushing Rolls

The maximum size of particle crushable is found by resolving the upward and downward forces on the particle. If R is the force acting at the point of contact of the roller and the particle then the upward force is,

$$R \sin \theta \quad \ldots (4.7)$$

and the downwards force is,

$$\mu R \cos \theta \quad \ldots (4.8)$$

so

$$\mu R \sin \theta > R \sin \theta \quad \ldots (4.9)$$

i.e.

$$\mu > \tan \theta$$

A typical value of the coefficient of friction would be $\tan^{-1} 16°$ so $\theta < 16°$

$$\theta = \cos^{-1} \frac{R + \delta}{R + r} \quad \ldots (4.10)$$

so,

$$\frac{R + \delta}{R + r} = \cos 16° = 0.961 \quad \ldots (4.11)$$

For rolls with R = 1 m and which are touching the maximum feed size is 8.2 cm which increases as the gap increases.

4.5.2 Relative Merits of the Jaw Crusher and Gyratory Crusher

Both jaw crusher and gyratory crushers are high duty equipments in wide use. The selection of a crusher for a particular duty is therefore very difficult. However, the specific features of these machines should be known to make a correct choice.

Features of Jaw Crusher:
(a) Large receiving opening per unit investment.
(b) Shape of receiving opening favours large block shaped feed. This gives the jaw crusher a definite advantage over the gyratory crusher except in very large sizes.
(c) The jaw crusher handles dirty or sticky feed more easily than the gyratory crusher.
(d) Routine maintenance is much more easy for the jaw crusher.
(e) For crushing extra tough materials extra strength can be built into a jaw at less cost.

Features of Gyratory Crusher:
(a) High capacity per unit investment.
(b) More cubical product is obtained.
(c) Method of feeding is very simple.
(d) Low flywheel effect minimizes the starting peaks.
(e) Higher pinion shaft speed allows use of higher speed motors and lower ratio drives.
(f) Lubrication is simpler and more economical.
(g) They have a wide range of adjustment for product size.
(h) Only small headroom and space is required.

4.5.3 Hammer Mills and Impactors

Many types of mills can be termed as impact mills. The hammer mills and stamping mills are the examples of such machines. The distinct features of an impact mill is that it has a fast moving part which transfers its kinetic energy to the particles when it hits them. This causes the particles to shatter and break into pieces of smaller size.

These mills all contain a high-speed rotor turning inside a cylindrical casing. The shaft is usually horizontal. Feed dropped into the top of the casing is broken and falls out through a bottom opening. In a hammer mill the particles are broken by sets of swing hammers pinned to a rotor disk. A particle of feed entering the grinding zone cannot escape being struck by the hammers. It shatters into pieces, which fly against a stationary anvil plate inside the casing and break into still smaller fragments. These in turn are rubbed into powder by the hammers and pushed through a grate or screen, which covers the discharge opening.

Several rotor disks 150 to 450 mm in diameter and each carrying four to eight swing hammers, are often mounted on the same shaft. The hammers may be straight bars of metal with plain or enlarged ends or with ends sharpened to a cutting edge. Intermediate hammer mills yield a product 25 mm to 20-mesh in particle size.

In hammer mills for fine reduction the peripheral speed of the hammer tips may reach 112 m/s; they reduce 0.1 to 15 tons/h to sizes finer than 200-mesh. Hammer mills grid almost anything-tough fibrous solids like bark or leather, steel turnings, soft wet pastes, sticky clay, hard rock. For fine reduction they are limited to the softer materials.

The capacity and power requirement of a hammer mill vary greatly with the nature of the feed and cannot be estimated with confidence from theoretical considerations. They are best found from published information or better from small-scale or full-scale tests of the mill with a sample of the actual material to be ground. Commercial mills typically reduce 60 to 240 kg/k Wh of energy consumed.

The hammer mills have the following advantages:
(a) The energy required is relatively smaller than for most size-reduction machines.
(b) Comparatively little space is required.
(c) Worn out part can be replaced easily.
(d) Machines can be built from a small size handling (50 kg per hour) to large size (5000 kg per hour).
(e) Soft minerals and fibrous materials such as bones, wood, asbestos can be broken efficiently in a hammer.
(f) Strainfree particles are produced that are not susceptible to cracking or breaking.

4.5.4 Ball Mill

In a ball mill or pebble mill most of the reduction is done by impact as the balls or pebbles drop from near the top of the shell. In a large ball mill the shell might be 3 m in diameter and 4.25 m long. the balls are 25 to 125 mm in diameter; the pebbles in a pebble mill are 50 to 175 mm in size. A tube mill is a continuous mill with a long cylindrical shell, in which material is ground for 2 to 5 times as long as in the shorter ball mill.

Tube mills are excellent for grinding to very fine powders in a single pass where the amount of energy consumed is not of primary importance. Putting slotted transverse partitions in a tube mill converts it into a compartment mill. One compartment may contain large balls, another small balls, and a third pebbles.

This segregation of the grinding media into elements of different size and weight aids considerably in avoiding wasted work, for the large, heavy balls break only the large particles, without interference by the fines. The small, light balls fall only on small particles, not on large lumps they cannot break.

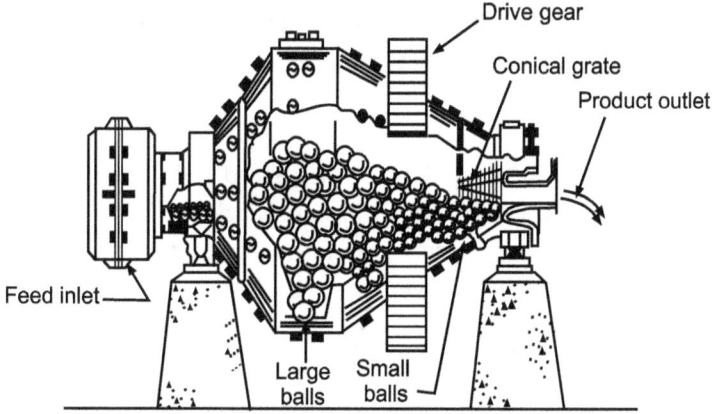

Fig. 4.4: Conical Ball Mill

Segregation of the grinding units in a single chamber is a characteristic of the conical ball mill. Feed enters from the left through a 60° cone into the primary grinding zone, where the diameter of the shell is a maximum. Product leaves through the 30° cone to the right. A mill of this kind contains balls of different sizes, all of which wear and become smaller as the mill is operated. New large balls are added periodically.

As the shell of such a mill rotates, the large balls move toward the point of maximum diameter, and the shall ball migrate toward the discharge. The largest balls dropping the greatest distance, therefore, do the initial breaking of the feed particles,; small particles are ground by small balls dropping a much smaller distance. The amount of energy expended is suited to the difficulty of the breaking operation, increasing the efficiency of the mill.

Grinding Parameters in Ball Mill: The most important grinding parameters are:
(a) Feeding arrangement.
(b) Particle size of the feed.
(c) Grinding media-material, size, quality.
(d) Mill size, its speed and power consumption.
(e) Solid-liquid ratio and circulating load in a closed circuit operation.

When the mill is rotated, the balls are picked up by the mill wall and carried nearly to the top, where they break contact with the wall and fall to the bottom to be picked up again. Centrifugal force keeps the balls in contact with wall and with each other during the upward movement.

While in contact with the wall, the balls do some grinding by slipping and rolling over each other, but most of the grinding occurs at the zone of impact, where the free-falling balls strike the bottom of the mill.

If the speed is too high, however, the balls are carried over and the mill is said to be *centrifuging*. The speed at which centrifuging occurs is called the critical speed. Little or no grinding is done when a mill is centrifuging, and operating speeds must be less than the critical. The critical speed of ball mill is given as,

$$n_c = \frac{1}{2\pi}\sqrt{\frac{g}{R-r}} \qquad \ldots (4.12)$$

where,

R = Radius of Ball mill;
r = Radius of ball
n_c = Critical speed of ball mill

Tumbling mills run at 65 to 80 percent of the critical speed, with the lower values for wet grinding in viscous suspensions.

The ball mill is used for the grinding of a wide range of materials, including coal, pigments, felspar for pottery and will take feed up to 2 inches in size. The efficiency of grinding increases with the hold-up in the mill until the voids between the balls are filled.

4.6 Equipment Operation

For the proper selection and economical operation of size-reduction machinery, attention must be given to many details of procedure and of auxiliary equipment. A crusher, grinder, or cutter cannot be expected to perform satisfactorily unless,
(1) the feed is of suitable size and enters at a uniform rate;
(2) the product is removed as soon as possible after the particles are of the desired size;
(3) unbreakable material is kept out of the machine; and
(4) in the reduction of low-melting or heat-sensitive products, the heat generated in the mill is removed. Heaters and coolers, metal separators, pumps and blowers, and constant-rate feeders are therefore important adjuncts to the size-reduction unit.

4.6.1 Open-Circuit and Closed-Circuit Operation

In many mills the feed is broken into particles of satisfactory size by passing it once through the mill. When no attempt is made to return oversize particles to the machine for further reduction, the mill is said to be operating in open circuit. This may require excessive amounts of power; for much energy is wasted in regrinding particles that are already fine enough. If a 50-mesh product is desired, it is obviously wasteful to continue grinding 100 or 200 mesh material.

Thus it is often economical to remove partially ground material from the mill and pass it through a size-separation device. The undersize becomes the product and the oversize is returned to be reground. The separation device is sometimes inside the mill, as in ultra fine grinders; or, as is more common, it is outside the mill. Closed-circuit operation is the term applied to the action of a mill and separator connected so that oversize particles are returned to the mill.

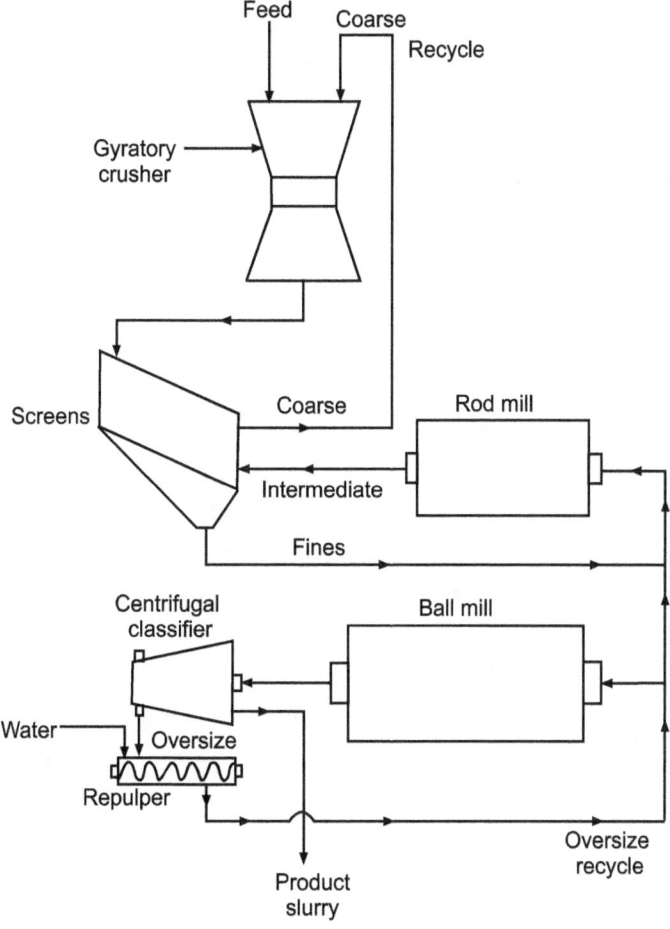

Fig. 4.5: Flowsheet for Closed-Circuit Grinding

For coarse particles the separation device is a screen or grizzly; for fine powders it is some form of classifier. A typical set of size-reduction machines and separators operating in closed circuit is shown in Fig. 4.4. The product from a gyratory crusher is screened into three fractions, fines, intermediate, and oversize. The oversize is sent back to the gyratory; the fines are fed directly to the final reduction unit, a ball mill. Intermediate particles are broken in a rod mill before they enter the ball mill. In the arrangement shown in the diagram the ball mill is grinding wet; i.e., water is pumped through the mill with the solid to carry the broken particles to a centrifugal classifier. The classifier throws down the oversize into a sludge, which is repulped with more water and returned to the mill.

The undersize, or product, emerges from the classifier as a slurry containing particles of acceptable size. Although screens are simpler to operate than classifiers, they cannot economically make separations when the particles are smaller then about 150 to 200 mesh. It is the over grinding of precisely these fine particles that results in excessive consumption of energy. Closed-circuit operation is therefore of most value in reduction to fine and Ultrafine sizes, which demands that the separation be done by wet classifiers or air separators. Energy must of course be supplied to drive the conveyors and separators in a closed-circuit system, but despite this, the reduction in total energy requirement over open-circuit grinding often reaches 25 percent.

4.6.2 Feed Control

Of the operations auxiliary to the size reduction itself, control of the feed to the mill is the most important. The particles in the feed must be of appropriate size. Obviously they must not be so large that they cannot be broken by the mill; if too many of the particles are very fine, the effectiveness of many machines, especially intermediate crushers and grinders, is seriously reduced. With some solids precompression or chilling of the feed before it enters the mill greatly increases the ease with which it can be ground. In continuous mills the feed rate must be controlled within close limits to avoid choking or erratic variations in load and yet make full use of the capacity of the machine. In cutting sheet material into precise squares or thread into uniform lengths for flock, exact control of the feed rate is obviously essential.

4.6.3 Mill Discharge

To avoid buildup in continuous mill the rate of discharge must equal the rate of discharge. Furthermore, the discharge rate must be such that the working parts of the mill can operate most effectively on the material to be reduced. In a jaw crusher, for example, particles any collect in the discharge opening and be crushed many times before they drop out. As mentioned before, this is wasteful of energy if many of the particles are crushed more than necessary.

Operation of a crusher in this way is sometimes deliberate; it is known as choke crushing. Usually, however, the crusher is designed and operated so that the crushed particles readily drop out, perhaps carrying some oversize particles, which are separated and returned. This kind of operation is called free-discharge crushing or free crushing. Choke crushing is used only in unusual problems, for it requires large amounts of power and may damage the mill.

With fairly coarse comminuted products, as from a crusher, intermediate grinder, or cutter, the force of gravity is sufficient to give free discharge. The product usually drops out the bottom of the mill. In a revolving mill it escapes through openings in the chamber wall at one end of the cylinder (peripheral discharge); or it is lifted by scoops and dropped into a cone, which directs it out through a hollow trunnion (trunnion discharge). A slotted grate or diaphragm keeps the grinding medium from leaving with the product. Peripheral discharge is common in rod mills, trunnion discharge in ball mills and tube mills.

In discharging mills for fine and ultra fine grinding the force of gravity is replaced by the drag of a fluid carrier. The fluid may be a liquid or a gas. Wet grinding with a liquid carrier is common in revolving mills. It causes more wear on the chamber walls and on the grinding medium than dry grinding, but it saves energy, increases capacity, and simplifies handling and classification of the product. A sweep of air, steam, or inert gas removes the product from attrition mills, fluid-energy mills, and many hammer mills. The powder is taken out of the gas stream by cyclone separators or bag filters.

4.6.4 Energy Consumption

Enormous quantities of energy are consumed in size-reduction operations, especially in manufacturing cement; crushing coal, rock, and shale; and preparing ores for making steel and copper. Size reduction is probably the most inefficient of all unit operations over 99 percent of the energy goes to operating the equipment, producing undesirable heat and noise, leaving less than 1 percent for creating new surface. As processes have been developed which require finer and finer particles as feed to a kiln or reactor, the total energy requirement has increased, for reduction to very fine sizes is much more costly in energy than simple crushing to relatively coarse products.

4.6.5 Removal or Supply of Heat

Since only a very small fraction of the energy supplied to the solid is used in creating new surface, the bulk of the energy is converted to heat, which may raise the temperature of the solid by many degrees. The solid may melt, decompose, or explode unless this heat is removed. For this reason cooling water or refrigerated brine is often circulated through coils or jackets in the mill. Sometimes the air blown through the mill is refrigerated, or solid carbon dioxide (dry ice) is admitted with the feed.

Still more drastic temperature reduction is achieved with liquid nitrogen, to give grinding temperature below – 75°C. The purpose of such low temperatures is to alter the breaking characteristics of the solid, usually by making it more friable. In this way substances like lard and beeswax become hard enough to shatter in a hammer mill; tough plastics, which stall a mill at ordinary temperatures, become brittle enough to be ground without difficulty.

4.7 Comparison between Crushing and Grinding Operations

In general, there is very difficult to differentiate between crushing and grinding both of which aim at size reduction. The difference is more of a degree than of kind. However certain differences may be highlighted.

(a) The reduction ratio (i.e. the ratio of the largest size in feed to the largest size in the product), seldom exceeds 6-8 inches crushing, where as, in a ball mill (grinding operation), a reduction ratio of 100 is possible.

(b) The primary crushing is always done in open circuit whereas secondary or tertiary crushing may be done in closed as well as open circuit. On the other hand, grinding is always done in closed circuit with a suitable classifier.

(c) Crushing is invariabley done on a dry feed. As a matter of fact, many crushers can not take up a moist feed. The grinding is possible with a dry feed or a pulp containing water. In process industires, most of the time wet grinding is practised.

(d) The force generated in crushing machiens are intense and are concentrated at a few points to achieve maximum effect. On the other hand, during grinding multipoint forces are generated by the tumbling of the loose balls or rods. Wehre as, crushing is a one shift operation, grinding is carried out continuouly in all the shifts. This is due to the residence time in crusher is *less* and throughputs are *large*. In grinding, however, the residence time is relatively *larger* and throughputs are *smaller*.

4.8 Principles of Size Enlargement

Scope and Applications:

Size enlargement is any process whereby small particles are gathered into larger, relatively permanent masses in which the original particles can still be distinguished. The term encompasses a variety of unit-operations or processing techniques dedicated to particle agglomeration. *Agglomeration* is the formation of aggregates through the sticking together of feed and/or recycle material. These processes can be loosely broken down into *agitation* and *compression* methods. Although terminology is industry specific, agglomeration by agitation will be referred to as *granulation*. Here, a particulate feed is introduced to a process vessel and is agglomerated, either batchwise and continuously to form a granulated product. Agitative processes include fluid-bed, pan (or disc), drum and mixer granulators. The feed typically consists of a mixture of solid ingredients, referred to as a *formulation*, which includes an active or key ingredient, binders, diluents, flow aids, surfactants, wetting agents, lubricants, fillers or end-use aids (e.g. sintering aids, colours or dyes, taste modifiers). The agglomeration can be induced in several ways. A solvent or slurry can be atomized onto the bed of particles which either coats the particle or granule surfaces promoting agglomeration, or the spray drops can form small nuclei in the case of a powder feed which subsequently can agglomerate. The solvent or slurry may contain a binder, or solid binder may be present as one component of the feed. Alternatively, the solvent may induce dissolution and recrystallization in the case of soluble particles. Slurries often contain the same particulate matter as the dry feed, and granules may be formed, either completely or partially, as the droplets solidify in flight prior to reaching the particle bed. **Spray-drying** is an extreme case with no further, intended agglomeration taking place after granule formation. Agglomeration may also be induced by heat, which either leads to controlled **sintering** of the particle bed or induces sintering or partial melting of a binder component of the feed for example, a polymer.

An alternative approach to size enlargement is by **compression agglomeration**, where the mixture of particulate matter is fed to a compression device which promotes agglomeration due to pressure. Either continuous sheets of solid material are produced or some solid form such as a **briquette** or **tablet.** Heat or cooling may be applied, and reaction may be induced as for example with sintering. Carrier fluids may be present, either added or induced by melting in which case the product is **wet extruded.** Continuous compaction processes include roll presses, briquetting machines, and extrusion, whereas batch-like processes include tableting. Some processes operate in a semicontinuous fashion, such as ram extrusion.

At the level of a manufacturing plant, the size-enlargement process involves several peripheral, unit operations such as milling, blending, drying or cooling, and classification referred to generically as an **agglomeration circuit**. In addition, more than one agglomeration step may be present as in the case of a pharmaceutical process which often involves both an agitative-granulation technique followed by the compressive technique of tableting.

Numerous benefits result from size-enlargement process, as will bution as well as feed-formulation properties. Often wetting agents such as surfactants are carefully chosen to enhance poorly wetting feeds. In the **coalescence** or **growth** stage, partially wetted primary particles and larger nuclei coalesce to form granules composed of several particles. The term **nucleation** is typically applied to the initial coalescence of primary particles in the immediate vicinity of the larger-wetting drop, whereas the more general term of **coalesence.**

Objectives of Size Enlargement:

(i) Production of useful structural forms, as in pressing of intricate shapes in powder metallurgy.
(ii) Provision of a defined quantity for dispensing and metering, as in agricultural chemical granules or pharmaceuticals tablets.
(iii) Elimination of dust handling hazards or losses, as in briquetting of waste fines.
(iv) Improved product appearance, or product renewal.
(v) Reduced caking and lump formation, as in granulation of fertilizer.
(vi) Improved flow properties, as in granulation of pharmaceuticals for tableting or ceramics for pressing.
(vii) Increased bulk density for storage.
(viii) Creation of non-segregating blends of powder ingredients, as in sintering of fines for steel or agricultural chemical granules.
(ix) Control of solubility as in instant food products.
(x) Control of porosity and surface-to-volume ratio, as with catalyst supports.
(xi) Improvement of heat transfer characteristics, as in ores or glass for furnace feed.

Removal of particles from liquid, as with polymer additives which induce clay flocculation.

Table 4.2: Enlargement method and application

Method	Product size (mm)	Granule density	Scale of operation	Additional comments	Typical applications
Tumbling granulators Drums Discs	0.5 to 20	Moderate	0.5-800 ton/hr	Very spherical granules	Fertilizers, iron ore, non-ferrous ore agricultural chemicals
Mixer granulators Continuous high shear (e.g. Shugi mixer) Batch high shear (e.g. paddle mixer)	0.1 to 2 0.1 to 2	Low to high High	Upto 50 ton / hr Upto 500 kg batch	Handles very cohesive materials well, both batch and continuous	Chemicals, detergents, clays, carbon black, Pharmaceuticals, ceramics
Fluidized granulators Fluidized beds Spouted beds Wurster coaters	0.1 to 2	Low (agglomerated) Moderate (Layered)	100-900 kg batch 50 ton / hr continuous	Flexible, relatively easy to scale, difficult for cohesive powders, good for coating applications	Continuous fertilizers, inorganic salts, detergents. Batch: Pharmaceuticals, agricultural chemicals, nuclear wastes.
Centrifugal granulators	0.3 to 3	Moderate to high	Upto 200 kg batch	Powder layering and coating applications	Pharmaceuticals, agricultural chemicals
Spray methods Spray drying Prilling	0.05 to 0.5 0.7 to 2	Low Moderate		Morphology of spray dried powders can vary widely	Instant food, dyes, detergents, ceramics Urea, ammonium nitrate
Pressure compaction Extrusion Roll press Tablet press Molding press Pellet mill Thermal processes Sintering	> 0.5 > 1 10 2 to 50	High to very high High to very high	Upto 5 ton / hr Upto 50 ton / hr Upto 1 ton / hr Upto 100 ton / hr	Very narrow size, distributions, very sensitive to powder flow and mechanical properties Strongest bonding.	Pharmaceuticals, catalysts, inorganic chemicals, organic chemicals, plastic preforms, metal parts, ceramics, clays, minerals, animal feeds. Ferrous and non-ferrous ores, cement clinker, minerals, ceramics
Liquid systems Immiscible wetting in mixers So-gel processes Pellet flocculation	< 0.3	Low	Upto 10 ton / hr	Wet processing based on flocculation properties of particulate feed	Coal fines, soot and oil removal from water. Metal dicarbide, silica hydrogels. Waste sludges and slurries

MECHANICAL OPERATIONS — SIZE REDUCTION

4.9 Solved Examples

Example 4.1:

A certain crusher employed in ore dressing unit accepts a feed having a volume-surface mean diameter of 20 mm and gives a product of volume-surface mean diameter of 5 mm. The power required to crush 15 tonnes per hour of this feed material is 10 HP. Determine the power consumption if the capcity is reduced to 10 tonnes per hour.

Solution: Rittinger's Law:

$$\frac{P}{\dot{m}} = K_r \left[\frac{1}{\bar{D}_{S_b}} - \frac{1}{\bar{D}_{S_a}} \right]$$

where,

P = Power consumption in HP

$\dot{m}$ = Feed rate in tonnes/hr.

$\bar{D}_{S_b}$ = Surface - volume mean diameter of product

$\bar{D}_{S_a}$ = Surface – volume mean diameter of feed

Case – I: Here, P = 10 HP; $\dot{m}$ = 15 tonnes/hour

$\bar{D}_{S_a}$ = 20 mm = 0.79 inch; $\bar{D}_{S_b}$ = 5 mm = 0.2 inch

$$\therefore \quad \frac{10}{15} = K_r \left[\frac{1}{0.2} - \frac{1}{0.79} \right]$$

$$\therefore \quad K_r = 0.178$$

Case – II: P =?; $\dot{m}$ = 10 tonnes/hour, $\bar{D}_{S_b}$ = 0.2 inch; $\bar{D}_{S_a}$ = 0.79 inch

$$\therefore \quad \frac{P}{10} = 0.178 \left[\frac{1}{0.2} - \frac{1}{0.79} \right]$$

$$\therefore \quad P = 6.65 \text{ HP} \qquad \text{(Ans.)}$$

Example 4.2:

What will be the power required to crush 150 tonnes per hour of limestone of 80% of the feed passes 2 inch screen and 80% of the product a $\frac{1}{8}$ inch screen? Take work index of limestone = 12.74.

Solution: We use equation:

$$\frac{P}{\dot{m}} = 0.3162 \, W_i \left[\frac{1}{\sqrt{\bar{D}_{P_b}}} - \frac{1}{\sqrt{\bar{D}_{P_a}}} \right]$$

where,

P = Power in kW

$\dot{m}$ = Feed rate

MECHANICAL OPERATIONS   SIZE REDUCTION

Work Index = W_i = Work Index
D_{P_b} = Particle size of product
D_{P_a} = Particle size of feed

Data given:
$\dot{m}$ = 150 tonnes/hour
Work Index = W_i = 12.74
$D_{P_b} = \frac{1}{8}$ inch = 3.175 mm
D_{P_a} = 2 inch = 50.8 mm

Bond's law:
$$\frac{P}{150} = 0.3162\,(12.74)\left(\frac{1}{\sqrt{3.175}} - \frac{1}{\sqrt{50.8}}\right)$$

P = 254.4 kW or
P = 341 HP   **(Ans.)**

Example 4.3:

A certain crusher takes rock whose average particle diameter is 0.025 m and crushes it to a product whose average particle diameter is 0.018 m, at the rate of 20 tonnes/hour. At this rate, the mill takes 9 HP of power and 0.46 HP power is required to run it empty.

(i) What would be the power consumption for same capacity, if the average particle diameter in the product is 0.008 m.
(ii) How much power would be required under conditions (i) by Kick's law?

Solution: Data given: Rate of crushing = $\dot{m}$ = 20 tonnes/hour.

Let, P = Power consumption for crushing only = $P_1 - P_0$
where, P_1 = Power consumption by the mill during crushing.
P_0 = Power consumption by the mill to run it empty.
So, P = 9 − 0.46 = 8.54 HP

Rittinger's Law:
$$\frac{P}{\dot{m}} = K_r\left[\frac{1}{\bar{D}_{S_b}} - \frac{1}{\bar{D}_{S_a}}\right]$$

where, P = is in HP, $\dot{m}$ is in tonnes/hour

So, $\frac{8.54}{20} = K_r\left[\frac{1}{0.018} - \frac{1}{0.025}\right]$

∴ K_r = 0.0275

(i) Let P' be the power consumption for this case.

$\bar{D}_{S_b}$ = 0.008 m

So,
$$\frac{P'}{20} = K_r \left(\frac{1}{0.008} - \frac{1}{0.025} \right)$$

or, $P' = 46.75$ HP

(ii) By Kick's Law,
$$\frac{P}{\dot{m}} = K_k \log \frac{D_{S_a}}{D_{S_b}}$$

$$\frac{8.54}{20} = K_k \log \frac{0.025}{0.018}$$

So, $K_k = 2.993$

Power required under conditions (i)

$$\frac{P'}{\dot{m}} = K_k \log \frac{0.025}{0.008}$$

$$P' = 20 \times 2.993 \times \log \left(\frac{0.025}{0.008} \right)$$

$$P' = 29.62 \text{ HP} \qquad \text{(Ans.)}$$

Example 4.4:

Calculate the energy required to crush 100 tonnes/hour of limestone if 80% of the feed passes through a screen 3.75 cm. aperture and 80% of the product passes through a screen with 0.03 cm. aperture. The work index for limestone is 12.74, when the capacity is expressed in tonnes/hour, energy required in HP and size of feed and product in feet.

Solution: Bond's Law:
$$\frac{P}{\dot{m}} = 0.3162 \, W_i \left[\frac{1}{\sqrt{\bar{D}_{P_b}}} - \frac{1}{\sqrt{\bar{D}_{P_a}}} \right]$$

Data given: Particle size of product $\bar{D}_{P_b} = 0.03$ cm $= \frac{0.03}{30.54}$ feet

Work Index $= W_i = 12.74$

Particle size of the feed $= \bar{D}_{P_a} = 3.75$ cm $= \frac{3.75}{30.54}$ feet

Feed rate $= \dot{m} = 100$ tonnes/hour $= \frac{100}{60}$ tonnes/min.

$= \frac{5}{3}$ tonnes/min.

So,
$$P = \frac{5}{3} \times 0.3162 \times 12.74 \left[\frac{1}{\sqrt{\frac{0.03}{30.54}}} - \frac{1}{\sqrt{\frac{3.75}{30.54}}} \right]$$

$P = 195$ kW or
$P = 261$ HP (Ans.)

MECHANICAL OPERATIONS — SIZE REDUCTION

Example 4.5:

A material is crushed in a Blake jaw crusher and the average size of particles is reduced from 5 cm to 1.3 cm, with consumption of 37 $\frac{\text{(watts) (hour)}}{\text{(metric ton)}}$. What will be the consumption of energy necessary to crush the same material of average size 8 cm to an average size of 3 cm? You may assume that the mechanical efficiency remains unchanged. Do the calculations using: (i) Using Rittinger's law, (ii) Using Kick's Law.

Solution: (i) Rittinger's law is, $\quad \dfrac{P}{\dot{m}} = K_r \left[\dfrac{1}{\overline{D}_{S_b}} - \dfrac{1}{\overline{D}_{S_a}} \right]$

Here, $\quad \overline{D}_{S_b} = 1.3$ cm

$\overline{D}_{S_a} = 5$ cm

$P = 37 \dfrac{\text{(watts) (hour)}}{\text{(metric ton)}}$

$\dot{m} = 1$ ton/hour

So, $\quad \dfrac{37}{1} = K_r \left(\dfrac{1}{1.3} - \dfrac{1}{5} \right)$ ... (1)

For the second case, let P' be the power consumption

So, $\quad \dfrac{P'}{1} = K_r \left(\dfrac{1}{3} - \dfrac{1}{8} \right)$ ... (2)

Dividing equations (2) by equations (1),

$$\dfrac{P'}{37} = \dfrac{\left(\dfrac{1}{3} - \dfrac{1}{8} \right)}{\left(\dfrac{1}{1.3} - \dfrac{1}{5} \right)}$$

Solving for P' we get, $\quad P' = 13.54 \dfrac{\text{(watts) (hour)}}{\text{(metric ton)}}$ **(Ans.)**

(ii) Expression for Kick's law is,

$$\dfrac{P}{\dot{m}} = K_k \log \dfrac{\overline{D}_{S_a}}{\overline{D}_{S_b}}$$

Here, $\dot{m} = 1$ tonnes/hour

$\overline{D}_{S_a} = 5$ cm

$\overline{D}_{S_b} = 1.3$ cm

$$P = 37 \frac{\text{(watts) (hour)}}{\text{(metric ton)}}$$

So, $\dfrac{37}{1} = K_k \log \dfrac{5}{1.3}$ ... (3)

For the second case, let P" be the power required

So, $\dfrac{P"}{\dot{m}} = K_k \log \dfrac{\bar{D}_{S_a}'}{D_{S_b}'} = K_k \log \dfrac{8}{3}$ ... (4)

Dividing equations (4) by equation (3),

$$\dfrac{P"}{37} = \dfrac{\log 8/3}{\log \dfrac{5}{1.3}}$$

Solving for P" we get, $P" = 26.94 \dfrac{\text{(watts) (hour)}}{\text{(metric ton)}}$ **(Ans.)**

Example 4.6:

A certain set of crushing rolls has rolls of 100 cm diameter by 38 cm width face. They are set so that crushing surfaces are 1.25 cm apart at the narrowest point. The manufacture recommends that they may be run at 50 to 100 rpm. They are to crush a rock having a specific gravity of 2.35 and the angle of nip is 30°. What are the maximum permissible size of feed and maximum actual capacity in tonnes per hour, if the actual capacity is 12% of the theoretical?

Solution: Let, A_n = Angle of nip = 30°

$$\cos(A_n/2) = \dfrac{\dfrac{D_p}{2} + r}{\dfrac{D_f}{2} + r}$$

where, $\dfrac{D_p}{2} = \dfrac{1}{2} \times$ space between the rolls = radius of the product.

r = radius of the rolls
D_f = Diameter of the feed (sphere) to be crushed

So, $\cos 15° = \dfrac{50 + \dfrac{1.25}{2}}{50 + \dfrac{D_f}{2}} = \dfrac{50.625}{50 + \dfrac{D_f}{2}}$

or, $0.966 \left(50 + \dfrac{D_f}{2}\right) = 50.625$

or, $\dfrac{D_f}{2} = \dfrac{2.325}{0.966}$

Hence, $D_f = 4.81$ cm

Maximum permissible size of feed = 4.81 cm.

Theoretical capacity of a set of crushing rolls is given by,

$$q = 60 \times (2d) \times (\pi ND) \times b$$

where,
q = volumetric capacity, cm³/hour
d = one half roll spacing, cm
N = rpm
D = Diameter of the rolls, cm

So, $q = 60 \times 1.25 \times \pi (100)(100) \times 38$

$= 8.954 \times 10^7$ cm³/hour

Density of material = $\rho_S = 2.35$ gm/cm³

Weight of material = $9 \times \rho_S$

$= \dfrac{8.954 \times 10^7 \times 2.35}{10^6}$

= 210.4 tonnes/hour

Actual capacity is 12% of the theoretical. Hence, actual capacity of the rolls

= 210.4 × 0.12 = 25.25 $\dfrac{\text{tonnes}}{\text{hour}}$.

Maximum feed size = 4.81 cm.

Actual capacity of rolls = 25.25 tonnes/hour **(Ans.)**

Example 4.7:

A certain set of crushing rolls has rolls of 150 cm in diameter by 50 cm width of face. They are set so that the crushing surfaces are 1.25 cm apart at the narrowest point. The manufacture recommends 100 rpm, as the roll speed. They are to crush a rock having a specific gravity of 2.35 and the angle of nip is 30°.

(a) What are the permissible size of the feed and the maximum actual capacity in metric tonnes per hour if the actual capacity is 12% of the theoretical?

(b) After long use, the tires on the rolls of mill have become roughened so that the angle of nip is 32° 30'. What will now be the maximum permissible size of feed and the capacity of the rolls?

Solution: (a) Let A_n = Angle of nip = 30°

$$\cos\frac{A_n}{2} = \frac{r + \frac{D_p}{2}}{r + \frac{D_f}{2}} = \frac{75 + \frac{1.25}{2}}{75 + \frac{D_f}{2}}$$

$$0.966\left(75 + \frac{D_f}{2}\right) = 75.625$$

or $\quad\quad\quad\quad\quad\quad\quad\quad \dfrac{D_f}{2} = \dfrac{3.175}{0.966}$

So, $\quad\quad\quad\quad\quad\quad\quad\quad D_f = 6.57$ cm

Maximum permissible feed size = 6.57 cm

Theoretical capacity = q = $60 \times 2d \times \pi DN \times b$

$\quad\quad\quad\quad\quad\quad\quad\quad = 60 \times 1.25 \times \pi \times 150 \times 100 \times 50$

$\quad\quad\quad\quad\quad\quad\quad\quad = 1.76 \times 10^8$ cm³/hour

$\quad\quad\quad\quad\quad\quad\quad\quad = 1.76 \times 10^8 \times \dfrac{2.35}{106}$

$\quad\quad\quad\quad\quad\quad\quad\quad = 415.28$ tonnes/hour

Actual capacity $\quad\quad = 415.28 \times 0.12 = 49.83$ tonnes/hour $\quad\quad\quad$ **(Ans.)**

(b) New angle of nip = A_n' = 32° 30'

$$\cos\frac{A_n'}{2} = \frac{r + \frac{D_p}{2}}{r + \frac{D_f'}{2}} = \frac{75 + 0.625}{75 + \frac{D_f'}{2}}$$

$$0.960\left(75 + \frac{D_f'}{2}\right) = 75.625$$

Solving, $\quad\quad\quad\quad\quad\quad D_f' = 7.55$ cm

Maximum permissible size of feed for new conditions = 7.55 cm

Since the capacity is independent of feed size, hence it remains unchanged. So, capacity for this case = 49.83 tonnes/hour $\quad\quad\quad\quad\quad\quad$ **(Ans.)**

Example 4.8:

A certain set of crushing rolls has rolls of 1000 mm diameter by 375 mm width of face. They are set so that the crushing surfaces are 12 mm apart at the narrowest point. What is the maximum permissible size of feed?

Data: Angle of nip = 30°

Solution: Data gives:

r = radius of roll = $\frac{1000}{2}$ = 500 mm

R = radius of feed particle = ?

d = gap between the rolls/2 = 12/2 = 6 mm

α = angle of nip/2 = 30/2 = 15°

∴ $\cos \alpha = \dfrac{r + d}{r + R}$

$\cos 15 = \dfrac{500 + 6}{500 + R}$

$0.9659 = \dfrac{500 + 6}{500 + R}$

∴ R = 23.86 mm

Size of feed particle = 2R = 2 × 23.86 = 47.72 mm **(Ans.)**

Example 4.9:

What should be the diameter of a set of rolls to take feed of size equivalent to 38 mm spheres and crush to 12.7 mm, if the coefficient of friction is 0.35?

Solution: We have $\mu = \tan \alpha$. Since $\mu > \tan \alpha$, α must be less than $\tan^{-1} 0.35$ or 19° 17'

$\cos \alpha = 0.944$

$\cos \alpha = \dfrac{r + d}{r + R}$ ... (1)

where,

r = radius of rolls = ?

R = radius of feed particle = $\dfrac{38}{2}$ = 19 mm

d = gap between rolls/2 = $\dfrac{12.7}{2}$ = 6.35 mm

from equation (1), $0.944 = \dfrac{r + 6.35}{r + 19}$

r = 206.92 mm

∴ Diameter of rolls = 2r
= 2 × 206.92 = 413 mm or 16 inch **(Ans.)**

Example 4.10:

A crusher crushes rock having a volume surface mean diameter of 0.2 m and discharges product of volume – surface means diameter of 0.04 m. To crush 3.5 kg/sec, 7 kW of power is required. Using Rittinger's law, calculate Rittigner's constant K_R.

Solution: Rittinger's law:

$$\frac{P}{\dot{m}} = K_r \left(\frac{1}{\overline{D}_{S_b}} - \frac{1}{\overline{D}_{S_a}} \right)$$

$$\frac{7}{3.5} = K_r \left(\frac{1}{0.04} - \frac{1}{0.2} \right)$$

∴ $K_r = 0.1$ kW.s.m/kg. (Ans.)

Example 4.11:

If the coefficient of friction μ between rock and roll material is 0.4. What is the minimum radius of crushing rolls to reduce 0.06 m pieces of rock to 0.02 m?

Solution:

$$\cos \alpha = \frac{r + d}{r + R} \quad \ldots (1)$$

$$\tan \alpha = 0.4$$

so,
$$\alpha = \tan^{-1} 0.4 = 21° 48'$$

and
$$\cos \alpha = 0.9285$$

∴ Putting known values in equation (1), we get,

$$0.9285 = \frac{r + \dfrac{0.02}{2}}{r + \dfrac{0.06}{2}}$$

Solving for r we get, $r = 0.2497 \cong 0.25$ m (Ans.)

Example 4.12:

Particles of average feed size 25×10^{-4} m are crushed to an average product size of 5×10^{-4} m at the rate of 15 tonnes/hour. At this rate the crusher consumes 32 kW of power of which 2 kW are required for running the mill empty. What would be the power consumption if 10 tonnes/hour of this product is further crushed to 1×10^{-4} m size in the same mill? Assume Rittinger's law is applicable.

Solution: Rittinger's law,

$$\frac{P}{\dot{m}} = K_R \left[\frac{1}{\overline{D}_{S_b}} - \frac{1}{\overline{D}_{S_a}} \right] \quad \ldots (1)$$

where,

$\overline{D}_{S_a}$ = Particle size of feed = 25×10^{-4} m

$\overline{D}_{S_b}$ = Particle size of product = 5×10^{-4} m

$\dfrac{P}{\dot{m}}$ = Actual power consumption = $32 - 2 = 30$ kw

∴ $K_R = \dfrac{30}{15} \left[\dfrac{1}{5 \times 10^{-4}} - \dfrac{1}{25 \times 10^{-4}} \right]$

$K_r = 12.5 \times 10^{-4}$

Substituting value of K_r in equation (1), for 10 tonnes of the product.

$$\frac{P}{10} = 12.5 \times 10^{-4} \left[\frac{1}{1 \times 10^{-4}} - \frac{1}{5 \times 10^{-4}} \right]$$

$$\boxed{P = 100 \text{ kW}}$$ (Ans.)

Example 4.13:

A pair of rolls is to take a feed equivalent to spheres of 3 cm in diameter and crush them to spheres having 1 cm diameter. If the coefficient of friction is 0.29, what would be the diameter of rolls?

Solution: The following formula relates the coefficient of friction (μ), radius of rolls (r), radius of product (d), and radius of feed (R):

$$\cos \alpha = \frac{(r + d)}{(r + R)} \qquad \ldots (1)$$

where α is related to the coefficient of friction by the relation,

$$\mu = \tan \alpha$$

$$\text{Angle of nip} = 2\alpha$$

We have, $\mu = 0.29$

Therefore, $\alpha = \tan^{-1}(0.29) = 16.17°$

And we have, $d = 0.5$ cm; $R = 1.5$ cm

Substituting for the known values in equation 1, we get,

$$\cos(16.17) = \frac{(r + 0.5)}{(r + 1.5)}$$

$$0.9604 = \frac{(r + 0.5)}{(r + 1.5)}$$

$$r + 0.5 = 0.9604 (r + 1.5)$$

$$r - 0.9604\, r = 1.4406 - 0.5$$

$$r = 23.753 \text{ cm}$$

Radius of rolls = 23.753 cm

Dia. of rolls = $2 \times 23.753 = 47.5$ cm. (Ans.)

Example 4.14:

In a ball mill of diameter 2000 mm, 100 mm diameter steel balls are being used for grinding. Presently, for the material being ground, the mill is run at 15 rpm. At what speed will the mill have to be run if the 100 mm balls are replaced by 50 mm balls, all the other conditions remaining the same?

Solution: The critical speed of ball mill is given by,

$$n_c = \frac{1}{2\pi} \sqrt{\frac{g}{R - r}}$$

Where, R = radius of ball mill;
r = radius of ball
For R = 1000 mm and r = 50 mm,
n_c = 30.7 rpm

But the mill is operated at a speed of 15 rpm. Therefore, the mill is operated at $100 \times \dfrac{15}{30.7}$ = 48.86% of critical speed. If 50 mm diameter balls, and the other replace 100 mm diameter balls conditions are remaining the same,

$$\text{Speed of ball mill} = \left[\dfrac{0.4886}{(2\pi)}\right] \times \left[\dfrac{9.812}{(1-0.025)}\right]^{0.5}$$

= 14.8 rpm **(Ans.)**

Example 4.15:

The rate of grinding of uniform sized particles is assumed to follow first order breakage of particles. 50 gms of powder of average diameter 215 microns was ground in a laboratory batch mill. The amount of unground material (215 microns) was measured at various times of grinding and the results are given in the table. Estimate the specific rate of grinding.

Weight (gm)	50	17	12	8	6	2
Time (sec.)	0	60	90	120	150	240

Solution: Rate of grinding (dx/dt) can be expressed as,

$$\dfrac{dx}{dt} = -kx \qquad \ldots (1)$$

where, k = Specific rate of grinding
x = Mass fraction of material unground at time t

Integrating equation (1), we get,

$$\ln x = -kt$$

$$x = \dfrac{\text{Weight}}{\text{Total weight}}$$

The specific rate of grinding k may be estimated for various time intervals as,

$$k = \dfrac{\ln x_1 - \ln x_2}{t_2 - t_1} \qquad \ldots (2)$$

Weight (gm)	Time (sec.)	Mass fraction retained (x)	ln x	k
50	0	1	0	
17	60	0.34	−1.08	0.018
12	90	0.24	−1.43	0.012
8	120	0.16	−1.83	0.013
6	150	0.12	−2.12	0.010
2	240	0.04	−3.22	0.012

$$\text{Average } k = \frac{(0.012 + 0.013 + 0.010 + 0.012)}{4}$$

$$= 0.0123 \text{ s}^{-1}$$

[**Note:** First value of k is not included in the average calculation as it deviates much from the other variables].

Example 4.16:

A Raymond mill consumes 800 kW in reducing 20 tonnes/h of a material from the feed 1 size distribution shown below to the product size distribution. It is found that a new consignment of feed has a slightly different size distribution; feed 2 below.

Calculate the Bond work index of the material and estimate:

(i) the new power consumption for the new feed if the throughput and product specification are unaltered.

(ii) the new throughput if the power cannot be altered and the product specification must be preserved.

(iii) the altered product specification if both power and throughput are held constant.

Data Table

Size (in µm)	Feed 1 Wt %	Product Wt %	Feed 2 Wt %
1190-1000	0	0	6
1000-840	7	0	14
840-710	13	0	32
710-590	35	0	42
590-500	25	0	5
500-420	12	0	1
420-350	6	3	0
350-250	2	5	0
250-149	0	12	0
149-105	0	25	0
105-74	0	35	0
74-53	0	15	0
53-44	0	5	0

Solution: The sizes used in Bond's law are defined as the size of screen through which 80% of the material will pass. Hence for the two feeds and the product the values of L used in the equation will be

	L (µm)
Feed 1	710
Product	149
Feed 2	840

The Bond work index E_i is calculated from Bond's Law:

$$E_{12} = E_i \sqrt{\frac{100}{L_2}} \left\{ 1 - \frac{1}{\sqrt{\frac{L_1}{L_2}}} \right\}$$

where,

$$q = \frac{L_1}{L_2}$$

Substituting data from the question, using feed 1 and the product

$$E_{12} = \frac{800 \times 10^3 \times 3600}{20 \times 10^3} = 144 \text{ kJ/kg}$$

$$E_{12} = 144 = E_i \sqrt{\frac{100}{149}} \left\{ 1 - \sqrt{\frac{149}{710}} \right\} = 0.444 \, E_i$$

$$E_i = 324.4 \text{ kJ/kg}$$

(i) The new power consumption for the new feed if the throughput and product specification are unaltered. The new value of L_1 is 840 μm, the value of L_2 is still 149 μm and the Bond work index is still as calculated above, hence:

$$E_{12} = 324.4 \times \sqrt{\frac{100}{149}} \left\{ 1 - \sqrt{\frac{149}{840}} \right\} = 153.8 \text{ kJ/kg}$$

at a feed rate of 20te/h or 5.56kg/s the power input is

$$5.56 \times 153.8 = 855.1 \text{ kW} \qquad \text{(Ans.)}$$

As expected this is a higher power consumption rate than for feed 1.

(ii) The new throughput if the power cannot be altered and the product specification must be preserved. The energy per unit mass required is 153.8kJ/kg, as calculated above. The power input is limited to 800 kW so the throughput is

$$\frac{800}{153.8} = 5.202 \text{ kg/s} = 18.7 \text{ t/h} \qquad \text{(Ans.)}$$

(iii) The altered product specification if both the power and the throughput are held constant.
The energy input rate is held at 144kJ/kg, L_1 is that of feed 2, 840 μm and L_2 is to be determined:

$$144 = 324.4 \sqrt{\frac{100}{L_2}} \left\{ 1 - \sqrt{\frac{L_2}{840}} \right\}$$

MECHANICAL OPERATIONS SIZE REDUCTION

$$0.444 = 10\left\{\frac{1}{\sqrt{L_2}} - \frac{1}{\sqrt{840}}\right\}$$

$$0.0444 = \frac{1}{\sqrt{L_2}} - 0.0345$$

$$\frac{1}{\sqrt{L_2}} = 0.0789$$

$$L_2 = 160.6 \text{ μm} \qquad \text{(Ans.)}$$

As we would expect this is larger than the original product size of 149 μm.

Example 4.17:

(a) The power required to crush 100 ton/hr of a material is 179.8 kW, if 80% of the feed passes through a 51 mm screen and 80% of the product passes through a 3.2 min screen. What is the work index of the material?

(b) What will be the power required for the same feed at 100 ton/hr to be crushed to a product such that 80% is to pass through a 1.6 mm screen?

Solution: Bond's Law:

$$\frac{P}{\dot{m}} = K_b\left(\frac{1}{\sqrt{D_p}} - \frac{1}{\sqrt{D_f}}\right)$$

where, P = Power required for crushing.

$\dot{m}$ = Mass flow rate of feed.

K_b = Bond's law constant.

D_f = Mean diameter of feed.

D_p = Mean diameter of product.

Work index W_1 is defined as the power required per ton of feed to reduce from very large size to such that 80% of product passes a 100 μm screen i.e. $W_i = K_b \sqrt{100}/K_b$ is calculated from the given data as:

$$K_b = \frac{(179.8/100)}{(1/\sqrt{3200}) - (1/\sqrt{51000})} = 135.7 \text{ kWhr.μm}^{1/2}/\text{ton}$$

And,

$$W_i = K_b/\sqrt{100} = 135.7/10 = 13.57 \text{ kWhr/ton} \qquad \text{(Ans.)}$$

Power to make a product size of 1.6 mm:

$$P = 100 \times 135.7 \times \left(\frac{1}{\sqrt{1600}} - \frac{1}{\sqrt{51000}}\right) = 279.16 \text{ kW (Ans.)}$$

MECHANICAL OPERATIONS — SIZE REDUCTION

Example 4.18:

A material is crushed in a jaw crusher and the average size of the particle reduced from 5 cm to 1 cm, with the consumption of energy 1.32×10^4 J/kg. What will be the consumption of energy to crush the same material of an average size of 7.5 cm to 2.5 cm, assuming (a) Rittinger's law, and (b) Kick's law.

Solution: Rittinger's Law:

$$\frac{P}{m} = K_r \left(\frac{1}{D_p} - \frac{1}{D_f} \right)$$

Kick's Law:

$$\frac{P}{m} = K_k \ln \frac{D_f}{D_p}$$

where,
- P = Energy required for crushing
- m = Mass of feed
- D_f = Mean diameter of feed
- D_p = Mean diameter of product
- K_r = Rittenger's law constant
- K_k = Kick's law constant

Rittinger's Law Constant:

$$K_r = \frac{P/m}{\left(\frac{1}{D_p}\right) - \frac{1}{D_f}} = \frac{1.32 \times 10^4}{(1/1 - 1/5)} = 1.65 \times 10^4 \text{ J.m/kg}$$

Kick's Law Constant:

$$K_k = \frac{P/m}{\ln \frac{D_f}{D_p}} = \frac{1.2 \times 10^4}{\ln(5/1)} = 8.202 \times 10^3 \text{ J/kg}$$

Energy consumption, from Rittenger's law:

$$\frac{P}{m} = 1.65 \times 10^4 \left(\frac{1}{2.5} - \frac{1}{7.5}\right) = 4.4 \times 10^3 \text{ J/kg} \qquad \textbf{(Ans.)}$$

Energy consumption, from Kick's law:

$$\frac{P}{m} = 8.202 \times 10^3 \times \ln \frac{7.5}{2.5} = 9.01 \times 10^3 \text{ J/kg} \qquad \textbf{(Ans.)}$$

Example 4.19:

A size reduction operation involves crushing and grinding. The feed ore has 90% passing a 36 mm screen and is crushed to 90% passing 2.5 mm screen in a cone crusher. The crushed material is further ground in a ball mill to 90% passing a 160 micron screen. Use the Bond method to calculate the power required for each stage of the size reduction operation if 100 t/hr of a) iron ore and (b) clay is processed. The Bond work index is given in the table.

Table: Typical values of W_i

Material	W_i kWhr/t
All Materials	15.19
Barite	6.86
Basalt	22.45
Cement Clinker	14.84
Clay	7.81
Coal	12.51
Copper Ore	14.44
Dolomite	12.44
Emery	64.00
Feldspar	12.84
Galena	10.68
Glass	3.39
Gold Ore	16.31
Granite	15.83
Iron Ore	16.98
Lead Ore	12.54
Limestone	12.77
Mica	148.00
Oil Shale	19.91
Phosphate Rock	11.14
Quartz	14.05
Taconite	16.36

Solution:

The power required for crushing the iron ore **(5 marks)**

$$P = 10 W_i \left\{ \frac{1}{\sqrt{D}} - \frac{1}{\sqrt{D_0}} \right\} \times (\text{Mass rate}) = 10 \times 16.98 \text{ kWh/t}$$

$$\left\{ \frac{1}{\sqrt{2.5 \times 10^3}} - \frac{1}{\sqrt{36 \times 10^3}} \right\} \times (100 \text{ t/h}) = 250.1 \text{ kW}$$

The power required for grinding the iron ore

$$P = 10 W_i \left\{ \frac{1}{\sqrt{D}} - \frac{1}{\sqrt{D_0}} \right\} \times (\text{Mass rate}) = 10 \times 16.98 \text{ kWh/t}$$

$$\left\{ \frac{1}{\sqrt{160}} - \frac{1}{\sqrt{2.5 \times 10^3}} \right\} \times (100 \text{ t/h}) = 1002.79 \text{ kW}$$

The power requires for crushing the clay sample:

$$P = 10\,W_i \left\{\frac{1}{\sqrt{D}} - \frac{1}{\sqrt{D_0}}\right\} \times (\text{Mass rate}) = 10 \times 7.81 \text{ kWh/t}$$

$$\left\{\frac{1}{\sqrt{2.5 \times 10^3}} - \frac{1}{\sqrt{36 \times 10^3}}\right\} \times (100 \text{ t/h}) = 115.04 \text{ kW}$$

The power required for grinding the clay sample:

$$P = 10\,W_i \left\{\frac{1}{\sqrt{D}} - \frac{1}{\sqrt{D_0}}\right\} \times (\text{Mass rate}) = 10 \times 7.81 \text{ kWh/t}$$

$$\left\{\frac{1}{\sqrt{160}} - \frac{1}{\sqrt{2.5 \times 10^3}}\right\} \times (100 \text{ t/h}) = 461.23 \text{ kW}$$

EXERCISE FOR PRACTICE

(1) A certain crusher accepts a feed of rock having a volume surface-mean diameter of 1.9 cm and discharges product of 0.5 cm. The power required to crush 12 tonnes/hour is 6.94 kW. What should be the power consumptions if the capacity is reduced to 10 tonnes/hour and the volume surface mean diameter of product is 0.38 cm. The mechanical efficiency remains unchanged Assume Rittinger's law is applicable.

(Ans.: 8.25 kW)

(2) A pair of rolls is to take a feed equivalent to spheres 4 cm. in diameter and crush them to spheres having a diameter of 2 cm. If the coefficient of friction between the roll surface and the feed is 0.3, calculate the diameter of the rolls. **(Ans.: 43.62 cm)**

(3) A material is crushed in a Blake jaw crusher and the average size of particle reduced from 50 mm to 10 mm with the consumption of energy at the rate of 13 Kw/(Kg/sec). What will be the consumptions of energy needed to crush the same material of average size 75 mm to an average size of 25 mm. (a) Assuming Rittinger's law applies? (b) Assuming Kick's law applies?

(Ans.: (a) Energy = 4.33 kW/(kg/sec);
(b) Energy = 8.88 kW/(kg/sec)

(4) (a) The power required to crush 100 ton/hr of a material is 179.8 kW, if 80% of the feed passes through a 51 mm screen and 80% of the product passes through a 3.2 mm screen. What is the work index of the material?

(b) What will be the power required for the same feed at 100 ton/hr to be crushed to a product such that 80% is to pass through a 1.6 mm screen?

(Ans.: Work Index = 13.57 kWhr/ton; Power = 279.16 kW)

(5) A material is crushed in a jaw crusher and the average size of the particle reduced from 5 cm to 1 cm, with the consumption of energy of 1.32×10^4 J/kg. What will be the consumption of energy to crush the same material of an average size of 7.5 cm to 2.5 cm, assuming (a) Rittinger's law; (b) Kick's law.

(Ans.: Rittinger's law power = 4.4 kJ/kg; Kick's law power = 9.01 kJ/kg)

(6) A ball mill 1.3 in dia is being run at 60 rpm. It is found that the mill is not working satisfactorily. Analyze the operation and suggest the remedy.

(7) A ball mill 1.2 m in dia. is being run at 0.85 Hz. It is found that the mill is not working satisfactorily. Suggest any modification in the conditions of operation

(8) 89.5 KW power is required to crush certain material from 50.8 mm to 6.35 mm. What will be the power required using the same feed to crush to 3.18 mm?

(9) Calculate the average recalculation load of a mill, which is closed circuit with a classifier and grinds 300 ton of dry ore per day. The screen analysis of the mill discharge, classifier overflow, and classifier underflow are as follows:

Mesh	Mill Discharge %	Classifier	
		Overflow %	Underflow %
− 65 + 150	15.2	19.6	13.8
− 150 + 200	6.1	12.4	4.1

(10) What rotational speed in r.p.m., would you recommend for a ball mill 1200 mm in diameter charged with 75 – mm balls?

(11) You need to mill a fine grain to an average particle diameter of 0.5 mm, with little size spread around this average. Discuss the types of milling equipment you might use, and the mode in which it may be operated. Provide reasons for your choices (and reasons for rejecting other options).

(12) What sorts of mechanisms might you use for the following size reduction tasks:
- Slicing potatoes for "fries"
- Slicing potatoes for "chips"
- Cutting sheeded material into individual muesli bars.

(13) You currently use a mill with a 5 kW motor to reduce the size of an ingredient from 3 mm diameter to around 1 mm diameter. You wish to reduce it further to 0.2 mm diameter. If you use the same type of mill for this second stage size reduction, what size motor would you estimate will be required?

(14) You currently use a hammar mill to reduce a product from an average diameter of 3 mm to an average diameter of 0.04 mm. What percentage decrease in throughput might you expect if you were to produce a finer product, average diameter half that of the current product, using the same equipment?

(15) The particle diameter of a material to be fed through a roll mill is 2 mm, and its coefficient of friction is 0.1. What is the minimum diameter of the rolls which could be used if a product diameter of 0.2 mm is required?

(16) A feed with 80% by weight less than 3 mm is crushed to a product with 80% less than 1.5 mm. The energy consumption per kg of feed for this process is 125 kJ/kg. This intermediate product is then further crushed to produce a final product with size 80% below 0.5 mm. What energy input is required for this second size reduction using:
(a) Rittinger's Law, (b) Kick's Law and (c) Bond's Law?

(Ans. (a) 375 mm kJ/kg, (b) 180.34 kJ/kg, and (c) 312.4 kJ/kg)

(17) Show that for a material, which obeys Bond's Law, where P in the equation below has a value of $-3/2$ the energy required for size reduction from L_1 to L_2 is given by:

$$E = E_i \sqrt{\frac{100}{L_2}} \left\{ 1 - \frac{1}{q^{1/2}} \right\}$$

where, q is the ratio of L_1 to L_2 and $K = 5E_i$, where K is the constant in the equation below and E_i is the Bond work index (Jkg^{-1}):

$$\frac{dE}{dL} = -KL^P$$

L is the size, in μm, of sieve mesh through which 80% of the material will pass.

(18) The initial size distribution of a feed material is:

Size range (cm)	Weight %
5-10	5
1-5	15
0.5-1	35
0.3-0.5	40
<0.3	5

Milling trials have been carried out on this material. The material was first separated into size fractions then milled. The results of these tests are as follows (all size ranges are given in cm):

Original size	wt. % of product in size ranges				
	5-10	1-5	0.5-1	0.3-0.5	<0.3
5-10	10	25	35	20	10
1-5	0	10	25	40	25
0.5-1	0	0	15	40	45
0.3-0.5	0	0	0	25	75

(a) Determine the size distribution of the product produced by milling a feed with the initial size distribution shown above.

(b) Estimate the sieve mesh size through which 80% of the product would pass (assume the distribution is linear between 0.3 and 0.5 cm).

(c) The energy required to mill 1 kg of the feed in this process was 60 kJ kg^{-1}. Determine E_i, the Bond work index, for this material.

(d) The feed rate to the process is increased by 50 %, with no increase in energy input. What would the resulting product size (i.e. value of L_2) be?

NOMENCLATURE

Symbol	
A_w	Specific surface of particles, m^2/gm; A_{wa}, for feed; A_{wb}, for product.
D_p	Particle size, mm; D_{Pa}, of feed; D_{Pb}, of product; $D_{P,\,max}$, maximum particle size nipped by rolls.
D_{Pn}	Mesh opening in screen n, mm, ($D_{P(n+1)}$, in screen n + 1; D_{Pu}, in screen u.
$\bar{D}_n$	Arithmetic average of D_{Pn} and $D_{P(n+1)}$, mm
$\bar{D}_s$	Mean volume-surface diameter, mm; $\bar{D}_{Sa}$, of feed; $\bar{D}_{Sb}$, of product
$\bar{D}_u$	Average particle diameter on screen u, which is coarser than screen n.
d	One-half distance between crushing rolls, m.
e_s	Surface energy per unit area, J/m^2
g	Acceleration of gravity, m/s^2
K	Constant; K_b, in Bond's law; K_k, in Kicks' law; K_r, in Rittinger's law
m	Mass of ball
$\dot{m}$	Feed rate to crusher, kg/s
n	Speed, r/min; screen number, couting from large screen of series; n_c, critical speed in ball mill.
P	Power, kW or hp
R	Radius of crushing rolls or ball mill, m

Symbol	
r	Radius of balls in ball mill, m
S_p	Area of particle, m²
t	Time, s; t_T, total grinding time
u	Number of screen coarser than screen n
V_p	Volume of particle, m³
W	Energy input to crusher, J/gm; W_n, energy absorbed by material during crushing.
W_i	Bond work index, kWh/ton
x	Mass fraction; x_n, on screen n; x_{n+1} on screen n after t time increments; x_u, on screen u; x_1, on coarsest screen; $x_{1,0}$, coarest fraction in feed.
Greek Letters:	
α	Angle between radius and vertical in ball mill.
Δt	Time increment, s.
Δx_n	Change in x_n, in time Δt.
η_c	Crushing efficiency.
η_m	Mechanical efficiency of crusher.
ρ_p	Density of particle, kg/m³.
ϕ_S	Sphericity; ϕ_a, of feed; ϕ_b, of product.
w	Angular velocity, rad/s.

Unit V

Chapter 5: MECHANICAL SEPARATIONS: SCREENING

5.1 Mechanical Separations

Mechanical separations can be divided into four groups – sedimentation, centrifugal separation, filtration and sieving.

In sedimentation, two immiscible liquids, or a liquid and a solid, differing in density, are separated by allowing them to come to equilibrium under the action of gravity, the heavier material falling with respect to the lighter. This may be a slow process. It is often speeded up by applying centrifugal forces to increase the rate of sedimentation; this is called centrifugal separation. Filtration is the separation of solids from liqids, by causing the mixture to flow through fine pores which are small enough to stop the solid particles but large enough to allow the liquid to pass. Sieving, that is interposing a barrier through which the larger elements cannot pass, is often used for classification of solid particles.

Mechanical separation of particles from a fluid uses forces acting on these particles. The forces can be direct restraining forces such as sieving and filtration, or indirect as in impingement filters. They can come from gravitational or centrifugal action, which can be thought of as negative restraining forces, moving the particles relative to the containing fluid. So the separating action depends on the character of the particle being separated and the forces on the particle which cause the separation. The important characteristics of the particles are size, shape and density; and of the fluid are viscosity and density. The reactions of the different components to the forces set-up relative motion between the fluid and the particles, and between particles of different character. Under these relative motions, particles and fluids accumulate in different regions and can be gathered as in:

- the filter cake and the filtrate tank in the filter press;
- the discharge valve in the base of the cyclone and the air outlet at the top;
- the outlet stream of a centrifuge;
- on the various sized sieves of a sieve set.

In the mechanical separations studied, the forces considered are gravity, combinations of gravity with other forces, centrifugal forces, pressure forces in which the fluid is forced away from the particles, and finally total restraint of solid particles where normally the fluid is of little consequence. The velocities of particles moving in a fluid are important for several of these separation.

5.2 Screening (Sieving)

Screening is a method of separating particles according to size alone. In industrial screening the solids are dropped on, or thrown against, a screening surface. The undersize, or *fines*, pass through the screen openings; oversize, or *tails*, do not. A single screen can make but a single separation into two fractions.

These are called unsized fractions, because although either the upper or lower limit of the particle sizes they contain is known, the other limit is unknown. Material passed through a series of screens of different sizes is separated into sized fractions, i.e. fractions in which both the maximum and minimum particle sizes are known. Screening is occasionally done wet but much more commonly dry.

Industrial screens are made from woven wire, silk or plastic cloth, metal bars, perforated or slotted metal plates, or wires that are wedge-shaped in cross-section. Various metals are used, with steel and stainless steel the most common. Standard screens range in mesh size from 4 mesh to 400-mesh, and woven metal screens with openings as small as 1 μm are commercially available.

Screens finer than about 150-mesh are not commonly used, however, because with very fine particles other methods of separation are usually more economical. Separation in the size range between 4-mesh and 48-mesh is called *"fine screening"*, and for sizes smaller than 48-mesh it is considered *"Ultrafine"*.

Screening Terminlogy:
Undersize: Fines or minus (–) material, material passing through a given screen.
Oversize: Tails or plus (+) material, material retained on a given screen.
Screen aperture: The space between the wires of a screen mesh. Screens are sometimes denoted by mesh number (number of wires per inch). In this case, aperture actually depends on the wire diameter, but for standard screens, wire size in specified.
Screen interval: The relationship between successively decreasing openings in a standard screen series. In the **Tyler Standard** the ratio between screen apertures in successive screens is $2^{0.5}$, though at finer sizes a screen interval of $2^{0.25}$ is used. In **British Standards** and **American Society for Testing Materials**, the screen interval is $2^{0.25}$.
Diameter of a sieve function: The average diameter of the fraction one screen, but retained on the next larger section. This is normally taken as the arithmetic average of the two screen apertures.
Diameter of solid particles: This is defined as the particle dimension controlling its retention on a particular sized screen. Since particles are usually irregularly shaped, so an average diameter is used. A number of methods of measurement may be used. In particle, average particle diameter is often determined by sieve analysis, with a spherical shape assumed for the sake of calculation.

Factors affecting the efficiency of a screening system:
1. **Rate of feeding:** If feed rate is too high, there is insufficient residence time. The screen becomes overloaded, and some "fines" leave with the oversize.
2. **Particle size:** Large particles can impede the path of smaller ones, and a preliminary separation may be required if a high proportion of larger particles are present.
3. **Moisture:** Moisture can cause adhesion of small particles to larger ones, so some undersize leave with the oversize.
4. **Worn or damaged screens:** Oversize may fall through damaged areas.
5. **Blinding (clogging) of screens:** Particularly likely when the size of particles is very close to the screen aperture. Result can be undersize leaving with oversize.
6. **Electrostatic charge:** When screening dry powders, surfaces can become charged, resulting in small particles clumping together and leaving with the oversize. Grounding of screens may be necessary.

5.3 Types of Screening Equipment

Many varieties of screens are available for different purposes, and only a few representative types are discussed here. In most screens the particles drop through the opening by gravity; in a few designs they are pushed through the screen by a bush or centrifugal force. Coarse particles drop easily through large openings in a stationary surface, but with fine particles the screen surface must be agitated in some way, such as by shaking, gyrating, or vibrating it mechanically or electrically. Typical screen motions are illustrated in Fig. 5.1.

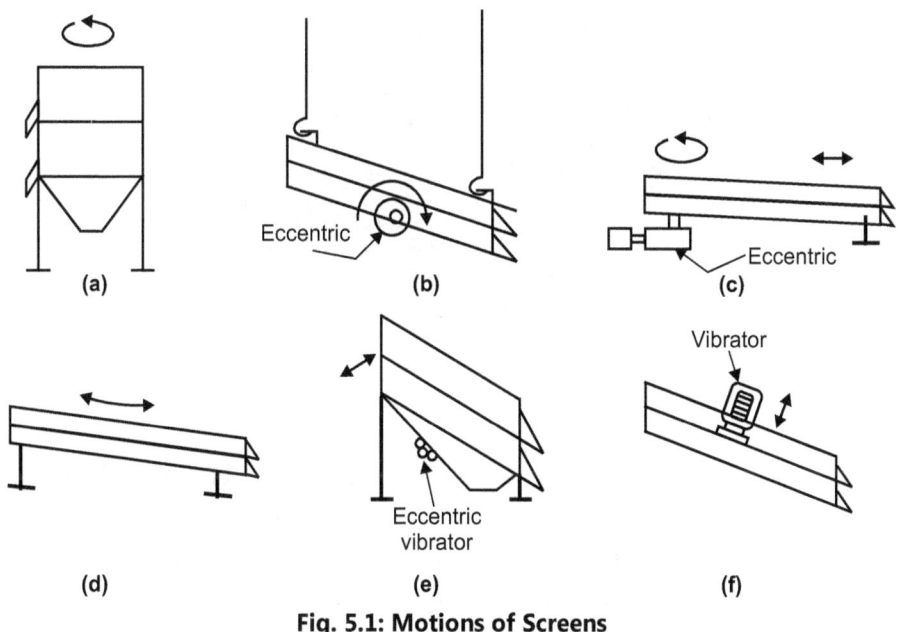

Fig. 5.1: Motions of Screens

(a) Stationary screens and grizzlies: A grizzly is a grid of parallel metal bars set in an inclined stationary frame. The slope and the path of the material are usually parallel to the length of the bars. Very coarse feed, as from a primary crusher, falls on the upper end of the grid. Large chunks Roll and slide to the tails discharge; small lumps fall through to a separate collector. In cross-section the top of each bar is wider than the bottom, is that the bars can be made fairly deep for strength without being choked by lumps passing partway through. the spacing between the bars is 50-200 mm. Stationary inclined woven-metal screens operate in the same way, separating particles 12-100 mm in size. They are effective only with very coarse free-flowing solids containing few fine particles.

(b) Gyrating screens: In nearly all screens which produce sized fractions the coarse material is removed first and the fines last. The gyrating flat screens shown in Fig. 5.2 illustrate this. These machines contain several decks of screens, one above the other, held in a box or casing. The coarsest screen is at the top and the finest at the bottom, with suitable discharge ducts to permit removal of the several fractions. The mixture of particles is dropped on the top screen. Screens and casing are gyrated to shift the particles through the screen openings.

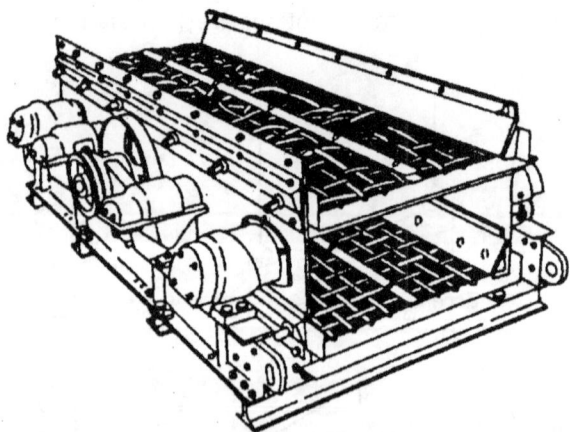

Fig. 5.2: Heavy-Duty Vertically Gyrated Screens

In the design shown in Fig. 5.2 the casing is inclined at an angle between 16° and 30° with the horizontal. The gyrations are in a vertical plane about a horizontal axis. An eccentric shaft set in the floor of the casing halfway between the feed point and the discharge causes them. The screens are rectangular and fairly long, typically 0.5 to 1.2 mm by 1.5 to 4.3 mm. The speed of gyration and the amplitude of throw are adjustable, as is the angle of tilt. One particular combination of speed and throw usually gives the maximum yield of desired product from a given feed. The rate of gyration is 600 to 1,800 rpm, the motor size is 1 to 3 hp. the angle of tilt greatly influences the capacity of the screen. It is best to use the steepest angle possible. Very steep angles, however, can be used only with coarse products; good separation into fine fractions usually requires an angle of not more than 20° with the horizontal.

The screen shown in Fig. 5.2 is gyrated in a horizontal plane. It contains rectangular slightly inclined screens, which are gyrated at the feed end. The discharge end reciprocates but does not gyrate. This combination of motions stratifies the feed, so that fine particles travel downward to the screen surface, where they are pushed through by the larger particles on top. Often the screening surface is double, as shown in the figure. Between the two screens are rubber balls held in separate compartments. As the screen operates, the balls strike the screen surface and free the openings of any material that tends to plug them. Dry, hard, rounded or cubical grains ordinarily pass without trouble through screens, even fine screens; but elongated, sticky, flaky, or soft particles do not. Under the screening action such particles may become wedged into the openings and prevent other particles from passing through. A screen plugged with solid particles is said to be *blinded*.

(c) Vibrating screens:

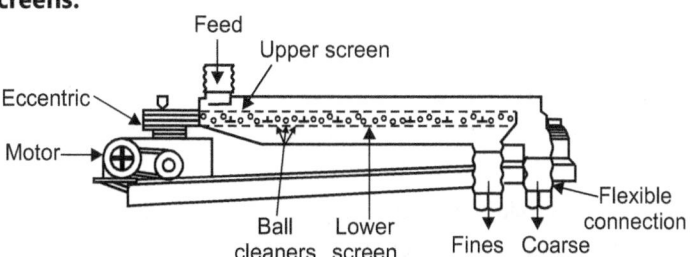

Fig. 5.3: Electrically Vibrated Screen

Screens that are rapidly vibrated with small amplitude are less likely to blind than are gyrating screens. The vibrations may be generated mechanically or electrically. Mechanical vibrations are usually transmitted from high-speed eccentrics to the casing of the unit and from there to steeply inclined screens.

Electrical vibrations from heavy-duty solenoids are transmitted to the casing or directly to the screens. Fig. 5.2 shows a directly vibrated unit. Ordinarily no more than three decks are used in vibrating screens. Between 1,800 and 3,600 vibrations per minute are usual. A screen 1.2 m wide and 3 m long draws about screen draws 4 hp. (3 kW).

(d) Centrifugal sifter: In centrifugal sifter the screen is a horizontal cylinder of woven metal or plastic. High-speed helical paddles on a central shaft impel the solids against the inside of the stationary screen; fines pass through, and oversize is conveyed to the discharge. Plastic screens stretch a little during operation, and the resulting minute changes in the dimensions of the openings tend to prevent clogging or blinding. In some designs brushes attached to the paddles assist the centrifugal action in pushing solids through the screen.

(e) Trommels: Many size separations are carried out on sieves or screens, the principle is exactly the same as in analytical sieves, but larger. Large rocks are graded on *grizzles*, which are often constructed from railway rails. Finer separations are carried out on *trommels*.

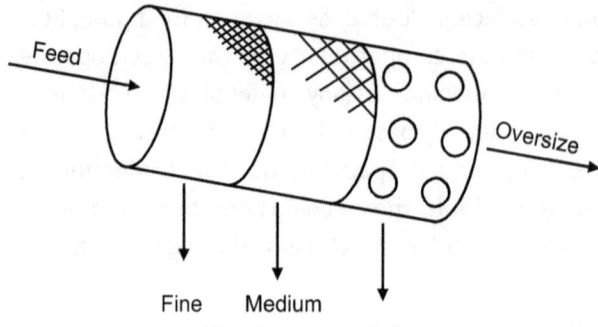

Fig. 5.4: Trommel

All the feed, including the largest has to pass over the finest screen, which can be a problem. One solution is to have concentric drums, the finest of the outside.

Vibrating screens are very similar to large analytical sieves. They are vibrated either by off-centre weights on a revolving shaft, mechanical tapping or electromagnetic vibration. They may be sloped to facilitate discharge or the oscillations can be controlled to provide a spiral paths. Balls or rings may be used to prevent blinding.

5.4 Comparisons of Ideal and Actual Screens

The objective of a screen is to accept a feed containing a mixture of particles of various sizes and separate it into two fractions, an underflow that is passed through the screen and an overflow that is rejected by the screen. An ideal screen would sharply separate the feed mixture in such a way that the smallest particle in the overflow would be just largest than the largest particle in the underflow. Such an ideal separation defines a cut diameter D_{pc} that marks the point of separation between the fractions. Usually, D_{pc} is chosen to be equal to the mesh opening of the screen.

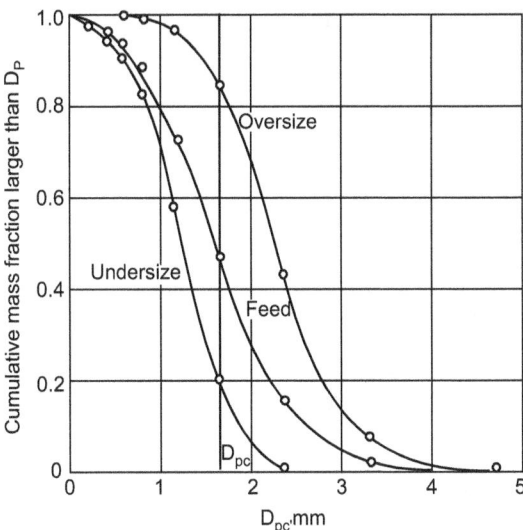

Fig. 5.5: Cumulative Screen Analysis of the Underflow, Overflow and Feed

Actual screens do not give a perfect separation about the cut diameter; instead the cumulative screen analysis of the underflow and overflow are like those shown in Fig. 5.3. In this typical example, the undersize contains about 19 percent of material coarser than D_{pc}, and the oversize about 15 percent that is smaller than D_{pc}. The closest separations are obtained with spherical particles on standard testing screens, but even there is an overlap between the smallest particles in the overflow and the largest ones in the underflow. The overlap is especially pronounced when the particles are needlelike or fibrous or where the particles tend to aggregate into clusters that act as large particles. Some long, thin particles may strike the screen surface endwise and pass through easily, while other particles of the same size and shape may strike the screen sidewise and be retained. Commercial screens usually give poorer separations than testing screens of the same mesh opening operating on the same mixture.

5.5 Material Balances Over Screen

Simple material balances can be written over a screen, which are useful in calculating the ratios of feed, oversize, and underflow from the screen analysis of the three stream and knowledge of the desired cut diameter. Let:

F = mass flow rate of feed
D = mass flow rate of overflow
B = mass flow rate of underflow
x_F = mass fraction of material A in feed.
x_D = mass fraction of material A in overflow.
x_B = mass fraction of material A in underflow.

The mass fractions material B in the feed, overflow, and underflow are $1 - x_F$, $1 - x_D$, and $1 - x_B$.

Since the total material fed to the screen must leave it either as underflow or as overflow.

$$F = D + B \qquad \ldots (5.1)$$

The material A in the feed must also leave in these two streams and

$$F\, x_F = D\, x_D + B\, x_B \qquad \ldots (5.2)$$

Elimination of B from equations (5.1) and (5.2) gives,

$$\frac{D}{F} = \frac{x_F - x_B}{x_D - x_B} \qquad \ldots (5.3)$$

Elimination of D gives,

$$\frac{B}{F} = \frac{x_D - x_F}{x_D - x_B} \qquad \ldots (5.4)$$

5.6 Screen Effectiveness

$$\text{Recovery} = \frac{\text{Mass flow of desired fraction in product stream}}{\text{Mass flow of desired product in feed}}$$

$$\text{Rejection} = 1 - \text{"Recovery" of undesired fraction}$$

$$\text{Effectiveness} = \text{Recovery} \times \text{Rejection}$$

The effectiveness of a screen (often called the screen efficiency) is a measure of the success of a screen in closely separating materials A and B. If the screen functioned perfectly, all of material A would be in the overflow and all of material B would be in the underflow. A common measure of screen effectiveness is the ratio of oversize material A that is actually in the overflow to the amount of a entering with the feed. These quantities are D_{x_D} and F_{x_F}, respectively. Thus,

$$E_A = \frac{D \cdot x_D}{F \cdot x_F} \qquad \ldots (5.5)$$

Where E_A is the screen effectiveness based on the oversize. Similarly, an effectiveness E_B based on the undersize material is given by,

$$E_B = \frac{B\,(1 - x_B)}{F\,(1 - x_F)} \qquad \ldots (5.6)$$

A combined overall effectiveness can be defined as the product of the two individual ratios, and if this product is denoted by E,

$$E = E_A\, E_B = \frac{D B x_D\,(1 - x_B)}{F^2\, x_F\,(1 - x_F)} \qquad \ldots (5.7)$$

Substituting D/F and B/F from equations (5.3) and (5.4) into this equation gives.

$$E = \frac{(x_F - x_B)(x_D - x_F) x_D (1 - x_B)}{(x_D - x_B)^2 (1 - x_F) x_F} \qquad \ldots (5.8)$$

Equation (5.8) is used to calculate efficiency of screen.

5.7 Capacity and Effectiveness of Screens

In addition to effectiveness, capacity is important in industrial screening. The capacity of a screen is measured by the mass of material that can be fed per unit time to a unit area of the screen.

Capacity and effectiveness are opposing factors. To obtain maximum effectiveness the capacity must be small, and large capacity is obtainable only at the expense of a reduction in effectiveness. In practice, a reasonable balance between capacity and effectiveness is desired. Although accurate relationships are not available for estimating these operating characteristics of screens, certain fundamentals apply, which can be used as guides in understanding the basic factors in screen operation.

The capacity of a screen is controlled simply by varying the rate of feed to the unit. The effectiveness obtained for a given capacity depends on the nature of the function of the number of times the particle strikes the screen surface and the probability of passage during a single contact. If the screen is overloaded, the number of contacts is small and the chance of passage on contact is reduced by the interference of the other particles. The improvement of effectiveness attained at the expense of reduced capacity is a result of more contacts per particle and better chances for passage on each contact.

5.8 Solved Examples

Example 5.1:

One ton per hour of dolomite is produced by a ball mill operating in a closed circuit grinding with a 100 mesh screen. The screen analysis (weight %) is given below. Calculate the screen efficiency.

Data from screen analysis:

Mesh	Feed (%)	Oversize (%)	Undersize (%)
35	7.07	13.67	0.00
48	16.60	32.09	0.00
65	14.02	27.12	0.00
100	11.82	20.70	2.32
150	9.07	4.35	14.32
200	7.62	2.07	13.34
−200	33.80	0.00	70.02
	100.00	100.00	100.00

MECHANICAL OPERATIONS — MECHANICAL SEPARATIONS : SCREENING

Solution: Screen efficiency is given by expression,

$$E = \frac{(x_F - x_B)(x_D - x_F) \cdot x_D (1 - x_B)}{(x_D - x_B)^2 \cdot x_F (1 - x_F)}$$

With a 100 - mesh screen, cumulative mass fraction are given as below:

Feed = 49.51
Oversize = 93.58 (from screen analysis table)
Undersize = 2.32

Therefore,
$x_F = 0.4951$
$x_D = 0.9358$
$x_B = 0.0232$

$$\therefore \quad E = \frac{(0.4951 - 0.0232)(0.9358 - 0.4951) \cdot 0.9358 (1 - 0.0232)}{(0.9358 - 0.0232)^2 \cdot 0.4951 (1 - 0.4951)}$$

$\therefore$ E = 0.9132

Efficiency of screen = 91.32% **(Ans.)**

Example 5.2:

One ton per hour of dolomite is produced by crushing and then screening through a 14 mesh screen. According to the screen analysis (in weight percent) given below, calculate (a) the total load to the crusher, (b) the effectiveness of the screen.

Screen analysis data

Mesh	Feed (%)	Undersize (%)	Oversize Circulations load (%)
4 on	14.3	–	20
8 on	20.0	–	28
14 on	20.0	0	28
28 on	28.5	40	24
48 on	8.6	30	(through 28 mesh)
100 on	5.7	20	–
100 through	2.9	10	–
	100.00	100.00	100.00

Solution: From screen analysis, the cumulative fractions for a 14 mesh screen are as under:

feed = 54.3
oversize = 76
undersize = 0

Therefore,
$x_F = 0.543$
$x_D = 0.76$
$x_B = 0$

We know that,
$$\frac{B}{F} = \frac{x_D - x_F}{x_D - x_B}$$

where B is the product (undersize)

$$B = 1 \text{ ton/hour}$$
$$x_D = 0.76$$
$$x_F = 0.543$$
$$x_B = 0$$

So,
$$\frac{1}{F} = \frac{0.76 - 0.543}{0.76 - 0}$$
$$F = 3.5 \text{ tonnes/hour}$$

The load to crusher = 3.5 tonnes/hour. **(Ans.)**

(b) Effectiveness of screen is given by:
$$E = \frac{(x_F - x_B)(x_D - x_F) x_D (1 - x_B)}{(x_D - x_B)^2 (1 - x_F) \cdot x_F}$$

$$= \frac{(0.543 - 0)(0.76 - 0.543)(0.76)(1 - 0)}{(0.76 - 0)^2 (1 - 0.543)(0.543)}$$

$$E = 0.6248$$

The effectiveness of the screen is 62.48%. **(Ans.)**

Example 5.3:

A quartz mixture having the screen analysis shown in the following table is screened through a standard 10 mesh screen. The cumulative screen analysis of overflow and underflow are given in table below. Calculate:

(a) the mass ratios of the overflow and underflow to feed,
(b) the overall effectiveness of the screen.

Screen analysis data

Mesh	D_p mm	Cumulative fraction smaller than D_p		
		Feed	Overflow	Underflow
4	4.699	0	0	–
6	3.327	0.025	0.071	–
8	2.362	0.15	0.43	0
10	1.651	0.47	0.85	0.195
14	1.168	0.73	0.97	0.58
20	0.833	0.885	0.99	0.83
28	0.589	0.94	1.00	0.91
35	0.417	0.96	–	0.94
65	0.208	0.98	–	0.975
PAN	–	1.00	–	1.00

Solution: (a) The cumulative analysis of feed, overflow and product are plotted as shown in Fig. 5.6.

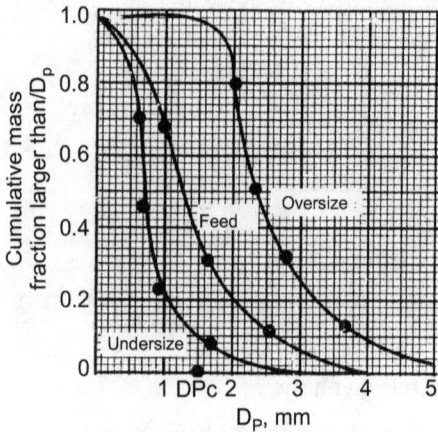

Fig. 5.6: Cumulative Analysis of Feed, Overflow and Product

The cut point diameter is the mesh size of the screen, which from data table is 1.651 mm. Also from data table, for this screen,

$$x_F = 0.47$$
$$x_D = 0.85$$
$$x_B = 0.195$$

The ratio of overflow to feed is,

$$\frac{D}{F} = \frac{0.47 - 0.195}{0.85 - 0.195} = 0.420 \quad \text{(Ans.)}$$

The ratio of underflow to feed is,

$$\frac{B}{F} = 1 - \frac{D}{F} = 1.042$$

$$\frac{B}{F} = 0.58 \quad \text{(Ans.)}$$

(b) The overall effectiveness is given by equation,

$$E = \frac{(x_F - x_B)(x_D - x_F) \cdot x_D (1 - x_B)}{(x_D - x_B)^2 (1 - x_F) x_F}$$

$$E = \frac{(0.47 - 0.195)(0.85 - 0.47)(1 - 0.195)(0.85)}{(0.85 - 0.195)^2 (0.53)(0.47)}$$

$$E = 0.669$$

So, overall effectiveness of screen = 66.9% \quad **(Ans.)**

Example 5.4:

Given the following sieve analysis:

Sieve size (mm)	% Retained
1.00	0
0.50	11
0.25	49
0.125	28
0.063	8
Through 0.063	4

Plot a cumulative sieve analysis and estimate the weight fraction of particles of sizes between 0.300 and 0.350 mm and 0.350 and 0.400 mm.

Solution: From the above table,

Less than aperture	(mm)	0.063	0.125	0.250	0.500	1.00
	(µm)	63	125	250	500	1000
Percentage (cumulative)		4	12	40	89	100

This has been plotted on Fig. 5.7 and the graph F(D) has been smoothed. From this, the graph of F(D) has been plotted, working from the slope of F(D), to give the particle size distribution.

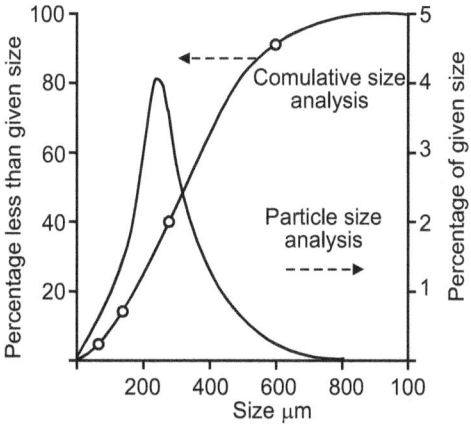

Fig. 5.7: Particle-Size Analysis

To find the fraction between the specified sizes, this will be given directly by the fraction, that the area under the F(D) graph and between the sizes of interest, is to the total area under the F(D) curve. Counting squares, on Fig. 5.7 gives:

between 300 µm (0.300 mm) and 350 µm) (0.350 mm) as 13%.
and 350 µm (0.350 mm) and 400 µm) (0.400 mm) as 9%.

Example 5.5:

Material is fed to a nominal 100 μm screen and separated into oversize and undersize streams. Size distributions for the feed and two product streams are shown below. Calculate the effectiveness of the sieve if the desired fraction of the material is the material, which is smaller than 100 μm.

Size range μm	Feed kg/h	Oversize kg/h	Undersize kg/h
160-180	5	5	0
140-160	10	10	0
120-140	10	9	1
100-120	20	16	4
80-100	15	4	11
60-80	15	2	13
40-60	10	0	10
<60	15	0	15

Solution: The effectiveness of the sieve can be calculated in two ways; by calculating the recovery and rejection and multiplying these figures or by using the formula derived in the notes. The first method is much more straightforward, referring to the sketch below:

Sketch with mass balance:

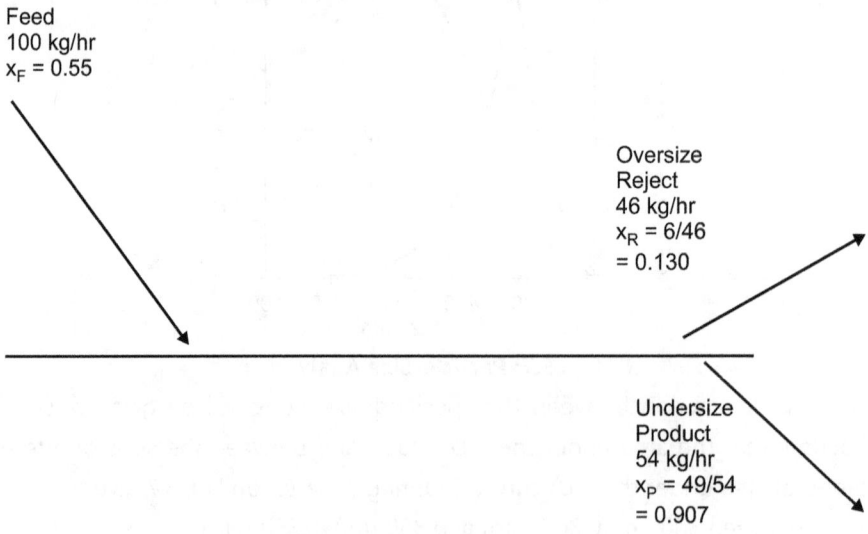

Feed
100 kg/hr
$x_F = 0.55$

Oversize Reject
46 kg/hr
$x_R = 6/46$
$= 0.130$

Undersize Product
54 kg/hr
$x_P = 49/54$
$= 0.907$

Fig. 5.8: Mass Balance Conditions

MECHANICAL OPERATIONS — MECHANICAL SEPARATIONS : SCREENING

$$\text{Recovery} = \frac{Px_P}{Fx_F} = \frac{(11 + 13 + 10 + 15)}{(15 + 15 + 10 + 15)} = \frac{49}{55} = 0.8909$$

$$\text{Rejection} = 1 - \frac{P(1 - x_P)}{F(1 - x_F)} = 1 - \frac{(P - Px_P)}{(F - Fx_F)} = 1 - \frac{(54 - 49)}{(100 - 55)}$$

$$= 1 - \frac{5}{45} = 0.8889$$

Effectiveness = $0.8909 \times 0.8889 = 0.792$

Alternatively Effectiveness is given by,

$$\eta = \frac{x_P(x_F - x_R)}{x_F(x_P - x_R)} \left(1 - \frac{(x_F - x_R)(1 - x_P)}{(x_P - x_R)(1 - x_F)}\right)$$

$$\eta = \frac{0.907(0.55 - 0.130)}{0.55(0.907 - 0.130)} \left(1 - \frac{(0.55 - 0.130)(1 - 0.907)}{(0.907 - 0.130)(1 - 0.55)}\right)$$

$$= 0.792$$

Note that the calculation of x_P and x_F has introduced rounding errors into the overall calculation. This formula is really only useful when flowrates are not available.

Example 5.6:

Anthracite coal from a pulverization unit has been found to contain an excess of fine material (75% by weight). In order to remove these fines, it is screened using a 1.5 mm. screen. Estimate the effectiveness of the screen from the following data:

Particle size, mm	Mass fraction	
	Oversize from screen	Undersize from screen
−3.33 + 2.36	0.143	0.00
−2.36 + 1.65	0.211	0.098
−1.65 + 1.17	0.230	0.234
−1.17 + 0.83	0.186	0.277
−0.83 + 0.59	0.196	0.149
−0.59 + 0.42	0.034	0.101
−0.42 + 0.29	0.00	0.141

Solution: Since the objective of screening is to remove the fine material, undersize from screen which will contain most of the fine material is the reject and the oversize material from the screen is the product. The aperture size of classifying screen is 1.5 mm. It is obviously not a standard screen, but is an industrial screen constructed specifically for the purpose. Our desired material is therefore the +1.5 material. Let X_D' and X_B' be cumulative mass fraction corresponding to the particle size of 1.5 mm in case of product (oversize from screen) and reject (undersize from screen) respectively. Therefore, by definition, X_D' is the total mass fraction of material having size less than 1.5 mm in the product. The mass fraction of +1.5 material (the desired material) in the product will be then $(1 - X_D')$. Thus, $X_D = [1 - X_D']$.

Similarly, $\qquad X_B = [1 - X_p']$

Since, the feed contains 75% fine material,

$$X_F = 0.25$$

To find the values X_D' and X_B', let us construct a cumulative mass fraction table from the data given:

Particle size, mm	X_D	X_B
3.33	1.0	1.0
2.36	0.857	1.0
1.65	0.646	0.902
1.17	0.416	0.668
0.83	0.230	0.391
0.59	0.034	0.242
0.42	0.0	0.141

We now plot both X_D and X_B against particle size on a semi-log graph paper. The plot is given in Fig. 5.9. From the figure, the cumulative mass fractions corresponding to a particle size of 1.5 mm are obtained as

$$X_D' = 0.57$$

$$X_B' = 0.85$$

Therefore, $\qquad X_D = (1 - X_D') = 0.43$

$$X_B = (1 - X_B') = 0.15$$

Substituting the values of X_D and X_B in equation (5.8), we can estimate the screen effectiveness.

$$E_C = 44.755\% \qquad \text{(Ans.)}$$

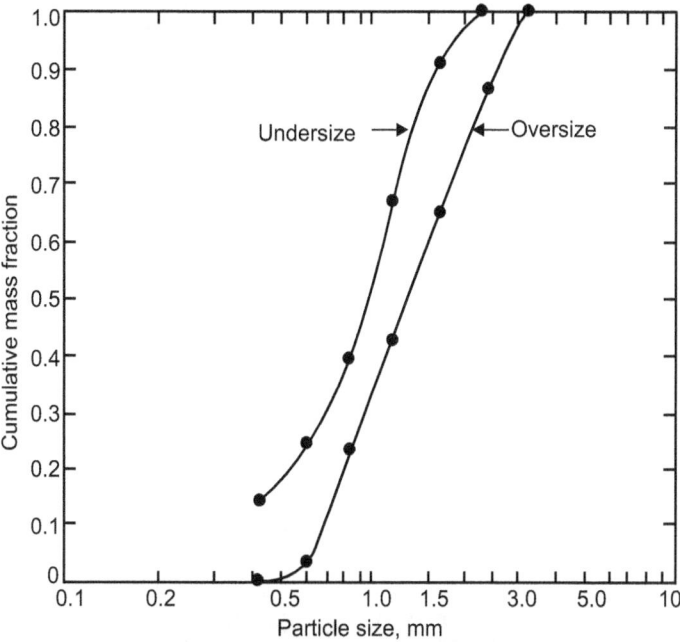

Fig. 5.9: Plots of Cumulative Mass Fraction Versus Particle Size on Semi-log Co-ordinates

Example 5.7:

Example Table salt is being fed to a vibrating screen at the rate of 150 kg/hr. The desired product is −30 + 20 mesh fraction. A 30 mesh and a 20 mesh screen are therefore used (double deck), the feed being introduced on the 30 mesh screen. During the operation, it was observed that the average proportion of oversize (from 30 mesh screen) : oversize (from 20 mesh screen) undersize (from 20 mesh screen) is 2 : 1.5 : 1. Calculate the effectiveness of the screener from the following data:

Mesh	Mass fraction			
	Feed	Oversize from 50 Mesh Screen	Oversize from 20 Mesh Screen	Oversize from 20 Mesh Screen
−85+60	0.097	0.197	0.026	0.0005
−60+40	0.186	0.389	0.039	0.0009
−40+30	0.258	0.337	0.322	0.0036
−30+20	0.281	0.066	0.526	0.3490
−20+15	0.091	0.005	0.061	0.2990
−15+10	0.087	0.006	0.026	0.3470

Solution: It is given that the desired product is the −30 + 20 fraction. Since the feed is introduced on the 30 mesh screen, only the −30 material will fall on the 20 mesh screen. Thus the oversize from the 20 mesh screen will be the −30 + 20 fraction (the product). However, since both screens are not 100% efficient, other sizes than desired are also present in the product and reject streams.

From the given table, mass fraction of the desired material (−30 + 20 material) in the feed is 0.281. Thus,

$$X_F = 0.281$$

Similarly, $X_D = 0.526$ (since oversize from 20 mesh screen is the product stream).

A material balance around the double-deck screener gives,

Feed (F) = Oversize from 30 mesh (B_1) + Oversize from 20 mesh (B_2) + Undersize from 20 mesh (B_2)

Since it is given that $B_1 = D$,

$$B_1 : D : B_2 = 2 : 1.5 : 1$$

$$\left(\frac{D}{F}\right) = \frac{D}{D + B_1 + B_2} = \frac{1.5}{4.5} = \frac{1}{3}$$

Now substituting the values of X_F, X_D and (D/F) in equation (5.8) we can compute the effectiveness of the screener.

$$E = 0.486 = 48.6\% \qquad \text{(Ans.)}$$

EXERCISE FOR PRACTICE

(1) A screen with an aperture of 6 mesh BSS is treating a feed with 66% of +6 mesh and producing an oversize fraction containing 89% of +6 mesh particles. If the undersize fraction contains 2% of +6 mesh particles, calculate the effectiveness of the screen.

(Ans.: 75.59%)

(2) Table salt is being fed to a vibrating screen at the rate of 150 kg/hour. The desired product is −39 + 20 mesh fraction. A 30 mesh and 20 mesh screen are therefore used (double deck), the feed being introduced on the 30 mesh screen. During the operation it was observed that the average proportion of oversize (from 30 mesh screen): oversize (from 20 mesh screen): undersize (from 20 mesh screen) is 2 : 1.5 : 1. Calculate the effectiveness of the screener from the following data.

Mesh	Feed	Mass Fractions		
		Oversize from 30 mesh screen	Oversize from 20 mesh screen	Undersize from 20 mesh screen
−85 + 60	0.097	0.197	0.026	0.0005
−60 + 40	0.186	0.389	0.039	0.0009
−40 + 30	0.258	0.337	0.322	0.0036
−30 + 20	0.281	0.066	0.526	0.349
−20 + 15	0.091	0.005	0.061	0.299
−15 + 10	0.087	0.006	0.026	0.347

(Ans.: 63.39%)

(3) Leonard defines the efficiency of screening as the ratio:

$$\frac{\text{(tonnes/hour of feed)} - \text{(tonnes/hour of material of size} < A \text{ in top product)} - \text{(tonnes/hour of material of size} > A \text{ in bottom product)}}{\text{(tonnes/hour of feed)}}$$

show that this leads to, Efficiency $= (1 - b) - \dfrac{a - b}{c - b}(1 - b - c)$

where, a, b and c are the fraction of material of size < A in the feed, top product respectively.

(4) Anthracite coal from a pulverization unit has been found to contain an excess of fine material (75% by weight). In order to remove these fines, it is screened using a 1.5 mm screen. Estimate the effectiveness of the screen from the following data.

Particle size mm	Oversize from screen	Undersize from screen
−3.33+2.36	0.143	0.00
−2.36+1.65	0.211	0.098
−1.65+1.17	0.230	0.234
−1.17+0.83	0.186	0.277
−0.83+0.59	0.196	0.149
−0.59+0.42	0.034	0.101
−0.42+0.29	0.00	0.141

(5) A mixture of spherical beads is to be separated by sieving. The mixture consists of two sizes of bead, of 0.500 mm and 0.794 mm in diameter. The mixture is 0.5 number fraction of each size.

If the separation were perfect what weight of 0.500 mm bead would you expect per 100 kg of feed to the sieve?

(6) The actual compositions of the product from the sieve are as shown below, these compositions are on a weight basis. Take the smaller beads to be the desired material where necessary in the following calculations:

(i) For 100 kg of feed, what mass of beads passes through the sieve?
(ii) Calculate the recovery, rejection and efficiency of the sieve.

	0.500 mm diameter	0.794 mm diameter
Retained on the sieve	0.5%	99.5%
Passed through the sieve	65%	35%

(7) 100 kg of the mixture is sieved on a sieve with nominal aperture size 1.5 mm. The smaller particles are the desired material in this case. The recovery of this sieve is 87% and the rejection is 95%. What mass of material passes through the sieve?

(8) A mixture of spherical particles consists of 60% number fraction 1 mm diameter particles and 40% number fraction 2 mm particles. Both sizes of particle have the same density. What is the mass fraction of large particles?

NOMENCLATURE

Symbol	
A	Area, m²;
B	Underflow from screen, kg/hr
D	Overflow from screen, kg/hr
D_P	Particle Size, m
E	Screen Effectiveness, Dimensionless; E_A, based on oversize, E_B, based on undersize
F	Feed rate, kg/hr
g	Acceleration of gravity, m/s²
m	Mass, kg
$\dot{m}$	Mass flow rate, kg/hr
r	Radius
S_P	Surface area of single particle, m²
V_P	Volume of single particle, m³
x	Mass fraction of cut in mixture of particles; x_B, in underflow from screen; x_D, in overflow from screen; x_F, in feed to screen.
Greek Letters:	
μ	Viscosity, cP
ρ	Density, kg/m³
ϕ_s	Shape factor or sphericity
ω	Angular velocity, rad/s

***

Unit VI

Chapter 6: FILTRATION

6.1 Introduction

Filtration is one of the oldest chemical engineering unit operations. Pictures of the straining of wine have been engraved on the tombs of ancient Pharaohs (ca 1450 B.C.) found. In the chemical industry, filtration is used when the feed slurry contains solids at concentrations as low as a few parts per million and when filtration rates with normal driving forces are above about 0.204 $m^3/m^2.hr$ (5 gallons/ft^2.hr). This unit operation gives fairly dewatered cakes and clear liquor. In general, filtration competes with centrifugation as a mechanical separation process since both these methods have similar characteristics. It is convenient to use centrifugation at higher temperatures and for toxic materials instead of filtration. Filtration can be performed using either gravity, pressure difference or a centrifugal force. Gravity filtration is used primarily in municipal water supply units where large volumes of the liquid, having solids concentration in the range of parts per million are to be filtered. Other than for his purpose, pressure (or vacuum) or centrifugal filtration is used.

Filtration is the removal of suspended particles from a fluid, performed by a filter medium, septum, cloth or bed of solids. In this chapter we will discuss only liquid filtration, the removal of particles from gases is covered in Chapter 10. Filtration is commonly encountered in chemistry laboratories on a Buchner funnel and within the kitchen during the making of filter coffee. It is a very important industrial process as it is often a key stage in product recovery: following reaction, precipitation and crystallization stages, but preceding thermal drying and packaging (For example, in pharmaceutical production). It is more economic to remove moisture from particles by mechanical means, including filtration, than by thermal means. Thus, domestic washing machines provide higher and higher spin speeds prior to thermal, or evaporative, drying. There is a vast range of filtration types; depending upon whether the objective is to produce a clean liquid, as in drinking water production, or solids retained in a filter cake, as in product recovery. The former process is called clarification, or clarifying filtration and is often performed in equipment containing packed beds.

There is a variety of types of filter used but all rely on the simple principle. The fluid is forced through some medium that the solids cannot pass through. Usually, the filter medium is a cloth that may not be impermeable to the smallest particles, in which case the cake of solids built up on the surface catches the smallest particles. At the beginning of a filtration run the federate may be kept low to avoid forcing solids through the cloth. If it is essential to have a clear filtrate for the entire run a pre-coat may be necessary. Sometimes, filter aids are used to increase the porosity of the cake and reduce the pressure drop through it.

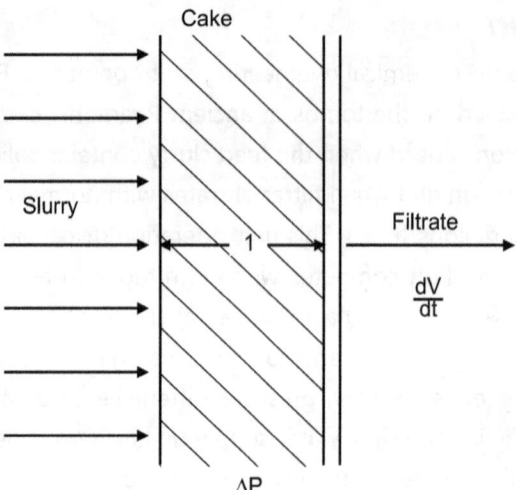

Fig. 6.1: Principles of Filtration

Filtration is the removal of solid particles from a fluid by passing the fluid through a filtering medium, or septum, on which the solids are deposited. The fluid may be a liquid or a gas; the valuable stream from the filter may be the fluid, or the solids, or both. Sometimes it is neither, as when waster solids must be separated from waste liquid prior to disposal. Filters are divided into three main groups: *cake filters, clarifying filters and crossflow filters*. Cake filters separate relatively large amount of solids as a cake of crystals or sludge. Often they include provisions for washing the cake and for removing some of the liquid from the solids before discharge. At the start of filtration in a cake filter, some solid particles enter the pores of the medium and are immbolised, but soon others begin to collect on the septum surface. After this brief period the cake of solids does the filtration, not the septum; a visible cake of appreciable thickness builds up on the surface and must be periodically removed. Clarifying filters remove small amount of solids to produce a clean gas or a sparkling clear liquid such as beverage. The solid particles are trapped inside the filter medium or on its external surfaces. Clarifying filters differ from screens in that the pores of the filter medium are must large in diameter than the particles to be removed. In a crosslow filter, the feed suspension flows under pressure at a fairly high velocity across the filter medium. A thin layer of solids may form on the surface of the medium, but the high liquid velocity keeps the layer from building up. The filter medium is a ceramic, metal or polymer membrane with pores small enough to exclude most of suspended particles. Some of the liquid passes through the medium as clear filtrate, leaving a more concentrated suspension behind.

6.2 Factors Affecting on Rate of Filtration

The rate of filtration depends on the following factors:

(1) Resistance offered by filter medium.

(2) Cake Compressibility: If the cake is rigid and incompressible as observed with hard granular particles, the compressibility of cake S = 0. For incompressible cakes, the rate of filtration is directly proportional to: (i) the pressure of filtration, (ii) the square of filtering surface and it is indirectly proportional to: (i) the viscosity of the filtrate, (ii) the total amount of cake. If the cake is composed of extremely soft, easily deformed particles, then compressibility factor S → 1. Under these conditions, the rate of filtration for very incompressible cakes is independent of pressure of filtration.

(3) Effect of Pressure: For filtration of granular of crystalline solids it is observed that increase in pressure always brings about a nearly proportionate increase in the rate of filtration. However, for cake composed of flocculent or slimy substances, rate of filtration increases only slightly with the increase of pressure.

(4) Cake Thickness: The cake thickness is also a key factor that determines the rate of filtration and cycle of operation. During the initial period when cake is porous, the rate of filtration for a given quantity of filtrate or cake is inversely proportional to the thickness of cake. However as the cake grows in thickness, bed porosity decreases and hence bed resistance rapidly increases. Thus, the rate of filtration for a given quantity of filtrate or cake is inversely proportional to the square of the thickness of the cake at the end of filtration.

(5) Effect of Viscosity: At any moment, the rate of filtration is inversely proportional to the viscosity of filtrate. Hence, to obtain high rate of filtration, high viscosity of filtrate is reduced by diluting with a low-viscosity solvent.

(6) Effect of Temperature: An increase of temperature brings about marked decrease in the viscosity of most liquids. So for filtering incompressible solids, higher filtration rate is ensured by higher temperature. For example, if the filtrate is water, the rate of filtration gets just doubled with increase in temperature from 20°C to 60°C (i.e. 40°C difference).

Other factors which affects on rate of filtration are:

(7) Effect of particle size,

(8) Effect of nature of filter medium, and

(9) Effect of solid concentration.

6.3 Clarifying Filters

Clarifying filters are also known as "deep-bed filters," because the particles of solid are trapped inside the filter medium, and usually no layer of solids can be seen on the surface of the medium. Clarification differs from screening in that the pores in the filter medium are much larger in diameter than the particles to be removed. The particles are caught by surface forces and immobilized within the flow channels, as shown in Fig. 6.2 and although they reduce the effective diameter of the channels, they normally do not block them completely.

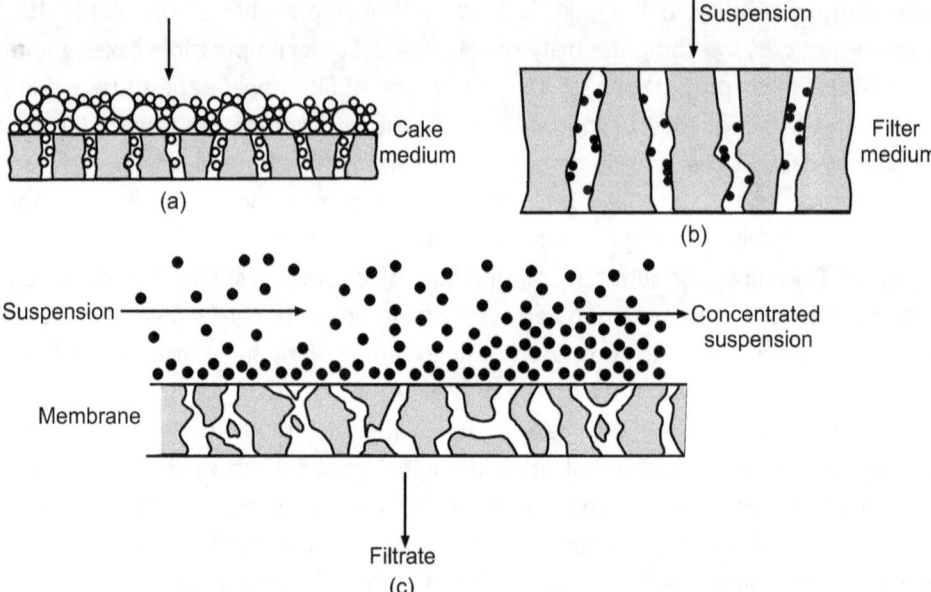

Fig. 6.2: Mechanisms of Filtration: (a) Cake Filter, (b) Clarifying Filter, (c) Crossflow Filter

6.3.1 Gas Cleaning

Filters for gas cleaning include pad filters for atmospheric dust, and granular beds and bag filters for process dusts. Passing it through pads of cellulose pulp, cotton, felt, glass fibre, or metal screening cleans air; the pad material may be dry or coated with a viscous oil to act as a dust holder. For light duty the pads are disposable, but in large-scale gas cleaning they are frequently rinsed and recoated with oil.

6.3.2 Liquid Clarification

Clarifying filters for liquids include the gravity bed filters for water treatment mentioned earlier and a variety of small cartridge filters containing filter elements of various designs and materials of construction. Some of the cake filters described later, especially tank filters and continuous precoat filters, and are used extensively for clarification. In a batch unit, the filtration rate and solids removal efficiency are typically almost constant for a considerable period of operation, but eventually the solids content of the effluent rises to an unacceptable "breakthrough" value, and backwashing of the filter element becomes necessary.

6.4 Cake Filters

The mechanism of cake filtration is shown in Fig. 6.2 (a). Here the filter medium is relatively thin, compared with that of a clarifying filter. At the start of filtration some solid particles enter the pores of the medium and are immobilized, but soon they begin to collect on the septum surface. After this brief initial period the cake of solids does the filtration, not the septum; a visible cake of appreciable thickness builds up on the surface and must be periodically removed.

Expect as noted under bag filters for gas cleaning, cake filters are used almost entirely for liquid-solid separations. As with other filters they may operate with above-atmospheric pressure upstream from the filter medium, or with vacuum applied downstream. Either type can be continuous or discontinuous, but because of the difficulty of discharging the solids against a positive pressure, most pressure filters are discontinuous.

6.5 Classification of Filters

The basic requirements for filtration equipment are:
- mechanical support for the filter medium,
- flow accesses to and from the filter medium and
- provision for removing excess filter cake.

In some instances, washing of the filter cake to remove traces of the solution may be necessary. Pressure can be provided on the upstream side of the filter, or a vacuum can be drawn downstream, or both can be used to drive the wash fluid through.

There are a number of ways to classify types of filtration equipment and it is not possible to make a simple classification that includes all types of filters. In one classification, filters are classified according to whether the filter cake is desired product or whether the clarified filtrate or outlet liquid is desired. In either case the slurry can have a relatively large percentage of solids so that a cake is formed or have just a trace of suspended particles.

Filters can be classified by operating cycle. Filters can be operated as batch, where the cake is removed after a run or continuous, where the cake is continuously removed. In another classification, filters can be of the gravity type, where the liquid simply flows by a hydrostatic head or pressure or vacuum can be used to increase the flow rates. An important method of classification depends upon the mechanical arrangement of the filter media. The filter cloth can be in a series arrangement as flat plates in an enclosure, as individual leaves dipped in the slurry or on rotating-type rolls in the slurry. In the following sections only the most important types of filters will be described.

6.5.1 Discontinuous Vacuum Filters

Pressure filters are usually discontinuous; vacuum filters are usually continuous. A discontinuous vacuum filter, however, is sometimes a useful tool. A vacuum filter is little more than a large Buchner funnel, 0.9 to 3 m in diameter and forming a layer of solids 0.1 to 0.3 m thick.

6.5.2 Continuous Vacuum Filters

In all continuous vacuum filters liquor is sucked through a moving septum to deposit a cake of solids. The cake is moved out of the filtering zone, washed, sucked dry, and dislodged from the septum, which then reenters the slurry to pick up another load of solids. Some part of the septum is in the filtering zone at all times, part is in the washing zone, and part is being relieved of its load of solids, so that the discharge of both solids and liquids from the filter is uninterrupted. The pressure differential across the septum in a continuous vacuum filter is not high, ordinarily between 10 and 20 in. Hg. Various designs of filter differ in the method of admitting slurry, the shape of the filter surface, and the way in which the solids are discharged. Most all, however, apply vacuum from a stationary source to the moving parts of the unit through a rotary valve.

6.6 Equipment for Filtration

6.6.1 Plate and Frame Filter Presses

One of the important types of filters is the plate-and-frame filter press, which is shown diagrammatically in Fig. 6.3 (a). These filters consist of plates and frames assembled alternatively with a filter cloth over each side of the plates. The plates have channel cut in them so that clear filtrate liquid can drain down along each plate. The feed slurry is pumped into the press and flows through the duct into each of the open frames to that slurry fills the frames. The filtrate flows through the filter cloth and the solids build up as a cake on the frame side of the cloth. The filtrate flows between the filter cloth and the face of the plate through the channel to the outlet. The filtration proceeds until the frames are completely filled with solids. In Fig. 6.3 (a) all the discharge outlets go to a common header. In many cases the filter press will have a separate discharge to the open for each frame. Then visual inspection can be made to see if the filtrate is running clear.

If one is running cloudy because of a break in the filter cloth or other factors, it can be shut off separately. When the frames are completely full, the frames and plates are separated and the cake removed. Then the filter is reassembled and the cycle is repeated.

If the cake is to be washed, the cake is left in the plates and through washing is performed, as shown in Fig. 6.3. In this press a separate channel is provided for the wash water inlet. The wash water enters the inlet, which has ports opening behind the filter cloths at every other plate of the filter press. The wash water then flows through the filter cloth, through the entire cake (not half the cake as in filtration), through the filter cloth at the other side of the frames and out the discharge channel. It should be noted that there are two kinds of plates in Fig. 6.3 (b) those having ducts to admit wash water behind the filter cloth, alternating with those without such ducts.

The plate-and-frame presses suffer from the disadvantages common to batch processes. The cost of labour for removing the cakes and reassembling plus the cost of fixed charges for downtime can be an appreciable part of the total operating cost. Some newer types of plate-and-frame presses have duplicate sets of frames mounted on a rotating shaft. Half of the frames are in use while the others are being cleaned, thus saving downtime and labour costs. Other advances in automation have been applied to these types of filters. Filter presses are used in batch processes but cannot be employed for high-throughput processes. They are simple to operate, very versatile and flexible in operation, and can be used at high pressures, when necessary, if viscous solutions are being used or the filter cake has a high resistance.

The plate and frame filter press is cheap but it is difficult to mechanize to any great extent. Variants of the plate and frame press have been developed which allow easier discharging of the filter cake. For example, the plates, which may be rectangular or circular, are supported on a central hollow shaft for the filtrate and the whole assembly enclosed in a pressure tank containing the slurry.

Filtration can be done under pressure or vacuum. The advantage of vacuum filtration is that the pressure drop can be maintained whilst the cake is still under atmospheric pressure and so can be removed easily. The disadvantages are the greater costs of maintaining a given pressure drop by applying a vacuum and the limitation on the vacuum to about 80 kPa maximum. In pressure filtration, the pressure driving force is limited only by the economics of attaining the pressure and by the mechanical strength of the equipment.

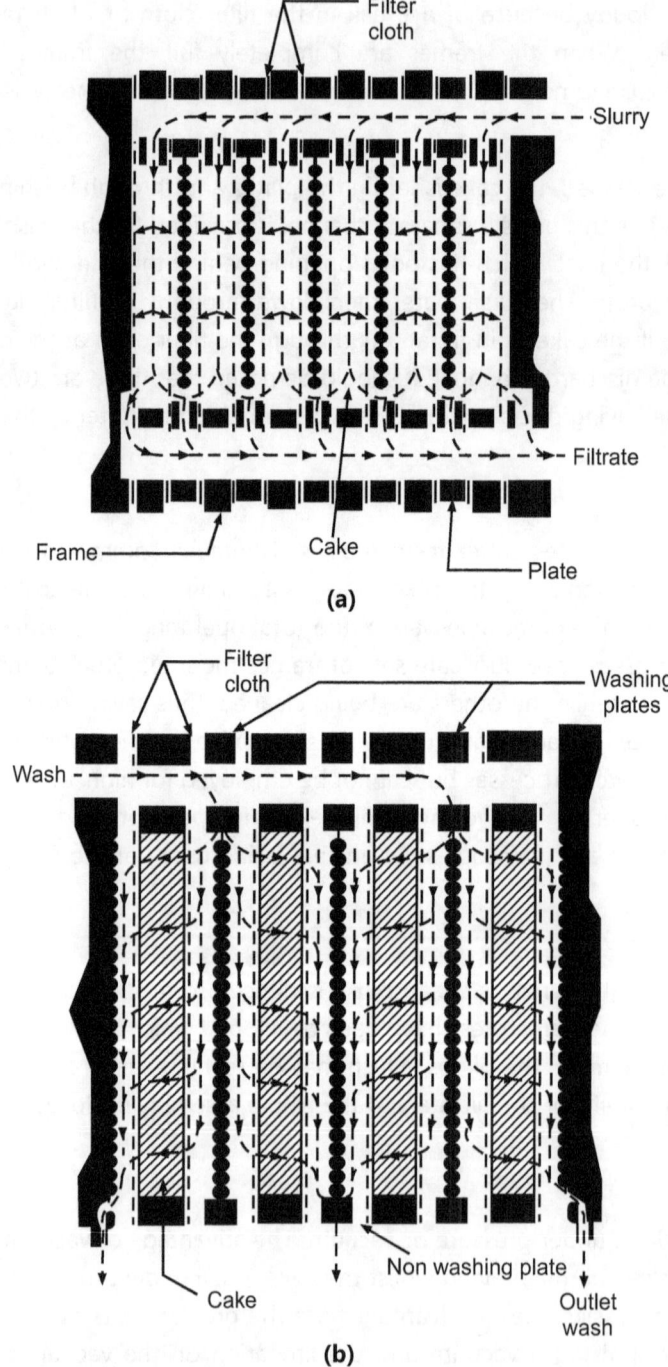

Fig. 6.3: Diagrams of Plate-and-Frame Filter Presses: (a) Filtration of Slurry with Closed Delivery, (b) Through Washing in a Press with Open Delivery

6.6.2 Leaf Filters

The filter press is useful for many purposes but is not economical for handling large quantities of sludge or for efficient washing with a small amount of wash water. The wash water often channels in the cake and large volume of wash water be needed. The leaf filter shown in Fig. 6.4 was developed for larger volumes and more efficient washing. Each leaf is a hollow wire framework covered by a filter cloth. A number of these leaves are hung in parallel in a closed tank. The slurry entry tank and is forced under pressure through the filter cloth, where the cake deposits outside of the leaf. The filtrate flows inside the hollow framework and out a head wash liquid follows the same path as the slurry.

Hence, the washing is more efficient through washing in plate-and-frame filter presses. To remove the cake, the opened. Sometimes air is blown in the reverse direction into the leaves to dislodging the cake. If the solids are not wanted, water jets can be used to simple away the cakes without opening the filter. Leaf filters also suffer from the disadvantage of batch operation. They automated for the filtering, washing and cleaning cycle. However, they are still and are used for batch processes and relatively modest throughput processes.

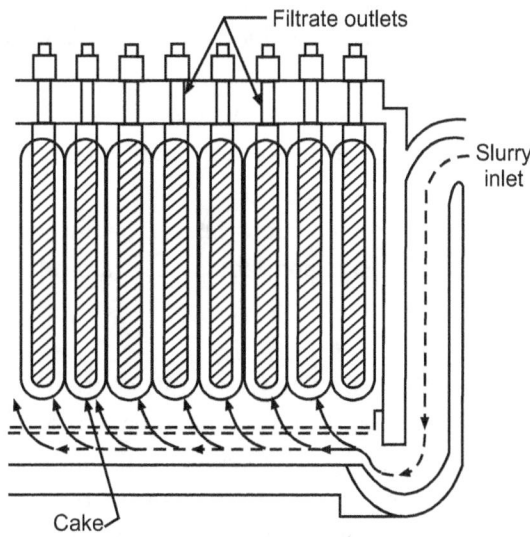

Fig. 6.4: Leaf Filter

6.6.3 Continuous Rotary Filters

The plate-and-frame filters suffer from the disadvantage common to all batch processes and can not be used for large capacity process number of continuous-type filters are available as discussed as follows.

(a) Continuous Rotary Vacuum-Drum Filter: This filter shown in Fig. 6.5 washes and discharges the cake in a continuous repeating sequence. The drum is provided with a suitable filtering medium. The drum rotates and an automatic valve in the serves to activate the filtering, drying, washing and cake discharge functions. The filtrate leaves through the axle of the filter. The automatic valve provides separate outlets for the filtrate and the wash liquid. Also, if needed, a connection for compressed air blow back just before discharge used to help in cake removal by the knife scraper. The maximum pressure difference in the vacuum filter is only 1 atm. Hence, this type is not suitable for viscous liquids.

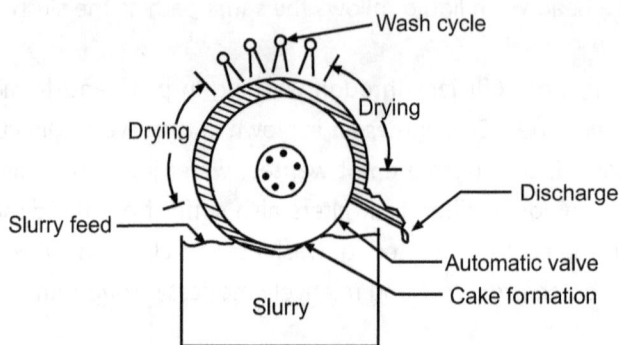

Fig. 6.5: Schematic of Continuous Rotary-Drum Filter

If the drum is enclosed in a shell, pressures above atmospheric can be used. However, the cost of a pressure type is about two times that of a vacuum-type rotary drum filter.

Modern, high-capacity processes use continuous filters. The important advantages are that the filters are continuous and automatic and labour costs are relatively low. However, the capital cost is relatively high.

(b) Continuous Rotary Disk Filter: This filter consist of concentric vertical disks mounted on a horizontal rotating shaft. The filter operates on the same principle as the vacuum rotary drum filter. Each disk is hollow and covered with a filter cloth and is partly submerged in the slurry. The cake is washed, dried and scrapped off when the disk is in the upper half of its rotation. Washing is less efficient than with a rotating drum type filter.

(c) Continuous Rotary Horizontal Filter: This type is a vacuum filter with the rotating annular filtering surface divided into sectors. As the horizontal filter rotates it successively receives slurry, is washed, dried and the cake is scrapped-off. The washing efficiency is better than with the rotary disk filter. This filter is widely used in ore extraction processes, pulp washing and other large-capacity processes.

6.7 Filter Media

The septum in any filter must meet the following requirements:
(1) It must retain the solids to be filtered, giving a reasonably clear filtrate.
(2) It must not plug or blind.
(3) It must be resistant chemically and strong enough physically to withstand the process conditions.
(4) It must permit the cake formed to discharge cleanly and completely.
(5) It must not be prohibitively expensive.

In industrial filtration a common filter medium is canvas cloth, either duck or twill weave. Many different weights and patterns of weave are available for different services. Corrosive liquids require the use of other filter media, such as woolen cloth, Monel or stainless steel, glass cloth, or paper. Synthetic fabrics like nylon, polypropylene, Saran, and Dacron are also highly resistant chemically.

In a cloth of a given mesh size, smooth synthetic or metal fibers are less effective than the more ragged natural fibers in removing very fine particles. Ordinarily, coarse particles containing no fines the actual filtering medium is not the septum but the first layer of deposited solids. Filtrate may first come through cloudy, and then grow clear. Cloudy filtrate is returned to the slurry tank for refiltration.

6.8 Filter Aids

Slimy or very fine solids, which form a dense, impermeable cake quickly, plug any filter medium that is fine enough to retain then. Practical filtration of such materials requires that porosity of the cake be increased to permit passage of the liquor at a reasonable rate. This is done by adding a filter aid, such as diatomaceous silica, perlite, purified wood cellulose, or other inert porous solid, to the slurry before filtration. The filter aid may subsequently be separated from the filter cake by dissolving away the solids or by burning out the filter aid. If the solids have no valve, they and the filter aid are discarded together.

Another way of using a filter aid is by precoating, i.e., depending a layer of it on the filter medium before filtration. In batch filters the precoat layer is usually thin; in a continuous precoat filter, as described previously, the layer of precoat is thick, and an advancing knife to expose a fresh filtering surface continually scrapes off the top of the layer. Precoats prevent gelatinous solids from plugging the filter medium and give a clearer filtrate. The precoat is really a part of the filter medium rather than of the cake.

6.9 Principles of Cake Filtration

Filtration is a special example of flow through porous media, which was discussed for cases in which the resistances to flow are constant. In filtration the flow resistances increases with time as the filter medium becomes clogged or a filter cake builds up, and the equations given below, must be modified to allow for this. The chief quantities of interest are the flow rate through the filter and the pressure drop across the unit. As time passes during filtration, either the flow rate dimension or the pressure drop rises. In what is called constant-pressure filtration the pressure drop is held constant and the flow rate allowed to fall with time; less commonly, the pressure drop is progressively increased to give what is called constant-rate filtration. Hermans and Bredee developed a general equation for all types of constant-pressure filtration in 1935. Their equation is:

$$\frac{d^2t}{dV^2} = k_1 \left(\frac{dt}{dV}\right)^n \qquad \ldots (6.1)$$

Where, V = Volume of filtered liquid, or filtrate, collected in time t
K_1, n = constants

In clarification filtration n may be 2, 3/2, or 1, depending on the mechanism of particle deposition. In cake filtration, n = 0.

For constant-rate filtration the Hermans-Bredee equation is:

$$\frac{d(\Delta p)}{dV} = K_2 (\Delta p)^n \qquad \ldots (6.2)$$

Where, Δp is pressure drop across the filter and n has the same values.

6.10 Principles of Clarification

If the solid particles being removed completely plug the pores of the filter medium, and the rate of plugging is constant with time, the mechanism is known as direct sieving, for which n. Directly sieving is rarely encountered. Much more commonly the particles partially block the pores, giving a gradual reduction in pore size; this is called standard blocking, for which n = 3/2. Occasionally during the transition between clarification and cake formation there may be a period during which n = 1. This is called intermediate blocking.

Standard blocking is the usual mechanism in clarifying filters. With n = 3/2, integration of the following equations for constant-pressure filtration:

$$q = Q_0 (1 - K_s V)^2 \qquad \ldots (6.3)$$

$$\frac{t}{V} = K_s t + \frac{1}{q_0} \qquad \ldots (6.4)$$

Where,
q = dV/t, volumetric flow rate through filter
q_0 = Flow rate at t = 0
K_s = Constant equal to $K_1/2q_0^{1/2}$

6.10.1 Membrane Filtration

In the context of particle technology, the most appropriate membrane filtration process is Microfiltration (MF), but it is quite common to filter very fine particles using an ultrafiltration (UF) membrane. Also, UF mathematical models are sometimes applied to MF applications. So, both techniques will be briefly described here. A general definition of a MF membrane is one that possesses filtering pores between 10 and 0.1 μm. A UF membrane has pores below 0.1 μm, but is usually rated in terms of molecular weight cut-off, and is employed to retain macro-molecular material. Membranes usually possess a thin filtering surface, which may be supported by a much thicker structure.

On the figure a variable pore structure is evident and the manufacturer's pore rating of the membrane is 0.2 μm, but surface openings up to 3 μm are evident. The filter is effective for the removal of all bacteria (sizes down to 0.2 μm), but it is obvious that these small particles will not be retained on the filter surface – at least some will penetrate the membrane matrix. The amount of penetration will depend upon the concentration of solids as, at high concentration, a cake may form. Thus, if all the fine particles are retained at all concentrations deposition must take place inside the filter and the micro filter is relying on depth filtration.

The consequence of internal deposition of particles within the membrane is that the filtration flux rate (or permeate rate) will decrease, if a constant pressure differential is being used. The permeate rate will also decrease as solids become deposited on the surface of the membrane, for similar reasons as described during cake filtration. In order to limit the occurrence of a cake cross flow filtration is often employed. This is illustrated in Fig. 6.6 (a).

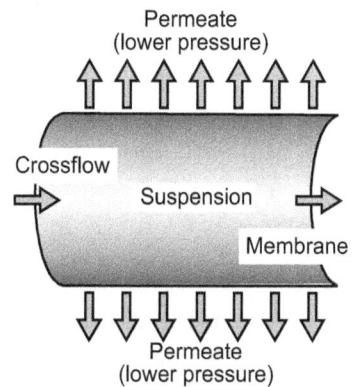

Fig. 6.6 (a): Illustration of Cross Flow Filtration – Shear at the Membrane Surface Helps Reduce Particle Deposition

The process selection of either cross flow operation or filtration in dead-end mode using, for example, a cartridge filter depends upon the process conditions. Cartridge membrane filters are used extensively in the electronics and medical industries to ensure sterility and particle free fluids (gases as well as liquids). In most of these applications the concentration of suspended material is very small and the filter operates in dead-end and it is discarded when the pressure drop required maintaining an acceptable flow rate becomes too great. However, these are high value industries that can afford to discard these products. A duplex system is often used: a second cartridge filter is used whilst the first is taken off-line for filter element changing. However, at higher concentrations of suspended solids the frequency of element changing would be too great and cross flow filtration may be appropriate. In this instance a clean liquid stream is still supplied, but a second liquid stream containing a higher concentration of suspended material is recycled. This stream is the retentate and the process is illustrated in Fig. 6.6 (b).

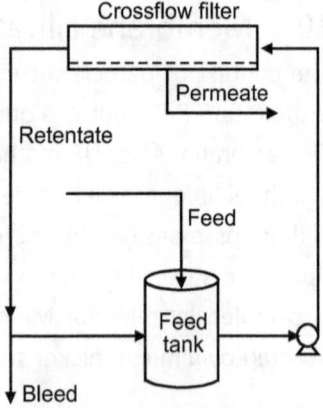

Fig. 6.6 (b): Illustration of Cross Flow Filtration Process Operation

6.11 Pressure Drop through Filter Cake

The overall pressure drop at any time is the sum of the pressure drops over medium and cake. If P_a is the inlet pressure, P_a the outlet pressure, and p' the pressure at the boundary between cake and medium,

$$\Delta p = P_a - P_b = (P_a - p') + (p' - P_b) = \Delta p_c + \Delta p_m \quad \ldots (6.5)$$

Where, Δp = Overall pressure drop.
Δp_c = Pressure drop over cake.
Δp_m = Pressure drop over medium.

Fig. 6.7 shows diagrammatically a section through a filter cake and filter medium at a definite time t from the start of the flow of filtrate. At this time the thickness of the cake, measured from the filter medium, is L_c. the filter area, measured perpendicularly to the direction of flow, is A. Consider the thin layer of cake of thickness dL lying in the cake at a distance L from medium. Let the pressure at this point be p. This layer consists of a thin bed of solid particles through which the filtrate is flowing. In a filter bed the velocity is sufficiently low to ensure laminar flow. Accordingly, as a starting point for treating the pressure drop through the cake, an equation can be used, noting that $\Delta p/L = dp/dL$. If the velocity of the filtrate is designated as u, equation becomes,

$$\frac{dp}{dL} = \frac{150 \, \mu u \, (1-\epsilon)^2}{g_c \, (\phi_s \, D_p)^2 \, \epsilon^3} \quad \ldots (6.6)$$

Often the pressure drop is expressed as a function of the surface-volume ratio instead of the particles size. Substitution of $6(v_p/S_p)$ for $\phi_s D_p$ equation gives.

$$\frac{dp}{dL} = \frac{4.17\ \mu u\ (1-\epsilon)^2\ (S_p/v_p)^2}{g_c\ \epsilon^3} \qquad \ldots (6.7)$$

Where, dp/dL = Pressure gradient at thickness L.

μ = Viscosity of filtrate.
u = Linear velocity of filtrate, based on filter area.
S_p = Surface of single particle.
v_p = Volume of single particle.
ϵ = Porosity of cake.
g_c = Newton's law proportionality factor.

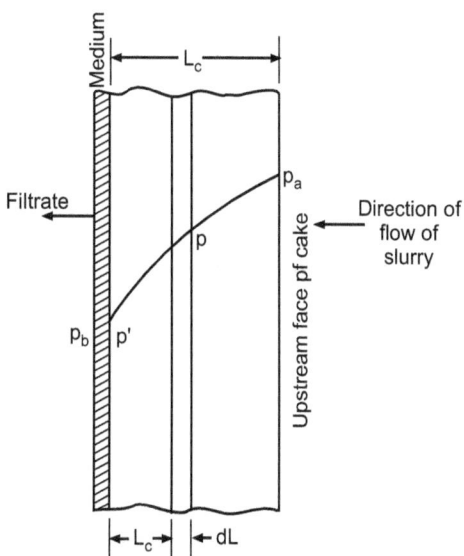

Fig. 6.7: Section Through Filter Medium and Cake

For beds of compressible particles or beds with a very low void fraction the coefficient in equation may be much larger than 4.17. The linear velocity u is given by the equation:

$$u = \frac{dV/dt}{A} \qquad \ldots (6.8)$$

Where V is the volume of filtrate collected from the start of the filtration to time t. Since the filtrate must pass through the entire cake, V/A is the same for all layers and u is independent of L. The volume of solids in the layer is $A(1-\epsilon)\ dL$, and if ρ_p is the density of the particles, the mass dm of solids in the layer is:

$$dm = \rho_p\ (1-\epsilon)\ A\ DL \qquad \ldots (6.9)$$

Elimination of dL, from equations (6.7) and (6.9) gives,

$$dp = \frac{k_1\ \mu u\ (S_p/v_p)^2\ (1-\epsilon)}{A g_c\ \rho_p\ A\epsilon^3} \qquad \ldots (6.10)$$

Where k_1 is used in place of the coefficient 6.17 in equation (6.7).

MECHANICAL OPERATIONS — FILTRATION

6.12 Compressible and Incompressible Filter Cake

In the filtration under low pressure drops of slurries containing rigid uniform particles, all factors on the right-hand side of equation (6.10) except m are independent of L, and the equation is integrable directly, over the thickness of the cake. If m_c is the total mass of solids in the cake, the result is:

$$\int_{p'}^{p_a} dp = \frac{k_1 \mu u (S_p/v_p)^2 (1 - \epsilon)}{A g_c \rho_p \epsilon^3} \int_0^{m_c} dm \quad \ldots (6.11)$$

$$P_a - P' = \frac{k_1 \mu u (S_p/v_p)^2 (1 - \epsilon) m_c}{A g_c \rho_p A \epsilon^3} = \Delta P_c \quad \ldots (6.12)$$

Filter cakes of this type are called *incompressible*. For use in equation (6.12) specific cake resistance α is defined by the equation:

$$\alpha + \frac{\Delta P_c\, g_c\, A}{\mu\, u\, m_c} \quad \ldots (6.13)$$

Where,
$$\alpha = \frac{k_1 (S_p/v_p)^2 (1 - \epsilon)}{\epsilon^3 \rho_p} \quad \ldots (6.14)$$

The cake resistance α may also be expressed in terms of the particle size D_p, with a new coefficient k_2.

$$\alpha = \frac{k_2 (1 - \epsilon)}{(\phi_s D_p)^2 \epsilon^3 \rho_p} \quad \ldots (6.15)$$

For incompressible cakes α is independent of the pressure drop and of position in the cake.

6.13 Filter Medium Resistance

A filter-medium resistance R_m can be defined by analogy with the cake resistance $\alpha m_c/A$.

The equation is:
$$R_m = \frac{(p' - p_b) g_c}{\mu u} - \frac{\Delta p_m g_c}{\mu u} \quad \ldots (6.16)$$

The dimension of R_m is L^{-1}.

The filter-medium resistance R_m may vary with the pressure drop, since the higher liquid velocity caused by a large pressure drop may force additional particles of solid into the filter medium.

6.14 Constant Pressure Filtration

We have
$$\frac{dt}{dV} = \frac{\mu}{A g_c (\Delta p)} \left(\frac{\alpha_c V}{A} + R_m \right) \quad \ldots (A)$$

When Δp is constant, the only variables in equation (A) are V and t. When $t = 0$, $v = 0$ and $\Delta p = \Delta p_m$; hence

$$\frac{\mu R_m}{A \Delta p\, g_c} = \frac{(dt)}{(dV)_0} = \frac{1}{q_0} \quad \ldots (6.17)$$

Equation (A) may therefore be written

$$\frac{dt}{dV} = \frac{1}{q} = k_c V + \frac{1}{q_0} \qquad \ldots (6.18)$$

where,
$$k_c = \frac{\mu u\,\alpha}{A^2\,\Delta p\,g_c} \qquad \ldots (6.19)$$

Integration of equation (6.18) between the limits (0, 0) and (t, V) gives:

$$\frac{t}{V} = \left(\frac{k_c}{2}\right)V = \frac{1}{q_0} \qquad \ldots (6.20)$$

Thus a plot of t/V vs. V will be linear, with a slope equal to $k_c/2$ and an intercept of $1/q_0$.

6.15 Empirical Equation for Cake Resistance

By conducting constant pressure experiments at various pressure drops, the variation of α with Δp may be found. If α is independent of Δp, the sludge is incompressible. Ordinarily α increases with Δp, as most sludge are at least to some extent compressible. For highly compressible sludges, α increases rapidly with Δp.

Empirical equations may be fitted to observed data for Δp vs. α, the commonest of which is,

$$\alpha = \alpha_0\,(\Delta p)^s \qquad \ldots (6.21)$$

Where, α_0 and s are empirical constant. Constant s is the compressibility coefficient of the cake. It is zero for incompressible sludges and positive for compressible ones. It usually falls between 0.2 and 0.8. Equation (6.21) should not be used in a range of pressure drops much different from that used in the experiments conducted to evaluate α_0 and s.

6.16 Constant-rate Filtration

If filtrate flows at a constant rate, the linear velocity u is constant and

$$u = \frac{dV/dt}{A} = \frac{V}{At} \qquad \ldots (6.22)$$

Equation (6.13) can be written, after substituting as $m_c = V_c$ and u from equation (6.22), we get,
$$\frac{\Delta p_c}{\alpha} = \frac{\mu c}{t g_c}\left(\frac{V}{A}\right)^2 \qquad \ldots (6.23)$$

The specific cake resistance α is retained on the left-hand side of equation (6.23) because it is a function of Δp for compressible sludges. If α is known as a function of Δp_c and if Δp_m, the pressure drop through the filter medium, can be estimated, equation (6.23) can be used directly to relate the overall pressure drop to time when the rate of flow of filtrate is constant. A more direct use of this equation can be made, however, if equation (6.21) is

MECHANICAL OPERATIONS — FILTRATION

accepted to relate α and Δp_c. If α from equation (6.21) is substituted in equation (6.23) and if $\Delta p - \Delta p_m$ is substituted for Δp_c, the result is:

$$\Delta p_c^{1-s} = \frac{\alpha_0 \mu c t}{g_c}\left(\frac{V}{At}\right)^2 = (\Delta p - \Delta p_m)^{1-s} \qquad \ldots (6.24)$$

Again, the simplest method of correcting the overall pressure drop for the pressure drop through the filter medium is to assume the filter medium resistance is constant during a given constant-rate filtration. Then, by equation (6.16), Δp_m is also constant in equation (6.24). Since the only variables in equation (6.24) are Δp and t, the equation can be written:

$$(\Delta p - \Delta p_m)^{1-s} = k_r t \qquad \ldots (6.25)$$

Where K_r is defined by:
$$k_r = \frac{\mu u^2 c \alpha_0}{g_c} \qquad \ldots (6.26)$$

6.17 Filter-cake Compressibility

With some filter cakes, the specific resistance varies with the pressure drop across it. This is because the cake becomes denser under the higher pressure and so provides fewer and smaller passages for flow. The effect is spoken of as the compressibility of the cake. Soft and flocculent materials provide highly compressible filter cakes, whereas hard granular materials such as sugar and salt crystals, are little affected by pressure. To allow for cake compressibility the empirical relationship has been proposed:

$$r = r'\Delta (P)^s$$

where, r is the specific resistance of the cake under pressure P, ΔP is the pressure drop across the filter, r' is the specific resistance of the cake under a pressure drop of 1 atm and s is a constant for the material, called its compressibility.

This expression for r can be inserted into the filtration equations and values for r' and s can be determined by carrying out experimental runs under various pressures.

6.18 Rate of Washing

When filtration is complete wash water is often passed through the cake to flush out any remaining mother liquor. The rate of water passage through the cake is calculated using the "packed-bed" equation.

$$\left(\frac{dV}{dt}\right)_{wash} = \frac{A^2 \Delta P_{wash}}{r \mu (vV_F + AL)}$$

where,

ΔP_{wash} = Pressure differential used in washing (constant pressure).

μ_w = Water viscosity.

V_F = Volume of filtrate passed in filtration.

If the wash is carried out at constant flowrate the pressure drop is easily calculated.

6.19 Principles of Centrifugal Filtration

The basic theory of constant pressure filtration can be modified to apply to filtration in a centrifuge. The treatment applies after the cake has been deposited and during flow of clear filtrate or freshwater through the cake. Fig. 6.8 shows such a cake. In this figure,

r_1 = Radius of inner surface of liquid.
r_i = Radius of inner face of cake.
r_2 = Inside radius of basket.

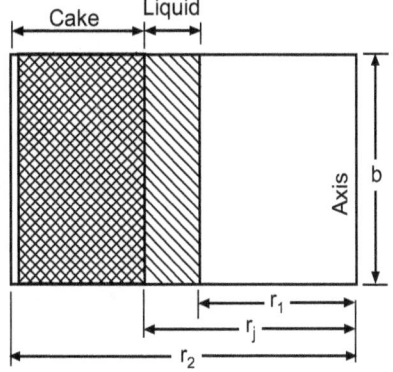

Fig. 6.8: Centrifugal Filter

The following simplifying assumptions are made. The effects of gravity and of changes in kinetic energy of the liquid are neglected, and the pressure drop from centrifugal action equals the drag of the liquid flowing through the cake; the cake is completely filled with liquid; the flow of the liquid is laminar; the resistance of the filter medium is constant; and the cake is nearly incompressible, so an average specific resistance can be used as a constant.

In the light of these assumptions the flow rate of liquid through the cake is predicted as follows. Assume first that the area A for flow does not change with radius, as would nearly be true with a thin cake in a large-diameter centrifuge. The linear velocity of the liquid is then given by:

$$u = \frac{dV/dt}{A} = \frac{q}{A} \qquad \ldots (6.27)$$

Where, q is the volumetric flow rate of liquid.

Also,

$$\Delta p = \frac{q\mu}{g_c}\left(\frac{m_c \alpha}{A^2} + \frac{R_m}{A}\right) = \frac{q}{A} \qquad \ldots (6.28)$$

The pressure drop from centrifugal action is given by:

$$\Delta p = \frac{\rho\bar{\omega}^2 (r_2^2 - r_1^2)}{2g_c} \qquad \ldots (6.29)$$

Where, ω = Angular velocity, rad/s
ρ = Density of liquid.

Combining equations (6.28) and (6.29) and solving for q gives.

$$q = \frac{\rho\bar{\omega}^2 (r_2^2 - r_1^2)}{2\mu (\alpha m_c /A^2 + R_m /A)} \qquad \ldots (6.30)$$

When the change in A with radius is too large to be neglected, it can be shown that equation (6.30) should be written.

$$q = \frac{\rho \bar{\omega}^2 (r_2^2 - r_1^2)}{2\mu (\alpha m_c/\bar{A}_L \bar{A}_a + R_m/A_2)} \quad \ldots (6.31)$$

Where, A_2 = area of filter medium (inside area of centrifuge basket)

$\bar{A}_a$ = Arithmetic mean cake area.

$\bar{A}_L$ = Logarithmic mean cake area.

The average areas $\bar{A}_a$ and $\bar{A}_L$ are defined by the equations:

$$\bar{A}_a = (r_i + r_2) \pi b \quad \ldots (6.32)$$

$$\bar{A}_L = \frac{2\pi b (r_2 - r_1)}{\ln (r_2/r_i)} \quad \ldots (6.33)$$

Where, b = Height of basket.
 r_i = Inner radius of cake

Note that equation (6.31) applies to a cake of definite mass and is not an integrated equation over an entire filtration starting with an empty centrifugal. The cake resistance is generally somewhat greater than that found in a pressure or vacuum filter under comparable conditions. Especially with compressible cakes, α increases with the applied centrifugal force.

6.20 Fundamentals of Microfiltration

Microfiltration is a form of filtration that has two common forms. One form is *crossflow separation*. In crossflow separation, a fluid stream runs parallel to a membrane. There is a pressure differential across the membrane. This causes some of the fluid to pass through the membrane, while the remainder continues across the membrane, cleaning it. The other form of filtration is called *dead-end filtration or perpendicular filtration*.

In dead-end filtration, all of the fluid passes through the membrane and all of the particles that can not fit through the pores of the membrane are stopped. Crossflow micro filtration is used in a number of applications, as either a prefiltration step or a process to separate a fluid from a process stream. Dead-end microfiltration is used commonly in stopping particles in either prefiltration or final filtration before a fluid is to be used. Cartridge filters are typically composed of microfiltration media.

Microfiltration is specifically the filtration of substances that range in size from 0.1 μm to μm. Often microfiltration is used to refer to the removal of microbes, such as in cold sterilization since bacteria, fungal spores, yeast and some viruses fall into this size range. Filters with a 0.2 μm or smaller pore size rating are frequently regarded as being able to sterilize solutions. Generally, this is only approximately true and then only if the filter itself is sterilized before use. Filters with later pore size rating may be used to clarify samples without necessarily sterilizing them.

Filtration is similar to dialysis in that both use a membrane to effect a separation based on the size of particles or molecules. Filtration uses pressure to drive the material through the membrane; this differs from dialysis where osmotic pressure is used to drive the separation. Because large pressures can be used to drive microfiltration separations, considerable concentration polarization can develop. In standard dead-ended separations (where the bulk fluid flow is toward the filter membrane) the concentration of retained species will increase most rapidly just behind the membrane.

This leads to a decreasing flow as the retained material forms a barrier just behind the membrane. As the concentration of retained material just behind the membrane increases, its solubility limit may be reached. This will result in the formation of a "gel" layer that further restricts the flow. Spectrum's microfiltration products are based on hollow fibre filters. In these filters, bundles of small tubes (hollow fibres) of filter media are used to filter. The use of many small tubes keeps the bulk flow moving along the surface of the membrane and not directly toward the filter surface. This lowers the concentration of retained material near the filter surface by continually washing it away and prevents the formation of a gel layer.

6.20.1 Basic Principles of Microfiltration

Microfiltration can be defined as the separation of particles of one size from particles of another size in the range of approximately 0.10 μm through 20 μm. The fluid may be either a liquid or a gas. Microfiltration media are available in a wide variety of materials and methods of manufacture. They can be rated either "Absolute" or "Nominal" depending upon the percentage of capture of particles of the same size or larger than the retention rating of the media. Membrane filters are generally rated as absolute media.

They can be manufactured of various polymeric materials, metals and ceramics. Nominal media includes filters made of glass fibres, polymeric fibres, discrete particles (diatomaceous earth), ceramics etc. However, even absolute media can be considered absolute only with a finite time span because of the possibility of bacterial grow-through.

Microfiltration membranes can be divided into two broad groups based on their pore structure. These are membranes with capillary-type pores, hereafter called screen membranes and membranes with tortuous-type pores, hereafter called depth membranes. The membrane has nearly perfect round cylindrical pores, more or less normal to the surface of the membrane, with even random pore dispersion over the surface.

Screen membranes are absolute and are commercially available in thin films of polycarbonate and polyester. They are manufactured in a two-step nuclear track and etch process. They are preferred in a wide variety of applications including optical and electron microscopy, chemotaxis, exfoliative cytology, particulate analyses, aerosol analyses, gravimetric analyses and blood rheology.

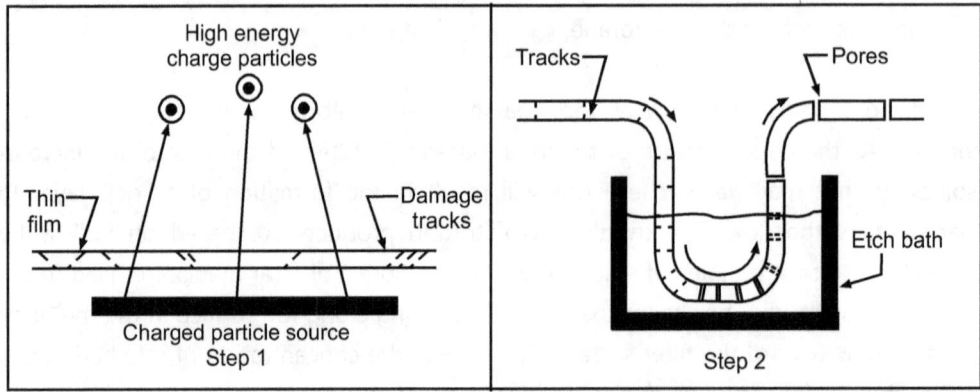

Fig. 6.9

How polycarbonate screen membrane filters are made: In the first step, thin plastic film is exposed to ionizing radiation forming damage tracks. In the second step, the tracks are preferentially etched out into pores by a strong alkaline solution.

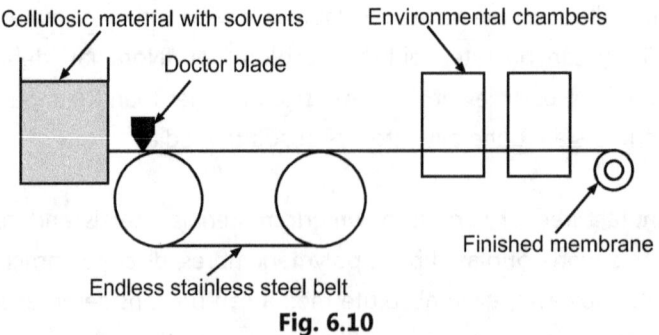

Fig. 6.10

Most depth membranes are manufactured of various polymeric materials using a casting machine. membranes cast with cellulosic esters are the most widely used membranes. Referring to Fig. 6.10 cellulosic membranes are manufactured by dissolving the cellulose esters in a mixture of organic solvents; adding various chemical agents for improved characteristics and casting the solution as a film approximately 150 µm thick onto a moving belt. As solvents are evaporated under controlled conditions, the tortuous pore structure is formed. The resulting open area ranges from 75% to 89%. Membranes of this highly-porous structure with its labyrinth of interconnecting isotropic pores are recommended for general precision filtrations, electrophoresis, sterilization of fluids, culturing of microorganisms and for many other uses.

PTFE depth membranes are manufactured by the controlled stretching of a fluorocarbon sheet. Some polypropylene membranes have also been manufactured by this method. The silver membrane is manufactured of pure metallic silver particles that are molecularly bonded to each other to form a uniform porous monolithic structure. A major application for silver membrane filter is inorganic material analyses. With the difference between screen and depth membranes, it is clear that the characteristics of the two types of membranes would allow each to have significant advantages and disadvantages. For optimum results, membrane users should consider all characteristics in selecting which (or both) of the two types of membranes should be used.

6.20.2 Particle Retention

Particles are captured directly on the surface of the screen membrane. However, screen membranes retain with certainty only those particles the same size or larger than the pore size of the membrane. Except for inertial imprecation and diffusion, most particles smaller than the pore size pass unimpeded through the screen membrane. The screen membrane should also be selected if the user wants low non-specific binding (maximum yield of particles or proteins in the filtrate). This is important, for example, when viruses are being separated from a growth solution and the maximum yield of viruses is desired. Binding of proteins in screen membranes has been found to be less than 10 percent that of depth membranes.

With depth membranes, most particles are captured within the interstices of the membrane except for relatively large particles. Since depth membranes depend upon the tortuously of their flow paths for capture, they will trap not only particles of the same size or larger than the rated pore size, but also many particles below that rated pore size. Should the user want maximum removal of all particles and/or a high binding capacity, the depth membrane should be selected. The depth membrane has a much larger available surface area than the screen membrane; therefore it has a much larger particle loading capacity and many more sites where proteins and viruses can bind.

6.21 Introduction to Biofiltration

Biofiltration is a relatively new pollution control technology. It consists of the removal and oxidation of compounds from contaminated air using micro-organisms. Biofiltration is the removal and oxidation of organic gases (volatile organic compounds, or VOCs) from contaminated air by beds of compost or solid (biofilter media). Billions of indigenous micro-organisms inherent within the biofilter media convert the organic compounds to carbon dioxide and water. These naturally occurring micro-organisms consume the offending compounds in a safe, moist, oxygen-rich environment.

A biofilter is an engineered bed of soil or compost under which lies a distribution system of perforated pipe and a layer of coarse distribution media. Contaminated air is blown into the perforated pipes and slowly diffuses up through the biofilter media. The contaminant molecules flow through the biofilter media like pebbles in a stream, until they settle out and are consumed by the micro-organisms. These same micro-organisms are responsible for the degradation of organics in nature. The biofilter media retains no residue from the original organic compounds found in the contaminated air stream. This is due to the extremely efficient microbial ecosystem that exists within the biofilter media. Enhancing and maintaining this rich microbial ecosystem is what biofiltration is all about. The choice of biofilter media is the key.

6.21.1 Principles of Biofiltration

Biofiltration uses micro-organisms to break down organic compounds (or to transform some inorganic compounds) into carbon dioxide, water and salts. When the biofilter is built, the micro-organisms are already on the material that is used as a filter bed. Nevertheless, in order to increase the degradation speed in the laboratories; the micro-organisms are introduced considering their efficiency in degrading the studied material.

The filter material is in general peat, soil, compost or heather, but granular activated carbon and polystyrene can also be used. The choice of the filter material is very important because it has to supply the micro-organisms in nutrients, to support biological growth and to have a good sorption capacity. The biological process is an oxidation by micro-organisms and can be written as follows:

$$\text{Organic Pollutant} + \text{Oxygen} \rightarrow CO_2 + H_2O + \text{Heat} + \text{Biomass}$$

The micro-organisms live in a thin layer of moisture, the biofilm, which is built around the particles of the filter material. The contaminated gas is diffused in the biofilter and absorbed onto the biofilm. This is the place where the oxidation process actually takes place. The contaminant is not permanently transferred to the filter material.

6.21.2 Advantages of Biofiltration

(1) The main advantage of using biofiltration over other more convention control methods are lower capital costs, lower operating costs, low chemical usage and no combustion source.
(2) Biofiltration units can be designed to physically fit into any industrial setting. A biofiltration unit can be designed as any shape, size or as an open field with the piping and delivery system underground. In addition, biofilters can be designed with stacked bed to minimize space requirements and multiple units can be run in parallel.
(3) Biofiltration is versatile enough to treat odors, toxic compounds and VOCs. The treatment efficiencies of these constituents are above 90% for low concentrations of contaminates (< 1000 ppm).
(4) Different media, microbes and operating conditions can be used to tailor a biofilter system for many emission points.

6.21.3 Disadvantages of Biofiltration

(1) Biofiltration can not successfully treat some organic compounds, which have low adsorption or degradation rates. This is especially true for chlorinated VOCs.
(2) Contaminant sources with high chemical emissions would require large biofilter units or open areas to install a biofiltration system.
(3) Sources with emissions that fluctuate severely or produce large spikes can be detrimental to the of a biofilter's microbial population and overall performance.
(4) Acclimation periods for the microbial population may take weeks or even months, especially for VOC treatment.

6.21.4 Commercial Applications

There have been over 50 commercial biofilters using compost-type material installed in Europe and the United States over the past 15 years.

VOC applications to date have included the following industries:
- Chemical and petrochemical industry.
- Oil and gas industry.
- Synthetic resins.
- Paint and ink.
- Pharmaceutical industry.
- Waste and waste water treatment.
- Soil and Ground water remediation.

Odor abatement applications to date have included the following industries:
- Sewage treatment.
- Slaughter houses.
- Rendering.
- Gelatin and glue plants.
- Agricultural and meat processing.
- Tobacco, cocoa and sugar industry.
- Flavour and fragrance.

6.22 Design of Filtration Units

In the design of filter presses, the following procedure is normally adopted:

(a) Study the slurry characteristics and process requirements and choose the type of filter press, filter medium, filter aids etc. to be used Table 6.1 and 6.2 can be of some help in this. Assume that it has been decided to use a plate and frame press (due to its low cost) and constant rate filtration (i.e. a positive displacement pump). Also, assume the cake to be incompressible.

(b) For constant rate filtration in a plate and frame press. The unknowns are α, R_m, cycle time (i.e., time of filtration + time of dismantling, cleaning and reassembling system), $-\Delta P$, area of filtration per frame, A' number of frames N, (i.e., A = NA') and dV/dt. μ and w' will be known from process conditions.

(c) Obtain α and R_m by a trial run on a small unit. Assume that the same values of α and R_m characterize the large-scale operation. This leaves cycle time, $-\Delta P$, A', N and dV/dt as the unknowns. (If it is preferred to work with V_e, the V_e/A in the large unit must be equated to the V_e/A obtained from small-scale runs, since V_e is directly proportional to the area of the filter medium).

(d) From the production rate desired (of filtrate or solids) and an assumed cycle time (time during which cleaning operations are carried out can be estimated from the time taken for individual operations), the desired dV/dt can be obtained. This leaves $-\Delta P$, A' and N as unknowns.

(e) Values of A' (usually based on available presses) and $-\Delta P_{maximum}$ can be assumed at the end of the filtration in each cycle (usually based on pumps available) and N computed.

Thus, there are three degrees of freedom which, in the above procedure, have been taken as cycle time, A' and $-\Delta P_{maximum}$. The optimum combination of these three variables is chosen.

Thereafter, the duties imposed by washing and drying of the cake may be checked.

Similar procedures can be written for other filter presses.

Table 6.1: Filtration Equipment Selection

	Slurry Characteristics	Fast Filtering	Medium Filtering	Slow Filtering	Dilute	Very Dilute
1.	Cake formation rate under vacuum	in the range of 25 mm/s (1 in./s)	in the range of 25 mm/min (1 in./min)	1.27 – 6.35 mm/min (0.05 – 0.25 in./min) 1–10%	< 1.27 mm/min (< 0.05 in./min)	very little
2.	Solids concentration	> 20%	10 – 20%	1 – 10%	< 5%	< 0.1%
3.	Settling rate of solids	very rapid	fast	slow	slow	negligible
4.	Filtrate rate under normal operation, m^3/m^2–hr (gallons/ft^2–min)	> 12.2 (>5)	0.49 – 12.2 (0.2 – 5)	0.025 – 0.05 (0.01 – 0.02)	0.025 – 4.9 (0.01 – 2)	0.025 – 4.9 (0.01 – 2)
	EQUIPMENT					
	Continuous Vacuum Filters					
	Multicompartment drum	x	x	x		
	Single compartment drum	x				
	Scroll discharge	x	x			
	Belt	x	x			
	Disc		x	x		
	Pre-coat				x	x
	Batch Vacuum Filters					
	Batch vacuum leaf		x	x	x	x
	Batch nutsche	x	x	x	x	x
	Continuous Pressure Pre-coat				x	x
	Batch Pressure Filters					
	Plate and Frame		x	x	x	x
	Vertical leaf		x	x	x	x
	Tubular		x	x	x	x
	Horizontal plate	x	x	x	x	x
	Catridge edge					x

MECHANICAL OPERATIONS — FILTRATION

Table 6.2: Characteristics of Various Filter Media

Type	Minimum Particle Size Retained, μm	Porosity %
Ceramics	1	30 – 50
Sintered metal	3	–
Perforated metal	100	20
Wire mesh	5	20
Plastic sheets	3	15 – 35
Plastic membranes	0.005	–
Synthetic cloths	10	50 – 60
Felt	10	–
Paper	5	60 – 95
Glass	2	–
Asbestos fibre	Sub-micrometer	80
Loose powders	–	80 – 90

6.23 Solved Examples

Example 6.1:

A plate and frame press filtering a slurry, gave a total of 25 m³ of filtrate in 30 minutes and 35 m³ in 60 minutes when filtration was stopped. Estimate the washing time in minutes if 10 m³ of wash water are used. The resistance of the cloth can be neglected and a constant pressure is used throughout.

Solution:

For constant pressure filtration with negligible cloth resistance, the basic equation becomes,

$$\frac{dV}{d\theta} = \frac{A^2 \, \Delta P}{2 \, C_v \, V}$$

with $\dfrac{A^2 \, \Delta P}{C_v}$ as a constant 'K',

$$\frac{dV}{d\theta} = \frac{K}{2V}$$

with integration, $\displaystyle\int_0^V 2V \, dV = \int_0^\theta K \, d\theta$

or
$$V^2 = K\theta$$

For, $\theta = 30$ minutes

$V = 25$ m³

∴ $(25)^2 = K(30)$

∴ $K = \dfrac{625}{30}$ m⁶/min

Filtration was complete at θ = 60 min. and V = 35 m³

∴ Final rate of filtration is,

$$\left(\frac{dV}{d\theta}\right)_f = \frac{K}{2V}$$

$$= \frac{625}{30 \times 2 \times 35} = 0.298 \text{ m}^3/\text{min.}$$

For a plate and frame press,

$$\text{Rate of washing} = \frac{1}{4} \times \text{Final rate of filtration}$$

$$= \frac{1}{4} \times 0.298 = 0.0745 \text{ m}^3/\text{min.}$$

$$\text{Washing time} = \frac{\text{Volume of wash water}}{\text{Rate of washing}}$$

$$= \frac{10}{0.0745} = 134.2 \text{ minutes} \quad \textbf{(Ans.)}$$

Example 6.2:

A rotary filter, operating at 2 r.p.m., filters 1000 lits/min. operating under the same vacuum and neglecting the resistance of the filter cloth at what speed must the filer be operated to give a filtration rate of 2000 lits/min. ?

Solution:

Let, V_R = Volume of filtrate collected per revolutions.

N_R = Number of revolutions/min.

$$\text{Volume of filtrate collected per unit time} = A_D \sqrt{\frac{2\phi N_R \Delta P}{\alpha \omega \mu}}$$

(where the terms have their usual meanings)

So,

$$(1000)^2 = A_D^2 \cdot \frac{2\phi N_R \Delta P}{\alpha \omega \mu}$$

$$= K N_R$$

where,

$$K = \frac{2 A_D^2 \phi \Delta P}{\alpha \omega \mu}$$

Let, N_R' = The new speed of the filter for the increased delivery.

So,

$$(2000)^2 = K \cdot N_R'$$

∴

$$\frac{(2000)^2}{(1000)^2} = \frac{K N_R'}{K N_R}$$

MECHANICAL OPERATIONS FILTRATION

or
$$\frac{4}{1} = \frac{N_R'}{N_R}$$

∴ $N_R' = 4 N_R = 4 \times 2 = 8$

So, the required speed of filter = 8 rpm. **(Ans.)**

Example 6.3:
A sludge forming a uniform non-compressible cake is filtered through a filter press out of which one frame is kept under study. At a constant pressure difference of 2.8 kg/cm², a 10 cm cake is formed in one hour with a filtrate volume of 6000 litres. Three minutes are needed to drain liquor from filter. Two minutes are needed to fill the filter with water. Washing proceeds exactly as filtration using 1200 litres. Opening dumpling and closing take 6 minutes. Assume the filtrate has the same properties of wash water and neglect the resistance offered by cloth and flow lines. How many liters of filtrate are produced in 24 hours on the average ?

Solution: It is constant pressure filtration processes,

$$\frac{dV}{d\theta} = \frac{A^2 \Delta P}{2 C_V (V + V_e)}$$

$$V_e = 0$$

with $\dfrac{A^2 \Delta P}{C_V} = K$

$$\frac{d_V}{d\theta} = \frac{K}{2V}$$

or, $\displaystyle\int_0^V 2V\, dV = K \int_0^\theta d\theta$

i.e. $V^2 = K\theta$
with $V = 6000$ liters
  $\theta = 1$ hour
  $(6000)^2 = K \cdot 60$

∴ $K = 6 \times 10^5$ (lit)²/min

Final rate of filtration = $\left(\dfrac{d_V}{d\theta}\right)_f = \left(\dfrac{K}{2V}\right)$

∴ $\left(\dfrac{d_V}{d\theta}\right)_f = \dfrac{6 \times 10^5}{2 \times 6000} = 50$ lit/min.

Rate of washing = $\dfrac{1}{4}\left(\dfrac{d_V}{d\theta}\right)_f = \dfrac{1}{4} \times 50$

| MECHANICAL OPERATIONS | FILTRATION |

$$= 12.5 \text{ lit/min.}$$

$$\text{Washing time} = \frac{1200}{12.5} = 96 \text{ min.}$$

Cycle time: Filtering time = 60 min.
Washing time = 96 min.
Draining time = 3 min.
Filling time = 2 min.
Opening, dumping and closing time = $\frac{6 \text{ min.}}{\text{Total time} = 167 \text{ min.}}$

In a cycle, which is completed in 167 minutes, amount of filtrate obtained = 6000 litres. Filtrate produced in 24 hours on the average is given by,

$$\frac{24 \times 60}{167} \times 6000 = 51736 \text{ liters} \qquad \text{(Ans.)}$$

Example 6.4:

A constant pressure filtrations test gave data that can fit an expression $\frac{dt}{dV} = 9.3\,V + 8.5$ (t = seconds, V = liters). If the resistance of the filter medium is assumed unaffected with pressure drop and the compressibility coefficient of the filter cake is 0.3, what will be the time taken for the collection of 3.5 liters of filtrate at a filtration pressure twice that used in the test?

Solution: Given:
$$\frac{dt}{dV} = 9.3\,V + 8.5 \qquad \ldots (1)$$

For filteration operation, we know
$$\frac{dt}{dV} = \frac{2V}{C} + \frac{2V_f}{C}$$

where, $\quad C = \dfrac{C_1 \Delta P}{\alpha}$

C_1 = Constant.
α = Specific cake resistance = $\alpha_0\,(\Delta P)^s$.
s = Compressibility coefficient.

Given that V_f is constant with changes in ΔP. Therefore,
$$C = \frac{C_1 \Delta P}{\alpha_0 (\Delta P)^{0.3}} = C_2 (\Delta P)^{0.7}$$

where, C_2 = Constant

Hence,
$$\frac{dt}{dV} = \frac{2V}{C_2\,(\Delta P)^{0.7}} + \frac{2V_f}{C_2\,(\Delta P)^{0.7}} \qquad \ldots (2)$$

Chp 6 | 6.31

On comparison of equations (1) and (2),

$$\frac{2V_f}{C_2 (\Delta P)^{0.7}} = 8.5 \text{ or } \frac{2V_f}{C_2} = 8.5 (\Delta P)^{0.7}$$

and $\quad \dfrac{2}{C_2 (\Delta P)^{9.3}}$ or $\dfrac{2}{C_2} = 9.3 (\Delta P)^{0.7}$

If pressure is doubled, $\Delta P_{new} = 2\Delta P$. Therefore,

$$\frac{2V_f}{C_2} = 8.5 (2\Delta P)^{0.7}$$

$$= 13.81 (\Delta P)^{0.7}$$

$$\frac{2V_f}{C_2 (\Delta P)^{0.7}} = 13.81 \qquad \ldots (3)$$

Similarly, $\quad \dfrac{2}{C_2} = 9.3 (2\Delta P)^{0.7}$

$$= 15.11 (\Delta P)^{0.7}$$

From equations (3) and (4), equation (2) becomes,

$$\frac{dt}{dV} = 15.11 \, V + 13.81$$

Integrating, and with the initial condition of $V = 0$ at $t = 0$,

$$t = 15.11 \frac{V^2}{2} + 13.81 \, V$$

Given: $V = 3.5$ litres. Therefore,

$$t = 15.11 \times \frac{3.5^2}{2} + 13.81 \times 3.5 = 140.9 \text{ seconds} \qquad \textbf{(Ans.)}$$

Example 6.5:

A filter press contains 20 frames, each of 0.6 m by 0.6 m inside dimensions. The frames are 0.025 m thick. The press is equipped with 1 and 3 button plates for washing. The volume of wash water used is 10% of the filtrate per cycle. The time required for filtering, at constant pressure, is 2 hours by which time the frames are full. Washing is done at the same pressure as filtering and the viscosity of wash water is nearly7 the same as that of filtrate. What is the time for washing? There is 0.05 m³ of final cake per m³ of filtrate. Neglect the resistance of the filter medium.

Solution: For constant pressure filtration:

$$\frac{d\theta}{dV} = K_p V + B$$

$$\therefore \quad \theta = K_p \frac{V^2}{2} + BV$$

$B = 0$ (Given: resistance of medium is negligible)

∴ $$\theta = \frac{K_p V^2}{2} \qquad \ldots (1)$$

∴ $$K_p = \frac{20}{V^2}$$

$$K_p = 2(2)/V^2 = 4/V^2$$

$$\theta = 2 \text{ hours}$$

$$V = \frac{0.6 \times 0.6 \times 0.025 \times 20}{0.05} = 3.6 \text{ m}^3$$

where, V = filtrate volume.
Numerator corresponds to cake volume.

∴ $$K_p = \frac{4}{V^2} = 0.3086$$

Now, washing rate for plate and frame filter is

$$\frac{dV_f}{d\theta} = \frac{1}{4} \times \frac{1}{K_p V_f + B}$$

$$= \frac{1}{4} \times \frac{1}{K_p V_f}$$

Now cake volume = $20 \times 0.6 \times 0.6 \times 0.025 = 0.18 \text{ m}^3$

Filtrate volume = $\frac{0.18}{0.05} = 3.6 \text{ m}^3$

Washing water used = $(0.1)(3.6) = 0.36 \text{ m}^3$

Equation (1) can be simplified to,

$$\frac{V_f^2}{2} = \frac{1}{4} \frac{\theta}{K_p}$$

$$V_f = 0.36 \text{ m}^3$$

$$K_p = 0.308$$

∴ $$\theta = (0.308)(0.36)^2 \times 2$$

$$\theta = 0.08 \text{ hours}$$

∴ time in min. = 0.08×60

$$t = 4.80 \text{ min.} \qquad \textbf{(Ans.)}$$

Example 6.6:

A rotary drum filter, operating at 0.03 Hz, filters 0.0075 m³/sec. operating under the same vacuum and neglecting the resistance of the filter cloth, at what speed must be filter be operated to give a filtration rate of 0.0160 m³/sec ?

Solution: For constant pressure filtration in a rotary filter:

$$V^2 = \frac{A^2 (-\Delta P)}{r \mu V} t$$

i.e.
$$V^2 \propto t \propto \frac{1}{N}$$

where, N is the speed of rotation

As $V \propto \frac{1}{\sqrt{N}}$ and the rate of filtration is $\frac{V}{t}$ then,

$$\frac{V}{t} \propto \left(\frac{1}{\sqrt{N}} \times \frac{1}{t}\right) \propto \left(\frac{1}{\sqrt{N}} \times N\right) \propto \sqrt{N}$$

$$\therefore \frac{(V/t)_1}{(V/t)_2} = \frac{\sqrt{N_1}}{\sqrt{N_2}}$$

$$\frac{0.0075}{0.0150} = \frac{\sqrt{0.03}}{\sqrt{N_2}}$$

$$\therefore N_2 = 0.12 \text{ Hz (7.2 rev/min.)} \qquad \textbf{(Ans.)}$$

Example 6.7:

A multi-compartment drum vacuum filter 1.83 m long and 1.22 m in diameter is used to filter the slurry. The drum rotates at 2 rpm and a fraction, f = 0.4 of the surface is immersed in the slurry. Find the rate of production of solids if the pressure inside the drum during the filtration part of the cycle is 6×10^4 N/m².

Data: $R_m = 9.4 \times 10^{-10}$ m^{-1},

$\propto = 3.34 \times 10^{10}$ m/kg.

Solution: Let the time for one rotations of drum be $t_c = 0.5$ min. During this rotation, any point on the filter medium remains immersed in the slurry for a time $t = f t_c$ during which it experiences a constant pressure filtration. In this case, the governing equations is,

$$\frac{1}{A} \cdot \frac{dv}{dt} = \frac{-\Delta P}{\mu\left[\frac{\propto w' V}{A} + R_m\right]} = -\frac{\Delta P}{\frac{\mu \propto w'}{A}[V + V_e]} \qquad \ldots (1)$$

Equation (1) may be integrated as,

$$\frac{\propto w'}{A} \int_0^V V dV + \frac{R_m}{A} \int_0^V dV = \frac{(-\Delta P)}{\mu} \int_0^t dt$$

or

$$\frac{\propto w'}{2}\left(\frac{V}{A}\right)^2 + R_m\left(\frac{V}{A}\right) = \frac{(-\Delta P) t}{\mu} = \frac{(-\Delta P)}{\mu} \times ft_c$$

$\left(\frac{V}{A}\right)$ gives the volume of filtrate collected per unit area of filter medium in one rotation. The above quadratic equation may be solved to give the positive root as,

$$\frac{V}{A} = \frac{\frac{-2R_m}{\propto w'} + \sqrt{\frac{4Rm^2}{\propto^2 w'^2} + \frac{4 \times 2 (-\Delta P) t_c f}{\mu \propto w'}}}{2}$$

Dividing by t_c, gives the average rate at which the filtrate is collected per unit area of medium.

$$\frac{1}{t_c}\frac{V}{A} = \left[\left(\frac{R_m}{\alpha w' t_c}\right)^2 + \frac{2(-\Delta P)f}{\mu \alpha w' t_c}\right]^{1/2} - \frac{R_m}{t_c \alpha w'}$$

Now,
$$t_c = 0.5 \text{ min}$$
$$f = 0.4$$
$$R_m = 9.4 \times 10^{-10} \text{ m}^{-1}$$
$$\frac{\mu \alpha w'}{2(-\Delta P)} = 1.025 \times 10^4 (0.186)^2 \frac{\text{min.}}{\text{m}^2} = 354 \frac{\text{min.}}{\text{m}^2}$$
$$\alpha w' = 3.34 \times 10^{10} \frac{\text{m}}{\text{kg}} \times 52.7 \frac{\text{kg}}{\text{m}^3} = 1.76 \times 10^{12} \text{ m}^{-2}$$

$$\frac{V}{A_{t_c}} = \left[\left(\frac{9.4 \times 10^{10} \text{ m}^2}{1.76 \times 10^{12} \text{ m} \times 0.5 \text{ min.}}\right)^2 + \frac{1 \text{m}^2}{354 \text{ min}} \times \frac{0.4}{0.5 \text{ min}}\right]^{\frac{1}{2}}$$

$$+ \frac{9.4 \times 10^{10} \text{ m}}{1.76 \times 10^{12} \times 0.5 \text{ min}} = 0.01 \frac{\text{m}^3}{\text{m}^2 \cdot \text{min.}}$$

∴ Mass of solids collected per minute

$= 0.01 \frac{\text{m}^3 \text{ filtrate}}{\text{m}^2 \cdot \text{min}} \times (3.142 \times 1.22 \times 1.83) \text{ m}^2 \times 52.7 \text{ Kg CaCO}_3/\text{m}^3 \text{ filtrate}$

$= 3.7 \text{ kg/min.}$ **(Ans.)**

Example 6.8:

A filtration is carried out for 10 min at a constant rate in a leaf filter and thereafter it is continued at constant pressure. This pressure is that attained at the end of the constant rate period. If one quarter of the total volume of the filtrate is collected during the constant rate period, what is the total filtration time? Assume that the cake is incompressible and the filter medium resistance is negligible.

Solution: We know,
$$\frac{d\theta}{dV} = \frac{2V}{C} + \frac{2V_f}{C} \qquad \ldots (1)$$

For filtration operation, where C is a function of DP and mean specific cake resistance (a).

i.e.,
$$C = \frac{C_1 DP}{a} \qquad \ldots (2)$$

C_1 is a constant. Specific cake resistance a is related to the compressibility coefficient (s) by the relation,

$$a = a_0 (DP)^s$$

where, a_0 is a constant. Equation (2) can be written as,

$$C = C_2 DP \text{ where } C_2 \text{ is a constant}$$

For an incompressible cake, s = 0; in other words, a is a constant.
If filter medium resistance is negligible, then, $V_f = 0$

$$\frac{d\theta}{dV} = \frac{2V}{C} \qquad \ldots (3)$$

$$\frac{d\theta}{dV} = \frac{2V}{C_2 \Delta P} \qquad \ldots (4)$$

Now the equation (1) can be written in the form,
For constant rate filtration,

$$\frac{dq}{dV} = \text{Constant} = \frac{q}{V}$$

Given: $\qquad q = 10$ min for $V = 0.25\ V_T$
Where, $\qquad V_T$ = total volume of filtrate
(filtrate collected in constant rate operation and constant pressure operation)

From equation (4), $\quad \dfrac{2V}{(C_2 DP)} = \dfrac{10}{(0.25\ V_T)} = \dfrac{40}{V_T}$

i.e. $\qquad DP = \dfrac{2V}{\dfrac{40 C_2}{V_T}} = V \dfrac{V_T}{(20 C_2)}$

DP at the end of constant rate operation

$$= \frac{0.25\ V_T^2}{(20 C_2)} = \frac{0.0125\ V_T^2}{C_2}$$

Constant Pressure Filtration:
For the given problem conditions,
$\qquad C_2 = $ Constant
and DP for the constant pressure operation is that obtained at the end of the constant rate operation. From equation (4),

$$\frac{dq}{dV} = \frac{2V}{(C_2 DP)}$$

$$= \frac{2V}{(0.0125\ V_T^2)} \qquad \ldots (5)$$

Integrating equation (5) between the limits
$\qquad V = 0.25\ V_T$ to V_T and $q = 10$ min to q_T

$$dq = \frac{\left(\dfrac{2}{0.0125\ V_T^2}\right)}{V dV}$$

$$q_T - 10 = \left(\frac{80}{V_T^2}\right) [V_T^2 - (0.25\ V_T)^2]$$

$$q_T = 10 + \left(\frac{80}{V_T^2}\right) \times 0.9375 \times V_T^2$$

$$q_T = 10 + 75 = 85 \text{ minutes}$$

Total filtration time = 85 minutes (Ans.)

Example 6.9:

In the production of a dyestuff, batches of product slurry are drained into a pressure filter, which is then pressurized to 600 kPa gauge with nitrogen, forcing the liquid through a pressure filter. The filtration takes 2 hours and 20 m^{-3} of filtrate is collected.

As part of a modernization scheme the pressure vessel is to be replaced by an unpressurized holding tank and a screw-type positive displacement pump. The rate of delivery of the latter is substantially independent of downstream pressure. The overall delivery rate of filtrate is to remain the same. If the filter medium will fail at a pressure differential of 900 kPa, is this proposal feasible?

Solution: Since there is no mention of cloth resistance, we will assume it is negligible. The original process is constant pressure filtration, described by the equation:

$$\frac{V_2^2}{2} = \frac{A^2 \Delta P}{r\mu\upsilon} t_2$$

Since in this case, $V_1 = 0$ at $t_1 = 0$. So,

$$\frac{A^2}{r\mu\upsilon} = \frac{V_2^2}{2\Delta P t_2} = \frac{20^2}{2 \times 600 \times 10^3 \times 7200} = 4.630 \times 10^{-8} \text{ m}^6/\text{Ns}$$

The new pump is a positive displacement one, so the filtration takes place at constant flow.

$$\max \Delta P = \frac{r\mu\upsilon}{A^2} \dot{V} V$$

$$\dot{V} = \frac{20}{7200} = 2.78 \text{ m}^2\text{s}$$

$$\Delta P = \frac{1}{4.630 \times 10^{-8}} \cdot 2.78 \times 10^{-3} \times 20$$

(Maximum pressure drop occurs at the end of filtration).

$$\Delta P = 1201 \times 10^3 \text{ N/m}^2$$

This operation will not be feasible because the pressure drop will be too great at the end of the filtration.

Example 6.10:

A rotary filter, operating at 2 rpm, produces 500 lit/min of filtrate. Operating with the same feed and under the same conditions of suction etc., at what speed must the filter be run to give a flowrate or 1000 lit/min? Ignore the resistance of the medium.

Solution: Consider an element of the filter. If the rotational speed of the filter is increased that element will spend less time per revolution immersed in the slurry. If the time spent per revolution in the slurry is θ then $\theta \propto \dfrac{1}{n}$ where, n is the rotational speed.

The volume of filtrate passing through the element per revolution will also decrease since, at constant ΔP.

Volume of filtrate per revolution $\propto \sqrt{\theta}$. So,

Volume of filtrate per revolution $\propto \dfrac{1}{\sqrt{n}}$.

However, there are also more revolutions in a given period so the total volume of filtrate collected, V, is related to speed by,

$$V \propto \dfrac{1}{\sqrt{n}} \cdot n \propto \sqrt{n}$$

Hence, to double filtrate flowrate the rotational speed must be quadrupled i.e. we need 8 rpm.

An Alternative Solution is as follows:

$$\text{Rate of filtration production} = \dfrac{\text{Rate of cake production}}{\upsilon}$$

$$= \dfrac{l \pi D_F \omega / 60}{\upsilon}$$

$$= \dfrac{\text{Thickness of cake} \times \text{Perimeter} \times \text{revs/s}}{\upsilon}$$

From the constant ΔP filtration equation,

$$V = \sqrt{\dfrac{2A^2 \Delta P t}{r \mu \upsilon}}$$

$$l = \dfrac{V \upsilon}{A}$$

where,

$$t = \dfrac{\alpha \times 60}{2 \pi \omega}$$

α = Angle of sector in slurry.

t = Time spent by an element in the slurry.

Therefore,

$$\text{Rate of filtrate production} = \dfrac{\pi D_F \omega}{60 \, \upsilon} \sqrt{\dfrac{60 \, \alpha \Delta P \upsilon}{\pi r \mu \omega}}$$

$$= \sqrt{\dfrac{\pi D_F^2 \omega \Delta P}{90 \, \upsilon r \mu}}$$

At present the flow rate of filtrate is 5001/min at 2 rpm so

$$\frac{0.5}{60} = \sqrt{\frac{2\pi D_F^2 \Delta P}{90 \upsilon r\mu}}$$

So, $\sqrt{\dfrac{D_F^2 \Delta P \pi}{60 \upsilon r\mu}} = 5.893 \times 10^{-3}$

Hence, to double production to 10001/min

$$\frac{1}{60} = 5.893 \times 10^{-3} \sqrt{\omega_2}$$

$$\omega_2 = 2.828^2 = 8 \text{ rpm} \qquad \text{(Ans.)}$$

Example 6.11:

A slurry is filtered in a plate and frame filter press comprising of 12 frames, each 0.3 m square and 0.025 m thick. During the first three minutes in each cycle the filtration pressure is slowly raised to the operating value of 4 bar, the rate of filtrate withdrawal is maintained at a constant value over this period.

Subsequently, filtration is carried out at constant pressure and the cakes are formed in another 15 min. They are then washed for 10 min at a constant pressure differential of 2.5 bar, using the same flow path as for the filtration.

Calculate the volume of filtrate collected and the volume of wash water consumed. The slurry had previously been subjected to a vacuum filter leaf test in which a 0.05 m² leaf was used with a constant vacuum of 0.7 bar. The volume of filtrate delivered in the first 5 minutes was 0.251 and after a further 5 minutes an additional 0.151 was collected.

Assume that the filter cake was incompressible and that the cloth resistance was the same for the leaf filter as for the full-scale filter. Also assume that filter and wash water viscosities are equal.

Solution: The filter leaf test allows $r\mu\upsilon$ and $r\mu L$ to be determined.

Constant pressure filtration equation is,

$$\frac{t_2 - t_1}{V_2 - V_1} = \frac{r\mu\upsilon}{2A^2\Delta P}(V_2 - V_1) + \frac{r\mu\upsilon V_1}{A^2\Delta P} + \frac{r\mu L}{A\Delta P}$$

In this case the second term on the right hand side of the equation, which has the term including V_1 can be eliminated by having V_1 and t_1 equal to 0. This gives the equation of a straight line of $\dfrac{t_2 - t_1}{V_2}$ Vs. V_2 with gradient $\dfrac{r\mu\upsilon}{2A^2\Delta P}$ and intercept $\dfrac{r\mu L}{A\Delta P}$.

For $t_2 = 5$ min and $V_2 = 0.251$.

$$\frac{5}{0.25} = \frac{r\mu\upsilon}{2A^2\Delta P} \cdot 0.25 + \frac{r\mu\upsilon}{A\Delta P} \qquad \ldots (1)$$

and for $t_2 = 10$ min and $V_2 = 0.41$

$$\frac{10}{0.4} = \frac{r\mu\upsilon}{2A^2\Delta P} \cdot 0.4 + \frac{r\mu\upsilon}{A\Delta P} \qquad \ldots (2)$$

NB you cannot use $t_1 = 5$ min and $t_2 = 10$ min without reintroducing the term eliminated from the original equation.

Subtracting equation (1) from (2)

$$25 - 20 = (0.4 - 0.25) \frac{r\mu\upsilon}{2A^2 \Delta P}$$

$$r\mu\upsilon = \frac{5}{0.15} \cdot 2A^2 \Delta P = 66.67 \times 0.05^2 \times 0.7 = 0.117$$

Substituting this value into equation (1),

$$20 = \frac{0.117}{2 \times 0.05^2 \times 0.7} \cdot 0.25 + \frac{r\mu L}{0.05 \times 0.7}$$

$$r\mu L = (20 - 8.357) \times 0.035$$
$$= 0.408$$

The units throughout have V in litres, t in minutes and ΔP in bars, for convenience.

Constant Rate Filtration equation for the first three minutes of filtration:

$$\Delta P = \frac{V_2 - V_1}{t_2 - t_1} \left\{ \frac{r\mu(\upsilon V + AL)}{A^2} \right\}$$

(Because $\dot{V}$ is constant and therefore, equal to $\frac{V_2 - V_1}{t_2 - t_1}$.)

$$\Delta P = \frac{r\mu\upsilon V}{A^2}\left(\frac{V_2 - V_1}{t_2 - t_1}\right) + \frac{r\mu AL}{A^2}\left(\frac{V_2 - V_1}{t_2 - t_1}\right)$$

$V_1 = 0$ at $t_1 = 0$ and $t_2 = 3$ min and $\Delta P = 4$ bar at the end of the filtration.

Filter area $= 2 \times 12 \times 0.3^2 = 2.16$ m² (each frame has 2 sides)

We want to find the value of $V_2 = V$ which satisfies these conditions.

$$4 = \frac{0.177\,V}{2.16^2} \cdot \frac{V}{3} + \frac{0.408}{2.16^2} \cdot 2.16 \cdot \frac{V}{3}$$

$$4 = 8.359 \times 10^{-3} + 0.063\,V$$

$$V = \frac{-0.063 \pm \sqrt{(0.063^2 + 4 \times 8.358 \times 10^{-3} \times 4)}}{2 \times 8.359 \times 10^{-3}} = 18.431$$

Subsequent constant pressure filtration:

Using the same equation as before:

$$\frac{t_2 - t_1}{V_2 - V_1} = \frac{r\mu\upsilon}{2A^2 \Delta P}(V_2 - V_1) + \frac{r\mu\upsilon V_1}{A^2 \Delta P} + \frac{r\mu L}{A \Delta P}$$

In this case V_1 is not equal to zero, $V_1 = 18.431$ and $t_1 - t_2 = 15$ min so:

$$\frac{15}{(V_2 - 18.43)} = \frac{0.117\,(V_2 - 18.43)}{2 \times 2.16^2 \times 4} + \frac{0.117 \times 18.43}{2.16^2 \times 4} + \frac{0.408}{2.16 \times 4}$$

$$\frac{15}{(V_2 - 18.43)} = 3.134 \times 10^{-3} V_2 - 0.0578 + 0.1156 + 0.04725$$

$$= 3.134 \times 10^{-3} V_2 + 0.105$$

$$15 = (3.134 \times 10^{-3} V_2 + 0.105)(V_2 - 18.43)$$

$$0 = 3.134 \times 10^{-3} V_2^2 + 0.0472 V_2 - 16.935$$

$$V_2 = \frac{-0.0472 \pm \sqrt{0.0472^2 + 4 \times 3.134 \times 10^{-3} \times 16.935}}{2 \times 3.134 \times 10^{-3}}$$

$$V_2 = \frac{-0.0472 \pm 0.463}{6.268 \times 10^{-3}}$$

Total filtrate delivered = 66.361

This includes the filtrate from the initial constant rate period.

Washing at constant pressure.

$$\left(\frac{dV}{dt}\right)_{wash} = \frac{A^2 \Delta P_{wash}}{r\mu\omega\upsilon V_F + r\mu AL}$$

$$\dot{V} = \frac{2.16^2 + 2.5}{0.117 \times 66.36 + 0.408 \times 2.16}$$

$$\therefore \quad \dot{V} = 1.35 \, l/min. \quad \textbf{(Ans.)}$$

So wash water used is 13.5 litres.

Example 6.12:

A filtration test was carried out, with a particular product slurry, on a laboratory filter press under a constant pressure of 340 kPa and volumes of filtrate were collected as follows:

Filtrate volume (kg)	20	40	60	80
Time (min)	8	26	54.5	93

The area of the laboratory filter was 0.186 m². In a plant scale filter, it is desired to filter a slurry containing the same material, but at 50% greater concentration than that used for the test, and under a pressure of 270 kPa. Estimate the quantity of filtrate that would pass through in 1 hour if the area of the filter is 9.3 m².

Solution: From the experimental data:

V (kg)	20	40	60	80
t (s)	480	1560	3270	5580
V/A (1/m²)	107.5	215	323	430
t/(V/A) (sm²kg⁻¹)	4.47	7.26	10.12	12.98

These values of t/(V/A) are plotted against the corresponding values of V/A in Fig. 6.11. From the graph, we find that the slope of the line is 0.0265, and the intercept is 1.6.

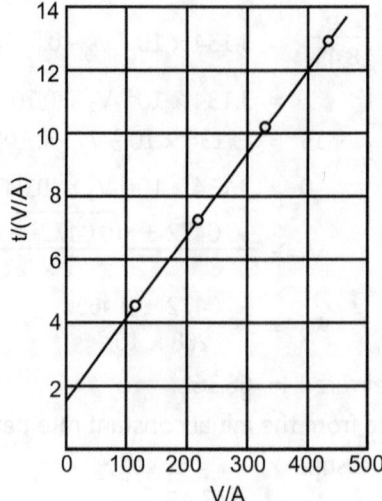

Fig. 6.11: Filtration Graph

Then substituting in equation we have,
$$t/(V/A) = 0.0265 (V/A) + 1.6$$
To fit the desired conditions for the plant filter, the constants in this equation will have to be modified. If all of the factors in equation except those which are varied in the problem are combined into constants, K and K', we can write
$$t/(V/A) = (w/\Delta P) K \times (V/A) + K'/\Delta P \qquad \ldots \text{(a)}$$
In the laboratory experiment $w = w_1$, and $\Delta P = \Delta P_1$
$$K = (0.0265\,\Delta P_1/w_1) \text{ and } K' = 1.6\,\Delta P_1$$
For the new plant condition, $w = w_2$ and $P = P_2$, so that, substituting in the equation (a) above, we then have for the plant filter, under the given conditions:
$$t/(V/A) = (0.0265\,\Delta P_1/w_1)(w_2/\Delta P_2)(V/A) + (1.6\,\Delta P_1)(1/\Delta P_2)$$
and since from these conditions:
$$\Delta P_1/\Delta P_2 = 340/270$$
and
$$w_2/w_1 = 150/100,$$
$$t/(V/A) = 0.0265\,(340/270)(150/100)(V/A) + 1.6\,(340/270)$$
$$= 0.05\,(V/A) + 2.0$$
$$t = 0.5\,(V/A)^2 + 2.0\,(V/A)$$
To find the volume that passes the filter in 1 hrs. which is 3600s, that is to find V for t = 3600.
$$3600 = 0.05\,(V/A)^2 + 2.0\,(V/A)$$
and solving this quadratic equation, we find that $V/A = 250$ kgm^{-2}
and so the slurry passing through 9.3 m² in 1 hrs. would be:
$$= 250 \times 9.3$$
$$= 2325 \text{ kg.} \qquad \textbf{(Ans.)}$$

Example 6.13:

The volumetric flow rate during constant pressure filtration is,

$$\frac{dV}{dt} = \frac{1}{K_cV + 1/q_0}$$

where, V is the total volume of filtrate collected in time t, and K_c and q_0 are constants.

(a) Integrate the above equation to obtain a relation between V and t.
(b) Make a sketch of t/V versus V from your results.
(c) Given V = 1.0 litre at t = 41.3 sec. and V = 2.0 litre at t = 108.3 sec, find K_c.

Solution: Given:
$$\frac{dV}{dt} = \frac{1}{K_cV + 1/q_0}$$

Let $Q_0 = 1/q_0$. Rearranging

$$(K_cV + Q_0)\, dV = dt$$

Integrating,

$$\int_0^V K_cV + Q_0\, dV = \int_0^t dt$$

$$K_cV^2/2 + Q_0V = t$$

$$K_c\frac{V}{2} + Q_0 = \frac{t}{V} \quad \ldots (1)$$

The above equation is represented in the sketch as given below:

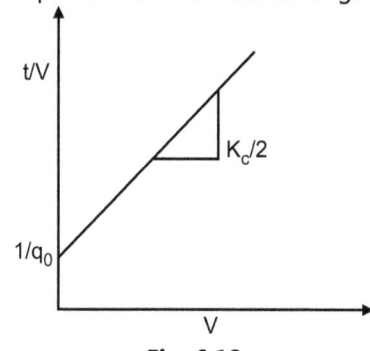

Fig. 6.12

Given: V = 1.0 litre at t = 41.3 sec and V = 2.0 litre at t = 108.3 sec. Substituting these in the equation (1)

$$K_c\frac{1}{2} + Q_0 = \frac{41.3}{1}$$

$$K_c\frac{2}{2} + Q_0 = \frac{108.3}{2}$$

Solving the above equations, K_c = 25.7 sec/ltr². **(Ans.)**

MECHANICAL OPERATIONS — FILTRATION

Example 6.14:
A leaf filter filtering a slurry, gave a total of 8 m³ filtrate in 30 minutes. Filtration was continued till 11.3 m³ of filtrate was collected. Estimate the washing time in minutes, if 11.3 m³ of wash water are used. The resistance of the cloth can be neglected and a constant pressure is used throughout.

Solution: Filteration equation:

$$\frac{d\theta}{dV} = \frac{2V}{C} + \frac{2V_f}{C}$$

Since filter-medium resistance is negligible, $V_f = 0$. Therefore,

$$\frac{d\theta}{dV} = \frac{2V}{C}$$

Integrating with the initial condition of $V = 0$ at $t = 0$,

$$\theta = V^2/C$$

Given: When $\theta = 30$ min, $V = 8$ m³. Therefore,

$$C = 8^2/30 = 64/30$$

Final rate of filtration = $(dV/d\theta)_{final} = \dfrac{C}{2V} = \dfrac{(64/30)}{2 \times 11.3} = 0.09$ m³/min.

Rate of washing = Final rate of filtration

Therefore,

$$\text{Washing time} = \frac{\text{Volume of wash water}}{\text{Rate of washing}} = \frac{11.3}{0.09} = 119.7 \text{ min.} \quad \textbf{(Ans.)}$$

(**Note:** Washing in 3-button plates is also referred to as through washing. If only 1 and 2 button plates are available, rate of washing equals the final rate of filtration).

Example 6.15:
Show that for a non-washing plate and frame filter press, operating at constant pressure with negligible filter medium resistance, the optimum cycle occurs when the time for filtering equals the time lost in opening, dumping, cleaning and reassembling the press.

Solution: For a filtration process

$$\frac{d\theta}{dV} = \frac{2V}{C} + \frac{2V_f}{C}$$

If filter medium resistance is negligible $2V_f/C$ term becomes zero. Therefore,

$$\frac{d\theta}{dV} = \frac{2V}{C}$$

Integrating $\qquad \theta = \dfrac{V^2}{C} = BV^2 \qquad \ldots (1)$

where, $B = 1/C$. Let θ' be the total time required in opening, dumping, cleaning and re-assembling the press, per cycle. Then,

$$\text{Overall rate of filtration (W)} = \frac{V}{\theta + \theta'}$$

MECHANICAL OPERATIONS   FILTRATION

where, V is the volume of filtrate collected per cycle.

$$W = \frac{V}{BV^2 + \theta'} \qquad \ldots (2)$$

W is maximum when dW/dV = 0. Hence, from equation (2),

$$\frac{dW}{dV} = \frac{(BV^2 + \theta') - V(2BV)}{(BV^2 + \theta')^2} = 0$$

Therefore, $BV^2 + \theta' - 2BV^2 = 0$

or $\theta' = BV^2$ ... (3)

Comparing equations (1) and (3)

$$\theta = \theta'$$

Therefore, optimum time cycle occurs while the time during which filtration is carried-out, is exactly equal to the time the filter press out of service.

In practice, in order to obtain the maximum overall rate of filtration, the filtration time must always be somewhat greater in order to allow for the resistance of the cloths.

Example 6.16:

In a filtration process, if V is the volume of filtrate collected in time t, a general relationship can be given as,

$$\frac{dt}{dV} = \frac{\mu}{A(\Delta P)}\left(\frac{\alpha cV}{A} + R_m\right)$$

where, α is the specific cake resistance, R_m is the filter medium resistance, A is the filter area, c is the concentration of solids in the slurry, μ is the viscosity of the filtrate and ΔP is the overall pressure drop.

(a) Filtration experiments were carried out at a constant pressure drop on a slurry containing 20 kg/m³ of $CaCO_3$ in water. The data obtained from the plots of t/V vs. V at two different pressure drops are given in the table below.

Pressure drop (N/m²)	Slope (s/litre²)	Intercpet (s/litre)
5 × 10⁴	12.5	26.5
35 × 10⁴	3.5	6.9

If the filter area is 0.09 m² and the viscosity of the filtrate is 0.001 kg/m.s, determine the specific cake resistance and the filter medium resistance corresponding to each pressure drop.

(b) Determine from the above data whether the cake is compressible.

Solution: Given:
$$\frac{dt}{dV} = \frac{\mu}{A(\Delta P)}\left(\frac{\alpha cV}{A} + R_m\right)$$

Chp 6 | 6.45

Substituting for the known quantities,

$$\frac{dt}{dV} = \frac{0.001}{0.09\,\Delta P}\left(\frac{\alpha \times 20 \times V}{0.09} + R_m\right)$$

$$= \frac{0.011}{\Delta P}(222.2\,V\alpha + R_m)$$

Rearranging and integrating the above equation,

$$t = \frac{0.011}{\Delta P}(111.1\,V^2\alpha + R_m V)$$

Rearranging,
$$\frac{t}{V} = \frac{1.22}{\Delta P}\alpha V + \frac{0.011}{\Delta P}R_m \qquad \ldots (1)$$

If $\Delta P = 5 \times 10^4$ N/m, equation (1) becomes,

$$\frac{t}{V} = \frac{1.22}{5 \times 10^4}\alpha V + \frac{0.011}{5 \times 10^4}R_m$$

$$= 2.44 \times 10^{-5}\,\alpha V + 2.2 \times 10^{-7}\,R_m \qquad \ldots (2)$$

From equation (2), slope = $2.44 \times 10^{-5}\,\alpha$.

Given: Slope = 12.5 s/ltr² = 12.5×10^6 s/m⁶. Therefore,

$$2.44 \times 10^{-5}\,\alpha = 12.5 \times 10^6$$

Solving, $\alpha = 5.123 \times 10^{11}$ m/kg. From equation (2), intercept = $2.2 \times 10^{-7}\,R_m$.

Given: Intercept = 26.5 s/ltr = 26.5×10^3 s/m³ Therefore,

$$2.2 \times 10^{-7}\,R_m = 26.5 \times 10^3 \qquad \ldots (3)$$

Solving, $R_m = 12.05 \times 10^{10}$ m⁻¹.

If $\Delta P = 35 \times 10^4$ N/m² equation (1) becomes,

$$\frac{t}{V} = \frac{1.22}{35 \times 10^4}\alpha V + \frac{0.011}{35 \times 10^4}R_m$$

$$= 34.86 \times 10^{-7}\,\alpha V + 0.314 \times 10^{-7}\,R_m$$

From equation (3), slope = $34.86 \times 10^{-7}\,\alpha$.

Given: Slope = 3.5 s/ltr² = 3.5×10^6 s/m⁶ Therefore,

$$34.86 \times 10^{-7}\,\alpha = 3.5 \times 10^6$$

Solving, $\alpha = 10 \times 10^{11}$ m/kg. From equation (3), intercept = $0.314 \times 10^{-7}\,R_m$.

Given: Intercept = 6.9 s/ltr = 6.9×10^3 s/m³. Therefore,

$$0.314 \times 10^{-7}\,R_m = 6.9 \times 10^3$$

Solving, $R_m = 21.97 \times 10^{10}$ m⁻¹.

Since α changes with ΔP, the cake is compressible. **(Ans.)**

EXERCISE FOR PRACTICE

(1) A sludge filtered in a washing plate and frame press, is of such a nature that the filtration equation is $V^2 = K\theta$, where V is the volume of filtrate obtained in time θ, when the pressure is constant 30 m³ of filtrate is produced in 10 hours.
  (a) 3 m³ of wash water is forced through the cake at the end of filtration. Estimate the washing time.
  (b) If the filtering surface of the press is doubled, all other conditions remains constant, how long would it take to produce 30 m³ of filtrate?

(Ans.: (a) 8 hours, (b) 2.5 hours)

(2) A plate and frame press, filtering a slurry, gave a total of 8m³ of filtrate in 1800 second and 11 m³ in 3600 seconds, when filtration was stopped. Estimate the washing time in seconds if 3m³ of wash water is used. The resistance of cloth can be neglected and a constant pressure is used throughout.

(Ans.: 8400 seconds (2.3 hours))

(3) A rotary drum filter 1.2 m diameter and 1.2 m long can handle 6 kg/sec of slurry containing 10% of solids when rotated at 0.005 Hz. By increasing the speed to 0.008 Hz, it is found that it can handle 7.2 kg/sec. What will be the percentage change in the amount of wash water which can be applied to each kg of cake caused by the increase of speed? What are the limitations to increased production by increase in the speed of rotation of drum and what is the theoretical maximum quantity of slurry which can be handled?

(Ans.: % increase = 4.17, the highest rate will be achieved when V tends to 0, 18 kg/s)

(4) The following filtrations data were obtained on a 5% (by weight) $CaCO_3$ slurry in water using 4.14×10^4 N/m² pressure differential.

Filtrate Collected (kg)	Time interval (min.)
0	0
2.275	0.70
4.55	0.52
6.825	0.65
9.08	0.75
11.37	1.00
13.65	1.08

The filtration area was 0.186 m². Calculate (a) α, (b) (Ve/A), and (c) Rm.

$$\text{Ans.}: \alpha = 3.34 \times 10^{10} \text{ m/kg}, \left(\frac{Ve}{A}\right) = 0.0529 \text{ m}, R_m = 9.40 \times 10^{-10} \text{ m}^{-1}$$

(5) A leaf filter, filtering a slurry, gave a total of 8 m³ of filtrate in 30 min. Filtration was continued till 11.3 m³ of filtrate was collected. Estimate the washing time in minutes, if 11.3 m³ of wash water are used. The resistance of the cloth can be neglected and a constant pressure is used throughout.

(6) A filter press contains 20 frames, each of 0.6 m by 0.6 m inside dimensions. The frames are 0.025 m thick. The press is equipped with 1 and 3 button plates for washing. The volume of wash water used is 10% of the filtrate per cycle. The time required for filtering at constant pressure is 2 hours by which time the frames are full. Washing is done at the same pressure as filtering and the viscosity of wash water is nearly the same as that of the filtrate. What is the time for washing? There is 0.05 m³ of final cake per m³ of filtrate. Neglect the resistance of the filter medium.

(7) A constant pressure filtration test gave data that can fit an expression, dt/dV = 9.3V + 8.5; (t in seconds; V in litres). If the resistance of the filter medium is assumed unaffected with pressure drop and the compressibility coefficient of the filter cake is 0.3, what will be the time taken for the collection of 3.5 litres of filtrate at a filtration pressure twice that used in the test?

(8) Show that for a no washing plate and frame filter press, operating at constant pressure with negligible filter medium resistance, the optimum cycle occurs when the time for filtering equals the time lost in opening, dumping, cleaning and reassembling the press.

(9) An experimental filter press having an area of 0.041 m² is used to filter aqueous BaCO₃ slurry at a constant pressure of 267 kPa. The filtration equation was obtained as:

$$t/V = 10.25 \times 10^6 V + 3.4 \times 10^6$$

Where, t is in sec and V is in m³. If the same slurry and conditions are used in a leaf press having an area of 6.97 m², how long will it take to obtain 1.00 m³ of filtrate?

(10) In a plate and frame filter (no cloth resistance) it takes 2 hour 15 minutes to filter 18 m³ of suspension. Filter cake is washed with 2 m³ of water having viscosity of filtrate. If washing velocity is 1/4ᵗʰ of the filtration velocity at the final moment, calculate washing time.

(11) Data for laboratory filtration of CaCO₃ slurry in water at 298 K are reported as follows at a constant pressure (–ΔP) of 338 kN/m². The filter area of the plate and frame press was 0.04329 m² and the slurry concentration was C_s = 23.4 kg/m³. Calculate the constant α and R_m from the experimental data given, where t is time in S and V is filtrate volume collected in m³.

t (s)	V (m²)
4.4	0.498 × 10⁻³
9.5	1.000 × 10⁻³
16.3	1.501 × 10⁻³
24.6	2.000 × 10⁻³
34.7	2.498 × 10⁻³
46.1	3.002 × 10⁻³
59.0	3.506 × 10⁻³
73.6	4.004 × 10⁻³
89.4	4.502 × 10⁻³
107.3	5.009 × 10⁻³

(Ans.: $\alpha = 1.86 \times 10^{11}$ m/kg; $R_m = 10.63 \times 10^{10}$ m⁻¹)

(12) The same slurry used in above example to filtered in a plate-and-frame press having 20 frames and 0.873 m² area per frame. The same pressure will be used in constant-pressure filtration. Assuming the same filter cake properties and filter cloth, calculate the time to recover 3.37 m³ filtrate. Use the experimental data of time, t and volume collected, V from above example. **(Ans.: 270 sec.)**

(13) A centrifuge having a radius of the bowl of 0.1016 m is rotating at speed, N = 100 r/min.
   (a) Calculate the centrifugal force developed in tempers in gravity forces.
   (b) Compare this force to that for a bowl with a radius of 0.2032 m rotating at the same r/min.

$$\left[\text{Ans.} : (a)\ \frac{F_c}{g} = 113.6\ \text{gravities};\ (b)\ \frac{F_c}{F_g} = 227.2\ \text{gravities} \right]$$

(14) The following filtration data were obtained on a 5% (by weight) $CaCO_3$ slurry in water using a 4.14×10^4 N/m² gauge (6 psig) pressure differential.

Filtrate Collection (kg)	Time Interval hour
0	0
2.275	0.70
4.55	0.52
6.825	0.65
9.08	0.75
11.37	1.00
13.65	1.08

The filtration area was 0.186 m² obtain α, (V_e/A) and R_m

$$\left[\text{Ans.} : \alpha = 3.34 \times 10^{10}\ \text{m/kg},\ V_e/A = 0.0529\ \text{m},\ R_m = 9.40 \times 10^{10}\ \text{m}^{-1} \right]$$

(15) In filtration the pressure drop through the cake and the flowrate of filtrate are related by –

$$\frac{1}{A}\frac{dV}{dT} = \frac{\Delta P}{r\mu l}$$

V = Volume of filtrate produced upto time t.
r = Specific cake resistance.
A = Filter area.
l = Cake thickness.

Show that –

$$\frac{dV}{dt} = \frac{A^2 \Delta P}{r\mu \upsilon V}$$

Given that V is the volume of cake deposited from unit volume of filtrate.

(16) The resistance of the filter medium can be represented by an equivalent thickness of cake. Use this representation to show that, for a constant pressure drop ΔP.

$$\frac{t_2 - t_1}{V_2 - V_1} = \frac{r\mu\upsilon}{2A^2\Delta P}(V_2 - V_1) + \frac{r\mu\upsilon V_1}{A^2\Delta P} + \frac{r\mu L}{A\Delta P}$$

If L is the cake thickness equivalent to the filter medium.
How is this equation used to evaluate rμL and rμL from experimental data?

(17) The data below was obtained from a vacuum filter leaf experiment. The pressure drop was a constant 0.8 bar and the filter areas was 0.06 m².

A full size filter is to be specified to filter the same slurry so that filtrate is produced at 1 m² per minute. The filter medium is known to the double the resistance of the material used in the filter leaf.

If the pressure drop across the filter cannot exceed 3 bar and the filter must operate for at least 30 minutes before cleaning, what filter area is required?

(18) The slurry contains 10% by weight solids with a density of 2400 kgm³. The cake voidage of 0.36 and the liquid may be taken to be water.

If the design of the filter is such that the cake thickness cannot exceed 15 cm what filter area is required?

DATA

Time (min)	Total Filtrate Volume
0	0
5	0.048
10	0.070
15	0.087
20	0.101

(19) In filtration the Carman-Kozeny equation relates filtrate delivery rate and pressure drop at any instant. Where the filter medium presents an appreciable resistance this equation takes the form:

$$\frac{1}{A}\frac{dV}{dt} = \frac{\Delta P}{r\mu(1+L)}$$

where,

A = Filter area
t = Filtration time
r = Specific cake resistance
1 = Cake thickness
V = Total volume of filtrate delivered
ΔP = Pressure drop across cake and medium
μ = Filtrate viscosity
L = Thickness of cake equivalent to medium resistance

Show that, for constant pressure filtration starting at $t = 0$ and $V = 0$, the following equation relates time and volume of filtrate delivered. v is the volume of cake produced per unit volume of filtrate delivered.

$$\frac{t}{V} = \frac{r\mu V}{2A^2\Delta P} + \frac{r\mu L}{A\Delta P}$$

(20) A sludge is filtered in a plate and frame press fitted with 25 mm frames.
(Case 1): For the first 10 min the slurry pump runs at maximum capacity. During this period the pressure rises to 415 kN/m² and a quarter of the total filtrate is obtained. The filtration takes a further 60 min to complete at constant pressure at 15 min is required for emptying and resetting the press. (Case 2): It is found that if the cloths are precoated with filter aid to a depth of 1.6 mm, the cloth resistance is reduced to a quarter of its former value. What will be the increase in the overall throughput of the press if the precoat can be applied in 3 min. ?
Case 1 gives a total cycle time of 5100s.
Case 2 gives a total cycle time of 4083s.

(21) A slurry is filtered in a plate and frame press containing 12 frames, each 0.3 m square and 25 mm thick. During the first 3 min, the pressure difference for the filtration is slowly raised to the final value of 400 kN/m² and during this period, the rate of filtration is maintained constant. After the initial period, filtration is carried out at a constant pressure and the cakes are completely formed in a further 15 min. the cakes are then washed with a pressure difference of 275 kN/m² for 10 min, using through washing. What is the volume of the filtrate collected per cycle and how much wash water is used? A sample of the slurry had previously been tested with a leaf filter of 0.05 m² filtering surface using a vacuum giving a pressure difference of 71.3 kN/m². The volume of filtrate collected in the first 5 min was 250 cm³ and, after a further 5 min, an additional 150 cm³ was collected. Assume the cake to be incompressible and the cloth resistance to the same as in the filter press.

NOMENCLATURE

Symbol	
A	Area, m²; A_T, total area of continuous filter; A_1, area of inner surface of material in centrifuge; A_2, Area of outer surface of material in centrifuge; $\bar{A}_L$, logarithmic mean of A_1 and A_2; $\bar{A}_a$, arithmetic mean of A_1 and A_2.
b	Width of centrifugal basket, m.
c	Mass of solid deposited in filter per unit volume of filtrate, kg/m³; also concentration of solids in suspension, kg/m³, gm/lit.
F	Feed rate, kg/hr; also force N; F_c, centrifugal force; F_g, force of gravity.
f	Fraction of filter cycle available for cake formation.
g	Acceleration of gravity, m/s²
k_c	Constant in equation for constant-pressure cake filtration, define by equation (6.18).
k_r	Constant in equation for constant-rate filtration, equation (6.26).

Symbol	
k_1, k_2	Constants in equations (6.14) and (6.15) respectively.
L	Distance in cake measured from filter medium, m; L_c, filter cake thickness.
m	Mass, kg, m_F, mass of filter cake; m_c, mass of solids in filter cake.
$\dot{m}$	Mass flow rate, kg/hr; $\dot{m}_c$, of solids from continuous filter.
n	Drum speed of continuous filter, r/s
p	Pressure, atm; pressure in cake at distance L from filter medium; p_a, at inlet to filter; p_b, at discharge from filter; p', at boundary between cake and medium in filter.
q	Volumetric flow rate, m³/s; corresponding to removal of particles of cut diameter; q_o, at start of filtration.
R_m	Filter-medium resistance, m^{-1}.
r	Radius, m; r_e, effective average value; r_i, of interface between cake and liquid layer in centrifuge; r_o, of particle; r_1; inner radius of material in centrifuge; r_2, outer radius of material in centrifuge.
s	Thickness of liquid layer in centrifuge, m; S_e, effective average value; also compressibility coefficient [Equation (6.21)].
T	Absolute temperature, K
t	Time, hr or s; t_T, residence time in centrifuge; t_c, cycle time in continuous filter.
V	Volume, m³, liter; also volume of filtrate collected to time t.
Greek Letters:	
α	Specific cake resistance, m/kg; $α_o$, constant in equation (6.13).
ΔP	Overall pressure drop through cake, p_a – p'. Pressure drop through filter medium, p' – p_b.
Δπ	Difference in osmotic pressure, atm.
ε	Porosity or volume fraction voids in bed of solids, dimensionless; $\bar{ε}$, average porosity of filter cake.
∝	viscosity, cP
≠	Osmotic pressure, atm.
ρ	Density; kg/m³; of fluid or filtrate; $ρ_p$, of particle; $ρ_{pA}$ of heavy particle; $ρ_{pB}$, of light particle.
ω	Angular velocity, rad/s.

***

Unit VII

Chapter 7: SEPARATION BASED ON MOTION OF PARTICLES THROUGH THE FLUIDS

(A) GRAVITY SETTLING PROCESS

7.1 Introduction

Many methods of mechanical separation are based on the movement of solid particles or liquid drops through a fluid. The fluid may be gas or liquid; it may be flowing or at rest. In some situations the objective of the process is to remove particles form a stream of fluid in order to eliminate contaminants from the fluid or to recover the particles, as in the elimination of dust and fumes from air or flue gas or the removal of solids from liquid wastes. In other problems, particles are deliberately suspended in fluids to obtain separations of the particles into fractions differing in size or density. The fluid is then recovered, sometimes for reuse, from the fractionated particles. The principles of particle mechanics that underlie the operations described here are discussed. It is evident that if a particle starts at rest with respect to the fluid in which it is immersed and is then moved through the fluid by an external force, its motion can be divided into two stages. The first stage is a short period of acceleration, during which the velocity increases from zero to the terminal velocity. The second stage is the period during which the particle is at its terminal velocity.

Since the period of initial acceleration is short, usually of the order of tenths of a second or less, initial acceleration effects are short range. Terminal velocities, on the other hand, can be maintained as long as the particle is under treatment in the equipment. Some separation methods, such as jigging and tabling, depend on differences in particles behavior during the acceleration period. Most common methods, however, including all those described here, make use of the terminal velocity period only.

7.2 Relative Motion Between Particles and Fluids

Particle-Fluid Systems:

For a small, spherical particle in a fluid stream the drag force F_D is usually expressed in terms of a drag coefficient C_D defined by:

$$C_D = \frac{F_D}{\frac{1}{2}\rho u_{fs}^2 (\pi/4) D_p^2} = \frac{2F_D}{A\rho u^2} \qquad \ldots (7.1)$$

where, u_{fs} is the relative velocity between the solid and the fluid, D_p is the particle diameter, A is the particle projected area and ρ is the fluid density. This is similar to the pipe friction factor. C_D is a function of the particle Reynolds number $Re' = \dfrac{uD_p\rho}{\mu}$.

In the viscous range, where $Re' < 2$.

$$C_D = \frac{24}{Re'} \qquad \ldots (7.2)$$

so
$$F_D = \frac{1}{2} C_D \rho u_{fs}^2 \frac{\pi D_p^2}{4} = \frac{1}{2} \frac{24\mu}{u_{fs} D_p \rho} \rho u_{fs}^2 \frac{\pi D_p^2}{4} \qquad \ldots (7.3)$$

and
$$F_D = 3\pi\mu D_p u_{fs} \text{ which is Stoke's Law} \qquad \ldots (7.4)$$

At larger values of Re' other relationships between C_D and Re' must be used.

For $Re' < 800$ (or above, with less accuracy).

$$C_D = \frac{24}{Re'} (1 + 0.15\, Re'^{0.687}) \qquad \ldots (7.5)$$

Alternatively for, $2 < Re' < 200$ $C_D = 18\, Re'^{-0.6}$

When $2000 < Re' < 200000$ $C_D = 0.44$

Somewhere between $Re' = 10^5$ and $Re' = 10^6$ C_D drops sharply, due to turbulence in the boundary layer. It is most unlikely that you will encounter this effect.

In order for Stokes' Law to apply particles must be small enough to have terminal velocities in the laminar region. The maximum particle size to be in the Stokes' Law regime, d_{max}, is derived as follows.

Terminal velocity in the Stokes' Law regime is found by equating drag and gravity forces on the particle.

From the definition of drag coefficient, C_D, the drag force is,

$$F_D = \frac{1}{8} D_p^2 \rho_f u_{fs}^2 \pi C_D \qquad \ldots (7.6)$$

The gravitational force is,

$$F_g = \frac{\pi D_p^3}{6} (\rho_s - \rho_p) g \qquad \ldots (7.7)$$

Equating these gives,

$$\frac{1}{8} D_p^2 \rho_f u_{fs}^2 \pi C_D = \frac{\pi D_p^3}{6} (\rho_s - \rho_p) g \qquad \ldots (7.8)$$

$$C_D = \frac{24}{Re'} \qquad \ldots (7.9)$$

MECHANICAL OPERATIONS SEPARATION BASED ON MOTION ......

Since this is the laminar region

$$\frac{1}{8} D_p^2 \rho_f u_{fs}^2 \pi \frac{24}{Re'} = \frac{\pi D_p^3}{6} (\rho_s - \rho_p) g \qquad \ldots (7.10)$$

which gives,

$$D = \frac{18 \rho_f u_{fs}^2}{Re' (\rho_s - \rho_f) g} \qquad \ldots (7.11)$$

We already know that if Stokes' law applies the terminal velocity is given by,

$$u_{fs} = u_t = \frac{D_p^2}{18 \mu} (\rho_s - \rho_f) g \qquad \ldots (7.12)$$

$$D = \frac{18}{Re'} \left(\frac{D_p^2 (\rho_s - \rho_f) g}{18 \mu} \right)^2 \frac{\rho_f}{(\rho_s - \rho_f)} \qquad \ldots (7.13)$$

$$\frac{D}{D^4} = \frac{1}{18 Re'} \frac{(\rho_s - \rho_f) g}{\mu^2} \rho_f \qquad \ldots (7.14)$$

$$D = \left[\frac{18 Re \, \mu^2}{(\rho_s - \rho_f) g \rho_f} \right]^{\frac{1}{3}} \qquad \ldots (7.15)$$

Setting Re' to its maximum value of 2 gives,

$$D_{max} = \left[\frac{36 \mu^2}{(\rho_s - \rho_f) g \rho_f} \right]^{\frac{1}{3}} \qquad \ldots (7.16)$$

This result is for spherical particles only.

For particles with diameter greater than D_{max} the terminal velocity will be such that Re' > 2 so that Stokes' law will not apply. It is more difficult to determine terminal velocity for particles outside the Stokes' region because in order to determine C_D and hence F_D one must know Re'. In order to calculate Re' u_{fs} is needed, which is what we were trying to find originally. For a spherical particle under gravity the terminal velocity is found by equating drag and gravity forces as before:

$$\frac{\pi}{6} D_p^3 (\rho_s - \rho_f) g = C_D \frac{1}{2} \rho_f u_t^2 \frac{\pi}{4} D_p^2 \qquad \ldots (7.17)$$

Hence,

$$\frac{D_p}{6} (\rho_s - \rho_f) g = \frac{C_D}{8} \rho_f u_t^2$$

So,

$$u_t = \left[\frac{4}{3} D_p \frac{(\rho_s - \rho_f) g}{C_D \rho_f} \right]^{\frac{1}{2}} \qquad \ldots (7.18)$$

And

$$C_D = \frac{4}{3} D_p \frac{(\rho_s - \rho_f) g}{u_t^2 \rho_f} \qquad \ldots (7.19)$$

This does not immediately solve the problem of C_D being a function of u_t. It is convenient to define a dimensionless group N_D which eliminates u_t from C_D and Re' as follows.

$$N_D = Re'^2 C_D = \left(\frac{\rho_f u_t D_p}{\mu}\right)^2 \frac{4}{3} \frac{D_p (\rho_s - \rho_f) g}{\rho_f u_t^2} \qquad \ldots (7.20)$$

$$N_D = Re'^2 C_D = \frac{4}{3} \frac{D_p^3 (\rho_s - \rho_f) g \rho_f}{\mu^2} \qquad \ldots (7.21)$$

N_D can be calculated and there are correlations between N_D and Re' and C_D available in the literature. Once N_D has been calculated Re' may be obtained from the correlation and hence u_t is calculated.

Classification:

Just as the fact that particles settle at different speeds is used in size determination it can also be used to separate different materials. The problem when separating different materials as that settling velocity depends on both size and density i.e. small dense particles fall as fast as large light ones. To achieve a perfect separation, the smallest particle of the larger density must have a terminal velocity greater than that of the largest particle of the lower density:

(Assuming Stokes' Law behaviour)

$$\frac{d_{min}^2 (\rho_1 - \rho_f) g}{18 \mu} > \frac{d_{max}^2 (\rho_2 - \rho_f) g}{18 \mu} \qquad \ldots (7.22)$$

where, ρ_1 and ρ_2 are the solid densities, with $\rho_1 > \rho_2$.

So,
$$\frac{d_{max}}{d_{min}} < \sqrt{\frac{(\rho_1 - \rho_f)}{(\rho_2 - \rho_f)}} \qquad \ldots (7.23)$$

This is known as the *Free-settling ratio*.

The term "classification" is used to designate separation of solid particles based on the difference in their terminal settling velocities in a fluid. Since the terminal settling velocity of a particle in a fluid depends both on its size as well as density, separation is affected based on both size and density. If particles of same density are separated according to their sizes, the operation is often termed as sizing. Sizing is thus a possible alternative to screening. If materials of same equivalent size are separated according to their densities, the operation is called sorting.

The basic criterion therefore required for separating two Materials by classification is that their terminal settling velocities in a given fluid must not be equal. Particles (say, A and B) having the same terminal settling velocity in a fluid are called "equally falling" particles. The ratio of sizes of A and B when they are equally falling is called the *settling ratio*. If the particles are spherical, the expression for settling ratio can be derived as follows:

Since, the particles are equally falling,

$$V_{tA} = V_{tB} \qquad \ldots (7.24a)$$

$$\left(\frac{4}{3}\right)\left[\frac{\rho_A - \rho_f}{\rho_f}\right]\frac{gd_A}{f_{DA}} = \left(\frac{4}{3}\right)\left[\frac{\rho_B - \rho_f}{\rho_f}\right]\frac{gd_B}{f_{DB}} \qquad \ldots (7.24b)$$

or
$$(d_A/d_B) = [(\rho_B - \rho_f)/(\rho_A - \rho_f)][f_{DA}/f_{DB}] \qquad \ldots (7.25)$$

If the settling zone is laminar, we know that $f_D = 24/Re_p$. Therefore,

$$(f_{DA}/f_{DB}) = (Re_p)_B/(Re_p)_A = (d_B/d_A) \qquad \ldots (7.26)$$

Substituting in equation (7.25) we get,

$$(d_A/d_B)^2 = (\rho_B - \rho_f)/(\rho_A - \rho_f) \qquad \ldots (7.27)$$

Similarly, in the turbulent zone ($1000 < Re_p < 200,000$), f_D is essentially, constant and independent of Re_p. Therefore, $f_{DA} = f_{DB}$.

Equation (7.25) then becomes,

$$(d_A/d_B) = (\rho_B - \rho_f)/(\rho_A - \rho_f) \qquad \ldots (7.28)$$

If the settling ratio of two particles is equal to that computed from equation (7.25) then these particles cannot be separated by classification using that particular fluid in question. A large settling ratio is therefore desirable to permit separation of material having wide size, ranges. One way of accomplishing this is to use a fluid of high density as the settling medium. Density of water can be increased by adding, salts to it, but this could increase corrosion problems. Use of suspensions such as magnetite suspensions in water or suspension of galena fines in water as the settling media helps in increasing the settling ratio (since the bulk density ρ_b of a suspension is much larger than that of a pure liquid) and thereby in achieving sharper separation of materials. It can be seen from equation (7.25) when the density of fluid approaches that of one of the solid materials, the settling ratio approaches infinity and therefore it will be possible to sort particles of any size range. The ratio of the average size of the largest particle in the mixture to that of the smallest particle is termed as the size ratio and if the settling ratio is equal to the size ratio, complete separation is possible.

7.3 Gravity Settling Processes

Particles heavier than the suspending fluid may be removed from a gas or liquid in a large setting box or settling tank, in which the fluid velocity is low and the particles have ample time to settle out. Simple devices of this kind, however, have limited usefulness because of the incompleteness of the separation and the labour required to remove the settled solids from the floor of the vessel. Industrial separators nearly all provide for the continuous removal of settled solids. The separation may be partial or very nearly complete. A settler that removes virtually all the particles from a liquid is known as a clarifier, whereas a device, which separates the solids into two fractions, is called a classifier. The same principles of sedimentation apply to both kinds of equipment.

7.3.1 Gravity Classifiers

Most classifiers in chemical processing separate particles on the basis of size, in situations in which the density of the fine particles is the same as that of the larger ones. The elutriation leg of the crystallizer is an example. By adjusting the upward velocity of the liquid so that it is smaller than the terminal settling velocity of acceptably large crystals, this device carries unwanted fine crystals back to the crystallizing zone for further growth. Mechanical classifiers are extensively used in closed circuit grinding especially in metallurgical operations. Here the relatively coarse particles are called sands and the slurry of fine particles is called slimes. Sufficient time is provided to allow the sands to settle to the bottom of the device; the slimes leave in the effluent liquid.

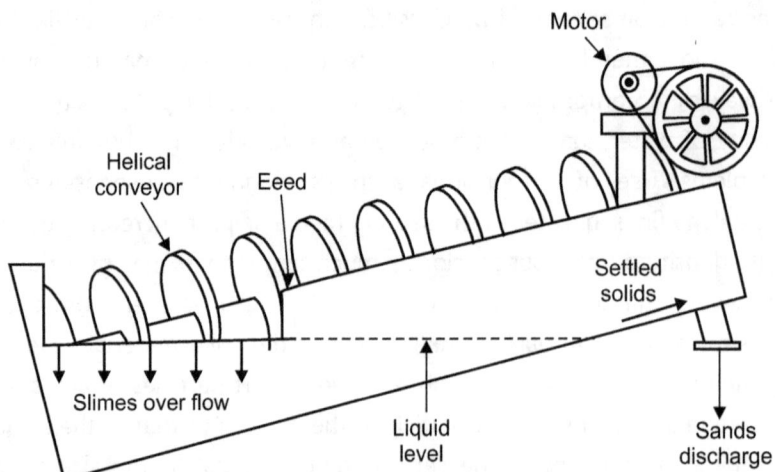

Fig. 7.1: Mechanical Classifier

A typical mechanical classifier is shown in Fig. 7.1. In this device the settling vessel is an inclined through with a liquid overflow at the lower end. Slurry is continuously fed to the trough at an intermediate point. The flow rate and slurry concentration are adjusted so that the fines do not have time to settle but are carried out with the liquid leaving the classifier. Larger particles sink to the floor of the trough, from which they must be removed. Different types of classifiers differ chiefly in the means by which they do this.

In the Crossflow classifier illustrated in Fig. 7.1 the trough is semi cylindrical, set at an angle of about 12° with the horizontal. A rotating helical conveyor moves the settled solids upward along the floor of the trough, out of the pool of liquid and up to the sands discharge chute. Such a classifier works well with coarse particles where exact splits are not required. Typical applications are in connection with ball or rod mills for reduction to particle sizes between 8 and 20 mesh. These classifiers have high capacities. They lift coarse solids for return to the mill, so that auxiliary conveyors and elevators are not needed. For close separations will finer particles, however, other types of classifier must be used. Modified forms of the settling basins and sedimenting centrifuges discussed later are used for this purpose.

7.3.2 Sorting Classifiers

Devices, which separate particles of differing densities, are known as sorting classifiers. They use one or the other of two principal separation methods sink and float and differential settling.

7.3.3 Sink and Float Methods

A sink and float method uses a liquid sorting medium, the density of which is intermediate between that of the light material and that of the heavy. Then the heavy particles settle through the medium, and the lighter ones float, and a separation is thus obtained. This method has the advantage that, in principle, the separation depends only on the difference in the densities of the two substances and is independent of the particle size. This method is also called heavy fluid separation.

Heavy fluid processes are used to treat relatively coarse particles, usually greater than 10 meshes. The first problem in the use of sink and float is the choice of a liquid medium of the proper gravity to allow the light material to float and the heavy to sink. True liquid scan be used, but since the specific gravity of the medium must be in the range 1.3 to 3.5 or greater, there are but few liquids that are sufficiently heavy, cheap, non-toxic, and no corrosive to be practicable. Halogenated hydrocarbons are used for the purpose. Calcium chloride solutions are used for cleaning coal. A more common choice of medium is a pseudo liquid consisting of a suspension in water of fine particles of a heavy mineral.

Magnetite (specific gravity = 5.17), ferrosilicon (specific gravity = 6.3 to 7.0), and galena (specific gravity = 7.5) are used. The ratio of mineral to water can be varied to give a wide range of medium densities. Provision must be made for feeding the mixture to be separated, for removing overflow and underflow, and for recovering the separating fluid, which may be expensive relative to the value of the materials being treated in the process particles fall or rise at their terminal velocities, and hindered settling is used. Cleaning coal and concentrating ores are the common application of sink and float. Under proper conditions, clean separations between materials differing in specific gravity by only 0.1 have been claimed.

7.3.4 Differential Settling Methods

Differential settling methods utilize the difference in terminal velocities that can exist between substances of different density. The density of the medium is less than that of either substance. The disadvantage of the method is that since the mixture of materials to be separated covers range of particle sizes, the larger, light particles settle at the same rate as the smaller, heavy ones and a mixed fraction is obtained. In differential settling, both light and heavy materials settle through the same medium. This method brings in the concept of equal settling particles. Consider particles of two materials A and B settling through a medium of density ρ. Let material A be the heavier; for example, component A might be galena (specific gravity = 7.5) and component B quartz (specific gravity = 2.65). The terminal velocity of a particle of size D_p and of density ρ_p settling under gravity through a medium of density ρ is given for settling in the Stoke's law regime. This equation can be written, for a galena particle of density ρ_{pA} and diameter D_{pA}

$$u_t A = \frac{gD_{pA}^2 (\rho_{pA} - \rho)}{18 \mu} \qquad \text{... (7.29)}$$

For a quartz particle of density ρ_{pB} and diameter D_{pB}.

$$u_t B = \frac{gD_{pB}^2 (\rho_{pB} - \rho)}{18 \mu} \qquad \text{... (7.30)}$$

For equal settling particles $u_{tA} = u_{tB}$, and therefore,

$$\frac{D_{pA}}{D_{pB}} = \sqrt{\frac{\rho_{pB} - \rho}{\rho_{pA} - \rho}} \qquad \text{... (7.31)}$$

For settling in the Newton's law range the diameters of equal settling particles are related by the equation.

$$\frac{D_{pA}}{D_{pB}} = \frac{\rho_{pB} - \rho}{\rho_{pA} - \rho} \qquad \text{... (7.32)}$$

The significance in a separation process of the equal settling ratio of diameters is shown by Fig. 7.2, in which curves of u_t vs. D_p are plotted for components A and B, for Stokes' law settling. Assume that the diameter range of both substances lies between points D_{p1} and D_{p4} on the size axis. Then, all particles of the light component B having diameters between D_{p1} and D_{p2} will settle more slowly than any particle of the heavy substance A and can be obtained as a pure fraction. Likewise, any particles of substance A having diameters between D_{p3} and D_{p4} settle faster than any particle of substance B and can also be obtained as pure fraction.

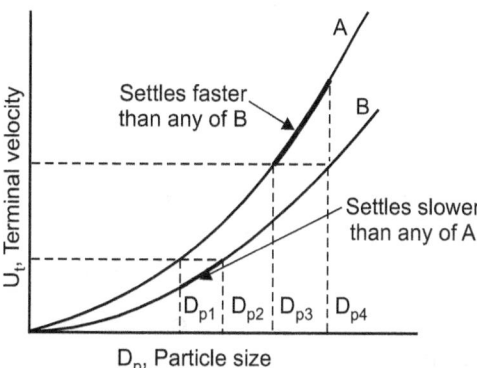

Fig. 7.2: Equal – Settling Particles

But any light particle having a diameter between D_{p2} and D_{p4} settles at the same speed as a particle of substance A in the size range between D_{p1} and D_{p3}, and all particles in these size ranges form a mixed fraction. Equations (7.29) and (7.30) show that the sharpness of separation is improved if the density of the medium is increased. it is also clear from Fig. 7.2 that the mixed fraction can be reduced or eliminated by closer sizing of the feed. For example, if the size range of the feed is from D_{p3} to D_{p4} in Fig. 7.2, complete separation is possible.

7.4 Free and Hindered Settling

Free Settling: When the particle is at sufficient distance from the boundaries of the container and from other particles, so that its fall is not affected by them, the process is called *free settling*.

Hindered Settling: If the motion of the particle is impeded by other particles, which will happen when the particles are nearer each other even though they may not actually be colliding, the process is called as *hindered settling*. The drag coefficient in hindered settling is greater than in free settling. Empirical correlations for hindered settling exist only for small spherical particles for which Stokes law is applicable. For such cases, the terminal settling velocity of a sphere, relative to the fluid, $v_{t,r}$, is given in terms of the density of the slurry, ρ_m, and its viscosity, μ_m,

$$v_{t,r} = \frac{(\rho_s - \rho_m) g D^2}{18 \mu_m} \qquad \ldots (7.33)$$

The bulk density of the slurry can be expressed in terms of the densities of the solid and the fluid and the volume fraction of fluid, ϵ, assuming that the volume of the mixture is the sum of the volumes of the ingredients. The viscosity of the mixture is obtained empirically in terms of the fluid viscosity, μ and ϵ, for small spherical particles in a fluid as:

$$\mu_m = \mu_e^{4.19(1-\epsilon)} \qquad \ldots (7.34)$$

Also, while considering the settling of any one particle, it must be remembered that because of the settling of neighbouring particles at the same plane, the fluid has a net upward velocity, v_{up}. This is illustrated in Fig. 7.3 (A). If $v_{t,w}$ represents the velocity of downward motion of the solid particles with respect to the wall and v_{up}, the upward velocity of the fluid (again with respect to the wall) due to the downward motion of the neighbouring solid particles, then

$$v_{t,r} = v_{t,w} + v_{up} \qquad \ldots (7.35)$$

If A is the area of cross-section of the tube in which settling is taking place, and if we assume that the fraction of area occupied by the solids at the plane shown in Fig. 7.3 is the same as the volume fraction of solids, $1 - \epsilon$, then the solid particles displace fluid at a rate of $A(1-\epsilon)V_{t,w}$ by virtue of their downward motion. This displaced fluid must flow upwards through area $A\epsilon$ available to it between the solids. The equation for terminal settling velocity of small spheres for hindered settling is given by:

$$V_{t,w} = \frac{(\rho_s - \rho_m) \epsilon \cdot g \cdot D^2 \cdot e^{-4.19(1-\epsilon)}}{18 \mu} \qquad \ldots (7.36)$$

No equivalent information is available in the literature for larger spheres and for irregular particles. In such cases, design of settling tanks for processing slurries must be based on actual experimental results on settling rates.

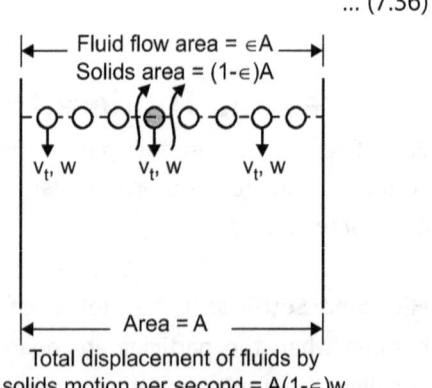

Fig. 7.3: Hindered Settling of Spheres

7.5 Sedimentation
7.5.1 Introduction
Settling and sedimentation can be found in industry quite frequently. It is valuable for the removal of solids from liquid sewage wastes, getting crystals from what they precipitated from, settling solid food particles from a liquid food and settling the slurry from a soyabean leaching process. Sedimentation or settling can be used to separate any particle from any fluid, whether it is a liquid from a gas, or a solid from a liquid.

There are actually two different styles of settling, known as free settling and hindered settling. The process of separating a suspension by gravity settling into a clear fluid and a slurry of solids is called *sedimentation*.

All the equipment so far has operated in the *Free Settling* regime; particles do not interact with each other because they are far apart. Stoke's Law or similar behaviour based on the behaviour of single, isolated particles may then be assumed. At high solid concentrations the regime is one of *Hindered Settling*. This change in behaviour is brought about because:
1. Solid particles settle relative to a mixture of liquid and smaller particles, reducing the effective density difference.
2. There is a significant upward flow of liquid as it is displaced by falling particles.
3. Velocity gradients in the fluid in the vicinity of the particles are enhanced due to obstruction of the flow path.
4. Small particles are dragged down by large particles.

Often a settling test is carried out to determine the settling characteristics of a suspension. This is generally done in a large measuring cylinder. There is a wall effect in the experiment, but in a large cylinder this may be neglected.

If the variation in particle size is such that,
$$d_{max} < 6d_{max}$$

A clear liquid-suspension interface is formed which moves downwards as the solid settle. After an initial acceleration period this boundary settles at constant speed, the local particle concentration remains constant.

Eventually, the interface reaches the variable concentration region and the settling rate slows down. Once all the sediment is consolidated the interface velocity drops to zero. This behaviour is not followed by all suspensions; there may be no constant rate period or no falling rate period.

Sedimentation uses gravitational forces to separate particulate material from fluid streams. The particles are usually solid, but they can be small liquid droplets, and the fluid can be either a liquid or a gas. Sedimentation is very often used in the food industry for separating dirt and debris from incoming raw material, crystals from their mother liquor and dust or product particles from air streams.

In sedimentation, particles are falling from rest under the force of gravity. Therefore, in sedimentation, takes the familiar form of **Stokes' Law:**

$$v_m = D^2 g(\rho_p - \rho_f)/18\mu$$

Note that equation (7.9) is not dimensionless and so consistent units must be employed throughout. For example, in the SI system, D in m, g in ms^{-2}, ρ in kgm^{-3} and μ in Nsm^{-2}, and then v_m would be in ms^{-1}. Particle diameters are usually very small and are often measured in microns (micro-metres) = 10^{-6} m with the symbol µm.

Stoke's Law applies only in streamline flow and strictly only to spherical particles. In the case of spheres, the criterion for streamline flow is that $(R_e) < 2$ and many particle cases occur in the region of stream line flow, or atleast where streamline flow is a reasonable approximation.

Separation of Solids and Liquids: In order to separate a solid-liquid mixture, there is often a two-step procedure that needs to occur. First is what is known as *thickening*, in which the particles in the mixture settle into a thickened, denser, underflow, with a clear overflow. This step is sometimes marked by the addition of a coagulant or other thickening agent. The second stage involves taking the underflow and further reducing it, attempting to convert it into a compact solid with relatively small amounts of liquid. The second stage is more or less defined by the first stage and as such, most attention is focussed on the original separation and thickening of the solid-liquid mixture.

Settling Mechanisms:
- Four distinct settling mechanisms have been identified.
- The fluid dynamics differ for each mechanism, which affects or dictates the method of data analysis.

1. **Type I:**
    ⇒ Individual particles settling without interaction with each other.
    ⇒ Dilute suspension → Unhindred settling.

2. **Type II:**
   ⇒ Flocculation particles settling in a dilute suspension.
   ⇒ Particle size grows as particle settles.
   ⇒ However, fluid dynamic analysis of a single particle continues to apply.
   ⇒ Dilute suspension → Unhindered settling.
3. **Type III:**
   ⇒ Zone or hindered settling due to high concentration of particles.
   ⇒ Particles interact with fluid dynamically.
4. **Type IV:**
   ⇒ Compression settling.
   ⇒ Squeezing water out rather than particle.
   ⇒ Settling particles are in contact.

Gravity Settling: Here is an experiment. Look at one of the "snow globes" you can buy at almost any gift shop. Take it, and shake it up and see all the particles of white "snow" flying around in the water. Then if you set it down and wait a few minutes, the "snow" will begin to start hitting the ground. In a few minutes, you will reach what is sometimes called a *critical point or critical sedimentation point*. At that point, everything has reached the ground state. It is all "sediment" so to speak. In a few more minutes, compression continues and eventually, everything settles back to normal; the water on top and the compacted white "snow" particles on the ground. However, this is just a very simplified version of settling and sedimentation.

Free Settling: Free settling occurs when a particle is sufficiently far away from walls and other particles that they do not affect its fall. It can be shown that for particles having a diameter of less than 1/200 that of the container or if the particle concentration is less than 0.2% by volume, that the interference is less than 1%.

Hindered settling is what occurs when particles are crowded and surrounding particles interfere with the motion of individual particles. It's the same principle that works when you try and fit your thousand cars coming home from work on a road that can only fit about five thousand. Things tend to move fairly slow or at least, not as fast as if there were only a few cars on the road.

Thickening is a mechanical method for creating more concentrated solid portions faster than simple gravity settling. Look in the reactor section for what a thickener can look like, schematically. Basically, all it does is remove the very bottom sediment from the batch, as well as removing the clear fluid from the very top and thus there will be a continual creation of new packed sediment as well as removal of clear liquid. Eventually, if we are running this as a batch process, all that will be left is that sludge.

Factors influencing Sedimentation:
1. Size and shape of tank
   ⇒ Rectangular vs. circular.
   ⇒ Number of tanks.
2. Flow arrangements
   ⇒ Inlet and outlet details.
   ⇒ Baffling.
3. Flow through rate
   ⇒ Surface loading or overflow rate.
   ⇒ Detention time.
   ⇒ Climate and density currents.
4. Particulate and water quality
   ⇒ Seasonal water quality.
   ⇒ Coagulation, polyelectrolytes and other chemimcal agents.
   ⇒ Flocculation.
5. Flow Distribution
   ⇒ Dead space $\quad \dfrac{\text{Mean t}}{\text{Theoretical t}} < 1$
   ⇒ No dead space $\quad \dfrac{\text{Mean t}}{\text{Theoretical t}} = 1$
   ⇒ Short circuiting $\quad \dfrac{\text{Median t}}{\text{Mean t}} < 1$
   ⇒ No short circuiting $\quad \dfrac{\text{Median t}}{\text{Mean t}} = 1$

7.5.2 Batch Settling Tests

In the operation of thickeners a basic assumption (not always accurate) is that the material to be settled consists of flocs (aggregates of much finer material) sufficiently uniform in size and shape so that they settle at uniform velocities under conditions of hindered settling in the initial stages. The process of settling is best described by batch-settling tests in glass cylinders. Figure 7.4 gives a series of observations of such tests.

Figure 7.4 shows a cylinder containing the uniformly mixed suspension (called pulp in metallurgical work). in Fig. 7.4 several things have occurred. First, any coarse material has already fallen to the bottom as shown by layer E. Next, there is a layer of settled solid D, with a transition zone of partly thickened material above it C. The boundary between C and D is usually obscure and is marked by vertical channels through which water is escaping from the lower layers, which are under compression. Next is a zone B of pulp at the original concentration; and finally a layer A of clear water. The boundary between A and B is usually sharp. As thickening progresses, layers B and C ultimately disappear, but layer D may shrink further because of compression.

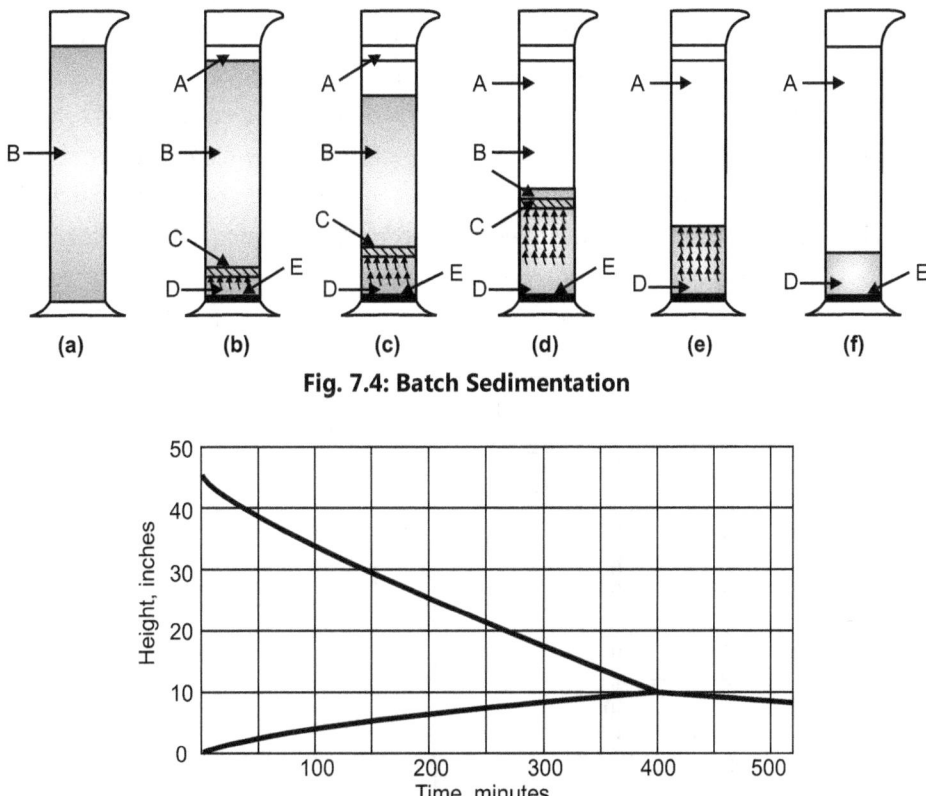

Fig. 7.4: Batch Sedimentation

Fig. 7.5: Progress of Settling with Time

The distribution of concentrations at a stage corresponding to Fig. 7.4 is shown in Fig. 7.6 (a) curve 1. The original height of the pulp was 44 inches, and the original concentration of solid was 45 g/liter. The uniform concentration in zone B is plain. Layers C and D are not yet well formed. Curve 2 still shows some of zone B, though its concentration has increased slightly.

This corresponds about to Fig. 7.6 (a) Curve 3 of Fig. 7.5 corresponds to the conditions of Fig. 7.4 and shows how zone D has become compressed during the settling process. In Fig. 7.5 the upper curve shows the position of the interface between zones A and B and the lower curve the interface between zones C and D. The point where these two curves unte corresponds to the conditions of Fig. 7.4. Such a test will give a different curve for every precipitate and a somewhat different one for different concentrations. Such laboratory batch-settling tests are the basis for the design of continuous thickeners.

In the operation of a continuous thickener the conditions are similar except for one feature. In batch settling, conditions and zone boundaries vary with time. In continuous settling a steady state is set up, in which there are the same zones as in batch settling, but their position and concentration are constant with time. Fig. 7.7 shows how the zones of Fig. 7.4 may be arranged in a thickener. The clarification zone of this figure corresponds to the clear-liquid layer of Fig. 7.4, and the others follow in order. Fig. 7.6 (a), which shows concentration ranges, shows that for curve 1 condition here were very like conditions in the batch-settling tests of Fig. 7.5. The precipitate was calcium carbonate. A much more nearly colloidal material (pot clay) gave quite different, conditions (curve 2). Nevertheless, both cases gave (1) a clear overflow, and (2) a thickened compression layer at the bottom.

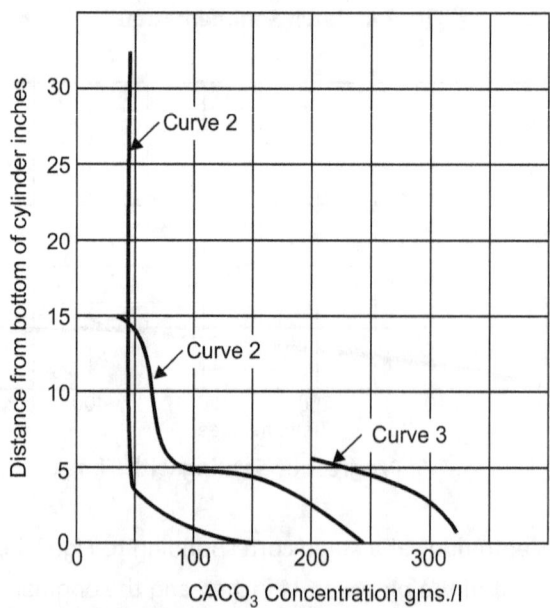

Fig. 7.6 (a): Relation between Concentration and Depth in Slurry – Settling Tests
(Curve 1, 2 and 3 are at Successive Times)

MECHANICAL OPERATIONS SEPARATION BASED ON MOTION ......

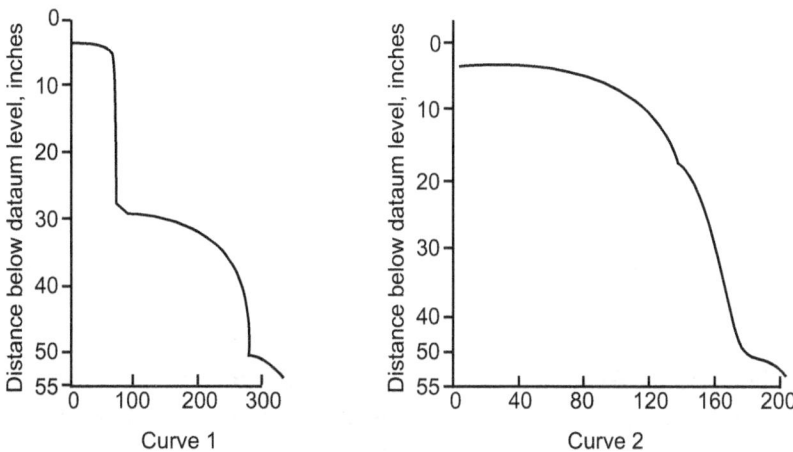

Fig. 7.6 (b): Relation between Concentration and Depth in a Continuous Thickner

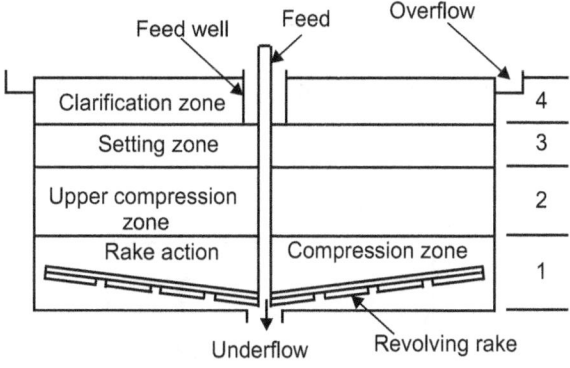

Fig. 7.7: Various Zones in Continuous Thickners

Thickener design:

A continuous thickener is a vessel with a feed, at low solid concentration, and two output streams: an overflow of clean liquid and an underflow suspension of much greater concentration than the feed. The vessel is normally circular, with a conical bottom that is raked to bring the solids into the discharge well. The design requirement is to deduce the plan area required for a given flow rate of solids entering and to achieve the desired degree of thickening. If insufficient area is provided then the concentration of solids within the vessel increases and will eventually leave in the overflow. The fluxes within a thickener include the batch flux, described above, but there is an additional flux due to the continual removal of material from the base; i.e. underflow.

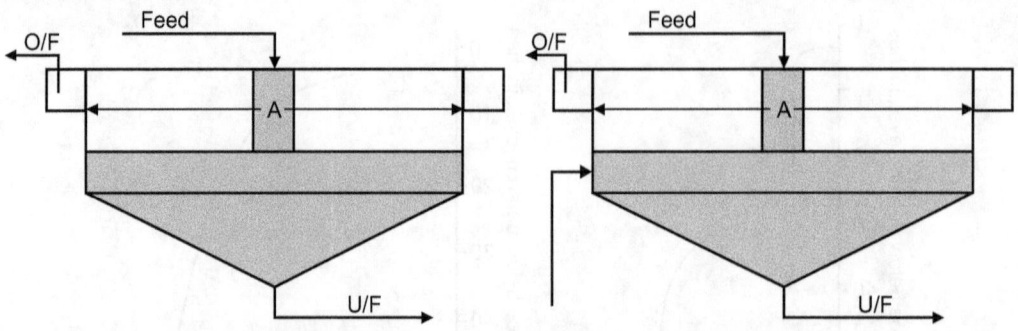

Underflow flux: $ATC_U \rho_s$
$m^2\ ms^{-1}\ v/v\ kg\ m^{-3}$
τ is the velocity induced in the thickener by underflow withdrawal

Flux in thickener: $G = A(U_s + T_p C_p)\ kg\ s^{-1}$
i.e. total flux is sum of batch settling flux and underflow withdrawal flux. We need to design the thickener to have an adequate area for the flux required when thickening from the inlet to outlet concentrations

Fig. 7.8: Fluxes in a Thickener

Feed flux: FC, ρ_s $m^3\ s^{-1}$ v/v $kg\ m^{-3}$ giving $kg\ s^{-1}$

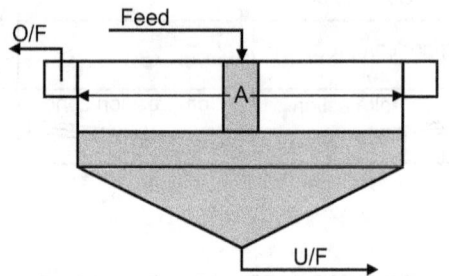

F is the suspension feed rate, C_f the Solids Concentration
Fig. 7.9: Flux (kg s^{-1} of solids) Fed to the Thickener

The fluxes are illustrated in Fig. 7.8, which includes a schematic diagram of the thickener. The thickener feed flux is illustrated in Fig. 7.9 and this is the mass feed rate entering the system. Equating all the flux terms provides, where F is the thickener feed rate ($m^3\ s^{-1}$).

$$G = A(U_0 + T)C\rho_s = FC_f \rho_s \qquad \ldots (7.37)$$

The flux at an arbitrary height within the thickener will be equal to the flux at the underflow (TC_a), which can be substituted into equation (7.37).

$$A = \frac{FC_f}{(U_0 + T)C_u} \qquad \ldots (7.38)$$

But the batch flux at the underflow will be negligible compared to the underflow withdrawal flux; hence we can write

$$A = \frac{FC_f}{TC_u} \quad \text{... (7.39)}$$

Equation (7.39) is the design equation and to use it we must determine the flux at the underflow concentration. The underflow withdrawal induces a downward velocity within the thickener which is constant for all the concentrations present from C_f to C_u. Hence, the underflow withdrawal flux is a straight line on a graph of flux against concentration, see Fig. 7.10. Adding the batch and underflow withdrawal flux together gives the composite flux curve; which has a minimum at a critical concentration between C_f and C_u. It is this concentration that has the minimum solids flux, or handling, ability. Hence, if too much solids are added to the thickener the critical concentration (Cc) will build up within the device and eventually overflow. The batch, underflow and composite flux curves are illustrated in Fig. 7.11.

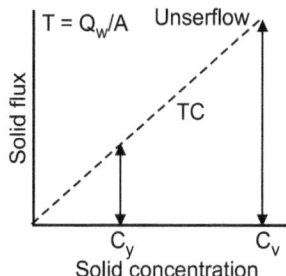
Fig. 7.10: Underflow Withdrawal Flux

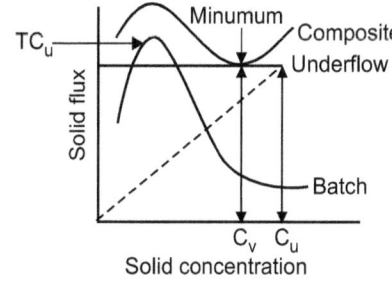
Fig. 7.11: All the Flux Curves

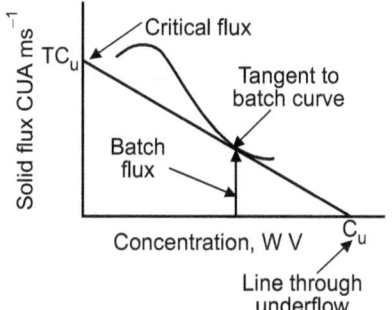
Fig. 7.12: Construction to Determine the Critical Flux – Equation (7.39)

In Fig. 7.12 the construction required to determine TC_u, for use in equation (3), is illustrated. The minimum composite flux occurs at Cc and is numerically equal to the underflow flux at

Cu; i.e. TCu. However, the composite flux at the critical concentration does have two components: that due to batch settling and underflow withdrawal, which are marked on the figure. Clearly, it is possible for the thickener to be operated under conditions that require a batch flux less than the value at the batch flux curve, at Cc, but batch fluxes greater are not possible. Hence, the limit of operation is where Cc meets the batch flux curve. So, for a required underflow concentration (Cu) a line drawn through the concentration axis at Cu and tangential to the batch flux curve will meet the flux curve at the value of TC_u. This value can then be used in equation (7.12) to determine the thickener area.

Thickener height is not determined by flux theory and, in general, thickeners are short vessels with diameters up to 50 meters. Minimum heights are allocated for the raked zone (0.5 m), solids storage zone (0.5 m) and clarification (0.5 m). Thus, a thickener is usually 1.5 to 4 m in height, unless solids compression is important.

An alternative design method to the use of the batch flux curve construction described above was originally described by Coe and Clevenger. A flux balance between the feed and underflow provides

$$G = ATC_u \rho_s = FC_f \rho_s \qquad \ldots (7.40)$$

Hence,
$$T = \frac{FC_f}{AC_u} \qquad \ldots (7.41)$$

which can be substituted in to equation (7.38) and rearranged to give

$$A = \frac{FC_f}{U_0}\left[\frac{1}{C} - \frac{1}{C_u}\right] \qquad \ldots (7.42)$$

Equation (7.13) is solved by selecting concentrations between C_f and C_u, where U_0 is required for the value of C selected, and using the greatest area for the design. Equation (7.42) is easier to apply than the graphical technique described earlier, but equation (7.39) and the graphical construction has the advantage that it can be used to predict the underflow concentration from an existing thickener under different operating loads; i.e. FC_f.

7.5.3 Application of Batch Settling Tests to Design of Continuous Thickeners

The capacity of a continuous thickener is determined by the fact that the solids initially present in the feed must be able to settle through all zones of slurry concentration, from that of the initial feed to that of the underflow, at a rate equal to that at which they are introduced into the thickener. If the area provided is not sufficient, the solids will build-up through the settling zone and into the clarification zone (see Fig. 7.7) until finally some solids are discharged in the overflow. Furthermore, it is not known at the start which zone will be the zone of minimum capacity.

The earliest method suggested for the design of continuous thickeners, and one which has been used until quite recently, was that proposed by Coe and Clevenger. For a given set of operating conditions (the solid material in the slurry feed, the size frequency distribution of the solid particles, and the liquid properties remain constant), it was assumed that the settling rate was a function only of the solids concentration expressed as volume of solids per unit volume of slurry. It was also assumed that if batch-settling tests were run at different initial pulp concentrations, the essential characteristics of the solids (degree of flocculation, for one) were unchanged. This assumption may not always be correct.

7.5.4 Equipment for Settling and Sedimentation

(1) Simple Gravity Settling Tank: In Fig. 7.13 a simple gravity settler is shown for removing by settling a dispersed liquid phase from another phase. The velocity horizontally to the right must be slow enough to allow time for the smallest droplets to rise from the bottom to the interface or from the top down to the interface and coalesce.

In Fig. 7.13 gravity settling chamber is shown schematically. Dust-laden air enters at one end of a large box-like chamber. Particles settle toward the floor at their terminal settling velocities. The air must remain in the chamber a sufficient length of time (residence time) so that the particles reach the floor of the chamber. Knowing the throughput of the air stream through the chamber and the chamber size, the residence time of the air in the chamber can be calculated. The vertical height of the chamber must be small enough so that this height, divided by the settling velocity, gives a time less than the residence time of the air.

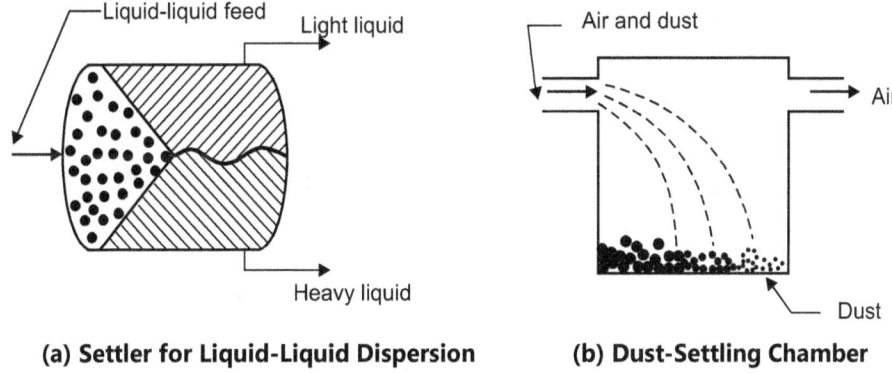

(a) Settler for Liquid-Liquid Dispersion   **(b) Dust-Settling Chamber**

Fig. 7.13: Gravity Settling Tanks

(2) Equipment for Classification: The simplest type of classifier is one in which a large tank is subdivided into several sections, as shown in Fig. 7.14.

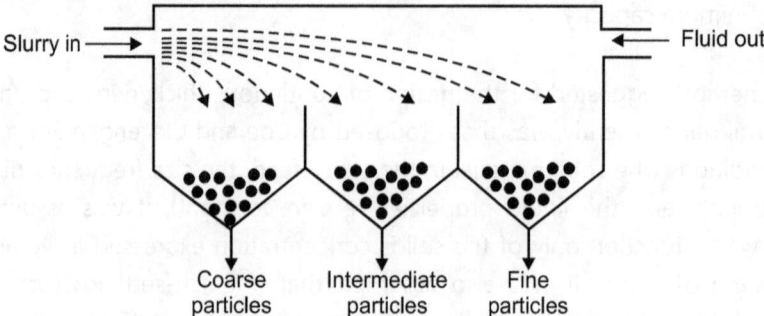

Fig. 7.14: Simple Gravity Settling Classifier

A liquid slurry feed enters the tank containing a size range of solid particles. The larger, faster-settling particles settle to the bottom close to the entrance and the slower-settling particles settle to the bottom close to the exist. The linear velocity of the entering feed decreases as a result of the enlargement of the cross-sectional area at the entrance. The vertical baffles in the tank allow for the collection of several fractions. The settling-velocity equations derived in this section hold.

(3) Spitzkasten Classifier: Another type of gravity settling chamber is the Spitzkasten, shown in Fig. (7.15), which consists of a series of conical vessels of increasing diameter in the direction of flow. The slurry enters the first vessel, where the largest and faster-settling particles are separated. The overflow goes to the next vessel, where another separation occurs. This continues in the succeeding vessel or vessels. In each vessel the velocity of upflowing inlet water is controlled to give the desired size range for each vessel.

(4) Sedimentation Thickener: The separation of a dilute slurry by gravity settling into a clear fluid and a slurry of higher solids concentration is called sedimentation. Industrially, sedimentation operations are often carried out continuously in equipment called thickness. A continuous thickener with a slowly revolving rake for removing the sludge or thickened slurry.

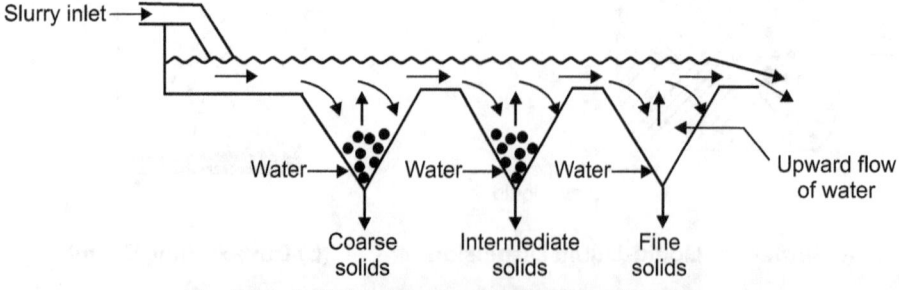

Fig. 7.15: Spitzkasten Gravity Settling Chamber

(5) Tubular Centrifuge: The bowl is tall and has a narrow diameter, 100 to 150 mm. Such centrifuges, known as super centrifuges, develop a force about 13,000 times the force of gravity. Some narrow centrifuges having a diameter of 75 mm and very high speeds of 60,000 or so rev/min are known as ultracentrifuges. These super centrifuges are often used to separate liquid-liquid emulsions.

(6) Disk Bowl Centrifuge:

The disk bowl centrifuge shown in Fig. 7.16 often used in liquid-liquid separations. The feed enters the actual compartment at the bottom and travels upward through vertically spaced feed holes, filling the spaces between the disks. The holes divide the vertical assembly into an inner section, where mostly light liquid is present and an outer section, where mainly heavy liquid is present. This dividing line is similar to an interface in a tubular centrifuge. The heavy liquid flows beneath the underside of a disk to the periphery of the bowl. The light liquid flows over the upper side of the disks and toward the inner outlet.

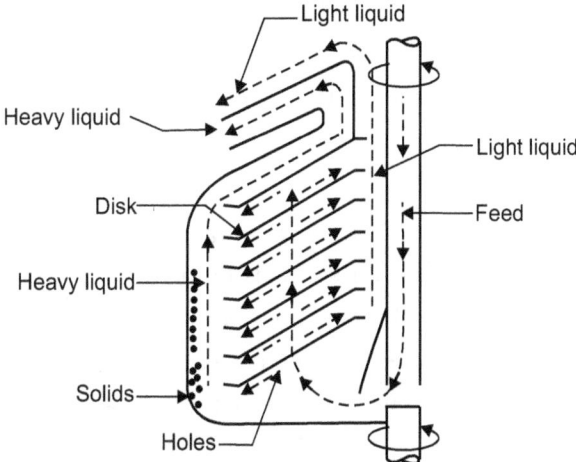

Fig. 7.16: Schematic of Disk Bowl Centrifuge

7.5.5 The Kynch Theory

More recently a method has been proposed which requires only the first of the two assumptions implicit in the Coe and Clevenger method. This method is based on a mathematical analysis of batch settling presented by Kynch, which showed that the settling rate, and the concentration of the zone that limits capacity, can be determined from a single batch-settling test (for a given pulp and temperature of operation). In a batch test started with a uniform initial concentration of solids, the concentration of solids in the zone C must

MECHANICAL OPERATIONS SEPARATION BASED ON MOTION ......

range between that of the initial slurry concentration in zone B and that of the final slurry in zone D. If the solids-handling capacity per unit area is lowest at some intermediate concentration, a zone of such concentration must start building up, since the rate at which solids enter this zone will be less than the rate at which they will leave this zone. It has been shown that the rate of upward propagation of such a zone is constant and is a function of the solids concentration:

$$\bar{v} = c\frac{dv}{dc} - v \qquad \text{... (7.43)}$$

Where, $\bar{v}$ = Upward velocity of propagation of concentration zone of minimum settling rate with respect to

Vessel:

v = Settling velocity of solids in concentration zone of minimum settling rate with respect to vessel.

c = Concentration of solids, weight of solids per unit volume of pulp.

From the assumption that the settling rate is a function only of the solids concentration, i.e., that = $v = f(c)$,

$$\bar{v} = cf'(c) - f(c) \qquad \text{... (7.44)}$$

Suppose that C_0 and Z_0 represent the initial concentration and height, respectively, of a pulp in a batch-settling test. The total weight of solids in this pulp is then $C_0 A z_0$, where A is the cross-sectional area of the column of pulp. Consider the test at the instant of time when the layer corresponding to the limiting settling rate has reached the interface between the clear supernatant liquid and the pulp. All the solids in the initial pulp must have passed through this layer since the layer was propagated upward from the bottom of the column. If the concentration of this layer is c_L and the time instant at which the layer reaches the interface is θ_L, then,

$$c_L A (v_L + \bar{v}_L) \theta_L = c_0 A z_0 \qquad \text{... (7.45)}$$

Where v_L and $\bar{v}_L$ refer to the respective velocities for a layer having a solids concentration of c_L. Let z_L correspond to the height of the interface at time θ_L then.

$$\bar{v}_L = \frac{z_L}{\theta_L} \qquad \text{... (7.46)}$$

Since from equation (7.15) $\bar{v}$ is constant if c is constant. Substituting equation (7.46) in (7.45) and simplifying, we get,

$$c_L = \frac{C_0 Z_0}{z_L + v_L \theta_L} \qquad \text{... (7.47)}$$

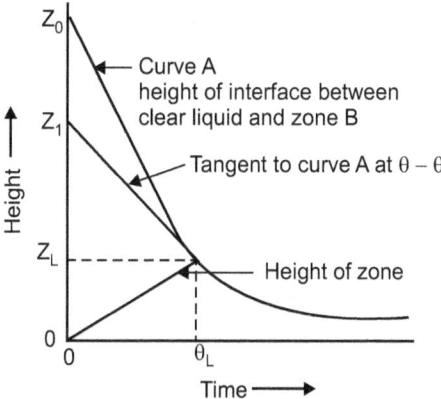

Fig. 7.17: Determination of Settling Velocities from Batch-Settling Curve

The value of the settling velocity v_L is the slope of the tangent to curve A at $\theta = \theta_L$. This tangent intersects the vertical axis at,

$$z = z_i$$

since,

$$\tan \alpha = \frac{z_i - z_L}{0 - \theta_L}$$

$$z_i - z_L = \theta_L \tan \alpha = \theta_L v_L$$

$$z_i = z_L + \theta_L v_L$$

$$c_L z_i = c_0 z_0 \qquad \ldots (7.48)$$

Equation (7.48), states that z_i is the height of a uniform slurry of concentration c_L which contains the same amount of solids as the initial slurry. The settling velocity as a function of concentration may be developed from a single settling test by use of the above relationships. Using arbitrarily chosen values of settling time θ, the corresponding tangents to the settling curve are located and the values of the slope and intercept determined. The values of the intercept are used in Equation (7.17) to determine the corresponding concentrations. The corresponding slopes give the respective settling rates.

7.5.6 Determination of Thickener Area

In the case of a continuous thickener, the area required is determined by that concentration layer for which the solids-handling capacity, expressed as weight of solids per (unit area) (unit time), is a minimum. the material balance for a thickener, operating with a slurry feed of concentration c_0 and an underflow concentration of c_u and containing no solids in the overflow, based on a slurry feed rate of F volumes per unit time is as follows:

Volume of solids entering thickener per unit time = Fc_0

Since no solids leave in the overflow, if L represents the volumes of underflow per unit of time,
$$L = \frac{Fc_0}{c_u} \quad \ldots (7.49a)$$
$$Fc_0 = Lc_u$$

From a balance for the liquid:
$$F(1-c_0) - L(1-c_u) = V \quad \ldots (7.49b)$$

Where V is overflow volume per unit time. Substituting equation (7.46) in (7.47),
$$F(1-c_0) - \frac{Fc_0}{c_u}(1-c_u) = Fc_0\left(\frac{1}{c_0} - \frac{1}{c_u}\right) \quad \ldots (7.50)$$
$$= V \quad \ldots (7.51)$$

If the cross-sectional area of the thickener be denoted by A, then
$$\frac{V}{A} = \frac{Fc_0}{A}\left(\frac{1}{c_0} - \frac{1}{c_u}\right) \quad \ldots (7.52)$$

The term V/A in Equation (7.52) represents the upward liquid velocity in the clarification zone of the thickener. When the thickener is operated at capacity the lowest settling rate encountered must be equal to or greater than this value, otherwise some solids will leave in the overflow. Consequently V/A may be replaced by v. Furthermore, Equation (7.46) may be written in terms of the concentration of the layer which limits the capacity rather than in terms of the feed concentration and rate which is set by this capacity, i.e.,
$$Fc_0 = L_L c_L$$
$$\frac{L_L c_L}{A} = \frac{v}{1/c_L - 1/c_u} \quad \ldots (7.53)$$

By using the settling velocity – concentration curve to obtain corresponding values of v and c_L and using these values in equation (7.50), various values of $\frac{L_L c_L}{A}$, which represents the solid-handling capacity per unit area may be calculated. The lowest value calculated is to be used in determining the area of thickener.

Continuous Settlers:

Taking the area below the feed to a continuous settler:

If the thickener is working correctly the weight flux, G, of solids moving downwards is constant and equal to G_{feed}.

There is also an upward flux of displaced liquid which varies with height in the settler, and with the rate of increase of solids concentration.

A water mass balance across the horizontal boundary at some level below the feed gives:
$$G_{feed}(D - D_B) = \rho_f u \qquad \ldots (7.54)$$

where, G is the mass of solid/area time
D is the mass of fluid per unit mass of solids in the downward flow.
ρ_f is the fluid density.
u is the upward fluid velocity.

So,
$$\frac{D}{\rho_f} - \frac{D_B}{\rho_f} = \frac{u}{G_{feed}} \qquad \ldots (7.55)$$

Bearing in mind that:
$$\frac{D}{\rho_f} = \frac{\text{Mass fluid per unit mass solid}}{\text{Mass fluid per unit volume liquid}}$$

$$= \text{Volume fluid per unit mass solids} = \frac{1}{c}$$

where, c is the concentration of solids (mass/unit volume)

Thus,
$$\frac{1}{c} - \frac{1}{c_B} = \frac{u}{G_{feed}}$$

or
$$uc = G_{feed}\left(1 - \frac{c}{c_B}\right) \qquad \ldots (7.56)$$

(which is a straight line)

The criterion for operation of a thickener is that the value of uc given by the equation above must not be greater than –
(hindered settling velocity of particles) × (local solids concentration)
$$= u_h(c) \times c$$

$u_h(c) \times c$ is the limiting mass flux of particles at concentration c and if the mass balance requires higher settlement rates the result in a thickner would be a build-up of solids.

If we plot $u_h(c)$ c vs. c the graph produces a maximum followed by a long tail off to zero. i.e. as c → 0 u_h reaches a maximum at u_t and as c → 0 u_h decreases to zero.

Referring back to the equation for uc above this line may be drawn on the graph $u_h(c)$ c vs. c, it has intercept on the $u_h(c)$ c axis at $u_h(c)$ c = G_{feed} and on the c line at c = c_B and will be tangent to the curve at some point.

In order to construct the graph of $u_h(c)$ c vs. c values of the settling velocity at different concentrations must be determined. Coe and Clevinger (1916) suggested that this could be done by measuring the initial settling velocities of a series of different concentrations of suspension.

Kynch (1952) pointed out that the falling rate part of the batch settling curve contains all the necessary information as it deals with steadily increasing concentrations to the ultimate final settled value. The necessary trick is to assign a concentration to each point in the falling rate region. Kynch's theory is very complex but the result is very easy to apply. Simply draw a tangent to the batch-settling curve - the intercept on the height axis is then z_i, the intercept on the time axis is t_i and the interface velocity is given by z_i/t_i. Concentration at the interface is given by $\dfrac{c_0 z_0}{z_i}$.

where, c_0 is the initial concentration of the suspension and z_0 is the initial height of the suspension. However $u(c)$ as measured from the diagram is not quite equal to $u_h(c)$, the hindered settling velocity. This is because in the batch experiment there is an appreciable upward velocity of fluid, u_f against which the solids have to settle because there is no solid removed from the bottom.

If ε do the solids occupy the voidage of the suspension then the volume fraction is $1 - \varepsilon$ and the downward flow of the particles is $(1 - \varepsilon) u(c)$.

Since there is no escape from the bottom this is equal to the upward volume flow of displaced fluid:

$$(1 - \varepsilon) u(c) = u_f \varepsilon$$

$$u_f = \frac{1-\varepsilon}{\varepsilon} u(c)$$

and
$$u_h(c) = u(c) + u_f = u(c)\left(1 + \frac{1-\varepsilon}{\varepsilon}\right) = \frac{u(c)}{\varepsilon} \qquad \ldots (7.57)$$

Remember that ε is given by,

$$c = (1 - \varepsilon)\rho_s \qquad \varepsilon = 1 - \frac{c}{\rho_s} \qquad \ldots (7.58)$$

The values of $u_h(c)$ and $u_h(c)c$ are used in the graphical construction above. c_B is usually fixed by design considerations so the design process boils down to finding a value of G_{feed} small enough (i.e. an area large enough) to obey the design criterion. This applies to the zone below the feed; the diameter above the feed is always equal to that below.

Depth: The usual way of fixing depth is to find from the batch experiment the time required to settle from the required initial to final concentration. This is set equal to the residence time and the minimum area is determined from the known flow rate and height.

$$t_{settling} = t_{res} = \frac{V}{Q} = \frac{Ah}{Q} \qquad \ldots (7.59)$$

This is very crude; the depth is usually much greater to allow for flow non-ideality.

(B) CENTRIFUGAL SETTLING PROCESSES
7.6 Cyclone Separator

Introduction:

The cyclone is a simple device, which causes the centrifugal separation of materials in a fluid stream. Unlike the slow setting within a settling tank, the pump and cyclone separator system yields fast separation and utilizes less space. Separations occur quickly because one "g" of gravitation force is replaced by many "g"s of centrifugal force. These materials may be particles of solid, bubbles of gas or immiscible liquids. In the case of two solids suspended in the feed liquid they may separate according to size, shape or density. The cyclone utilizes the energy obtained from fluid pressure to create rotational fluid motion. This rotational motion causes the materials suspended in the fluid to separate from one another or from the fluid quickly due to the centrifugal force. The rotation is produced by the tangential or involutes introduction of fluid into the vessel.

A hydrocyclones is a cyclone separator that uses water as the bulk fluid. Hydrocyclones are becoming well established in industrial applications. Applications of hydrocyclones fall into several broad categories: clarification, thickening, classification, sorting.

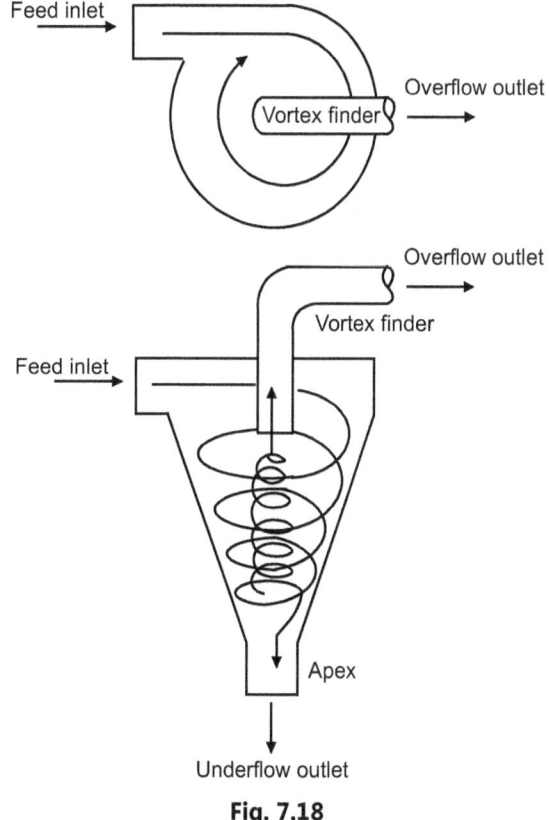

Fig. 7.18

Washing, liquid-liquid separation, liquid degassing and particle size measurement. They are frequently used as protection or pre-treatment devices to improve the performance or decrease the cost of down stream equipment. The target industries include mineral processing, mining, petrochemicals, oil production, wastewater and effluent treatment, food processing, pharmaceuticals, and other industries dealing with slurries.

(1) Definition of cyclone separators: A cyclone separator is a very useful piece of equipment for the removal from air streams of particles above 10 micrometer in diameter. The equipment is a settling chamber in the form of a vertical cylinder, so arranged that the particle laden air spirals round the cylinder to create centrifugal forces which throw the particles to the outside walls.

(2) Cyclone types most commonly used: Cyclone separators can be classified according to either geometrical configuration in (tangential inlet axial discharge, tangential inlet peripheral discharge, axial inlet and discharge and axial inlet peripheral discharge, Figures a-d below, respectively) or their efficiency in (high efficient (98-99%), moderate efficient (70 80%) and low efficient (50%).

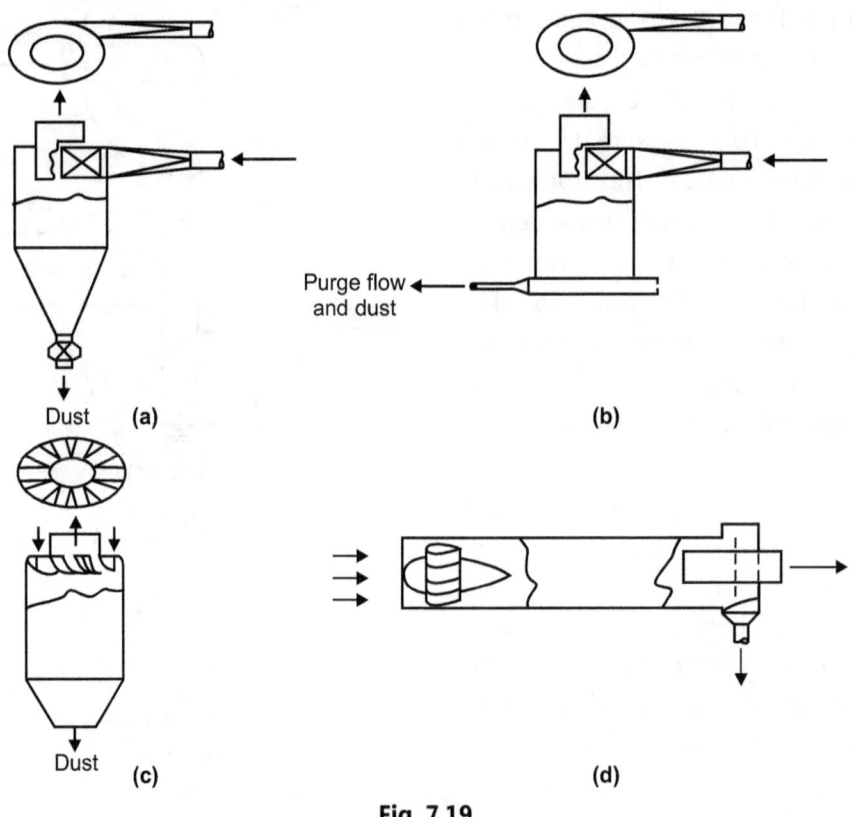

Fig. 7.19

Figure (a): Tangential inlet, axial discharge.
Figure (b): Tangential inlet, peripheral discharge.
Figure (c): Axial inlet, axial discharge.
Figure (d): Axial inlet, peripheral discharge.

(3) Operating principles of cyclone separators: Although there are four commonly used cyclone separators, their operating principles based on that of the conventional cyclone, are very similar. In the conventional cyclone, the gas enters a cylinder tangentially, where it spins in a vortex as it proceeds down the cylinder. A cone section causes the vortex diameter to decrease until the gas reverses on itself and spins up the center to the outlet pipe or vortex finder. A cone causes flow reversal to occur sooner and makes the cyclone more compact. Dust particles are centrifuged toward the wall and collected by inertial impingement. The collected dust flows down in the gas boundary layer to the cone apex where it is discharged through an air lock or into a dust hopper serving one or more parallel cyclones. Although conventional cyclones can be built to larger diameter, they are commonly 600 to 915 mm in diameter.

In axial inlet and discharge cyclones, the operating principles are similar to those of the conventional cyclone, the differences being the smaller diameter (25 to 305 mm) of the former cyclone. Because of their smaller diameters, axial inlet and discharge cyclones have higher collection efficiency but low gas capacity. Regarding the tangential inlet peripheral discharge and the axial inlet peripheral discharge cyclones, the functioning principles are the same as those in the conventional cyclone. However, in the tangential inlet peripheral discharge and the axial inlet peripheral discharge cyclones, the dust is not completely removed from the gas stream but is concentrated into about 10% of the total flow. The collection efficiency is increased by removing the dust in airborne from and reducing its entertainment losses which occur at the cone apex. In the tangential inlet peripheral discharge cyclone the gas reverses internally as in the conventional cyclone, but the axial inlet peripheral discharge straight through flow which is convenient for connecting to large volume sources where changes in gas direction could be inconvenient.

(4) Applications of cyclone separators: Cyclones can be used for separating particles from liquids as well as from gases and they can also be used for separating liquid droplets from gases. The first cyclones used for dust separation probably were built about 1885 by the Knickerbockers Company. In industries such as food industries, cyclones are used for removing the dry product from the air. In synthetic detergent production, fast reactor cyclones are used in separating a cracking catalyst from vaporized reaction products. Cyclones are used for classification as for example, in the digressing of kaolin clay where sand is removed from the crude clay suspension before finer classification in a conveyor discharge centrifuge and final product recovery in a disk centrifuge.

(5) Sizing and selection of cyclone separators:
   (a) Sizing: The key parameters (collecting efficiency and the pressure drop) of a cyclone are governed chiefly by its dimensions, that is to say the cross sectional areas and lengths of the individual flow channels. The diameter of a cyclone strongly influences its collecting efficiency. Smaller diameters (200 to 600 mm) provide greater collecting efficiency. The dust discharge opening should be as small as possible to forestall its clogging. The ratio

between the discharge port diameter do and the cyclone diameter D normally ranges between 0.18 and 0.40. the higher ratios are usually found on the large diameter cyclones intended of trapping coarser dusts. Cyclone overall height affects not only flow resistance but also collecting efficiency. increasing cyclone overall height will increase both its flow resistance and collecting efficiency. Overall heights of cyclones generally vary between 2D and 6D. The cone apex angle mostly lies between 10 and 20 degrees with the smaller angles being more usual on high efficiency units.

(b) Selection of cyclone separators: Selecting a cyclone type for a given application seems to be based on only the collecting efficiency or performance of the cyclone. However, many other factors which tend to impair the performance of the cyclones or the amount of service one can get out of them have to be considered. Among these detrimental factors one can mention the (1) mechanical defects of the cyclone, (2) the clogging of the unit by dust deposits and (3) the excessive wear, usually by abrasion.

(c) Mechanical defects: The mechanical defaces in alone are usually due to negligence or error in designs, manufacture or installation of the unit. These defects can cause the cyclone to fill up with trapped matter or the ingress of moisture which leads to clogging. Preventing the occurrence of such defects is preferable.

(d) Clogging: It results from the chemistry of the dust and its physical properties such as grain size. The chemistry of the dust can cause it to bond or cement. This type of clogging is prevented by improving thermal insulation, stricter observance of the specified operating conditions and meticulous maintenance of the equipment. The distribution of grain size can cause a clogging which commonly occurs when high efficiency cyclones are used to deal with dust of the minus 10 to minus 15 micron fractions. Such clogging is very complicated to deal with and can lead to the replacement of the cyclone.

(e) Excessive wear: Excessive abrasion in a cyclone will ultimately wear a hole in the equipment. The critical zones where holes are commonly encountered are the cylinder part just beyond the tangential inlet opening and the conical part at its very bottom (Othmer, 1980). With multicyclones any hole in the inlet chamber will affect the cyclone's whole flow pattern and reduce collecting efficiency. Although it is impossible to prevent wearing, it can be limited by providing the critical zones of the cyclone with thicker walls or ceramic inserts.

(6) Key parameters of cyclone separators: The most important parameters of a cyclone as for any separating device are its collecting efficiency and the pressure drop across the unit. The collecting efficiency of a cyclone is defined as its ability to capture and retain dust particles whereas the pressure drop is the amount of power that the unit needs to do so.

Circular Motion of Particles:

In many cases, the terminal velocity under gravity alone is too slow for practical purposes. If a rotary motion is imposed on the system the effective force on the particles is increased and separation may be achieved in much smaller equipment.

Consider a particle in a rotational field, the centrifugal acceleration on the particle is,

$$\omega^2 r = \frac{u_\theta^2}{r} \qquad \ldots (7.60)$$

where, u_θ is the tangential velocity of the particle.

The force on a spherical particle of diameter d, density ρ_s in a fluid density ρ_f is then,

$$\frac{\pi}{6} d^3 (\rho_s - \rho_f) \frac{u_\theta^2}{r} \qquad \ldots (7.61)$$

If the particle is no longer accelerating this equals the drag force exerted by the fluid on the particle.

$$\frac{\pi}{6} d^3 (\rho_s - \rho_f) \frac{u_\theta^2}{r} = 3\pi \mu d u_r \qquad \ldots (7.62)$$

where, u_r is the radial velocity of the particle.

Hence, $$u_r = \frac{d^2}{18\mu} (\rho_s - \rho_f) \frac{u_\theta^2}{r} = u_t \frac{u_\theta^2/r}{g} \qquad \ldots (7.63)$$

i.e. the terminal velocity under gravity, u_t scaled up the ratio of the centripetal acceleration to gravity. Hence, if we know the distance a particle must travel to be collected the residence time and hence the equation size may be calculated (in an ideal situation).

Design Cyclone of Separator:

Cyclones are not sized from theory but are normally designed by set procedures. One set of sizes of various parts is as follows:

$D_e = D_e/2$
$H_e = D_e/2$
$S_e = D_e/8$
$L_e = 2D_e$
$Z_e = 2D_e$
$B_e = D_e/4$
$J_e = D_e/4$

$B_c = D_c/4$
$D_c = D_c/2$
$H_c = D_c/2$
$L_c = 2/D_c$
$S_c = D_c/8$
$Z_c = 2/D_c$
$J_c =$ Arbitrary usually $D_c/4$

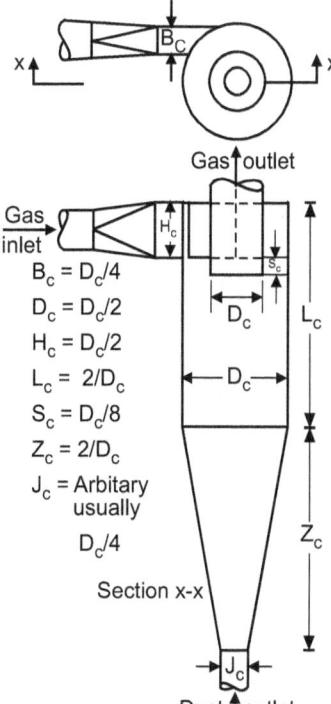

Fig. 7.20: Typical Cyclone Showing Design Proportions

The minimum diameter of a particle which can theoretically be completely separated from the gas stream is given by,

$$D_{p, min.} = \left[\frac{9 \mu B}{\pi V N_t (\rho_v - \rho)}\right]^{1/2} \quad \ldots (7.64)$$

μ = Viscosity of the fluid (poise).
B = Width of cyclone inlet duct (cm).
V = Average inlet velocity (cm/s).
N_t = Number of turns made by gas stream in cyclone.
ρ_p = Density of the particle (g/cc).
ρ = Density of fluid (g/cc).

The design factor having the greatest effect on the collection efficiency is the cyclone diameter. For a given pressure drop, smaller the diameter, higher is the efficiency, because centrifugal action increases with decreasing radius of rotation.

Centrifugal forces employed in modern designs vary from 5 to 2500 times gravity depending on the diameter of the cyclone. Cyclone efficiencies are greater than 90% for particles with diameter of the order of 10 µ. For particles with diameter higher than 20 µ, efficiency is about 95%.

In practice, cyclonic separators may be designed for the satisfactory collection of particles over wide ranges of sizes and concentration, and over wide ranges of pressure and temperature. They can be operated at temperatures as high as 1000°C and pressures 500 atmospheres. They can handle gas volumes ranging from about 0.85 to 700 cubic metres per minute. Particles of diameter 5-10 µ can be easily separated. If particles are large (5-200 µ), a properly designed cyclone will perform adequately with moderate power requirement. For particles larger than 200 µ, a settling chamber is desirable, as it is more resistant to abrasion. An important precaution to be taken in operating a cyclone is to prevent gas leakage. A 15% gas leakage can bring down the efficiency to virtually zero.

Today, various cyclone designs are being developed covering a wide range in size, geometry, and method of gas entry. Gas entries may be tangential, or involute or may employ guide vanes to impart a spiral motion to the gas stream.

Efficiency:
Cyclones are generally, divided into two classes, 'conventional' and 'high efficiency'. High efficiency cyclones merely have a smaller body diameter to create greater separating forces, and there is no sharp dividing line between the two groups. High efficiency cyclones are generally considered to be those with body diameters up to about 0.25 m.

One particular cyclone efficiency problem is the formation of eddies at the top of the unit where the dirty gas is introduced. The turbulence in the eddies causes some of the incoming dirty gas to be mixed with the outgoing clean gas stream. The exit gas stream at a point below the zone of maxium turbulence. This is done by adding a central tube called a vortex finder which projects into the cyclone body below the turbulent entry region to cofine the rising inner gas spiral.

In general, increase in collection efficiency will result if there is an increase in any of the following: dust particle size, dust particle density, gas inlet velocity, inlet dust loading, cyclone body length (number of gas revolutions), and ratio of body diameter to gas outlet tube diameter.

On the contrary, collector efficiency will decrease if there is an increase in gas viscosity or density, cyclone diameter, gas outlet diameter, inlet width and inlet area.

To get increased efficiency, especially for the collection of smaller sized particles, a small diameter, long taper cyclone should be used.

Table 7.1 indicates the efficiency range of cyclones.

Table 7.1: Efficiency Range of Cyclones

Particle size range (μ)	Efficiency percentage	
	Conventional	High efficiency
Less than 5	Less than 50	50-80
5-20	50-80	80-95
15-40	80-95	95-99
Greater than 40	95-99	95-99

Tangential Inlet and Involute Inlet – A Comparison:

Inlets are of two types - tangential and involute. A straight tangential entry creates quite a bit of turbulences which will lead to back mixing and loss of efficiency even when a vortex finder is included in the cyclone design. On the other hand, the involute design (Fig. 7.16) brings in the gas parallel to the outer edge of the cyclone (tangent at that point) and leads it around a spiral for 180° to enter the top section with minimum turbulence. The other advantages of the involute design are better particle projection to the wall and a decrease in the loss of finer particles. The higher velocity in the central core can cause a slight increase in the Bernoulli effect, drawing more fine particles from the wall towards the central core. However, fines losses at the top and the pressure loss are much less and the efficiency much higher for the involute design than for the tangential entry design.

Operating Problems:

There are three important operating problems associated with cyclones. They are erosion, corrosion and material build-up.

(i) Erosion: Heavy, hard, shard-edged particles, in a high concentration, moving at high velocity in the cyclone, continuously scrape against the wall and can erode the metallic surface unless suitable materials are used.

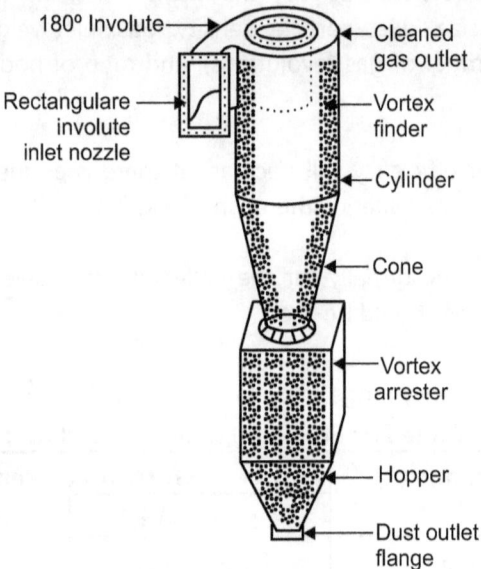

Fig. 7.21: Involute cyclone

(ii) Corrosion: It is a problem if the cyclone is operating below the condensadtion point when the reactive gases are present in effluent stream. The best solution to any corrosion problem in a cyclone is to keep the product above the dew point. If the gas and dust are corrosive at low temperatures then perhaps the only alternative is to use a stainless alloy.

Build-up: Build-up of dust cake on the cyclone walls, especially around the vortex finder, at the ends of any internal vanes, and opposite the entry can become a severe problem. It occurs most frequently with hygroscopic dusts.

In case the dust builds-up on the wall of the cyclone cone, a simple solution is to pound on the cone with a sledge hammer. Another solution is to hang chains inside; this works, but reduces efficiency. A better solution is to flange a section between the dust collecting hopper and the cyclone body. It can be removed periodically and scraped.

Advantages of Cyclones:
1. Low initial cost.
2. Simple construction and operation.
3. Low pressure drop.
4. Low maintenance requirements.
5. It has no moving parts.
6. Continuous disposal of solid particulates.
7. They can be constructed of any material which will meet the temperature and pressure requirements and the corrosion potential of the carrier gas stream.

Disadvantages of Cyclones:
1. Low collection efficiency for particles below 5-10 µ in diameter.
2. Equipment is subject to severe abrasive deterioration.
3. Decreasing collection efficiencies for decreasing dispersoid concentrations in the gas stream.

Applications:
Cyclones are used widely for the control of gas-borne particulates in such industrial operations as cement manufacture, feed and grain processing, food and beverage processing, mineral processing, paper and textile industries, and wood working industries.

Cyclones are also used to separate dust in disintegration operations, such as rock crushing, ore handling and sand conditioning in industries. They are also used in the recovery of catalyst dusts in the petroleum industry, and in the reduction of fly ash emissions.

Gas and solids down an *outer spiral*, the circular motion throws the particles outwards, towards the wall of the cyclone. The gas then passes up and out of the cyclone in an inner spiral, leaving via. the *vortex finder*. Solids leave at the lower outlet. Cyclones will work at any attitude, not just vertical.

If N_t is the number of turns in the outer spiral then

$$\text{Path length} = \pi N_t D_c \quad \ldots (7.65)$$

(Treating the cyclone as a parallel cylinder).

If the tangential fluid velocity is u_θ, then the residence time is given by,

$$\frac{\pi N_t D_c}{u_\theta} \quad \ldots (7.66)$$

Radial distance moved in this time is radial velocity x residence time,

$$\frac{d^2}{18\mu}(\rho_s - \rho_f)\frac{u_\theta^2}{r} \cdot \pi N_t \frac{D_c}{u_\theta} \quad \ldots (7.67)$$

Putting the radius of rotation, $r = \dfrac{D_c}{2}$ we get the distance travelled.

$$\dfrac{d^2}{9\mu}(\rho_s - \rho_f)\pi N_t u_\theta \qquad \text{... (7.68)}$$

If the particles are initially uniform distributed across the inlet duct the fraction collected of a particular size of particle is,

    Radial distance travelled/Breadth of inlet duct

So, if 50% of particles are to be collected of a particular size the distance travelled will be $B_c/2$ so

$$\dfrac{B_c}{2} = \dfrac{d_{50}^2}{9\mu}(\rho_s - \rho_f)\pi N_t u_\theta \qquad \text{... (7.69)}$$

d_{50} is the particle size of which 50% is collected.

Rearranging for d_{50} gives,

$$\boxed{d_{50} = \sqrt{\dfrac{9\mu B_c}{2(\rho_s - \rho_f)\pi N_t u_\theta}}} \qquad \text{... (7.70)}$$

For a standard cyclone the dimensions have ratios as follows:

$$H_c = 2B_c = \dfrac{D_c}{2} \qquad \text{... (7.71)}$$

Length = $4D_c$ (including the conical section, cylindrical portion length = $3D_c$, N_t is usually about 5.

Centrifuges:

There are two main types: Tube-Bowl and Disc-Bowl. Both can be used to separate either solids from liquids or two liquids of different density. The tube bowl is simply a tube rotated about its axis; either the liquids separate as they flow along the centrifuge or the solids are thrown towards the wall. Overflow dams at the outlet and end allow the two phases to be collected separately.

The Disc-bowl feed is admitted near the base and passes up through holes in the disc (which are actually inverted cones). The discs are about 5 mm apart. The solids do not have to travel far before hitting a disc and effectively being separated. Solids then continue to move outwards and are either removed manually or through nozzles on the periphery as concentrated slurry. Disc centrifuges range from 10 cm to 75 cm in diameter, spin speeds are in the 1000's or rpm range.

Operating Equations (Tube-Bowl Type):

The radial velocity, u_r of the denser droplets or the particles is given by,

$$u_r = \frac{r\omega^2}{18\mu}(\rho_1 - \rho_2)d^2 \quad \ldots (7.72)$$

where, ω is the rotational speed of the centrifuge.

The liquid layer thickness is small compared to the tube diameter; hence, we can treat the radius of rotation as a constant $\bar{r}$. This gives the travelled in the residence time t_{res} as,

$$u_r t_{res} = \frac{\bar{r}\omega^2}{18\mu}(\rho_1 - \rho_2)d^2 t_{res} \quad \ldots (7.73)$$

If the feed is homogeneous and the distance moved is equal to half the total thickness of the liquid layer, then half the particles with diameter d will be collected. In this case $d = d_{50}$ (this only applies if the concentration of 1 phase in the other is very small).

So,

$$u_r t_{res} = \frac{r_2 - r_1}{2} \quad \ldots (7.74)$$

where, r_1 and r_2 are the radii of the inner and outer overflow dams, respectively.

In order to compare centrifuges of different design it is convenient to use a relationship which links the throughput with a term, which accounts for the nature of the materials and one, which accounts for the physical design of the machine.

$$t_{res} = \frac{V}{Q} \quad \ldots (7.75)$$

where, V is the volumetric holdup and q is the volumetric throughput.

$$Q = \frac{V}{t_{res}} = \frac{d_{50}^2 \bar{r}\omega^2 (\rho_1 - \rho_2) V}{9\mu(r_2 - r_1)} \quad \ldots (7.76)$$

$$Q = 2 \cdot \frac{g(\rho_1 - \rho_2)d_{50}^2}{18\mu} \cdot \frac{V\bar{r}\omega^2}{g(r_1 - r_2)} \quad \ldots (7.77)$$

$$Q = 2u_t{}_{50} \Sigma \quad \ldots (7.78)$$

where, u_t is the terminal velocity under gravity of the d_{50} particle.

$$\Sigma = \frac{V\bar{r}\omega^2}{g(r_1 - r_2)} \quad \ldots (7.79)$$

Σ is a characteristics of the centrifuge design only and is equal to the area of gravitational settler required to do the same duty.

For scale up on the same duty

$$\frac{Q_1}{\Sigma_1} = \frac{Q_2}{\Sigma_2} \quad \ldots (7.80)$$

Values of Σ are given by manufacturers.

For a Disc-Bowl centrifuge,

$$\Sigma = \frac{2n\pi (r_2^3 - r_1^3) \omega^2}{3g \tan \Omega} \qquad \ldots (7.81)$$

where, r_1, r_2 are the inner and outer radii of the disk stack.

n is the number of spaces between the disc and Ω is the cone half-angle.

7.7 The Hydrocyclone

Hydroclone operate on a similar principle as reverse flow gave a high tangential velocity by means of a specially designed inlet and the solids are collected at the walls. The Hydrocyclone is normally used in the range of particle sizes of 0.004 mm (where it competes with the centrifuge) to 0.6 mm (where it competes with screens). The advantages of the Hydrocyclone are that there are no moving parts involved. The cone angle is usually in the range of 20-25°. The separation efficiency, η, has been obtained by Bennett as a function of the particle diameter, D, as:

$$\eta = 1 - \left\{ -\left(\frac{D}{D_{50}} - 0.115\right)^3 \right\} \qquad \ldots (7.82)$$

Where D_{50} is the 50 percent cut-off diameter (D for which $\eta = 0.5$). Equation (7.53) has been found to agree with experimental data on hydro cyclones having diameters, D_c, beyond about 4 cm. D_{50}.

Hydrocyclone: Hydrocyclone is fast replacing the mechanical classifiers as a sizing device. A Hydrocyclone is a device, which by utilizing a centrifugal force causes the separation of solids in the slurry. It has a tremendous capacity and yet it is very simple in construction as can be seen form Fig. 7.22.

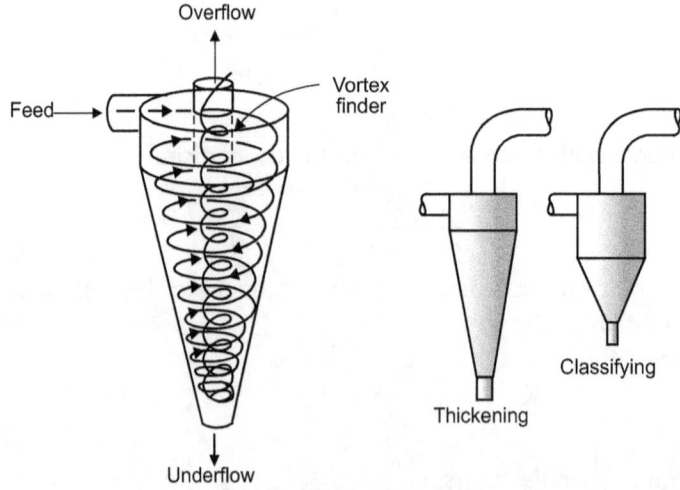

Fig. 7.22: Hydrocyclone

It is essentially a cyclindroconical shell with a tangential feed inlet, lower discharge giving under flow and upper discharge called vortex finder giving overflow. The coarser particles report in the under flow whereas the fines report in the overflow.

7.8 Centrifugal Settling

We have discussed the processing methods of settling and sedimentation where particles are separated from a fluid by gravitational forces acting on the particles. The particles were solid, gas, or liquid and the fluid was a liquid or a gas. In the present section we discuss settling or separation of particles from a fluid by centrifugal forces acting on the particles.

Use of centrifuges increases the forces on particles manyfold. Hence, particles that will not settle readily or at all in gravity settlers can often be separated from fluids by centrifugal force. The high settling force means that practical rates of settling can be obtained with much smaller particles than in gravity settlers. These high centrifugal forces do not change the relative settling velocities of small particles, but these forces do overcome the disturbing effects of Brownian motion and free convection currents.

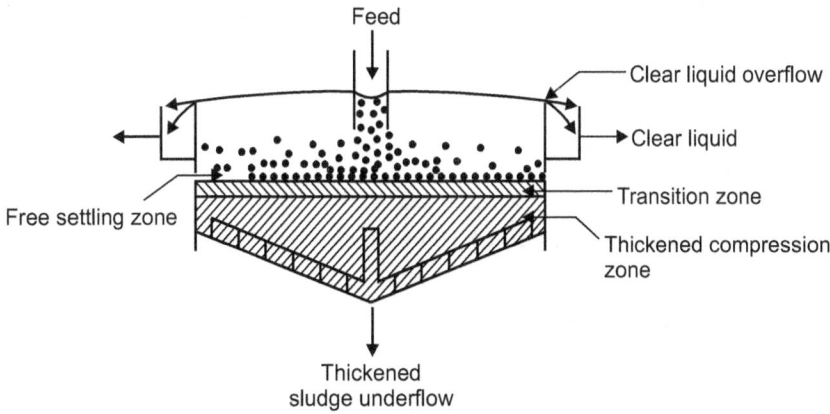

Fig. 7.23: Continuous Thickener

Sometimes gravity separation may be too slow because of the closeness of the densities of the particle and the fluid, or because of association forces holding the components together, as in emulsions. An example in the dairy industry is the separation of cream from whole milk, giving skim milk. Gravity separation takes hours, while centrifugal separation is accomplished in minutes in a cream separator. Centrifugal settling or separation is employed in many food industries, such as breweries, vegetable oil processing, fish protein concentrate processing, fruit juice processing to remove cellular materials, and so on. Centrifugal separation is also used in drying crystals and for separating emulsions into their constituent liquids or solid-liquid.

7.9 Selection of Separation Equipment

The choice of separation equipments primarily depends on the size and concentration of solids, though other factors like space requirement and pressure drops may also play some role. The ranges of operation of some common equipment 2-5 have been listed in Fig. 7.24 Sargent 4 also gives the approximate values of the gas velocity, solids collection efficiency, pressure drop and size ranges of equipment available commercially for several gas-solid separation units.

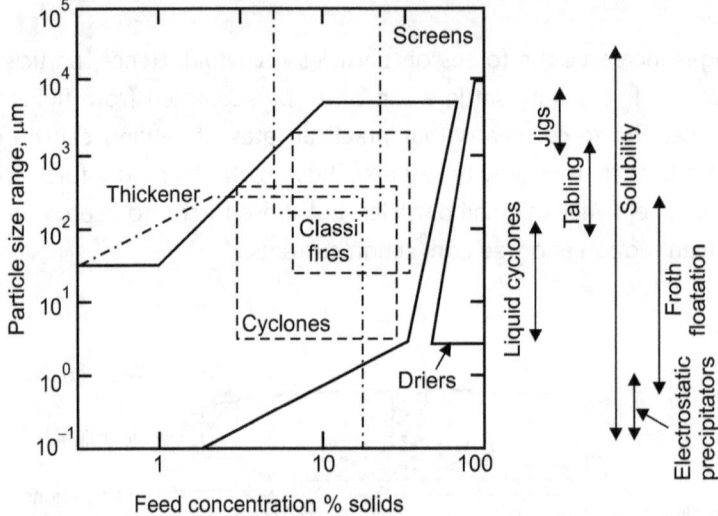

Fig. 7.24: Range of Operation of Some Mechanical Separation Equipment

7.10 Solved Examples

Example 7.1:

Calculate the maximum velocity at which a spherical particle of galena 0.15 cm in diameter will fall in water.

Data: Special gravity of galena = 7.5,
Special gravity of water = 1.0,
Viscosity of water = 0.82 C_p,
For sphere drag coefficient, Q_D = 0.45

Solution: Since the size of the particle is above 1000 microns, Newtonian conditions may be assumed.

So,
$$V_m = \sqrt{\frac{4}{3} \frac{(\rho_S - \rho_L) g \cdot d}{\rho_L (Q_D)}} = \sqrt{\frac{4}{3} \frac{(7.5 - 1)(980 \times 0.15)}{1 \times 0.45}}$$

V_m = 53 cm/sec. **(Ans.)**

MECHANICAL OPERATIONS
SEPARATION BASED ON MOTION ......

Now Reynolds number $N_{Re} = \dfrac{\rho_L \cdot V_m \cdot d}{\mu}$

$= \dfrac{1 \times 53 \times 0.15}{0.0082} = 1000$

Thus, $N_{Re} >> 600$

Hence, the assumption that conditions are Newtonian is valid.

Example 7.2:

Calculate the maximum velocity at which spherical particles of silica of 0.05 mm in diameter will fall through still water of temperature 75° C.

   Data given: Special gravity of silica = 2.70,
   Special gravity of water = 1.0, Viscosity of water at 75° C = 0.30 C_p.

Solution: Since, the particle size is 50 microns, Stokesian condition may be assumed.

So, $V_m = \dfrac{gd^2 (\rho_S - \rho_L)}{18\mu} = \dfrac{980 \, (5 \times 10^{-3})^2 \, (2.7 - 1.0)}{18 \times 0.0030}$

$V_m = 0.77$ cm/sec. **(Ans.)**

Now, Reynolds Number,

$N_{Re} = \dfrac{\rho_L V_m d}{N} = \dfrac{1 \times 0.005 \times 0.77}{0.77} = 1.26 \cong 1$

Hence, assumption of condition being Stokesian is justified.

Example 7.3:

Obtain the velocity of hindered settling for glass spheres of 200 mesh size in water. Assume ρ_S = 2600 kg/m³ and the volume fraction glass as 0.2.

   Data: (i) Density of fluid = ρ_f = 1000 kg/m³,
   (ii) Viscosity = N = 1C_p = 10^{-3} kg/m.sec,
   (iii) ϵ = porosity = 0.8,
   (iv) Diameter = 74 μm = 7.4×10^{-5} m.

Solution: We first obtain ρ_m. If we consider 1 m³ of slurry, 0.2 m³ of it is glass, having a mass of 0.2 × 2600 = 520 kg and 0.8 m³ of water having mass 800 kg. The total mass of the slurry is thus 1320 kg.

∴ ρ_m = 1320 kg/m³

We have, $V_{t, w} = \dfrac{(\rho_S - \rho_m) \epsilon \cdot 9 D^2 \, e^{-4.19} \, (1 - \epsilon)}{18\mu}$

∴ $V_{t, w} = (2600 - 1320) \times \dfrac{(7.4 \times 10^{-5})^2}{10^{-3}} \times 0.8 \times e^{-4.19 \times 0.2} \times 9.80$

$\boxed{V_{t, w} = 1.32 \times 10^{-3} \text{ m/s}}$ **(Ans.)**

Chp 7 | 7.43

MECHANICAL OPERATIONS — SEPARATION BASED ON MOTION

Example 7.4:
Calculate the terminal velocity of a steel ball, 2 mm diameter (density 7870 kg/m³) in oil (density 900 kg/m³, viscosity 50 mNs/m²).

Solution: For a sphere, $\left(R_o/\rho u_o^2\right) Re_o^2 = (2d^3/3\mu^2)\,\rho\,(\rho_s - \rho)\,g$

$$= (2 \times 0.002^3 / 3 \times 0.05^2)\, 900\, (7870 - 900 \times 9.81)$$
$$= 131.3$$
$$\log_{10} 131.3 = 2.118$$
$$\therefore\quad R_{eo} = 6.80$$
$$\therefore\quad \mu_o = 6.80 \frac{0.05}{(900 \times 0.002)}$$

$\boxed{\mu_o = 0.189 \text{ m/sec}}$ **(Ans.)**

Example 7.5:
In a hydraulic jig a mixture of two solids is separated into its components by subjecting an aqueous slurry of material to a pulsating motion and allowing the particles to settle for a series of short-time intervals such that they do not attain their terminal falling velocities. It is desired to separate materials of special gravities 1.8 and 2.5 whose particle size ranges from 0.3 to 3 mm diameter. It may be assumed that the particles are approximately spherical and that Stoke's law is applicable. Calculate approximately the maximum time interval for which the particles may be allowed to settle so that no particle of the less dense material falls a greater distance than any particle of the dense material. Data: Viscosity of water = 1 mNs/m².

Solution: For Stoke's law to apply, $N_{Re} < 0.2$ and resistance is due to skin friction only.

We have equation,
$$y = \frac{b}{a}t + \frac{v}{a} \cdot \frac{b}{a^2} + \left(\frac{b}{a^2} - \frac{v}{a}\right) e^{-at}$$

or, assuming the initial velocity, $v = 0$

$$y = \frac{b}{a}t - \frac{b}{a^2} + \frac{b}{a^2} e^{-at}$$

where
$$b = \left(1 - \frac{\rho}{\rho_s}\right) g$$

and
$$a = \frac{18\mu}{d^2 \rho_s}$$

For small particles of the dense material,
$$b = \left(\frac{1 - 1000}{2500}\right) 9.81 = 5.89 \text{ m/s}^2$$

$$a = \left(\frac{18 \times 0.001}{(0.3 \times 10^{-3})^2}\right) \times 2500 = 80/s$$

For large particles of the light material

$$b = \left(\frac{1-1000}{1800}\right) 9.81 = 4.36 \text{ m/s}^2$$

$$a = \frac{(18 \times 0.001)}{(3 \times 10^{-3})^2} \times 1800$$

$$a = 1.11/s$$

In order that these particle should fall the same distance,

$$\left(\frac{5.89}{80}\right)t - \left(\frac{5.89}{80^2}\right)(1 - e^{-80\,t}) = \frac{4.36}{1.11} t - \frac{4.36}{1.11^2}(1 - e^{-1.11\,t})$$

$$\therefore \quad 3.8504\,t + 3.5316\,e^{-1.11\,t} - 0.00092\,e^{-80\,t} = 3.5307 \text{ and solving by trial and error,}$$

$$\boxed{t = 0.01 \text{ sec.}} \tag{Ans.}$$

Example 7.6:

Two very small silica particles are settling at their respective terminal velocities through a highly viscous oil column. If one particle is twice as large as the other, how much time the larger particle will take than the smaller particle to fall through the same height?

Solution: Terminal velocity, u_t is given as, $u_t = \sqrt{\dfrac{4g\,(\rho_p - \rho)\,D_p}{3\,C_D\,\rho}}$

at low $N_{Re,\,P}$ (as in present case), $N_{Re,\,P} = \dfrac{D_p\,\rho\,u_t}{\mu}$

Since D_p is very small and μ is very high, $N_{Re,\,P}$ is low.

$$\therefore \quad C_D = \frac{24}{N_{Re,\,P}} \text{ and}$$

$$F_D = \frac{3\,\pi\,\mu\,u_c\,D_p}{g_c}$$

$$\therefore \quad u_t = \frac{g \cdot D_p^2\,(\rho_p - \rho)}{18\,\mu}$$

$$\therefore \quad u_t \propto D_p^2 \text{ for otherwise identical condition time for settling, } t \propto \frac{1}{u_t}$$

Thus, larger particles takes *one fourth* time as the time taken by smaller particles to fall through the same height. (Ans.)

Example 7.7:

A mixture of coal and sand particles having size smaller than 1×10^{-4} m in diameter is to be separated by screening and subsequent elutriation by water. recommended a screen aperture such that the oversize from the screen can be separated completely into sand coal particles by elutriation. Calculate also the required water velocity. Assume that Stoke's law is applicable. Density of sand = 2650 kg/m²; Density of coal = 1350 kg/m³; Density of water = 1000 kg/m³; Viscosity of water = 1×10^{-3} kg/m.s; g = 9.81 m/s².

Solution: For Stoke's law to be valid, $N_{Re, P} \leq 0.1$

Thus by Stoke's law,
$$V_t = \frac{(\rho_S - \rho) g \cdot D_P^2}{18 \mu L} \quad \ldots (1)$$

where V_t = Terminal settling velocity

and
$$N_{Re, P} = \frac{D_P \rho_P V_t}{\mu_L} = 0.1 \quad \ldots (2)$$

Now, in elutriation, terminal velocity of the largest particle (of lower density) should be the velocity of water. Thus, all the particles of lighter substance are carried away by water and all heavier particles settle.

So, we consider in calculation of D_P and V_t, the properties of coal

∴ $\rho_S = 1350$ kg/m³

$\mu_L = 1 \times 10^{-4}$ kg/m.s

Substitute for V_t in equation (2) from equation (1),

$$N_{Re, P} = \frac{D_P \rho_P}{\mu_L} \times \frac{(\rho_S - \rho) g \cdot D_P^2}{18 \mu_L} = 0.1$$

∴ $$0.1 = \frac{1350 \times (1350 - 1000) \times 9.81 \times D_P^3}{18 \times 10^{-4} \times 10^{-4}}$$

∴ $D_P^3 = 3.88 \times 10^{-15}$

∴ $D_P = 1.57 \times 10^{-5}$ m **(Ans.)**

∴ $$V_t = \frac{(1350 - 1000) \times 9.81 (1.57 \times 10^{-5})^2}{18 \times 10^{-4}}$$

$V_t = 4.71 \times 10^{-4}$ m/s **(Ans.)**

∴ Size of screen aperture = 1.57×10^{-5} m **(Ans.)**

∴ Velocity of water = 4.71×10^{-4} m/s **(Ans.)**

Example 7.8:

A particle of radius R and density ρ_S is moving radically out in a centrifuge. The angular velocity of centrifuge is ω. The density and viscosity of the fluid are ρ and μ. It is expected that Stoke's law is valid.

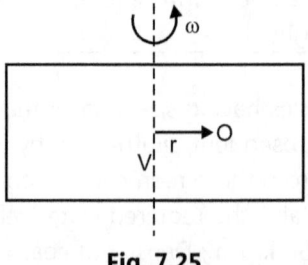

Fig. 7.25

Assuming that the particles move only radically, derive an expression for the radial velocity of the part at any radial location r in the centrifuge.

Solution: Taking a force balance around the centrifuge we have,

$$m \cdot \frac{dy}{dt} = F_e - F_b - F_D$$

where,
F_e = Gravitational force
F_b = Buoyancy force
F_D = Drag force

$$F_e = \frac{C_D \cdot u^2 \rho A_P}{2}$$

$$F_b = \frac{m \cdot \rho \cdot a_e}{\rho_P}$$

$$C_d = \frac{24}{N_{Re,P}} \text{ (Stoke's law)}$$

∴ $$m \cdot \frac{dy}{dt} = m \cdot a_e - m \cdot \frac{\rho}{\rho_P} a_D - \frac{24 \, u^2 \rho A_P}{N_{Re\,p} \times 2}$$

∴ $$\frac{du}{dt} = a_e \left[\frac{\rho_P - \rho}{\rho_1}\right] - \frac{24 \, u^2 \, r \, A_P}{N_{Re\,P} \cdot 2m}$$

$$\frac{du}{dt} = \omega^2 r \left[\frac{\rho_P - \rho}{\rho_P}\right] - \frac{12 \, u \, A_P \, \mu}{d_{Pm}}$$

or $$\frac{du}{dt} + \frac{12 \, u \, A_P \, \mu}{d_{P\,m}} = \omega^2 r \left[\frac{\rho_P - \rho}{\rho_P}\right]$$

$\frac{dy}{dt}$ is negligible as comparison to other forms of the above equation and it depends on the radial distance.

∴ $$\boxed{u = \omega^2 r \left[\frac{\rho_P - \rho}{\rho_P}\right] \frac{d_{Pm}}{12 \, A_P \, \mu}}$$ **(Ans.)**

Example 7.9:

A slurry containing 5 kg of water per kg of solids is to be thickened to a sludge containing 1.5 kg of water per kg of solids in a continuous operation. Laboratory tests using five different concentrations of the slurry gave the following results:

Concentration (kg water/kg solid)	5	4.2	3.7	3.1	2.5
Rate of sedimentation (mm/s)	0.17	0.10	0.08	0.06	0.042

Calculate the minimum area of a thickener to effect the separation of 0.6 kg of solids per seconds.

Solution: Basis: 1 kg of solids: 1.5 kg water is carried away in underflow, balance in overflow, V = 1.5.

Concentration U	Water to Overflow (U – V)	Sedimentation rate, u_c (mm/s)	$(U - V)/u_c$ (sec./mm)
5.0	3.5	0.17	20.56
4.2	2.7	0.10	27.0
3.7	2.2	0.08	27.5
3.1	1.6	0.06	26.67
2.5	1.0	0.042	23.81

Maximum velocity of $\dfrac{(U-V)}{u_c} = 27.5$ s/mm = 27,500 s/m

and $A = \left[\dfrac{(U-V)}{u_c}\right]\dfrac{w}{\rho} = 27{,}500 \dfrac{0.6}{1000}$

$\boxed{A = 16.5 \text{ m}^2}$ **(Ans.)**

Example 7.10:

The daily output of a continuous cone-bottom settling tank (diameter 10 m) should be 36 tonnes of solid phase. Show how the settling tank height will vary with change in dilution of the compression zone as follows:

  1 : 1.2, 1 : 1.3, 1 : 1.4, 1 : 1.5, 1 : 1.6, 1 : 1.7, 1 : 1.8.

The liquid phase is water (Density = 1000 kg/m²) The density of solid phase = 2600 kg/m³, Height of feed zone = 60 cm, Height of settling tank zone = 75 cm, Plot the results graphically.

Solution: The amount of solid settling per unit area of settling surface,

$$Q = \dfrac{36}{\dfrac{\pi}{4}(10)^2}\left(\dfrac{16}{24}\right) = 0.3055 \text{ tonne/m}^2 \text{ of settling area}$$

$h_1 + h_3 = 0.6 + 0.75 = 1.35$ m

m'	Δ_{sus}, Relative density of suspension (kg/m³)	$[M_{sus}]$ mass concentration of suspension	solid $\dfrac{}{m^3}$ of suspension (Tonne)	H_2 (m)	$H = h_1 + h_2 + h_3$ (m)
1.2	1.388	0.454	0.630	0.3055/0.630 = 0.4842	1.834
1.3	1.365	0.434	0.593	0.5147	1.864
1.4	1.344	0.416	0.559	0.5455	1.89
1.5	1.326	0.400	0.530	0.5759	1.92
1.6	1.310	0.384	0.503	0.6063	1.95
1.7	1.295	0.370	0.479	0.6369	1.98
1.8	1.281	0.357	0.457	0.6677	2.07

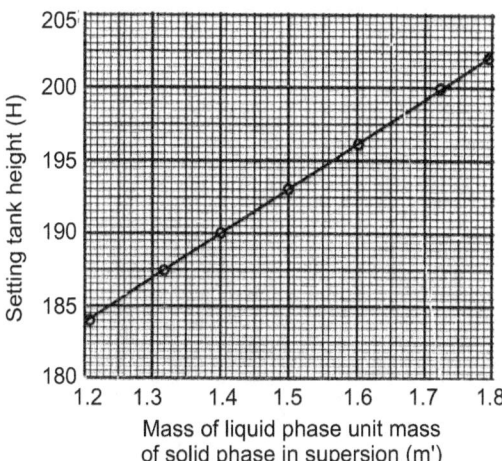

Fig. 7.26: Dependence of Settling Tank Height with the Change of Dilution in the Compression Zone

Example 7.11:

A mixture of coal and sand particles having sizes smaller than 1×10^{-4} m in diameter is to be separated by screening and subsequent elutriation with water. Recommend a screen aperture such that the oversize from the screen can be separated completely into sand and coal particles by elutriation. Calculate also the required water velocity. Assume that Stokes law is applicable. Density of sand = 2650 kg/m³; density of coal = 1350 kg/m³; density of water = 1000 kg/m³; viscosity of water = 1×10^{-3} kg/m.s; g = 9.812 m/s².

Solution: For laminar settling regimes, terminal-settling velocity is given by

Stokes law: (valid for $N_{Re, p} < 0.1$)

$$u_t = \frac{D^2 (\rho_s - \rho) g}{(18 \mu)}$$

where, D is the dia of particle, ρ_s is the density of solid.

where, $$N_{Re, p} = \frac{D u_t \rho}{\mu}$$

u_t of larger dia. coal particle $= \dfrac{(1 \times 10^{-4})^2 \times (1350 - 1000) \times 9.812}{(18 \times 0.001)}$

$= 1.9079 \times 10^{-3}$ m/sec

Diameter of sand particle corresponding to the u_t of larger dia coal particle:

$$1.9079 \times 10^{-3} = D^2 \times \frac{(2650 - 1000) \times 9.812}{(18 \times 0.001)}$$

$$D = 4.6056 \times 10^{-5} \text{ m} \qquad \text{(Ans.)}$$

The size of screen aperture needed so that the oversize particles can be separated completely into sand and coal by elutriation = 4.6056×10^{-5} m.

The required water velocity
= 1.9079 × 10⁻³ m/sec **(Ans.)**

By operating at the water velocity of 1.9079 × 10⁻³ m/sec, coal particles will be carried along with water and sand particles will settle down.

This calculation is aided with the following figure:

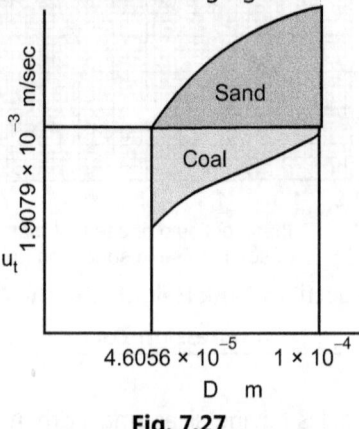

Fig. 7.27

Example 7.12:
In a mixture of quartz (sp. gr. = 2.65) and galena (sp. gr. = 7.5), the size of the particles range from 0.0002 cm to 0.001 cm. On separation in a hydraulic classifier using water under free settling conditions, what are the size ranges of quartz and galena in the pure products? (Viscosity of water = 0.001 kg/m.s; density = 1000 kg/m³).

Data: Density of quartz (ρ_{sa}) = 2650 kg/m³
Density of galena (ρ_{sb}) = 7500 kg/m³
Particle size range (D_{min} to D_{max}): 0.0002 cm to 0.001 cm
Viscosity of water (m) = 0.001 kg/m. sec
Density of water (ρ) = 1000 kg/m³

Solution: For laminar settling regimes, terminal-settling velocity is given by,

Stokes law: (valid for $N_{Re, p} < 0.1$).

$$u_t = D^2 \frac{(\rho_s - \rho) g}{(18 \mu)}$$

where, D is the diameter of particle. r_s is the density of solid.

$$N_{Re, p} = \frac{D u_t \rho}{\mu}$$

for turbulent regime, $u_t = \left[\frac{4D (\rho s - \rho) g}{(3 C_D \rho)}\right]^{0.5}$

C_D is the drag coefficient. If C_D is assumed to be same for the two different density particles of the same diameter (assumption is valid in high turbulent velocities and practically assumed to be correct for laminar regimes also), for laminar flow, for equal settling velocities, we have,

$$\frac{D_a}{D_b} = \left[\frac{(\rho_{sb} - \rho)}{(\rho_{sa} - \rho)}\right]^{0.5} \quad \ldots (1)$$

Similarly for turbulent flow, for equal settling velocities,

$$\frac{D_a}{D_b} = \left[\frac{(\rho_{sb} - \rho)}{(\rho_{sa} - \rho)}\right]$$

First let us check for the flow regime for the given particle size range of particles: For the largest dia particle of higher density to follow laminar regime,

$$N_{Re, p} = \frac{D u_t \rho}{\mu} = D D^2 \frac{(\rho_s - \rho) g \rho}{(18 \mu^2)} \text{ should be less than 0.1.}$$

i.e., the maximum size of particle is,

$$D^3 = 0.1 \times \frac{18 \mu^2}{(\rho_s - \rho) g}$$

$$r = \frac{0.1 \times 18 \times 0.001^2}{[(7500 - 1000) \times 9.81 \times 1000]}$$

$$= 3.05 \times 10^{-5} \text{ m} = 0.00305 \text{ cm}$$

which is well above the maximum size of the particles.

Therefore, laminar flow equations can be used for this problem. The fractions obtained after separation are: (i) Pure Galena only, (ii) Galena and quartz, (iii) Quartz only. The terminal settling velocity of minimum dia galena in fraction (i) corresponds to the settling velocity of maximum dia quartz particles.

From equation (1), $\quad \dfrac{D_a}{D_b} = \left[\dfrac{(\rho_{sb} - r)}{(\rho_{sa} - \rho)}\right]^{0.5}$

$$\frac{D_a}{0.001} = \left[\frac{(2.65 - 1)}{(7.5 - 1)}\right]^{0.5} \quad \textbf{(Ans.)}$$

$$D_a = 0.0005 \text{ cm}$$

The fraction (i) consists of pure galena in the size range 0.0005 cm to 0.001 cm. The terminal settling velocity of maximum dia quartz in fraction (ii) corresponds to the settling velocity of minimum dia galena particles.

From equation (1),

$$\frac{D_a}{0.0002} = \left[\frac{(7.5 - 1)}{(2.65 - 1)}\right]^{0.5} \quad \textbf{(Ans.)}$$

$$D_a = 0.0004 \text{ cm}$$

The fraction (iii) consists of pure quartz in the size range 0.0002 cm to 0.0004 cm.

The fraction (ii) consists of quartz in the size range 0.0004 cm to 0.001 cm, and galena in the size range 0.0002 cm to 0.0005 cm. This result is shown in Fig. 7.28.

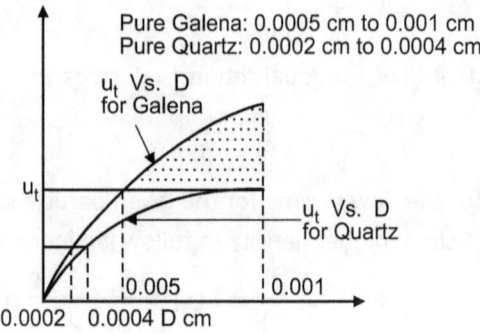

Fig. 7.28

Example 7.13:

Derive expressions for the unhindered gravitational settling velocity:

(a) In laminar flow for which $C_D = \dfrac{K}{Re}$

(b) In fully developed turbulent flow where C_D = constant = K'

In each case find the expression for the free settling ratio of particles of densities ρ_1 and ρ_2 in a fluid of density ρ_f.

Calculate the free settling ratios for separation of galena and quartz (densities 7500 and 2800 kgm^{-3} respectively) in water. Which is more restrictive condition?

Solution: Derive expressions for the unhindered gravitational settling velocity:

(a) in laminar flow for which $C_D = \dfrac{K}{Re}$

Rearranging the definition of C_D gives,

$$F_D = C_D \cdot \dfrac{1}{2} \rho_f u_{fs}^2 \dfrac{\pi d^2}{4}$$

So,

$$F_D = \dfrac{K}{Re} \dfrac{1}{2} \rho_f u_{fs}^2 \dfrac{\pi d^2}{4}$$

So,

$$F_D = \dfrac{\pi}{8} K d \mu_f u_{fs}$$

Gravitational force $= mg = V(\rho_s - \rho_f) = \dfrac{\pi d^3}{6}(\rho_s - \rho_f) g$

Equating gravitational and drag forces then gives terminal velocity:

$$\dfrac{\pi}{8} K d \mu_f u_t = \dfrac{\pi}{6} d^3 (\rho_s - \rho_f) g$$

So,

$$u_t = \dfrac{4}{3} \dfrac{d^2}{K\mu_f}(\rho_s - \rho_f) g$$

(b) in fully developed turbulent flow where C_D = Constant = K'

$$C_D = K'$$

$$F_D = \frac{K'}{2} \rho_f u_{fs}^2 \cdot \frac{\pi d^2}{4} = \frac{\pi}{6} d^3 (\rho_s - \rho_f) g$$

$$u_t^2 = \frac{4}{3} \frac{d}{K' \rho_f} (\rho_s - \rho_f) g$$

and
$$u_t = \sqrt{\frac{4}{3} \frac{d}{K' \rho_f} (\rho_s - \rho_f) g}$$ (Ans.)

In each case find the expression for the free settling ratio of the particles of densities ρ_1 and ρ_2 in a fluid of density ρ_f.

The free settling ratio is the ratio of the diameter of the largest less dense particle and the smallest more dense particle which will have equal terminal velocities.

For case (a):

$$d = \sqrt{\frac{3}{4} \frac{u_t K \mu_f}{(\rho_s - \rho_f) g}}$$

So,
$$\frac{d_{max}}{d_{min}} = \left(\frac{(\rho_1 - \rho_f)}{(\rho_2 - \rho_f)}\right)^{\frac{1}{2}}$$

where, $\rho_1 > \rho_2$

For case (b):
$$d = \frac{3}{4} \frac{K' \rho_f u_t}{4(\rho_s - \rho_f) g}$$

$$\frac{d_{max}}{d_{min}} = \frac{(\rho_1 - \rho_f)}{(\rho_2 - \rho_f)}$$

For ρ_1 = 7500 kg/m³ and ρ_2 = 2800 kg/m³

(a) $\frac{d_{max}}{d_{min}} = 1.900$ (Ans.)

(b) $\frac{d_{max}}{d_{min}} = 3.611$ (Ans.)

(b) Is the more restrictive case, because in (b) the larger particle must be 3.6 times the diameter of the smallest, while in (a) it needs only be 1.9 times the diameter of the smallest.

Example 7.14:

Calculate the terminal velocity of a spherical particle of diameter 1 mm and density 3000 kg/m³, falling through atmospheric air.

Solution: It cannot be assumed that Stokes' Law applies, this is a relatively large particle in a relatively low viscosity/density fluid. In this case the terminal velocity calculated from the

MECHANICAL OPERATIONS
SEPARATION BASED ON MOTION ......

equation derived from Stokes' Law would be of the order of 100 m/s. This should immediately strike you as being high. What you have to do instead is to calculate $C_D Re^2$ and use the graph to determine Reynolds number and hence the velocity. The equation for $C_D Re^2$ is,

$$C_D Re^2 = \frac{4}{3} \frac{d^3 (\rho_s - \rho_f) g \rho_f}{\mu^2}$$

Substituting the values for this example,

$$C_D Re^2 = \frac{4}{3} \times \frac{0.001^3 (3000 - 1.25) \times 9.81 \times 1.25}{(0.018 \times 10^{-3})^2}$$

So, $C_D Re^2 = 151.326$

From graph, which gives values of $\frac{F}{A \rho u^2} \cdot Re^2$ vs. Re, this is not equal to $C_D Re^2$ vs. Re, since,

$$C_D = \frac{F_D/A}{\frac{1}{2} \rho_f u_{fs}^2}$$

$$\frac{F}{A \rho u^2} \cdot Re^2 = \frac{1}{2} C_D Re^2$$

Hence, $Re = 600$ and

$$u_t = \frac{600 \times 0.018 \times 10^{-3}}{1.25 \times 0.001}$$

$$u_t = 8.64 \text{ m/s} \quad \text{(Ans.)}$$

Example 7.15:

In an experiment, 1 kg/s of a particulate material was transported 4 m through a horizontal 0.038 m I.D. pipe by an air stream with mean velocity 5.0 m/s. The material had a density of 2000 kg/m³ and a terminal velocity in atmospheric air of 1.5 m/s. The pressure drop in the pipe was found to be 0.38 bar. Find the mean particle velocity and the voidage of the solid-air mixture.

What pressure of air supply would be necessary to transport the same solid flowrate to a hopper on the roof of a building 30 m high? What would be the air consumption (std. m³/min) for this service ?

Solution:
- W = solids rate = 1.0 kg/s
- l = 4 m
- ρ = density of atmosphere in which v_t was determined
- v_t = terminal velocity = 1.5 m/s
- ρ_f = density of air in experiment
- ρ_s = 2000 kg/m³
- u_f = fluid velocity = 5.0 m/s

If the pipe discharges to atmosphere, (1.0 bara) entering air pressure = 1.38 bara and mean pressure = 1.19 bara. If the operation is isothermal:

$$\frac{\rho_f}{\rho} \simeq \frac{P_f}{P} = 1.19$$

$$\frac{\rho}{\rho_s} \simeq 0$$

So, $\quad \frac{\pi}{4}(0.038)^2 \times 0.38 \times 10^5 = \frac{1 \times 4}{u_s} \times 9.82 \times 1 \times 1.19 \left(\frac{5 - u_s}{1.5}\right)^2$

$$2.076\, u_s = (5 - u_s)^2 = 25 - 10\, u_s + u_s^2$$

$$u_s^2 - 12.076\, u_s + 25 = 0$$

and $\quad u_s = \dfrac{12.076 \pm (145.84 - 4 \times 25)^{\frac{1}{2}}}{2} = 9.42 \text{ or } 2.65 \text{ ms}^{-1}$

Since the first of these is greater than the gas velocity u_s must be 2.65 m/s

Mass of solids per m of tube $= \dfrac{W}{u_s} = 12.65 = 0.377$ kg

Volume of solids $= \dfrac{0.377}{2000} = 1.885 \times 10^{-4}$ m³

Volume of 1 m of pipe $= \dfrac{\pi}{4}(0.038)^2 = 1.134 \times 10^{-3}$ m³

So, $\quad \varepsilon = \dfrac{1.134 \times 10^{-3} - 1.885 \times 10^{-4}}{1.134 \times 10^{-3}} = 0.834$

For vertical transport the pressure drop will be the scaled up pressure drop from the horizontal experiment –

$$0.38 \times \frac{30}{4} = 2.85 \text{ bar}$$

Plus a contribution due to the hydrostatic head of suspended solids equal to

$$\frac{Wl}{u_s} g \left(1 - \frac{\rho_f}{\rho_s}\right) \div \frac{\pi}{4}(0.038)^2 = 9.8 \times 10^4 \text{ Nm}^{-2} = 0.98 \text{ bar}$$

So the total pressure drop = 2.85 + 0.98 = 3.83 bar

In order to have a velocity at the pipe entry of 5 m/s under these conditions gas flowrate must be,

$$5 \times \frac{\pi}{4}(0.038)^2 \times 4.831 \times 60 = 1.64 \text{ stdm}^3/\text{minute} \quad \text{(Ans.)}$$

Example 7.16:

A solid material is to be recovered from water by gravity settling. Describe the experiment, you would carry out to establish the settling characteristics of the material. Using sketches outline the different zones present in the settling experiment over time. Sketch a typical graph of height of clear liquid-suspension interface vs. time.

A 3% (weight) slurry of $CaCO_3$ $\left(I = \sqrt{\dfrac{\mu(1-\mu)(N-1)}{n\sum_i (x_i - \bar{x})^2}} = 2630 \text{ kgm}^{-3}\right)$ in water was subjected to a batch sedimentation test. The result are given below.

Time (minutes)	0	20	40	60	80	100	120	140
Interface height (m)	1.76	1.00	0.74	0.57	0.42	0.34	0.26	0.22

Determine the area and depth of a continuous thickener required to handle 100 tonnes of solid per day. The initial solids concentration is 3% (weight) and the thickened slurry is to be 10% (weight).

Solution: The relevant graphs are given.

t(min)	h(m)	z_i(m)	t_i(min)	$C(kg/m^3)$ $C_0 z_0/z_i$	$u(m/min)$ z_i/t_i	Σ C/ρ_s
0	1.76	1.76	25	30.9	0.070	0.988
20	1.00	1.44	68	37.8	0.021	0.986
40	0.74	1.14	113	47.7	0.010	0.982
60	0.57	1.08	126	50.4	0.009	0.981
80	0.42	0.85	160	64.0	0.005	0.976
100	0.34	0.77	174	70.6	0.004	0.973
120	0.26	0.61	206	89.2	0.003	0.966
140	0.22					

Values of z_i and t_i are taken from graph 1, a plot of interface height vs. time.

$$C_0 = \dfrac{\text{mass solid}}{\text{volume liquid}} = \dfrac{3}{97 \times 10^{-3}} = 30.9 \text{ kg/m}^3$$

t	$C(kg/m^3)$	$u_h(u/\Sigma)$ (m/min)	$u_h C$ (kg/min m^3)
0	30.9	0.071	2.194
20	37.8	0.021	0.794
40	47.7	0.010	0.477
60	50.4	0.009	0.454
80	64.0	0.005	0.320
100	70.6	0.004	0.282
120	89.2	0.003	0.277

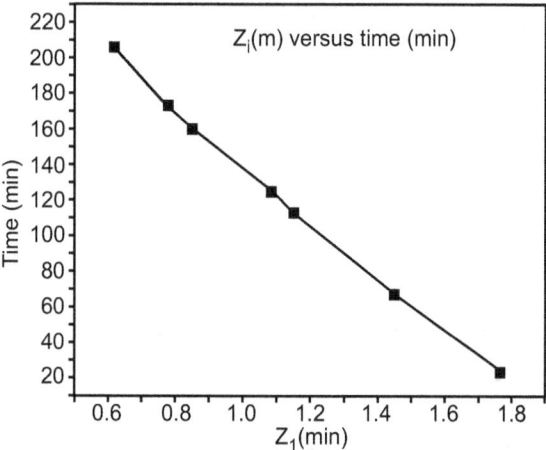

Fig. 7.29: Plot of Interface Height Versus Time

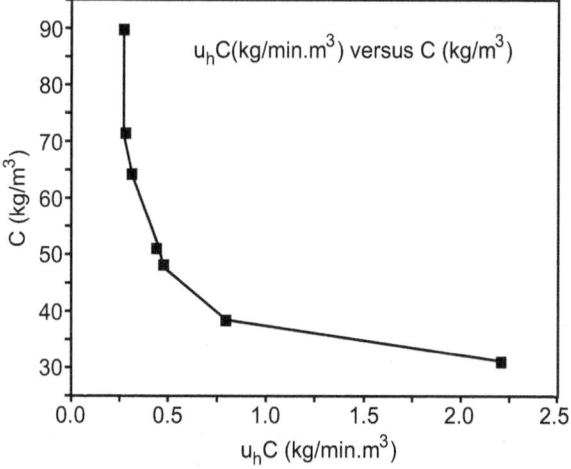

Fig. 7.30: Plot of u_h C (kg/min. m³) Versus C (kg/m³)

Plot u_hC vs. C (graph 2)

$$C_{feed} = 30.9 \text{ kg/m}^3$$

$$C_B = C_{prod} = \frac{10}{90 \times 10^{-3}} = 111.1 \text{ kg/m}^3$$

For maximum G_{feed} and hence minimum area draw the line joining C_B and G_{feed} such that it just touches the graph.

This gives G_{feed} as 0.74 kg/min m² or 0.0123 kg/s m².

Hence, a rate of 100 tonne/day requires an area of 94 m².

$$t_{res} = 140 \text{ min}$$

Q is the volumetric flowrate of solids plus the volumetric flowrate of liquid.

$$Q = \frac{100 \times 10^3}{2630} + \frac{3233 \times 10^3}{1000} = 3271 \text{ m}^3/\text{day} = 0.0379 \text{ m}^3/\text{s}$$

$t_{res} = \dfrac{V}{Q}$ so $V = 318 \text{ m}^3$

And minimum depth is $318/94 = 3.4$ m (Ans.)

Example 7.17:
Calculate the settling velocity of dust particles of (a) 60 μm and (b) 10 μm diameter in air at 21°C and 100 kPa pressure. Assume that the particles are spherical and of density 1280 kgm³, and that the viscosity of air = 1.8×10^{-5} Ns m^{-2} and density of air = 1.2 kgm^{-3}.

Solution: (a) For 60 μm particle:

$$v_m = \frac{(60 \times 10^{-6})^2 \times 9.81 \times (1280 - 1.2)}{(18 \times 1.8 \times 10^{-5})}$$

$$= 0.14 \text{ ms}^{-1}$$

(b) For 10 μm particles since v_m is proportional to the squares of the diameters,

$$v_m = 0.14 \times (10/60)^2$$

$$= 3.9 \times 10^{-3} \text{ ms}^{-1}$$

Checking Reynolds number for the 60 μm particles,

$$(Re) = (Dv\rho_f/\mu)$$

$$= (60 \times 10^{-6} \times 0.14 \times 1.2)/(1.8 \times 10^{-5})$$

$$= 0.56$$

Stokes' Law applies only to cases in which settling is free, that is where the motion of one particle is unaffected by the motion of other particles.

Example 7.18:
Calculate the terminal radial velocity of a soluble coffee particle (ρ = 1050 kgm^{-3}) 60 μm in diameter in air at 260°C (μ = 2.7×10^{-5} kg m^{-1}s^{-1} and ρ = 0.658 kgm^{-3}) entering a cyclone 0.45 m in diameter at a tangential velocity of 2m s^{-1}.

What would the gravitational terminal velocity of the same particle be, in the same fluid? What fraction of these particles would be collected if this is a 'standard' cyclone?

Solution: Calculate the terminal radial velocity of a soluble coffee particle (ρ = 1050 kgm^{-3}) 60 μm in diameter in air at 260°C (μ = 2.7×10^{-5} kg m^{-1}s^{-1} and ρ = 0.658 kgm^{-3}) entering a cyclone with cylindrical section 0.45 m in diameter at a tangential velocity of 2m s^{-1}.

$$u_r = \frac{d^2}{18 \, \mu_f}(\rho_s - \rho_f)\frac{u_\theta^2}{r}$$

$$u_r = \frac{(60 \times 10^{-6})^2}{18 \times 2.7 \times 10^{-5}}(1050 - 0.658)\frac{4}{0.225}$$

$$u_r = 0.138 \text{ ms}^{-1}$$

It would make very little difference here if we had taken $\rho_f \approx 0$ since it is so much smaller than the solid density.

What would the gravitational terminal velocity of the same particle be, in the same fluid?

Under gravity
$$u_t = u_r \cdot g \cdot \frac{r}{u_t^2}$$

$$u_t = 0.138 \times 9.81 \times \frac{0.225}{4}$$

$$u_t = 0.076 \text{ ms}^{-1} \qquad \text{(Ans.)}$$

What fraction of these particles would be collected if this is a 'standard' cyclone? A standard cyclone has

$$B_C = \frac{D_C}{4} = 0.1125 \text{ m} \qquad \text{(Ans.)}$$

The residence time in the cyclone is,

$$\frac{\pi N_t D_c}{u_\theta} = \frac{\pi \cdot 5 \cdot 0.45}{2} = 3.53 \text{ s}$$

Distance travelled radially = Residence time × u_r

$$= 3.53 \times 0.138 = 0.49 \text{ m}$$

Since this distance is greater than the width of the duct the fraction collected will be 1. If the distance travelled had been less than width of the duct the fraction collected would be,

$$\frac{\text{Distance travelled radially}}{B_D}$$

Example 7.19:

Flue gases from a thermal power station, flowing at the rate of 1000 m³/min and containing particles in the size range of 1 to 100 microns, are sent to a multi-tray settling chamber for preliminary separation of particles. The settling unit, 5 m long and 5 m wide, contains 25 trays including the bottom shelf, spaced uniformly 30 cm apart. Determine the minimum particle size that can be separated in the unit. Assume Stroke's law to be applicable.

Data: Temperature of gases = 200°C
Density of gases = 0.001 g/cm³
Viscosity of gases = 0.035 cp
Density of particles = 2.2 g/cm³

Solution: Height of the unit = 25 × 30 = 750 cm

$$(d_p)_{min} = \left[\frac{18\,\mu\,Q}{g\,(\rho_s - \rho)\,LB}\,\frac{h}{H}\right]^{1/2}$$

$$= \left[\frac{18 \times (0.035 \times 10^{-2})\,(1000 \times 10^6 \times 30)}{981 \times 2.2 \times 60 \times 500 \times 500 \times 750}\right]^{1/2}$$

$$= 2.79 \times 10^{-3}\text{ cm}$$

$$= 27.9\text{ microns} \qquad \text{(Ans.)}$$

Example 7.20:

Specify a cyclone separator to handle 60 m³/min. of gases containing particles of density 2.0 g/cm³ and size distribution.

Particle size (microns)	Mean size (microns)	Weight (%)
<5	2.5	15
5-10	7.5	15
10-30	20	30
30-50	40	25
>50	50	15

For the standard configuration chosen, the effective number of swirls equals 5. The efficiency and reduced diameter are given by the following table:

d_p/d_{pc}	0.20	0.30	0.50	0.70	1.0	1.5	2.0	3.0	5.0	7.0	10
% efficiency	4	8	20	33	50	69	80	90	96	98	99

If 20 cyclones of equal size in a multicyclone are used to handle the gas, estimate their dimensions and efficiency of separation.

Solution:
Temperature of gases = 80°C
Density of gases = 0.00095 g/cm³
Viscosity of gases = 0.025 cp
Width of the inlet, B = $D_c/4$
Height of the inlet, H = $D_c/2$
Inlet velocity heads lost in the cyclone = 8
Pressure loss across the cyclone = 7.5 cm water

Take the head available, in a multicyclone, to be 10 percent less than that in a single unit.

$$= \frac{60 \times 10^6}{60}$$

$$= 10^6 \text{ cm}^3/\text{s}$$

Density of gases = 0.00095 g/cm³
Head loss across the cyclone = 7.5 cm water

$$= \frac{7.5}{0.00095} = 7894.75 \text{ cm gas}$$

$$= 8 \text{ times the inlet velocity heads}$$

If D_c is the diameter of the cyclone separator,

$$\text{Inlet area} = \frac{D_c^2}{8} \quad \left(\because A = B \times N = \frac{D_C}{2} \times \frac{D_C}{4} = \frac{D_C^2}{8}\right)$$

$$\text{Inlet velocity, } v_1 = \frac{8Q}{D_c^2} \quad \left(\because V = \frac{Q}{A} = \frac{Q}{\frac{D_c^2}{8}} = \frac{8Q}{D_c^2}\right)$$

where, Q is the flow rate, cm³/s

$$\text{Inlet velocity head} = \frac{v_i^2}{2g_c}$$

$$= \frac{7894.74}{8}$$

$$\therefore \quad v_i = \left(\frac{7894.74 \times 2 \times 981}{8}\right)^{1/2}$$

$$= 1391.47 \text{ cm/s}$$

$$= 13.915 \text{ m/s}$$

$$\text{Area of inlet} = \frac{D_c^2}{8} = \frac{60 \times 10^6}{60 \times 13.915} = 718.648 \text{ cm}^2$$

Diameter of cyclone separator = $(718.65 \times 8)^{1/2}$

$$= 75.82 \text{ cm} \quad \text{(Say 76 cm)}$$

Width of inlet, $B = \frac{D_c}{4} = 18.96 \text{ cm}$ (Say 19 cm)

Height of the inlet $= \frac{D_c}{2} = 37.91 \text{ cm}$ (Say 38 cm)

$$\text{Cut diameter} = \left[\frac{9\mu B}{2\pi N v_i (\rho_s - \rho)}\right]^{1/2}$$

$$= \left[\frac{9 \times 0.02 \times 10^{-2} \times 19}{2\pi \times 5 \times 1391.5 \times 2}\right]^{1/2}$$

$$= 0.625 \times 10^{-3}$$

$$= 6.25 \text{ microns}$$

Mean size	d_p/d_{p_c}	% Efficiency η_i	Weight fraction W_i	$\eta_i W_i$
2.5	0.4	15	0.15	2.25
7.5	1.2	58	0.15	8.70
20	3.2	91	0.30	27.30
40	6.4	97	0.25	24.25
50	8.0	98	0.15	14.70
				$\sum \eta_i W_i = 77.2$

Average efficiency of separation = 77.2 percent.

Multicyclones:

$$\text{Head available} = \frac{7.5}{1.1} = 6.82 \text{ cm water}$$

$$= \frac{6.82}{0.00095} = 7177 \text{ cm gas}$$

$$\text{Volume flow rate per unit} = \frac{60 \times 10^6}{60 \times 20} = 5 \times 10^4 \text{ cm}^3/\text{s}$$

$$V_i = \left(\frac{7177 \times 2 \times 981}{8}\right)^{1/2}$$

$$= 1326.713 \text{ cm/s}$$

$$\text{Area of the inlet} = \frac{5 \times 10^4}{1326.713} = 37.69 \text{ cm}^2$$

$$\frac{D_c^2}{8} = 37.69$$

$$D_c = 17.36 \text{ cm}$$

$$B = 4.34 \text{ cm}$$

$$d_{p_c} = \left(\frac{9 \times 0.02 \times 10^{-2} \times 4.34}{2\pi \times 5 \times 1326.713 \times 2}\right)^{1/2}$$

$$= 3.06 \times 10^{-4} \text{ cm} = 3.06 \text{ microns}$$

Mean size Microns	d_p/d_{p_c}	% Efficiency η_i	Weight fraction W_i	$\eta_i \times W_i$
2.5	0.817	40	0.15	6.0
7.5	2.45	85	0.15	12.75
20	6.536	98	0.30	29.40
40	13.07	99	0.25	24.75
50	16.34	99	0.15	14.85
				$\sum \eta_i W_i = 87.75$

Efficiency of multicyclone = **87.75 per cent.** (Ans.)

Example 7.21:

A binary mixture of 100 μm size having densities of 2 g/cm³ and 4 g/cm³ is to be classified by elutriation technique using water. Estimate the range of velocities that can do the job and recommend a suitable value.

Solution: Assuming the applicability of Stoke's law (valid for $Re_p < 1$)

$$v_t = \frac{D_p^2 (\rho_s - \rho) g}{18 \mu}$$

Therefore, Re_p of heavy density particles is,

$$\frac{D_p v_t \rho}{\mu} = \frac{D_p D_p^2 (\rho_s - \rho) g \rho}{18 \mu^2}$$

$$= \frac{(100 \times 10^{-6})^3 \times (4000 - 1000) \times 9.812 \times 1000}{18 \times (0.001)^2}$$

$$= 1.64 \text{ (which is nearly equal to 1;}$$
hence the assumption is valid).

Therefore, v_t is given by Stoke's law. Minimum v_t is obtained for low density particles; and Maximum v_t is obtained for heavy density particles.

$$v_{t,min} = \frac{(100 \times 10^{-6})^2 \times (2000 - 1000) \times 9.812}{18 \times 0.0001}$$

$$= 5.45 \times 10^{-3} \text{ m/s}$$

$$v_{t,max} = \frac{(100 \times 10^{-6})^2 \times (4000 - 1000) \times 9.812}{18 \times 0.001}$$

$$= 16.35 \times 10^{-3} \text{ m/s}$$

The recommended range of velocities is between 5.45×10^{-3} and 16.35×10^{-3} m/s.

(Ans.)

Example 7.22:

Compute the maximum velocity at which particles of silica 0.04 mm in diameter (specific gravity = 2.65) will fall through quiet water that fills a 50 mm ID glass cylinder, if
  (a) the slurry is so dilute that free settling prevails.
  (b) the mass ratio of water to silica is 2.0.

Assume the particles to be essentially spherical.

Solution: Since the particle size is quite small and the liquid is water, there is every possibility that the settling zone is laminar. However, we have to first verify this. For settling zone to be laminar,

$$Re_p < 0.1$$

or $$\left(\frac{d_p V_t \rho_f}{\mu_f}\right) < 0.1 \quad \ldots \text{(i)}$$

For laminar settling of spherical particles, from Stokes' law,
$$V_t = (\rho_s - \rho_f) g d_p^2 / 18 \mu_f$$

Substituting this in equation (i),
$$\frac{(\rho_s - \rho_f) g d_p^3 \rho_f}{18 \mu_f^2} < 0.1$$

The left hand side of above equation can be now computed by substituting $\rho_s = 2.65 \times 10^{-3}$ kg/m³, $\rho_f = 1000$ kg/m³, $d_p = 0.04 \times 10^{-3}$ m and $\mu_f = 0.001$ kg/(m.s.). Thus,

$$\frac{(\rho_s - \rho_f) g d_p^3 \rho_f}{18 \mu_f^2} = \frac{(2.65 - 1.0) \times 10^3 (9.80) (0.04 \times 10^{-3})^3 \, 1000}{18 (0.001)^2}$$

$$= 0.05749$$

Since this is less than 0.1, the settling zone is laminar. Therefore, the terminal free settling velocity is given by,

$$V_t = \frac{(0.05794) \mu_f}{d_p \rho_f} C_f \qquad \ldots \text{(ii)}$$

The correction factor C_f to incorporate wall effects can be computed from equation (3.3.1):

$$C_f = [1.0 - (d_p/D_c)]^{2.25}$$
$$= [1.0 - (0.04/50)]^{2.25} = 0.998$$

It can be seen that the correction factor is very close to unity since the particle size is much smaller than the vessel diameter. Substituting in equation (ii),

$$V_t = \frac{(0.05749)(0.001)}{(0.04 \times 10^{-3}) \, 1000} (0.998)$$

$$= 0.14343 \times 10^{-2} \text{ m/s}$$

(b) If hindered settling prevails, since particles are essentially spherical we can still use Stokes law after replacing ρ_f by ρ_b and μ_f.

Example 7.23:

A mixture of an ore (specific gravity = 2.0) and the gangue (specific gravity = 7.0) has to be separated in a hydraulic free settling elutriator. If the mixture has the following size distribution (valid for both ore and the gangue) and the relation $f_D = 18.5/Re_p^{0.6}$ is valid for the flow zone under consideration, estimate the upward velocity of hydraulic water to be used in the elutriator so that the entire ore is collected in the overflow. Will the overflow be gangue-free?

Particle size (mm)	Mass fraction
− 0.58 + 0.49	0.62
− 0.49 + 0.40	0.21
−0.40 + 0.36	0.17

Solution: If the upward velocity of the hydraulic water is more than the terminal free settling velocity of the largest ore particle, we can be certain that the entire ore will be carried over and collected in the overflow. Since from the size distribution table the largest possible size is 0.58 mm, let us estimate the terminal free settling velocity V_{tA} of 0.58 mm ore particle. Neglecting wall effects, V_{tA} can be computed from equation

$$V_{tA} = \left[\frac{4}{3}\left(\frac{\rho_A - \rho_f}{\rho_f}\right)\frac{gd_A}{f_{DA}}\right]^{1/2} \quad \ldots (i)$$

It is given that, $f_{DA} = 18.5/Re_p^{0.6}$.

$$= \frac{18.5\,(\mu_f)^{0.6}}{(d_A V_{tA} \rho_A)^{0.6}} \quad \ldots (ii)$$

Substituting for f_{DA} in equation (i) and solving for V_{tA}, we get,

$$V_{tA}^{1.4} = \frac{4}{3}\left[\frac{\rho_A - \rho_f}{\rho_f^{0.4}}\right]\frac{gd_A^{1.6}}{18.5\,\mu_f^{0.6}} \quad \ldots (iii)$$

where, ρ_A density of ore = 2000 kg/m³
ρ_f = density of water = 1000 kg/m³
d_A = 0.58 mm = 5.8×10^{-4} m
μ_f = viscosity of water = 0.001 kg/(m.s)

Substituting these values in equation (iii), we get,

$$V_{tA} = 0.058 \text{ m/s}$$

Thus, upward velocity of hydraulic water must be equal to (or more than) 0.058 m/s to yield all the ore particles in the overflow.

To find out whether the overflow will be gangue-free, let us determine the terminal settling velocity V_{tB} of the smallest gangue particle.
Thus,

$$d_B = 0.36 \text{ mm} = 3.6 \times 10^{-4} \text{ m}$$
$$\rho_B = 7000 \text{ kg/m}^3$$

Equation (iii) can be rewritten as,

$$V_{tB}^{1.4} = \left(\frac{4}{3}\right)\left(\frac{\rho_B - \rho_f}{\rho_f^{0.4}}\right)\frac{gd_B^{1.6}}{18.5\,\mu_f^{0.6}} \quad \ldots (iv)$$

Substituting numerical values of ρ_B, ρ_f, d_B and μ_f we get, $V_{tB} = 0.121$ m/s.

Since the settling velocity of even the smallest gangue particle is much more than 0.058 m/s, no gangue particles will be carried over into the overflow and thus the overflow will be gangue-free.

Example 7.24:

A mixture containing 30% (by weight) of galena (specific gravity = 7.5) and balance silica (specific gravity = 2.65) is to be elutriated with water flowing at 0.006 m/s. If the size distribution of the mixture (valid for both components) is as given below and the flow zone is essentially laminar, what fraction of galena fed will be in the overhead and bottom products and what will be the mass fraction of galena (on dry basis) in these products?

Particle size	20	30	40	50	60	70	80	90	100
Mass fraction (cumulative)	0.33	0.53	0.67	0.77	0.83	0.88	0.91	0.93	0.95

Solution: Let us first find out the size of galena particles whose terminal free settling velocity is equal to the upward velocity of water. Since the flow zone is given to be laminar, we can apply Stokes' Law. Thus, neglecting wall effects,

$$V_t = \frac{(\rho_s - \rho_f) g d_p^2}{18 \mu_f} \text{ or, } d_P = \left[\frac{18 \mu_f V_t}{(\rho_s - \rho_f) g}\right]^{1/2}$$

Given that:
$\rho_s = 1000 \text{ kg/m}^3$
$\rho_f = 0.001 \text{ kg/m.s}$
$V_t = 0.006 \text{ m/s}$

Therefore, $d_p = d_{P1} = 4.12 \times 10^{-5}$ m = 41.2 microns

We now plot a graph of cumulative mass fraction versus particle size (on rectangular co-ordinates). The plot is given in Figure 7.31. From the figure, the cumulative mass fraction corresponding to a particle size of 41.2 microns is- 0.685. This means, 68.5% of galena particles have a size less than 41.2 microns. Since all galena particles having size less than 41.2 microns will have a settling velocity less than 0.006 m/s (upward velocity of water), we can conclude that 68.5% of galena fed will be in the overflow. Obviously, the remaining 31.5% will be in the bottom product.

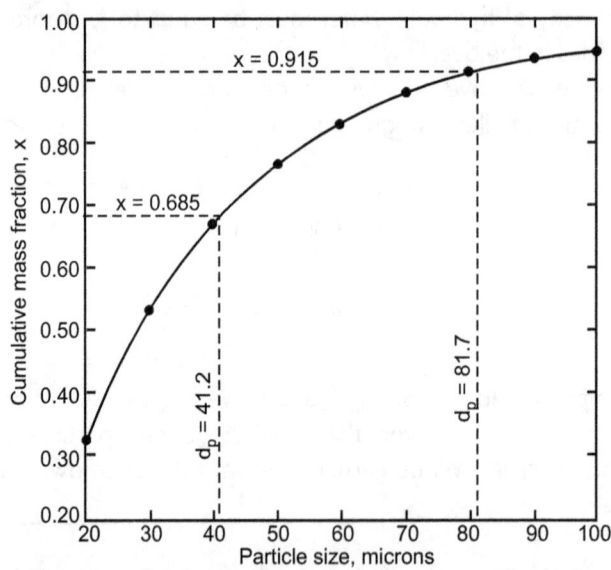

Fig. 7.31: Plot of Cumulative Mass Fraction Versus Particle Size

To find out the mass fraction (on dry basis) of galena in the overhead and bottom products, we require to know the amount of silica in these products. Therefore, following a similar procedure, the diameter of silica particles having terminal free settling velocity equal to upward velocity of water (0.006 m/s) will be,

$$d_{p2} = \left[\frac{18 \times 0.001 \times 0.006}{(2.65 - 1.0) \times 10^3 \times 9.8} \right]^{1/2}$$

$$= 8.17 \times 10^{-5} \text{ m} = 81.7 \text{ microns.}$$

From Fig. 7.31, corresponding to a particle size of 81.7 microns, the cumulative mass fraction = 0.915. Therefore, 91.5% of silica fed will be in the overhead and the rest in the bottom product.

Let the total feed be 100 kg.

Mass of galena fed = 30 kg

Since 68.5% of galena fed has been found to be present in the overflow,

$$\text{Galena in overflow} = (30) \frac{68.5}{100} = 20.55 \text{ kg}$$

Similarly, $\quad$ Silica in overflow $= (70) \frac{91.5}{100} = 64.05$ kg

Therefore, mass fraction (on dry basis) of galena in overflow

$$= \frac{20.55}{(20.55 + 64.05)} = 0.243$$

Similarly, galena in bottom product

$$= \frac{30 \times 31.5}{100} = 9.45 \text{ kg}$$

$$\text{Silica in bottom product} = \frac{70 \times 8.5}{100} = 5.95 \text{ kg}$$

Therefore, mass fraction (on dry basis) of galena in the bottom product

$$= \frac{9.45}{9.45 + 5.95} = 0.614 \qquad \textbf{(Ans.)}$$

EXERCISE FOR PRACTICE

(1) Find the weight of a sphere of material of specific gravity 7.5 which falls with a steady velocity of 0.6 m/s in a large deep tank of water. **(Ans.: 0.029 gm)**

(2) What will be the settling velocity of a spherical particle 0.40 mm diameter in an oil of special gravity 0.82 and viscosity 10 mN/sm^2 ? The specific gravity of steel is 7.87.

(Ans.: 0.051 m/s)

(3) Calculate the minimum area and diameter of a thickener with a circular basin to treat 0.1 m^3/sec of a slurry of solids concentration of 150 kg/m^3. The results of batch settling tests are as follows:

Solid Concentration (kg/m³)	Settling Velocity (μm/sec)
100	148
200	91
300	55.33
400	33.25
500	21.40
600	14.50
700	10.29
800	7.38
900	5.56
1000	4.20
1100	3.27

(Ans.: A = 974 m², d = 35.2 m, volumetric flow rate of underflow = 0.0116 m³/sec)

(4) A slurry containing 0.2 kg of solids per kg of water is to be thickened to a sludge containing 0.70 kg solids per kg of water in a continuous settling process. With five different concentrations of the slurry the following tests results were obtained:

Slurry concentration (kg solids/kg water)	0.2	9.235	0.266	0.333	0.4
Sedimentation rate (m/min)	0.001	0.0075	0.006	0.0042	0.003

What would be the minimum area of thickener to effect a separation at the rate of 0.625 kg of solids per second. **(Ans.: 14.571 m²)**

(5) A concentrated suspension of spherical quartz particles in water settles under gravity. The particle diameter is $D_p = 10^{-5}$ m and the particle density is $r_p = 2650$ kg/m³. The initial voidage in the suspension is e = 0.8.
   (a) Obtain the expression for the terminal velocity (u_t) of a single particle assuming Stoke's law to be valid.
   (b) Find the initial settling velocity (u_s) of the particles in the suspension given
   $$u_s = u_t \, e^{4.6}$$
   (c) Calculate the upward velocity of water in the suspension resulting from the settling of the particles for e = 0.8

(6) The size analysis of a powder is carried out by sedimentation in a vessel having sampling point 180 mm below the liquid surface. If the viscosity of liquid is 2 mNs/m² and the density of the powder and liquid are 2500 and 1100 kg/m³ respectively. Determine the time which must elapse before any sample will exclude particles larger than 20 mm size.

(7) A mixture of silica and galena particles having a size range of 5.21 mm to 2.50 mm is to be separated by hydraulic classifier. The specific gravity of silica is 2.65 and that of galena is 7.5. Calculate the size range of the various fractions obtained in settling.

(8) Solid spherical particles of coffee extract from a dryer having a diameter of 400 μm are falling through air at a temperature of 422 K. The density of particles is 1030 kg/m³.

Calculate the terminal settling velocity and distance of fall in 5 seconds. Assume the pressure in this case is 101.32 kPa. **(Ans.: V_t = 1.49 m/s; 7.45 m fall)**

(9) Oil droplets having a diameter of 200 µm are settling from still air at 294 K and 101.32 kPa. The density of oil is 900 kg/m³. A settling chamber is 0.457 m high. Calculate the terminal settling velocity. How long will it take the particles to settle?
[Hint: If the Reynold number is about 100, the equations and form drag correlation for rigid spheres can not be used.]

(10) A batch settling test on a slurry gave the following results, where the height z in meters between the clear liquid and the suspended solids is given in time t hours.

t (hr)	z (m)
0	0.360
0.50	0.285
1.00	0.211
1.75	0.150
3.00	0.125
5.00	0.113
12.0	0.102
20.0	0.090

The original slurry concentration is 250 kg/m³ of slurry.
(a) Determine the velocities of settling and concentrations.
(b) Make a plot of velocity versus concentration.

(11) The data given below were obtained from a single batch-sedimentation test on an ore slurry. The true density of solids in the slurry was 2.50 gm/cm³ and density of the liquid was 1.00 gm/cm³. Determine the area required for a thickener to handle 100 tons of solids per day from a feed concentration of 65 gm/liter to an underflow concentration of 485 gm/liter.

Data from Batch-Sedimentation Test

Concentration, $\dfrac{\text{gm solids}}{\text{liter of slurry}}$	65	70.9	94.3	11.7	139.9	173.9	222	331
Settling rate cm/hr	139.9	103.6	71.9	49.4	27.1	16.8	10.0	6.40

(12) Show that for a standard cyclone d_{50} (the particle size of which 50% is collected) is given by:

$$d_{50} = \sqrt{\dfrac{9\,\mu B_c}{2(\rho_s - \rho_f)\,\pi N_t u_\theta}}$$

where,
B_c = Inlet duct breadth
N_t = The number of turns in the outer spiral
u_θ = The tangential fluid velocity
ρ_s, ρ_f = Solid and fluid densities
μ = Fluid viscosity

MECHANICAL OPERATIONS   SEPARATION BASED ON MOTION ......

(13) A solid material is to be fed to a reactor. This feed stream contains 30 kg/hr of material greater than 30 μm in diameter and this must be reduced to a maximum of 3 kg/hr before it enters the reactor. It is proposed that a cyclone with 5 turns in the outer spiral could be used to achieve this separation.

The inlet duct breadth is 15 cm, the conveying fluid is air, viscosity 1.8×10^{-5} Nsm^{-2}, and the solid density is 1300 kgm^{-3}. What inlet velocity is needed to achieve the required separation? Assume all the oversize material has diameter 30 μm for the purpose of this calculation.

NOMENCLATURE

Symbol	
A	Area, m^2
B	Constant
C_c	Critical concentration in thickener
D_p	Particle size, m; D_{p_A}, of heavy particle; D_{p_B}, of light particle.
F	Force.
N_{Re}	Reynolds number, $Du\rho/\mu$
u	Linear velocity, m/s, u_g, settling velocity in gravity field; u_t, terminal settling velocity; u_{t_A}, of heavy particle; u_{t_B}, of light particle.
v	Settling velocity of solid.
V	Volume, m^3, liter, $\bar{V}$, upward velocity of a zone in a thickener.
Z	Height of liquid-solid interface in sedimentation test, m; z_i, intercept in kynch method for sedimenter design; z_o, initial height.
Subscripts:	
a	refers to material a.
b	refers to material b.
i	refers to interface.
L	refers to a particular layer.
u	refers to underflow.
S	refers to solid.
t	refers to terminal velocity.
0	refers to conditions in an infinite extent of fluid; initial conditions.
Greek Letters:	
ε	volume fraction of voids.
θ	time.
μ	viscosity.
ρ	density; without subscript, density of liquid.
φ, φ'	a function.

***

Unit VIII

Chapter 8: MIXING AND AGITATION

8.1 Introduction

What is Mixing (or blending)?

Mixing is a unit operation in which a relatively uniform mixture is obtained from two or more components. Mixing has no preservative effect (on food) but is meant only as a processing aid, though in some cases mixing is required to promote some other objective such as mass transfer or chemical reaction. The degree of uniformity achievable varies widely. It is easy to achieve virtually complete homogeneity when mixing miscible liquids or mixing a soluble solids into a liquid, but it can be difficult to achieve a homogeneous result when mixing two solids, mixing two highly viscous liquids or mixing items with widely varying densities, especially if the amount of one component is very small compared to the amounts of the others. The efficiency of mixing depends on the efficient use of energy to generate flow of the components. Important aspects in the design of a mixer include:

(i) Provision of adequate input energy (for an appropriate time).
(ii) Design of the mechanism for introducing the energy.
(iii) Properties of the components.

Mixing and agitation are the most common operations in chemical engineering practice and play a significant role in several important industrial processes like liquid-liquid extraction, leaching, crystallization, absorption etc. Details of such applications are listed in Table 8.1.

Table 8.1: Some Common Chemical Engineering Processes Requiring Agitation and Mixing

Process	Phases Present
Batch and continuous stirred tank reactors	Two or more liquids
	liquid + solid (e.g. catalyst)
	liquid + gas
Liquid-Liquid Extraction	Two immiscible liquids
Leaching	solid + liquid
Crystallization	solid (crystals) + liquid (mother liquor)
Slurrying	solid + liquid, solid insoluble
Dissolution	solid + liquid, solid soluble
Blending	Two or more solids, solids + liquids, two or more miscible liquid
Absorption	gas + liquid
Heat transfer	liquids, liquid + gas, liquid + solid
Mass transfer	gas + liquid, liquid + liquid

In general these two terms mixing and agitation, are often used synonymously in the literature, *agitation* conventionally refers to the induced motion of material in some manner, apart from any mixing accomplished. The term *mixing* is the random distribution of two or more initially separate phases (miscible or immiscible or of elements of single phase material having temperature or concentration gradients. This may be achieved either by agitation or by other means such as mixing of two gases by molecular diffusion by just keeping them together for some time.

8.2 Agitation Equipment

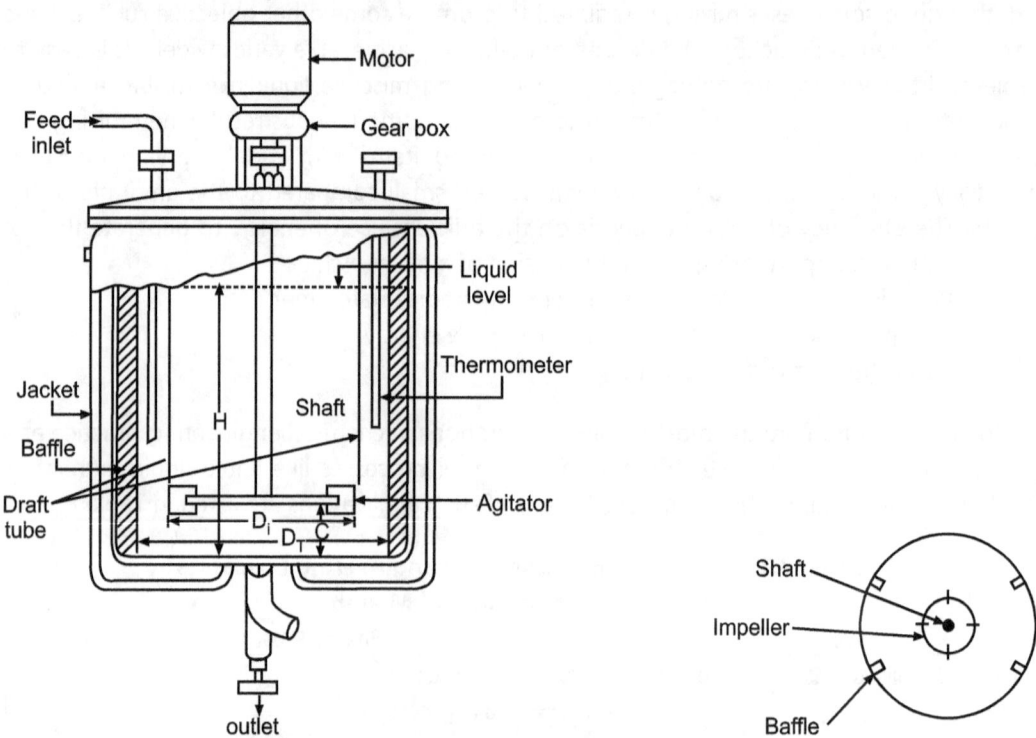

Fig. 8.1: Typical Mixing and Agitation set-up

A typical mixing and agitation set-up is as shown in Fig. 8.1. Liquids may be agitated in some type of vessel, usually cylindrical shape. A motor, generally mounted on the tank cover, rotates a shaft carrying an impeller at its bottom, through a gear box.

In order to prevent vortex formation, small rectangular solid strips, called baffles, extending from the tank to the liquid level are attached to the tank, as shown in Fig. 8.1. Several types of impellers are available, each having its own characteristic flow pattern for specific purpose.

Vessels: Usually, cylindrical in shape with vertical axis are quite common. The tank bottom is slightly rounded, and not flat so as to eliminate sharp corners and dead regions which may not get mixed, with rest liquid depth may usually be equal to tank diameter although this may not be so in certain situations.

Vessels may be jacketed to supply steam or cooling water. The vessel may also have supported legs or lugs. This agitator (also called as impeller) is generally introduced from the top but in some special applications it may be introduced from side or bottom, in which case a good quality seal is essential. Agitators produce flow patterns and circulate the liquid.

Flow Pattern: All the agitators will produce radial, axial and circumferential flow patterns, but one of them is more predominant Radial, axis (parallel to the shaft) and circumferential flow patterns are shown in Fig. 8.2.

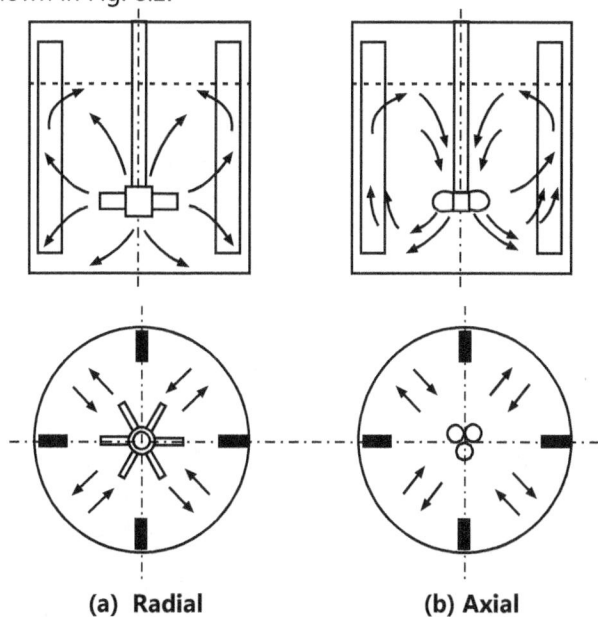

(a) Radial   (b) Axial
Fig. 8.2: Flow Patterns in Agitated Vessels (a) Radial, (b) Axial

Draft tube: This accessory may be used to aid to generation of axial flow pattern. This may be necessary in operations such as crystallization or blending viscous fluids. Draft tube is a hollow cylinder of a short length suspended in a vessel. The agitator may be located at the end or just inside this tube.

8.3 Impellers and their Characteristics

Impellers may be divided into two broad categories:
(I) High speed, low surface area impellers suitable for low viscosity fluids, and
(II) Low speed high surface area impellers suitable for high viscosity fluids.

Type I includes number of impellers such as turbines, paddles and propellers. Plane discs or shrouded disc may also be used.

Turbines: Different types of turbines are shown in figure 8.3. The turbines are used for liquids having viscosities upto 10^4 cP. Pitched turbines are sometimes also called as "fan type" (or even "propellers").

The angle of blade to the horizontal is between 30° to 60°, 45° being quite common. Turbines produce mainly radial flow pattern. The pitched blades enhance the axial flow pattern while curved blades help to generate circulatory pattern.

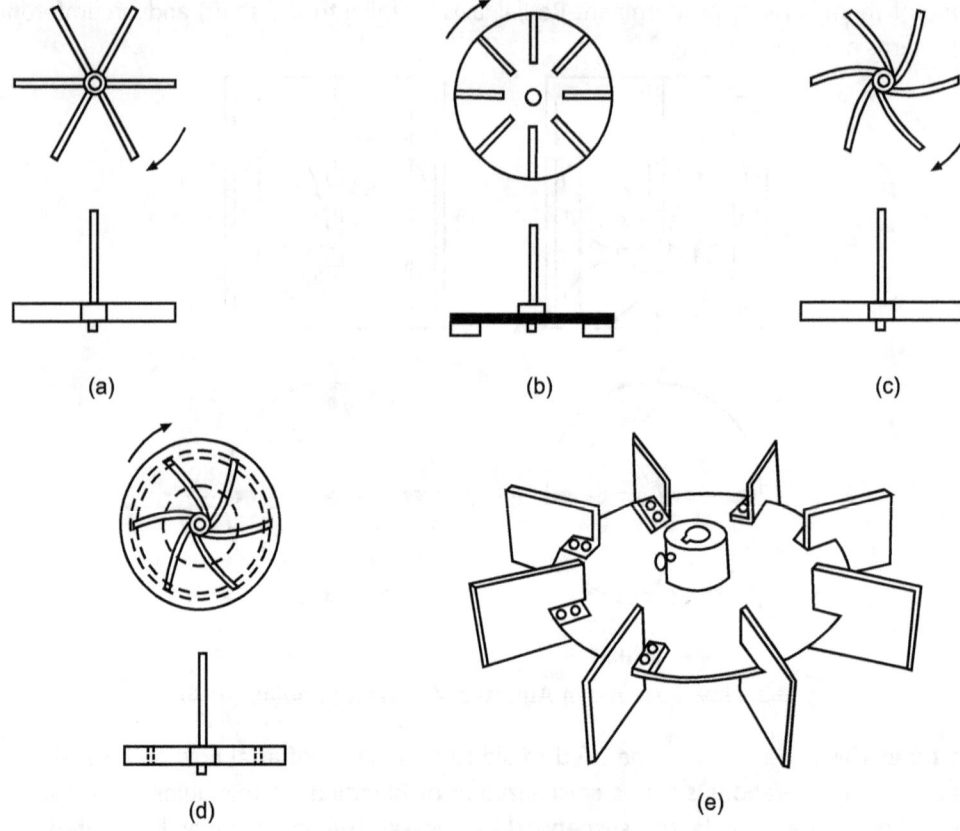

Fig. 8.3: Turbine Agitators

Propellers: These are shown in figure 8.4. They are also termed as *marine propellers*. Three blades are almost an universally accepted practice. The driving face of the blade is flat or concave while the backside is convex. *Pitch* of the propeller is defined as the ratio of the longitudinal distance fluid may move due to one full rotation of the agitator to its diameter. Usually, a square pitch i.e. equal to the diameter of the propeller is very common.

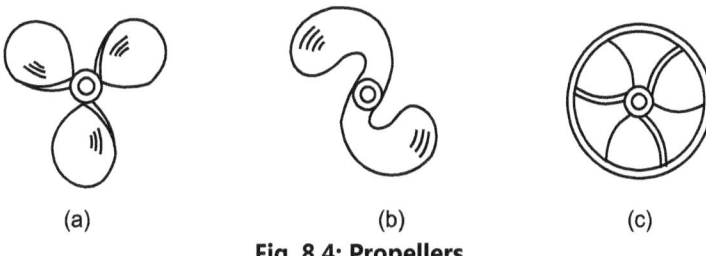

Fig. 8.4: Propellers

Propellers generally produce axial flow pattern. Propellers which thrust the fluid upwards when rotating in clockwise direction are called as *right hand propellers* and those which thrust the liquid downward under identical condition are termed as *left hand propellers*. Propellers are also used for liquids with viscosities upto 10^4 cP.

Paddles: These are shown in figure 8.5. Simple and pitched paddles are commonly used for liquids with viscosities upto 10^4 cP. Although anchor, helical screws or helical ribbons etc., are termed as modified paddles.

Another type of agitator is also shown in Figure 8.5. Anchor diameter is very close to the diameter of vessel. Their main function is to "wipe" the cylindrical wall surface of the vessel. It does not help in generating velocity patterns to assist mixing as in the case of turbines, paddles or propellers.

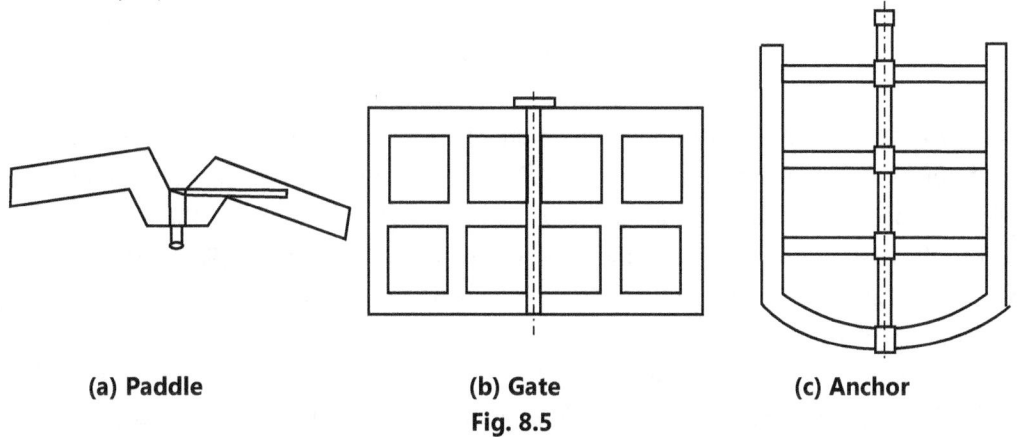

(a) Paddle **(b) Gate** **(c) Anchor**

Fig. 8.5

The rotational speed for the turbines, propellers or paddles is (but not the anchor) quite high and the tip speed (i.e. product of rotational speed, N, and impeller diameter, D, written as ND) can vary from 10 m/min to 30 m/min. Rotational speeds can be from 100 to 1500 rpm. Another type includes the impellers suitable for viscous fluids.

Modified paddles: Fig. 8.6 show number of such agitators. Helical screw or a helical ribbon of their combination may be used for liquids of viscosities between 10^3 cP to 10^6 cP. The diameter of such impellers is very close to the diameter of the vessel.

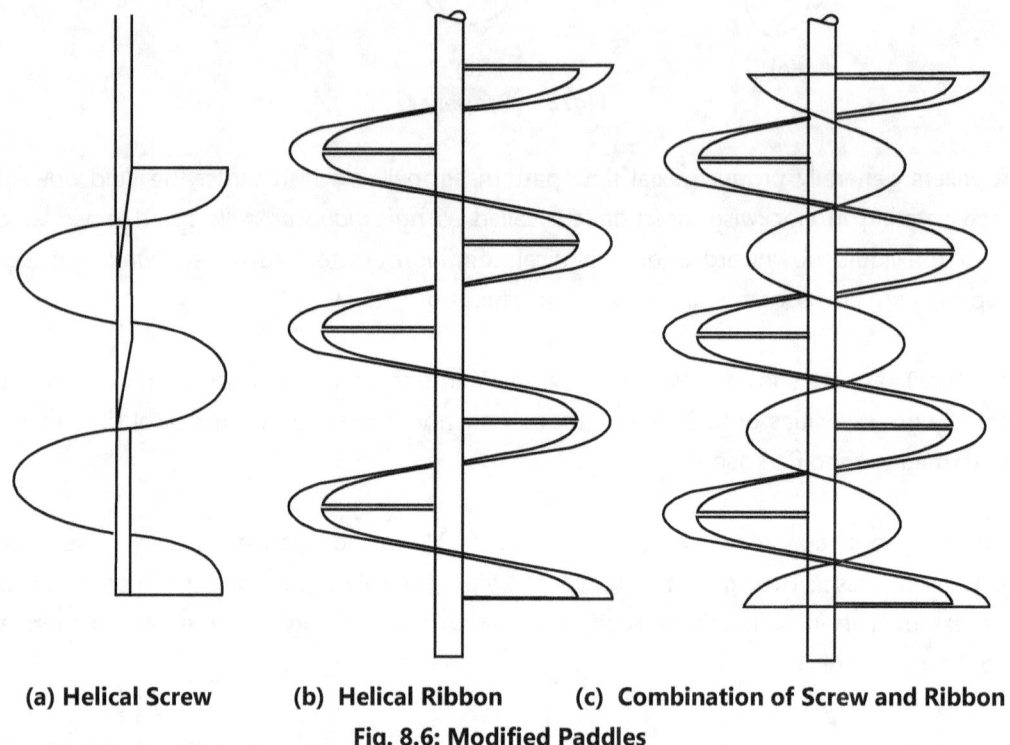

    (a) Helical Screw   **(b) Helical Ribbon**   **(c) Combination of Screw and Ribbon**

Fig. 8.6: Modified Paddles

Other type of agitators includes extruders, sigma mixers, roll mixers, etc. These may be used for materials having viscosities above 10^5 cP. The agitators such as anchor, helical screw, helical ribbon etc. are also called as *close proximity agitators*. The two or three roll mills are used to disperse pigment etc. Into the vehicle such as rubber latex or alkali resins etc. as in the paint industry. There may be several other shapes and types which may be designed to perform a specific duty.

Static Mixers: These are also called as *in-line mixers*. There are no moving parts in these types of mixers. Basically in-line mixers consist of a conduit with some form of "packing", called element. The elements are so arranged that the flow direction is made to change continually which causes mixing of different streams. For a given job the number of elements are arranged one after the other in the same conduit. Usually, the static mixers are available in the sizes ranging from about 10 mm to 80 mm.

Powder Mixers: In this type of equipment the solids are mixed by causing random movement of particles and inter mixing of large groups. The vessel may be made to rotate or an agitator of a specific design may be used. Generally, the particles are "lifted" and "showered" into each other. Powder mixing or solid mixing is encountered mainly in food, pharmaceutical and cosmetic industry. Uniform mixing of solids is more difficult and may be compared with mixing of very viscous materials. Double cone or 'Y' shaped mixers revolves around their axis. The internal fights or baffles aid the random movement. Muller may have a stationary pan and rotating turrets or vice versa. It sometimes has pan moving clockwise and muller turrets rotating in anticlockwise direction as shown in Fig. 8.7. Helical ribbon in cylindrical vessel may also be used but vertical screw in a conical vessel rotating about its own axis and orbiting around central axis is quite effective. It may be noted that muller may have two muller turrates. The vertical screw type or such a combination of planatory movement is very suitable for paste like materials. The essential feature of these types of mixers is that they break the agglomerates.

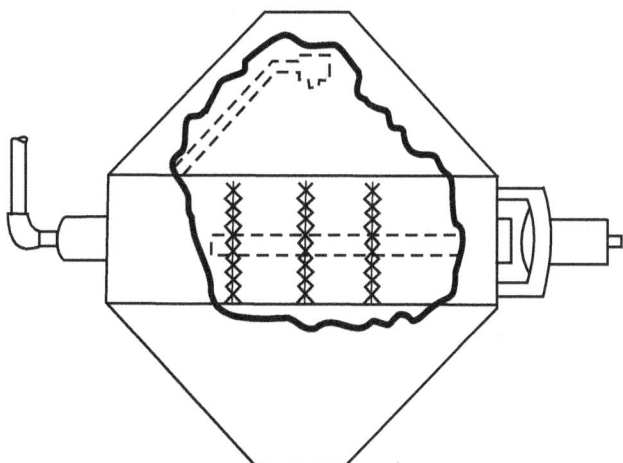

Fig. 8.7: Powder Mixers

8.4 Power Requirements for Agitation

For any type of agitator this is one of the most important characteristics. The power required is a function of geometrical details such as diameter, thickness, width etc., of an impeller; type of impeller; geometrical details of the vessel such as its diameter, numbers of baffles and their dimensions etc., rotational speed and fluid properties i.e. viscosity, density, and for multiphase system the interfacial tension. Location of the impeller in a vessel also affects the power consumption. Thus it may be possible to write:

$$P = f_1 [D_i, H, C, S, L, W, \rho, \mu, N, g, B, R, \ldots \ldots] \quad \ldots (8.1)$$

All linear dimensions such as diameter of vessel, depth of fluid etc. are made dimensions by dividing these by diameter of impeller. From dimensional analysis,

$$\frac{P}{\rho D_i^5 N^3} = f_2 \left[\left(\frac{(\rho D_i^2 N)}{\mu}\right), \left(\frac{D_i^2 N}{g}\right), \frac{H}{D_i}, \frac{C}{D_i} \right] \quad \ldots (8.2)$$

Rest of the terms in equation (8.2) is geometrical details, which are constant for a given system. Thus for a given system,

$$P_o = [(R_e), (F_r)] \quad \ldots (8.3)$$

The Froude number, F_r affects the power consumption only if vortex is present. If the speed of an impeller is increased the free surface of the liquid assumes a paraboloid form as shown in Fig. 8.8, which is called as *vortex*. Generally, vortex is avoided by employing baffles. In some instances the closed system or off centered impeller is also employed to suppress the vortex. It must be noted here that at lower speeds of agitation i.e. for values of Reynolds number less than 300 or so, overtaxing may not be observed even for vessel without baffles.

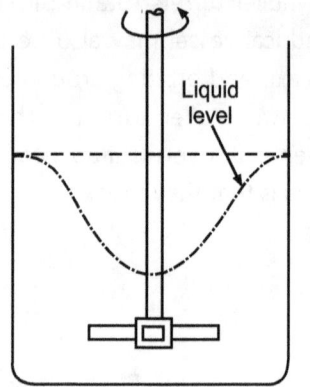

Fig. 8.8: Vortex in Agitated Vessel

Thus is vortex is absent, then for a given system,

$$P_o = f(R_e) \quad \ldots (8.4)$$

A typical power number variation with Reynolds number is shown in Fig. 8.9. Two limiting cases are seen.

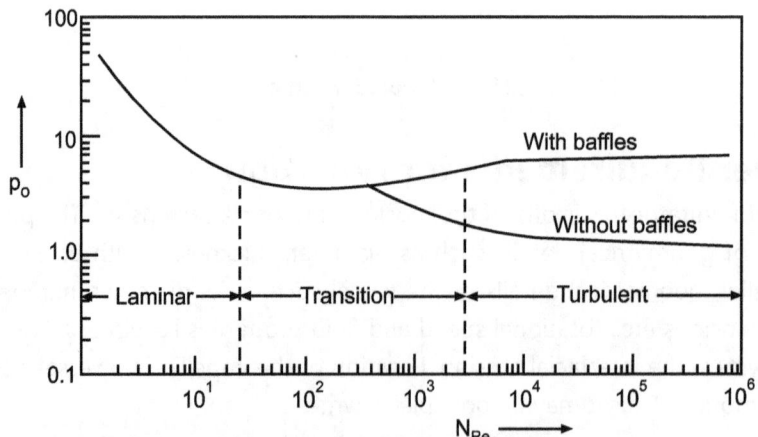

Fig. 8.9: Variation of Power Number with Reynolds Number

Laminar Flow: In this regime, relationship between Reynolds number and the Power number, is given as,
$$P_o = \frac{C_o}{R_e} \quad \ldots (8.5)$$
Where C_0 is a constant for a given impeller and for given geometrical details. From the definitions of these two numbers it is seen that
$$P_o \times R_e = C_o \quad \ldots (8.6)$$
Power consumed, P, is then
$$P = C_o \mu D_i^3 N^2 \quad \ldots (8.7)$$
Thus if speed is doubled power consumption will increase by a factor of four.

Turbulent Flow: In this regime the power number is constant.
Thus,
$$P_3 = C_t \quad \ldots (8.8)$$
Which means, power consumed,
$$P = C_t \times \rho \times D_i^3 \times N^3 \quad \ldots (8.9)$$
Thus in turbulent flow if the speed is doubled the power consumption is increased by a factor of eight.

8.5 Selection of Impellers

Several methods of selecting an impeller are available. One of these, based on liquid viscosity and tank volume, is shown in Fig. 8.10 and another based on the liquid viscosity alone, is depicted in Table 8.2. Over viscosity ranges where several types of impellers are suitable, an impeller is chosen based on various other characteristics like circulation, shear stress, power requirements etc. Mersmann et al. suggest that the propeller is very good for blending and solids-suspending, flat blade turbines for dispersing and helical impellers for blending high viscosity fluids whereas for heat exchangers, generally any impeller is suitable.

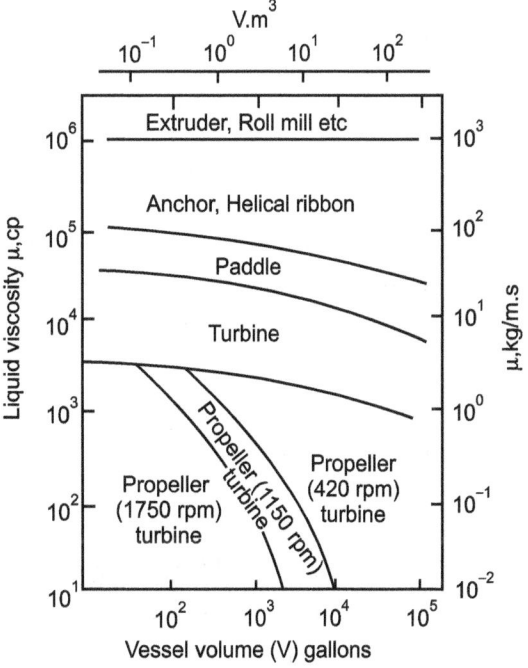

Fig. 8.10: Impeller Selection

Table 8.2: Impeller Selection Guide

Type of Impeller	Range of Liquid Viscosity	
	c_p	kg/m-s
Anchor	$10^2 - 2 \times 10^3$	$10^{-1} - 2$
Propeller	$10^0 - 10^4$	$10^{-3} - 10^1$
Flat-blade turbine	$10^0 - 3 \times 10^4$	$10^{-3} - 3 \times 10^1$
Paddle	$10^2 - 3 \times 10^1$	$10^{-1} - 3 \times 10^1$
Gate	$10^3 - 10^5$	$10^0 - 10^2$
Helical screw	$3 \times 10^3 - 3 \times 10^5$	$3 - 3 \times 10^2$
Helical ribbon	$10^4 - 2 \times 10^6$	$10^1 - 2 \times 10^3$
Extruders	$> 10^6$	$> 10^3$

8.6 Scale-up of Mixing Systems

Scaling a mixing operation: When changing the scale of equipment with the goal of obtaining the same mixing performance at the new scale:

(i) *Geometric similarity should be preserved* – Dimensional ratios should be the same in the large tank as in the small.

(ii) *Dynamic similarity should be preserved* – Reynolds numbers should be the same in the large tank as in the small.

Note: The above analysis is correct for *Newtonian fluids only* – it becomes more complex when the non-Newtonian behaviour of food materials is taken into account.

Mixing of low and moderate viscosity liquids: Turbulence should be induced to entrain slow-moving parts within faster – moving parts. Turbulence is highest near the impeller and liquid should be circulated through this region as much as possible.

A vortex should be avoided because adjoining layers of circulating liquids travel at a similar speed and entertainment does not take place – the liquids simply rotate around the mixer.

Calculation of the power requirements for agitation of a system is only part of the total problem. In any mixing problem, there is always a *process* or *mixing result* which is of prime importance. The process result can be a well defined, measurable quantity like the time required for blending two miscible liquids, rate of heat transfer from a heated jacket per unit volume of the agitated liquid, mass transfer rate from gas bubbles dispersed by agitation in a liquid, rate of dissolution of a solid in an agitated solid-liquid slurry, etc. Sometimes it may not be as precisely defined as for example, in the stirring of a liquid detergent in a tank;

where if the rpm of the stirrer is increased, the detergent becomes very watery (because the molecules may get degraded due to the high shear stresses) and if the rpm is too low, the blending may not be uniform. The process result of interest is then to obtain a 'good' batch with an optimum combination of efficient blending and an absence of thinning.

The process results are related, in general, to variables characterizing mixing, viz., geometrical dimensions, rpm of stirrer, power, μ, ρ, the surface tension, σ, in a two phase system, etc., or their dimensionless combinations like Reynolds number, Fourde number, Weber number ($\rho N^2 D^3/\sigma$), etc. In general small experimental mixing units using the same materials as desired on the large scale are taken and the desired process result is obtained on this smaller set-up. By varying N, dimensions, geometrical ratios, etc., optimal experimental conditions for achieving the same process result are obtained. The system must now be scaled-up, i.e., predict process *conditions* on the larger system, based on *results* on the smaller unit, in order to duplicate the process results if possible (or at least get decent process results if identical results are not practical or uneconomical on a large scale).

In order to simplify the scale-up procedure, normally geometric similarity is assumed. Thus, if the exact configuration and dimensions of the small scale mixing system denoted by subscript S, are known, the same configuration and geometrical ratios will be present in a larger system denoted by subscript L. Mathematically, we can write:

$$\frac{T_S}{D_S} = \frac{T_L}{D_L}$$

$$\frac{Z_S}{D_S} = \frac{Z_L}{D_L}, \text{etc.} \qquad \ldots (8.10)$$

Thus, once the volume of the liquid to be handled in the larger system is known, it is possible to calculate all the dimensions characterizing the larger mixing tank. The only quantity then left to be determined is the rpm of the agitator, N_L (the importance of the assumption of geometric similarity can be overemphasized; to reduce the number of independent variable to one, i.e. N_L.) In general, the following equation may be written:

$$\frac{N_L}{N_S} = \left(\frac{D_L}{D_S}\right)^x \qquad \ldots (8.11)$$

We must choose x such that the process results are duplicated in larger system. This rate which gives us x is called *scale-up rate* and ratio of $\frac{D_L}{D_S}$ is called as *scale-up ratio*. Examples of scale-up rules would be, matching the Reynolds number for the larger and small systems, matching N_{FR} or N_{Weber}, matching the power etc. Each of these scale-up rules will gives a different value of x and hence the design engineer must descide which scale-up rule be used. Common mixing scale-up rules in chemical engineering practice are shown in Table 8.3.

Table 8.3: Common Mixing Scale-Up Rules in Chemical Engineering Practice $\dfrac{N_L}{N_S} = \left(\dfrac{D_L}{D_S}\right)$

No.	x	Scale-up rule and Chemical Engineering operations used in	Effect on W/V (W/V increases by what factor for scale-up ratio of 10)
1	$\dfrac{1}{4}$ to 0	equal blending time, seldom used	(W/V) increases tremendously (~ 100)
2.	–1/2	equal Froude number	W/V increases slightly only (~ 3)
		equal heat transfer coefficient used in cases where vortex behaviour is important and in scale-up of heat transfer to agitated vessels	
3	–2/3	W/V constant. Used in cases of: mass transfer between immiscible liquids (liquid-liquid extraction)	W/V constant (~ 1)
		mass transfer in gas-liquid dispersions (absorption)	~
		solids dissolution in liquid if dissolution is fast	~
		heat transfer with agitation, blending of liquids (non-equal blending times) most popular scale-up rule	~
4	–3/4	equal solids suspension used in scale-up of systems involving suspension of solids insoluble in liquids, also in cases where solids, are being dissolved in an agitated liquid and rate of dissolution is slow	W/V decreases (~1/3)
5	–1	tip speed constant. Used in single-phase liquid blending	W/V reduces (~ 1/100)
6	–2	equal N_{Re}: seldom used	W/V reduces drastically
		where W = power	
		V = volume	

8.7 Liquid Mixing

Food liquid mixtures could in theory be sampled and analysed in the same way as solid mixtures but little investigational work has been published on this, or on the mixing performance of fluid mixers. Most of the information that is available concerns the power requirements for the most commonly used liquid mixer - some form of paddle or propeller stirrer. In these mixers, the fluids to be mixed are placed in containers and the stirrer is rotated. Measurements have been made in terms of dimensionless ratios involving all of the physical factors that influence *power consumption*. The results have been correlated in an equation of the form –

$$(P_o) = K(R_e)^n (Fr)^m \quad \ldots(8.12)$$

where, $(R_e) = (D^2N\rho/\mu)$, $(P_o) = (P/D^5N^3\rho)$ and this is called the Power number (relating drag forces to inertial forces), $(Fr) = (DN^2/g)$ and this is called the Froude number (relating inertial forces to those of gravity); D is the diameter of the propeller, N is the rotational frequency of the propeller (rev/sec), ρ is the density of the liquid, μ is the viscosity of the liquid and P is the power consumed by the propeller.

Notice that the Reynolds number in this instance, uses the product DN for the velocity, which differs by a factor of π from the actual velocity at the tip of the propeller.

The Froude number correlates the effects of gravitational forces and it only becomes significant when the propeller disturbs the liquid surface. Below Reynolds numbers of about 300, the Froude number is found to have little or no effect, so that equation (8.12) becomes,

$$(P^o) = K(R_e)^n \quad \ldots(8.13)$$

Experimental results from the work of Rushton are shown plotted in Fig. 8.11.

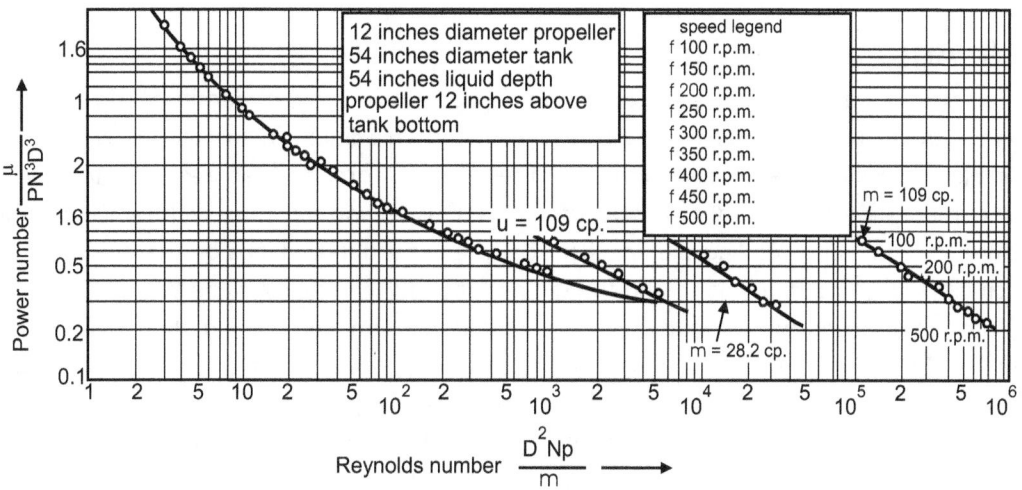

Fig. 8.11: Performance of Propeller Mixers Adapted from Rushton (1952)

Unfortunately, general formulae have not been obtained, so that the results are confined to the particular experimental propeller configurations that were used. If experimental curves are available, then they can be used to give values for n and K in equation (8.13) and the equation then used to predict power consumption. For example, for a propeller, with a pitch equal to the diameter, Rushton gives n = –1 and K = 41.

In cases in which experimental results are not already available, the best approach to the prediction of power consumption in propeller mixers is to use physical models, measure the factors, and then use equation (8.12) or equation (8.13) for scaling up the experimental results.

8.8 Design of Mixing Systems

In the design of a mixing tank, the following procedure may be adopted:
(1) Study properties of liquid, physical requirements etc. and choose the type of impeller.
(2) Select size ratios (preferably the same as standard values to avoid experimentation or else based on small scale studies).
(3) Select D for the larger system (to accommodate the system to be mixed). This leaves N as the only independent variable.
(4) Choose N based on scale-up studies or rules commonly used.
(5) Calculate W, mixing time, etc. Account for mechanical losses etc., to select motor.
(6) Change N and W to standard values.
(7) Integrate and see if alternative designs requiring lower W exist.
(8) Do mechanical design, for example, obtain shaft diameter, supports, bearing designs etc.

8.9 Agitator Design

Let us consider a turbine impeller of diameter D_a agitating a liquid of density ρ_f and viscosity μ_f tank of diameter D_t (see Fig. 8.12). The height of the liquid in the tank is H and the impeller is positioned at an elevation E from the tank bottom. It is also necessary to specify the number of impeller blades, number of baffles (if used) and the baffle width J. Clearly, the power P required for driving the impeller at a given speed n depends on the these factors such as D_a, D_t, H, E, J, μ_f and ρ_f and the dimensions of the impeller blade W and L. Also, if baffles are not used or no provision has been made to eliminate swirling, then a vortex will appear at the surface of the liquid and, some of the liquid must have to be lifted above the average level of the liquid surface against the force of gravity. As a result, gravitational acceleration g will also become an influencing factor. Thus, we can write,

$$P = f_n [n, D_a, D_t, E, L, W, J, H, \mu_f, \rho_f, g] \quad \ldots (8.14)$$

where f_n means "function of".

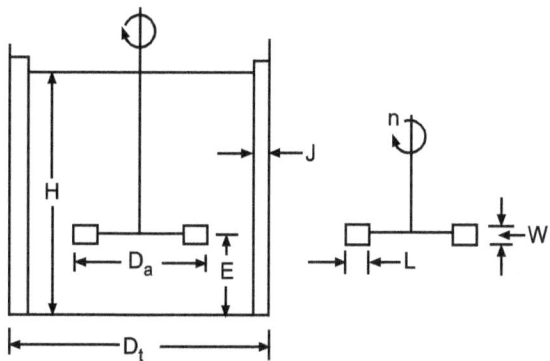

Fig. 8.12: Agitator Design

To rearrange the above equation in a more workable form, let us perform a dimensional analysis. Incidentally, the linear dimensions such as D_t, E, L, W, J and H can be made dimensionless by dividing each of them by a suitable chosen characteristic length. Normally, the impeller diameter D_a is used as the characteristic length. Thus,

$$S_1 = D_t/D_a,\ S_2 = E/D_a,\ S_3 = L/D_a,\ S_4 = W/D_a$$
$$S_5 = J/D_t \text{ and } S_6 = H/D_t = \text{or } H/(S_1 D_a) \qquad \ldots (8.15)$$

These dimensionless factors S_1, S_2, S_3, S_4, S_5 and S_6 are called shape factors. If we temporarily exclude these shape factors, then equation (8.14) can be rewritten as,

$$P = f_n\,(n,\ D_a,\ \rho_f,\ \mu_f,\ g) \qquad \ldots (8.16)$$

It is to be noted that we have assumed the liquid to be Newtonian. If the liquid is Newtonian, then its rheological parameters also will have to be included in the above equation. For the purpose of dimensional analysis, equation (8.16) can be expressed as,

$$P = K_1\, n^a\, D_a^b\, \rho_f^c\, \mu_f^d\, g^e \qquad \ldots (8.17)$$

where, K_1 is a dimensionless constant.

Let us now express all the quantities in the above equation in terms of the fundamental dimensions such as mass (M), length (L) and time (T). For example,

$$P = \text{Watts} = \text{Joules/sec} = \text{Nm/s}$$
$$= \text{kg}\,(m/s^2)\,(m/s)$$
$$= ML^2/T^3$$

Similarly, expressing all quantities on the right hand side also in terms of M, L and T, we get,

$$\frac{ML^2}{T^3} = K_1 \left(\frac{1}{T}\right)^a (L)^b \left(\frac{M}{L^3}\right)^c \left(\frac{M}{LT}\right)^d \left(\frac{L}{T^2}\right)^e \qquad \ldots (8.18)$$

Now, we equate the sum of the exponents of each fundamentals dimension on the right hand side to the exponent of that dimension on the left hand side, as given below.

For $\quad$ M: $1 = c + d$
For $\quad$ L: $2 = b - 3c - d + e$
For $\quad$ T: $-3 = -a - d - 2e$

Solving for a, b and c in terms of d and e, we get,
$$a = 3 - d - 2e$$
$$b = 5 - 2d - e$$
$$c = 1 - d$$

Thus, equation (8.18) becomes,
$$P = K_1 n^{3-d-2e} D_a^{5-2d-e} \rho_f^{1-d} \mu_f^d g^e \quad \ldots (8.19)$$

Grouping variables having like exponents together we get,
$$P = K_1 \left[(n^3 D_a^5 \rho_f) \left(\frac{nD_a^2 \rho_f}{\mu_f} \right)^{-d} \left(\frac{n^2 D_a}{g} \right)^{-e} \right]$$

or
$$\left[\frac{P}{n^3 D_a^5 \rho_f} \right] = K_1 \left[\left(\frac{nD_a^2 \rho_f}{\mu_f} \right)^{-d} \left(\frac{n^2 D_a}{g} \right)^{-e} \right] \quad \ldots (8.20)$$

Incorporating the shape factors also, we can write,
$$\left[\frac{P}{n^3 D_a^5 \rho_f} \right] = f_n \left[\left(\frac{nD_a^2 \rho_f}{\mu_f} \right) \left(\frac{n^2 D_a}{g} \right), S_1, S_2, S_3, S_4, S_5, S_6 \right] \quad \ldots (8.21)$$

Table 8.4

	Impeller type	S_1	S_2^1	S_3	S_6	a	b
1.	Three bladed marine propeller, pitch = 2	3.3	0.75-1.3	–	1.0	1.7	18.0
2.	Three bladed marine propeller, pitch = 1.04	4.5	0.75-1.3	–	0.6-0.9	0.0	18.0
3.	Three bladed marine propeller, pitch = 1.05	2.7	0.75-1.3	–	1.0-1.45	2.3	18.0
4.	Flat-bladed turbine with six blades	3.0	0.75-1.3	0.25 (S_4 = 0.2)	0.9-1.3	1.0	40.0
5.	Three bladed marine propeller, with square pitch	3.0	0.75-1.3	–	0.9-1.3	2.1	18.0

The dimensionless group on the left hand side of the above equation is called the power number, P_o. It is analogous to the drag coefficient we discussed. It represents the characteristic ratio of the drag force acting on a unit area of the impeller to the inertial stress. The dimensionless groups on the right hand side are,

$$\left[\frac{nD_a^2 \rho_f}{\mu_f}\right] = Re_m = \text{Mixing or impeller Reynolds number}$$

$$\left[\frac{n^2 D_a}{g}\right] = Fr_m = \text{Mixing Froude number}$$

We know that Reynolds number represents the characteristic ratio of inertial stress to viscous stress whereas Froude number gives the relative magnitude of inertial stress to gravitational force acting on unit area of the fluid. Thus, we can rewrite equation (8.21) as,

$$P_o = f_n [Re_m, Fr_m, S_1, S_2, S_3, S_4, S_5, S_6] \qquad \ldots (8.22)$$

It must not be forgotten that though not included in the above equation, the power consumption P depends not only on the impeller diameter D_a and blade dimension V and L, but also on the number of impeller blades and apart from the baffle width J, the number of baffles used as well. If a propeller is used, the pitch of the propeller should also be specified. Equation (8.22) is normally re-expressed in a more convenient form as,

$$\frac{P_o}{Fr_m^m} = \phi = f_n [Re_m, S_1, S_2, S_3, S_4, S_5, S_6] \qquad \ldots (8.23)$$

where, ϕ is called the power function. The exponent m is defined as,

$$m = (a - \log Re_m)/b \qquad \ldots (8.24)$$

where, a and b are impeller constants. The magnitudes of a and b depend on the type of impeller and the shape factors S_1 to S_4 and S_6. Some typical values of a and b are given in Table 8.40.

Standard plots of ϕ versus Re_m on log-log co-ordinates are available in the literature. One such family of plots is shown in Fig. 8.13. It is to be noted that each curve in the figure corresponds to a particular type of impeller and a given set of values of S_1 to S_6. Since many curves overlap on each other, the plots should be utilised with great care.

The effect of Froude number Fr_m becomes significant only when there is vortex formation and at large values of Reynolds number ($Re_m < 300$). At low Reynolds number ($Re_m < 300$) or when baffles are used or with off-center inclined and side-entering impellers (when vortex formation is eliminated), Fr_m will not be a factor and its effect can be neglected. In such cases,

$$\phi = P_o$$

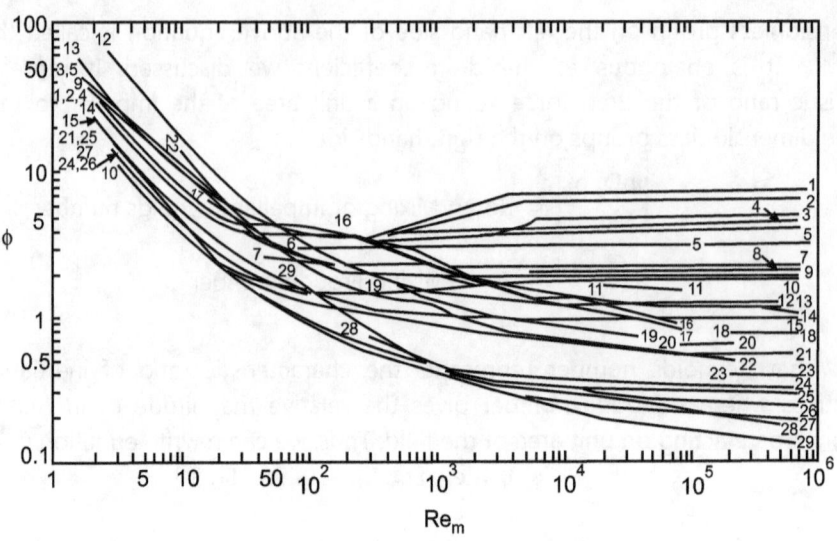

Fig. 8.13: Power Function Versus Reynolds Number Plots

Equation (8.23) then reduces to,
$$P_0 = f_n [Re_m, S_1, S_2, S_3, S_4, S_5, S_6] \qquad \ldots (8.25)$$

It can be seen from Fig. 8.13 that the plot is essentially linear with a slope of –1 when Re_m is very low (less than 10). The impeller is then said to be operating in the laminar zone and in this zone,
$$\phi \, Re_m = K_L = \text{Constant} \qquad \ldots (8.26)$$

Since Re_m is very low, Frounde number will not be a factor therefore we can write,
$$P_o \, Re_m = K_L \qquad \ldots (8.27)$$

Substituting for P_o and Re_m we get,
$$\frac{P}{n^2 D_a^3 \mu_f} = K_L = f_n (S_1, S_2, S_3, S_4, S_5, S_6)$$

or
$$P = K_L \, n^2 \, D_a^3 \, \mu_f \qquad \ldots (8.28)$$

It can be seen that the power consumption in the laminar zone is independent of fluid density but varies with the square of the impeller speed. It is to be noted that the value of K_L depends on the impeller type and the magnitude of the shape factors. For example, for a vessel fitted with four baffles (baffle width = 0.1 D_t) K_L = 41.0 for a three bladed propeller with square pitch, whereas it is 68.0 for a six bladed (flat blades) turbine and for a shrouded turbine with diffuser ring operating in an unbaffled vessel, K_L is as high as 172.5.

If the Reynolds number Re_m very large (> 10,000), then the impeller is said to be operating in a fully developed turbulent zone. In such a case, for baffled vessels, ϕ can be seen to be essentially constant and independent of Re_m. Thus,

$$\phi = K_T = \text{Constant} \qquad \ldots (8.29)$$

Since the vessel is baffled, P_o. Therefore,

$$P_o = \frac{P}{n^3 D_a^5 \rho_f} = K_T$$

or
$$P = K_T n^3 D_a^5 \rho_f \qquad \ldots (8.30)$$

Thus, the power consumption is independent of fluid viscosity in the fully developed turbulent zone. However, it is more dependent on the impeller speed as it varies with the cube of n. Once again the value of K_T depends on the impeller type and the magnitude of shape factors. For a four-baffled vessel (baffle width = 0.1 D_t), K_T = 0.32 when a three bladed propeller with square pitch is used, but K_T = 0.9 if the pitch of the propeller is 2.0. For a six bladed (flat blades) turbine operating in the same tank, K_T = 6.30 while for a two bladed paddle, K_T is only 1.7.

The values K_L and K_T can be deduced from the standard plots given in Fig. 8.13.

Once the impeller Reynolds number Re_m is specified, the value of power function or power number can be obtained from the standard plot and the power required for driving the impeller at the given speed can be computed therefrom. For example, let us consider baffled tank. Now,

$$\phi = P_o = P/n^3 D_a^5 \rho_f$$

Since,
$$Re_m = nD_a^2 \rho_f/\mu_f, \quad n = Re_m \mu_f/\rho_f D_a^2$$

Substituting for n in the expression for P_o we get,

$$P_o = P \rho_f^2 / Re_m^3 \mu_f^3 \qquad \ldots (8.31)$$

Taking logarithm on both sides,

$$\ln(P_o) = \ln\left[\frac{P \rho_f^2}{\mu_f^3}\right] - 3 \ln(Re_m) \qquad \ldots (8.32)$$

Thus, a plot of P_o versus Re_m on log-log co-ordinates will yield a straight line of slope-3. The point of intersection of this straight line with the standard plot of P_o versus Re_m. (Fig. 8.13) gives the value of Re_m, from which the impeller speed n can be easily computed.

8.10 Agitator Selection

The most suitable agitator for a given industrial operation is the one that produces the given degree of mixing within a reasonably low time and with a reasonably low power consumption. It is therefore convenient to define two additional dimensionless groups such as the *mixing number* N_t and the *modified power number* N_L, the former being a function of the blending time t_T but is independent of the power consumption P whereas the latter decides the power consumption but is independent of t_T. Thus,

$$N_t = (nt_T)/(Re_m S_1^2) \qquad \ldots (8.33)$$

Since $Re_m = (nD_a^2 \rho_f/\mu_f)$ and $S_1 = (D_t/D_a)$, the expression for N_t becomes,

$$N_t = \frac{t_T \mu_f}{D_t^2 \rho_f} \qquad \ldots (8.33)$$

It can be seen that N_t is proportional to the blending time t_T, but is independent of P.

$$N_L = P_o (Re_m)^3 S_1 \qquad \ldots (8.34)$$

Substituting for P_o, Re_m and S_1, we get,

$$N_L = \frac{P \rho_f^2 D_t}{\mu_f^3} \qquad \ldots (8.35)$$

Thus, N_L is proportional to P but is independent of t_T. It is possible to prepare plots of N_t versus N_L for the different impellers used in commercial practice. These plots will help us in choosing the agitator that is most satisfactory for a given industrial application. For example, consider the plots sketched in Fig. (8.14). Let the process criterion be that the blending time t_T should not exceed a value t_1. Let the value of N_t at $t_T = t_1$ be at (a) as shown in the figure. It can be seen that the value of N_L (and thereby the power consumption P) is lower for impeller-2 than that for impeller-1, corresponding to $t_T = t_1$.

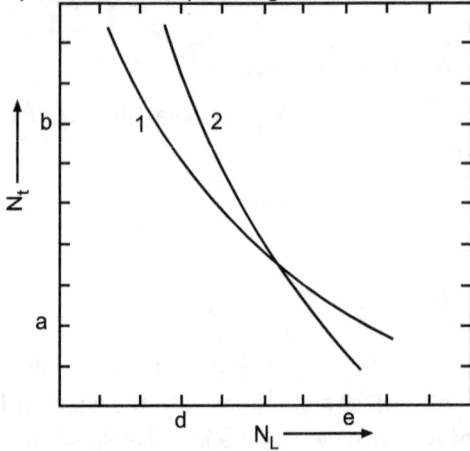

Fig. 8.14: Plots of Mixing Number versus Modified Power Number

Thus, impeller-2 will produce the same degree of mixing within the same time but consuming lesser power and therefore it must be preferred for the final application. If a larger blending time t_2 is available (may be for lowering the power consumption or for achieving a higher degree of mixing) and at $t_T = t_2$, N_t is at (b), then it can be seen that impeller-1 will produce the same effect with a lower power consumption and therefore it is to be preferred here. Conversely, we may fix the maximum permissible power consumption and thereby the value of N_L [say at (d) or (e)] and find out which of the impellers shall do the work within a lesser amount of time. If N_L is fixed at (d), then the value of N_t and thereby the blending time required for impeller-1 is lower and it is to be our final choice. However, if a larger power consumption is permissible so that N_L is fixed at (e), then impeller-2 is to be preferred since it will do the job within a lesser duration of time.

Example:
A pilot plant vessel using a 400 rpm (optimum speed determined experimentally) six-bladed turbine impeller and four longitudinal baffles (each of width 0.1 D_t) is of such size that 1 kg of a material charged to it is equivalent to 512 kg of same material charged to the production unit. The specifications of the production vessel are, diameter = height = 2m, impeller diameter = 0.3 D_t, baffle width = 0.1 D_t, number of baffles = 4. The process consists of blending of two miscible liquids and the reaction mass may be assumed to be having same physical and transport properties as water. The criteria for scale up are either to keep the blending time constant or the power input per unit volume constant. Determine which condition would you recommend and why. For blending of miscible liquids, a dimensionless blending time factor ft is commonly used which is defined as,

$$f_t = \frac{t_T (nD_a^2)^{2/3} g^{1/6} D_a^{1/2}}{H^{1/2} D_t^{3/2}}$$

The above factor varies linearly with impeller Reynolds number Re_m in the laminar zone and becomes essentially constant (independent of Re_m) in the fully developed turbulent zone.

Solution: For the scale-up of process equipment, we utilize what is called the "similarity criteria". This can be broadly classified into three such as geometric similarity, kinematic similarity and dynamic similarity. Two process vessels are said to be geometrically similar when their like dimensions bear a constant ratio. Mixers and agitators are possibly the only equipment that obey geometric similarity almost precisely, though not always. If kinematic similarity exists between two systems, then the radii of curvature of the flow lines or flow paths at corresponding points in the two systems occur in a fixed ratio regardless of the path or point selected. At these corresponding points the velocity ratios will also be constant regardless of which particular point is selected. If the ratios of the accelerations (and thereby forces) at corresponding points are also fixed independent of the position of the points selected, then the systems are said to be dynamically similar. Geometric similarity is a prime requisite for dynamic similarity. Often, though geometric similarity may be obtained between laboratory and plant equipment, kinematic and dynamic similarities are hardly achieved and the designer has to depend on judgement based on experience.

For the present case, we assume the pilot plant vessel and the final production unit are geometrically similar. This means,

$$\left(\frac{D_{a1}}{D_{a2}}\right) = \left(\frac{D_{t1}}{D_{t2}}\right) = \left(\frac{H_1}{H_2}\right) \text{ and so on}$$

or
$$\frac{D_{t1}}{D_{t2}} = \frac{D_{t2}}{D_{t2}} = S_1 \text{ (shape factor)}$$

Similarly,
$$\frac{H_1}{D_{t1}} = \frac{H_2}{D_{t2}} = S_6$$

Suffixes "1" and "2" refer to pilot plant vessel and final production vessel respectively. We can therefore rewrite the expression for f_t in terms of D_a by substituting for D_t and H as $D_t = S_1 D_a$ and $H = S_6 D_t = S_6 S_1 D_a$:

$$f_t = \frac{t_T (nD_a^2)^{2/3} g^{1/6} D_a^{1/2}}{(S_1 D_a)^{1/2} (S_1 S_6 D_a)^{3/2}}$$

Since S_1 and S_6 are constants,

$$f_t = C_1 t_T n^{2/3}/D_a^{1/6} \quad \ldots (i)$$

where,
$$C_1 = \left(\frac{g^{1/6}}{S_1^2 S_6^{3/2}}\right) = \text{Constant}$$

Since it is given that 1 kg of a material charged to the pilot reactor is equivalent to 512 kg of same material charged to the production unit, we can write

$$\frac{(\pi D_{t1}^2/4) H_1}{(\pi D_{t2}^2/4) H_2} = \frac{1}{512}$$

or
$$\frac{(S_1 D_{a1})^2 (S_1 S_6 D_{a1})}{(S_1 D_{a2})^2 (S_1 S_6 D_{a2})} = \frac{D_{a1}^3}{D_{a2}^3} = \frac{1}{512}$$

Therefore,
$$\frac{D_{a1}}{D_{a2}} = \left(\frac{1}{512}\right)^{1/3} = \frac{1}{8}$$

or $D_{a1} = D_{a2}/8 = 0.6/8 = 0.075$ m
Similarly, $D_{t1} = D_{t2}/8 = 2/8 = 0.25$ m
$H_1 = H_2/8 = 2/8 = 0.25$ m

The impeller Reynolds number for the pilot plant vessel can be now estimated as,

$$(Re_m)_1 = \frac{n_1 D_{a1}^2 \rho_f}{\mu_f} = \frac{\left(\frac{400}{60}\right)(0.075)^2 (1000)}{(0.001)} = 37{,}500$$

The value of Re_m for the production vessel will obviously be larger than this and since $Re_m > 10{,}000$, impellers in both vessels are operating in fully developed turbulent zone. Since f_t is constant and independent of Re_m in turbulent zone,

$$f_{t1} = f_{t2}$$

or, from equation (i),

$$\frac{C_1 \, t_{T1} \, n_1^{2/3}}{D_{a1}^{1/6}} = \frac{C_1 \, t_{T2} \, n_2^{2/3}}{D_{a2}^{1/6}}$$

or $\quad (t_{T1}/t_{T2}) = \left[\dfrac{D_{a1}}{D_{a2}}\right]^{1/6} = \left[\dfrac{n_2}{n_1}\right]^{2/3}$ ... (ii)

Let us now consider the first criterion, that is the blending time is kept constant. Thus, $t_{T1} = t_{T2}$. Then, from equation (ii),

$$\left(\frac{n_2}{n_1}\right) = \left[\frac{D_{a2}}{D_{a1}}\right]^{1/4} = (8)^{1/4} = 1.68$$

So, $\quad n_2 = (1.68)\, n_1 = (1.68)(400) = 672$ rpm

The impeller speed in the production vessel is therefore not very large. However, to ascertain the suitability of the criterion, we must determine the power consumption per unit volume. Since the impeller is operating in fully developed turbulent zone,

P (from equation 7.1.15) = $K_T \, n^3 \, D_a^5 \, \rho_f$

The power input per unit volume P' therefore becomes,

$$P' = \frac{P}{\frac{\pi}{4} D_t^2 H} = \frac{K_T \, n^3 \, D_a^5 \, \rho_f}{(\pi/4) \, S_1^3 \, S_6 \, D_a^3}$$

$$= C_2 \, n^3 \, D_a^2 \quad \text{... (iii)}$$

where, $\quad C_2 = (4 K_T \, \rho_f / \pi \, S_1^3 \, S_6) = $ Constant

Thus, $\quad \dfrac{P_1'}{P_2'} = \left(\dfrac{n_1}{n_2}\right)^3 \left(\dfrac{D_{a1}}{D_{a2}}\right)^2$

Since $\quad (n_2/n_1) = (D_{a2}/D_{a1})^{1/4}$

$$(P_1'/P_2') = \left(\frac{D_{a1}}{D_{a2}}\right)^{11/4} = (1/8)^{11/4}$$

or $\quad P_2' = P_1' \, (8)^{11/4} = (304.44)\, P_1'$

Thus, the power consumption per unit volume in the production unit will be more than 300 times that for the pilot plant vessel. This could turn out to be uneconomical and therefore the criterion of keeping blending time constant cannot be considered acceptable.

MECHANICAL OPERATIONS — MIXING AND AGITATION

Let us now consider the second criterion. If power input per unit volume is kept constant,

$$P_1' = P_2'$$
$$C_2 \, n_1^3 \, D_{a1}^2 = C_2 \, n_2^3 \, D_{a2}^2$$

or
$$\frac{n_1}{n_2} = \left(\frac{D_{a2}}{D_{a1}}\right)^{2/3}$$

Substituting in (ii), we get,
$$\frac{t_{T1}}{t_{T2}} = \left(\frac{D_{a1}}{D_{a2}}\right)^{11/18} = (1/8)^{11/18}$$

or
$$t_{T2} = t_{T2} \, (8)^{11/18} = (3.56) \, t_{T1}$$

Thus, the blending time required in the production vessel is only 3.56 times that required in the pilot plant vessel, with the same power consumption per unit volume. Therefore, this can be considered as an acceptable criterion.

8.11 Solved Examples

Example 8.1:

A six blade turbine is installed centrally in a cylindrical tank with flat bottom. The diameter of turbine is 60 cm. The vessel diameter is 180 cm and it is filled with a solution of viscosity 10 C_p and density of 1.45 gm/cm^3. The speed of agitation is 90 rpm. The turbine is located centrally and at a height of 60 cm from the bottom of the vessel. The vessel is fully baffled. Calculate the horse power (HP) required.

Data: Power number, P_o = 1.05 for R_e > 300

$\dfrac{315}{R_e}$ for R_e < 300

Solution: Reynolds number,
$$R_e = \frac{60 \times 60 \times \frac{90}{60} \times 1.5}{0.1}$$
$$= 81000$$

So flow is turbulent, Power number = 1.05 (given for turbulent flow)

Power, $P = C_t \, u \times \rho \times D_L^5 \times N^3$

Here,
$C_t = P_3 = 1.05$
$\rho = 1.45$ gm/cc
D_i = Diameter of impeller = 60 cm
$N = \dfrac{90}{60} = 1.5$ rev/sec.

$\therefore \quad P = 1.05 \times 60^5 \times 1.5^3 \times 1.45$
$= 13.7 \times 10^9$ rev/sec = 1370 J/sec
$= 1370$ Watt

$\therefore \quad$ Power in HP $= \dfrac{1370}{746} = 1.84$ HP **(Ans.)**

Example 8.2:

A helical screw has a diameter of 50 cm and rotating at 80 rpm in a solution of viscosity 140 poise and density of 0.95 gm/cm³. Calculate the HP required.

Data: $P_o = \dfrac{100}{R_e}$, $R_e < 30$

$P_o = 3.5$, $R_e > 30$

Solution:

Reynolds number $= \dfrac{50 \times 50 \times 80/60 \times 0.95}{140} = 22.62$

So flow is laminar,

$P_o = \dfrac{C_o}{R_e}$ = Power number $= \dfrac{100}{22.62} = 4.42$

∴ $P = C_o \, \mu \, D_i^3 \, N^2$

Here, $P_o = C_o = 4.42$

∴ $P = 4.42 \times (50)^5 \times \left(\dfrac{80}{60}\right)^2 \times 0.95 \times 10^{-7}$ watt

$P = 233$ watt

H.P. required $= \dfrac{233}{746} = 0.31$ HP. **(Ans.)**

Example 8.3:

A flat blade turbine with six blades is installed centrally in a vertical tank. The tank is 1.83 m in diameter; the turbine is 0.61 m in diameter and is positioned 0.61 m from the bottom of the tank. The tank is filled to a depth of 1.83 m with a solution of 50% caustic soda which has a viscosity of 12 cP and density of 1.5 gm/cm³. The turbine is operated at 90 rpm. The tank is fitted with 4 baffle, each having a width of 19 cm. Estimate the power consumption for the operation of the baffled mixer.

Data: The value of power function ϕ may be approximated from the following table for ϕ vs N_{Re}.

N_{Re}	ϕ
10,000	5.8
60,000	6.0
80,000	6.0

Solution:

D_a = Diameter of impeller = 0.61 m

N = rps = $\dfrac{90}{60}$ = 1.5 rev/sec

$\mu = 12\ C_p = 0.12$ gm/cm/sec.

$\rho = 1.5$ gm/cm³

Reynolds number = $N_{Re} = \dfrac{D_a^2 \, N \, \rho}{\mu} = \dfrac{(61)^2 \times 1.5 \times 1.5}{0.12} = 69769$

MECHANICAL OPERATIONS   MIXING AND AGITATION

In a battled-mixer, with $N_{Re} > 10000$, N_{Fr} (Froude Number) has no effect. From N_{Re} v/s ϕ table given, $\phi = 6.0$ for N_{Re} 69769.

So, Power required,
$$P = \frac{\phi N^3 D_a^5 \rho}{g_c}$$

$$= \frac{6 \times (1.5)^3 \times (0.61)^5 \times 1500}{9.81} = 261.5 \text{ m.kgf/sec}$$

$$\boxed{P = 3.43 \text{ HP}} \quad \text{(Ans.)}$$

Example 8.4:

For geometrically similar baffled stirred tanks, the power number is known to remain constant at high Reynolds number.

(a) Let P be the power supplied per unit volume of fluid. N the revolutions per second of the agitator, ρ the density of the fluid, μ the viscosity of the fluid and D the diameter of the impeller. Determine α, β, γ and δ in the following equation $= P = N^\alpha \rho^\beta \mu^\gamma D^\delta$

(b) What is effect of Froude number on P?

Let us write the Dimensions of various quantities.

Solution:

Symbol	Unit	Dimension
ρ	W/m³ = kg/(m.s³)	$ML^{-1} t^{-3}$
N	s^{-1}	t^{-1}
ρ	kg/m³	ML^{-3}
μ	kg/(m.s)	$ML^{-1} t^{-1}$
D	m	L

Given:
(a) Let, $P = N^\alpha \rho^\beta \mu^\gamma D^\delta$

P = Power supplied per unit volume of fluid
N = Revolution per second of the agitator
ρ = Density of fluid
μ = Viscosity of fluid
D = Diameter of the impeller
$P = N^\alpha \rho^\beta \mu^\gamma D^\delta$

Converting the units of each of these quantities into fundamental quantities (M, L,

We have,
$$\frac{K}{m \cdot S^3} = \left[\frac{1}{S}\right]^\alpha \left[\frac{Kg}{m^3}\right]^\beta \left[\frac{Kg}{m \cdot S}\right]^\gamma [m]^\delta$$

$$\frac{M}{LT^3} = T^{-\alpha} \left[\frac{M}{L^3}\right]^\beta \left[\frac{M}{LT}\right]^\gamma \cdot \delta$$

$$ML^{-1} T^{-3} = T^{-\alpha-\gamma} \cdot M^{\gamma+\beta} \cdot L^{-3\beta-\gamma+\delta}$$

Hence, comparing LHS and RHS,

$$1 = \gamma + \beta \quad \ldots \text{(a)}$$

$$-1 = -3\beta - \gamma + \delta \quad \ldots \text{(b)}$$
$$3 = \alpha + \gamma \quad \ldots \text{(c)}$$

put, $\delta = 0$

Then,
$$\gamma + \beta = 1$$
$$-\gamma - 3\beta = -1$$
$$\alpha + \gamma = 3$$

∴ $\beta = 0, \gamma = 1, \alpha = 2$. Put in equation (b), then $\delta = 0$

∴ $\alpha = 2, \beta = 0, \gamma = 1$ and $\delta = 0$ is the original solution.

(b) In power correlation for agitated vessels, the effect of Froude number appears for unbaffled vessels and when Reynolds number is greater than 300.

Example 8.5:

For producing an oil-water emulsion, two portable three-bladed propeller mixer are available. 0.5 m diameter impeller rotating at 1 Hz and 0.35 m impeller rotating at 2 Hz. Assuming turbulent condition prevail, which unit will have the lower power consumption?

Solution: Under turbulent conditions, the power required for mixing is given by:
$$P = K N^3 D^5$$

In this case,
$$P_1 = (K \times 1^3 \times 0.5^5)$$
$$P_1 = 0.03125 \, K$$
$$P_2 = (K \times 2^3 \times 0.35^5)$$
$$P_2 = 0.0420 \, K$$

Thus the 0.5 m diameter impeller will have the lower power consumption; some 75% of that of the 0.35 m diameter impeller.

Example 8.6:

Vitamin concentrate is being blended into molasses and it has been found that satisfactory mixing rates can be obtained in a small tank 0.67 m diameter, height 0.75 m, with a propeller, 0.33 m diameter rotating at 450 rev min^{-1}. If a large-scale plant is to be designed which will require a tank 2 m diameter, what will be suitable values to choose for tank depth, propeller diameter and rotational speed, if it is desired to preserve the same mixing conditions as in the smaller plant? What would be the power requirement for the motor driving the propeller? Assume that viscosity of molasses is 6.6 N sm^{-2} and its density is 1520 kgm^{-3}.

Use the subscripts S for the small tank and L for the larger one. To preserve geometric similarity the dimensional ratios should be the same in the large tank as in the small.

Solution: Given that the full-scale tank is three times larger than the model,
$$D_L = 3D_S$$
$$H_L = 3H_S = 3 \times 0.75 = 2.25 \text{ m} = \text{Depth of large tank}$$

and
$$D_L = 3D_S = 3 \times 0.33 = 1 \text{ m} = \text{Propeller diameter in the large tank}$$

For dynamic similarity, $(R_e)_L = (R_e)_S$

$$D_L^2 N_L = D_S^2 N_S$$
$$N_L = (1/3)^2 \times 450$$
$$= 50 \text{ rev. min}^{-1}$$
$$= 0.83 \text{ rev. sec}^{-1}$$
$$= \text{Speed of propeller in the large tank}$$

For the large tank,

$$(R_e) = (D_L^2 N_L \rho/\mu)$$

So, $(R_e) = (12 \times 0.83 \times 1520)/6.6$
$$= 191$$

Equation (8.13) is applicable, and assuming that K = 41 and n = –1, we have,
$$(P_o) = 41 \, (R_e)^{-1} = (P/D^5 N^3 \rho)$$
$$P = (41 \times 1^5 \times (0.83)^3 \times 1520)/(191)$$
$$= 186 \text{ Js}^{-1}$$

And since 1 horsepower = 746 Js^{-1}

Required motor = 186/746, say 1/4 horsepower

Apart from deliberate mixing, liquids in turbulent flow or passing through equipment such as pumps are being vigorously mixed. By planning such equipment in flow lines, or by ensuring turbulent flow in pipelines, liquid mixing may in many instances be satisfactorily accomplished as a by product of fluid transport.

Example 8.7:

An agitated baffle vessel is being used to prepare a uniform solution of viscosity 2 cP, running the agitator at 100 rpm, so as to obtain a Reynolds number of 50,000. If the contents of the vessel are replaced by a solution of viscosity 4 cP, and the agitator rpm is increased to 200, by how much will the power requirement change?

Solution: Theory: For agitated vessel, the following dimensional relationship is applicable.

$$Po = \psi \, (Re, Fr, S_1, S_2, ..., S_n)$$

where, Po = Power Number = $\dfrac{P}{n^3 D_\alpha^5 \rho}$

Re = Reynolds Number = $\dfrac{n D_\alpha^2 \rho}{\mu}$

Fr = Froude Number = $\dfrac{n^2 D_\alpha}{g}$

$S_1, S_2, ..., S_n$ = Shape factors

n = rotation per unit time of agitator

D_α = Diameter of impeller

ρ = Density of fluid

μ = Viscosity of fluid

MECHANICAL OPERATIONS — MIXING AND AGITATION

If the shape factors are remaining constant, then
$$Po = \psi(Re, Fr)$$
For baffled vessel, Po is a function of only Re provided the shape factors are remaining at constant value, i.e.
$$Po = \psi(Re)$$
For various impeller configurations, and system geometry, Po Vs. Re chart is available to estimate the power required. From the charts available, it could be seen that, for Re > 10000, Po is independent of Re, and remains at a constant value i.e. Po = constant, (for Re > 10000), and viscosity is not a factor.

Calculations:

For the given problem, for the case 1:
$$\mu_1 = 2 \text{ cP}; \; n_1 = 100; \; Re_1 = 50000$$
$$Re_1 = \frac{n_1 D_\alpha^2 \rho}{\mu_1} = 50000$$
Therefore, $D_\alpha^2 \rho = 50000 \times 2/100 = 1000$

For the case 2:
$$\mu_2 = 4 \text{ cP}; \; n_2 = 200$$
$$Re_2 = \frac{(D_\alpha^2 \rho) n_2}{\mu_2} = \frac{1000 \times 200}{4} = 50000$$

Here, R_e is more than 10000. Therefore, P_o = constant = K.
$$P_o = \frac{P}{n^3 D_\alpha^5 \rho} = K$$
i.e.
$$P = K n^3 D_\alpha^5 \rho$$

Since D_α and ρ are same for the two cases, we can group $K D_\alpha^5 \rho$ as a constant, say M i.e. $P = M n^3$.

The ratio of power required for case 2 to 1 is,
$$\frac{P_2}{P_1} = \frac{n_2^3}{n_1^3} = \frac{(200)^3}{(100)^3} = 8$$

The power required for the second case will be 8 times that of the first case. In other words, the power requirement will rise by, $100 \times (8 - 1)/1 = 700\%$.

Example 8.8:

A small model reactor is to be built for scale up studies of the behaviour of a proposed large industrial stirred tank reactor having 1000 times capacity. The bigger unit of 2 m diameter will have a liquid depth of 2 m. This will be fitted with a four bladed Rushton turbine of 0.6 m diameter.

(a) Estimate the dimensions of the smaller unit.

(b) For the optimum stirrer speed of 330 rpm observed in the smaller model, what will be the recommended speed in the industrial unit under the following conditions:

   (i) Power per unit volume is kept constant.

   (ii) Reynolds number does not change.

(c) What design criteria would you recommend for this type of study.

Solution: (a) Dimensions of model (smaller unit):

$$\text{Capacity of bigger unit} = (\pi/4) D_B^2 L_B = (\pi/4) \times 2^2 \times 2 = 6.283 \text{ m}^3$$

$$\text{Capacity of model} = 6.283/1000 \text{ m}^3 = 6.283 \times 10^{-3} \text{ m}^3$$

Diameter of model:

$$\pi/4 \, D_M^3 = 6.283 \times 10^{-3} \text{ m}^3$$

$$D_M = 0.2 \text{ m}$$

For geometric similarity between the model and bigger unit,

$$\frac{D_B}{D_M} = \frac{D_{\alpha B}}{D_{\alpha M}}$$

Here, $\dfrac{D_B}{D_M} = \dfrac{2}{0.2} = 10$

Therefore, $D_{\alpha M} = \dfrac{D_{\alpha M}}{10} = \dfrac{0.6}{10} = 0.06 \text{ m}$

i.e. Diameter of impeller of model unit = 0.06 m

$$\text{Power per unit volume} \propto \frac{n^3 D_\alpha^5}{D_\alpha^3} \propto n^3 D_\alpha^2$$

Therefore, if power per unit volume is to be kept constant,

$$[n^3 D_\alpha^2]_B = [n^3 D_\alpha^2]_M$$

$$n_B^2 = \frac{300^3 \times 0.06^2}{0.6^2}$$

$$n_B = 71 \text{ rpm}$$

Recommended speed of bigger unit = 71 rpm

$$\text{Reynolds number} = \frac{n D_\alpha^2 \rho}{\mu}$$

If Reynolds number should not change (and if fluid is not changed),

$$Re_B = Re_M$$
$$[nD_\alpha^2]_B = [nD_\alpha^2]_M$$
$$n_B = \frac{330 \times 0.6^2}{0.06^2} = 3.3 \text{ rpm}$$

Tip speed = $\pi D_\alpha n$ = $\pi \times 0.06 \times 3.3$ = 6.22 m/min. This tip-speed will give very low degree of agitation. Hence, the design criteria should be based on "Power per unit is to be kept constant".

EXERCISE FOR PRACTICE

(1) Calculate the power consumption of an agitator of diameter 60 cm, rotating at 30 r.p.m., in a fluid of viscosity of 70 poise and density of 1.05 gm/cm³. The power number is related by the correlation: $\frac{75}{R_e}$, for laminar flow (upto Re = 100) and power number is 1.1, for turbulent flow (R_e > 100) **(Ans.: 0.038 HP)**

(2) It is required to agitate a liquid having a viscosity of 1.5×10^{-3} pa. sec. and density of 969 kg/m³ in a tank having a diameter of 0.91 m. The agitator will be a six-blade open turbine having a diameter of 0.305 m operating at 180 rpm. The tank has 4 vertical baffles each with a width J of 0.076 m. Also W = 0.0381 m. Calculate the required kW.
(Ans.: N_P = 2.5, Power = 0.172 kW (0.231 HP))

(3) A three-bladed propeller is used to mix a fluid in the laminar region. The stirrer is 0.3 m in diameter and is rotated at 1.5 Hz. Due to corrosion, the propeller has to be replaced by a flat two bladed paddle 0.75 m in diameter. If the same motor is used, at what speed should be paddle rotate? **(Ans.: N = 0.403 Hz (24 rpm))**

(4) You are blending a number of ingredient to produce a dry instant soup mix. It includes some noodles and dried diced vegetables. Suggest types of mixers which you would use and some you wouldn't. Explain your answers.

(5) For the soup mix above, describe how you would determine when the product is adequately mixed?

(6) You have determined the mixing time for a blend of liquids in a pilot scale mixer. The diameter of the mixing tank is 1.2 m, and it is filled to a depth of 0.5 m. The mixer uses a paddle agitator 1 m in diameter, rotating at 8 rpm. Determine the tank and agitator dimensions and speed of rotation for a full scale mixer of equivalent performance capable of mixing a 1500 litre batch.

NOMENCLATURE

Symbol	
A_p	Area of cylinder swept out by tips of impeller blades, m^2
a	Interfacial area per unit volume, m^{-1}
D	Diameter of pipe m; D_a, diameter of impeller; D_t, tank diameter
E	Height of impeller above vessel floor, m
E_k	Kinetic energy of fluid, J/m^3
F	Force N; F_D, drag force; F_b, buoyant force; F_g, gravitational force
g	Gravitational acceleration, m/s^2
H	Depth of liquid in vessel, m
J	Width of baffles
L	Length of impeller blades, m
N_{Ae}	Aeration number, $q_g/n D_a^3$
N_{Fr}	Froude number, $n^2 D_a/g$
N_P	Power number $p/n^3 D_a^5 \rho$
N_Q	Flow number, q/nD_a^3
N_{Re}	Agitation Reynolds number, $n D_a^2 \rho/\mu$
N_{We}	Weber number, $\dfrac{D\rho \bar{V}^2}{\sigma}$ or $\dfrac{D_a^3 n^2 \rho_c}{\sigma}$
n	Rotational speed, r/s; n_c, critical speed for complete solids suspension
p	Power, kW
q	volumetric flow rate, m^3/s
r	Radial distance from impeller axis, m
t_T	Blending time, s
u	Velocity, m/s; u_2, velocity of impeller blade tip
W	Impeller width
Greek Letters:	
$\Delta\rho$	Density difference, kg/m^3
μ	Absolute viscosity, poise
υ	kinematic viscosity, m^2/s
ρ	Density, kg/m^3
σ	Interfacial tension, dyne/cm

***

Unit IX

Chapter 9: FLUIDIZATION

9.1 Introduction

Fluidization refers to those gas-solids and liquid-solids systems in which the solid phase is subjected to behave more or less like a fluid by the upwelling current of gas or liquid stream moving up through the bed of solid particles. Both the forces of gravity and the fluid friction act simultaneously to effect fluidization of the bed of solid particles. Fluidized bed combustion and catalytic cracking of heavy crude-oil fractions of petroleum are the two good examples of fluidization.

Many important industrial processes rely upon intimate contact between a fluid (liquid or gas) and a granular material. These processes vary from grain drying, to a wide range of chemical reactions, including combustion.

In early applications, the fluid flowed through a static bed of granules supported on a grid. Provided the material is suitable, great improvement in mixing and contact is achieved if the granule size is properly matched to the upward velocity of the fluid. If they are matched well, the drag forces will support the particles of material. When this occurs, the bed is said to be "fluidized".

A gas-fluidized bed may have the appearance of a boiling liquid. It has bubbles, which rise and appear to burst. The bubbles result in vigorous mixing and a generally horizontal free surface. The motion of the bed varies with the fluid flow rate. At high velocities, particles may become entrained and transported by the fluid.

9.2 Principles of Fluidization

Whenever a fluid stream moves up through a bed of particulate-solid phase, transfer of momentum from the fluid to the solid particles takes place. If the fluid is flowing at low velocities, the momentum transfer does not cause the particles to move. The fluid just passes through narrow, tortuous channel, losing pressure energy.

However, with the increase of stream velocity, the rate of momentum transfers from the fluid to the solid particles and hence the pressure drop for the flow through the bed increases gradually. Eventually, as the fluid velocity is increased, a point is reached where the momentum transferred from the fluid to the solid particles balances the opposing gravitational force on the particles i.e. the bed pressure drop equals the sum of the weight of the bed per unit cross-sectional area plus the friction of the bed against the vessel wall. Two distinct cases may arise at this point:

(1) The entire bed may get lifted up like a piston, the top surface of the bed forming an arch from wall to wall. This situation is encountered with solid particles, which are not freely flowing. However, the arch, in most cases, breaks away and drops down as aggregates creating a stable channel through which the upgoing fluid escapes.

(2) The bed expands and assumes a more open arrangement. This condition arises if the particles are free flowing. No further pressure drop exceeding the unit bed weight is observed in the expanded bed with a further increase of fluid velocity. The pores and channels of already expanded bed enlarge and the particles get widely dispersed. They vibrate or circulate locally in a semi-stable arrangement with the effect that the entire bed resembles, in many ways, a boiling liquid. This point is called Fluidization and the bed is called Fluidized-Bed System.

The physical characteristics of gas-fluidized beds differ significally from those of liquid-fluidized beds. Whereas in the latter, solids are almost uniformly distributed, in the former two phases can be identified – a "bubble" phase having a low concentration of solids, rising up through a continuous "emulsion" phase characterized by a much higher concentration of solids and a lower voidage (Fig. 9.1). This significant difference in the quality of fluidization leads to differences in the correlations for the other characteristics of fluidized beds.

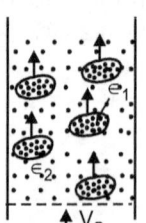

Fig. 9.1 : Bubbles in Gas Fluidized Beds, $\varepsilon_2 < \varepsilon_1$

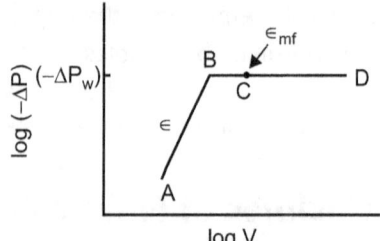

Fig. 9.2 : Pressure Drop Characteristics of an Ideal Bed of Solids

9.3 Flow Through Packed Beds

When a fluid is passed upwards through a bed of particles the pressure loss in the fluid due to frictional resistances increases with increasing fluid flow. A point is reached when the upward drag force exerted by the fluid on the particles is equal to the apparent weight of particles in the bed. At this point the particles are lifted by the fluid, the separation of the particles increases, and the bed becomes fluidized. The force balance across the fluidized bed dictates that the fluid pressure loss across the bed of the particles is equal to the apparent weight of the particles per unit area of the bed. Thus:

$$\text{Pressure drop} = \frac{\text{Weight of particles} - \text{Upthrust on particles}}{\text{Bed cross-sectional area}}$$

If a fluid is forced up through a stationary bed of particulate or porous solids, the pressure drop for the flow due to fluid friction is given by:

$$\frac{(-\Delta P_b)}{\rho \cdot g} = \frac{4f \cdot L \cdot v^2}{2 \cdot g \cdot D} \qquad \ldots (9.1)$$

where, f = Fanning's friction factor and is related by
$f = \phi(Re)$.

Therefore, the above equation becomes,

$$f = \frac{(-\Delta P_b)}{4L \cdot \rho \cdot v^2} = \phi(Re) = \phi\left(\frac{D \cdot v \cdot \rho}{\mu}\right) \qquad \ldots (9.2)$$

where,

$(-\Delta_b)$ = Bed pressure drop due to fluid friction N/m².
D = Diameter of vessel, m. It should be replaced by an equivalent diameter, D_{eq} for non-circular vessel.
D_{eq} = $4S/P_m$.
S = Surface area of the vessel, m².
P_m = Wetted perimeter, m.
V = Velocity of fluid, m/s.
L = Bed height or bed depth, m.

For packed bed we can write,

$$D_{eq} = \frac{(4S)(L)}{(P_m)(L)} = \frac{\text{Total volume of voids}}{\text{Total surface area of particles}}$$

$$= \frac{4\varepsilon}{1-\varepsilon} \cdot \frac{N \cdot V_p}{N \cdot A_p} \qquad \ldots (9.3)$$

Where,

ε = Voidage or porosity of the bed i.e. the fraction of the total bed volume that is void.
N = Total number of bed particles.
V_p = Average volume of a single solid particle, m³
A_p = Average surface area of a single solid particle, m².

Upon substituting D_{eq} for D in equation (9.1) and putting its value from equation (9.2), we get,

$$f = \frac{2(-\Delta P_b)}{4L \cdot \rho \cdot v^2} \cdot \frac{4\varepsilon}{1-\varepsilon} \cdot \frac{V_p}{A_p} = \phi\left(\frac{4\varepsilon}{1-\varepsilon} \cdot \frac{V_p}{A_p} \cdot \frac{v \cdot \rho}{\mu}\right) \qquad \ldots (9.4)$$

Now for spherical particles,

$$\frac{V_p}{A_p} = \frac{(\pi/6) d_o^3}{(\pi) d_o^2} = d_o/6 \qquad \ldots (9.5)$$

where, d_o = diameter of spherical particles

$$\therefore \qquad d_o = \frac{6}{A_p/V_p} \qquad \ldots (9.6)$$

However, the granular particles in a packed bed are irregular in most cases. For an irregular particle of known A_p/V_p ratio there exists only one size of sphere having this same ratio. The diameter of this sphere is taken as the characteristic of the particles.

$$\therefore \qquad \frac{V_p}{A_p} = \frac{d_o}{6} = \frac{d}{6}$$

where, d = particle diameter

Replacing V_p/A_p by $d/6$ and v by v_s (superficial velocity, $v_s = \varepsilon \cdot V$. It is the velocity which would occur with the actual mass flow rate through the vessel holding the bed if the vessel were empty) in equation (9.4) we get,

$$f = \frac{2(-\Delta P_b)}{L \cdot \rho \cdot v_s^2} \cdot \frac{\varepsilon^3}{1-\varepsilon} \cdot \frac{d}{6}$$

$$= \phi\left(\frac{4\varepsilon}{1-\varepsilon} \cdot \frac{d}{6} \cdot \frac{v_s \cdot \rho}{\varepsilon \cdot \mu}\right) \qquad \ldots (9.7)$$

If the flow is laminar (i.e. for low value of soaring velocity)

$$f = \frac{k_1}{Re} \text{ where } k_1 = \text{proportionality constant}$$

Combining this equation with equation (9.7) results.

$$\frac{k_1}{Re} = \frac{2\varepsilon^3}{1-\varepsilon} \cdot \frac{(-\Delta P_b)}{L \cdot \rho \cdot v_s^2} \cdot \frac{d}{6} \qquad \ldots (9.8)$$

or, $$\frac{k_1}{\frac{4\varepsilon}{1-\varepsilon} \cdot \frac{V_p}{A_p} \cdot \frac{v_s \rho}{\varepsilon \cdot \mu}} = \frac{2\varepsilon^3}{1-\varepsilon} \cdot \frac{(-\Delta P_b)}{L \cdot \rho \cdot v_s^2} \cdot \frac{d}{6} \qquad \ldots (9.9)$$

$$\frac{(-\Delta P_b)}{L} = \frac{k_1}{2}\left[\frac{1-\varepsilon}{4} \cdot \frac{6}{d} \cdot \frac{\mu}{v_s \cdot \rho}\right]\left(\frac{1-\varepsilon}{\varepsilon^3}\right)(\rho \cdot v_s^2) \cdot \frac{6}{d}$$

$$= 4.5 \, k_1 \frac{(1-\varepsilon)^2}{\varepsilon^3} \cdot \frac{\mu \cdot v_s}{d^2} \qquad \ldots (9.10)$$

MECHANICAL OPERATIONS — FLUIDIZATION

$$\boxed{\frac{(-\Delta P_b)}{L} = k_2 \frac{(1-\varepsilon)^2}{\varepsilon^3} \cdot \frac{\mu \cdot v_s}{d^2}} \qquad \ldots (9.11)$$

where, k_1 and k_2 are constant. $K_2 = 4.5\, k_1$.

The equation (9.11) is known as **Carman-Kozeny equation**.

This expression has successfully been employed to calculate the bed pressure drop per unit bed height. Kozeny used a simplified model of a number of parallel capillary tubes of equal length and diameter to describe the packed bed. For exact model, $k_1 = 64$.

Carman on the other hand applied this equation (9.11) to account for the experimental results on flow through packed beds and founds.

$$k_2 = 180$$

Equation (9.11) gives the pressure drop caused by form drag due to laminar flow. If the flow velocity is sufficiently large, i.e. as Re is high, kinetic-energy losses become significant that solely accounts for bed pressure drop $(-\Delta P_b)_k$ where,

$$(-\Delta P_b)_k = \rho \cdot v^2 = \rho \cdot \frac{v_s^2}{\varepsilon^2} \qquad \ldots (9.12)$$

If the energy loss occurs repeatedly in unit channel length, then

$$\frac{(-\Delta P_b)_k}{L} = \left(\frac{1}{2}\right) n \cdot \rho \cdot (v_s/\varepsilon)^2 \qquad \ldots (9.13)$$

Where, n = Number of repetitive kinetic energy losses per unit bed height.
Using 'n' inversely proportional to D_c, then channel diameter.

$$\frac{(-\Delta P_b)_k}{L} k_3 \cdot \frac{\rho}{D_c} (v_s/\varepsilon)^2 \quad \text{where, } k_3 \text{ is proportionality constant} \qquad \ldots (9.14)$$

Now,
$$\frac{A_p}{V_p} = \frac{6}{d}$$

But,
$$\frac{A_p}{V_p} = \frac{N_c\,(\pi D_c \cdot L)}{\frac{\pi}{4} \cdot D^2 \cdot L\,(1-\varepsilon)} = 4 N_c \cdot \frac{D_c}{D^2} \cdot \frac{1}{(1-\varepsilon)}$$

Where, N_c = number of channels is the bed cross-section. The bed is supposed to be composed of a large number of capillary tubes (channels) of fixed length and diameter. The particle surface are (A_p) has been taken equal to the surface area of the walls of these capillaries.

$$D = \text{bed dia, m.}$$

Again
$$N_c \left[\frac{\pi}{4}(D_c)^2\right] = \left[\frac{\pi}{4} \cdot D^2\right] \cdot \varepsilon$$

$$\therefore \quad \frac{D_c}{D^2} = \frac{\varepsilon}{(N_c \cdot D_c)}$$

$$\therefore \quad \frac{A_p}{V_p} = 4N_c \cdot \frac{\epsilon}{N_c \cdot D_c} \cdot \frac{1}{1-\epsilon} = \frac{4}{D_c} \cdot \frac{\epsilon}{1-\epsilon} \qquad \ldots (9.15)$$

or,
$$\frac{6}{d} = \frac{4}{D_c} \cdot \frac{\epsilon}{1-\epsilon}$$

$$\therefore \quad D_c = \frac{4}{6} \cdot d \cdot \frac{\epsilon}{1-\epsilon}$$

$$\frac{(-\Delta P_b)_k}{L} = k_3 \cdot \frac{6}{4} \cdot \frac{\rho}{d} \cdot \left(\frac{1-\epsilon}{\epsilon}\right) \cdot \left[\frac{v_s}{\epsilon}\right]^2 = \frac{3}{2} \cdot k_3 \cdot \frac{\rho \cdot v_s^2}{d} \cdot \frac{1-\epsilon}{\epsilon^3} \qquad \ldots (9.16)$$

Upon substitution of the value of D_c in equation (9.14) it becomes.

$$\frac{(-\Delta P_b)_k}{L} = k_3 \cdot \frac{6 \rho}{4 d} \left(\frac{1-\epsilon}{\epsilon}\right) \cdot \left(\frac{v_s}{\epsilon}\right)^2$$

$$= k_4 \frac{\rho \cdot v_s^2}{d} \frac{1 \epsilon}{\epsilon^3} \qquad \ldots (9.16\ a)$$

where,
$$k_4 = \frac{3}{2} k_3 = \text{constant}$$

Equation (9.16 a) represents the expression for bed pressure drop due to turbulent flow through packed beds. Equation (9.11) gives bed pressure drop caused by form-drag and equation (9.16 a) expresses bed pressure drop caused by kinetic-energy losses. Combining these two gives total pressure drop. Resulting from flow through packed bed.

$$\frac{(-\Delta P_b)}{L} = k_2 \frac{(1-\epsilon)}{\epsilon^3} \cdot \frac{\mu \cdot v_s}{d^2} + k_4 \frac{1-\epsilon}{\epsilon^3} \cdot \frac{\rho \cdot v_s^2}{d} \qquad \ldots (9.17)$$

However, equation (9.17) is based on the assumption that velocity of flow of the fluidizing media is constant throughout the bed height. However for a gas flowing at high-pressure drop this would not be. In such cases, the equation (9.17) is modified to

$$\frac{(-\Delta P_b)}{L} = k_2 \frac{(1-\epsilon)^2}{\epsilon^3} \cdot \frac{\mu \cdot v_{sm}}{d^2} + k_4 \frac{(1-\epsilon)}{\epsilon^3} \cdot \frac{G \cdot v_m}{d} \qquad \ldots (9.18)$$

where,

V_{sm} = Superficial velocity computed at the average of inlet and outlet pressure.

G = Mass rate of flow per unit bed cross-section, $kg/m^2 \cdot S$

= $\rho \cdot V_s$.

The values of k_2 and k_4 can be determined by rearranging equation (9.18) to:

$$\frac{(-\Delta P_b)}{L} \cdot \frac{\epsilon^3}{(1-\epsilon)^2} \cdot \frac{d^2}{\mu \cdot v_m} = k_2 + k_4 \frac{Re}{1-\epsilon} \qquad \ldots (9.19)$$

And plotting the left hand side against $Re/(1-\epsilon)$ whereupon a straight-line of slope k_4 and intercept k_2, [at $Re/(1-\epsilon) = 0$] results Fig. 9.3.

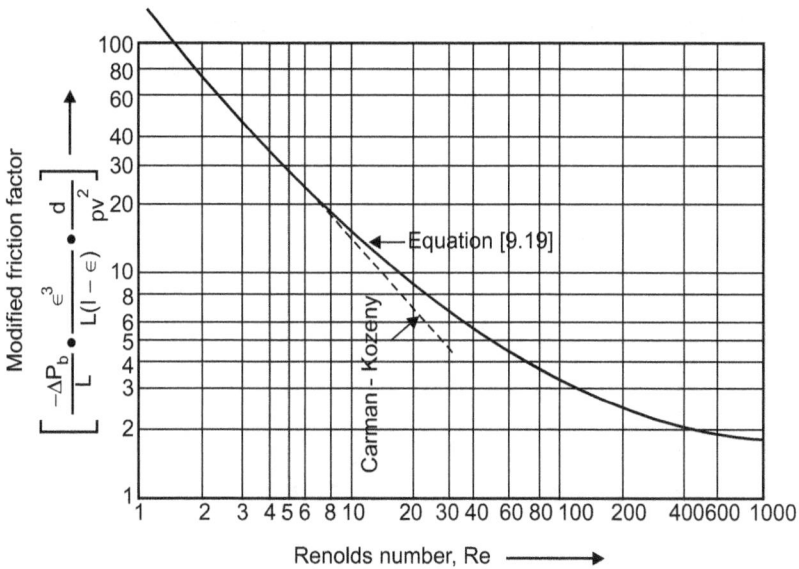

Fig. 9.3: Pressure Drop for Flow through Packed Beds

A large amount of experimental results show $k_2 = 150$ and $k_4 = 1.75$.

Introducing these values in equation (9.18) results

$$\boxed{\frac{(-\Delta P_b)}{L} = 150 \frac{(1-\epsilon)^2}{\epsilon^3} \cdot \frac{\mu \cdot v_{sm}}{d^2} + 1.75 \frac{(1-\epsilon)}{\epsilon^3} \cdot \frac{G \cdot v_m}{d}} \quad \ldots (9.20)$$

This is known as **Ergun's equation**.

9.4 Pressure Drop in Packed Beds

We can think of a packed bed as large number of solid particles in contact with one another or as a network of tortuous passages formed by the spaces between the particles.

A fluid flowing though the bed does so under the influence of a pressure drop ΔP over unit length of bed.

Carman and Kozeny (1937 and 1927 respectively) attempted to model the tiny passages by an "equivalent" large pore with equal surfaces area and volume.

When a fluid flows through a parallel-sided passage, the friction factor C_f is related to the Reynolds Number Re:

$$C_f = \frac{2\tau_0}{\rho\mu^2} \quad Re = \frac{\rho\mu d_H}{\mu} \quad \ldots (9.21)$$

τ_0 = Shear stress at the wall.

d_H = Hydraulic mean diameter = $4 \times$ Flow Area + Wetted Perimeter.

MECHANICAL OPERATIONS — FLUIDIZATION

We assume that these relationships apply to our "equivalent pore". However, the velocity we know is the "superficial velocity", based on the cross-sectional area of the empty bed i.e.

$$\mu = \frac{Q}{A_{bed}} \qquad \ldots (9.22)$$

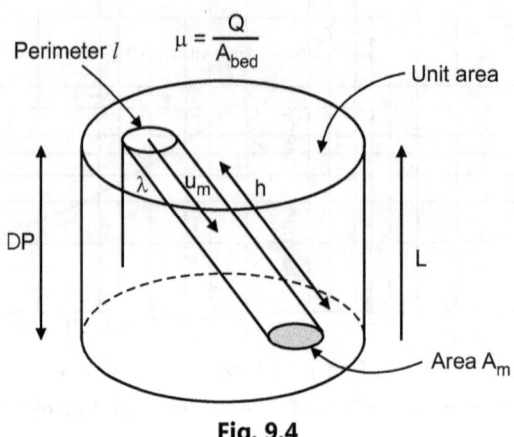

Fig. 9.4

The illustration shows the equivalent pore in unit area of bed, depth L. The pore has cross-sectional area A_m, perimeter l and length $h = L/\cos \lambda$, as it is inclined to the mean flow direction by angle λ.

Equvality of Pore Volume:

$$\text{Volume of Pore} = A_M h = \frac{A_M L}{\cos \lambda} = \text{Pore volume in bed section} = 1 \times L \times \varepsilon$$

$$\Rightarrow A_M = \varepsilon \cos \lambda \qquad \ldots (9.23)$$

Equality of Surface Area:

$$\text{Area of equivalent pore surface} = lh = \frac{lL}{\cos \lambda}$$

$$= \text{Surface area of solids in bed section}$$

$$= 1 \times L \times a$$

$$\Rightarrow l = a \cos \lambda \qquad \ldots (9.24)$$

a is the surface area of solids per unit volume.

The mean velocity in the passage is the total volume flow per unit area divided by A_m. The first term is simply the superficial velocity, u. So:

$$u_m = \frac{u}{A_m} = \frac{u}{\varepsilon \cos \lambda} \qquad \ldots (9.25)$$

Pressure force exerted on fluid in pore = $\Delta P A_m$.

Since the surface area is given by La the shear stress resisting the pressure force is,

$$\frac{\Delta P A_m}{La} = \frac{\Delta P}{L} \cdot \frac{\varepsilon \cos \lambda}{a} = \tau_o \qquad \ldots (9.26)$$

$$C_f = \frac{2\tau_o}{\rho u_m^2} \qquad \ldots (9.27)$$

By definition:
$$C_f = \frac{2\tau_o}{\rho u_m^2} = \frac{2\Delta P}{L} \cdot \frac{\varepsilon \cos \lambda}{a} \cdot \frac{1}{\rho u_m^2}$$

$$= \frac{2\Delta P}{L} \cdot \frac{\varepsilon \cos \lambda}{a} \cdot \frac{\varepsilon^2 \cos^2 \lambda}{\rho u^2}$$

$$= \frac{2 \Delta P}{L} \cdot \frac{\varepsilon^3 \cos^3 \lambda}{\rho \mu^2 a} \qquad \ldots (9.28)$$

$$Re = \frac{\rho u_m d_H}{\mu} \quad d_H = \frac{4 A_m}{l} = \frac{4\varepsilon}{a}$$

where, $Re = \frac{\rho u}{\varepsilon \cos \lambda} \cdot \frac{4\varepsilon la}{\mu} = \frac{4\rho u}{\rho u \cos \lambda}$ ... (9.29)

Assuming the flow in the equivalent pore in laminar then by definition,

$$C_f = \frac{16}{Re} = \frac{4\rho u \cos \lambda}{\rho u}$$

$$\frac{4 \rho \mu \cos \lambda}{\rho u} = 2 \frac{\Delta P}{L} \frac{\varepsilon^3 \cos^3 \lambda}{\rho u^2 a}$$

i.e. $\qquad \frac{\Delta P}{L} = \frac{2 \rho u a^2}{\varepsilon^3 \cos^2 \lambda} \qquad \ldots (9.30)$

The above equation, the Carman-Kozeny equation is general. For spheres in a packed bed containing N spheres per unit volume, with diameter d.

$$a = N \pi d^2$$

$$1 - \varepsilon = \frac{\pi}{6} N d^3 \text{ dividing to eliminate } N$$

$$a = 6(1-\varepsilon)/d$$

$$\frac{\Delta P}{L} = \frac{2 \rho u \cdot 36(1-\varepsilon)^2/d^2}{\varepsilon^3 \cos^2 \lambda}$$

$$= \frac{72 \rho u(1-\varepsilon)^2}{\cos^2 \lambda \varepsilon^3 d^2} \qquad \ldots (9.31)$$

Substituting for spheres Carman (1956) gives values of the constant $(72/\cos^2\lambda)$ between 162 and 184 (average 173) corresponding to $48° < \lambda < 51°$ which is physically possible, the transition to turbulence occurs when,

$$Re' = \frac{4\rho u}{\rho u \cos \lambda} > 1.5 \text{ or so}$$

i.e. $\dfrac{\rho u d}{\mu(1-\varepsilon)} > 1.5$ ... (9.32)

For transitional and higher Reynolds number Ergun gives,

$$f = \frac{\Delta P d \, \varepsilon^3}{\rho u^2 L(1-\varepsilon)} = \frac{150}{Re'} + 1.75 \quad \ldots (9.33)$$

NB this value of f is proportional to but not equal to C_f.

$$Re' = \frac{\rho u d}{\mu(1-\varepsilon)} \quad \ldots (9.34)$$

This gives a very satisfactory fit; the first term predominates at low, the second at high Re'.

9.5 Pressure Drop-Flow Rate Diagrams

An ideal bed of solids has pressure drop vs superficial velocity characteristics as shown in Fig. 9.5. Between points A and B, the bed is a fixed bed and equations derived in the previous chapter hold good. The $(-\Delta P)$ vs. v_s graph has a slope of unity, for low Reynolds numbers (due to the small particle sizes normally used). The voidage of the bed is ε. At point B, the $(-\Delta P)$ is large enough to balance the buoyant weight of the bed, $-\Delta P_w$, and the bed expands slightly as v_s is increased.

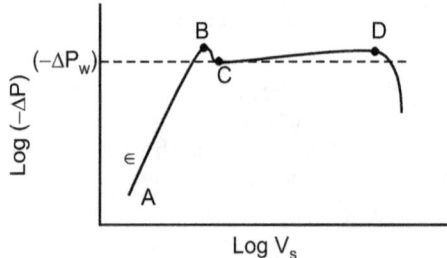

Fig. 9.5: Pressure – Drop Characteristics of Real Beds of Solids

At some point C, the solids lose contact with each other and begin to oscillate at their own positions. Point C is called the incipient or *minimum fluidization point* and is characterized by a voidage, ε_{mf}. Beyond point C, the pressure drop remains almost constant and as v_s is increased, ε and the height of the bed increases. On lowering v_s, the path DCBA is reversibly traced back. Real beds of solids, however, show a slightly different behaviour as shown in Fig. 9.5, probably due to the effect of channeling. Between points A and B, fixed bed conditions hold good and the porosity is ε. A maximum in the pressure drop (point B) is usually observed, this pressure drop being slightly larger than the value $-\Delta P_w$ required to balance the buoyant weight of the bed. On increasing the superficial velocity of the fluid, the bed suddenly expands and the pressure drop falls immediately to a value of $-\Delta P_w$ (point C).

The voidage at point C is ϵ_{mf}. The reason why point B is slightly above – ΔP_w is not precisely known and it has been explained intuitively, to be because of some energy required to "unlock" the solid particles from each other. After point C, there is a slight increase in the pressure drop. At high superficial fluid velocities, entertainment of solids starts (point D) and the pressure drop falls. Non-idealities like channelling lead to much lower pressure drops whereas 'slugging' (gas bubbles coalesce and become large enough to spread across the entire tube, carrying the solids above it as if a piston were moving upwards; this slug finally disintegrates at the top and a new slug is formed at the bottom) leads of fluctuations in the (–ΔP) vs. v_s curve with time. Even though the physical characteristics of the bed differ for liquid and gas fludized beds, the –ΔP vs. v_s diagram is similar for both these systems.

9.6 Types of Fluidization

Fluidization without solids entrainment or with very little entrainment is called dense-*phase fluidization*. However, fluidization accompanied by the total entrainment of solids is called *lean-phase fluidization with pneumatic transport*.

On the basis of the experiments two main types of dense-phase fluidization have been identified:
(1) Particulate Fluidization.
(2) Aggregative Fluidization.

9.6.1 Particulate Fluidization

This is characterized by even bed fluidization with each particles moving individually through a relatively uniform mean-free path. This occurs in those cases where the density difference of the solids and the fluid is narrow and where the particles are small. Therefore, bed fluidization takes place at low velocity of flow. And the dense phase attains many of the characteristics of a liquid.

$$\text{Particulate fluidization occurs if } (Fr)(Re)\left(\frac{\rho_s - \rho}{\rho}\right)\left(\frac{L}{D}\right) < 100 \quad \ldots (9.35)$$

where,
Fr = Froude number = $V^2/g.d$
Re = Reynolds number = $dV\rho/\mu$
ρ_s = density of solids, kg/m^3
ρ = density of the fluid, kg/m^3
D = bed dia, m.
L = bed height, m.

9.6.2 Aggregative Fluidization

This is characterized by uneven bed fluidization with considerable number of large bubbles bursting out at bed surface. This occurs where the density difference of the solid and the fluid is too great or where the particles are large. The velocity of flow must be considerably large to induce fluidization. The uneven fluidization is associated with a large number of large bubbles, which burst at the surface spraying solid particles on the bed. Within the bed the particles move in distinct aggregates, which are lifted by bubbles. The bed behaves like a liquid while the fluid phase acting as a gas bubbling through it.

Aggregative fluidization occurs if: $(Fr)(Re)\left(\dfrac{\rho_s - \rho}{\rho}\right)\left(\dfrac{L}{D}\right) > 100$ ... (9.36)

9.6.3 Determination of Minimum Fluidizing Velocity

Ergun derived a correlation for the prediction of U_{mf} by equating a correlation for pressure drop through a packed bed at the voidage corresponding to that at minimum fluidization, ϵ_{mf}, to the weight of the bed per unit area and obtained the following form:

$$Ar = 150\dfrac{1 - \epsilon_{mf}}{\phi^2 \epsilon_{mf}^3} Re_{mf} + \dfrac{1.75}{\phi \epsilon_{mf}^3} Re_{mf}^2 \quad \ldots (9.37)$$

Ar – Archimedes number.

Re_{mf} – Reynolds number in terms of U_{mf}.

ϵ_{mf} – Voidage at minimum fluidization.

ϕ – Particle shape factor.

The first term of the correlation in Re_{mf} tends to dominate under laminar flow conditions, whereas, the second term in Re_{mf}^2 dominates in beds of very large particle for which the interstitial flow is turbulent. Under transitional conditions, the contributions of both terms are important. The correlation is obviously very sensitive to the value of ϵ_{mf} used. To use the correlation for predictive purposes, ϵ_{mf} may be estimated from measurements on a loosely packed bed, but it has been shown that ϵ_{mf} varies with operating temperature under some conditions. It is also difficult to estimate the particle shape factor, ϕ, so large errors in the estimation of U_{mf} are likely (typically ± 30%).

Estimation of Voidage:

For materials which have no internal porosity, the voidage can be estimated from the density of the solid ρ_b and the density of the bed ρ_b.

$$\rho = 1 - \dfrac{\rho_b}{\rho_p} \quad \ldots (9.38)$$

$$\varepsilon_{mf} = 1 - \frac{\rho_{bmf}}{\rho_p} \qquad ...(9.39)$$

$$\rho_{bmf} = \frac{\text{Mass of particles in bed}}{\text{Volume of bed at } U_{mf}} \qquad ...(9.40)$$

Shape Factor:

The shape factor (ϕ) is a ratio of surface area:

$$\phi = \frac{\text{(Surface area of sphere of given volume)}}{\text{(Surface area of particle of same volume)}} \qquad ...(9.41)$$

This is easily calculated for regular geometric shapes but is more difficult to assess for irregular particles.

The shape factor for the granular material supplied with this unit is about 0.73.

9.6.4 Observation of General Bed Behaviour

Measurement of Minimum Fluidization Velocity, U_{mf}

If the value of U_{mf} required is that found under ambient conditions, it is best to measure it directly. To do this, charge a sufficient quantity of particle into the container to form a bed, then fluidize the bed vigorously for a few minutes to break down any particle interlocking. Make measurements of the pressure drop across the bed as the fluidizing gas velocity is reduced in stages. Plot the results in the form of bed pressure drop against superficial gas velocity. At the higher gas flow rates the pressure drop is expected to have a value equal to that of the weight of the bed per unit area, but it may be less than this because some of the weight of the bed is being supported by the column wall through particle or wall interactions. At low gas flow rates, the pressure drop across the bed should increase from zero (with zero gas flow rate), linearly, with increase in superficial gas velocity, until the bed approaches the conditions of fluidization. This is because the gas flow through the bed will be laminar.

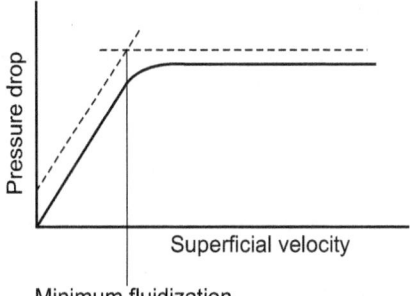

Fig. 9.6: Superficial Velocity (Decreasing) Versus Bed Pressure Drop

Fig. 9.6 illustrates a typical plot of bed pressure drop against superficial gas velocity. The minimum fluidizing velocity corresponds to the velocity at the point of intersection between the rising and flat portions of the curve. If the experiment is performed with beds of much larger/denser particles, for example, alumina of mean diameter ~ 1 mm, the increase in pressure drop will increase more rapidly because the flow conditions will be changing from laminar to transitional to turbulent.

If the experiment is repeated in the reverse direction by incremental increasing the gas velocity from zero and noting the corresponding bed pressure drops, it may not follow the earlier curve, and it certainly will not do so if the bed has been tapped. Tapping encourages the bed to compact into the static condition with gas flow through it. This condition is because the bed voidage, ϵ, is reduced to below that of its condition at minimum fluidization, ϵ_{mf}. A measurement under these conditions will lead to an underestimate of the minimum fluidizing velocity. Also, when making incremental measurements from the packed bed condition, the bed pressure drop may initially exceed that of the weight of the bed per unit area as the bed begins fluidization, because the drag force has first to increase to break down the particle interlocking within the bed (Fig. 9.7).

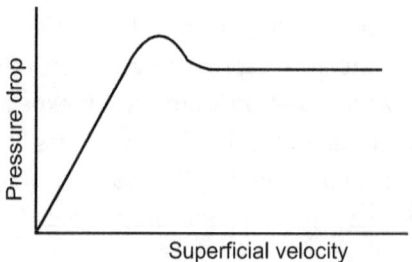

Fig. 9.7: Increasing Superficial Velocity

The transition from packed to fluidized conditions will be sharper if the bed material is closely sized than if the bed consists of wide particle size distribution. In the latter instance, as the gas flow rate is increased, there will be a tendency for the finer particles to become fluidized first, and the approach to the fluidized condition will be more gradual. Under such conditions where the fines tend to fluidized and come to the top of the bed, segregation is occurring. If there is a wide particle size distribution, beds should be fluidized vigorously to produce a bubbling bed thus, quickly reaching a well mixed condition and reducing the tendency for segregation to occur. Once segregation has occurred, it is much more difficult to remix the bed material. These properties will be seen in Experiment E.

Bed Height:

In these experiments the bed height should be measured as a function of superficial gas velocity. At higher velocities this can only be measured approximately, because the surface will fluctuate rapidly as bubbles burst through the surface. The degree of bed expansion beyond that seen at U_{mf} is due to flow of bubbles through the bed.

(**Note:** Although the bubbling bed may look turbulent, the interstitial gas flow between the particles is laminar except the fluidizing beds of large/dense particles).

Bubble Behaviour:

It is instructive to look at the bubbling behaviour. Bubbles usually grow as they rise through the bed. Partly this is a spontaneous process, but mostly it occurs by larger bubbles, rising more quickly than a smaller. They overtake the smaller bubbles and coalesce with them. With beds of large/dense particles, however, this coalescence behaviour is different. These bubbles will tend to grow by cross-wise coalescense. The rising bubbles draw a streak of particles after them and carry some particle in their wake. This is the mechanism by which solids circulation is generated. The influence of the wall surface, makes the bubbles tend to move inwards into the bed. One can plainly see the return flow of solids descending at the wall in stick/slip flow to replace those which have been carried upward within the bulk of the bed by the rising bubbles. Again, with beds of larger/denser particles, the bubbling action that occurs is not so effective in generating particle mixing as with the other bubbling beds. The higher the fluidizing velocity, the larger and more numerous the bubbles, because most of the excess gas flows as bubbles.

9.7 Applications of Fluidization Technique

Fluidization lends a very useful mean to carry out such diverse processes as solid-catalyzed reactions, coal/solid fuel combustion, particulate drying, and heat and mass transfer operations.

The largest-scale industrial application of fluidization is the catalytic cracking of heavy crude oil fractions to manufacture gasoline. Developed during World War II, the process feeds the vapourized feedstock and regenerated catalyst at about 840°K into the reactor where the coke is burnt off the catalyst, which is recycled. Only about 1% of the catalyst is entrained by the product, which is free from it in cyclones.

(1) Ore roasting:
  (a) Roasting of pyrite, pyrrhotite or other sulfur ores to provide SO_2 for the manufacture of sulfuric acid.

(b) Roasting of such ores (viz. Sulfidic, arsenical or antimonial ores) as will facilitate the release of gold or silver values.
(c) Roasting of copper, cobalt and zinc sulfide ores.
(d) Calcination of lime, dolomite and clay.
(2) Manufacturing cement.
(3) Extraction of oil from oil shale.
(4) The manufacture of ethylene oxide from ethylene.
(5) The production of phthalic anhydride by oxidation of naphthalene.
(6) The combustion of low-grade fuels and combustible wastes to generate steam. Besides, fluidized bed is used to ensure heat transfer:
   (i) To and from the bed by installing heat-exchange surfaces, usually, in the form of vertical tubes at top, or bottom of the bed or exterior to the vessel.
   (ii) From solids to gas and gas to solids. A correction for particle-fluid heat transfer coefficient is

$$h/G = 0.043 \left[k \cdot C_p^{1/2} / \mu \right]^{2/3} \left[d \left(\frac{1-\epsilon}{G} \right)^2 \cdot g \, (\rho_s - \rho) \cdot \rho \right]^{0.25} \quad \ldots (9.42)$$

For temperature control accomplished through:
(i) Control of gas flow and/or solids feed rate.
(ii) Regulating solids circulation.
(iii) Regulating gas circulation.
(iv) Injecting volatile liquid to the bed so that latent heat of vapourization takes care of excess heat.
(v) Installation of a heat exchange surface in the bed.

Mixing of solids can be achieved in fluidized beds by maintaining high ratios of fluidizing velocity to minimum fluidizing velocity. Under these conditions, tremendous solid circulation takes place from top to bottom of the bed and that ensures rapid mixing of solids. Fluidized-bed units are commonly used for drying solids such as coal, cement, rock, limestone, dolomite etc.

9.8 Design of Fluidized Beds

The design of fluidized beds is similar to packed beds (as long as there is particulate fluidization) and a simple example of a fluidized bed reactor is discussed. The parameters of interest (independent degrees of freedom) are tube diameter, bed height or catalyst weight, solids particle size, in addition to the temperature and pressure of the reactor etc., which are determined primarily on the basis of reaction engineering, thermodynamics and heat transfer.

The size of the particles can usually be fixed from reaction engineering (the larger the size, the less is the surface of catalyst particles per unit volume for non-porous catalysts). The height of the bed or the catalyst weight, can gain be determined as for fixed bed reactors by the conversion desired. This leaves only the diameter of the bed to be determined.

This can be obtained by optimization (the larger the diameter, the larger will be the cost of the tube but the lower will be the compressor cost since the pressure drop due to reduced height will be lower). Gas fluidized beds, however, generally behave very erratically due to bubble formation, slugging, etc. and scale-up is very uncertain and a subject of intense current research activity. The study of bubble formation is very important in this context.

In many liquid-solid systems an increase in velocity above V_{om} results in a smooth progressive expansion of the bed. Large scale instabilities and heterogeneites are not observed. A bed such as this is called a *homogenous* fluidized bed. This is typically observed when the fluid and solids have similar intrinsic densities. When there is a large difference in the densities of the fluid and solid phases an increase in fluid velocity typically causes large bubbles or other such instabilities. Several types of instabilities are described by Kunii and Levenspeil. (Kunii and O. Levenspeil, Fluidization Engineering, 2ed., Butterworth-Heineman, Boston, 1991).

In turbulent and pneumatically mobilized beds a significant part of the bed may be carried out of the vessel. For steady-state operations the particles must be recovered such as with a cyclone. A spouted bed is a variation on the fluidized bed in which the flow of the fluid is localized along the center axis and the solids move downward along the vessel walls.

Fluidized beds display a number of liquid-like properties:
- Lighter objects float on top of the bed (i.e., objects less dense than the bulk density of the bed),
- The surface stays horizontal even in titled beds,
- The solids can flow through an opening in the vessel just like a liquid,
- The beds have a "static" pressure head due to gravity, given by $\rho_o gh$,

Levels between two similar fluidized beds equalize their static pressure heads.
There are a number of ways in which to design and operate gas-fluidized systems for continuous operations. Fig. 9.8 shows a counter current column and a cross flow system.

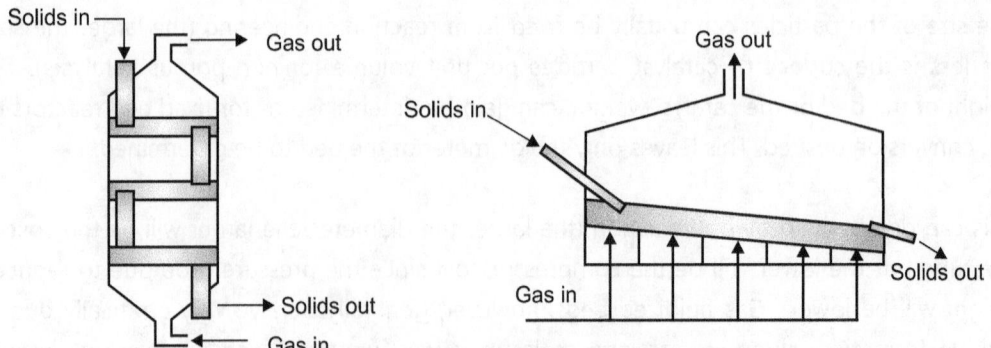

Fig. 9.8: Counter Current and Cross Flow Methods of Continuous Contacting in Fluidized Bed Designs

9.8.1 Comparison of Contacting Methods

Kunii and Levenspiel provide a table comparing different types of fluidized beds to the fixed bed. Beds include:

- Fixed bed
- Moving bed
- Bubbling/turbulent bed
- Fast fluidized bed
- Rotary cylinder
- Flat hearth

9.8.2 Advantages and Disadvantages of Fluidized Beds

The advantages of fluidized beds includes:

- Liquid like behaviour, easy to control and automate,
- Rapid mixing, uniform temperature and concentrations,
- Resists rapid temperature changes, hence responds slowly to changes in operating conditions and avoids temperature runaway with exothermic reactions,
- Circulate solids between fluidized beds for heat exchange,
- Applicable for large or small scale operations,
- Heat and mass transfer rates are high, requiring smaller surfaces.
- The large surface area between particles and fluid promotes heat transfer operations.
- The ease with which fluidized solids can be transported.
- The excellent heat transfer properties of the gas-fluidized bed. The bubble generated mixing keeps the bulk of the bed isothermal, and high heat transfer rates are obtainable between the bed and immersed surfaces.

Fluidized bed reactors are most often used in the temperature regulation of highly exothermic reactions and in continuously recycling a catalyst between a reactor and regenerator. Currently, there is much interest in the potential advantages of fluidized bed combustors.

The disadvantages of fluidized beds includes:
- Bubbling beds of fine particles are difficult to predict and are less efficient,
- Rapid mixing of solids causes non-uniform residence times for continuous flow reactors,
- Particle comminuting (breakup) is common,
- Pipe and vessel walls erode due to collisions by particles.
- Fluid throughput rates are limited to the range over which the bed is fluidized. If the velocity is much higher than U_{mf}, there can be excessive loss of material carried out from the bed and there may also be unacceptable particle damage due to excessive operating velocity.
- The pumping power supplied to fluidize the bed can excessive for very large, deep beds.
- Size and type of particles which can be handled by this technique are limited.
- Due to the complexity of fluidized bed behaviour, there are often difficulties in attempting to scale-up smaller scale to industrial units.

9.8.3 Uses of Fluidized Bed
The uses of fluidized beds are limited to our imaginations. Typical uses include:
- Reactors:
  - Cracking hydrocarbons
  - Carbonization
  - Coal gasification
  - Calcination
- Heat exchange
- Drying operations
- Coating (example, metals with polymer)
- Solidification/Granulation
- Growth of particles
- Adsorption/desorption
- Bio fluidization

9.9 Pneumatic Conveying
Pneumatic conveying involves the transport of particulate materials by air or other gases. It is generally suitable for the transport of particles in the size range 20 μ m to 50 mm. Finer particles cause problems arising from their tendency to adhere together and to the walls of the pipe and ancillary equipment. Sticky and moist powders are the worst of all. Large particles may exceed excessively high velocities in order to maintain them in suspension or to lift them from the bottom of the pipe in horizontal systems. The successful operation of a pneumatic conveyor may well depend much more on the need to achieve reliable operation, by removing the risks of blockage and of damage by erosion, than on achieving conditions

which optimize the performance of the straight sections of the pipeline. It is important to keep changes in direction of flow as gradual as possible, to use suitable materials of construction (polyurethane lining is frequently employed) and to use velocities of flow sufficiently high to keep the particles moving, but not so high as to cause serious erosion.

In hydraulic conveying the densities of the solids and the fluid are of the same order of magnitude, with the solids usually having a somewhat higher density than the liquid. Practical flow velocities are commonly in the range of 1 to 5 m/sec. In pneumatic transport, the solids may have a density two to three orders of magnitude greater than the gas and velocities will be considerably greater - up to 20-30 m/sec.

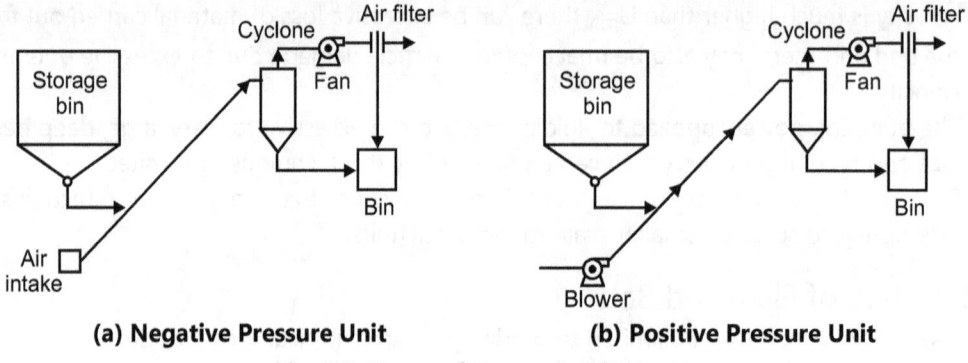

(a) Negative Pressure Unit   (b) Positive Pressure Unit

Fig. 9.9: Types of Conveying Systems

Conveying Systems for Solids: One of the methods used in industry for transporting solids from one place to another is by the use of air at high velocities. In this process, air is made to flow through ducts at high velocities either by means of blowers or by vacuum devices and carries forward the solids introduced into these ducts. Two common types of pneumatic conveying systems, the positive and the negative pressure types are indicated in Fig. 9.9. The negative pressure types are limited by the amounts of vacuum that can be created and are preferred when solids have to be conveyed from several points in a plant to one single point. Positive pressure systems are normally used when conveying solids from a single point to several points., From the design point of view, there is no basic different between two basic types of units.

9.10 Solved Examples

Example 9.1:
A tube of 0.05 m² cross-sectional area is packed with spherical particles up to a height of 0.25 m. The porosity of the bed is 0.35. It is desired to fluidise the particles with water (ρ = 1000 kg/m³, μ = 10^{-3} pa.sec.). Calculate the minimum velocity of fluidization given the Ergan's equation:

$$-\frac{\Delta P}{L}\frac{D_P}{\rho_f V^2}\frac{\epsilon}{1-\epsilon} = \frac{150\,\mu\,(1-\epsilon)}{D_P \rho_f V} + 1.75$$

Data: Diameter of particles = 0.01 m, Density of solid particles = 2600 kg/m³.

Solution: Minimum fluidization velocity:

$$\frac{\Delta P}{L}\frac{D_P}{\rho_f V^2}\frac{\epsilon^3}{1-\epsilon} = \frac{150\,\mu\,(1-\epsilon)}{D_P \rho_f V} + 1.75$$

Substituting values, we have,

$$\frac{(2800-100)}{0.25}\frac{0.01}{1000\times V^2}\frac{0.35^3}{1-0.35} = \frac{150\times 10^{-3}(1-0.035)}{0.01\times 1000\times V} + 1.75$$

$$\frac{0.686}{162.5\,V^2} = \frac{0.0975}{10\,V} + 1.75$$

$$\frac{0.00422}{V^2} = \frac{0.00975}{V} + 1.75$$

$$0.00422 - 0.00975\,V - 1.75\,V^2 = 0 - 1.75\,V^2 - 0.0975\,V + 0.00422 = 0$$

Using quadratic formula,

$$\frac{-b\pm\sqrt{b^2-4ac}}{2a} = \frac{-0.00975\pm\sqrt{0.00975^2 + \sqrt{4\,(1.75)\,(0.00422)}}}{2\times 1.75}$$

$$= \frac{-0.00975\pm 0.172}{2\times 1.75} = 0.046\ \text{m/s} \qquad \text{(Ans.)}$$

Example 9.2:

Air flows through a packed bed of a powdery material of 1 cm depth at a superficial gas velocity of 1 cm/sec. A manometer connected to the unit registers a pressure drop of 1 cm of water. The bed has a porosity of 0.4. Assuming that Kozeny – Carman equation is valid for the range of study, estimate the particle size of the powder.

Data: ρ_{air} = 1.23 kg/m³, μ_{air} = 1.8 × 10⁻⁵ kg/m.s

Solution: Given: $\bar{V}_o$ = 1 cm/sec, ΔP = 1 cm of water, ρ_{air} = 1.23 kg/m³ = 1.23 × 10⁻³ gm/cm³

μ_{air} = 1.8 × 10⁻⁵ kg/m.s = 1.8 × 10⁻⁴ gm/cm.sec, ϵ = 0.4, ϕ_S = 1 (assume)

Kozeny–Carman equation,

$$\frac{\Delta_P\,\phi_S^2\,D_P^2\,\epsilon^3}{L\,\bar{V}_o\,\mu\,(1-\epsilon)^2} = 150$$

$$\frac{D_P^2\,(0.4)^3}{1\times 1\times 1.8\times 10^{-4}\,(1-0.4)^2} = 150$$

Solving for D_P $\boxed{D_P = 0.3897\ \text{cm}}$ (Ans.)

Example 9.3:

Obtain a relationship for the ratio of the terminal falling velocity of a particle to the minimum fluidising velocity for a bed of similar particles. Assume that the stoke's law and the Carman-Kozeny equation are applicable. What is the value of the ratio if the bed voidage at the minimum fluidising velocity is 0.4?

Solution: Stoke's law equation is given by:

$$u_o = \frac{d^2 g (\rho_s - \rho)}{18 \mu} \qquad \ldots (1)$$

Carman-Kozeny equation is given by:

$$u = \frac{1}{K} \frac{\epsilon^3}{S^2 (1-\epsilon)^2} \frac{1}{\mu} \frac{(-\Delta P)}{l} \qquad \ldots (2)$$

In a fludisied bed, the total frictional force must be equal to the effective weight of the bed. Then, $\quad -\Delta P = (1-\epsilon)(\rho_s - \rho) lg \qquad \ldots (3)$

Substituting equation (3) in equation (2) and putting K" = 5 gives

$$u_f = 0.0055 \frac{\epsilon^3}{1-\epsilon} \frac{d^2 (\rho_s - \rho) g}{\mu}$$

Hence,

$$\frac{u_o}{u_f} = \frac{d^2 g (\rho_s - \rho)(1-\epsilon)}{18 \mu \times 0.0055 \epsilon^3} \frac{\mu}{d^2 (\rho_s - \rho) g}$$

$$= \frac{1-\epsilon}{18 \times 0.005 \, \epsilon^3}$$

$$= 10.1 \frac{(1-\epsilon)}{\epsilon^3}$$

If, $\qquad \epsilon = 0.4$

$$\boxed{\frac{u_o}{u_f} = 94.7} \qquad \text{(Ans.)}$$

Example 9.4:

The Ergun equation for pressure drop in a packed bed takes the form:

$$f = \frac{d \Delta P \, \epsilon^2}{\rho U^2 L (1-\epsilon)} = \frac{150}{Re'} + 1.75 \qquad \ldots (1)$$

where, $\qquad Re' = \frac{\rho U d}{\mu (1-\epsilon)} \qquad \ldots (2)$

ΔP is the pressure drop across a bed of depth L, percolated by a fluid of density ρ, viscosity μ with superficial velocity U. d is the equivalent particle diameter, defined as the diameter of a sphere with the same volume as the particle, ϵ is the voidage of the bed.

A packed bed reactor is 2 m in diameter with a packed height of 5 m. The catalyst pellets are used cylinders 1 mm in diameter and 3 mm long with true density 2250 kg m^{-3}.

The bed is to process 6 kgs^{-1} of a gaseous reactant stream with viscosity 2.5×10^{-5} kgm^{-1} s^{-1} and density 2 kgm^{-3}. The direction of flow is downward and the bed voidage is 0.45. What will the pressure drop be over this bed?

The particles will suffer damage at a compressive stress of greater than 0.5 bar. How many separate bed sections and bed supports should there be in the reactor?

MECHANICAL OPERATIONS — FLUIDIZATION

The compressive stress in a packed bed without flow asymptotes to:

$$\sigma_2 = \frac{D_B \rho_S (1-\epsilon) g}{4 k \tan \phi} \quad \ldots (3)$$

where, D_B is the bed diameter, ρ_S is the solid density, k is the Poisson's ratio for the solid (= 0.4) and ϕ is the angle of friction at the wall (35°).

Solution: The Ergun equation for pressure drop in a packed bed takes the form:

$$f = \frac{d \Delta P \epsilon^3}{\rho U^2 L (1-\epsilon)} = \frac{150}{Re'} + 1.75$$

where,

$$Re' = \frac{\rho U d}{\mu(1-\epsilon)}$$

ΔP is the pressure drop across a bed of depth L, percolated by a fluid of density ρ, viscosity μ with superficial velocity U. d is the equivalent particle diameter, defined as the diameter of a sphere with the same volume as the particle. ϵ is the voidage of the bed.

A packed bed reactor is 2 m in diameter with a packed height of 5 m. The catalyst pellets used as cylinders 1 mm in diameter and 3 mm long with true density 2250 kg m^{-3}. The bed is to process 6 kg s^{-1} of a gaseous reactant stream with viscosity 2.5×10^{-5} kgm^{-1} s^{-1} and density 2 kgm^{-3}. The direction of flow is downward and the bed voidage is 0.45. What will be the pressure drop over this bed ?

First the equivalent diameter of the particle is calculated:

$$\frac{\pi d^3}{6} = \frac{\pi (10^{-3})^2 \times 3 \times 10^{-3}}{4}$$

$$d^3 = \frac{9}{2} \times 10^{-9}$$

$$d = 1.65 \text{ mm}$$

If the equation given is used i.e.

$$\frac{d \Delta P \epsilon^3}{\rho U^2 L (1-\epsilon)} = \frac{150}{Re'} + 1.75$$

and Re is calculated then the pressure drop can be found, since all the other variables are known or can be calculated.

$$Re' = \frac{\rho u d}{\mu(1-\epsilon)}$$

u is the superficial velocity, the volumetric flowrate divided by the cross-sectional area of the bed. The superficial velocity is the velocity of the fluid would have if it were passing through the bed with no particles present. So,

$$u = \frac{6}{2} \cdot \frac{4}{2^2 \pi} = 0.955 \text{ m/s}$$

$$Re' = \frac{2 \times 0.955 \times 1.65 \times 10^{-3}}{2.5 \times 10^{-5} \times (1 - 0.45)}$$

$$= 229.2$$

Hence, ΔP is given by,

$$\Delta P = \frac{\rho u^2 L(1-\varepsilon)}{d\varepsilon^3}\left\{\frac{150}{229.2} + 1.75\right\}$$

$$\Delta P = \frac{2 \times 0.955^2 \times 5 \times 0.55}{1.65 \times 10^{-3} \times 0.45^3} \times 2.404$$

$$\Delta P = 80158.9 \text{ N/m}^2$$

Clearly the pressure due to the fluid alone is greater than the permitted stress, however we must also allow for the weight of the solids:

$$\sigma_z = \frac{D_B \rho_s (1-\varepsilon)g}{4 k \tan\phi}$$

$$= \frac{2 \times 2250 \times (1-2.45) \times 9.81}{4 \times 0.4 \times \tan 35°}$$

$$= \frac{24279.75}{1.120}$$

$$= 21499.9 \text{ N/m}^2$$

Hence, the total pressure is the sum of these two pressures, 1.02 bar.

This is too high, therefore, more than one bed section is required, if three are used the fluid pressure is reduced to 26738.8 N/m². The pressure due to the weight of solids is not so straightforward since the formula is for the asymptotic pressure when the bed is relatively deep. However, it is possible that 2 bed sections would be too few, given that the fluid pressure would then be 40108.25 so three is the sensible choice, given the available information.

The compressive stress in a packed bed without flow asymptotes to:

$$\sigma_z = \frac{D_B \rho_z (1-\varepsilon)g}{4 k \tan\phi}$$

where, D_B is the bed diameter, ρ_s is the solid density, k is the Poisson's ratio for the solid (= 0.4) and ϕ is the angle of friction at the wall (35°). **(Ans.)**

Example 9.5:

A tube of 0.05 m² cross-sectional area is packed with spherical particles upto a height of 0.25 m. The porosity of the bed is 0.35. It is desired to fluidize the particles with water (density = 1000 kg/m³, viscosity = 10^{-3} Pa.s). Determine the minimum fluidization velocity by Ergun's equation.

Data: Diameter of particles = 0.01 m, Density of particles = 2600 kg/m³.

Solution: At minimum fluidization,

Pressure drop required = (Gravity force) − (Buoyancy force)

$$\Delta P = g(1-\varepsilon)(\rho_p - \rho)L$$

$$\Delta P = 9.812(1-0.35)(2600-1000) \times 0.25$$

$$= 2551.12 \text{ N/m}^2$$

Ergun's equation is given by,

$$\frac{\Delta P}{\rho} = \frac{1.75 \, V_s^2 \, L \, (1-\epsilon)}{D_p \, \epsilon^3} + \frac{150 \, \mu \, V_s \, (1-\epsilon)^2 \, L}{D_p^2 \, \epsilon^3 \cdot \rho}$$

Substituting the known values in the Ergun's equation,

$$\frac{2551.12}{1000} = \frac{1.75 \, V_s^2 \times 0.25 \times (1-0.35)}{0.01 \times 0.35^3}$$
$$+ \frac{150 \times 10^{-3} \times V_s \times (1-0.35)^2 \times 0.25}{0.01^2 \times 0.35^3 \times 1000}$$

$$2.5512 = 663.3 \, V_s^2 + 3.7 \, V_s$$

Solving for V_s from above equation,

V_s = Minimum fluidization velocity = **0.0593 m/s.** (Ans.)

Example 9.6:
A 1 m high bed made up of 2 mm particles is to be fluidized by an oil (density = 900 kg/m³; viscosity = 0.01 Pa.s). If at the point of incipient fluidization, the bed voidage is 39% and the pressure drop across the bed is 10 kPa. Estimate the density of particles.

Solution: Given Data:
ΔP = 10 KPa
h = 1 m
ϵ = 0.39
ρ = 900 kg/m³

We have,

Pressure drop required = (Gravity force) – (Buoyancy force)

$$\Delta P = (1-\epsilon) \, \rho_s \, gh - (1-\epsilon) \, \rho gh$$

Substituting the known values in above equation,

$$10 = (1-0.39) \times \rho_s \times 9.812 \times 1 - (1-0.39) \times 900 \times 9.812 \times 1$$

Solving for ρ_s, we get,

Density of particles = ρ_s = 2571 kg/m³ (Ans.)

Example 9.7:
Estimate bed pressure drop (expressed in cm of water (manometer) particles (density = ρ_p = 2000 kg/m³; D_p = 0.05 cm) of 60 cm bed depth and bed porosity of 0.5.

Solution: Data Given:
ρ_p = 2000 kg/m³
D_p = 0.05 cm
ϵ = 0.5
h = 60 cm

Pressure drop required = (gravity force) – (buoyancy force)

We have,

$$\Delta P = (1-\epsilon) \, \rho_s \, gh - (1-\epsilon) \, \rho \cdot gh$$
$$= (1-0.5) \times 2000 \times 9.812 \times 0.6 - 0$$
$$= 5887 \, N/m^2$$

Manometer head $\Delta h = \dfrac{\Delta P}{\rho g}$

$= \dfrac{5887}{1000 \times 9.812}$

$= 0.6$ m

$= 60$ cm   **(Ans.)**

Example 9.8:

A 0.5 m high bed made-up of 1 mm diameter glass spheres (density = 2500 kg/m³) is to be fluidized by water (density = 1000 kg/m³). If at the point of incipient fluidization, the bed voidage is 40%, calculate the pressure drop across the bed.

Solution: Data Given: $h = 0.5$ m

$\rho_s = 2500$ kg/m³

$\rho = 1000$ kg/m³

$\epsilon = 0.4$

We have, pressure drop = (Gravity force) − (Buoyancy force)

$\Delta P = (1-\epsilon)\, \rho_s\, gh - (1-\epsilon)\, \rho gh$

$= (1-\epsilon)(\rho_s - \rho)\, gh$

$= (1 - 0.4)(2500 - 1000) \times 9.812 \times 0.5$

$\Delta P = 4415$ Pa   **(Ans.)**

Example 9.9:

A bed consists of particles of density 2000 kg/m³. If the height of the bed is 1.5 m and porosity is 0.4, calculate the pressure drop required to fluidize the bed.

Solution: Data Given: $\rho_s = 2000$ kg/m³

$h = 1.5$ m

$\epsilon = 0.4$

Pressure drop required = (Gravity force) − (Buoyancy force)

$\Delta P = (1-\epsilon)\, \rho_s\, gh - (1-\epsilon)\, \rho gh$

where, $(1 - \epsilon)$ is the fraction of solid

Substituting the known values,

$\Delta P = (1 - 0.4) \times 2000 \times 9.812 \times 1.5 - 0$

$\Delta P = \mathbf{1177\ Pa}$ **(Ans.)**

Example 9.10:

Water trickles by gravity over a bed of particles, each 1 mm diameter in a bed of diameter 6 cm and height 2 m. The water is fed from a reservoir whose diameter is much larger than that of the packed bed, with water maintained at a height of 0.1 m above the top of the bed. The bed has a porosity of 0.3%. Calculate the volumetric flowrate of water if its viscosity is 1 cP.

Solution: Available pressure drop for the water is given by,

$$\Delta P = \rho g h = 1000 \times 9.812 \times (2 + 0.1)$$
$$= 20605.2 \text{ N/m}^2$$

Ergun's equation:

$$\frac{\Delta P}{\rho} = \frac{1.75 \, V_s^2 \, L \, (1-\epsilon)}{D_p \, \epsilon^3} + \frac{150 \, \mu \, V_s \, (1-\epsilon)^2 \, L}{D_p^2 \, \epsilon^3 \cdot \rho}$$

Substituting the value of ΔP and the available data in Ergun's equation.

$$\frac{20605.2}{1000} = \frac{1.75 \, V_s^2 \times 2 \times (1-0.31)}{1 \times 10^{-3} \times 0.31^3} + \frac{150 \times 0.001 \times V_s \times (1-0.31)^2 \times 2}{(1 \times 10^{-3}) \times 0.31^3 \times 1000}$$

$$20.6052 = 81065 \, V_s^2 + 4794.4 \, V_s$$

Solving for $V_s = 4.021 \times 10^{-3}$ m/s

Volumetric flow rate, $Q = \frac{\pi}{4} D^2 \, V_s$

$$= \frac{\pi}{4} \times 0.06^2 \times 4.021 \times 10^{-3}$$

$$= 11.38 \times 10^{-6} \text{ m}^3/\text{sec}$$

$$= 11.38 \text{ cm}^3/\text{sec.} \hspace{4em} \textbf{(Ans.)}$$

EXERCISE FOR PRACTICE

(1) Oil of specific gravity 0.9 and viscosity 3 mNs/m² passes vertically upwards through a bed of catalyst consisting of approximately spherical particles of diameter 0.1 mm and special gravity 2.6. At approximately what mass rate of flow per unit area of bed will (a) fluidization and (b) transport of particles occur.

(Ans.: (a) 2.78 kg/m² sec, (b) 2.7 kg/m² .sec)

(2) Calculate the minimum velocity at which spherical particles (specific gravity 1.6) of diameter 1.5 mm will be fluidised by water in a tube of diameter 10 mm.
Data: Viscosity of water = 1 mNs/m², Kozeny's Constant = 5.   **(Ans.: u_f = 0.0163 m/s)**

NOMENCLATURE

Symbol	
A	Area, m²; A_p, projected area of particle.
a_e	Acceleration of particle from external force, m/s².
D	Diameter, m; D_p, diameter of spherical particle.
F	Force, N; F_D, total drag force; F_b, buoyant force; F_e, external force.
f_b	Volume fractions of fludizied bed occupied by gas bubbles.
G_o	Superficial mass velocity in packed bed.
g	Gravitational acceleration, m/s².
L	Length of cylindrical particle, m; length of channels in packed bed; also total height of paced or fluidized bed.
m	Mass, kg.
N_{Re}	Reynolds number, dimensionless, $N_{Re,p}$, particle Reynolds number, $D_p G_o/\mu$, dimensionless.
p	Pressure, N/m².
S	Cross-sectional area, m²; S_o, of empty tower.
S_p	Surface area of single particle, m².
T	Temperature, K.
t	Time, s.
u	Velocity of fluid or particle, m/s; ub, average bubble velocity in fluidized bed; us, settling velocity of uniform suspension.
V_s	Velocity of solids in pneumatic conveyor, m/s.
$\bar{V}$	Volumetric average fluid velocity, m/s; $\bar{V}_o$, superficial or empty tower velocity; $\bar{V}_{OM}$, minimum superficial velocity for fluidization.
Greek Letters:	
Δp	Pressure drop in packed or fluidized bed.
ϵ	Porosity or volume fraction of voids in beds of solids; ϵ_M, minimum porosity for fluidisation.
μ	Absolute viscosity, cP.
ρ	Density, kg/m³; ρ_p, density of particle.
ϕ_S	Sphericity.
φ	Function.
ω	Angular velocity, rad/s.

***

Unit X

Chapter 10: BENEFICIATION PROCESSES

10.1 Introduction

The choice of collection equipment for a specific purpose depends on number of factors: the properties of the material, such as particle size and physical and chemical properties, the concentration and volume of particulate to be handled; the temperature and humidity of the gaseous medium and most importantly; the collection efficiency required.

In this chapter we will discuss the following beneficiation processes:
(i)   Filters (Gas, fibre and fabric filters).
(ii) Jigging.
(iii) Tabling.
(iv) Magnetic separation.
(v)   Electrostatic separation.
(vi) Forth floatation.

10.2 Which Beneficiation Process is right for your plant ?

Enough research work is done about beneficiation technologies to understand how these processes work, how various types of particulate material responds to efforts to beneficiate it and what general results should be expected. A very recent beneficiation technologies have been brought to commercial application. These have enjoyed success for good reasons, their developers have pursued the technologies through diligent investigation and development, they have the keen interest, support and commitment of demonstration host. These commercial processing technologies are very suitable in many cases.

Some applications may require some creativity to find a cost-effective solution. The best choice from these emerging technologies perhaps a combination of them, might provide a cost effective solution of your situation. Once several likely processes have been identified, some straightforward characterization test can be chosen to narrow the field of technologies to those most promising. Selection, analysis and interpretation of characterization tests are of course, a critical part of finding the best beneficiation method.

Gas cleaning:
The examples of unit operations that cause particles to become entrained in gas stream were include fluidization, pneumatic conveying and grinding. In certain workplaces removal

of particles down to very low sizes and concentrations is essential, such as within operating theatres, during fabrication of electronic equipment and production of pharmaceutical grade materials. Hence, a critically important task is the removal of particles from gas streams. The subject is significantly different from solid-liquid separation because the fluid medium is much less viscous than a liquid and this influences the forces that are most relevant to the trajectory analysis. In many industrial processes sedimentation is the primary mechanism for particle removal from a gas stream. Thus, gas fluidized beds have the characteristic shape (see chapter 9), the increase in the bed diameter leads to a decrease in the gas velocity above the bed and particles will fall back into the fluidized bed. However, finer particles may still be carried over with the gas, i.e. entrained in the gas flow, and additional particle/gas separation equipment is required.

Table 10.1: Industrial Gas Cleaning Devices and Mechanisms

Equipment	Collection efficiency (%) at following sizes				
	50 µm	5 µm	1 µm	High temperature	Relative cost*
Inertial collector	95	16	3	Yes	1
Medium efficiency cyclone	94	27	8	Yes	3
Low resistance cellular cyclone	98	42	13	Yes	2
High-efficiency cyclone	96	73	27	Yes	4
Impingement scrubber	98	83	38	No	7
Self-induced spray deduster	100	93	40	No	5
Void spray tower	99	94	55	No	11
Fluidised bed scrubber	> 99	99	60	No	8
Irrigated target scrubber	100	97	80	No	6
Electrostatic precipitator	>99	99	86	Yes	9
Irrigated electrostatic precipitator	>99	98	92	No	13
Flooded-disc scrubber-low energy	100	99	96	No	10
Flooded-disc scrubber-medium energy	100	>99	97	No	15
Venturi scrubber-medium energy	100	>99	97	No	14
High efficiency electrostatic precipitator	100	>99	98	Yes	16
Venturi scrubber-high energy	>100	>99	98	No	18
Shaker type fabric filter	>99	>99	99	No	12
Reverse jet fabric filter	100	>99	99	No	17
Ceramic filter elements	100	>99	>99	Yes	18

*relative cost per 1000 m³ of gas treated - the lower value the better.

10.3 Filters

Filtration is one of the most reliable efficient and economic methods by which particulate matter can be removed from gases. Filters can be broadly divided into the following two types:

(i) Fabric or cloth filters,   (ii) Fibrous or deep-bed filters.

In cloth filters, the filter is in the form of a fabric bag arrangement-tabular bags or as cloth envelopes, and is suitable for a dust loading of the order of 1 gm/m³. In case of deep bed filters, a fibrous medium like mats of wool, cellulose etc., acts as a separator and the collection takes place in the interstics of the bed. They are suitable for light duct loads of the order of 1 mg/m³.

10.3.1 Bag Filters

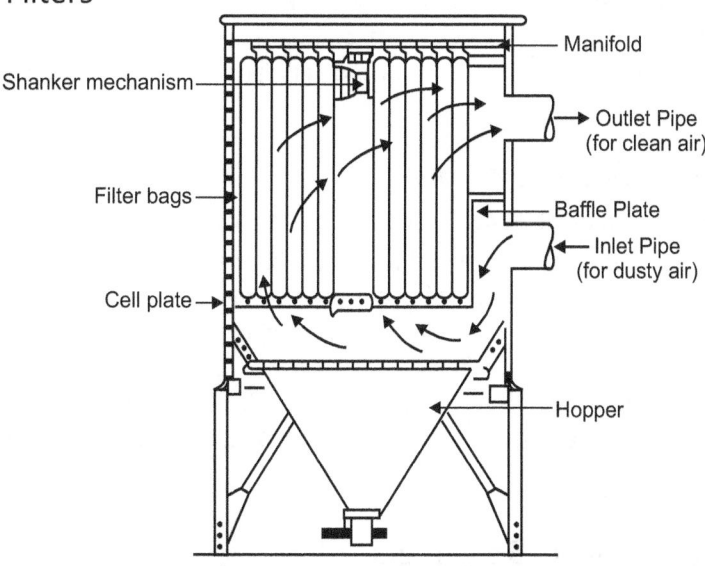

Fig. 10.1: Bag House Filter

These are not essentially the size separators but are included here because they often form an essential part of a sizing operation. For instance, a cyclone may take out coarse particles, and the bag filter removes the fines from the cyclone discharge. Air separators may be designed so that an air stream carrying the very finest particles is discharged to a bag filter. In this case the air separator makes two size fractions, and the dust removal equipment the third. In such a filter the air to be filtered is passed into long, cylindrical bags of cotton or wool fabric, so that the dust that is removed stays inside the bag. Some provision is then made for cutting off the air at intervals and shaking the bags in such a way that the dust will be discharged into a collecting hopper. The *ordinary household* vacuum cleaner is a very simple bag filter.

One design of bag filter is shown in Fig. 10.1. A number of cylindrical fabric bags are suspended in a sheet-metal container. During ordinary operation, or filtering period, the gas to be filtered enters the Hooper at passes up inside the bags, through the fabric, and out of the top of the casing to a main leading to a suction fan. The suction fan is so designed that the whole apparatus is under less than atmospheric pressure. During the filtering operation the bags are suspended so that they are drawn taut. The shaft rotates very slowly, so that at intervals of a few minutes the cam presses against the bell-crank lever, rotating it about its fulcrum, and changes the position of the damper as "shaking period". Since the unit shown in only one of several, and since all the units are under diminished pressure, this cases air to enter the casing and to pass into the bags, assisting in the displacement of the dust. Such dust laden air passes into the hopper and hence to the other units to be filtered. At the same time, the depression of the horizontal arm of the bell-crank lever brings the bar against the cams on the rapidly rotating shaft and this results in violently jerking the bags so that they are freed from dust. The greater portion of the dust falls into the hopper, from which it is removed at intervals by a gate attached at such devices are entirely automatic in their action and can be designed so as to afford very large filtering surfaces per unit of floor space.

Factors Affecting Efficiency of Bag Filters:
Efficiency of bag filters may decrease on account of the following factors:
 (1) **Excessive Filter Ratios:** "Filter ratios" is defined as the ratio of the carrier gas volume to gross-filter area; per minute flow of gas. Excessive filter ratios lower particulate removal efficiently and result in increased bag ware. Hence, *low filter ratios* are recommended for *high concentration* of particulates.
 (2) **Improper Selection of Filter Media:** While selecting filter media, properties like resistance to higher temperature, chemical attack and abrasion should be taken into consideration.

10.3.2 Fibrous or Deep-Bed Filters

In the deep-bed filters, a fibrous medium acts as the separator and the collection takes place in the interstics of the bed. They may be composed of mats of wool, cellulose, glass or iron fibres. They find their most extensive application in air conditioning and heating and ventilating systems. However, high efficiency mat filters are also employed as after cleaners and less efficient ones as roughing units to protect still more efficient equipment for pollution control purposes. They are most suitable for light dust loads, of the order of 1 mg/m^3. A peculiar advantages and less efficient ones as roughing units to protect still more efficient equipment for pollution control purposes. They are most suitable for light dust loads, of the order of 1 mg/m^3. A peculiar advantages of deep bed filter is that they are generally very good for service in a corrosive atmosphere because of their 'throwaway' nature.

High efficiency dry fibrous filters have been developed for special applications such as removal of radioactive or toxic particles or cleaning of air in industrial plants manufacturing photographic films or fine instruments.

Advantages of Bag Filters:
(1) High collection efficiency for all particle sizes, especially for particles smaller than 10 μ in diameter.
(2) Simple construction and operation.
(3) Nominal power consumption.
(4) Dry disposal of collected material.

Disadvantages of Bag Filters:
(1) Operating limits due to high carrier gas temperature, high humidity etc.
(2) High maintenance and fabric replacement costs. (Bag houses are difficult to maintain because of difficulty in finding and replacing even a single leaking bag. In general, about 25% of the bags will need replacement every year).
(3) Large size equipment.
(4) Problems in handling dusts which may abrade, corrode or blind the cloths.

Applications of Bag Filters:
Bag filters find extensive applications in the following industries and operations:
(1) Metallurgical industry   (2) Foundries   (3) Cement Industry
(4) Ceramic Industry   (5) Chalk and Lime Plants   (6) Flour Mills.

10.4 Jigging

Introduction:
Mineral jigs are widely used in industry to separate materials of different specific gravities. Typically, the particles are being transported via. slurry and are comparable in size due to milling in prior unit operations. Mineral jig separation is based on pulsations of water through a bed of coarse materials causing heavy particles to sink as light materials pass across the bed; then each product can be collected separately. These coarse particles, ragging, hinder the light particles from falling to the bottom, yet still allow the heavier particles to move downward. This device is typically used to concentrate coal and to treat metallic and heavy non-metallic ores such as iron and barite, respectively; refer to Table 10.2 below.

Table 10.2: Examples of mineral jig applications

Industry	Heavy particle	Light particle
Coal	Coal	Ash
Iron	Iron	Barite
Diamond	Diamond	Coal
Gold	Gold	Quartz

Jigging is a form of gravity concentration carried out by pulsing water through a screen on which lies a bed of crushed solids. Stratification of the particles is achieved by repeatedly affording a very thick suspension an opportunity to settle for very short period of time. The stratified layers are subsequently removed. Due to very short period of settling maximum settling velocity is not achieved and initial velocities cause the separation. In the initial stages the fluid resisting force, $F_R = 0$. Hence, we have a force balance.

$$ma = mg - m'g \qquad \ldots(10.1)$$

or
$$a = \left(\frac{m - m'}{g}\right)g = \left(\frac{\rho_S - \rho_L}{\rho_S}\right)g = \left(1 - \frac{\rho_L}{\rho_S}\right)g \qquad \ldots(10.2)$$

Thus, 'a' is the initial acceleration depends on the force of gravity and densities of the particles and fluid. It is independent of the size and shape of the particles. Hence, separation according to densities is possible. Jigs are essentially tanks of rectangular cross-section fitted with a screen placed below overflow in slightly sloping position as shown in Fig. 10.2. The pulsating motion is given to the water with the help of a plunger or diaphragm. A typical fixed screen diaphragm and its mechanism as shown in Fig. 10.2.

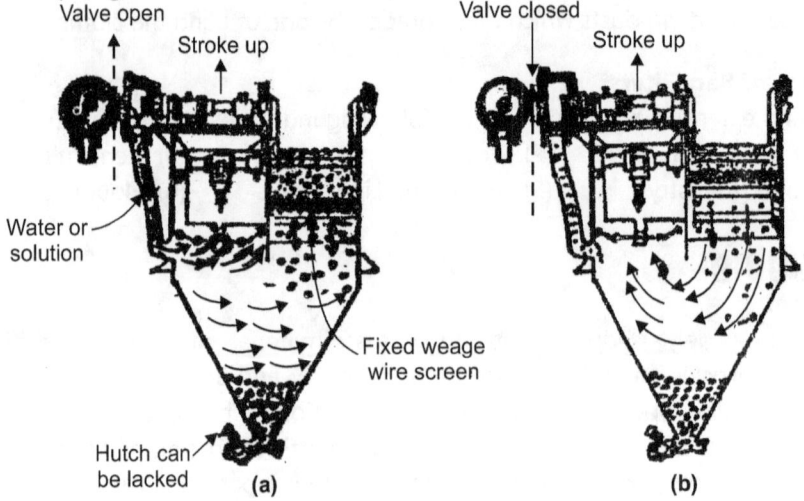

Fig. 10.2: Typical Jig

Theory:

A mineral jig is designed to separate materials varying in density through the oscillation of ragging, which is a bed of particles larger than the feed, in a pool of water. A diaphragm pulsing the water upward and drawing it downward causes the vibration with a frequency variant that is optimized for the feed being separated. A harmonic wave illustrates the effect of the pulsation and suction of water in the ragging. Four steps, dilation, differential initial acceleration, hindered settling, and consolidation trickling, describe this process of particle separation. Once the diaphragm creates a pulse in the water, all particles **dilate** (a) to a maximum height. Then, as suction occurs, during the **differential initial acceleration** step (b), the particles begin to separate, but only according to density and not size. As a result, some less dense particles pass over the ragging while more dense particles settle faster through the water than the remaining less dense particles. Following is the **hindered settling** step (c), in which the particles settle according to density and size. For instance, more dense particles, in addition to heavier particles, settle faster than less dense and lighter particles.

At this point, the less dense particles have either passed over the ragging and into a sieve or remained above the more dense particles. Therefore, during the last step, known as **consolidation trickling** (d), the larger particles interlock and the ragging begins to compact, allowing the smaller particles to move downward through the interlocking spaces. Refer to the following diagrams for a visual understanding of this separation process. The ragging of the jig is not pictured in Fig. 10.3, so that the motion of the heavy and light particles can be better visualized in the sequential steps of the theory. The ragging is pictured with the feed in Fig. 10.5 and Fig. 10.6.

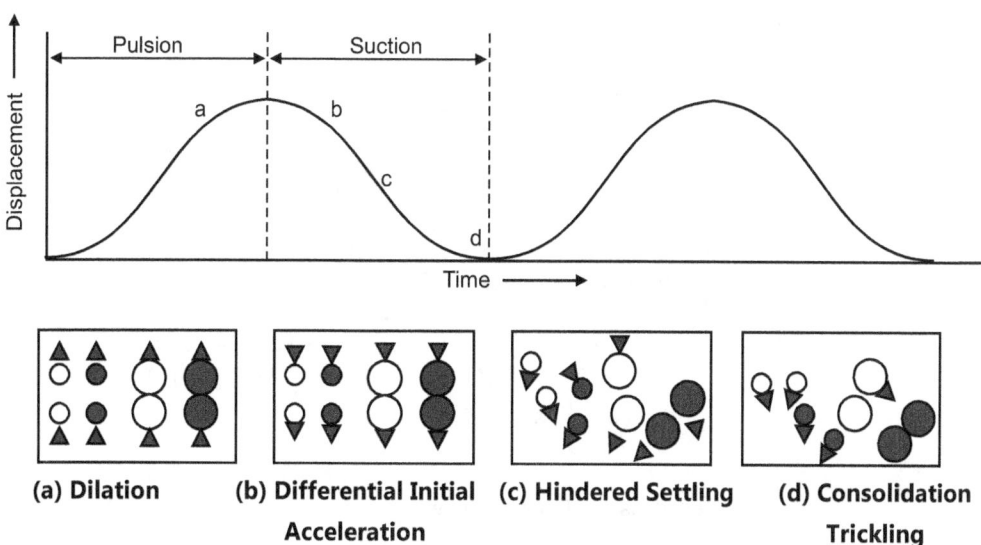

Fig. 10.3: Time Elapsed Cartoon of Feed Movement (Assuming only Two Types of Particles) During the Jigging Process. Larger Circles Denote Larger Particles of Corresponding Density as Indicated by Colour where the Less Dense are White and More Dense are Black

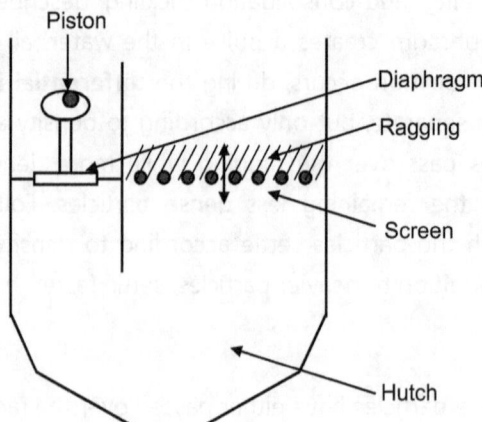

Fig. 10.4: Schematic of Jig not including the Feed Chute which is Situated Perpendicular to the Plane of the Page

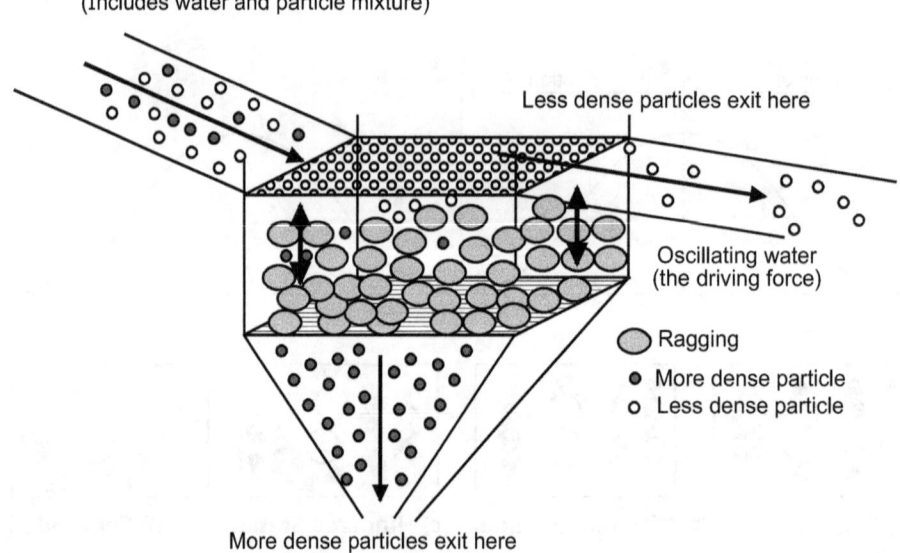

Fig. 10.5 Separation in the Mineral Jig

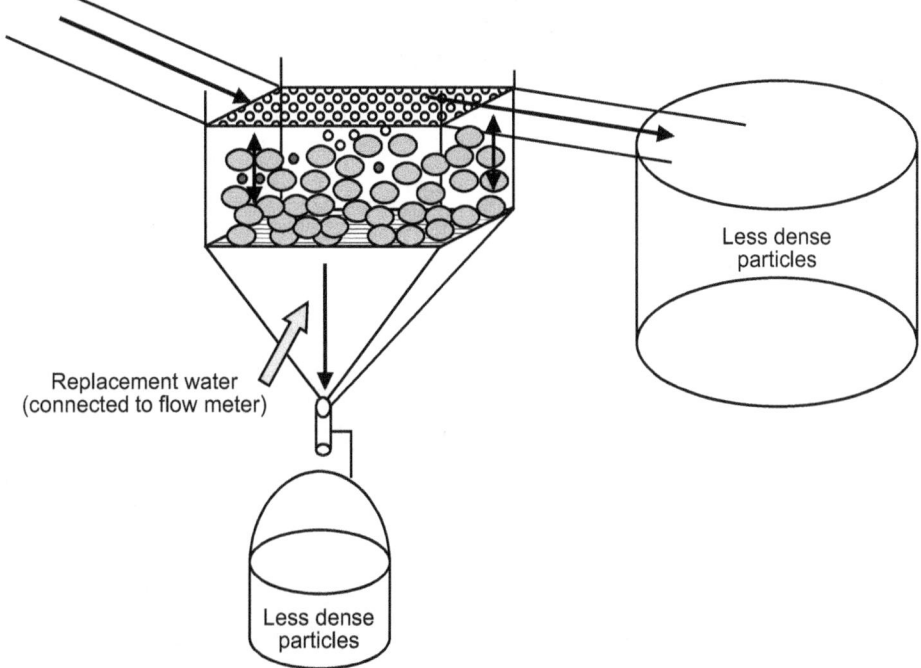

Fig. 10.6: Overall Schematic of the Process

10.5 Tabling

Introduction:

The Mineral Separator is an approach to concentration that involves the gravity system of tabling. Tabling is the method of concentration and separating particles of different sizes, shapes, and specific gravities by using the force of gravity. For many centuries, sorting by hand and gravity concentration were the only methods available to sort combined particles. However, in the early part of the twentieth century, gravity methods waned in popularity with the introduction of froth floatation, which has superior selectivity and capacity to concentrate finely ground ores. A revival of gravity methods soon occurred because of the simplicity, high capacity, low cost, and advances made in the equipment.

The primary focus of this equipment is to perform solid-solid separation. The separation process is based on differences in the specific gravity, shape and size of the mineral sample to be separated. The process is carried out in a wet state. It is most widely used for the processing of coal and ore minerals. The process is best suited for the separation of materials containing atleast one valuable mineral, where the valuable mineral can be recovered and the gangue mineral can be discarded. Table 10.3 presents the current applications in which the shaking table is used.

Table 10.3

Industry	Dense Material	Light Material
Coal	Ash	Coal Particles
Food	Stones	Corn
Tantalum	Tantalum	Tantalite
Chromium	Chromium	Chromite
Iron	Iron	Magnetite

Shaking Tables:

The modern shaking tables have evolved out of the panning of the gold containing sand to separate heavy gold particles. Shaking tables are used for the gravity separation of sands which are too fine be treated by jigging. A dilute pulp of solids containing two materials of different densities is passed over an inclined table (inclination 2 to 5 degrees from the horizontal). The table is given a reciprocating shaking motion at a rate of 150 to 350 per minute. The surface of the table is covered with linoleum and is provided with wooden riffles, which are wooden strips 1/4 to 1/2 inch wide and 1/8 to 1/16 inch thick and are placed about 1 inch apart.

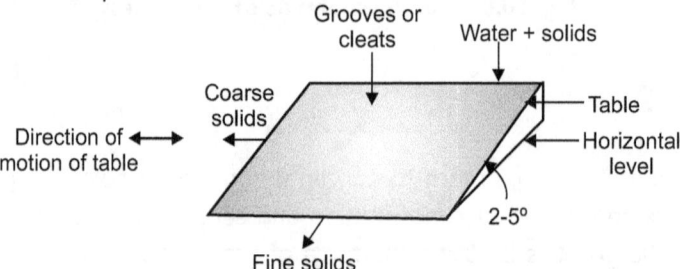

Fig. 10.7: Schematic Illustration of Wilfley Table

Two types of forces affect the particle movement under conditions of tabling (i) Movement of particles on an inclined plane in a fluid film flow (ii) Sideways movement of the table deck resulting in horizontal displacement of particles. It is evident that the heavy particles move farthest away from the feed end while the lighter gangue particles overflow along the lower margin of the table.

Although tables can be used to sort materials from 6 meshes to 300 meshes. They are more appropriate for particle sizes coarse than 100 meshes. The success of the process depends on the wide differences in the density of the solid particles to be sorted. The capacity of a table of 6 feet may be as high as 60 tons of solids per 24 hours.

Water requirement varies from mineral to mineral as also with operating conditions. A typical Wilfley Table is as shown in Fig. 10.7. The table is given a horizontal reciprocating motion at right angles to the direction of the incline. The forward motion is slow but the reverse motion is very rapid. Because of this motion of the table, the settled solids get carried to one side of the table where they are collected.

10.6 Magnetic Separation

Introduction:

A magnetic separator is a device used to separate a mixture of fine, dry materials based upon their magnetic properties. The principles governing this process are magnetism and the interaction between magnetic, gravitational, and centripetal forces. Magnetic properties of a material are based upon atomic structure and magnetic field intensity. The principles involved in the separation apparatus include: feed rate, velocity of the particles and magnetic field strength. Magneitc separation has two general applications, purification of feeds via. the magnetic removal impurities or the collection of the magnetic components from the mixture. A few examples of industrial use appear in the chart below.

Table 10.4: Industrial Applications for Magnetic Separators

Industry	Application	Magnetic Component	Non-magnetic Component
Food	Removal of Tramp Iron	Tramp Iron	Food
Mining	Used to purify the feed and to collect minerals	Ore	Gangue
Recycling	Separation of metals from glass and plastics	Aluminium, Iron	Plastics, Glass

Background and Theory:

Magnetic separation is a process in which two or more materials are separated from each other. The primary driving force of the separation is magnetization, however there are also other forces that act upon the particles as well. These forces are centripetal force and the gravitational force. These forces, in relation to a particle of material on the separator, are illustrated in Fig. 10.8.

As a particle approaches the magnetic roll at the end of the conveyor belt of the magnetic separator, it enters into the magnetic field. As the particle travels with the rotation of the magnetic roll, centripetal, gravitational, and magnetic forces are acting upon the particle.

There are two possible relationships that the forces satisfy in correlation with the path of the particle:

$$F_{gravitational} + F_{centripetal} > F_{magnetic} \quad \ldots (10.3)$$

or

$$F_{gravitational} + F_{centripetal} < F_{magnetic} \quad \ldots (10.4)$$

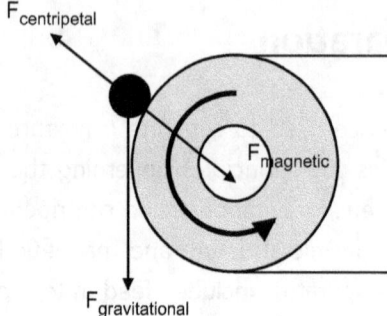

Fig. 10.8: Forces Exerted on a Particle

Equation (10.3) describes the disengagement of the particle from the magnetic roll and conveyor. In order for the particle to be released from the conveyor the sum of the centripetal force and a component of the gravitational force acting upon the particle must be greater than the force felt by the particle due to magnetic attraction. Note, the affect of gravity on the particle will be a function of the position of the particle in relation to the magnetic roll. Equation (10.4) decribes the contrasting relation. For the particle to remain in contact with the conveyor and to travel further as the magnetic roll rotates, the magnetic force must be greater than the sum of the centripetal force and a component of the gravitational force acting upon the particle. A better understanding of how the three forces act upon the particle may be gained through an explaination of each force in further detail.

The centripetal force is exerted on a particle that is located on the surface of a spinning object. This force tends to pull the particle away from the surface of the object. This resulting force acts in the direction of the circular path. It must be noted that the name of this force depends on the perspective of the observer. A centripetal force is observed when an outside spectator watches the particle spin with the object, where the force would be referred to as centrifugal if the force was being observed from the view of the particle on the spinning object. Gravitational force is exerted on a particle as a result of gravity, which pulls the particle towards the Earth's center. Centripetal and gravitational forces are easily explained, but the magnetic force due to a magnetic field requires a much more detailed explanation. The magnetic field produced by the magnet is the means for the exertion of a magnetic force on a substance. An example of a particle and its magnetic force is shown in Fig. 10.9.

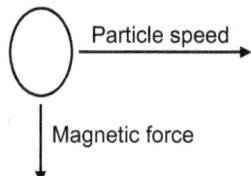

Fig. 10.9: Illustration of Magnetic Force with Respect to a Particle

Fig. 10.9 shows that the magnetic force acting on a particle is always perpendicular to the particle's speed. Therefore, the magnetic force cannot affect a particle's speed, but it can affect the direction of the particle. This was also illustrated in Fig. 10.8 as the particle rotated around the magnetic roll.

The magnetic field is the area surrounding a magnet that is marked by a detectable magnetic force in every part of the region. Magnetic field can be produced in two ways: as a result of the movement of electrically charged particles, such as a current in a wire, or due to the elementary particles of a substance, which have an intrinsic magnetic field surrounding them. In other words, the latter result explains that a particle's magnetic field strength is a basic characteristic of the particle itself.

The magnetic separator operates with a permanent magnet. A permanent magnet does not require a current to create a magnetic field. It utilizes the electrons in conjunction with the magnet and their respective magnetic fields. The magnetic field of a permanent magnet may be created in one of the two ways: it may be a natural occurrence in the material or it may be induced by another force. In the case of the magnet used for this laboratory, the magnetization occurs naturally within the material.

This method is based on the difference in the magnetic properties of the minerals. Magnetic separation is mostly used for separating ferromagnetic materials such as magnetite, pyrrhotite, etc. The separation is carried out both in dry and wet conditions the former being preferred for coarse particles.

A typical magnetic separator is shown Fig. 10.10. As shown in the figure, a drum rotates around stationery magnets. The feed is admitted at the top and is allowed to fall on the rotating drum. When the drum passes from near the magnet, the magnetic particles remain aligned to the drum whereas the non-magnetic particles follow a normal trajectory thus separating the magnetic material from the non-magnetic. In wet magnetic separator the lowest portion of the rotating drum is immersed in slurry kept in through.

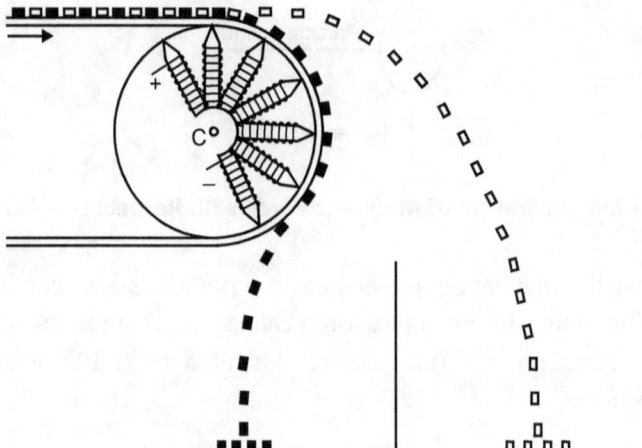

Fig. 10.10: Magnetic Separator Schematic

For separating weakly paramagnetic materials high intensity high gradient (HGMS) magnetic separator is used. Whereas low intensity magnets generate a field of 1500 gauss the high intensity magnets generate a field of 20,000 gauss. The relative magnetic character of several minerals with respect to iron whose magnetic attract ability is taken as 100 is given in Table 10.5.

Table 10.5: Relative Magnetic Attract Ability of Minerals Relative to that of Iron

Characteristics	Substance	Relative Attract ability
Strongly magnetic	Iron	100.00
	Magnetite	40.18
	Franklinite	35.38
	Ilmenite	24.70
Weakly magnetic	Pyrrhotite	6.63
	Hematite	1.32
	Zircon	1.01
	Pyrolusite	0.71
	Mangnite	0.52
	Garnet	0.40
	Quartz	0.37
Non-magnetic	Pyrite	0.23
	Sphalerite	0.23
	Magnetite	0.15
	Cryolite	0.05
	Galena	0.04
	Calcite	0.03

10.6.1 Magnetic Separation of Free Metals

Introduction: There are minerals that are attracted, repulsed and unaffected by magnetic fields, based on their "permeability" to magnetic fields. This is often illustrated by show in a picture of magnetic field lines and grains which attract lines by bending them into the grain (concentrating), grains which repel the liens and grains which are not affected. The degrees of magnetic permeability differ from mineral to mineral. Particles which concentrate the lines of force and become polarized and consequently attracted are called "paramagnetic". Those which disperse the liens are called "diamagnetic".

Based on magnetic behaviour, paramagnetic materials are sub-classified as ferro-magnetic and feebly magnetic. Magnetic separators are classified as drum, pulley, disc, ring and belt separators. They are all based on the same principle, and all use a provision for feed to run into and through the magnetic field and various means for discharging separator. Magnetic beneficiation can be used not only for separating pure nickel-iron metal granules, but also for minerals which have weak magnetic properties. This is done at earthiness. In space, where gravity is lower and more sensitive processes are possible, magnetic beneficiation can play a significantly greater role. After grinding, the streams of material are put through magnetic fields to separate the nickel-iron metal granules from the silicate grains. Repeated cycling through the magnetic field gives highly pure bags of free nickel iron metal. One of several alternative ways is to drop a stream of material onto magnetic drums, as shown in Fig. 10.11.

This method also shows an impact grinder discussed in the next paragraph. The silicates and weakly magnetic material deflect of the drum whereas the magnetic granuals and material holding magnetic grains stick to the magnetic drum until the scrape off point. This is shown in Fig. 10.11. An optional additional piece of equipment is an "impact grinder" or "centrifugal grinder" whereby a very rapidly spinning wheel accelerates the material down its spokes and flings it against an impact block. Any silicate impurities still attached to the free metal are shattered off. It's feasible to have drum speeds sufficient to flatten the metal granules by impact. A centrifugal grinder may be used after merchant grinding and sieving and before further magnetic separation. In fact, most of the shattered silicate will be small particles which could be sieved out.

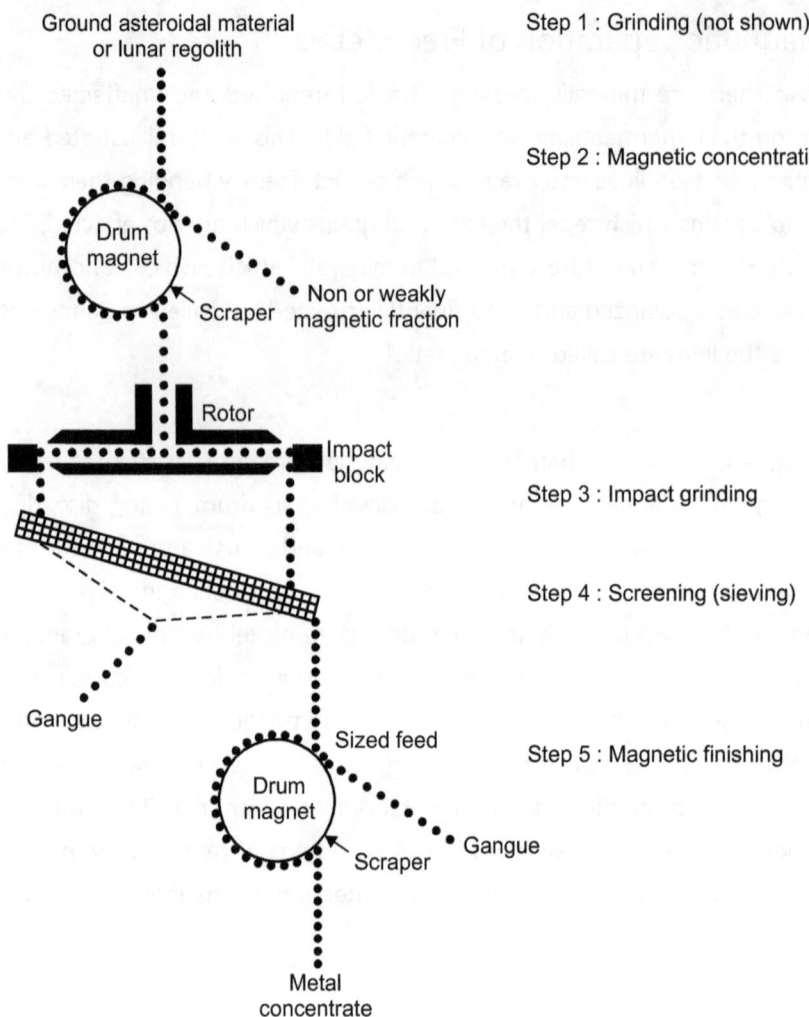

Fig. 10.11: Magnetic Separation of Free Metals

10.7 Electrostatic Separation

Principle of Electrostatic Separation: Particles of different minerals acquire varying surface changes in an electrostatic field. The forces acting on the particles are therefore different. The difference may also arise out of the differences in the dielectric constants. Forces due to an electric charge are parallel to the field while forces due to differences in dielectric constants are parallel to the direction of maximum variation in the field intensity and are zero in uniform electric field. In an electrostatic separator a particle acquires charge by being made to come in contact with a charged wire, screen or surface. The charged particle while falling is made to pass near an attracting surface while the uncharged particles fall down straight diagrammatic representation given in Fig. 10.12. The electrostatic precipitators used for the removal of solids in gases or smoke or fine liquid droplets (i.e. mist) also operate on similar principle.

Minerals come in grains. For example, a scoop of lunar dirt will typically contain a number of minerals, but the different minerals will come in the form of different grains, each grain being a glob of mostly one particular mineral. Usually, two ore more different mineral grains will be fused together into one, which requires grinding the material in order to separate the grains. However, like sand on a beach, you often see free pure grains beside different free pure grains or grains predominantly of one kind or another, depending upon origins. The naturally pulverized lunar soil is like a fine sandy beach. At the time, it is easy to scoop up a mix of fine grains and separate pure grains of a particular mineral from the rest and grains of predominantly one kind or another, using one or more of the following processes:

The material will be initially sieved by screens to separate grains by size. Optionally, the grains of each given size can be passed through the appropriately sized mechanical grinders and sieved again for uniformity. The next step is to separate the mineral grains by a process called "electrostatic beneficiation", which means charging them with static electricity and separating them by passing them through an electric field, as pictured in the next figure. An electrostatic beneficiator works because different minerals have different electrostatic affinities – will absorb different amounts of charge depending upon their composition and hence are deflected amounts by an electric field. After grains are sieved by size, they are placed through a beneficiator. After a few passes through benefactors, we have separated different minerals fairly well. (There's no change in physical or chemical identity; there's only separation of minerals.). Beneficiators typically use free-fall of grains through electric fields. However, some beneficiators slide the grains down a ramp and some put them across a rotating drum with a certain electrostatic charge so that grains of a certain affinity will stick to the drum and others will fall to the ground due to gravity or the centrifugal force. Thus, beneficiation separates minerals according to their electrostatic affinity, as well as their different densities (with gravity or the centrifugal force).

The grains are charged by any of the following methods: Charging the screen that sieves them or charging another surface which they slide over, or a diffuse electron beam as they fall. The charging method can depend upon which minerals we want to separate, since different minerals have different responses to different methods (and indeed to different temperatures, too). The resultant material is collected in different bins whereby the enriched portion of the desired mineral is called the "concentrate" and the rest of the output is called the "gangue" or "tailings."

MECHANICAL OPERATIONS | BENEFICIATION PROCESSES

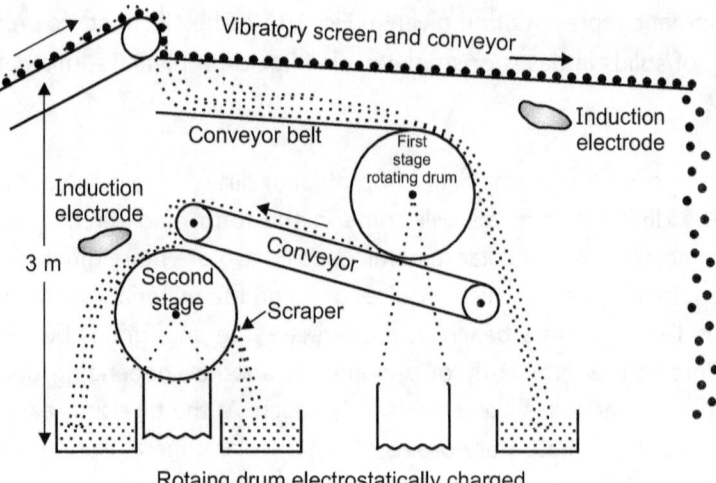

Fig. 10.12: Electrostatic Beneficiation Process

While on Earth we are usually interested in just one mineral and one bin, on the Moon we will often be interested in using more of the material. With an electrostatic benefactor we could have multiple bins at the bottom, as the mineral stream will split up into multiple steams depending upon the degree of attraction or repulsion of each mineral. Whereas electrostatic beneficiation is commonly used at miens on Earth, it world work even better in orbital space or on the Moon, dramatically so. The vacuum of space and the Moon means no air turbulence in the drop chamber. Air does not tolerate electric fields as well as vacuum and in fact electric field scan be ten times stronger in vacuum. In space and on the Moon, there is no moisture to make grains stick together.

Moisture also changes minerals electric conductivity and reduces the differences between minerals, hence on Earth we often have to roast the material before beneficiation. The one sixth lunar gravity dramatically slows the fall of the material through the electric field, thereby greatly enhancing the separation. If we beneficiate minerals in orbit (e.g., asteroidal minerals), the centrifuges could create artificial gravity of any sensitivity, which would be superior to the Moon's surface as well. Notably, the naturally fine lunar powder on the surface of the Moon was of keen interest in the early days, as grains would stick to things and sometimes show leviational properties such as gliding when kicked. This is due to the very high electrostatic affinity of some of the grains. Indeed, lunar dust was a nuisance.

Experiments with simulated lunar soil have produced excellent results using beneficiators in a regular air environment. (Notably, there's also a lot of experience at earth miens in separating the valuable mineral ilmentite, or particular interest and abundance on the Moon.

Some engineering companies focus on ilmentite in their first lunar mission scenarios). Metal-producing minerals are not the only targets of beneficiation. Quick production of some kinds of simple glass products are also of interest.

Beneficiation could occur either at a central processing area on the lunar base or at the mine. As is often the case on Earth, locating the beneficiator at the lunar mines could significantly reduce hauling of ore and hence the cost of bigger haulers and more energy but would require that the beneficiator be mobile. Some designs in the literature have a mobile beneficiator as part of the mobile excavation equipment whereby the waste is left behind in the same spot it was dug up, as landfill.

10.8 Gravity Concentrator

Introduction:

The gravity separator apparatus operates by applying gravitational, centrifugal and frictional forces to a particle-slurry with components of varying specific gravities. These individual force vectors are applied with separate directions in such a way that the more dense particles will migrate to the bottom of the collecting cone and the less dense particles will work their way upward and over the surface of a spinning cone to be discarded or collected. The spinning motion of the collecting cone applies the centrifugal force, frictional forces and applied via. water flow into the cone through small holes and gravity acts on the heavier particles to pull them toward the bottom of the cone. This device is typically used in the heavy mineral industry for the concentration of the desired mineral from a mixture that contains unwanted particles.

Industrial Applications for Gravity Separation	Laboratory Applications for Gravity Separation
- Coal - Mercury - Tin - Zircon - Chromite - Tantalum - Copper - Iron Ore - Precious metals including gold, silver and platinum - Heavy Minerals - Decontamination	- Experimentation for larger scale separation. - Biological separations.

Theory:

The gravity concentrator is designed to concentrate and separate dense particles within a slurry of lighter particles for maximum recovery. A classic example of this process is the concentration of gold from alluvial sand.

When the slurry is introduced into the cone, the centrifugal force produced by rotation pushes the solids towards the walls of the collection cone. The slurry fills each ring of the cone to capacity to create a bed of particles that are fluidized by water flow in the direction of the symmetrical center of the cone. When the slurry reaches the bottom of the cone frictional forces provided by the water flow into the cone force it outward and upward against the cone wall. Also, this fluidization process prevents compacting of the concentrating bed, which, if this occurs, could plug the holes provided for the introduction of water with the smallest solid particles.

Gravity pulls the heaviest particles into the bottom of the cone, while the frictional forces drive the lightest particles (usually the undesired particles) upward throughout the rings of the cone until they eventually get spun from the top of the spinning collection cone and out of the system. The bed is held in place by the centrifugal forces as it is fluidized. All three of the forces govern the separation process in the gravity concentration apparatus but only two of these forces can be controlled for optimal concentration.

The centrifugal force will need to be controlled such that the bed containing the heavier desired particles will not move upward throughout the cone because it will then spin away to be wasted. The centrifugal force on the heavies should be stronger than the frictional force acting on the heavies such that the desired bed will remain firmly in place. The water flow into the cone should be adjusted so that it will be sufficient enough to force the unwanted light particles upward through the successive rings of the cone so that they will be wasted, but should also be low enough so that it effect is too small to push the heavier particles upward. This optimal range will be dependent on the density difference between the types of particles in the slurry if their sizes are roughly the same; otherwise, a slurry of greatly varying size will be more difficult to separate. This usually is not the case with the laboratory apparatus as there is a mesh screen that prevents particles of diameter greater than 10 mesh from being introduced into the system.

MECHANICAL OPERATIONS — BENEFICIATION PROCESSES

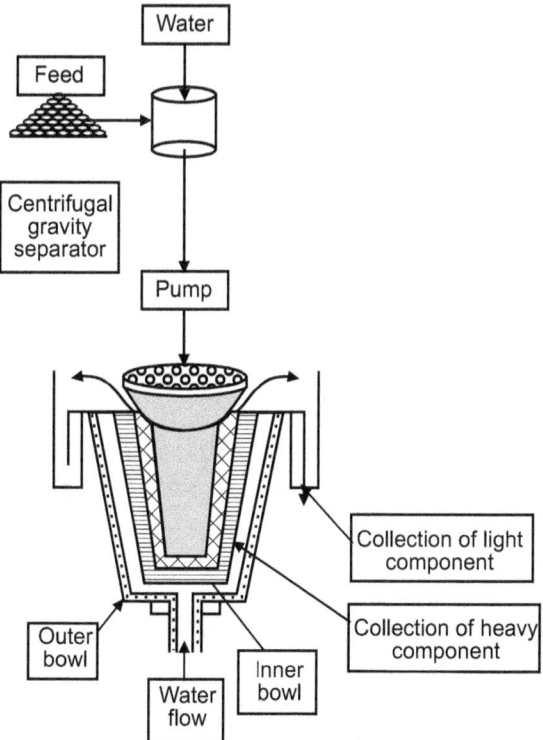

Fig. 10.13: Schematic of Gravity Concentrator

Description of Equipment:
The concentrator used in these experiments is essentially a high-speed centrifuge that combines a specialized fluidization process. The concentrator consists of a few major components and systems, which are describes in the following paragraphs.

Concentrating Cone:
This cone is made of a polyurethane compound and has a series of horizontal rings increasing in diameter toward the top of the cone. Fluidization holes, which must remain unclogged, enable water to be injected into each ring of the cone. When solids are introduced to the cone, they begin filling the rings starting with the bottom and working their way upward. When completely filled, a concentrating bed exists, which becomes subsequently fluidized with additional injection of water. Lighter particles, called "tailings", are sloughed off the bed and ejected into the multi-port hub.

Fluidization Water:
This water is introduced via. a water supply and controlled with a control valve. The water comes through the rotor shaft, into the chamber, and then forced through the fluidization holes in a counter-clockwise direction.

Rotor Assembly:
During operation, a rotor assembly including an electric motor with controls and a V-belt drive spins in a clockwise direction, with a maximum speed of sixty gravities. The rotatory union aids in transferring the fluidization water into the rotating cone.

Feed Tube and Mesh Screen:
A stationary feed tube introduces the feed slurry into the rotor assembly and is deflected outward into the rings of the concentrating cone. The mesh screen helps to sift the feed slurry and to help ensure a constant feed flow. A water washing system is also included to help force the feed slurry into the feed tube.

Multi-port Hub and Launder:
The multi-port hub receives the flushed concentrates and directs them to the tailings launder and ultimately the launder outlet port. A receiver is usually placed at the outlet port to capture the tailings for analysis.

Accessories:
The concentrator may incorporate many useful accessories to aid in the collection and analysis of proper operating parameters. A flow valve and pressure gauge may be placed downstream of the control valve for the fluidization water. A water filter upstream of the control valve may be installed to collect foreign debris that may impede optimal operation. Also, a variable speed motor can provide the operator with greater control.

10.9 Froth Floatation

Introduction:
Froth floatation is a surface-chemistry based process of separation of fine solids that takes advantage of the differences in wettability at solid particle-surfaces. Solid surfaces are often naturally wettable by water and termed hydrophilic. A surface that is non-wettable is water repelling and termed hydrophobic. If a surface is hydrophobic, it is also typically air attracting, termed aerophilic, and is strongly attached to an air interface, which readily displaces water at the solid's surface. In froth floatation, separation of a binary solids mixture may be accomplished by the selective attachment of hydrophobic solid particles to gas bubbles (typically air). The other hydrophilic solid particles remain in the liquid (typically water). The difference in the density between the air bubbles and water provides buoyancy that preferentially lifts the hydrophobic solid particles to the surface where they remain skimmed away, thus, effecting the separation. Froth floatation is often used to separate solids of similar densities and sizes, which prevent other types of separations based upon gravity that might otherwise be employed. It is especially useful for particle sizes below 100 μm (150 mesh), which are typically too small for gravity separation using jigging and tabling. The lower-size limit for floatation separation is approximately 35 μm (400 mesh);

however, particles as small as 1 µm have been separated. At these small particles sizes, it may be difficult to take advantage of surface-property differences to induce selective hydrophobicity. On the other hand, particles greater than 200 µm (mesh) tend to be readily shared from the bubble surfaces by collision with other particles or vessel walls. However, relatively low-density materials, such as coal, may be successfully separated upto 1600 µm (10 mesh) in some systems.

Froth floatation has been used in the minerals processing industry since the mid-1800's with many of its broad-based applications to mineral recovery extensively developed between 1900 and 1925. Today, atleast 100 different minerals, including almost all of the world's copper, lead, zinc, nickel, silver, molybdenum, manganese, chromium, cobalt, tungsten, and titanium, are processed using froth floatation. In 1997, the estimated worldwide mineral production, using froth floatation, was two billion tons. Another major usage of forth floatation is by the coal industry for desulferization and the recovery of fine coal, once discarded as waste. Since the 1950's, floatation has also been applied in many non-mineral industries including sewage treatment; water purification; paper de-inking; and chemical, plastics, and food processing. The development of froth floatation continues today with the need to recover minerals from increasingly poorer grades of ore, as well as its non-traditional application to other types of materials.

There are several different types of froth floatation systems in the use today including the mechanical type, of which there are many subtypes, and the floatation column. The type of froth floatation apparatus to be used in this experimentation is the batch, sub-aerated mechanical type shown in Fig. 10.14. While this is a laboratory scale unit capable of handling upto 5 L (5×10^{-6} m^3), the same equipment type and principals are used at the industrial level upto 7,000 ft^3 (200 m^3).

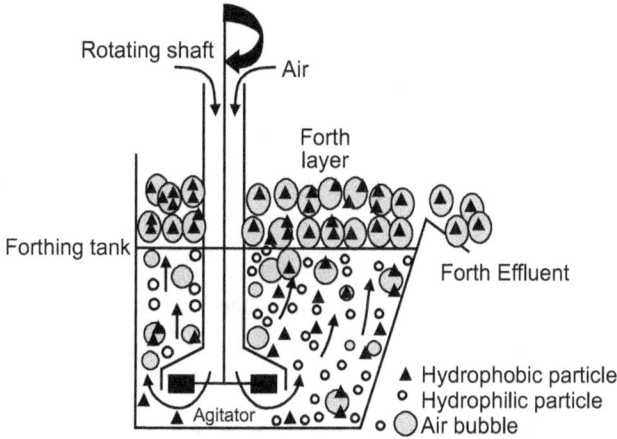

Fig. 10.14: Sub-aerated Mechanical Froth Floatation Apparatus

The froth floatation apparatus to be used consists of a frothing tank containing the solution and solid-particle mixture. A shrouded impeller or agitator provides continuous recirculatory mixing of the solids and solution. Air is introduced through the shaft and exists into the solution at the bottom of the agitator (sub-aerated). The introduction of air creates bubbles that are stabilized by an added frothing agent. The hydrophobic particles, activated by an added collector agent, adhere to the air bubbles (frothers and collectors will be discussed in subsequent sections). Due to the density differences, the air bubbles rise to the surface of the solution where they collect as a froth layer (the concentrate stream) which spills over into a froth-collection tray. The froth may also be mechanically skimmed-off. The hydrophilic particles remain in solution, which is eventually decanted off as waste (the tailing stream). Typically, the concentrating stream contains the desired, or more valuable, component and the tailing stream, the gangue.

Collectors:

To invoke selective hydrophobicity, substances know as *collectors* are used. Collectors are typically heteropolar organic substances - they contain both non-polar and polar chemical groups. The non-polar end is almost always a long-chain or cyclic hydrocarbon group that is hydrophobic. The collector must be able to attach to the solid, and it does so through its polar end, which is typically an ionic group termed the solidophil group.

Frothers:

In addition to collectors, another important component is successful floatation is the presence of *frothers*. Once its surface is rendered hydrophobic, a solid particle must be able to attach to an air bubble. While it may be possible to initially obtain solid particle attachment to air bubbles in an agitated liquid under aeration alone, these air bubbles are unstable and quickly break down due to collisions with other bubbles, solid particles, and the vessel walls. In addition, the bubble size may not be sufficient to effectively carry a solid particle to the surface of the liquid. Consequently, additional materials, termed frothers, are added to promote the formation of stable air bubbles under aeration. Frothers like collectors, are typically comprised of both a polar and non-polar end. The non-polar hydrophobic ends orient themselves into the air phase. Bubble wall strength is enhanced by simultaneous strong polar-group and water-dipole reaction (hydration) at the air-liquid interface resulting in greater bubble stability due to a localized increase in surface tension.

Table 10.6: Examples of Frothers

Frother	Formula
Aliphatic Alcohols	$CH_3(CH_2)_nCH_2OH, n = 3 - 5$
MIBC (4-methyl-2-pentanol)	$CH_3CH(CH_3)CH_2CH(OH)CH_3$
di-acetone alcohol	$(CH_3)_2(OH)CH_2COCH_3$
2-ethyl 3-hexanol	$CH_3(CH_2)_3CH(C_2H_5)CH_2OH$
Cyclic Alcohols	
Pine oil (terpineol)	$C_{10}H_{17}OH$
Xylenol (for example, xylitol)	$C_{10}H_{16}O$
Pherols	$CH_3C_6H_4OH$
Cresols	$HOCH(CHOH)_3 CH_2OH$
Xylenal (for example, xylitol)	
Alkoxyparaffins	
1, 1, 3-triethoxybutane	$CH_3CH_2CH(OC_2H_5)CH(OC_2H_5)_2$
Polyglycols	
poly(propylene glycol) monalkyl ethers	$R(OC_3H_6)_nOH, n = 2 - 5, R = CH_3, C_4H_9$
poly(ethylene glycol)s	$R(OC_2H_4)_nOC_2H_4OH, n = 2 - 5$
Other	
sulfo-cetyl alcohol	$CH_3(CH_2)_{14}CH_2OSO_2OH$

Modifiers:

Additional modifers such as activators, depressants, dispersants and pH regulators are also commonly used in froth floatation. *Activators* may be added to chemically "resurface" the solid to increase the interaction with collectors that are otherwise ineffective alone. *Depressants* form a polar chemical envelope around the solid particle that enhances hydrophilicity or selectively prevents interaction with collectors that may induce unwanted hydrophobicity. *Dispersants* act to break agglomerated particles apart so that single particles interact with the collectors and air bubbles. *Regulators* are commonly used to control the pH since the hydrophobicity of systems is often optimal within a certain pH range. Frothers also often need a certain pH range in order to form stable bubbles. The presence of reducing agents may also serve to prevent the presence of soluble ions due to oxidation that may undesirably activate certain minerals.

The term 'floatation' is a generalization of a number of processes known collectively as *'adsorptive bubble techniques'*. Floatation is used to separate one solid from the other on a large scale. It is also used to separate a solid from the liquid on a limited scale. In both the cases the solid surface has to be hydrophobic or made one by the addition of appropriate surface-active reagents.

10.9.1 Hydrophobicity and Floatation

Almost all the minerals and inorganic solids have a strong affinity for water. Therefore, the surfaces of these solids are easily wetted by water and hence they are known as hydrophillic. Hydrophillic solids are unfloatable because air bubbles cannot stick to the solid surface to form particle bubble aggregate. However, these solids can be made hydrophobic, with the help of surface-active reagents known as collectors. These collectors adsorb on the solid surface and make the surface more amenable to displacement of water film by air bubble, which now sticks to the solid surface.

The condition for good Hydrophobicity is shown in Fig. 10.15. The angle θ shown in the figure is called *contact angle*. It is an angle between the solid surface and the tangent to the bubble at the point of three-phase contact between the bubble solid and liquid. For the surface to be hydrophobic the contact angle $\theta > 0$ and the attachment of air bubble to the solid surface is feasible. Contact angle of over 30° is required for good floatation to take place.

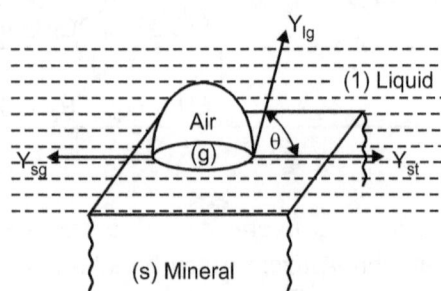

Fig. 10.15: Condition for Good Hydrophobicity

Floatation Reagents: Several types of reagents are used in floatation. Collectors are the most essential reagents and the function of these surface-active chemicals is to render selectively the desired mineral surfaces hydrophobic so that these minerals can be selectively floated. A characteristic feature of most collectors is a non-symmetrical molecule consisting of two parts-one polar and one non-polar. The non-polar part is usually a long hydrocarbon chain, which has pronounced water repellent properties. In contrast to the non-polar part of the molecule, the polar part can react with water. Thus, in case of sodium oleate, $C_{17}H_{33}$ COONa, collector the hydrocarbon radical is the non-polar part while the polar part is the carboxylic group COONa. Some of the important collectors are given in Table 10.5.

Table 10.5: Floatation Collectors

	Anionic Collectors	**Active Group**	**Remarks**
1.	Carboxylic aids and salts for example, oleate, stearate, linoleate	$-C\underset{O^-}{\overset{O}{\diagup}}$	Used for non-sulfide minerals
2.	Xanthates; for example, K, Na salts of ethyl, butyl amyl xanthates	$-O-C\underset{S^-}{\overset{S}{\diagup}}$	Used for sulfide minerals
3.	Dithiophosphate	$\underset{O}{\overset{O}{\diagup}}P\underset{S^-}{\overset{S}{\diagup}}$	Used for sulfide minerals
	Cationic Collectors		
4.	Amines, primary, secondary and tertiary, long chain aliphatic	$R - NH_2$ $R_2 - NH$ $R_3 - N$	Used for non-sulfide minerals

Apart from collectors frothing reagents are also used to from stable froth. Frothers are heteropolar surfaces active organic substances, which are preferentially adsorbed on the air-water interface. The most effective frothers are pine oils $C_{16}H_{17}OH$, cresols $CH_3C_6H_4OH$, methyl isobutyl carbinol and propylene glycol amyl ester. Other reagents are used either to activate or depress the floatation or to modify the pH of the pulp.

Thus, lime, soda ash, acids and caustic soda are used for pH control. Salts of Ba, Ca, Cu, Pb, Zn, as well as salts containing anions like $SiO_3 = CN -, CO_3 = S =, PO_4$ are used to condition the surface to make it more amenable to floatation or to depress floatation. Organic modifiers such as starch, dextrin, and sucrose are also used.

10.9.2 Physical Processes in Floatation

The physical unit steps involved in bubble particle attachment are:

(1) Collision between bubble and particle.

(2) Thinning of the film between the bubble and particle.

(3) Rupture of the liquid film.

(4) Expansion of the air meniscus resulting in stable attachment.

All the above steps together determine the *rate of floatation*.

10.9.3 Floatation Machines

A floatation unit or cell essentially consists of a tank provided with a feed at one end, an overflow for forth removal and a discharge for tailings at the other end. It has a provision for introducing air bubbles and for agitation. A typical cell is shown in Fig. 10.16. The modern cells incorporate a mechanical agitator which draws in air and distributes it throughout the pulp in the form of bubbles. It also agitates the pulp. There is a provision for auxiliary external air in some cells. the useful cell volume can be varied from 1000 to 10,000 litres whereas the power consumption may vary from 10 Hp to 25 Hp.

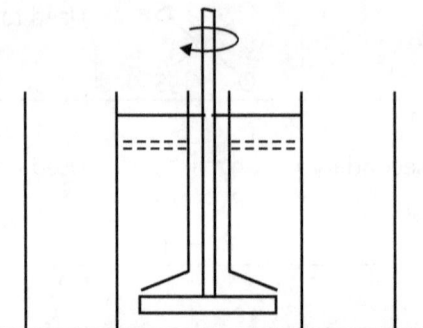

Fig. 10.16: Floatation Cell

The solid floatation recovery in a batch test is given by:

$$R_B = \frac{(C_o - C)}{C_o} = 1 - e^{-kt} \quad \ldots (10.5)$$

Where R_B = Solids recovery,
 C_o = Initial solids concentration, weight of solids per weight of liquid.
 C = Solids, concentration at time t.
 k = Constant, s^{-1}

If 'n' individual floatation machines were arranged in series then overall solids recovery is R_c^n and is $R_B = R_c^n$. Then,

$$\frac{\bar{t_c}}{t} = \frac{n}{kt}\left[\exp\left(\frac{kt}{n}\right) - 1\right] \quad \ldots(10.6)$$

Knowing the recovery in a batch test kt can be calculated from which the ratio t_c/t is evaluated by equation (10.6) $\bar{t_c}$ represents the mean residence time.

10.10 Flocculation

Flocculation:
Another means by which primary particles are brought together to form aggregates, that is easier to remove from suspension than primary particles, is by flocculation, see Fig. 10.17.

In this process the aggregation is caused by bridges from one particle to another, usually formed by high molecular weight polymers in solution. The polymers may be man-made, or they can be naturally occurring; examples of the latter are found with several biological compounds. The resulting aggregate is called a *floc, which* is formed by adding a flocculant (usually a polymer) in solution. The process of flocculation forms flocs that may be broken by the application of shear, such as during pumping, and the physical bridges linking the particles do not usually reform when the shear field is removed. Thus, unlike coagulation, the process of flocculation is shear sensitive. So, when flocculants are used in high shear applications, such as to assist dewatering in a scroll discharge decanter centrifuge a special shear resistant flocculant is required. These are normally very high molecular weight polymers. However, the higher the molecular weight the more difficult it is to dissolve the polymer and it may be more difficult to disperse the flocculant within the feed suspension to be treated.

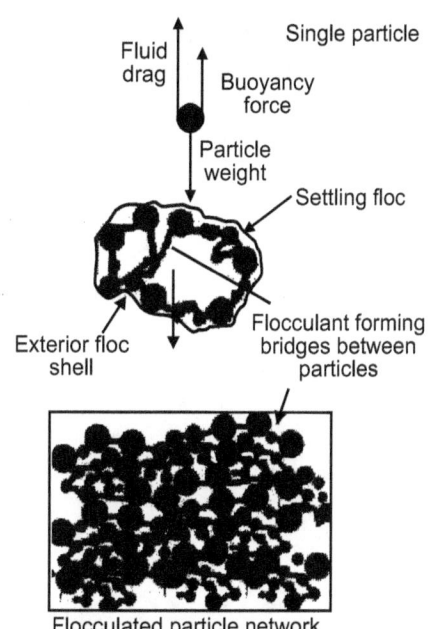

Fig. 10.17: A floc is Much Bigger Than a Particle and is Easier to Remove from Suspension, but a Floc Network Settles Slowly

Synthetic polymer flocculants (polyelectrolyte) are supplied in three forms: non-ionic, anionic and cationic. The first has no net charge, the second is negatively charged in solution and the latter is positively charged. Hence, when treating mineral suspensions cationic flocculants are preferred because they can more easily bind on to the negatively charged mineral surface. For similar reasons anionic flocculants are applied to biological suspensions. There are many instances when flocculation follows a primary coagulation stage. The coagulation is designed to destabilize the suspension and the flocculation stage to then form aggregates that are even easier to settle, filter etc. Hence, anionic polymers may be applied to mineral systems after coagulation and cationic to biological systems. So, the optimum flocculant and coagulant dose, and strategy, is one that can only be Fig. 10.17. A floc is much bigger than a particle and is easier to remove from suspension, but a floc network settles slowly determined by experimental testing. The quickest way to achieve this is by the simple settling jar test, fast settling times are desired. However, the optimum dose is usually provided by the cost of flocculant purchase, rather than any physical consideration, as these chemicals constitute a significant recurrent cost.

Conventionally coagulants and flocculants are added to the feed launder to the thickener, however, in the floc blanket clarifier (popular in the potable water industry) the feed is introduced, with flocculant, into the flocculated and settling bed of solids, see Fig. 10.18. Likewise the high rate thickener applies the same principle; the clarifier is used for dilute feeds and the thickener at higher concentrations usually found in the minerals industry.

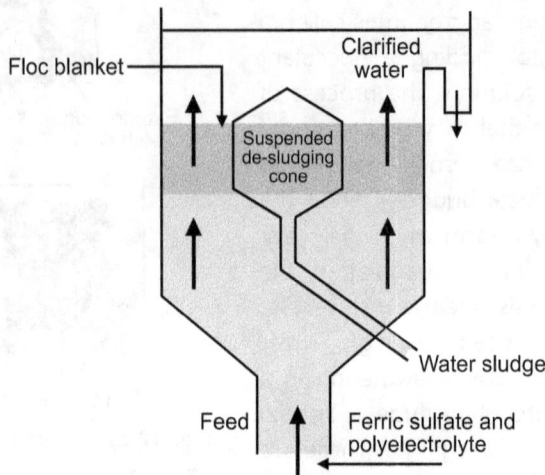

Fig. 10.18: Floc Bed Clarifier

NOMENCLATURE

Symbol	
A	Area, m².
a	Initial acceleration, m/s².
C	Solid concentration at time t.
C_o	Initial solid concentration, weight of solids per weight of liquid.
F	Feed rate, kg/hr; F_c, centrifugal force; F_g, force of gravity; F_R, resisting force.
g	Acceleration of gravity, m/s².
K	constant, s^{-1}.
m	mass, kg.
R_B	Solid recovery.
t	time, hr.
Greek Letters:	
ρ	Density, kg/m³; $ρ_S$, of particle, $ρ_L$, of liquid.
μ	Viscosity, cP.

***

MODEL QUESTION PAPERS
SET NO. 1

1. (a) For flow of solids out of a bin which opening is preferable, slide opening or a bottom opening ? Why ? **[6]**

    (b) What are the factors on which the rate of flow of granular solids by gravity, through a circular opening in the bottom of a bin, depends upon ? **[5]**

    (c) Discuss about various devices for the transportation of solids. **[6]**

2. (a) Discuss about axial mixing in paste mixers. **[6]**

    (b) A silty soil containing 14 percent moisture was mixed in a large muller mixer with 10.0 weight percent of a tracer consisting of dextrose and picric acid. After 3 min of mixing, 12 random samples were taken from the mix and analyzed colorimetrically for tracer material. The measured concentrations in the sample were in weight percent tracer 10.24, 9.30, 7.94, 10.24, 11.08, 10.03, 11.91, 9.72, 9.20, 10.76, 10.97, 10.55. Calculate the mixing index I_p and the standard deviations. **[10]**

3. (a) What is an Agitated mill ? Explain its operation. **[6]**

    (b) Discuss, with the aid of a schematic sketch of a colloid mill, the working of a colloid mill. **[6]**

    (c) What type of material can be handled in it ? **[4]**

4. (a) Explain the working of plate and frame press with a neat diagram. **[10]**

    (b) Discuss about shell-and-leaf filters. **[6]**

5. (a) Discuss about the types of membranes and the material of construction. **[8]**

    (b) Discuss about the rejection curve for some membranes based on molecular weight of membranes. **[8]**

6. (a) Write about the principles of centrifugal sedimentation and explain its mechanism of operation. **[8]**

    (b) Sink and float method with suitable example. **[8]**

7. (a) Describe power consumption in agitated vessels with relevant equations. **[8]**

    (b) Explain the term "vortex formation" in agitated tank with neat diagram. How can swirling be prevented ? **[8]**

***

SET NO. 2

1. (a) Explain how cohesive solids flow out of bins. **[6]**
   (b) The discharge opening for flow of solids out of bins plays an important role in maintaining a proper control of the flow rate. Explain. **[5]**
   (c) What causes the solids to arch or bridge in the container and prevent flow ? How is it overcome ? **[5]**

2. (a) Describe the construction and working of the Banbury mixer with a neat sketch. What are its uses ? **[6]**
   (b) A large Banbury mixer masticates 816 kg of scrap rubber with a density of 1121.26 kg/m^3. The power load is 1182 kW/m^3 of rubber. How much cooling water in m^3/min is needed to remove the heat generated in the mixer if the temperature of the water is not to rise more than 27°C ? **[10]**

3. A material is crushed in a Blake jaw crusher such that the average size of particle is reduced from 50 mm to 10 mm with a consumption f energy at the rate of 13 kJ/kg. What will be the consumption of energy needed to crush the same material of average size of 75 mm to an average size of 25 mm ?
   (a) Assuming Rittinger's law applies ? **[6]**
   (b) Assuming Kick's law applies ? **[6]**
   (c) Which of these results would be regarded as being more reliable and why ? **[4]**

4. Explain the principle of continuous vacuum filtration and describe the functioning of Rotary-Drum filter with a neat diagram. **[16]**

5. Write short notes on :
   (a) Partial rejection of solutes. **[4]**
   (b) Microfiltration **[8]**
   (c) Different types of membranes used for ultrasiltration **[4]**

6. (a) Describe the different stages of the hatch sedimentation process. **[8]**
   (b) Write about the rate of sedimentation and explain the relation between the interface height and settling time. **[8]**

7. A flat-blade turbine with six blades is installed centrally in a vertical tank. The tank is 1.5 m in diameter; the turbine is 0.5 m in diameter and is positioned 0.5 from the bottom of the tank. The turbine blades are 125 mm wide. The tank is filled to a depth of 1.5 m with rubber-latex compound at 65°C having a viscosity of 1200 P and a density of 1129 kg/m^3. The turbine is operated at 95 rpm. The tank is unbaffled ? What power will be required to operate the mixer (Make suitable assumptions) ? **[16]**

***

MECHANICAL OPERATIONS   MODEL QUESTION PAPERS

SET NO. 3

1. (a) What are the distinctive properties of particulate masses ? [8]

   (b) Explain how free flowing solids flow out of bins. [8]

2. Discuss about different mixers for free flowing solids. [16]

3. (a) What are the various laws of size reduction ? State each one of them with their limitations. [10]

   (b) Which law is more realistic in estimating power requirement of a commercial comminuting machine ? Give answer with justification. [3]

   (c) State the generalized relation for all the laws of size reduction. [3]

4. (a) What are the major requirements for selection of filter media ? [8]

   (b) Write short notes on : [8]
      (i) Filter aids
      (ii) Washing filter cakes

5. (a) Classify the membranes based on size range of the particles. [6]

   (b) Distinguish between micro and macrofiltration. [4]

   (c) Explain the solution diffusion mechanism under membrane based separations. [6]

6. Write notes on :

   (a) Axial flow conveyor centrifuges [8]

   (b) Centrifugal classifiers. [8]

7. (a) Show by dimensional analysis that the power required by mixer impeller can be correlated by means of power number as a function of Reynolds number and Froude number. [10]

   (b) Explain the physical significance of each number in the above correlation. [6]

***

MECHANICAL OPERATIONS MODEL QUESTION PAPERS

SET NO. 4

1. (a) State the similarities and differences between the properties of solid particles and fluids. [6]
   (b) How are particulate solids classified depending on their flow properties ? Give examples. [4]
   (c) Write in detail about bin storage and bulk storage. [6]
2. Write about the power consumption for different types of mixing equipment. [16]
3. (a) What are various laws of size reduction ? State each one of them with their limitations. [10]
   (b) Which law is more realistic in estimating power requirement of a commercial comminuting machine ? Give answer with justification. [3]
   (c) State the generalized relation for all the laws of size reduction. [3]
4. Write short notes on :
   (a) Ideal and actual screens. [8]
   (b) Capacity and effectiveness of screens. [8]
5. What are the different types of membranes and discuss them in detail with their applications ? [16]
6. (a) Write a note on sludge-separators. [8]
   (b) Describe helical-conveyor centrifuge with a neat diagram. [8]
7. What do you understand from the pitch of the agitator ? Mention the applications of flat bladed turbine, pitched turbine and propeller agitator. [16]

***

REFERENCE BOOKS

The number of references in each chapter has been kept to an absolute minimum. Where provided, they are given in the text. An intelligent search of the Internet will result in excellent equipment illustrations and pictures and these have also been kept to a minimum. However, for the purpose of further in-depth study of the topics introduced here the following books are recommended. All these books are currently available from well-known Internet retailers. (e.g. www.amazon.com)

1. M. Rhodes, Paperback, "Introduction to Particle Technology", 1998, 336 pages, John Wiley and Sons Ltd.; ISBN : 0471984833.
2. J. Seville, U. Tuzun, R. Clift, "Processing of Particulate Solids", Hardcover, 1997, 384 pages, 1997 Kluwer Academic Publishers; ISBN: 0751403768.
3. Brian H. Kaye, Characterization of Powders and Aerosols, Hardcover, 1999, 312 pages John Wiley & Son Ltd.; ISBN: 3527288538
4. Terence Allen, "Particle Size Measurement (Powder Technology Series)", 5th Edition, Hardcover, 1996, Kluwer Academic Publishers, Hardbound Set of 2 volumes
5. Rushton, A. S. Ward, R. G. Holdich, "Solid-Liquid Filtration and Separation Technology", 2nd Edition, Hardcover, 2000, 587 pages, Wiley-VCH; ISBN: 3527296042.
6. Maria Cristina Bustos, Fernando Concha, Raimund Bürger, Elmer M. Tory, "Sedimentation and Thickening : Phenomenological Foundation and Mathematical Theory Book Series : Mathematical Modeling : Theory and Applications", Volume 8, Hardbound, 1999, 304 pages, Kluwer Academic Publishers, Dordrecht, ISBN 0-7923-5960-7.
7. Fellows, P., "Food Processing Technology : Principles and Practice", 2nd Edition Woodhead Publishing Ltd., 2000, pp 98-110. *This is a good review of a range of methods of size reduction.*
8. Brennan, J. G., "Food Engineering Operations," 3rd Edition, Elsevier Applied Science, London, 1990, Chap. 4, pp 67-85.
9. Earle, R. L., "Unit Operations in Food Processing", 2nd Edition, Pergamon Press, 1983 pp 129-163.
10. Brennan, J. G., Butters, J.R., Cowell, N. D., and Lilley, A. E. V., " Food Engineering Operations", Elsevier Applied Science, London & New York, 1990, Chap. 4, pp 85 - 90.
11. C. Orr, "Particulate Technology", McMillan, New York, 1966.
12. Svarovsky, " Powder Testing Guide : Methods of measuring the physical properties of bulk powders", 1987. Published on behalf of the British Materials Handling Board by Elsevier Applied Science, London.
13. Badger and Banchero, "Introduction to Chemical Engineering", Tata McGraw Hill, New Delhi, 1997.

14. Brown et al., " Unit Operations", Wiley, New York, 1950.
15. McCabe and Smith, "Unit Operations of Chemical Engineering", 5th Edition, McGraw Hill, New York, 1993.
16. Perry and Chilton (Editors), "Chemical Engineer's Handbook", 7th Edition, McGraw Hill, 1997.
17. Brown C.G., "Unit Operations", Wiley New York, 1956.
18. Svarovsky, "Solid-Liquid Operations", Butterworths, London, 1977.
19. Coulson and Richardson, "Chemical Engineering", Volume 2 Butterworths, London, 1997.
20. Baumeister et.al. (Editors), "Standard Handbook for Mechanical Engineers", 8th Edition, McGraw Hill, New York, 1979.
21. Philip Schweitzer (Editor), "Handbook for Separation Processes for Chemical Engineers," McGraw Hill, New York, 1979.
22. S. K. Gupta, "Momentum Transfer Operations", Tata McGraw Hill, New Delhi, 1980.
23. P. Chattopadhya, "Unit Operations of Chemical Engineering" (Vol-I), Khanna Publishers, Delhi, 1996.
24. C. J. Geankoplis, "Transport Processes and Separation Processes Principles", 4th Edition, PHI, New Delhi, 2004.
25. M. G. Larian, "Fundamentals of Chemical Engineering Operations", Englewood Cliffs, New Jersey, 1958.
26. D. D. Kale, " Unit Operations", Pune Vidyarthi Griha Prakashan, 1990.
27. C. Orr (Editor), "Filtration : Principles and Practice (Two Volumes), Marcel Dekker, 1977.
28. R. J. Wakeman, "Filters and Filtration", Elsevier, 1975.
29. G. D. Dickey, " Filtration", Reinhold, New York, 1961.
30. P. Meares (Editor), "Membrane Separation Processes", Elsevier, 1976.
31. P. Meares (Editor), "Process Engineering Technique Evaluation : Filtration", McGraw Hill, 1984.
32. Kunnii and Levenspiel, "Fluidization Engineering", Wiley, New York, 1969.
33. Davidson et al., "Fluidization", 2nd Edition, Academic Press, London, 1985.
34. Geldar (Editor), "Gas Fluidization Technology", Wiley-Interscience, Chichester, 1986.
35. H.C. Perkins, "Air Pollution", McGraw Hill 1979.
36. S.P. Mahajan, "Pollution Control in Process Industries", Tata McGraw Hill, New Delhi, 1993.
37. G.G. Chase, "Beneficiation Process", Workshop arranged by the University of Akron, 1997.

***

Appendix – A
UNITS FOR PARTICULATE MEASUREMENT

A.1 : UNITS FOR PARTICULATE MEASUREMENT

- One angstrom unit (A. O. or Å) = 0.1 manometers, or one ten- thousandth of a micron (10^{-4} microns), or one hundred - millionth of centimeter (1×10^{-8}). One angstrom is the diameter of a hydrogen atom - the smallest element.

Definitions :

- Flow Rate = Time in seconds per 50 grams.
- Mesh = Number of openings per linear inch, starting with a ruler zeroed on the centre of any wire.
- Micron = One micron (μ) equals 10^{-4} centimeters or 0.001 millimeters.
- Nano = A prefix meaning one billionth or 10^{-9}. The symbol is n.
- Nanometer = One nanometer (nm) equals ten angstroms or 1 millimicron.
- **Sieve Analysis** refers to the particle size distribution, usually expressed as weight percentage retained upon each of a series of standard sieves of decreasing size and the percentage passed by the sieved of finest size.
- Surface Area = A measure of the surface area per unit weight.
- Wavelength = One wavelength (at 5500 Å) equals 21.8×10^{-6} inches.

A.2 : INTERNATIONAL SIEVE CHART

ASTME-11	JIS	BSI	Particle Diameter	AFNOR	DIN	Tyler	Angstrom Units (Å)
USA USS Mesh	JPN Microns (μ)	GBR Mesh	USA Microns (μ)	FRA Microns (μ)	DEU Microns (μ)	USA Mesh	Global Angstroms (Å)
3 in.	71		75 mm				
2 in.	50		50				
1. 06 in.	26.5		26.5		26.5	1.05 in	
7/ 8 in.	22.4		22.4	22.4	22.4	0.883 in.	
3/4 in.	19		19.0		19	0.742 in.	
5/ 8 in.	16		16.0	16	16	0.624 in.	
1/2 in.	12.5		12.5	12.5	12.5		
7/16 in.	11.2		11.2	11.2	11.2	0.441 in.	
3/8 in.	9.5		9.5	11.2	9.5	0.371	
5/16 in.	8		8.0	8	8	2.5	
0.265 in.	6.7		6.7		6.7	3	
3.5	90		5.6	5.6	5.6	3.5	
5	5		4.00	4	4	5	
8	8		2.36		2.36	8	
12			1.70		1.7	10	
14	1.4	12	1.40	1.4	1.4	12	

MECHANICAL OPERATIONS   APPENDIX – A: UNITS OF PARTICULATE MEASUREMENT

ASTME-11	JIS	BSI	Particle Diameter	AFNOR	DIN	Tyler	Angstrom Units (Å)
USA USS Mesh	JPN Microns (µ)	GBR Mesh	USA Microns (µ)	FRA Microns (µ)	DEU Microns (µ)	USA Mesh	Global Angstroms (Å)
16			1.18		1.18	14	
18			1.00	1.0	1.0	16	
20	850	18	850		850	20	
25	710	22	710	710	710	24	
30	600	25	600		600	28	
35	500	30	500	500	500	32	
40	425	36	425		425	35	
45	355	44	355	355	355	42	
50	300	52	300		300	48	
60	250	60	250	250	250	60	
70	212	72	212		212	65	
80	180	85	180	180	180	80	
100	150	100	150		150	100	
120	125	120	125	125	125	115	
140	106		106		106	150	
170	90	170	90	90	90	170	
200	75	200	75		75	200	
230	63	240	63	63	63	250	
270	53	300	53		53	270	
325	45	350	45	45	45	325	
400	38	400	38		38	400	
450	32	440	32	32	32	450	
500			25	25	25	500	
635			20	20	20	63.5	
			16		16		
			10		10	1,250	
			5		5	5,000	
					1	10,000	
1			**Particle Diameter (µ)**				**Angstrom Units (Å)**
			0.1				1,000
			0.01				100
			0.001				10
			0.0001				1
			0				0

A.3 : SIZE CONVERSION CHART

1 cm	1mm	100 micrometers	10 micrometers	1 micrometer	100 nanometers	10 nanometers	1 nanometer
0.01 meter	0.001 meter	0.0001 meter	0.00001 meter	0.000001 meter	0.0000001 meter	0.00000001 meter	0.000000001 meter

***

Appendix – B
FRONTIERS IN PARTICLE TECHNOLOGY

This section gives an overview of latest advancement in particle technology research for the following major topics:
1. Mixing Mechanics
2. Preventing and solving some common pneumatic conveying problems
3. Silo Problems: Prevention hurts less than the cure
4. Size Reduction Overview: Shear, Compression and Impact
5. The Three R's of Analyzing particle size

B.1 MIXING MECHANICS

Mixing and specifying: A lot of factors are involved in determining the best mixer to use, the most efficient batch size and mixing time, and how your material's particle size distribution, bulk density, and shape will affect your mixing. If you mix many different formulations, you quickly realize that your mixer isn't optimum for each, so you have to work within your equipment's limits.

What is mixing? The whole idea of mixing is to distribute different ingredients within a batch in such a way that when you divide the batch each division has the same proportion of each ingredient. This sounds easy. What's difficult is determining just how uniform the mixture has to be. What does your next process, next department, or customer really need? Will the mixing end product be used to make tablets or capsules, will you produce 10-pound divisions that don't have to be quite as precise, or will you produce a 50-pound bag that your customer will divide into smaller batches? These kinds of questions should be addressed in the mixing specification, which sometimes doesn't get the scrutiny it deserves.

Mixing specifications: When you start out with a new formulation, what do you do? You send it out to the mixing department and say, "Mix this." The mixer operator will determine how the ingredients are added, in what order, and how long they're mixed. The operator bases these decisions on personal experience, which might be 20 years or 1 week. With a well-planned mixing specification, you can minimize the difference between batches of the end product, no matter how much -- or how little -- experience the mixer operator has. Ingredients are classified as majors, minors, and micros. A major is more than 5 percent of the batch, a minor is from 1 to 5 percent, and a micro is less than 1 percent. Often a major is divided into two parts. One half is the first ingredient put into the mixer and the other half is the last. The minors and micros are added in between. If your product has several majors, you can put one or more in first, then the minors and micros, followed by the remaining majors.

If you have many minors and micros, you may want to consider specifying a premix (also called a *master batch*). This allows you to mix the minors and micros together first, and then add them to the mixer as you would one ingredient, either in one addition, or, if they make up a large quantity, in portions. Preparing a premix reduces operator exposure to hazardous fines by requiring less weighing, but sometimes it's not economical.

If there's no clear mixing specification, each time the batch is made, different operators might change the order of addition. And each time this changes, the batch can vary. Thus the ingredient addition order becomes a variable that can change the product's consistency. The value of a mixing specification is that it makes the ingredient addition order a constant instead of a variable. This means that if your operators follow the mixing specification, each operator will load the ingredients the same way every time. Your mixing specification should also tell how each ingredient is to be handled. For example, when minors or micros are added, they shouldn't just be added to the top. When the mixer is started, they may be thrown to a side or a lid, and if they stick, they aren't in your batch.

Sampling: Another element to include in your mixing specification is how sampling should be done. You take samples to ensure that your batch has the right mixture. Knowing what size sample to take is critical. Sample size is particularly important when the end product is tiny. For instance, if the end product will be a 1-gram vitamin pill that will be taken two at a time three times a day, a 6-gram sample would be suitable. But if the user will take only one pill once a day, your sample size should be only 1 gram. That's the only way you'll know that each vitamin pill contains the correct proportion of ingredients. On the other hand, if the end product is going to be used 10 pounds at a time, then your sample size can be up to 10 pounds.

In some applications, such as pharmaceuticals, the key ingredient is only a small percentage of the total mixture and has to be within a certain percentage or a certain minimum percentage. Your sample must be measured for that key ingredient to determine whether it's on spec or not. How this measurement is made varies from industry to industry, and your mixing specification should describe the appropriate tests for your application. Your mixing specification should also state where the samples are to be taken from. The sample not only determines if a batch is good, it also determines if a rework is required. Therefore, you want it to be based on a correctly taken sample. Samples taken near the mixer's sidewall, from the middle, and from the discharge area will be significantly different. Ensuring that your samples are taken in the same way every time eliminates another variable from the process.

Other factors: Your mixer operator shouldn't be exposed to hazardous ingredients during mixing. Consulting MSDS (Material Safety and Data sheets) for each ingredient and stating their safety precautions in your mixing specification will keep your operator safe.

It's also wise to talk to your plant's experienced operators to get their input on a mixing specification. They know how your materials handle in bulk and can give you valuable advice for putting together a good mixing specification.

B.2 PREVENTING AND SOLVING SOME COMMON PNEUMATIC CONVEYING PROBLEMS

If your pneumatic conveying system has problems -- such as being unable to convey multiple materials at the desired capacity, degrading your material, or creating safety hazards -- the cause is probably a flawed system design. This article's first section details how you can prevent such problems by running conveying tests on your materials during the system design process. The remaining sections explain how you can diagnose and solve problems in a poorly designed existing pneumatic conveying system. Designing a pneumatic conveying system that effectively conveys your material and operates without problems requires accurately understanding your application and, in particular, knowing your material's conveying properties.

These conveying properties depend primarily on the material's physical characteristics, including particle size and shape, bulk density, softness or hardness, elasticity, temperature sensitivity, moisture sensitivity, and permeability. Unfortunately, published theoretical calculation methods for designing pneumatic conveying systems don't take all of these material-conveying properties into account. While the calculation methods can produce an approximate system design, they're unlikely to produce a correct system design unless you use your past conveying experience and knowledge of your material's conveying properties to adjust these calculations.

Preventing conveying problems through testing: One common method for obtaining system design data is to run lab tests on a small pilot-plant conveying system and then use the results to design the production-scale conveying system. This requires using scale-up factors to convert the pilot plant's conveying line diameters, line lengths, and line routing to production size. The problem with this method is that it's typically impractical to run lab tests under your actual conveying conditions. For example, if you have a heat-sensitive material, you need to test the material when it's hot to determine operating pressures and conveying velocities. But even if you heat the material for the test, it will cool off very quickly when it's conveyed in the pilot plant's cold conveying lines.

Even if you insulate and heat the lines, keeping the material hot will be difficult. As a result, the test may not accurately reflect your real conveying conditions. The problem of accurately reflecting real conditions also affects tests of hygroscopic materials and friable materials, as well as tests of a conveying system's ability to handle multiple materials. It's also almost impossible to recreate the production conveying line's actual length and routing in the pilot plant because the line lengths and diameters that can be installed in a test lab are limited. While scale-up factors can help you adjust your test results, scale-up isn't a perfect science and will only produce an approximate system design.

Because of these problems, it's better -- whenever possible -- to use an existing conveying system in your plant to test your material under real conveying conditions and for sufficiently long conveying periods. The conveying line diameter and length generally will be closer to those in your final system too, so you can use much smaller scale-up factors in adjusting your test results. However, your existing conveying system probably isn't designed for running tests. This means that the system may not have blowers and rotary valves that can run at different speeds. It also may not have the instrumentation required for your test. Installing additional instrumentation typically doesn't cost much, but making changes to your blowers and rotary valves can be expensive. As a result, testing your material on an existing conveying system may give you only limited data. But this data will be far more accurate than that you derive from theories or lab tests.

If you don't have an existing conveying system in your plant, you can test your material in a supplier's test lab, but select a test lab whose pilot-plant design comes close to your system design. Also run the tests for a sufficiently long time to get as many data points as possible. *Design the system so that the conveying velocity throughout the conveying line is higher than the hardest-to-convey material's saltation velocity.* If you won't be designing a pneumatic conveying system in the near future but, instead, you have an existing system that exhibits problems, you can still use conveying tests. Running such tests can often help you correct the underlying system design errors that created the problems. The following sections describe how to diagnose and solve some common pneumatic conveying problems, including lost capacity when conveying multiple materials, material cross-contamination, material degradation, safety hazards, and limited conveying capacity.

Lost capacity when conveying multiple materials: To convey several materials in the same conveying system without excessive operating complexity, you can always run the system at the same conveying rate that will move all the materials. But this low rate may result in lost production capacity with your easy-to-convey materials. This problem usually occurs because the conveying system wasn't originally designed to handle the hardest-to-convey material. Consider, for example, a system designed to convey various grades of polyethylene pellets. Each grade has different properties, such as particle shape, particle size distribution, density, bulk density, melt index, particle temperature, modulus of elasticity, additive content, hardness, and permeability.

In general the hardest-to-convey polyethylene grade is the one with the largest particle size distribution, lowest density, highest melt index, highest temperature, and highest modulus of elasticity. As long as the system was designed for conveying some other material, its capacity when moving this hardest-to-convey material will be much lower than its capacity when conveying the material it was designed to handle. To solve this problem, improve your conveying system's design to handle the hardest-to-convey material. You can do this by running conveying tests on each material you'll convey and then modifying the system design based on the test data for the hardest-to-convey material. You must also allow large enough safety margins in the system's design to ensure that the system achieves your required conveying capacity. Typical safety margins are:

- 10 percent for the conveying rate.
- 10 percent for data collection or system calculation errors.
- 10 percent between the maximum allowable conveying pressure and system interlocks (which automatically shut down the feeder or blower).
- 10 percent between the blower's pressure-relief valve set point and the system's maximum conveying pressure. (A good rule of thumb: If the blower's pressure rating is 15 psig, the conveying system's pressure drop for the hardest-to-convey material should be about 10 psi.).

Also consider conveying velocity. Design the system so that the conveying velocity throughout the conveying line is higher than the hardest-to-convey material's saltation velocity. This will prevent the material from salting out (that is, dropping out) of the conveying gas when the conveying velocity is too low. As a safety factor, use a minimum conveying velocity at least 25 percent higher than the material's saltation velocity.

Material cross-contamination: If some material is contaminated by another material during pneumatic conveying, it can cause problems in your downstream process. For example, even a few particles of a black powder can contaminate a white powder conveyed in the same system. Or if low-density polyethylene is used in a blown-film production line (which produces a bubble of extruded polyethylene to make polyethylene film), even a few particles of high-density polyethylene can cause the blown-film bubble to collapse, which will shut down the entire production line.

If, as in these cases, cross-contamination is completely unacceptable in your process, it's best to improve the system's design by providing a dedicated conveying line for each of your conveyed materials. But this is very costly. A less costly option is to design and operate one common conveying system with sanitary construction. Such a system can handle multiple materials but can be fully cleaned between materials and has mechanical components that are designed to prevent material accumulation. Follow these guidelines when designing the system:

- Install a check valve immediately upstream of the material feed point to prevent any material from flowing backward into the system's gas-only line.
- Install a sanitary-construction rotary valve at the material feed point.
- Use conveying line couplings and flanges designed to prevent collecting or trapping particles.
- Install metal detectors in the system's receiving hoppers to detect any metal contaminants.
- Install the receiving hopper's vent filter outside the hopper so that any dust discharged by the filter doesn't contaminate the next material entering the hopper.
- Use mass-flow bins and silos to supply material to or receive material from the system. Such vessels empty completely even during continuous system operation. These vessels should have no internal components that can collect or trap even a few particles.
- Wash the bins and hoppers before introducing another material to the system.

Material degradation: Pneumatically conveying a material can cause it to wear, break up, or smear, resulting in dust, fines, or streamers. Streamers are usually formed in plastics conveying as the plastic is heated and softened during conveying, leaving plastic residue inside the conveying line that eventually peels off in strips; streamers generally cause more significant conveying problems than dust or fines. But dust, fines, and streamers can all cause a range of problems, including plugging the outlets of bins and silos, feed hoppers, dust collectors, cyclones, and other vessels; jamming rotary valves; preventing slide gates from fully closing; and causing cross-contamination between conveyed materials.

Dust and fines usually result from these conditions in a pneumatic conveying system:
- The conveying velocity is very high.
- The conveying line's internal surface is rough.
- The conveying line has too many bends.
- The material-to-gas ratio is too low.
- The conveyed material is brittle.

Streamers usually result from these conditions:
- The conveyed material is soft.
- The conveying line's internal surface is smooth.
- The conveying velocity is very high.
- The conveying gas temperature is high.
- The conveying line temperature is high.
- The conveying line has too many long radius bends.

The best way to avoid these problems is to design a conveying system -- or improve an existing system design -- to prevent the formation of dust, fines, and streamers. A properly designed dense-phase conveying system can prevent the formation of all three. A properly designed dilute-phase conveying system can prevent streamers, but won't prevent dust and fines generation. However, a process called *elutriation* can remove dust and fines in a dilute-phase system. In this process, the conveying line passes through an elutriator, installed before the filter receiver, in which a properly designed stream of upward-moving gas separates the dust and fines from the conveyed material and carries them to the filter receiver. To prevent or substantially reduce streamer formation when conveying plastics, use the following techniques:
- Minimize the conveying velocity by using stepped lines, if necessary.
- Minimize the conveying gas temperature by using a gas cooler (for a pressure conveying system).
- Use a conveying line with a rough internal surface.
- Use as few bends as possible and, instead of long radius bends, use special bends and tees that reduce friction between the material and the bend's outer surface as the material moves through the bend.

Safety hazards: Pneumatic conveying system safety hazards can take the form of dust leaks in conveying lines, dust clouds inside enclosed vessels, electrostatic shocks, and hydrocarbon gases. Your conveying system's design must protect your plant personnel and property from these hazards.

Dust leaks in conveying lines: If your conveyed material is combustible and leaks from the conveying line, it can form a dust cloud. Such a cloud can lead to a dust explosion in an enclosed space if the material's minimum ignition energy is low (less than 10 millijoules) and a source of high-enough ignition energy (greater than 10 millijoules) is present in the area. Poor housekeeping practices can also result in the buildup of dust layers on flat surfaces inside your plant. When an explosion occurs, these dust layers will form another dust cloud and lead to a more violent secondary dust explosion. Dust leaks typically occur with a pressure conveying system. To stop such emissions from your pressure conveying system, improve the system's design by making it gas-tight. Concentrate on using gas-tight conveying line components, such as couplings and flanges that can hold the line's internal pressure without leaking. Improve your maintenance and housekeeping practices to keep plant surfaces free of dust.

Dust clouds inside enclosed vessels: Enclosed vessels -- including dust collectors, bin vent filters, filter receivers, bins, and silos -- can be explosion hazards under certain conditions. Dust collectors, bin vent filters, and filter receivers are intrinsically more susceptible to dust explosions because they collect dust and fines from the conveying gas. If these units are under an air atmosphere and have a sufficiently high source of ignition energy, a dust explosion can occur inside them. This is more likely to happen when the dust and fines have low minimum ignition energy. For example, in a pulsejet dust collector that uses bag filters and wire cages, electrostatic charge can accumulate on the filter surfaces because of the friction between each bag filter and wire cage during pulsejet cleaning. Unless the resulting charge is dissipated to ground, this charge will become concentrated on the filters, where it can become an ignition source.

Enclosed vessels -- including dust collectors, bin vent filters, filter receivers, bins, and silos -- can be explosion hazards under certain conditions.

The most common way to protect your dust collector, bin vent filter, and filter receiver from explosions is to install an explosion-relief panel on each unit. The panel will release or break open immediately after an explosion initiates in the unit, venting the explosion's quickly developing pressure into an area outside the plant or safely away from workers and other equipment. For help in determining how to select and install the relief panels, follow the guidelines in the National Fire Protection Association (NFPA) standards 68 and 69. Also make sure that in a unit with bag filters, each filter has an exposed sewn-in grounding strap that makes a firm contact with the metal cage.

This grounds the cage assembly through the unit's tube sheet. A dust explosion can also occur in a bin or silo handling a combustible dust if the vessel is under air atmosphere and an ignition source with ignition energy higher than that of the dust is present in the vessel. These conditions are more likely when the material is a granular or powdered plastic, food, chemical, or agricultural product because such materials can contain particles under 200 mesh, which are easily ignited. To prevent an explosion in your bin or silo, follow the guidelines in NFPA standards 68 and 69 for explosion-relief panels, inserting explosion suppression, electrical area classification, and grounding.

Electrostatic shocks: A worker can experience a severe electrostatic shock by contacting a conveying line whose surface has accumulated a high electrostatic charge. Such a charge can develop as the result of friction created by conveying a synthetic material or by conveying virtually any material in a plastic conveying line. Unless the charge is dissipated to ground, it will accumulate on the line's surface. In most plants, conveying lines are located in pipe racks above ground level; a worker who contacts one of these high lines and receives a severe shock can fall to the ground and be injured. An electrostatic discharge is also a hazard in an area classified as hazardous for electrical installations. If the area contains a combustible gas, such as hydrocarbon gas, an electrostatic discharge from the conveying line surface can cause the gas to ignite and lead to a potentially serious explosion. To prevent worker injuries and explosions, make sure your conveying lines are fully grounded and bonded, the grounding is continuous, and the line's resistance to ground is less than 10 ohms. Also check the grounding's continuity as part of your regular maintenance program.

Hydrocarbon gases: Materials such as plastics can produce hydrocarbon gases as they react in process vessels. When such materials are pneumatically conveyed just after they are produced, they usually contain residual hydrocarbon gases. These can evolve in the conveying system and accumulate in downstream bins and silos, where the gases create an explosion hazard in these vessels and the system's dust collector. When combined with the fine dust particles present in the vessels, the hydrocarbon gases form hybrid mixtures that are more explosive than dust or hydrocarbon gases alone. To prevent explosion hazards when conveying such a material, use an inert gas such as nitrogen instead of air for conveying. Maintain an inert atmosphere in your bins and silos to prevent a dust explosion in them. Provide enough purging countercurrent flow of inert gas into the space above the material in each vessel to reduce the hydrocarbon gas concentration to one-third of the hydrocarbon gases' lower explosivity limit.

Because inert gas is more expensive than air, you can reduce operating expenses by using a closed-loop conveying system to recycle the gas. The system also prevents excessive hydrocarbon gas buildup by removing some of the old inert gas and adding fresh gas; the system also adds more inert gas to make up for rotary valve leakage. Be aware, however, that designing a closed-loop pneumatic conveying system is more complicated than designing a conventional pressure or vacuum conveying system. The need to both recycle and add fresh inert gas to the closed-loop system while it safely handles and vents hazardous gas buildup creates a more complex system, with more components and instrumentation.

Limited conveying capacity: Limited conveying capacity in your existing conveying system is generally caused by one of three conditions: the system's blower has reached its pressure limit; the system's feeder, typically a rotary valve, has reached its feeding limit; or the conveying velocity is too low, causing the material to salt out of the conveying gas.

The blower can reach its pressure limit for any of these reasons:
- The system was originally designed for a different, easier-to-convey material.
- The conveying rate has been increased from the original design rate.
- The line routing has been changed from the original system layout.
- Additional bends or flexible hoses have been added to the conveying line.
- The original conveying system design was incorrect.

The only way to improve the conveying capacity is to thoroughly study the conveying system to determine which condition is to blame so you can correct it.

If the rotary valve can't feed material into the conveying line at your desired rate, it has reached its feeding limit. The valve's feeding capacity depends on the valve's speed, volumetric displacement per revolution, leakage rate, and fill efficiency. A very high valve speed actually reduces the feedrate because it doesn't allow enough time for each returning empty pocket to fill with material. As a general guideline, limit the rotary valve's tip speed to about 100 fpm. Also, for a pressure conveying system, properly vent your rotary valve to release leakage and displacement gases, which otherwise can reduce the valve's feeding capacity. If your existing rotary valve's fill efficiency can't be improved, install a larger rotary valve to restore your desired feeding capacity. A low material velocity in any conveying line section can limit your system's conveying capacity. The material velocity is typically about 20 percent less than the conveying gas velocity.

For a constant-diameter conveying line the gas velocity continues to increase toward the system's endpoint, but the material velocity may decrease by 20 percent or more as the material goes through a bend. If the material velocity is too close to the material's saltation velocity, the material can salt out after going through a bend. A conveying system with a few bends close to each other can make this situation worse, most likely reducing the material velocity and limiting the system's conveying velocity? To restore conveying capacity, increase the system gas flow by increasing the blower speed, but ensure that the blower pressure doesn't exceed your system design limits.

B.3 SILO PROBLEMS: PREVENTION HURTS LESS THAN THE CURE
Poorly maintained silos can end up with flow problems, contaminated material, and reduced storage space. You can prevent these problems by regular inspection and cleaning.

Whether you are storing corn flour, cement, dog food, or other dry bulk materials in silos, it's critical to consider what problems these innocuous storage towers can cause in your plant. And the biggest problems tend to come from ignoring two simple steps: regular inspection and cleaning. Here are some basic questions and answers about silo maintenance.

How regularly should silos be cleaned?: A number of factors have to be considered, including your material and the cost-to-benefit ratio. If you are storing food materials, good hygiene is essential, so you will probably have to clean food silos more frequently than silos containing other materials. Also, some nonfood materials can cake and eventually clog the silo if it's not maintained, while other nonfood materials will sit quietly for a long time and then flow easily no matter how infrequently the silo is cleaned.

Common problems in food silos: *Of course, each stored material presents its own set of problems. What kinds of problems do you run into with silos storing foods?* One of the problems that can show up in flour silos and other food silos is insects or other vermin. Even though the FDA permits some insect presence in flour, the American Institute of Baking (AIB) guidelines say that to be in compliance with AIB inspection standards, there can't be a single beetle showing up in a sifter, typically located just downstream from the silo discharge. *Bugs and other vermin seldom occupy well-maintained storage and handling equipment.*

Most of the companies routinely inspect each sifter after every shift. That's a good practice for any food manufacturer to follow. Bugs and other vermin seldom occupy well-maintained storage and handling equipment. Moisture is another problem. Material can arrive warm and moist at a plant. When it's pumped into a cold silo, condensation can occur. A dehumidifier can help prevent this, as can routine cleaning. If you don't clean regularly, moisture can present a very destructive surprise. At a silo our company was asked to clean, our workers began scraping flour from the silo's walls.

As we scraped, moisture began to appear. Soon there was so much water that it was running down the walls. The flour had been holding the condensation in place for many months. But that wasn't the worst. All that hidden moisture had caused the silo's interior coating to rust through. In some places the coating was completely gone. In others, it was flaking and could easily have flaked off into the flour as it was fed from the silo into a process. When moisture damages a silo coating, you'll sometimes see coating particles showing up in your sifter. It's a good practice to recoat your silo every few years to prevent these problems and maintain a sanitary operation. Recoating not only prevents problems like flaking, it makes the silo easier to clean.

Common problems in non-food silos:
What are the most common problems you find in silos that store materials other than foods? Buildup and clumping are two common problems. Many materials tend to stick to the silo walls. If this goes on too long, the "walls" get thicker and thicker and the storage and flow areas become smaller. At some point you might discover that you can fill the silo with half the amount of new material that you used to put in it. So you've not only lost the use of the material that's built up on the walls, but you've lost a substantial amount of your storage space as well. Depending on the material, buildup that remains in place can sometimes be difficult to remove. Some materials clump together in lumps that can clog the flow area or contaminate the material. If you start seeing small clumps in your discharged material, you would better check it out and see if you have bigger clumping problems inside the silo.

Inspect regularly: *How can you prevent these problems?* Make regular inspections part of your routine silo maintenance. One thing to look for is leaks. Leaks in a silo can be disastrous. A typical full capacity of about 130,000 pounds in a medium-sized silo can be wasted if rain or dirt gets in. Leaks can also be a source of vermin. Also look for contaminants in the discharged material. These might be biological (bugs or mold, for example), coating flakes, chunks of old material, or foreign matter. And don't forget about flow. If your flow starts to decrease or become erratic, you need to find the source of that problem early so that it doesn't get to the point where you have to shut down production for a substantial length of time to fix it.

What causes silos to leak?: Leaks can be caused by silo wall deterioration, hail or other environmental damage, or even weird accidents -- one client hired us to clean a contaminated silo that had been pierced by gunfire.

Should your inspection include anything besides looking for leaks in the silo wall?: If your silo has breather bags at the top of the silo, check them too. They allow filtered air in and out of the silo, but insects sometimes gather in them as well. Small holes in the bags can permit larger insects to enter. A good practice is to regularly examine gaskets, silo doors, and even the space under the silo if you discharge there. Look for signs of material leaks, insects, or spoiled material.

Cleaning silos: *How can you decide whether to clean a silo yourself or hire a cleaning company?*

Two key questions can help you decide: First, does the material build-up come-off the silo walls and bottom easily, or do you need to scrape or use an even tougher removal method? We once cleaned a silo for a major roofing materials manufacturer. The silo held a wet, tar-like substance that left a hard residue about 3 feet deep at the bottom and 8 inches thick on the sides. We had to "clean" the bottom with 90-pound jackhammers and chisel the sides with 30-pound jackhammers. We also had to set-up scaffolding inside the silo for the workers to stand on. This is not the kind of job most manufacturers are equipped to handle themselves.

How is silo cleaning done?: Cleaning a silo may sound simple, but it takes practice and preparation. For some jobs, it's prudent to hire an experienced contractor. One reason is the safety factor. In most cases cleaning a silo involves brushing or scraping the interior walls first. Confined-space entry regulations apply. You need to take proper personal ventilation precautions when lots of dust or volatile chemicals are present or an oxygen shortage can occur. Many silos have platforms or "cages" in the top so a worker can climb in and clean or service the area.

Before using such a cage, check it for deterioration and breakage. Even if it looks perfectly safe, make sure your workers are using a harness and a lifeline before stepping into the silo. Sometimes, instead of a built-in cage, you may need to use a "bosun's chair" to drop down from the top. The chair is attached to a rope that's lowered into the silo by a motor-driven winch or a hand-controlled winch on the chair. Any time you use a bosun's chair, make sure it's secured outside the silo and that you follow applicable OSHA (Occupational Safety and Health Standards) safety standards.

Check your silo regularly for potential troubles like insects, leaks, mold, or residue buildup, and keep small problems from becoming big ones. Commonly, you must vacuum debris from the silo bottom. This can stir up a lot of static electricity around certain materials, such as flour, creating visible sparks or even explosions. Be sure you have a way to ground the vacuum equipment. Even something as simple as a wooden pole that's in constant contact with the silo wall and is attached to the vacuum hose can safely discharge the electricity.

When does a silo require wet cleaning?: Most silos are cleaned dry. However, you can use wet washing when the stored material is easily dissolved, like sugar. Wet cleaning may take longer, and it means the silo must thoroughly dry out and the removed material will likely be lost. This can cost production time. The added moisture also invites mold. Nevertheless, in some instances wet cleaning is the only method that can be used. For example, our company once had to prep a flour silo for welding, and the only way to completely remove the explosive flour dust was by wet cleaning the silo.

Do the upkeep: *What if you don't inspect and clean your silo regularly?*

Any plant with silos should closely consider whether the vessels need cleaning or other care. Inadequate silo cleaning can rob you of storage capacity. This can cost money when a silo empties too quickly or requires more frequent visits from material suppliers. Inadequate cleaning can cause safety hazards or contamination problems and can also put you out of compliance with federal, state, and industry association regulations. Check your silo regularly for potential troubles like insects, leaks, mold, or residue buildup, and keep small problems from becoming big ones. With some hard work, a neglected silo can be restored to a decent condition, as long as it hasn't been allowed to go too long without some upkeep. The better choice? Do the upkeep all along.

B.4 SIZE REDUCTION OVERVIEW: SHEAR, COMPRESSION AND IMPACT

Whether your material must be reduced to a particle size measured in millimeters or microns, there is a machine that can handle the job. This article introduces size reduction methods and describes common examples of equipment based on each method.

Most powders that are part of our everyday lives -- in the medicines we use, the foods we eat, and the plastic parts in the appliances and computers we operate -- start out as larger particles or agglomerates that must be reduced to a specified size. But each dry bulk material has its own characteristics, and these determine which type of size reduction machine is suited to reducing it. Dry bulk materials can be reduced by equipment based on one of three methods: *shear milling, compression milling,* or *impact milling.* Shear milling produces relatively larger particles. Compression milling produces smaller particles, and impact milling typically produces the smallest particles. However, impact milling is the most energy-intensive. In fact, the smaller the particles you need, the more energy you will typically use to produce them. The following information describes common machines that apply these methods.

Shear milling equipment: In shear milling, material is cut into particles as small as a few millimeters by a machine that operates like a pair of scissors. One common example is a rotary knife cutter. This machine handles only soft materials with a Mohs hardness of less than 3, such as corn husks, plastic film and sheets, gum rubber, and tires. The feed is typically at least several inches in diameter or width. The rotary knife cutter has a set of stationary knife blades, a rotor mounted with another set of knife blades, and, typically, a perforated screen at the outlet below the rotor. The diameter of the screen holes matches the desired final top particle size. In operation, material is fed into the machine's top as the rotor spins inside the housing. The stationary and rotating blades intermesh with a clearance of typically less than 0.020 inch, cutting the material into pieces as small as 1 to 6 millimeters. On-size particles pass through the screen while oversize particles are retained until they are cut to the desired size. The cutter, depending on its size, can achieve a throughput rate of about 30 lb/hp/h.

Compression milling equipment: Compression milling applies mechanical energy to compress particles against a surface, fracturing them to sizes typically ranging from 0.5 to 100 millimeters. Conical screen mills, rotor-and-screen mills, and crushing mills are common examples of compression milling equipment. A related unit -- the media mill -- uses a combination of compression and attrition to produce sub micron particles.

Conical screen and rotor-and-screen mills: Common examples of compression milling equipment for relatively soft materials -- with a Mohs hardness of up to 3 or 3.5 -- are conical screen mills and rotor-and-screen mills. The mills are commonly applied in the food and pharmaceutical industries. Both mills use a rotor and perforated screen. In the conical screen mill, the screen is cone-shaped and the rotor is mounted with blades that match the conical screen's slope. In the rotor-and-screen mill, the screen is cylindrical and the rotor is mounted with solid. The screen's hole diameter matches the final powder's desired top particle size. The hole shape -- round, square, or rectangular -- determines the particle shape and throughput rate. In both units, the final powder's particle size is also affected by the clearance between the rotor blades or bars and the screen. In operation, material chunks up to 2 or 3 inches in diameter are fed into the mill's top, and as the rotor spins, the blades or bars compress the chunks against the screen and fracture them. On-size particles pass through the screen, and oversize particles are retained for further reduction. The mills can achieve a top particle size of about 0.5 to 3.0 millimeters and, depending on the mill size, can provide throughput rates from 1.75 to 3.5 ounces (50 to 100 grams) per batch up to 11,000 lb/h (5,000 kg/h) in continuous operation.

Crushing mill: A crushing mill (also called a *crusher* or *roll crusher*) uses compression milling to reduce relatively harder materials, including those with a Mohs hardness up to 7, such as quartz and other minerals. The mill has two large, parallel, counter-rotating rolls (or wheels). In operation, material chunks up to 2 or 3 inches in diameter are fed between the rolls, which exert high external force on the chunks as they pass between the rolls. The force compresses and fractures them to a top particle size from 1 to 100 millimeters. The mill can provide throughputs of many tons per hour.

Media mill: A media mill (also called a *ball mill*) uses both compression and *attrition* (grinding by friction) to achieve ultrafine grinding. The mill typically handles 1- to 4-millimeter mineral feeds with a maximum Mohs hardness of 8. The mill usually consists of a chamber lined with wear-resistant material and filled with wear-resistant media (0.5- to 5.0-millimeter spheres called *balls, pearls, beads,* or *sand*). The media can be dry or dispersed in a liquid, such as water, for wet-milling applications. The mill can be configured for batch or continuous milling. In operation, the feed flows into the chamber and the interstitial space between the media. A mechanical stirring device, vibratory energy, or the chamber's rotation sets the media into motion. The particles are reduced as they're compressed and ground by friction between the moving media. The smaller the media, the smaller the interstitial space between the media, and thus the greater the media contact area and the finer the ground particles will be. The mill can achieve a top particle size of less than 1 micron and throughput rates from 2.2 lb/h (1 kg/h) for a lab-size mill to 3,300 lb/h (1,500 kg/h) for a production-size unit.

Impact milling equipment: In impact milling, which can be mechanical or pneumatic, high-energy impacts fracture the particles, reducing them to sizes from 1 to 500 microns. Common impact milling equipment includes hammer mills, pin mills, air-classifying mills, and jet mills. With some of the mills, the final powder's top particle size is controlled by either a static classifier (a screen) or a dynamic classifier, which separates the on-size from oversize particles.

Hammer mill: A hammer mill is available in two types: high speed and low speed. Both have a rotor assembly consisting of several hammers or bars on a shaft inside a horizontal housing. A perforated metal screen forms a half or full circle around the rotor assembly; the screen hole size and shape control the top particle size of the final powder.

A multideflector liner (or flow deflector) is mounted above the rotor assembly, and in some cases breaker plates are mounted inside the housing close to the hammer tips.

The high-speed hammer mill, which has a hammer-tip speed from 18,000 to 22,000 fpm, typically handles foods, fine minerals, chemicals, and pharmaceuticals. The feed can have maximum size of about 3/8 to 1/2 inch and a maximum Mohs hardness of 3. The unit can handle materials with a Mohs hardness up to 6, but this requires more frequent wear inspections and parts replacement. The low-speed hammer mill, which uses a hammer-tip speed of about 12,000 fpm or less, typically handles foods, wood waste, cardboard, and similar materials as large as 3 or 4 inches with a maximum Mohs hardness of 3.

In operation, material is fed into the hammer mill's top or side, and as the rotor assembly spins, the material flows in the direction of the hammer rotation. The swinging hammers impact the airborne particles, providing most of the reduction, and then cause the particles to impact the breaker plates (if so equipped), further reducing the particles. The multideflector liner deflects the material back into the grinding zone for further reduction. As the on-size particles pass through the screen, oversize particles are retained and impacted again by the hammers until they reach the desired final size. The high-speed hammer mill can produce particles with a top size less than 75 to 250 microns; the low-speed unit produces a top size of 1.5 to 2 millimeters. Throughput rates depend on the hammermill's size; a small mill can reduce materials at a rate from 50 to 100 lb/h (22.5 to 45 kg/h), and a large one can operate at up to 12,000 lb/h (5,400 kg/h).

Pin mill: A pin mill handles feeds up to 7 to 10 millimeters with a Mohs hardness up to 2.5 or 3, including plastics, chemicals, pharmaceuticals, spices, and minerals. Because the mill has no screen, the unit is often specified for reducing cohesive or sticky materials such as pigments and materials with a high oil or moisture content. The mill housing encloses two discs, each equipped with several rows of pins, as shown in Figure (3a). One disc is stationary and the other rotates so that the pins on both discs intermesh. Another set of stationary pins can be located outside the discs. In operation, material is fed into the rotating disc's center, where centrifugal force causes the particles to accelerate outward. They pass through the rotating disc's pins, then impact the stationary disc's pins, then impact the rotating disc's pins again. This continues until the particles are reduced enough to exit through the last row of pins, which is typically stationary. Particle-to-particle impact also aids in size reduction during this process. The ground particles discharge at the disc edges and drop from the mill outlet. Controlling the rotating disc's speed and the material feedrate can produce a top particle size of less than 500 microns.

A small pin mill can reduce materials at rates as low as 22 lb/h (10 kg/h); a large unit can produce from 8,000 to 10,000 lb/h (3,600 to 4,500 kg/h).

In another version of this mill both discs rotate, either in the same or opposite directions. When the discs counter-rotate, the pin-to-pin approach velocity in the mill becomes very high, enabling the particles to be ground to less than 40 to 250 microns, depending on the material and operating conditions. A related mill, called a *universal mill*, can be fitted with various grinding components for different impact milling applications, offering more flexibility for plants that grind several materials. The mill can serve as a pin mill, as shown in Figure 3a, when equipped with discs mounted with pins. The mill can also be fitted with bars to serve as a *cage mill*, another impact mill that handles larger feeds. For other applications, the universal mill can be fitted with hammers or other grinding components.

Air-classifying mill: An air-classifying mill provides size reduction and classifying in one pass. It can handle somewhat heat-sensitive feeds, such as sugar, as well as resins, chemicals, pharmaceuticals, spices, and minerals with a maximum Mohs hardness of 3. Harder feeds require that the mill's wear parts be made of wear-resistant materials, such as ceramic or tungsten, and that the mill be inspected more frequently for wear. Feed size is typically less than 3/8 inch, depending on the mill's size. The mill consists of a circular, typically vertical, housing with a rotor assembly that has hammers (or bars). The rotor assembly is located below a variable-speed classifying wheel, and a blower is located downstream from the mill.

In operation, material is fed into the mill's side. The hammers on the spinning rotor assembly impact the particles, reducing them before they pass through the spinning classifying wheel. As they pass through the wheel, the particles reach the wheel's rotational speed; this *centripetal acceleration* throws the particles outward. The blower draws airflow from outside the wheel toward the center, drawing on-size particles through the wheel and out of the mill. Oversize particles can't pass through the wheel and are returned to the mill for further grinding. The mill's dynamic classification enables the mill to produce finer particles, typically with a top size less than 20 to 150 microns. The feedrate, rotor assembly speed, classifying wheel speed, and airflow rate control the final powder's particle size. The throughput rate depends on the mill size, with a small unit producing about 44 lb/h (20 kg/h) and a large one up to 22,000 lb/h (10,000 kg/h).

Jet mill: A jet mill can handle harder, more abrasive materials than other impact mills and can achieve a top size of less than 10 microns. It uses compressed air or another gas (such as nitrogen) as a grinding fluid. Two common types are a spiral jet mill, which doesn't use dynamic classification, and a fluidized-bed jet mill, which does.

A *spiral jet mill* (also called a *pancake mill*) handles feeds such as pharmaceuticals, cosmetics, and pigments with a particle size less than 250 microns and a Mohs hardness typically under 3. The mill consists of a flat, circular housing that encloses a grinding chamber and is equipped with an injector tube, several tangentially mounted air nozzles, and a central outlet. The mill has no moving parts. In operation, material is fed through the injector tube into the grinding chamber. The air nozzles inject compressed air (or another gas) into the grinding chamber, creating a spiral flow pattern inside the chamber.

As the particles pass these nozzles, they accelerate and impact other particles and the chamber wall, which fractures the particles. On-size particles exit the central outlet with the airflow, while centrifugal force retains oversize particles inside the chamber against the wall until they are reduced to the desired size. The mill's lack of moving parts makes it suitable for highly reactive materials such as solid rocket propellant and pyrotechnic powders. Varying the material feedrate, air pressure, and air nozzle diameter and angle can control the final powder's particle size. A small jet mill can achieve a throughput rate of 17 oz/h (500 g/h), and a large unit can produce up to 440 lb/h (200 kg/h).

A *fluidized-bed jet mill* can handle hard feeds with a Mohs hardness of 10 and a particle size up to 3 or 4 millimeters, including minerals, ceramics, tungsten carbide, and diamonds. The mill is similar to a spiral jet mill. However, instead of tangential air nozzles, this mill has several opposing nozzles that direct airflow into the grinding chamber's center, and instead of a central outlet, the mill has a rotating classifying wheel at the chamber's top to provide dynamic classification of the ground particles.

In operation, material is fed into the mill's side and, as the air flows at high speed through the nozzles, it fluidizes the particles in the grinding chamber. The opposing airstreams contact the fluidized particles and accelerate them to the chamber's center, where they collide at very high speeds and, in effect, grind each other. The air and particles flow upward to the rotating classifying wheel; air and on-size particles exit through the wheel and oversize particles fall back into the grinding chamber for further reduction. Unlike other mills, the entire mill typically rests on load cells so the material weight in the grinding chamber can be monitored and maintained for process control. The final powder's particle size distribution, which is typically narrower than that provided by the spiral jet mill, can be controlled by varying the quantity of material in the grinding chamber, air pressure, air nozzle type and diameter, and classifying wheel speed. A small unit can process 2.2 lb/h (1 kg/h); a large unit can produce up to 5 t/h.

Choosing the right machine: Work closely with a size reduction equipment supplier to determine which machine is best for your material and production requirements. Preliminary questions to expect from the supplier include those about your feed particle size and other feed characteristics (such as explosivity), your desired final particle size, and the required production rate. During the selection process, you will need to indicate how much headroom and floor space is available for the equipment in your plant and how the equipment will fit into your overall operation -- for instance, whether it will handle the first, middle, or final step in your process line and what other equipment is included in the line.

The supplier will recommend a size reduction machine based on the information you supply. In most cases, the supplier will run a series of lab tests with your feed on a pilot- or production-scale unit to determine precisely which model, features, and motor size are best suited to your application. The test results can also help fine-tune your milling process for maximum efficiency

B.5 THE THREE R'S OF ANALYZING PARTICLE SIZE

Controlling your product's particle size distribution can be a challenge, but meeting this challenge can provide big rewards when it comes to the product's performance. This article explains how using a particle size analyzer that satisfies the three Rs -- resolution, repeatability, and "right on" accuracy -- can help you meet your product specifications. The information concentrates on analyzers based on laser light-scattering technology.

Particles that meet your product's target size ensure that the product reacts, as it should during subsequent processing or use by your customer. Off-spec particles can have the opposite effect. If your chemically reactive product's particle size is too small, the product can cause a dangerously fast reaction during processing or use. For example, a pharmaceutical containing an active ingredient that has smaller particles than specified can dissolve too fast in the human body and release too much medication. If your product's particles are too large, the product can either react too slowly or not react at all. For example, gunpowder with overly large particles can react too slowly to propel a bullet out of a gun. Off-spec particles can also cause your production process to go out of control, even bringing the process to a halt.

One way to prevent these problems and effectively control your particle size is to use a particle size analyzer that satisfies the three Rs -- *resolution, repeatability,* and *"right on" accuracy*. The analyzer type we will be discussing is based on laser light-scattering (also called *laser diffraction*) technology, which is the one of the most popular sizing methods because of its speed and versatility. In a laser light-scattering particle size analyzer, a laser light beam irradiates particles in a representative sample of your product. The particles are dispersed in dry or wet form in a transparent sample cell; for a dry sample, the particles are suspended in air, and for a wet sample, the particles are diluted in liquid. As the light from the laser passes through the sample cell, detector elements inside the analyzer measure the intensity of light scattered by the particles. The analyzer's computer determines the sample's particle size distribution based on the measured light from the scattering pattern and Mie theory calculations Let's explore how an analyzer can provide the resolution, repeatability, and "right on" accuracy you need to effectively control your product's particle size.

Resolution: Resolution is the particle size analyzer's ability to see very small differences in your product's measured particle size distribution from one batch to another. Measuring such differences is important because the differences can cause the product to perform differently from one batch to the next. The analyzer should also provide enough resolution to show small differences in two very similar particle size distributions. Why is this baseline-to-baseline resolution important? You need to know exactly what particle sizes are in your product to ensure that it performs to your expectations and, if off-spec particles are shown, to help you determine where they're coming from. Sizing tests that provide baseline-to-baseline resolution can clearly show any off-spec particle sizes. An analyzer with lower resolution may only show a lump or bump in the distribution curve, making the exact sizes of these off-spec particles and, hence, their origin, much less certain. In fact, if two ingredients in the same product have similar distribution curves, a low-resolution particle size analyzer may not even be able to show that the two distributions exist.

Repeatability: Repeatability is the particle size analyzer's ability to produce the same sizing results for the same sample no matter who performs the sizing test or when or where the test is done. An analyzer is of little use if different operators get different sizing results for the same sample. The results should match whether the tests are performed by one or many different operators, whether they are performed two or more times at 1-hour or 6-month intervals, and whether the product is tested in your lab or your customer's lab (which requires that both labs use the same analyzer model).*You need to know exactly what particle sizes are in your product to ensure that it performs to your expectations.*

"Right on" accuracy: Accuracy is the particle size analyzer's ability to give the correct sizing results without external prompting or setting controls on the analyzer. For example, assuming that a sample from a given product batch has a monomodal particle size distribution (that is, the distribution curve has one peak -- one average particle size) and then setting your analyzer to test the sample under this assumption can provide incorrect sizing results if your batch's size distribution has changed for some reason during processing and become bimodal or polymodal (producing a distribution curve with two or more peaks). Of course, the same inaccuracy can result if you set the analyzer to measure a bimodal distribution and your sample ends up having a monomodal distribution. The end result, depending on the magnitude of the error introduced by the operator's assumption and its effect on the product's properties, could be that an entire product batch is out of specification.

Table B.1
Reported and measured particle sizes for three reference materials

1	400	404.0	4.0	1.0
2	764	782.5	18.5	2.4
3	1,004	1,010.0	6.0	0.6

Thus, to produce accurate results, the analyzer shouldn't depend on the operator's assumptions. For example, in the sizing tests of the three sets of standard reference polystyrene beads the operator made no assumptions about the particle size distributions of each sample. The reported particle sizes of the three samples are listed in Table I, along with the particle sizes measured by the analyzer. The table shows that the measured sizes agree closely with the samples' reported sizes. Thus, the analyzer was able not only to correctly identify the three size distributions and produce correct sizing results for each, but it did so without relying on any assumptions by the operator. Such accuracy can help you maintain your product's particle size consistency from batch to batch.

Another factor that affects accuracy is the analyzer's ability to inform the operator that the prepared sample's particle concentration in the sample cell is adequate for performing the sizing analysis and for reporting the particles' dispersion level in the sample cell. Most laser light-scattering analyzers have monitors and controls for automatically adjusting the particles' concentration level and the energy used to properly disperse the sample in the cell. If an analyzer fails to make these adjustments, its conclusions about the sample's fitness for size analysis can be wrong, which will produce inaccurate sizing results.

Choosing an analyzer to achieve the three Rs: To choose a laser light-scattering particle size analyzer that will provide resolution, repeatability, and "right on" accuracy, you need to consider how the instrument processes the information the scattered light reveals about your sample and how it calculates sizing results.

How it processes the information: Some laser light-scattering analyzers use a photodiode array to process the light scattered by the particles in the sample. In this method, fewer than 150 detector elements with a limited light-sensitivity range sense the scattered light. The result can be a possible loss of detail due to over- or underexposure of the detector elements, depending on the laser beam's intensity.

To avoid this problem, you can select a light-scattering analyzer with a charge-coupled device (CCD) for collecting the scattered light from the laser beam. Instead of fewer than 150 detector elements, the CCD has 1.3 million, which are called *pixels*. Although the CCD isn't large enough to intercept all of the scattered light at once, the laser beam -- and, hence, the scattered light -- is moved through as many as 10 different angles to cover the entire required size analysis range. When the scattered light moves to a new angle, the CCD is remapped (that is, the appropriate CCD pixels are directed to sense the scattered light based on where the center of the laser beam is now located) to maintain the results' accuracy. Thus, moving the laser beam 10 times, which moves the scattered light through 10 angles, has the effect of yielding 13 million detector elements.

The analyzer should be able to detect any and all particle size distributions in a sample and be able to resolve them into individual distribution curves.

Not only does this increase the analyzer's sensitivity and accuracy, it eliminates a need to check the laser beam's alignment with the analyzer's other components, which must be done with a photodiode array analyzer. The CCD can also make multiple exposures of the scattered light at one angular position. For instance, if one area in the particle sample is underexposed at one angle, the CCD sends this information to the computer. The computer then orders the analyzer to make another exposure at a higher light level. This procedure continues until the CCD captures all information in the scattered light, preventing data losses by over- or underexposure. All the gathered information is used to calculate the sample's particle size distribution.

How it calculates sizing results: For best results, the analyzer should be able to detect any and all particle size distributions in a sample and be able to resolve them into individual distribution curves. As discussed previously, the analyzer should be able to do this without requiring the operator to make any assumptions about the sample's particle size distribution.

To have this capability, the analyzer's method for calculating sizing results must conform as closely as possible to the theoretical model on which the analyzer's operation and calculation method are based. The analyzer's distribution calculations should be based on the Mie light-scattering theory. A subset of this theory includes Fraunhofer calculations for light-scattering phenomena, which makes the Mie theory more inclusive than the Fraunhofer calculations alone. For a given sample, the analyzer's light-scattering curve -- which plots the relative intensity of light sensed by the analyzer against the laser beam angle (in degrees from the beam's center) -- should match the Mie theoretical light-scattering pattern for the sample.

Using your sizing results for process control: A laser light-scattering particle size analyzer that satisfies the three Rs -- resolution, repeatability, and "right on" accuracy -- provides benefits for both you and your customer. When you both use an analyzer model that meets these requirements, you can agree on your product's particle size, no matter which operator is doing the analysis or when and where the analysis is done.

The analyzer's sizing results also allow you to monitor your process and spot any particle size distribution trends that can lead to an out-of-specification product. To do this, install statistical process control (SPC) software in your analyzer's computer or your process control system. The software can automatically plot the data from your particle size analyzer in SPC chart form to show how closely your product's size distribution matches your expected control level. This allows you to make corrections to your process before serious problems have a chance to develop.

Appendix – C
BULK SOLIDS FOR STORAGE AND HANDLING

C.1 INTROUCTION

The controlled flow of particulate solids is a fundamental requirement for reliable and efficient operation of virtually all bulk storage, handling and processing installations. The scale and manner of bulk storage and the means to regulate the flow of solids rates varies widely. So do the ways in which flow reliability, flow uniformity and feed accuracy deviate from required standards of performance. Despite advances in powder technology, many types of problems arise in the field of storage and feeding of bulk materials. The root of these problems is that loose solids exist in a vast range of conditions and possess wide-ranging and complex rheological properties. These inherent difficulties are further aggravated by the multitudinous duties and extensive range of ambient conditions that have to be accommodated in industrial applications.

The key to efficient storage and feeding of bulk solids is securing reliable and consistent flow. When the chosen material is free flowing and in a suitable condition under all conditions of use, control of the flow rate is usually simple. Difficulties in solids feeding mainly revolve around attaining a stable density and a satisfactory flow state of the material being handled. Good design is founded upon a systematic understanding of powder behaviour, flow patterns and equipment mechanics. Means to achieve this end are explored in these papers, together with a review of the varied forms of problems that are commonly encountered and how these may be resolved.

C.2 SPECIFICATION OF BULK SOLIDS FOR STORAGE AND HANDLING

A prerequisite of any design study and a sound basis for plant specification, is to establish firm parameters for the duty and specification of the equipment. Whilst flow related properties of bulk solids could be measured, they rarely figure in contractual documents connected with the specification for supply of solids storage and handling equipment for various reasons. In some cases the material is not available for testing before production commences. Powder testing devices are not widely available and sometime the cost of comprehensive tests is not considered viable in relation to the equipment value. More usually however, the method adopted is to provide the name and a brief description of the material, and supply 'typical' samples on request.

The host of features that characterize how a bulk material will behave within a particular storage and handling situation exacerbates these handicaps to a scientific approach. Basic information as to bulk density and wall friction are relatively simple to define and measure. Information as to the bulk strength and deformation behaviour of a bulk solid is inherently more complex. Fundamental to the problem is that there is no single or 'once only' flow property measurement for any given bulk material. Even if there were one for given conditions, the interaction of equipment geometry, materials of construction, and variables of operation and environmental conditions, could lead to this generalized information being misleading. It is most important to appreciate that measurements of the flow properties of a bulk materials refer only to one specific condition of the material, and that any physical change in the material totally invalidates the design value of these measurements. Tests must be conducted for different product conditions if the material is likely to vary in any physical manner, such as particle size composition or moisture content, and measurements taken for the 'worst' condition used as a basis for relevant design features.

It is also important to note that the characteristics of interest differ widely according to the application. Aspects of material quality and hygiene, safety and operator considerations, features of the site and preferred form of equipment are all application related. The supply consistency of the bulk material must also be taking into account. The effect of multiple sourced products, operation and process variables, constituent changes, homogeneity of the bulk and the stability of the material with time or ambient variables, are vitally important with respect to how the material will behave.

To address this awkward situation the Bulk Solids Handling Committee of the Institution of Mechanical Engineers produced a document, setting out a format for the specification of bulk solids for storage and handing purposes [I. Mech. E. 1996]. The publication includes basic fact sheets (Tables C.1 and C.2), supplemented with queries concerning differing features of possible interest.

Table C.1: Specification of a Bulk Solid

For a storage or mechanical handling application (as recommended by the I. Mech. E. Bulk Materials Handling Committee)

Client / Ref	Company ....
Process Duty	Location ....
Special Ambient Condition	**Equipment under consideration**
....	....
Properties of the Bulk Material	**Density** [kg/m^3]
- Generic Name	- Loosely Poured . . . .
- Source or Sample	- Lightly Tapped . . . .
- Trade Name	- Aerated . . . .
- Size of Sample	- Material Compactable - Yes/No
- Clients Ref	**Flow Condition**
- Date of Sample	- Free Flowing - Yes/No
Individual Product - Yes/No	- Cohesive - Yes/No
Description	- Interlocking - Yes/No
- Appearance	- 'Cakes' - Yes/No
- Colour	Pour angle of Repose

MECHANICAL OPERATIONS — APPENDIX – C : BULK SOLIDS FOR STORAGE AND HANDLING

- Ambient Temp . . . . °C - Texture **Uniformity** - Homogeneous - Yes/No - Stable - Yes/No - Consistent - Yes/No **Physical Composition** - Particle Size Range: Min . . . . . Max . . . . . - Particle Shape **Moisture Content** [W/W basis] - Total . . . . % - Free . . . . % - Inherent . . . . % - Bound . . . . % **Melting / Softening temperature**	- Variable Yes/No - degrees . . . . . Slip Properties - Contact Face - Surface Finish - Friction angle Shear cell test results: Particle size distribution: Known handling problems: . . . . Sensitive product properties : Any other relevant information : . . . . Signed : _____

Table C.2: Features of the Bulk Material

The features are to be graded according to the following scales:

	IMPORTANCE	HAS EFFECTS ON
	1 Insignificant	1 Health and Safety
	2 Significant	2 Performance of the Equipment
	3 Important	3 Value or use of the Product
	4 Extreme	4 Design/Durability of Equipment
		5 Environment

	IMPORTANCE Circle One Only	HAS EFFECTS ON Circle ALL relevant
Segregates readily	1 2 3 4	1 2 3 4 5
Tends to 'Flood'	1 2 3 4	1 2 3 4 5
Cohesive / Sticky	1 2 3 4	1 2 3 4 5
Fibrous / Interlocking	1 2 3 4	1 2 3 4 5
Degrades / Deteriorates	1 2 3 4	1 2 3 4 5
Agglomerates	1 2 3 4	1 2 3 4 5
Abrasive	1 2 3 4	1 2 3 4 5
Melts at .... °C	1 2 3 4	1 2 3 4 5
Hygroscopic Deliquesces	1 2 3 4	1 2 3 4 5
Cakes / Sets Hardens	1 2 3 4	1 2 3 4 5
Reactive	1 2 3 4	1 2 3 4 5
Flammable	1 2 3 4	1 2 3 4 5
Explosive	1 2 3 4	1 2 3 4 5
Corrosive	1 2 3 4	1 2 3 4 5
Radioactive	1 2 3 4	1 2 3 4 5
Prevention of Contamination	1 2 3 4	1 2 3 4 5
High / Low Temperature	1 2 3 4	1 2 3 4 5

Ambient Gas	1 2 3 4	1 2 3 4 5
At Pressure ..... Bar	1 2 3 4	1 2 3 4 5
Hygiene requirements	1 2 3 4	1 2 3 4 5
Dusty, Dirty	1 2 3 4	1 2 3 4 5
Irritant	1 2 3 4	1 2 3 4 5
Odours / Fumes / Vapours	1 2 3 4	1 2 3 4 5
Toxic / Ingestion Hazard	1 2 3 4	1 2 3 4 5
Sharp / Penetrating	1 2 3 4	1 2 3 4 5
Unpleasant	1 2 3 4	1 2 3 4 5
Valuable	1 2 3 4	1 2 3 4 5

It is essential to supply all fire, safety, health, and environmental impact information and any other relevant details.

Quantified values are essential for predictable designs and tend to figure increasingly with quality programmes and design verification procedures. There remain certain features that are judgement related and essentially must fall within the province of the user to rank as to their importance. For these it is necessary to utilise a grading system indicating the degree to which the suitability of equipment may be effected. Whereas some aspects may not be relevant in particular cases, a systematic review of this type prompts attention so that no feature is overlooked by default. Guide notes outlining test procedures and their relevance are also included in the publication.

Two comprehensive studies of plants that handle bulk solids have shown that their performance efficiency compares very unfavourably with plants handling liquids and gasses [Merrow 1981 and 1985]. More significantly, this discrepancy has shown little signs of improvement compared with plant built in the sixties, despite the advances made in bulk technology since that time. It is clear that steps taken to introduce the use of more quantified values for equipment design must progress alongside the diffusion of knowledge in particulate solids technology, for performance standards to improve in the ubiquitous industries that handle bulk solids. Hence, one reason for this article and the means adopted for its propagation.

References:
1. Mech. E. (Bulk Materials Handling Committee), "Guide to the Specification of Bulk Materials for Storage and Handling Applications" (1996).
2. Jenike, A. W., "Storage and Flow of Solids", Engg. Exp. Station Bulletin 123 (Univ. of Utah, 1970).
3. Merrow E. W., K. E. Phillips, and C.W. Myers, "Understanding Cost Growth and Performance Shortfalls in Pioneering Process Plants", in Rand Corporation Report, Section V (1981).
4. Merrow E. W., "Linking R & D to Problems Experienced in Solids Processing", *Chem. Eng. Processing*, May 1985, pp. 14-22.

Appendix – D
BIN AND HOPPER DESIGN

D.1 INTRODUCTION

Bins are used by a wide range of industries throughout Europe to store bulk solids in quantities ranging from a few tonnes to over one hundred thousand tonnes. Bins are also called bunkers and silos. They can be constructed of steel or reinforced concrete and may discharge by gravity flow or by mechanical means. Steel bins range from heavily stiffened flat plate structures to efficient unstiffened shell structures. They can be supported on columns, load bearing skirts, or they may be hung from floors. Flat bottom bins are usually supported directly on foundations.

For structural design, it is convenient to classify bins using the BMHB system into the following four categories:

Class 1: Small bins holding less than 100 tonnes are simply and robustly constructed often with substantial reserves of strength.

Class 2: Intermediate bins, between 100 and 1000 tonnes, can be designed using simple hand calculations. Care is required to ensure reliable flow and predictable wall pressures.

Class 3: Large bins, over 1000 tonnes. Specialist knowledge of bins is required to prevent problems due to uncertainties of flow, pressure and structural behavior. Sophisticated finite element analyses of the structure may be justified.

Class 4: Eccentrically discharging bins where the eccentricity of the outlet e_o is greater than 0, 25 times the silo diameter, d_c.

Bin Design Procedures:

It consists of four parts as follows:

1. Determine the strength and flow properties of the bulk solid.
2. Determine the bin geometry to give the desired capacity, to provide a flow pattern with acceptable flow characteristics and to ensure that discharge is reliable and predictable. Specialized mechanical feeder design may be required.
3. Estimate the bin wall loads from the stored material and other loads such as wind, ancillary equipment, thermal etc.
4. Design and detail the bin structure.

Before the structural design can be carried out, the loads on the bin must be evaluated. Loads from the stored material are dependent, amongst other things, on the flow pattern, the properties of the stored material and the bin geometry while the methods of structural analysis and design depend upon the bin geometry and the flow pattern. The importance of Stages (1) and (2) of the design should not be underestimated.

2. Bin Classification:

For design purposes, their size, geometry, and the type of flow classify bins during discharge of the contents, and the structural material of the wall. The importance of each of these parameters in design is discussed below.

D.2 BIN SIZE AND GEOMETRY

The bin size and geometry depend on the functional requirements such as the storage volume and the method and rate of discharge, the properties of the stored material, available space and economic considerations. Bins usually consist of a vertical sided section with a flat bottom or a bottom with inclined sides, known as the hopper. They are usually circular, square or rectangular in cross-section and may be arranged singly or in groups. Typical bin geometries are shown in Fig. D.1.

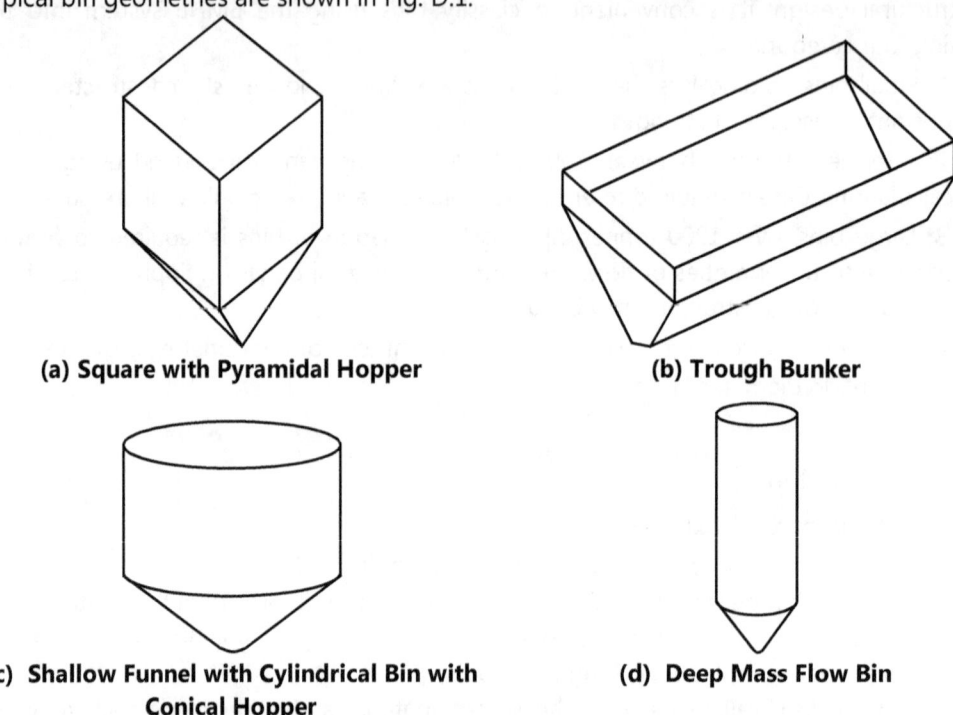

(a) Square with Pyramidal Hopper
(b) Trough Bunker
(c) Shallow Funnel with Cylindrical Bin with Conical Hopper
(d) Deep Mass Flow Bin

Fig. D.1: Typical Bin Geometries

Circular bins are more efficient structures than square or rectangular bins, leading to lower material costs. For the same height, a square bin provides 27% more storage than a circular bin whose diameter equals the length of the side of the square bin. Flat-bottom bins require less height for a given volume of stored material. The bin size is determined by feeding and discharge rates and the maximum quantity of material to be stored. High discharge rates require deep hoppers with steep walls. Flat-bottomed bins usually have low discharge rates and are used when the storage time is long, the discharge is infrequent and the storage volume is high.

The ratio of bin height to diameter influences the loads from the stored material and hence the structural design. Squat bins are defined as those where the height does not exceed 1.5 times the diameter or smallest side length. Slender bins have a height to diameter ratio greater than 1.5.

Hoppers are usually conical, pyramidal or wedge shaped. Pyramidal hoppers have the advantage of being simple to manufacture although they may lead to flow problems due to the building up of stored material in the corners. Outlets may be either concentric or eccentric to the centre of the bin. Eccentric outlets should be avoided because the pressure distribution is difficult to predict and there may be problems due to segregation of the stored material. The angle of inclination of the hopper sides is selected to ensure continuous discharge with the required flow pattern.

D.3 TYPE OF FLOW

Two types of flow are described and shown in Fig. D.2. They are mass flow and funnel flow. Discharge pressure is influenced by the flow pattern and so the flow assessment must be made before the calculation of loads from the stored material. In mass flow bins, all the contents of the bin flow as a single mass and flow is on a first-in first-out basis. The stored material in funnel flow bins flows down a central core of stationary stored material and flow is on a last-in, first-out basis.

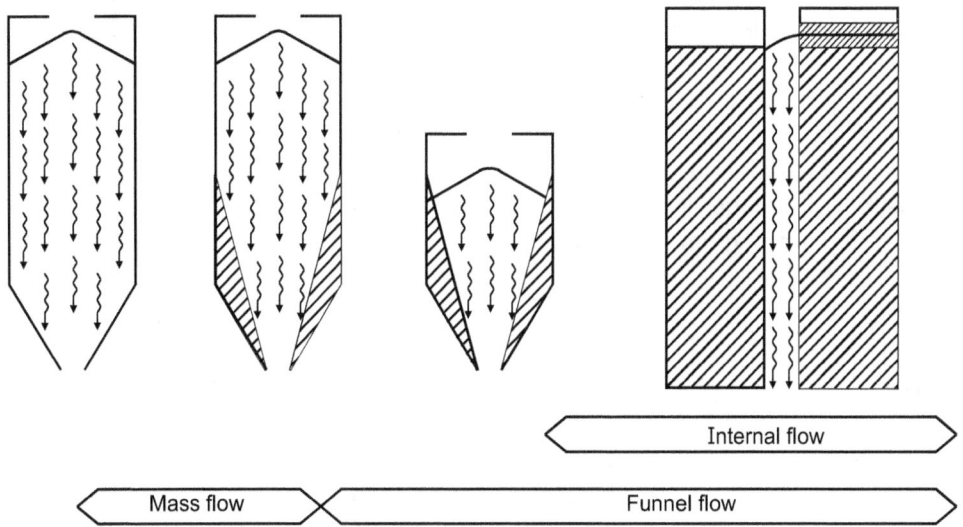

Fig. D.2: Flow Patterns

The flow type depends on the inclination of the hopper walls and the coefficient of wall friction. Mass flow occurs in deep bins with steep hopper walls whereas funnel flow occurs in squat bins with shallow hopper walls.

D.4 FLOW PROBLEMS

Typical problems, which occur at the storage of bulk solids, are:

- **Arching:** If a stable arch is formed above the outlet so that the flow of the bulk solid is stopped, then this situation is called arching (Fig. D.3 (a)). In case of fine grained, cohesive bulk solid, the reason of arching is the strength (unconfined yield strength) of the bulk solid which is caused by the adhesion forces acting between the particles. In case of coarse-grained bulk solid, blocking of single particles causes arching. Sufficiently large outlets can prevent arching.

Fig. D.3 (a): Arching

- **Ratholing** occurs in case of funnel flow if only the bulk solid above the outlet is flowing out, and the remaining bulk solid - the dead zones - keeps on its place and forms the rathole. The reason for this is the strength (unconfined yield strength) of the bulk solid. If the bulk solid consolidates increasingly with increasing period of storage at rest, the risk of ratholing increases. If a funnel flow silo is not emptied completely in sufficiently small regular time intervals, the period of storage at rest can become very large thus causing a strong time consolidation.

Fig. D.3 (b): Ratholing

- **Irregular flow** occurs if arches and ratholes are formed and collapse alternately. Thereby fine grained bulk solids can become fluidized when falling downwards to the outlet opening, so that they flow out of the silo like a fluid. This behaviour is called flooding. Flooding can cause a lot of dust, a continuous discharge becomes impossible.
- **Wide residence time distribution:** If dead zones are formed (funnel flow), the bulk solid in these zones is discharged only at the complete emptying of the silo, whereas bulk solid, which is filled in later, but located closer to the axis of the silo, is discharged earlier. Because of that, a wide distribution of residence time appears which is disadvantageous in some cases (e.g. in case of storage of food or other products changing their properties with time).

- **Segregation:** If a heap is formed on the bulk solids' surface at filling of the silo, segregation is possible according to particle size or particle density (Fig. D.3 (c)). In case of centric filling as shown in Fig. D.3 (c), the larger particles accumulate close to the silo walls, while the smaller particles collect in the centre. In case of funnel flow, the finer particles, which are placed close to the centre, are discharged first while the coarser particles are discharged at the end. If such a silo is used, for example, as a buffer for a packing machine, this behavior will yield to different particle size distributions in each packing. In case of a mass flow, the bulk solid will segregate at filling in the same manner, but it will become "remixed" when flowing downwards in the hopper. Therewith, at mass flow the segregation effect described above is reduced significantly.

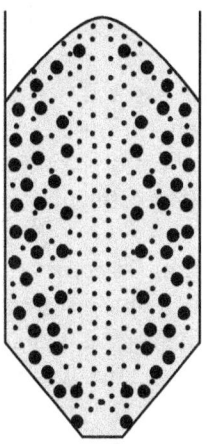

Fig. D.3 (c): Segregation

In a funnel flow silo, all problems mentioned above can occur generally, while in case of mass flow only arching has to be considered: segregation, ratholing, irregular flow and flooding of the bulk solid do not appear in a well designed mass flow silo. Two steps are necessary for the design of mass flow silos: The calculation of the required hopper slope, which ensures mass flow, and the determination of the minimum outlet size to prevent arching.

D.5 STRUCTURAL MATERIAL OF THE BIN WALL

Most bins are constructed from steel or reinforced concrete. The economic choice depends upon the material costs as well as the costs of fabrication and erection. Other factors such as available space also influence the selection. The main advantages of steel bins over cost in-situ concrete bins are:
- Small and medium sized steel bins and bunkers can be prefabricated and, therefore, their erection time is considerably shorter;
- Bolted bins are relatively easy to disassemble, move, and rebuild in another location;

The main disadvantages of steel bins are the necessity of maintenance to prevent corrosion, the steel walls may require lining to prevent excessive wear, and the steel walls are prone to condensation, which may damage stored products such as grain and sugar etc., which are moisture sensitive.

The selection of structural material for the wall may depend upon the bin geometry. A bin wall is subject to both vertical and horizontal forces. The vertical forces are due to friction between the wall and stored materials, while the horizontal forces are due to lateral thrust from the stored materials. Reinforced concrete bins carry vertical compressive forces with ease and so tend to fail in tension due to the high lateral thrusts. Steel bins, circular in plan, usually carry the lateral forces by hoop tension. They are more prone to failure by buckling under excessive vertical forces. The increase of horizontal and vertical pressure with depth is shown in Figure D.4. Increases in horizontal pressure are negligible beyond a certain depth and therefore concrete bins are more efficient if they are tall, whereas steel bins tend to be shallower structures.

Hopper Design:

Mankind have stored powdered materials for thousands of years, at least as far back as man has harvested and stored crops. Prior to the 1960s storage bins were designed largely by guessing. This was all changed by the research of Andrew W. Jenike in the 1960s. His work identified the criteria that affect material flow in storage vessels. Jenike developed the theory and methods to apply the theory, including the equations and measurement of the necessary material properties. His primary works are published in "Gravity Flow of Bulk Solids", Bulletin 108, University of Utah Engineering Experiment Station, October 1961, and Bulletin 123, November 1964.

Hoppers are used in industry for protection and storage of powdered materials. Hoppers must be designed such that they are easy to load. More importantly, hoppers must be designed such that they are easy to unload.

The way the hopper is designed affects the rate of flow of the powder out of the hopper, *if it flows at all*. Also, the way the hopper is designed affects how much of the stored material can discharge and whether there mixing of solid sizes or dead space that reduces the effective holding capacity of the hopper. These issues and others discussed here are important to consider when designing storage hoppers.

Flow Modes:

There are two primary and distinct types of flow of solids in hoppers, *mass flow* and *funnel flow*. There is also a special case that is a combination of these two flows called *expanded flow*. These flows get their names from the way in which solids move in the hoppers. The characteristics and differences between the flows are depicted in Figure 10-1.

The primary difference between mass and funnel flow is that in mass flow all of the material in the bin is in motion, though not necessarily all with the same velocity. In funnel flow only a core of material in the center above the hopper outlet is in motion while material next to the walls is stationary (stagnant).

Hoppers come in a variety of shapes and designs, not just conical. Figure D.5 shows some of the more common designs found for mass flow hoppers. Also, a variety of designs are possible for funnel flow hoppers, shown in Fig. 10.

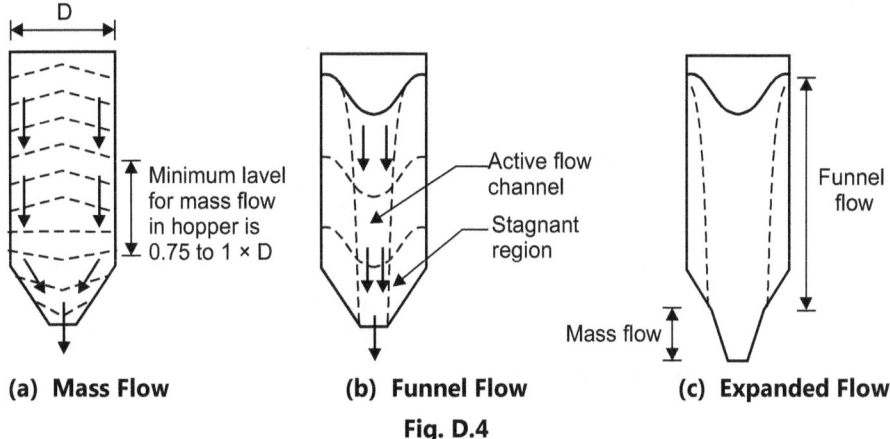

Fig. D.4

In mass flow (A) all material moves in the bin including near the walls. In funnel flow (B) the material moves in a central core with stagnant material near the walls. Expanded flow (C) is a combination of mass flow in the hopper exit and funnel flow in the bin above the hopper (normally used in retrofit situations).

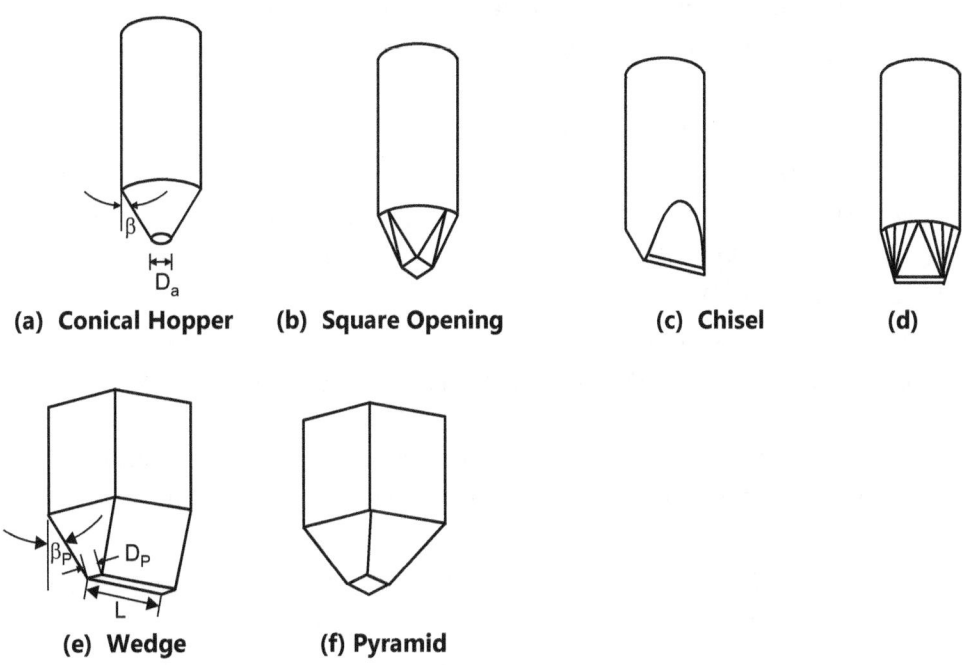

Fig. D.5: Common Designs for Mass Flow Hoppers

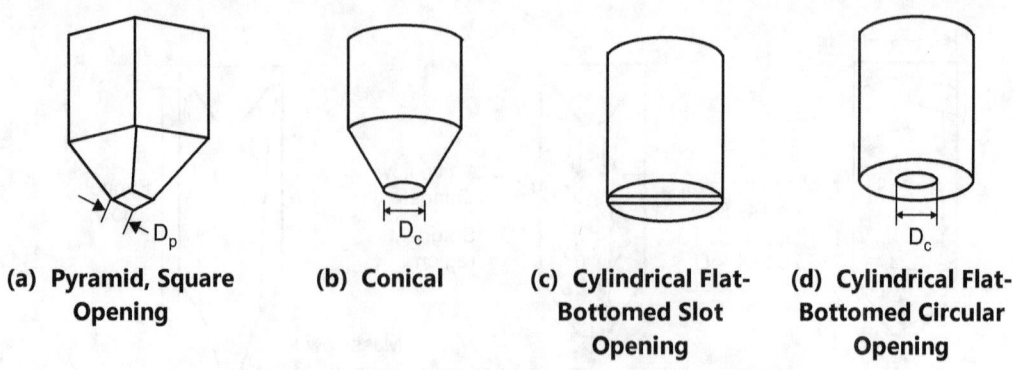

Fig. D.6: Common Designs for Funnel Flow Hoppers

Hopper Design Problems:

Hopper design problems are normally one of two types; either the material does not discharge adequately from the opening in the hopper or the material segregates during the flow. The problems that we would like to solve or avoid are –

- *RATHOLING/PIPING*. Ratholing or piping occurs when the core of the hopper discharges (as in funnel flow) but the stagnant sides are stable enough to remain in place without flowing, leaving a hole down through the center of the solids stored in the bin (See Fig. D.7 (a)).
- *FLOW IS TOO SLOW*. The material does not exit from the hopper fast enough to feed follow on processes.
- *NO FLOW DUE TO ARCHING OR DOMING*. The material is cohesive enough that the particles form arch bridges or domes that hold overburden material in place and stop the flow completely (Fig. D.7 (a)).
- *FLUSHING*. Flushing occurs when the material is not cohesive enough to form a stable dome, but strong enough that the material discharge rate slows down while air tries to penetrate into the packed material to loosen up some of the material. The resulting effect is a sluggish flow of solids as the air penetrates in a short distance freeing a layer of material and the process starts over with the air penetrating into the freshly exposed surface of material (Fig. D.7 (c)).
- *INCOMPLETE EMPTYING*. Dead spaces in the bin can prevent a bin from complete discharge of the material.
- *SEGREGATION*. Different size and density particles tend to segregate due to vibrations and a percolation action of the smaller particles moving through the void space between the larger particles.

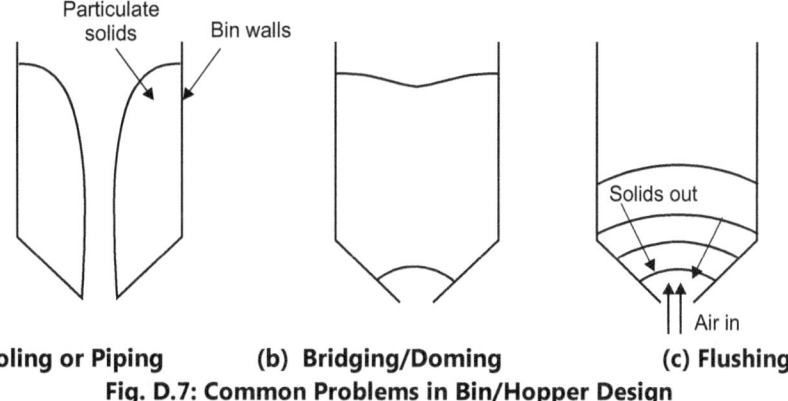

(a) Ratholing or Piping   (b) Bridging/Doming   (c) Flushing

Fig. D.7: Common Problems in Bin/Hopper Design

- *TIME CONSOLIDATION.* For many materials, if allowed to sit in a hopper over a long period of time the particles tend to rearrange themselves so that they become more tightly packed together. The consolidated materials are more difficult to flow and tend to bridge or rat hole.
- *CAKING.* Another important effect is called caking. Caking refers to the physiochemical bonding between particles what occurs due to changes in humidity. Moisture in the air can react with or dissolve some solid materials such as cement and salt. When the air humidity changes the dissolved solids re-solidify and can cause particles to grow together. A good description of this effect is given by Griffith (E. J. Griffith, *Cake Formation in Particulate Systems*, VCH Publishers, NY, 1991).

Predicting Mass Flow:

Many of the problems associated with bin and hopper design can be avoided by designing the hopper to operate in mass flow mode. The required cone angle from the vertical axis for mass flow to occur ranges from 40° to 0°.

Mass flow is not necessary in all cases. In some situations a mass flow hopper design is not practical due to the headroom required. Following table summarizes the key advantages and disadvantages of both mass flow and funnel flow hoppers. In most applications if you have a choice you want mass flow. But in the extreme cases or in cases in which mass flow is not really necessary then you may opt for the shorter funnel flow hopper design.

Table D.1: Advantages and Disadvantages of Mass and Funnel Flow Hoppers

	Mass Flow	Funnel Flow
Advantages	• Flow is more consistent. • Reduced radial segregation. • Stresses on walls are more predictable. • Effective use of full bin capacity. • First-in = First-out	• Low head room required.

	Mass Flow	**Funnel Flow**
Disadvantages	• More wear of wall surfaces. • Higher stresses on the walls. • More head room required.	• Rat holing. • Segregation. • First-in = Last-out. • Time consolidation effects can be severe. • Poor distribution of stresses on walls may cause silo collapse. • Flooding. • Reduction of effective storage capacity.

Binding Mechanisms:

There are a number of mechanisms that cause solid materials to bind together and thus make flow difficult if not impossible. Some of these have been mentioned above. Binding mechanisms include:

1. *Solids Bridge (i.e. Caking):*
   - Mineral Bridges
   - Chemical reactions
   - Partial melting
   - Binder hardening
   - Crystallization of dissolved substances
2. *Adhesions and Cohesion:*
   - There are a number of effects that are lumped together and are termed adhesion and cohesion. These include mechanically deformable particles that can plastically deform and bind to each other or with bin walls. Usually, very small particles display adhesion properties.
3. *Interfacial forces:*
   - Interfacial forces include liquid bridges and capillary forces between particles. These effects are due the contact surfaces between three phases (solid, liquid and gas) and interfacial tensions.
4. *Attractive forces:*
   - Attractive forces include intermolecular forces such as van der Waal's force, as well as longer range electrostatic and magnetic forces. There are also short-range repulsive forces, but if the particles are in close enough contact the attractive forces are stronger.
5. *Interlocking forces:*
   - Interlocking forces are due to the geometric entanglement that occurs with fibrous materials, analogous to what happens when you store coat hangers in a box - they become entangled.

Many earlier bin designs were based upon the angle of repose. However, the angle of repose alone is not sufficient to account for all of the mechanisms affecting hopper performance. The angle of repose is only useful in determining the contour of a pile, and its popularity among engineers is not due to its usefulness but due to the ease with which it can be measured.

TESTING REQUIREMENTS

To design storage hoppers, the following material properties are needed:
- Internal friction coefficient
- Wall friction coefficient
- Permeability
- Compressibility

Other factors that should be considered include temperature and moisture content along with phase diagrams if caking may be a problem.

One of the more common test apparatus is the Jenike Shear Tester. The powder sample is placed in a sample holder. The movement of the sample holder causes shear between a powder sample and a sample of the hopper wall to determine the wall friction coefficient. Or, the movement causes a shear internally in the powder sample to determine the internal coefficient of friction.

ANGLE AND OUTLET SIZE FOR MASS FLOW HOPPERS

To size and design a hopper we determine the design necessary for mass flow operation based upon the material properties. The properties that are used in the design of a mass flow hopper are the effective angle of internal friction, the material flow function, and the angle of wall friction between the powder material and the wall material.

In a mass flow hopper during discharge the stress distribution is such that stable arch or funnel flows do not occur and therefore the flow will not stop. This analysis can be used in the design of a new hopper or to check the suitability of an existing hopper for use with a particular material.

The Angle of Wall Friction:

The last property needed is the wall friction, ϕ_w between the powder and the wall of the hopper. This property is determined from experiments run with the shear tester where the measured shear force is plotted versus to the normal load (Fig. D.8). Often the data are linear. If they are non-linear then the smallest angle is used.

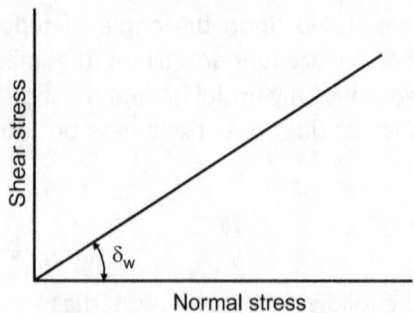

Fig. D.8: Plot to Determine the Wall Angle

References:

1. Eurocode 1: "Basis of design and actions on structures, Part 4, Actions in silos and tanks", ENV 1991-4, CEN.
2. British Materials Handling Board, "Silos - Draft design code", 1987.
3. Gaylord, E. H. and Gaylord, C. N., "Design of steel bins for storage of bulk solids", Prentice Hall, Englewood Cliffs, 1984.
4. Reimbert, M. and Reimbert, A., "Silos: Theory and practice", Trans Tech Publications, 1987.
5. Troitsky, M. S., "On the structural analysis of rectangular steel bins", Powder and Bulk Solids Technology, Vol 4, No. 4, 1980, pp 19-25.
6. Trahair, N. S. et al, "Structural design of steel bins for bulk solids", Australian Institute of Steel Construction, 1983.
7. Lambert, F. W., "The theory and practical design of bunkers", The British Construction Steelwork Association Limited, 1968.
8. Wozniak, S., "Silo design" in Structural Engineers Handbook.

Appendix – E
THE VALUE OF SIZE REDUCTION

E.1 INTRODUCTION

The breakdown of solid materials by the application of mechanical forces is also referred to as comminution. Size reduction operations can include grinding and cutting.

Size reduction in liquid foods (for example homogenisation) is covered in the "emulsification" topic in this series of articles.

The value of size reduction comes from:
- aiding the extraction of a constituent from a composite structure -- for example in making sugar from sugar cane.
- satisfying consumer or functional requirements -- for example in manufacturing of icing sugar, pineapple rings or pieces.
- increasing the ratio of surface area to volume so as to –
  -- reduce drying time.
  -- increase extraction rate.
  -- decrease heating, cooking time etc.
- improving mixing/blending -- for example in packaged soups, cake mixes etc.

E.2 GRINDING EQUIPMENT

Principles:

Forces for comminution can be applied in three basic ways:
- compressive for example, crushing rolls.
- impact for example, hammer mills.
- shear for example, attrition mills.

Often, size has to be reduced through a number of stages (for example, flour milling).

$$\text{Reduction Ratio} = F/P$$

where
F = Average size of feed.
P = Average size of product.

Coarse crushers have reduction ratios of less than 8 : 1, but fine grinders can have reduction ratios as high as 100 : 1.

Crushing rolls:
- two or more heavy steel cylinders revolve towards each other.
- an overload compression spring protects the roller surfaces from damage, but hard foreign bodies should be removed.
- the distance between the surfaces of the rollers is termed the nip.
- force applied to the product is mainly compressive, but the use of "fluted" rollers and/or differential speeds of rotation can also introduce shear forces.
- size reduction ratios are normally below five.
- volumetric capacity is affected by speed, nip, diameter and length of the rollers.

Calculations: For the limiting case, when the particle is just pulled into the rolls by friction:
$$\tan(A/2) = \mu$$
where, A = Angle of nip (the angle formed by the tangents to the roll faces at the points of contact with the particle).
μ = Coefficient of friction between the particle and the rolls.

The relationship of required roll diameter, D_r, to diameter of feed particles, D_g and diameter of product particles, D_p, is given by:
$$\cos(A/2) = (D_r + D_p)/(D_r + D_f)$$

Example: A roll mill is available with rolls of 400 mm diameter, and capable of milling to an average product particle diameter of 0.05 mm. If the coefficient of friction for the material on the rolls is 0.12, what is the largest average diameter of feed particle which could be fed to the mill?

Answer: Since $\tan(A/2) = \mu$, $A/2 = \tan^{-1} 0.12$ and thus $A/2 = 6.84°$. That is, maximum angle of nip is 13.7°. Since $\cos(A/2) = (D_r + D_p)/(D_r + D_f)$, then for 400 mm diameter rolls producing an average product particle diameter of 0.05 mm and

$$\cos(6.84) = (0.4 + 0.00005)/(0.4 + D_f)$$
$$0.993 = 0.40005/(0.4 + D_f)$$
$$0.4 + D_f = 0.40005/0.993$$
$$D_f = 0.4029 - 0.4$$
$$D_f = 0.0029$$

and so the maximum diameter of feed material would be 2.9 mm.

Hammer Mill:
- a high speed rotor carries a number of hammers around its periphery, inside a close fitting case containing a toughened breaker plate.
- reduction is mainly by impact as the hammers drive the material against the breaker plate (shear may also have a role under "choke" feeding conditions).
- final size is largely determined by the size of the retention screen through which discharge material must pass.
- regarded as general purpose mill, handling crystalline solids, fibrous materials, vegetable matter, sticky materials etc.
- due to excessive wear, hammer mills are not recommended for the fine grinding of very hard materials.

See http://www.mpd-inc.com/prod02.htm for more details.

Attrition Mills:
- mainly utilise shear between a plate and a stationary surface, or between two plates for fine grinding.

- in a single disc mill the feed stock passes between a high speed rotating grooved disc and the stationary casing of the mill.
- in a double disc mill, two discs are required, rotating in opposite directions. The pin-disc mill carries pegs or pins which intermesh on the rotating elements, so that impact forces also play a significant part in the size reduction process.
- in the Bhur mill, originally used in flour milling, the discs (or stones) are horizontal. The feed passes through the centre of the upper (stationary) disc, while the lower disc rotates. The material is subjected to shear between the two stones and exists around the periphery.

Ball Mills and Rod Mills:
- A rotating (tumbling) or vibrating chamber is filled with steel balls or rods.
- Feed material is subjected to impact and shear due to the movement of the balls or rods. Shear predominates at low speeds, while impact becomes more important at higher speeds (if speed is too high, balls can be carried around the periphery and grinding ceases).
- A variation is the use of a vibrating rather than rotating chamber.

A listing of a range of mill types (dry and wet milling) is available on the WWW through http://www.glenmills.com/

E.3 PRODUCT FACTORS INFLUENCING EQUIPMENT SELECTION

Hardness and abrasiveness of feed:

In general harder materials required more energy to comminute, therefore a longer residence time (lower throughput) or higher capacity equipment will be required. More robust construction is also required. Hard material also tends to be more abrasive, so that more wear resistant materials may be desirable (for example, manganese steel) and wearing parts should be easily replaceable. Slower speed is also desirable to reduce wear.

Internal structure of feed:

If the material is crystalline or friable in nature, compressive forces are likely to be suitable. If few lines of weakness are present and new "cracks" have to be formed, impact or shear may be more effective.

Moisture content:

Moisture can either aid or hinder comminution. With some materials, moisture above 2-3% may cause clogging of the mill, or agglomeration may occur. Too dry a condition can result in excessive dust. For some products milling may be carried out as a free flowing slurry for example, wet milling of maize.

Temperature sensitivity:

The heat generated by grinding can result in loss of heat sensitive components. Softening or melting may also be important - leading to clogging. In some cases cryogenic comminution may be necessary - cooling during milling using liquid nitrogen or dry ice for example, in milling spices or size reduction of meat.

E.4 MODES OF OPERATION OF GRINDING EQUIPMENT

Open Circuit Grinding:
- Simplest method of operating a mill. Product passes straight through, no classifying screens, no recycling of oversize.
- Wide size distribution results as some particles pass through quickly, others stay for some time (also resulting in higher energy consumption).

Free crushing:
- As with open circuit, but residence time kept to a minimum, often by material falling through action zone under influence of gravity.
- Production of undersize reduced, and lower energy consumption, but large size range.

Choke feeding:
- Discharge is restricted by inserting a screen in the outlet, so material stays choked in the action zone until reduced to a small enough size.
- Long residence time results in undersize particles and additional energy consumption.
- Useful to prevent oversize, and a large reduction ratio can be achieved.

Closed circuit grading:
- Residence time kept short, but classifier system at the outlet separates oversize material and recycles it.
- More energy efficient, with narrower range of final particle size.
- Additional cost of classifier system.

Wet milling:
- If material can be wet without harm, it may be advantageous to mill it as a slurry with a carrier liquid, often water.
- Eliminates dust problems and allows use of hydraulic separating techniques
  For example, centrifugation.
- Often used where extraction of a soluble component is also required for example, maize milling.
- Energy consumption high but tends to produce finer particles.

Reference:
1. G. Young, Size Reduction of Particulate Material, Education Resources for Particle Technology, 2003.

***

Appendix – F
ELUTRIATION OF PARTICLES FROM FLUIDIZED BEDS

Elutriation is the process in which fine particles are carried out of a fluidized bed due to the fluid flow rate passing through the bed. Typically, fine particles are elutriated out of a bed when the superficial velocity through the bed exceeds the terminal velocity of the fines in the bed. However, elutriation can also occur at slower velocities.

Fine particles are present in fluidized beds from several sources :
- Feed streams.
- Mechanical attrition or breakage of larger particles.
- Temperature stress cracking.
- Size reduction due to chemical reactions, shrinkage etc.

When fines elutriation is a significant problem and modifications to the bed design cannot aid in reducing the problem, fines can often be recovered such as with cyclones or hydrocyclones.

Leva (Chem. Engr. Prog., 47, 39, 1951) measured the rate of elutriation (total mass per time) from a bed of particles with a bimodal size distribution. He found that –

(1) When the column height above the bed is small, the elutriation rate is high. But if the height exceeds a certain minimum size then the rate is a constant minimum value (Fig. F.1). This occurs because small particles that are expelled from the top of the bed have high velocities and they require greater distance to slow down and turn around to return to the bed.

(2) The elutriation process causes a decrease in particle concentration. The concentrations may be empirically modelled by an Arrhenius type expression as –

$$C = C_0 \, e^{-Mt} \qquad \ldots (F.1)$$

where, C = Concentration at time, t;
C_0 = The initial concentration; and
M = An empirical constant.

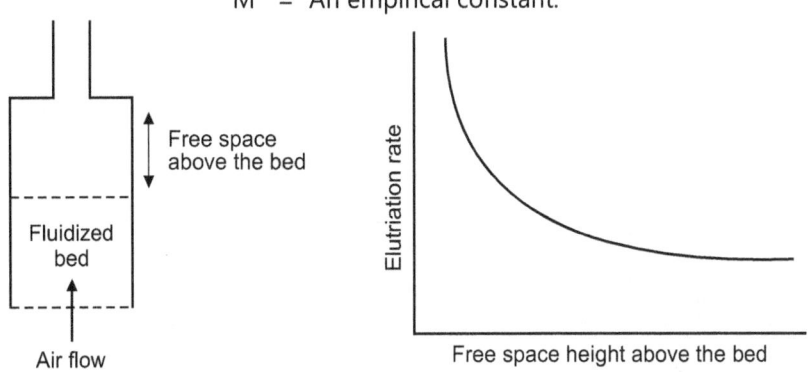

**Fig. F.1 : Elutriation Rate (total mass/time) vs. the free space height above the bed.
A fluidized bed behaves similar to a mixture of liquids with different volatilities. In the liquid-liquid mixture, the more volatile material leaves at the lower boiling temperature**

By analogy with boiling of liquid mixtures, finer particles have a lower boiling temperature than larger particles. The boiling temperature is analogous to the fluidization velocity. The free space height above the bed serves as a condenser, to cool and slow down the elutriated particles and return them to the mixture. The greater the boiling rate, the greater capacity that is needed of the condenser, hence the greater free space height. Not all elutriation bad. Sometimes elutriation can be helpful. For example, elutriation may be used to remove dusts or very fine particles from coarser particles.

Definition of Terms :

Lets define some terms that we can use to describe the elutriation process.

The **flux of solids** carried out of the top of the column is called **entrainment**,

G_s [kg/m²/s]

The **bulk density** of the solids in the existing gas stream is called the **holdup.**

ρ^0 [kg/m³]

We note that the entrainment is related to the holdup and the superficial velocity by,

$$G_s = \rho^0 V_0 \qquad \ldots (F.2)$$

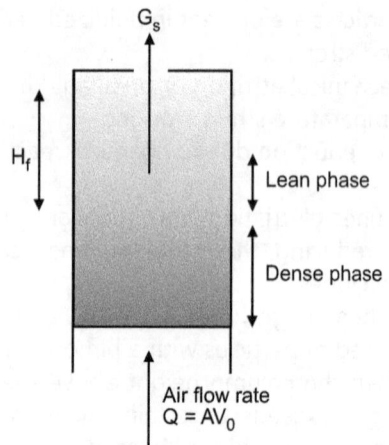

Fig. F.2 : Fluidized Bed with Flux Rate G

Free Board Height, H_f, is defined to be the measure of the free space above the boundary between the dense phase and the lean phase (Fig. F.3).

For design, we need to know the rate of entrainment and the size distribution of the entrained particles in relation to the size of the particles in the bed. A fluidized bed usually has two regions or phases : dense bubbling phase and lean dispersed phase (Fig. F.2).

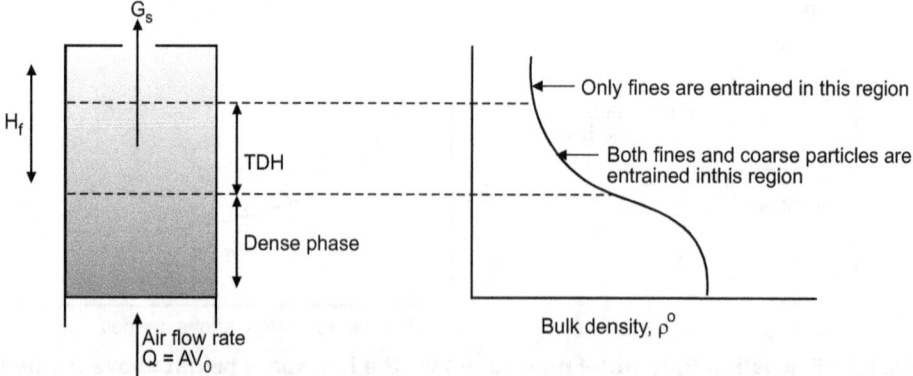

Fig. F.3 : Both Fines and Coarse Particle are Entrained in the Transport Disengagement Height (TDH) Region. Above the TDH only Fines are Entrained

MECHANICAL OPERATIONS — APPENDIX – F : ELUTRIATION OF PARTICLES FROM FLUIDIZED BEDS

The Transport Disengagement Height (TDH) is the height above the dense-phrase/lean-phase boundary above which entrainment and bulk density do not change appreciably. TDH depends upon the superficial velocity and the particle properties. The TDH is the height at which the kinetic energies of particle due to the collisions in the bed has been expended against gravity potential, and the coarse particles whose terminal velocities are greater than the superficial velocity are able to fall back down to the bed. The fine particles, whose terminal velocities are less than the superficial velocity, continue to be entrained out of the column.

When H_f > TDH then the holdup and entrainment rates are close to their minimums. Usually, H_f = TDH is the most economical design height for the fluidized bed. If H_f < TDH then coarse particles will be carried out of the column.

Estimation of TDH for Geldard A Particles :

Fr beds of fine particles there are several methods discussed in literature. Kunii and Levenspiel give a good review of this literature.

Method 1: Zenz and Weil (AICHE J. 4, 472, 1958) proposed a correlation between dimensionless TDH and the vessel diameter. For catalyst pellets in 20 to 150 micron size range, on a log-log plot, the relation between the dimensionless TDH and the vessel diameter are nearly linear (See Kunii and Levenspiel Fig.) as indicated in Fig. F.4.

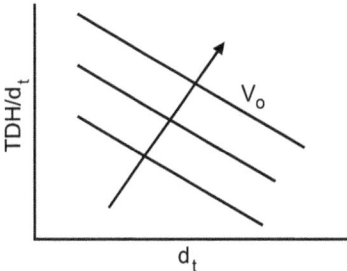

Fig. F.4: Dimensionless TDH/d_t vs. Vessel Diameter, d_t

We can model the data on the chart in the form of –

$$\text{Log} (TDH/d_t) = m \,\text{Log}(d_1) + \text{Log}(b) \qquad \ldots \text{(F.3)}$$

where, d_t is the vessel diameter.

Taking data points from the chart and curve fit to find the parameters m and b:

$$m = -0.115 V_0 - 0.587 \quad \text{...(F.4)}$$
$$b = 4.64 V_0 \quad \text{...(F.5)}$$

Finally, we take above equations and try to compress the chart by plotting the dimensionless TDH/d_t versus the Froude Number, $F_r = V_0^2/d_t/g$ to get the plot shown in Fig. F.5.

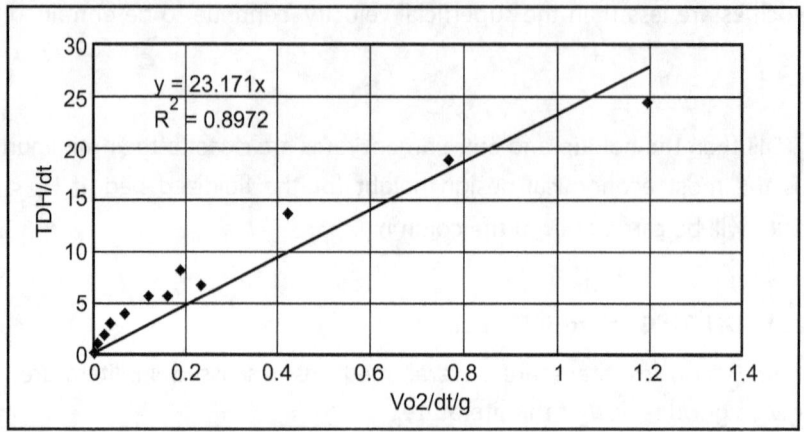

Fig. F.5 : Dimensionless TDH/d_t Versus Froude Number

If we take the linear fit in Fig. F.5 to represent the material behaviour, then we can relate,

$$\frac{TDH}{d_t} = 23.171 \frac{V_0^2}{d_t g} \quad \text{...(F.6)}$$

or, upon rearrangement, we get,

$$\frac{V_0^2}{TDH\, g} = \text{Constant} = 0.0432 \quad \text{...(F.7)}$$

The constant in equation (F.7) is likely to be material specific. Fournol *et. al.* (Can. J. Chem. Engr., 51, 401, 1973) independently determined, for a fluidized bed of fine catalyst particles, d_p = 58 microns, the TDH for this material to be given by –

$$\frac{V_0^2}{TDH\, g} = 0.001 \quad \text{...(F.8)}$$

Entrainment Rate from Tall Vessels :

There are several methods for estimating entrainment rates. Following the work by Zenz *et. al.* (AICHE J., 4, 472, 1958; and *Fluidization III*, Grace and Matsen, eds., Plenum, N.Y. 1980) we assume that the flux rate of solid size d_{pi} is proportional to its mass fraction, x_i,

$$G_{si} = x_i\, G_{si}^* \quad \text{...(F.9)}$$

where, G_{si}^* is the flux rate from an imaginary bed of all particles of size d_{pi}. This approach extends the analogy between fluidized beds and boiling of a liquid mixture. Raoult's Law for an ideal fluid mixture (R.E. Balzhiser, M. R. Samuels, and J. D. Eliassen, *Chemical Engineering Thermodynamics*, Prentice Hall, Englewood Cliffs, New Jersey, 1972) equates the partial pressure of component *i* in the vapour phase to themole fraction in the liquid phase times the pure fluid vapour pressure.

$$P_i = x_i P_i^* \qquad \ldots (F.10)$$

Hence, the flux rates are analogous to the vapour pressure.

The procedure to determine the flux rate from a bed with known particle size distribution is as follows.

1. Divide the size distribution into narrow intervals and find which intervals have terminal velocities greater than the superficial velocity (these are the particles that are entrained, because H_f > TDH).

2. Find G_{si}^* for each size range.

3. The total entrainment is given by,

$$G_s = \sum x_i G_{si}^* \qquad \ldots (F.11)$$

In terms of a continuous size distribution, $P(d_p)$, the total entrainment rate is given by,

$$G_s = \int G_{si}^* P(d_p) (d_p) \, dd_p \text{ (integration overall particles entrained)} \qquad \ldots (F.12)$$

To apply this procedure, a correlation such as shown in Fig. F.6 is required to find G_{si}^*.

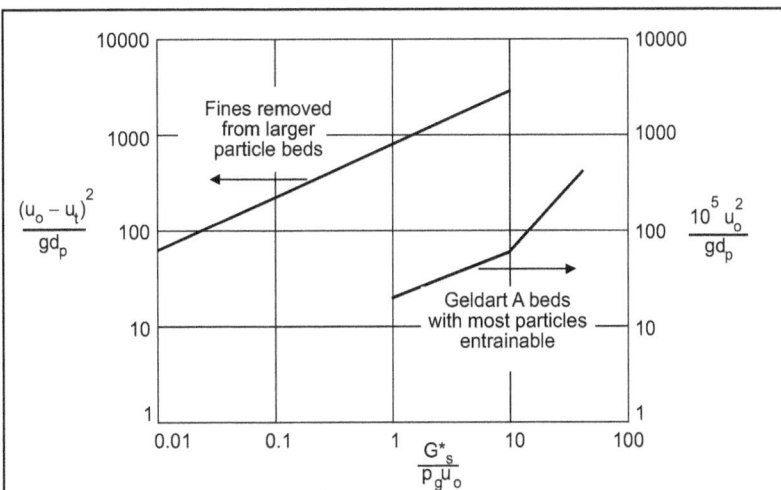

Fig. F.6 : Data taken from Kunii and Levenspiel, Fluidization Engineering, 2ed, Butterworth, Boston, 1991 (Fig. 6 page 175). From this plot the value of G_s^* may be determined for Geldart A Particles and for Fines Removed from Larger Particles Beds

For Geldart class B, C or D particles (the larger particles) other predictive models are available. Recommended references.

References:
1. Kunii and Levenspiel, *J. Chem. Eng. Japan*, 2, 84, 1969).
2. Lewis *et. al.*, *Chem. Eng. Prog. Symposium Series*, 58, (38), 65, 1962.
3. Wen and Chen, *AICHE J.*, 28, 117, 1982.
4. Kunii and Levenspiel, *Fluidization Engineering*, 2nd Ed., Butterworth, Boston, 1991.

✳✳✳

OBJECTIVE TYPE QUESTIONS

1. Shape factor for cylinder whose length equals its diameter is ....
   (a) 1.5 (b) 0.5 (c) 1 (d) none of these

2. The ratio of the actual mesh dimensions of Tayler series to that of the next smaller screen is ....
   (a) 2 (b) 1.5 (c) none of these

3. The opening of 200-mesh screen (Tayler series) is
   (a) 0.0074 cm (b) 0.0074 mm (c) 0.0047 cm (d) none of these

4. The ratio of the area of openings in one screen (Tayler series) to that of the openings in the next smaller Screen is ....
   (a) 1.5 (b) 1 (c) $\sqrt{2}$ (d) none of these

5. Cumulative analysis for determining size distribution is more precise than differential analysis because of ....
   (a) assumption that all particles in single fraction are equal in size
   (b) fact that screening is more effective
   (c) assumption that all particles in single fraction are equal in size is not needed
   (d) none of these

6. Equivalent diameter of particle is the diameter of the sphere having the same ....
   (a) ratio of surface to volume as the actual volume
   (b) ratio of volume to surface as the particle
   (c) volume as the particle (d) none of these

7. Ultrafine particles are sometimes described in terms of their ....
   (a) surface area per unit mass, usually in m^2/gm
   (b) volume per unit mass (c) microns (d) screen size

8. In practice, the angle of repose is .... the angle internal friction
   (a) smaller than (b) greater than (c) equal to (d) none of these

9. When hundreds or thousands of tons of material are to be stored, the most economical method is ....
   (a) Bin storage (b) Bulk storage (c) none of these.

10. For temporary storage before feeding solids to a process, the type of equipment used is ....
    (a) bin (b) silo (c) hopper (d) none of these

11. For transportation of sticky, gummy liquids like molasses, hot tar and sugar we may use a ....
    (a) screw conveyor (b) ribbon conveyor (c) flight conveyor (d) slat conveyor

12. For transportation of grain, asphalt, crushed coal, gravel and sand to a short distance we may use ....
    (a) screw conveyor
    (b) ribbon conveyor
    (c) flight conveyor
    (d) slat or drag conveyor

13. Non-abrasive loose materials like grain, food waste, garbage can be transported in short distance by a
    (a) screw conveyor
    (b) flight conveyor
    (c) slat conveyor
    (d) ribbon conveyor

14. Handling of ashes and similar materials can be achieved by a ....
    (a) screw conveyor
    (b) flight conveyor
    (c) ribbon conveyor
    (d) slat conveyor

15. For transportation of materials, which are lumpy, abrasive and hot we use ....
    (a) belt conveyor
    (b) apron conveyor
    (c) either
    (d) neither

16. The main objectives of crushing and grinding are to obtain products to meet ....
    (a) specific-size requirement
    (b) specific-surface requirement
    (c) both
    (d) neither

17. Dressing of metalliferrous ores prior to smelting results in ....
    (a) savings in freight and total smelting cost
    (b) reduction in losses of metal at the smelter
    (c) neither
    (d) both

18. Reduction of large pieces to intermediate or substantially smaller sizes is called ....
    (a) breaking, crushing, or grinding
    (b) breaking, crushing, or cutting
    (c) crushing, grinding, or comminution
    (d) crushing, grinding, or disintegration

19. Reduction to fine sizes or powders is called ....
    (a) grinding and comminution
    (b) pulverization
    (c) disintegration and dispersion
    (d) all the above

20. The constants K_r, K_k and K_b in the laws of crushing depends on ....
    (a) type of machine
    (b) feed material
    (c) both
    (d) neither

21. Due to compression size reduction occurs in ....
    (a) jaw crushers
    (b) gyratory crushers
    (c) smooth-roll crusher
    (d) all the above

22. A Ideal crusher or grinder should ....
    (a) have large capacity
    (b) consumes less power per unit mass or product
    (c) give highest percentage of desired product size
    (d) all the above

23. Size reduction in grinders (Intermediate and fine) is generally due to ....
    (a) compression
    (b) tearing and compression
    (c) impact and attrition, sometimes combined with compression
    (d) cutting action

24. Size reduction in toothed-roll crushers occurs due to ....
    (a) compression
    (b) tearing (shear), attrition, impact and compression
    (c) impact and attrition
    (d) cutting action

25. Cutting machines are ....
    (a) knife cutters
    (b) dicers
    (c) slitters
    (d) all the above

26. Use of grinding aids results in ....
    (a) finer products
    (b) higher production rate
    (c) both
    (d) neither

27. The energy consumption decrease with increase in ....
    (a) size of feed (at constant reduction ratio) and size of product (at constant size feed)
    (b) capacity of machine
    (c) both
    (d) neither

28. Length of ball mill is ....
    (a) 1.5 times ,ore than its diameter
    (b) slightly more than its diameter
    (c) equal to its diameter
    (d) less than its diameter

29. Size reduction of talc, soapstone, carbonates and sulfates can be achieved by using ....
    (a) ring-roll mills
    (b) compartment mill
    (c) either
    (d) neither

30. Basic slag can be ground in ....
    (a) ball mills
    (b) tube mills
    (c) compartment mills
    (d) all the above

31. A fluid energy mill is used for ....
    (a) cutting
    (b) grinding
    (c) ultragrinding
    (d) crushing

MECHANICAL OPERATIONS   OBJECTIVE TYPE QUESTIONS

32. As the product becomes finer, the energy required for grinding ....
    (a) decreases   (b) increases
    (c) is same as for coarser grinding   (d) is twice that for coarser grinding
33. Pick out the material having minimum Rittinger's number ....
    (a) Calcite   (b) Pyrite   (c) Quartz   (d) Galena
34. Paddle agitator ....
    (a) is suitable for mixing low viscosity liquids
    (b) produces axial flow
    (c) moves at very high speed
    (d) none of these
35. Highly viscous liquids and pastes are agitated by ....
    (a) propellers   (b) turbine agitators
    (c) multiple blade paddles   (d) none of these
36. A propeller agitator ....
    (a) produces mainly axial flow   (b) is used for mixing high viscosity pastes
    (c) runs at very slow speed (2 rpm)   (d) all (a), (b) and (c)
37. Helical screw agitator is used for ....
    (a) mixing highly viscous pastes   (b) blending immiscible liquids
    (c) mixing liquids at very high temperature (> 250°C)
    (d) none of these
38. Which of the following is most suitable for handling fibrous and dense slurries :
    (a) propeller agitator   (b) cone type agitator
    (c) radial propeller agitator   (d) turbine agitator
39. The capacity of screen ....
    (a) has no relationship with the screen aperature
    (b) is directly proportional to the screen aperature
    (c) is inversely proportional to the screen aperature
    (d) is directly proportional to the square of the screen aperature
40. A gravity settling process is the removal of ....
    (a) coarse particles from gases (gravity settling chamber)
    (b) coarse particles from liquid
    (c) fine particles from liquids (classifier)
    (d) all the above
41. In hindered settling, the drag coefficient is ....
    (a) equal to in free settling   (b) greater than in free settling
    (c) less than in free settling   (d) none of the above

MECHANICAL OPERATIONS   OBJECTIVE TYPE QUESTIONS

42. In sugar mill we use ....
    (a) suspended batch basket centrifuge
    (b) perforated horizontal – basket continuous centrifuge
    (c) tubular-bowl centrifuge   (d) disc-bowl centrifuge

43. For separation of isotopes one uses ....
    (a) disc-bowl centrifuge   (b) ultra centrifuge
    (c) either   (d) neither

44. Increasing the capacity of screen .... the screen effectiveness
    (a) decreases   (b) increases   (c) doesn't affect   (d) none of these

45. Screen efficiency is ....
    (a) recovery/rejection   (b) recovery
    (c) rejection   (d) none of these

46. A screen is said to be blinded when ....
    (a) oversize are present in undersize fraction
    (b) undersize are retained in oversize fraction
    (c) the screen is plugged with solid particles
    (d) its capacity is abruptly increased ....

47. Filter aid is used ....
    (a) to increase the rate of filtration   (b) to decrease the pressure drop
    (c) to increase the porosity of the cake   (d) as a support base for the septum

48. Filter medium resistance is that offered by the ....
    (a) filter cloth
    (b) embedded particles in the septum
    (c) filter cloth and embedded particles collectively
    (d) none of these.

49. Vacuum filter is most suitable for ....
    (a) removal of fines from liquid   (b) liquids having high vapour pressure
    (c) liquids if high viscosity   (d) none of these

50. The unit of specific cake resistance is ....
    (a) gm/cm^2 (b) cm/gm   (c) gm/cm^2 (d) gm/gm

51. The filter medium resistance is controlled by ....
    (a) the pressure drop alone   (b) the flow rate alone
    (c) both pressure drop and flow rate (d) the cake thickness

52. Compressibility coefficient for an absolutely compressible cake is ....
    (a) 0   (b) 1   (c) 0 to 1   (d) none of these

(O.5)

53. Filtration of water in a paper mill is done by ....
    (a) open sand filter (b) plate and frame press
    (c) vacuum leaf filter (d) sparkler filter
54. The speed of a rotary drum filter in rpm may be ....
    (a) 1   (b) 50   (c) 100   (d) 500
55. To remove dirt from flowing fluid, we use a ....
    (a) coagulant (b) gravity settler
    (c) strains (d) clarifier
56. Froth flotation is most suitable for treating ....
    (a) iron ores (b) sulfide ores
    (c) quartzite (d) none of these
57. For benefication of ore, the most commonly used method is ....
    (a) flocculation (b) froth flotation
    (c) jigging and tabling (d) none of these
58. Cyclones are used primarily for separating ....
    (a) solids (b) solids from fluids
    (c) liquids (d) solids from solids
59. Sedimentation on commercial scale occurs in ....
    (a) classifiers (b) rotary drum filters (c) thickeners (d) cyclones
60. Filtration rate through filter cake is ....
    (a) directly proportional to S
    (b) inversely proportional to 1/R
    (c) inversely proportional to 1/μ ....
    (d) all (a), (b) and (c); where S = Filtering surface; R = Specific cake resistance; μ = Viscosity of the filtrate
61. Which is continuous filter ....
    (a) plate and frame filter (b) cartridge filter
    (c) shell and leaf filter (d) none of these
62. The most efficient equipment for removal of sub microns dust particles from blast furnace gas is ....
    (a) venturi atomizer (b) gravity settling chamber
    (c) electro-static precipitator (d) cyclone separator
63. In froth flotation, chemical agent added to cause air adherence is called ....
    (a) collector (b) frother (c) modifier (d) none of these
64. During particle size analysis, the important characteristics of individual particle is ....
    (a) composition (b) size
    (c) shape (d) all of above

65. The composition of individual particle will determine its ....
    (a) density
    (b) conductivity
    (c) both (a) and (b)
    (d) none of these

66. The rate of chemical reaction between a solid and fluid is roughly proportional to the ....
    (a) surface involved between solid and fluid
    (b) density of both materials
    (c) friction between materials
    (d) all of above.

67. The best operated speed of revolving screen is usually ....
    (a) equal to critical speed
    (b) 0.1 to 0.2 times the critical speed
    (c) 0.33 to 0.45 times the critical speed
    (d) 0.8 to 0.9 times the critical speed

68. In screen analysis, the notation + 20 mm/– 30 mm means passing through ....
    (a) 20 mm screen and retained on 30 mm
    (b) 30 mm screen and retained on 20 mm
    (c) both 20 mm and 30 mm screens
    (d) neither 20 mm nor 30 mm screen.

69. The opening of 400 mesh screen (Taylor screen) is ....
    (a) 0.38 mm
    (b) 0.038 mm
    (c) 0.0038 mm
    (d) 3.8 mm

70. The material which passes the 100 mesh screen but was retained on 150 mesh, can be represented as ....
    (a) 100/150
    (b) – 100 + 150
    (c) either (a) or (b)
    (d) none of these

71. Dry screening refers to the treatment of a material containing ....
    (a) natural amount of moisture
    (b) material that has been dried before screening
    (c) both (a) and (b)
    (d) either (a) or (b)

72. Which of the following is an industrial screening equipment ?
    (a) Grizzlies
    (b) Trommels
    (c) Vibratory screen
    (d) All of above

73. Screen analysis can be presented ....
    (a) in tabular form
    (b) by fractional plots of the mass fraction retained on each screen versus average screen aperture
    (c) by cumulative plot of the mass fraction passing each screen versus particular screen aperture
    (d) any one of above

74. For a irregular particle, the sphericity ....
    (a) is the ratio of surface area of sphere of same volume as particle to the actual surface area of particle
    (b) is always less than one.
    (c) is the ratio of volume of a sphere having the same surface area as the particle to the actual volume of the particle
    (d) none of these

75. When a particle is passed through a screen aperture, it depends upon its ....
    (a) size of particle
    (b) orientation of particle
    (c) both (a) and (b)
    (d) density of particle

76. Which of the following screen has the maximum capacity ?
    (a) Grizzlies
    (b) Trommels
    (c) Vibrating screen
    (d) Stationary screen

77. The object of size reduction is to ....
    (a) increase the surface area
    (b) more intimate mixing of solids
    (c) influenced considerably the characteristics of a material
    (d) all of above.

78. The object of size reduction is to ....
    (a) produce solid with desired size range
    (b) produce solid of specific surface
    (c) to break apart minerals or crystals of chemical compounds which are intimately associated in the solid state

79. The size of fine particle is closely connected to the ....
    (a) internal structure of material
    (b) process by which size reduction is effected
    (c) either (a) or (b)
    (d) both (a) and (b)

80. Explosive materials can be crushed by ....
    (a) dry-grinding
    (b) wet grinding
    (c) either (a) or (b)
    (d) none of these

81. The choice of the crushing machine for a given crushing operation can be influenced by ....
    (a) nature of the product
    (b) size of the material
    (c) quantity of the material
    (d) all of above

82. Point out the law which is applicable for fine grinding.
    (a) Kick's law
    (b) Rittinger's law
    (c) Bond's law
    (d) Fick's law

83. The mechanical energy supplied to the crusher is always greater than the indicated by Rittinger's number, due to ....
    (a) friction losses
    (b) inertia effects
    (c) heat losses
    (d) all of above

84. Which of the following is not a fine crusher?
    (a) Ball mill
    (b) Pin mill
    (c) Tube mill
    (d) Babcock mill

85. As the product becomes finer, the energy required for grinding ....
    (a) decreases
    (b) increases
    (c) is same as for coarse grinding
    (d) is same as for intermediate grinding

86. According to Bond's law, the size of the material is taken as the size of square holes through which _____
    (a) 30% of it will pass
    (b) 50% of it will pass
    (c) 80% of it will pass
    (d) more than 95% of it will pass

87. Crushing efficiency of a process can be influenced by ....
    (a) the manner in which load is applied
    (b) magnitude of force
    (c) nature of force
    (d) all of above

88. Name the method which is used to feed the mateiral to a crusher.
    (a) Free crushing
    (b) Choke feeding
    (c) Either (a) or (b)
    (d) By the combination of (a) and (b)

89. Point out wihch is not true for wet grinding.
    (a) The power consumption is high about 20-30%
    (b) The capacity of the plant is increased
    (c) Dust formation is eliminated
    (d) The solids are more easily handled.

90. Which of the following is a course crusher ?
    (a) Crushing rolls   (b) Gyratory crusher
    (c) Ball mill   (d) Pin mill
91. For the crushing of big lumps of hard rock, we use ....
    (a) Crushing rolls   (b) Gyratory crusher
    (c) Tube mill   (d) Roller mill
92. Name the crusher in which one jaw is fixed and the other jaw is movable and pivotted at the bottom.
    (a) Black jaw crusher   (b) Simon roll crusher
    (c) Dodge jaw crusher   (d) Disc crusher
93. Fibrous material can be broken by ....
    (a) crushing rolls   (b) squirrel-cage disintegrator
    (c) tube mill   (d) ball mill
94. For ordinary rock crushing in smooth steel crushing rolls, the angle of nip is usually ....
    (a) 10°   (b) 20°
    (c) 32°   (d) 60°
95. Point out which is not true for ball mill.
    (a) The cost of installation and power consumption is low.
    (b) Only dry grinding is possible.
    (c) The mill is suitable for materials of all degree of hardness.
    (d) It can be used for open or close circuit grinding.
96. During size reduction, the optimum speed of ball mill must be ....
    (a) 10-15% of critical speed   (b) 30-35% of critical speed
    (c) 50-75% of critical speed   (d) more than 90% of critical speed
97. Colloidal mill is used to get ....
    (a) colloidal suspensions   (b) emulsions
    (c) solid dispersions   (d) any one of above
98. Grizzlies are used for screening ....
    (a) large size   (b) small size
    (c) very small size   (d) any one of above
99. For the transportation of 300 mesh particles, the equipment used is ....
    (a) screw conveyor   (b) belt conveyor
    (c) pneumatic conveyor   (d) any one of above
100. For the transportation of pasty material, one will use ....
    (a) ribbon conveyor   (b) screw conveyor
    (c) helical conveyor   (d) any one of above
101. Point out which is not true for belt conveyor.
    (a) It requires relatively low pressure and can transport solids to long distance
    (b) This consists of endless belt suitably supported and driven, which transport solids from place to place

(c) Changes in loading, temperature and humidity does not affect the length of belt. Hence, no provision is required for keeping the belt from sagging and become loose.
(d) Belts of strip steel is employed for conveying materials through furnaces.

102. The separation of solids from a suspension in a liquid by means of porous medium or screen which retains the solids and allows liquid to pass is known as ....
(a) distillation
(b) filtration
(c) leaching
(d) extraction

103. In general the size of pores of the medium during filtration must be ....
(a) very small as compared to particle
(b) slightly smaller than the particles
(c) larger than the particles
(d) either (b) or (c)

104. Point out the characteristics of liquid which are responsible for equipment selection and operating conditions.
(a) Viscosity
(b) Density
(c) Corrosive properties
(d) All of above

105. Point out the wrong statements in the selection of equipment and operating conditions for filtration.
(a) Concentration of solids in suspensions.
(b) The quantity of material to be handled does not affect equipment selection and operating conditions.
(c) Whether the valuable product is solid, liquid or both.
(d) Whether it is necessary to wash the filtration cake.

106. The rate of filtration depends upon ....
(a) drop in pressure from the feed to the far side of the filter medium
(b) area of filtering surface
(c) viscosity of filtrate
(d) ressitance of filter cake
(e) all of above

107. Point out the characteristics of suspended solids which are responsible to select the filtration equipment and operating conditions.
(a) Packing characteristics
(b) Particle size
(c) Particle shape
(d) Particle size distribution
(e) All of above

108. For the separation of abrasive solids in corrosive liquids, can be filtered by ....
(a) vacuum filters
(b) bag filters
(c) bed filters
(d) the plate and frame press filter

109. In order to maintain the flow rate during filtration, pressure must ....
(a) be gradually increased
(b) be gradually decreased
(c) remain constant
(d) none of above.

110. Batch filter can be operated by ....
    (a) pressure is to be kept constant
    (b) flow rate is to be kept constant
    (c) either (a) or (b)
    (d) none of these
111. Filter medium must be ....
    (a) mechanically strong
    (b) resistant to the corrosive action of fluid
    (c) offer to little resistance as possible to the flow of filtrate
    (d) all of above
112. Filter medium resistance is important during ....
    (a) the early stage of filtration   (b) every stage of filtration
    (c) final stage of filtration   (d) none of these
113. The most suitable filter in a given operation must fulfil ....
    (a) minimum overall cost
    (b) high overall rate of filtration
    (c) ease of discharge of the filter cake
    (d) all of above
114. Generally, the most satisfactory filter for free filtering material is ....
    (a) rotary filter   (b) rotary vacuum filter
    (c) bed filter   (d) none of these
115. During the initial stage of filtration of dilute slurry in upward-facing surface giving rise to a cake deposition at a ....
    (a) low resistance   (b) high resistance
    (c) constant resistance   (d) none of these
116. During the initial stage of filtration of dilute slurry in downward-facing surface giving rise to a cake deposition at a ....
    (a) low resistance   (b) high resistance
    (c) constant resistance   (d) none of these
117. The initial stages in the formation of cake is important because ....
    (a) the rate of flow is maximum at the beginning of the process
    (b) plugging of the pores of filter cloth and causes a very high resistance of flow
    (c) the orientation of the particles in the initial layer can appreciably influence the structure of the whole filter cake
    (d) all of above
118. The voidage of filter cake depends on ....
    (a) the nature of support   (b) rate of deposition
    (c) both (a) and (b)   (d) none of these
119. Specific resistance of cake depends upon ....
    (a) voidage of cake   (b) specific surface of the particles
    (c) either (a) or (b)   (d) both (a) and (b)

120. With the use of moving blade technique in filtration ....
    (a) much higher rate of filtration than conventional process is obtained
    (b) relatively low porosity of cake is obtained
    (c) both (a) and (b)
    (d) either (a) or (b)
121. Volumetric rate of deposition of cake is equal to ....
    (a) $\dfrac{\text{Rate of filtrate} \times \text{Solid per kg. of water}}{\text{Voidage} \times \text{Specific gravity of solid}}$
    (b) $\dfrac{\text{Rate of filtrate} \times \text{Solid per kg. of water}}{\text{Voltage} \times \text{Specific gravity of solid}}$
122. Cake resistance is ....
    (a) significant in the preliminary stage of filtration
    (b) increased with time of filtration
    (c) independent for pressure drop
    (d) all of above
123. For incompressible cakes, the resistance depends on ....
    (a) the rate of deposition
    (b) the nature of particles
    (c) the force between the particles
    (d) all of above
124. In incompressible cakes, the resistance to flow for a given volume of cake ....
    (a) is appreciably affected by pressure drop across the cake
    (b) is appreciably affected by the rate of deposition of material
    (c) is appreciably affected by pressure drop and the rate of deposition of material
    (d) is not appreciably affected by pressure drop and the rate of deposition of material
125. For incompressible cake ....
    (a) voidage can be taken as constant
    (b) specific resistance of the cake can be taken as constant
    (c) both (a) and (b)
    (d) either (a) or (b)
126. In a compressible filter cake –
    (a) compressibly is a function of the pressure difference across the cake
    (b) comspressibility may be a reversible or irreversible process
    (c) most filter cakes are in elastic and greater resistance offered to flow at high pressure difference
    (d) all of above
127. If the cake is compressible, then ....
    (a) voidage will increase progressively in the direction of filtrate
    (b) the local value of specific resistance of filter cake increases
    (c) either (a) or (b)
    (d) both (a) and (b)

128. Compressibility coefficient for an absolute compressible cake is ....
    (a) 0
    (b) 1
    (c) 100
    (d) infinite

129. The rate of flow of wash liquid and the volume of liquid needed to reduce the solute content of the cake to a desired degree is important in ....
    (a) the design of filter
    (b) the operation of a filter
    (c) both (a) and (b)
    (d) none of these

130. Sometimes, it is found that much of the cake is incompletely washed. It may be due to ....
    (a) voidage
    (b) channelling
    (c) both (a) and (b)
    (d) either (a) or (b)

131. In plate and frame press, the plate has ....
    (a) ribbed surface
    (b) plain surface
    (c) curved surface
    (d) none of these

132. In plage and frame press, the slurry is introduced through a pot in ....
    (a) the centre of press
    (b) one side of press
    (c) each frame
    (d) none of these

133. Point out which is not true for filter press.
    (a) Maintenance cost is low
    (b) It is continuous in operation
    (c) It can be used for a wide range of materials under varying operating conditions of cake thickness and pressure
    (d) It is equally suitable whether the cake or the liquid is the main product

134. Pressure leaf filtters are designed for final dicharge of cake in ....
    (a) dry state
    (b) wet state
    (c) either (a) or (b)
    (d) none of these

135. Pressure leaf filter is widely used for filtering ....
    (a) domestic water
    (b) organic solvents
    (c) oils
    (d) all of above

136. Moore filter is a ....
    (a) bag filter
    (b) the plate and frame filter press
    (c) leaf filter
    (d) none of these

137. For large scale filtration, rotatory filter must be used when ....
    (a) specific resistance is high
    (b) efficiency washing is not required
    (c) small quantity of solids are present in the liquid
    (d) all of above

138. Vacuum filter is most suitable for ....
    (a) removal of very fine solid particles from suspensions
    (b) liquids having high vapour pressures
    (c) liquids of very high viscous polymer
    (d) none of these

139. The speed of a rotatory drum vacuum filter may be ....
    (a) 1 rpm   (b) 100 rpm
    (c) 500 rpm   (d) 50 rpm
140. Point out which is not true for vacuum rotatory drum filter.
    (a) Vacuum is applied to the whole of the interior of the drum
    (b) Vacuum is created within compartments formed on the periphery of the drum
    (c) It is similar to gravity filter
    (d) It consists of a drum rotating about a horizontal axis and drum is partially submerged in the trough into which the material to be filtered in fed
141. Agitation produces motion in the process of liquid. This process is responsible for ....
    (a) blending   (b) dissolution
    (c) heat transfer   (d) all of above
142. Which of the following impeller is responsible to produce laminar flow during agitation ?
    (a) Helix impeller   (b) Disk-blade turbine
    (c) Curved blade turbine   (d) Any one of above
143. Highly viscous liquids and pastes can be agitated by ....
    (a) anchor impeller   (b) multiple blade paddles
    (c) helix impeller   (d) all of above
144. Turbine with pitched blade in baffled tank produces ....
    (a) radial flow   (b) axial flow
    (c) tangential flow   (d) any one of above
145. A propeller agitator ....
    (a) is used for mixing two immiscible high viscosity pastes
    (b) produces mainly axial flow
    (c) runs at very low speed (1 rpm)
    (d) all of above
146. In unbaffled tank, formation of vortex is not desirable because ....
    (a) very poor mixing between adjacent fluid layers
    (b) air be easily entrained into the liquid even at modest impeller speed
    (c) the liquid level at the top edge of the tank is raised significantly
    (d) all of above
147. Design variables during agitation process, are ....
    (a) agitating equipment variables (b) fluid properties
    (c) impeller rotational speed   (d) all of above
148. The practical approach to the design of a plant scale agitation equipment is to obtain data from ....
    (a) an appropriate experiment in a plant scale apparatus
    (b) laboratory scale equipment
    (c) scale-up technique
    (d) any one of above

149. The scale-factor (R) in terms of volume (V) is equal to ....

    (a) $\dfrac{V_2}{V_1}$
    (b) $\left(\dfrac{V_2}{V_1}\right)^{1/3}$
    (c) $\dfrac{V_1}{V_2}$
    (d) $\left(\dfrac{V_1}{\sqrt{2}}\right)^{1/3}$

    where, subscript 1 and 2 represents the smaller unit and large agitator respectively.

150. During agitation, power consumption during turbulent flow is proportional to the ....

    (a) density of liquid
    (b) viscosity of liquid
    (c) interface tension of liquid
    (d) thermal conductivity of liquid

151. In laminar flow, power (P) is proportional to ....

    (a) $\rho N^2 D^5$
    (b) $\mu N^2 D^3$
    (c) $\mu N^2 D^5$
    (d) $\rho N^2 D^3$

    where, N is rotational speed, D is impeller diameter, ρ is fluid density and μ is fluid viscosity.

152. For turbulent flow, scape-up procedure required experimental observations of ....

    (a) three or more test volumes
    (b) two test volumes
    (c) single test volume
    (d) either (a), (b) or (c)

153. The Reynolds number is defined as the inertial force to ....

    (a) viscous forces
    (b) surface tension forces
    (c) gravity forces
    (d) none of these

154. At high Reynolds number ....

    (a) power number tends to be independent of impeller Reynolds number
    (b) power number is dependent on the geometry of the impeller
    (c) both (a) and (b)
    (d) none of these.

155. At high Reynolds number (i.e. constant power number and impeller diameter), the power consumption increases with ....

    (a) speed
    (b) cube of speed
    (c) square of speed
    (d) none of these

156. Kinetic similarity is obtained when ....

    (a) equal liquid motion
    (b) equal solid suspension
    (c) equal mass transfer
    (d) equal surface behaviour

157. The Froude number may be defined as the ratio of ....

    (a) pressure forces to surface tension forces
    (b) pressure forces to inertial forces
    (c) inertial forces to gravity forces
    (d) gravity forces to inertial forces

158. The Froude number ....
    (a) is used to account for the effect of surface (for example, the centre vortex) on the power number
    (b) is included in the correlation of Reynolds number and power number for unbaffled system
    (c) in baffled system is independent for the curves between power number of Reynolds number
    (d) all of above
159. Paddel agitator ....
    (a) produces axial flow
    (b) is suitable for mixing of low viscosity liquids
    (c) moves at very high speed
    (d) none of these.
160. Inertial force are obtained when elastic forces are multiplied by ....
    (a) Reynolds number
    (b) Mach number
    (c) Froude number
    (d) Euler number

ANSWERS

1. (a)	2. (b)	3. (a)	4. (d)	5. (c)
6. (a)	7. (a)	8. (a)	9. (b)	10. (c)
11. (b)	12. (a)	13. (b)	14. (c)	15. (b)
16. (c)	17. (d)	18. (b)	19. (d)	20. (c)
21. (d)	22. (d)	23. (c)	24. (b)	25. (d)
26. (c)	27. (c)	28. (d)	29. (a)	30. (d)
31. (c)	32. (b)	33. (c)	34. (a)	35. (c)
36. (a)	37. (a)	38. (b)	39. (b)	40. (d)
41. (b)	42. (a)	43. (b)	44. (a)	45. (d)
46. (c)	47. (c)	48. (c)	49. (d)	50. (b)
51. (c)	52. (b)	53. (a)	54. (a)	55. (c)
56. (b)	57. (c)	58. (b)	59. (c)	60. (d)
61. (d)	62. (c)	63. (a)	64. (d)	65. (c)
66. (a)	67. (c)	68. (b)	69. (b)	70. (c)
71. (d)	72. (d)	73. (d)	74. (a)	75. (c)
76. (c)	77. (d)	78. (d)	79. (a)	80. (b)
81. (d)	82. (b)	83. (d)	84. (b)	85. (b)
86. (c)	87. (d)	88. (c)	89. (a)	90. (b)

MECHANICAL OPERATIONS   OBJECTIVE TYPE QUESTIONS

91. (a)	92. (c)	93. (b)	94. (c)	95. (b)
96. (c)	97. (d)	98. (a)	99. (c)	100. (d)
101. (c)	102. (b)	103. (c)	104. (d)	105. (b)
106. (e)	107. (e)	108. (a)	109. (a)	110. (c)
111. (c)	112. (a)	113. (d)	114. (b)	115. (a)
116. (b)	117. (d)	118. (c)	119. (d)	120. (c)
121. (b)	122. (b)	123. (d)	124. (d)	125. (c)
126. (d)	127. (b)	128. (b)	129. (c)	130. (b)
131. (a)	132. (c)	133. (b)	134. (c)	135. (d)
136. (a)	137. (b)	138. (d)	139. (a)	140. (c)
141. (d)	142. (a)	143. (d)	144. (b)	145. (b)
146. (d)	147. (d)	148. (c)	149. (b)	150. (a)
151. (b)	152. (d)	153. (a)	154. (c)	155. (b)
156. (a)	157. (c)	158. (d)	159. (b)	160. (b)

TRY YOURSELF

(A) Fill in the Blanks Type :

(1) In size reduction machines, solids generally break in ___ ways.

(2) Jaw crushers and Gyratory crushers are ___ crushers whereas crushing rolls (smooth roll crushers and toothed roll crushers) are called ___ crushers.

(3) Between the Blake jaw and the Dodge jaw crushers, ___ is more common.

(4) The ___ jaw crusher combines the principles of the Blake and the Dodge jaw crushers.

(5) Size reduction in cutting machines takes place principally by ___ (Ans-Cutting Action).

(6) Stamp mills are well suited for crushing ___

(7) Bradford breakers are widely used to reduce size of ___

(8) ___ crushers can be employed to reduce size of materials like coal, gypsum and ice.

(9) A ball mill may have ___ baffles.

(10) Ball charge equal to ...... % of the mill volume gives the maximum capacity.

(11) Minimum-size balls capable of grinding the feed in a ball mill give ___ efficiency.

(12) α (half the angle of nip) is generally about ___

(13) Coarse material returned to a mill by a classifier is known as the ___

(14) Grinding aids are used in the ___ grinding.

(15) Wear in dry crushing is ___ when compared to wet crushing.

(16) The surface shape factor K_a for spheres is ___
(17) The volume shape factor K_v for spheres is ___
(18) Oldest dressing method was ___
(19) ___ is the operation dealing with separation of solid particles according to their densities.
(20) ___ means separation of materials into products characterized by difference in size.
(21) A tangent to the gas-liquid interface forms the ___ angle (always measured through the more dense phase).
(22) Separation of solid particles into two or more fractions on the basis of their velocities of flow through fluids is called ___
(23) ___ is a classification operation to determine the grain size distribution or sizing of particles in the range 5 to 10 microns or below the finest screen size.
(24) Separation of two materials of different densities by passing dilute pulp over a table or a deck inclined about 2 to 5 degrees from the horizontal is called ___
(25) The separation of suspension into a supernatant clear fluid and a rather dense slurry containing a higher concentration of solid is called ___
(26) A ___ is a simple enlargement in a pipe line which reduces the velocity enough to permit the solids to settle out.
(27) Separation of solids and fluids of different densities using a force greater than that of gravity is called ___
(28) When the different rates of flow are used to separate materials of same density according to their size, the process is called ___
(29) For collection of sulfuric acid mist, we use a ___
(30) Opposite of ___ is dispersion.
(31) Opposite of size reduction is ___
(32) Materials like sulfur and coal are generally stored ___
(33) Screw and helical flight conveyors are called ___
(34) An apron conveyor's trough is made from ___ or ___
(35) ___ elevators are used for vertical travel.
(36) Spherical particles of limestone (d_p = 0.16 mm, density = 2800 kg/m^3) take 5 minutes to settle under gravity through a 6 m column of a fluid of density 1200 kg/m^3. The drag coefficient is equal to ___
(37) The sphericity of a non-spherical particle is defined as the ratio of ___ to ___ The sphericity of a cylindrical particle of diameter 3 mm and length 3 mm is ___
(38) The maximum diameter of a spherical sand particle (density = 2650 kg/m^3) that will settle in the Stokes law region in water (density 1000 kg/m^3, viscosity 0.001 kg/m.s) is ___ mm.

(39) The vacuum leaf filter gives a total volume of 10 m³ of filtrate in 30 minutes. If the resistance of filter cloth is negligible, the time taken for the collection of 20 m³ of filtrate is ___ minutes and for the collection of 30 m³ of filtrate is ___ minutes.

(40) For two-fold increase in pressure the specific resistance of a filter cake increases by ___, if the compressibility coefficient is 0.5 and increases by ___, if the compressibility coefficient is 0.8.

(41) Two very small silica particles are settling at their respective terminal velocities through a highly viscous oil column. If one particle is twice as large as the other, the larger particle will take ___ the time than by the smaller particle to fall through the same height.

(42) Froude number = (___) / (gravitational force per unit ___ of ___).

(43) In the design of storage bins, one important characteristic property of the solid being stored is ___

(B) Multiple Choice Questions :

(1) For a sphere falling in a constant drag coefficient regime, its terminal velocity depends on its diameter (d) as ___

(A) d (B) $d^{0.5}$ (C) d^2 (D) $1/d$

(2) The sphericity of a solid particle of cubical shape is

(A) p (B) $(p/6)^{1/3}$ (C) $(p/6)^{1/2}$ (D) p/3

(3) A 30% (by volume) suspension of spherical sand particles in a viscous oil has a hindered settling velocity of 4.4 mm/s. If the Richardson-Zaki hindered settling index is 4.5, then the terminal settling velocity of sand grain is

(A) 0.9 mm/s (B) 1 mm/s (C) 22.1 mm/s (D) 0.02 mm/s

(4) For a turbine-agitated and baffled tank, operating at low Reynolds number (based on impeller diameter), the power number (N_P) varies with N_{Re} as

(A) N_P a N_{Re} (B) N_P a $N_{Re}^{0.5}$ (C) N_P = Constant (D) N_P a $1/N_{Re}$

(5) The work index in Bond's law for crushing of solids has the following dimensions

(A) No units (dimensionless) (B) kWh/ton
(C) kW/ton (D) kW $m^{1/2}$/ton

(6) At low Reynold's numbers the power (P) required for agitating a fluid in a stirred tank becomes independent of intertial forces. In this limit, indicate which of the following relations is satisfied :

(A) P_o a Re^{-1} (B) P_o a Re^0 (C) P_o a $Re^{0.5}$ (D) P_o a Re^1

$P_o = P/(rN^3D^5)$: Power Number, $Re = rND^2/m$: Reynolds Number
N is the impeller rotational speed, and D is the impeller diameter.

MECHANICAL OPERATIONS   OBJECTIVE TYPE QUESTIONS

(7) The distribution given by microscopic analysis of powder is ___
   (A) Number   (B) Length   (C) Area   (D) Volume
(8) Stokes equation is valid in the Reynolds number range ___
   (A) 0.01 to 0.1   (B) 0.1 to 2   (C) 2 to 10   (D) 10 to 100
(9) To produce talcum powder use ___
   (A) Ball mill   (B) Hammer mill   (C) Jet mill   (D) Pin mill
(10) The sphericity of a cylinder of 1 cm diameter and length 3 cm is ___
   (A) 0.9   (B) 0.78   (C) 0.6   (D) 0.5
(11) For separating particles of different densities, the differential settling method uses a liquid sorting medium of density ___
   (A) Intermediate between those of the light and heavy ones
   (B) less than that of either one
   (C) greater than that of either one
   (D) of any arbitrary value
(12) At very low r.p.m (N_{Re} less than 5), the power required for agitation is proportional to
   (A) D   (B) D^2 (C) D^3 (D) D^5
(13) An electrostatic precipitator is normally used for separating particles from gases when
   (A) particle size is greater than 1 mm
   (B) particle size is less than 1 micron
   (C) gases contain high concentration of carbon monoxide
   (D) gases contain very high concentration of solids
(14) A particle A of diameter 10 microns settles in an oil of specific gravity 0.9 and viscosity 10 poise under Stokes law. A particle B with diameter 20 microns settling in the same oil will have a settling velocity ___
   (A) same as that of A   (B) one-fourth as that of A
   (C) twice as that of A   (D) four-times as that of A
(15) During washing of filter at the end of constant pressure filtration, the rate of washing equals the
   (A) rate of filtration at time zero
   (B) rate of filtration at the end of filtration
   (C) rate of filtration when half the filtrate has been obtained
   (D) rate of filtration at the end of filtration, but decreases with time subsequently
(16) In a gyratory crusher the size reduction is effected primarily by :
   (A) compression   (B) impact   (C) attrition   (D) cutting action
(17) In power correlations for agitated vessels the effect of Froude number appears :
   (A) for baffled vessels when Reynolds number is less than 300
   (B) for unbaffled vessels when Reynolds number is greater than 300
   (C) when there is no vortex formation
   (D) when the Reynolds number is less than 300

(O.21)

(18) The angle formed by pouring a powder as a heap on a flat surface is known as :
    (A) Contact angle   (B) Angle of nip
    (C) Angle of repose   (D) Critical angle

(19) During storage of coal
    (A) pile low, compact hard   (B) pile high, compact loose
    (C) pile high, compact hard   (D) pile low, compact loose

(20) The sphericity for a catalyst pellet of dia 6 mm and length 6 mm is
    (A) 0.5   (B) 0.36   (C) 1   (D) 0.67

(C) Match the following pairs :

(1)

(I)	Flow factor	(A)	Comminution
(II)	Grade efficiency	(B)	Storage silo
		(C)	Hydrocyclone
		(D)	Mixing

(2)

(I)	Saltation velocity	(A)	Filtration
(II)	Compressible cake	(B)	Fluidization
		(C)	Pneumatic conveying
		(D)	Screw conveyor

(3)

(I)	Gyratory crusher	(A)	Shear force
(II)	Hammer mill	(B)	Attrition
(III)	Buhrstone mill	(C)	Compression force
(IV)	Fluid energy mill	(D)	Impact

(4)

(I)	Cut diameter	(A)	Filtration
(II)	Specific cake resistance	(B)	Cyclone separators
(III)	Size reduction ratio	(C)	Storage of solids
(IV)	Angle of internal friction	(D)	Kick's law

✱✱✱

QUESTION BANK

1. Give the shape factor for a cylinder whose length equals its diameter.
2. In screen analysis notation + 5 mm/–10 mm means what?
3. Define sphericity for a non-spherical particle.
4. Which is the most suitable equipment for removing the fine dust particle of less than one-micron diameter from air?
5. Define crushing efficiency.
6. What is the advantage of wet grinding over dry grinding?
7. Define work index.
8. What are the factors that affect energy consumption in a ball mill?
9. Explain the term sedimentation.
10. Define hindered settling.
11. Explain the principle and application of centrifuge.
12. What is froth flotation? Discuss its applications.
13. The rate of filtration depends on what?
14. What are the good qualities of a filter media?
15. What are filter aids? Name few commonly used filter aids.
16. Differentiate between incompressible cake and compressible cake.
17. What are the purposes of agitation?
18. Define flow number.
19. Name the agitator which is suitable for mixing low viscosity fluids.
20. What are the types of mixers suitable for pastes and plastic masses?
21. Classify screening equipment and discuss any one with neat sketch.
22. Explain the principle of magnetic separation methods.
23. Give the various methods for storage of solids. Discuss them briefly.
24. What are the various types of crushers? Give some type of crusher and explain any one of them with neat diagram.
25. Explain the term "Terminal settling velocity" of a particle.
26. Discuss the basic principles involved in the beneficiation of ores by Froth Floatation. Explain with suitable examples the role of collectors, frothers and modifiers in the operation.
27. Explain with a neat sketch the working of a plate and frame filter press.
28. Discuss the basic principles of centrifugal filtration.
29. Classify mixers for dry powders and state their specific application.
30. What are the different ways adopted for size reduction in process industries?
31. Explain the Bond's crushing law and work index.
32. Explain differential screen analysis.
33. What is the ratio of actual mesh dimension in one screen to that of the next smaller screen as per Tayler's standard scale?

34. Explain the terms 'Capacity' and 'Effectiveness' of screens.
35. What is mixing index? Explain its significance.
36. What are the different methods adopted for prevention of swirling in an agitated tank?
37. What is the difference between a clarifier and classifier?
38. Define the terms 'Critical speed' and 'Centrifuging' in a ball mill.
39. What are the different types of impellers commonly used for agitation of liquids?
40. Write the relationships between drag coefficient and Reynolds number in various regimes of settling.
41. Explain the different types of filtration.
42. Explain the principle of centrifugal sedimentation.
43. What are open circuit and closed circuit operations?
44. Classify the particle size measuring techniques on the basis of size range.
45. Explain briefly the various flotation methods.
46. Explain the principle of electrical precipitation.
47. What are the requirements for selecting a suitable filter media?
48. What are sorting classifiers?
49. Classify screening equipment with the help of neat sketches. Compare between ideal and actual screens.
50. (a) State the basic laws of crushing and derive them from the following equation:

$$\frac{dE}{dL} = -CL^P$$

Where the terms have their standard nomenclature? Indicate the limitations of these laws.

51. Prove that the critical speed of a ball mill follows the following relationship:

$$n_c = \frac{1}{2\pi}\sqrt{\frac{g}{R-r}}$$

Where R and r represent the radius of the mill and ball respectively, g = acceleration due to gravity.

52. Explain the process of sedimentation and derive an expression for calculating the minimum thickener required by a batch sedimentation test.
53. What are the various types of flotation equipment commercially employed in industry? With the help of a neat sketch, discuss any one of them in detail.
54. What are filter aids and filter media?
55. Define 'sphericity' for a non-spherical particle.
56. What is 'blinding' of screens?
57. Cumulative analysis for determining surface is more precise than differential analysis. Why?
58. Differentiate between Grizzlies and Trommels.

MECHANICAL OPERATIONS   QUESTION BANK

59. Define Rittinger's law of crushing.
60. The operating speed of a ball mill should be less than the critical speed. Why?
61. Define angle of nip for a roll crusher.
62. Name the commonly used centrifuges for industrial applications.
63. Differentiate between a thickener and a clarifer.
64. What are filter aids? Name few commonly used filter aids.
65. Give the classification to filters.
66. Explain the Kozeny's equation for determining the pressure drop across the cake for batch filtration.
67. Differentiate between agitation and mixing.
68. What are the main types of impellers?
69. What are the three types of industrial screens and how they are employed?
70. Explain the principle of electrostatic precipitation in gas cleaning.
71. With the help of a neat sketch explain the working of a conical ball mill.
72. What is critical speed of grinding mill? Deduce a relation between the critical speed and diameter of a ball mill.
73. Discuss how the area of a thickener can be calculated from batch sedimentation data.
74. Explain the working of a vacuum drum filter with a neat sketch and specify the fields of application.
75. Give the sphericity of rasching ring whose length and diameter are equal.
76. Define effectiveness of screen.
77. Name the different methods of particle size measurement for fine particles.
78. List out any three equipment used for storage of solids.
79. Give the various methods of braking solids.
80. What are crushers? Give any three types.
81. What do you mean by closed circuit grinding?
82. What is size reduction?
83. What is the principle of comminution?
84. What are the characteristics of an ideal crusher?
85. What is the ratio of the diameters of the smallest and the largest particles in the comminuted product?
86. What is crushing efficiency?
87. What are the different laws of comminution associated with size reduction?
88. How is work index (wi) related to Bond's constant (kb)?
89. Classify size reduction equipment in detail.
90. What are the applications of crushing and grinding in chemical processing industry?
91. What is the basic principle of jaw crusher?
92. State the type of jaw crushers.
93. Given: Mineral rocks of 1.5 feet diameters, equipment capacity 1500 tons/hr to be crushed to a maximum product size of 10 cm. Which type of crusher will you recommend and why?

(Q.3)

94. What is the difference between Jaw crusher and Gyratory crusher?
95. What is the working principle of a ball mill?
96. What is centrifuging in a ball mill?
97. What is the critical speed of a ball mill?
98. Enlist the raw materials (feed) to the size reduction equipment.
99. What is the exact difference between particle size and particle shape?
100. What are the methods of particle size distribution of powder?
101. Give the formulae for the following:
    (a) Volume Surface Mean Diameter
    (b) Arithmetic Mean Diameter
    (c) Mass Mean Diameter
    (d) Volume Mean Diameter
102. How will you find the number of particles in a mixture?
103. What is volume shape factor?
104. What are the common equipments for mechanical separations?
105. What do you understand by undersize (fines) and oversize (tails) particles in connection with sedation by screen?
106. State material of construction for the screens.
107. What does fine screening mean? What is ultrafine screen?
108. Define ideal screen and cut-point diameter (d_{pc}).
109. What is grade efficiency? State its significance in particle size analysis.
110. How is batch separation carried out?
111. Compare free settling and hindered settling.
112. Give construction of continuous thickeners.
113. What is Kynch theory for sedementation?
114. What is the basic principle of cyclone separator?
115. What is the working principle of magnetic separators?
116. Which materials are treated in magnetic separators?
117. What is the basic principle on which an electrostatic separator works?
118. Enlist the different types of equipments used of size separation by centrifugal action.
119. Give the types of cyclones.
120. What is the advantage of cyclones over other size separation devices?
121. Enlist the applications of a cyclone separator.
122. Differentiate between clarifier and classifier.

123. What are sorting classifiers?
124. What is heavy fluid separation?
125. What is differential settling method?
126. What is flocculation? State its applications.
127. What is froth flotation? State its applications.
128. What is role of collectors and frothers in froth flotation?
129. What is basic principle of cake filtration?
130. What is the basic principle and working of filter press. State its application, merits and demerits.
131. Comment on "Jamming of filter press".
132. What is the doctor's blade "in connection with the rotary drum filter".
133. Give the examples of filter media.
134. What is meant by precoat filtration?
135. What are filter aids? Give examples.
136. What do you understand by – (i) Standard blocking, (ii) Intermediate blocking
137. What is Biofiltration? State the applications.
138. What is the principle of microfiltration?
139. What is the specific cake resistance?
140. Differentiate between constant rate of filtration and constant pressure filtration.
141. What is cross flow-filtration?
142. Differentiate clearly between agitation and mixing.
143. What is the purpose of agitation?
144. What are the types of impellers?
145. What are the applications of agitators in the industry?
146. What are the types of agitators commonly available?
147. What is the purpose of baffling in an agitator system?
148. What is Power number, Froude number, Reynolds number in connection with power requirement for agitation?
149. Enlist mixer for paste and plastic masses.
150. What are the types of mixers for dry powders?
151. List the applications of pug mill.
152. How will you determine the power required for an agitator system?
153. What is the selection criterion for agitators?
154. What is application Banbury mixer?
155. Explain the difference between Silo, Bin and Hoppers.
156. What are the applications of conveying in the industry? Give suitable examples.
157. Classify conveyers.

158. Recommend suitable device for transportation finely divided material and pastes.
159. Which type of conveyer is used in powerhouses?
160. What are the merits and demerits of scraper conveyer over belt conveyer?
161. For short runs and heavy loads, recommend a suitable conveyer.
162. What is the principle of pneumatic conveying?
163. State the advantages and disadvantages of pneumatic conveyers over other conveyers.
164. When you recommend for pneumatic conveyer over other types?
165. What is drag?
166. What are types of drag? Explain.
167. Define drag coefficient.
168. State Stoke's law.
169. State Ergun's equation.
170. What is Dracy's law?
171. State Kozeny-Carman equation.
172. What is terminal settling velocity? Give its significance.
173. State applications of fluidization in chemical industries.
174. What is the minimum fluidization velocity?
175. List the equipments available for gas solid separation in chemical industry.
176. Comment on the following statements giving reasons.
    You may agree with or contradict against any of the statements, but do justify your answers. Give examples and/or brief sketches wherever necessary.
    (a) The volumetric diameter of a cubical particle is less than its Sauter diameter,
    (b) For a cylindrical particle of length equal to its diameter, d_v, $d_{vs} < d_s$.
    (c) Sphericity of +100 mesh galena will always be larger than that of −100 mesh,
    (d) A trommel should always be operated above its critical speed,
    (e) A low Rittinger's number indicates easy crushability,
    (f) Maximum crushing takes place in a ball mill at its critical speed of rotation,
    (g) Size ratio will always be less than the settling ratio,
    (h) Hindered settling velocity is more than the free settling velocity,
    (i) Dense medium separation and jigging differ from each other in the sense that the former separates particles on the basis of size as well as density, whereas the latter separates on the basis of density only,
    (j) A batch filter is first operated at constant pressure and then at constant rate,
    (k) The rate of batch filtration increases with increase in filtration pressure if the sludge is incompressible, but not so if it is compressible,
    (l) A spare cross-section is preferred for the gas inlet in a gas cyclone,

(m) Separation is maximum in a hydrocyclone when flow rates of light and heavy phases are equal,

(n) Electrostatic precipitators are best suitable for separating submicron particles from gases and their collection efficiency is highly dependent on particle size,

(o) Increase in inlet Reynolds number increases the separation efficiency of a hydrocyclone, but not that of a gas cyclone,

(p) Work of adhension in flotation is independent of particle size, but depends very, much on the p_H of the medium,

(q) Solids exert more pressure on the vessel floor in a storage bin than a liquid of same density.

Distinguish between :

(a) Classification and jigging,
(b) Open-circuit and closed-circuit grinding units,
(c) Jaw crusher and a Gyratory crusher,
(d) Sphericity and wetted sphericity,
(e) Vibrating screen and trommel,
(f) Shape factor and specific surface ratio,
(g) Rittinger's law and Bond's law,
(h) Screening efficiency and screen effectiveness,,
(i) Mixing index and mixing number,
(j) Compressible and incompressible sludges,
(k) Hindered settling and free settling,
(l) Power number and power function,
(m) Hydrocyclone and gas cyclone,
(n) Centrifuge and centrifugal,
(o) Radial flow and axial flow impellers,
(p) Belt conveyor and screw conveyor,
(q) Gravity sedimentation and centrifugal sedimentation,
(r) Particulate and aggregative fluidisation.

Discuss what happens when,

(a) near-mesh particles are fed to a screen,
(b) the speed of a ball mill is gradually increased,
(c) the inlet Reynolds number is increased in (i) a gas cyclone, (ii) a hydrocyclone.

177. **Answer briefly:**

(a) You are familiar with Newton's law and Stokes law that are used for computing the terminal velocity of spherical particles settling in a liquid. Discuss how would you modify these laws for applying to, (i) gas bubbles rising in a quiescent liquid, (ii) liquid drops falling in a gas, (iii) fine dust particles (having size less than a micron) settling in a gas.

Discuss how would you use a fluidises as, (i) an elutriator (ii) a pneumatic conveyor.

178. **Outline the significance and applications of the following equations/laws:**
    (a) Gaudin-Schumann distribution law;
    (b) Kynch's theory,
    (c) Janssen's equation,
    (d) Kick's law.

179. **Discuss on the following:**
    (a) Washing and dewatering of filter cakes in a rotary drum filter,
    (b) Charging and migration of dust particles in a electrostatic precipitator,
    (c) Effect of particle size on the collection efficiency of a gas cyclone,
    (d) The significance of Σ factor in the design of centrifugal sedimentors.
    (e) Flooding in a packed bed.

180. **Name the type of separation technique (and outline its principle) you would recommend for separating.**
    (a) Particles of same size but having densities wide apart,
    (b) Particles equally falling but of different densities and sizes,
    (c) Particles of same density and size,
    (d) Particles of the same material having different sizes,
    (e) Two immiscible liquids of different densities.

181. **Explain how would you proceed to compute,**
    (a) Free settling velocity (at any instant) of a spherical particle in water,
    (b) Air requirement of a rotary drum filter,
    (c) Pressure drop in a pneumatic conveyor,
    (d) Effectiveness of a classifying screen.

182. **Recommend a suitable equipment for each of the following operations and outline its working principle**
    (a) Breaking of run-of-mine coal,
    (b) Fine grinding of explosives,
    (c) Separation of a kerosene-water emulsion,
    (d) Drying of ammonium sulphate crystals in a fertiliser plant,
    (e) Removal of precipitated wax from a heavy gas, oil in a petroleum refinery,
    (f) Mixing of dry salt and sand,
    (g) Washing of extraneous mineral matter associated with coal meant for a carbonisation unit,
    (h) Conveying of catalyst particles to the top of a tall column,
    (i) Crushing of wood and asbestos,
    (j) Transportinghot molasses from a sugar plant to a distillery that is around 5 km away,
    (k) Mixing of a rubber compound,
    (1) Separation of fine dust of fly ash from an exhaust gas stream,
    (m) Transporting coal from the mine to a thermal power plant situated at more than 100 km away,
    (n) Separation of coarse and fines from a slurry.

183. **Determine the surface mean diameter and harmonic mean diameter of an ore sample that has the following size distribution:**

ISS mesh	Percentage retained
− 480 + 340	3.4
− 340 + 240	6.3
− 240 + 160	8.1
− 160 + 120	10.2
− 120 + 85	16.5
− 85 + 60	13.1
− 60 + 40	10.1
− 40 + 30	9.5
− 30 + 20	7.0
− 20 + 15	4.7
− 15 + 10	3.1
− 10 + 8	2.0
− 8	6.0

Tests show that the specific surface ratios of the ore are -identical with those of calcite.

184. **The following data were collected when a crushed ore was screened using a 3.0 mm screen to separate the undercrushed material so that it can be returned to the crusher for further processing. Compute the effectiveness of the screen.**

| ISS mesh | Feed | Mass fraction | |
		Oversize from screen	Undersize from screen
+ 480	0.548	0.596	0.00
− 480 + 340	0.146	0.168	0.113
− 340 + 120	0.109	0.096	0.147
− 120 + 60	0.045	0.039	0.086
− 60 + 30	0.034	0.029	0.033
− 30	0.118	0.072	0.621

MECHANICAL OPERATIONS   QUESTION BANK

185. **Quartz is fed at the rate of 25,000 kg/hr to a ball mill that is operating in closed circuit with a hydraulic classifier. The screen analyses of known streams are given below:**

ISS mesh	Mass fraction		
	Raw feed to mill	Overflow material from classifier	Underfloor material from classifier
− 480 + 340	0.548	0.0	0.0
− 340 + 240	0.086	0.0	0.308
− 240 + 160	0.055	0.0	0.030
− 160 + 120	0.047	0.0	0.154
− 120 + 85	0.027	0.0	0.169
− 85 + 60	0.035	0.0	0.207
− 60 + 40	0.029	0.042	0.034
− 40 + 30	0.019	0.127	0.028
− 30 + 20	0.020	0.193	0.014
− 20 + 15	0.097	0.137	0.022
− 15 + 10	0.022	0.117	0.018
− 10 + 8	0.015	0.098	0.016
− 8	0.0	0.286	0.0

The mill is being operated with a recycle of 75,000 kg/hr. If the total power supplied to drive the mill is 75 kW, determine the energy efficiency of the mill,

(a) from Rittinger's law, (b) from Bond's law.

186. Estimate the power consumption of comminuting 20,000 kg/hr of a hard rock (specific gravity = 3.8, Rittinger's number = 0.0175 m^2/J) in a hammer mill of efficiency 18%, operating in closed circuit with a 100 micron screen from the following data:

Average size, mm	Mass fraction		
	Raw feed to mill	Oversize from screen	Undersize from screen
0.25	0.818	0.730	0.0
0.18	0.104	0.207	0.123
0.1296	0.065	0.043	0.142
0.0933	0.013	0.020	0.135
below 0.0933	0.0	0.0	0.60

Tests hate shown that the average ratio of undersize to oversize from screen is 1.0 and the specific surface ratios are identical with those of sphalerite. What will be the Sauter diameter of the product ? What will be the classifying screen effectiveness?

(Q.10)

187. Determine the time required for ore particles each weighing 4 gm (specific gravity = 7.5) to settle in water from an initial velocity of 0.2 m/s until a velocity of 0.7 m/s is attained relative' to the fluid. Assume that the particles are isometric (sphericity = 0.8) and free settling prevails.

188. For the beneficiation of tungsten oxide that is contaminated with silica, it is first elutriated in a rising stream of water at 30°C. The feed mixture has the size distribution given below:

Size, cm	Mass fraction
− 0.068 + 0.045	0.25
− 0.045 + 0.027	0.33
−0.027 + 0.013	0.22
− 0.013 + 0.0078	0.20

Determine the upward velocity of water that is to be maintained in the elutriator so as to obtain an uncontaminated tungsten oxide as the product. What will be the size range of this product ? Specific gravity of pure tungsten oxide = 7.2.

189. A sample of coal weighing 18 gm was tested in the laboratory by feeding it separately to different solutions, collecting the floated material and checking its ash content. The following data were collected:

When fed to a solution of	Amount floated, gm	Its ash content, gm
Specific gravity = 1.43	14.5	1.343
1.40	11.0	0.835
1.30	4.44	0.120
1.35	7.36	0.363
1.25	0.99	0.009

If the above coal is to be cleaned in a coal washery until its ash content reduces to 4.5%, specify what specific gravity of dense medium is to be employed. What shall be the percentage yield of clean coal?

190. A limestone-water slurry is to be thickened to 50% solids (by weight) within 3.4 hours in a Dorr thickener of cross-sectional area 1000 m². The slurry is fed to the thickener at the rate of 200 m³/hr. Estimate the depth of the thickener you shall recommend for final industrial design from the following batch sedimentation test data:

Time, (hr)	Height of interface, (cm)
0.0	36.0
0.25	32.4
0.50	28.6
1.00	21.0
1.75	14.7
3.00	12.3
4.75	11.55
12.00	9.80
20.00	8.80
∞	7.70

Data: Specific gravity of limestone: 2.1.

191. A coal-water suspension is to be clarified at the rate of 5000 kg/hr to provide an underflow sludge that contains 85% solids in a 1050 m² continuous thickener. However, the thickener broke down and the job has to be done in a centrifuge 600 mm in diameter and 400 mm in height. Estimate the speed of the centrifuge if it is to have the same sedimentation characteristics as the above thickener. The thickness of liquid layer, inside the centrifuge basket may be taken to be extremely small.
State and explain any assumptions made.

192. The causticizing of soda ash follows the reaction

$$Na_2CO_3 + Ca(OH)_2 \rightarrow 2\ NaOH + CaCO_3 \downarrow$$

After the reaction is complete, the product liquor containing 2 kg of calcium carbonate per kg of NaOH-free water is fed continuously at the rate of 1000 kg/hr to a series of thickeners in which it is washed countercurrently with neutral water. It is desired to recover 95 per cent of NaOH and the final solution obtained from the system is to contain 0.128 mass fraction NaOH.

(a) Compute the amount of neutral water required and the number of thickeners if the thickened sludge from each thickener contains 40 per cent solids. It is observed that the leach solution (overflow) from each stage (thickener) is clear. Equilibrium is attained at each stage and the compositions of the overflow solution and the solution leaving with the underflow are the same.

(b) How many thickeners would be required if the underflow sludge from each thickener contains 1 kg of solids per 1.5 kg of water?

193. A plate and frame press of 1.2 m² filtering area handling a homogeneous slurry containing 10 per cent (by weight) of solids (specific gravity = 2.33) in water gave the following results:

Time (min):	10	30	60	110
Volume of filtrate (m³):	80	115	152	200

MECHANICAL OPERATIONS QUESTION BANK

Tests show that the following relation is valid for the present case (for $t_f > 0$):

$$V_f^2 = K_1 t_f + K_2$$

where, V_f is the volume of filtrate (m^3) delivered in filtering time t_f hours and K_1 and K_2 are constants.

The cake is washed with water at a constant rate of one-third of final rate of filtration. The volume of wash water used is equal to one-twelveth of the volume of filtrate delivered per cycle. Opening, closing and reassembling take 45 minutes. Determine the optimum cycle time that will produce maximum daily output of filtrate.

194. A leaf filter handling a compressible sludge at 0.5 kg/(m^{2}s) gave the following results:

Time (seconds):	10	40	60	90
Pressure drop (kPa):	2.8	24.5	43.4	78.4

If the filter is operated at constant rate until the pressure difference becomes 70 kN/m^2, then at constant pressure until the filtrate collected is 2000 lit./m^2, estimate the total cycle time. Assume the filter medium resistance is negligible and the time for washing, cleaning and dumping is 60 minutes.

195. A 2000 rpm centrifugal filter 0.75 in diameter and 0.45 in height used to filter an incompressible sludge gave the following results. The final thickness of cake and liquid layer inside the bowl were 0.15 m and 0.025 in respectively.

Filtrate volume (litres):	1.0	1.5	2.0	2.5	3.0
Time (seconds):	40	70	105	150	200

If the same sludge is to be filtered in a filter press at a constant rate of 0.49 litres/(m^{2}s), estimate the pressure difference that should be maintained across the filter at the end of 60 seconds. Assume the filter medium resistance is constant and is the same for both the centrifugal filter and the filter press.

196. A rotary drum filter 2 m diameter and 4 in long is used to filter a slurry containing 10 mass per cent solids. The particles are 0.075 mm cubes (sphericity = 0.81, specific gravity = 1.85). Compute what volume of filtrate will be delivered in one hour of operation from the following data:

Submergence = 40 per cent

Cake voidage = 0.35

Pressure inside the drum = 60 kN/m^2

Rotational speed = 0.33 rpm

Specific gravity of filtrate = 1.0

Viscosity of filtrate = 12.5 centipoises.

MECHANICAL OPERATIONS — QUESTION BANK

197. A flotation unit concentrates 1000 kg/min of an ore containing 20% pyrite (specific gravity = 4.9) and balance silica (specific gravity = 2.65) to 95% pyrite. The rougher, scavenger and cleaner contain four, three and two Denver cells respectively, each cell (L/D = 1.5) being fitted with four baffles (width = 0.1 D_t) and a 300 rpm six-bladed turbine impeller (diameter = 0.33 D_t). Rougher concentrate has 60% silica and tailings from rougher, scavenger and cleaner,-ontain 95%, 99.5% and 80% silica respectively. If pulp consistency is 4.0 in.scavenger and 6.0 in cleaner and contact time 10 minutes in scavenger and 8.0 minutes in cleaner, estimate the hourly power consumption.

    State and explain any assumptions made.

198. A three-bladed marine propeller (pitch = 2.0) is used to agitate a solution of specific gravity 1.3 and viscosity 12.5 centipoises in an unbaffled tank of 1.0 m diameter and 1.5 m deep. The tank is filled to a depth of 1.0 m with the solution and the impeller (diameter = 0.3 D_t) is set at one impeller diameter above the vessel floor. Estimate the speed of the impeller if the power consumed to drive it is 0.34 W. What will be the impeller speed if the tank is fitted with four longitudinal baffles each having a width equal to 10 per cent of tank diameter?

199. Determine the power consumption for transporting coal particles of average size 1.0 mm (specific gravity = 1.5) in the form of a coal-water slurry through a commercial steel pipe of 0.5 m in diameter. In all, 2700 tonnes of coal are to be transported per hour over a distance of 20 km. The solid concentration in the slurry is maintained at 25 per cent (by weight).

200. In a chemical plant, dry catalyst particles (specific gravity 2.35) are to be delivered to the top of a tower 15 m high at the rate of 3000 kg/hour. The following two options are available. Determine which would you recommend and why.

    (a) A bucket elevator employing 2 litre buckets (mass of each 3.38 kg) running at an average bucket speed of 1.0 m/s (coefficient of pulley resistance = 1.075).

    (b) A pneumatic conveyor employing a commercial steel pipe of 10 cm in diameter and an air to solid ratio of 1 : 3.

    Assume that the catalyst particles are essentially spherical and of average size 0.8 mm.

    State and explain your assumptions, if any.

www.ingramcontent.com/pod-product-compliance
Lightning Source LLC
Chambersburg PA
CBHW080941300426
44115CB00017B/2902